Y0-ACB-013

THE CAMBRIDGE ECONOMIC HISTORY
OF LATIN AMERICA

The Cambridge Economic History of Latin America provides access to the current state of expert knowledge about Latin America's economic past from the Spanish conquest to the beginning of the twenty-first century. It includes work from diverse perspectives, disciplines, and methodologies from qualitative historical analysis of policies and institutions to cliometrics, the new institutional economics, and environmental sciences. Each chapter provides a comparative analysis of economic trends, sectoral development, or the evolution of the institutional and policy environment.

Volume II treats the "long twentieth century" from the onset of modern economic growth to the present. It analyzes the principal dimensions of Latin America's first era of sustained economic growth from the last decades of the nineteenth century to 1930. It explores the era of inward-looking development from the 1930s to the collapse of import-substituting industrialization and the return to strategies of globalization in the 1980s. Finally, it looks at the long-term trends in capital flows, agriculture, and the environment.

Volume I treats the colonial and independence eras up to 1850.

Victor Bulmer-Thomas is the Director of Chatham House, the London home of the Royal Institute of International Affairs, and Professor Emeritus at the University of London. From 1992 to 1998, he was Director of the Institute of Latin American Studies (now the Institute for the Study of the Americas) at London University. He is the author of *The Economic History of Latin America since Independence* (Second edition, 2003) and editor of *Regional Integration in Latin America and the Caribbean: The Political Economy of Open Regionalism* (2001).

John H. Coatsworth is Monroe Gutman Professor of Latin American Affairs in the Department of History at Harvard University. In addition to serving as the Director of the David Rockefeller Center for Latin American Studies since its founding in 1994, he chairs the Harvard University Committee on Human Rights Studies. His recent books include *Latin America and the World Economy since 1800*, edited with Alan M. Taylor (1998), and *Culturas encontradas: Cuba y los Estados Unidos*, edited with Rafael Hernández (2001).

Roberto Cortés Conde is Professor Emeritus of Economics at the Universidad de San Andrés in Buenos Aires, Argentina, and a corresponding member of the Royal Academy of History of Spain. A former Guggenheim Fellow, he has published numerous books and scholarly articles. His most recent books include *La economía argentina en el largo plazo (siglos xix y xx)* (1997); *Transferring Wealth and Power from the Old to the New World: Monetary and Fiscal Institutions in the 17th through the 19th Centuries* (2002), edited with Michael D. Bordo; and *Historia económica mundial* (2003).

THE CAMBRIDGE ECONOMIC HISTORY
OF LATIN AMERICA

VOLUME I

The Colonial Era and the Short Nineteenth Century

VOLUME II

The Long Twentieth Century

THE CAMBRIDGE ECONOMIC HISTORY OF LATIN AMERICA

VOLUME II

The Long Twentieth Century

Edited by

VICTOR BULMER-THOMAS
Royal Institute of International Affairs

JOHN H. COATSWORTH
Harvard University

ROBERTO CORTÉS CONDE
Universidad de San Andrés

CAMBRIDGE
UNIVERSITY PRESS

ARCHBISHOP ALEMANY LIBRARY
DOMINICAN UNIVERSITY
SAN RAFAEL, CALIFORNIA 94901

CAMBRIDGE UNIVERSITY PRESS
Cambridge, New York, Melbourne, Madrid, Cape Town, Singapore, São Paulo

Cambridge University Press
40 West 20th Street, New York, NY 10011-4211, USA

www.cambridge.org
Information on this title: www.cambridge.org/9780521812900

© Cambridge University Press 2006

This publication is in copyright. Subject to statutory exception
and to the provisions of relevant collective licensing agreements,
no reproduction of any part may take place without
the written permission of Cambridge University Press.

First published 2006

Printed in the United States of America

A catalog record for this publication is available from the British Library.

Library of Congress Cataloging in Publication Data

The Cambridge economic history of Latin America / edited by Victor
Bulmer-Thomas, John H. Coatsworth, Roberto Cortés Conde.
v.   cm.
Includes bibliographical references and index.
Contents: v. 1. The colonial era and the short nineteenth century –
v. 2. The long twentieth century.
ISBN-13: 978-0-521-81289-4 (hardback : v. 1)
ISBN-10: 0-521-81289-5 (hardback : v. 1)
ISBN-13: 978-0-521-81290-0 (hardback : v. 2)
ISBN-10: 0-521-81290-9 (hardback : v. 2)
1. Latin America – Economic conditions.   2. Latin America – Economic policy.
I. Bulmer-Thomas, V.   II. Coatsworth, John H., 1940– .   IV. Cortés Conde, Roberto.
V. Title: Economic history of Latin America.
HC125.C29   2006
330.98 – dc22   2005015006

ISBN-13   978-0-521-81289-4 (hardback : v. 1)
ISBN-10   0-521-81289-5 (hardback : v. 1)
ISBN-13   978-0-521-81290-0 (hardback : v. 2)
ISBN-10   0-521-81290-9 (hardback : v. 2)
ISBN-13   978-0-521-85716-1 (hardback : set)
ISBN-10   0-521-85716-3 (hardback : set)

Cambridge University Press has no responsibility for
the persistence or accuracy of URLs for external or
third-party Internet Web sites referred to in this publication
and does not guarantee that any content on such
Web sites is, or will remain, accurate or appropriate.

CONTENTS

v

PREFACE

The Cambridge Economic History of Latin America began with conversations among colleagues, later the editors, but would never have passed from idle chatter to intellectual and material substance without the collaboration of numerous scholars and institutions. The editors wish to thank the distinguished contributors to these two volumes for the chapters they contributed, for traveling great distances to discuss them, and for responding with dispatch and good cheer to requests to review texts, check citations, and correct translations.

Most of the papers that became chapters in these two volumes were presented in original and then revised form at one or more of three meetings. First draft papers were presented and discussed at the Congress of the Latin American Studies Association in Washington, DC, in September 2001 and at the Institute for Latin American Studies (now the Institute for the Study of the Americas [ISA]) at the University of London, hosted by ISA Director James Dunkerley, in February 2002. Revised papers, and some additional chapter drafts, were discussed at a presidential session of the Congress of the International Economic History Association (IEHA), organized by IEHA president Roberto Cortés Conde, in Buenos Aires in July 2002.

This project could not have come to fruition as it has without the generous support of the William and Flora Hewlett Foundation. The editors wish to thank the Foundation for its support and to acknowledge with special thanks the efforts of David Lorey, whose vision and hard work, in addition to his own distinction as a historian of Mexico, helped to make the Hewlett Foundation's program on U.S.–Latin American Relations a major contributor in the reconstruction of academic institutions and intellectual networks in the western hemisphere in the past decade. The Hewlett

Foundation grant was administered without cost to the project by the David Rockefeller Center for Latin American Studies at Harvard University, whose assistance is also gratefully acknowledged.

The editors also wish to thank Frank Smith of Cambridge University Press (CUP) for his encouragement and patience, CUP's anonymous reviewers for helpful comments and suggestions, and Daniel Gutierrez of Harvard University for his hard work and expert editorial assistance.

While these volumes were still in preparation, the editors learned of the death of Enrique Tandeter from pancreatic cancer on April 24, 2004, at the age of fifty-nine. Enrique died seven months after the death of his wife, historian Dora Schwarzstein, also from cancer and at an even younger age. Enrique was a scholar of exceptional rigor and intelligence, whose research contributed in fundamental ways to our understanding of the social and economic history of the Andes during the colonial era. All who knew Enrique and Dora remember them for their warmth and sophistication, their courage in the face of exile and tragedy, the high standards of integrity and professionalism they set for themselves and their students, and their joy in the achievements of their talented children, Leah and Frederico.

INTRODUCTION

In the past two decades, new research has transformed the economic history of Latin America. The pioneering work of the structuralist and dependency school historians, often collaborating with the United Nations Economic Commission for Latin America and the Caribbean (ECLAC),[1] produced a huge outpouring of new economic data in the 1950s and the 1960s, including the first historical (and in some cases current) estimates of Gross Domestic Product (GDP) for a number of countries. Statistical agencies and central banks, often founded and staffed by ECLAC graduates, undertook further work. The search for economic historical data was also stimulated by historians trained in the Anglo-American empirical tradition and in the methods of the French *Annales* School, and by heterodox development economists schooled in England and the United States. In the 1970s, these currents were joined by historians and economists trained mainly in the United States and often associated with the New Economic History. The ensuing debates over approaches and paradigms were fueled by the shifting fortunes of competing economic strategies – socialism, import substitution, freer trade – and by the rise of repressive military regimes throughout much of Latin America.

Latin America's economic history took a decisive turn with the 1982 financial and economic crisis and the ensuing transition to democracy throughout the region. Theoretical debates over competing economic strategies diminished in intensity. As democracies consolidated and the Cold War ended, ideological conflicts subsided or became muted. Economic history,

---

[1] ECLAC was known as ECLA (or CEPAL in Spanish) until the Caribbean was added to its name in 1973.

like the social sciences in general, professionalized in an environment that demanded better data and more sophisticated and coherent arguments. The impact of these changes in the Latin American intellectual landscape included notable advances in the study of the economic past marked by a series of general works and anthologies as well as an outpouring of original and often path-breaking monographic research.

The goal of these two volumes is to provide access to the current state of expert knowledge about the history of economic development in Latin America, here taken to include all of the western hemisphere from the "southern cone" of South America to the southern border of the United States. At the outset of the project, the three editors made two decisions that to some readers will inevitably appear at least arbitrary and possibly reckless. The first was to put aside the national and regional boundaries that have traditionally defined the scope of historical scholarship in order to commission chapters that address comparative topics with data and analysis on the entire region. The essays in these volumes focus on major trends and developments and confirm the utility of comparative work in economic history. The trade-off, of course, is that idiosyncratic experiences and smaller economies do not appear as often as they would in geographically delimited case studies.

The second decision was to break the two volumes at roughly 1850, a division that defies conventional periodizations. The logic of this division is economic and institutional rather than political. The transition from colonialism to independence in the 1820s coincided with economic fragmentation, but the economic and institutional legacy of the colonial economy continued to weigh heavily on the new countries. Not until the economic globalization of Latin America that commenced with massive inflows of capital and immigrants after 1850 did the region achieve sustained economic growth for the first time in history. The institutional modernization needed to sustain modern economic growth also took shape in the mid- to late nineteenth century. Finally, the onset of growth also coincided with the increases in the inequality of incomes and fortunes that were to characterize the region throughout the twentieth century.

THE LONG TWENTIETH CENTURY

In the last three decades of the nineteenth century, exports of commodities increased significantly in Latin America, laying the foundation for modern economic growth. Colonial exports had been limited to a small number of readily accessible natural resources. As these traditional exports recovered after the independence wars, a few new exports joined the list of colonial products, notably copper in Chile and guano in Peru. However, the commodity export boom of the last decades of the nineteenth century was both larger and deeper. The integration of the Latin American economies into the world economy between 1850 and World War I was unprecedented in scale and complexity.

The fall in transportation costs attributable to technological innovations was the key factor in Latin American exports reaching the European and North American markets. The Latin American countries did not trade much with each other, either because of scarce population and low income, or because their natural resource–based economies could not supply the manufactured goods that their neighbors sought to import. Instead, they sought access to markets outside the region.

This became possible through the dramatic fall in ocean freight rates (Chapter 1) and in land transportation costs from the interior to the ports made possible by the construction of a very wide railway network (Chapter 8). Capital flows from more developed countries to Latin America beginning in the last decades of the nineteenth century played a key role both in railroad construction and in exploiting newly accessible land and mineral resources (Chapter 2).

The wave of foreign investments that started around 1870 and – after a break in the 1890s – continued until the 1930s was the result of the higher profitability of investments in countries in need of capital. It was also attributable to the oversupply of capital, especially in Great Britain, the leader in international capital exports. However, capital was not the only scarce factor of production. In several sparsely populated countries of the South American temperate zones, labor was also needed. The latter came from across the Atlantic thanks to the income differentials between Latin America and Southern and Eastern Europe. Immigration was, in some cases, encouraged by official policies, as in Brazil, or occurred spontaneously, as in Argentina and Uruguay (Chapter 10).

The nature of the resources and geography determined the type of productive activity each country would undertake. In most cases, concentration on one or two activities was very marked, although in other cases (e.g., Argentina) exports were more diversified. In the Southern Andes, mining predominated (copper and nitrates in Chile, tin in Bolivia, guano and oil in Peru). Along the Atlantic coast and in the Caribbean, two types of agriculture were prevalent. Tropical production, usually organized in plantations, included coffee in Brazil, Colombia, and Costa Rica; sugar in Brazil and Cuba; and bananas in Central America, Colombia, and Ecuador. Temperate-zone agriculture in the south of the continent (Argentina, Chile, and Uruguay) specialized in grain and cattle production, which was more intensive in land use and less intensive in capital and labor (Chapter 9). These differences in production technology affected each country's subsequent development (Chapter 1). Growth was not limited to the export enclaves, but extended to other sectors. Industrial growth was significant although uneven and mainly centered on industries related to the processing of natural resources (Chapter 7).

Globalization, that is to say, the integration with international markets because of falling transportation costs, rising capital flows, and increased labor mobility, was a necessary condition for the exploitation of natural resources. Another necessary condition for growth was the establishment of relatively stable institutions and governments capable of inspiring the confidence of local capitalists as well as foreign investors. Political stability and institutional reform were, in turn, strengthened by economic expansion. The consolidation of national governments under constitutional regimes, with authority over the whole territory and respect for property rights, became widespread (Chapter 5). The possibility of receiving capital and labor for the exploitation of vast natural resources was an important incentive to the development of political consensus, leading (though not always) to the end of constant wars and conflicts.

Thus, the growth in foreign trade brought about an increase in tax revenues, which became the basis for the consolidation of increasingly powerful central governments. In the larger countries with federalist constitutions (Argentina, Brazil, and Mexico), subnational entities (states and provinces) continued to receive a major part of these revenues (Chapter 6). These same countries adopted the gold standard at the end of the century, and this not only allowed a more fluid trade thanks to the multilateral payments system, but also guaranteed foreign investors (those whose profits were generated in local currency) that they would have a stable currency at the moment they remitted their profits (Chapters 6 and 7).

World War I interrupted these globalization processes both in Latin America and elsewhere (Chapter 1). Inflationary financing during the war caused imbalances that prevented a successful return to the gold standard in the 1920s. Protectionist policies in North America and most of Europe, which caught up with Latin America's traditionally high tariffs, thwarted fluid trade. While the capital streams continued to flow into Latin America – no longer so much from Great Britain, but mainly from the United States (Chapter 2) – to finance balance of payments deficits of those countries trading with the capital-exporting countries, the protection of agricultural activities and the accumulation of inventories contributed to a significant fall in agricultural and raw material prices that, in indebted countries, meant a higher exposure to the catastrophic decrease in demand and prices caused by the Great Depression.

At the end of the 1920s, Latin American countries had all re-established the primacy of the export sector after the disruptions of World War I and the brief 1920–1 depression. Most republics had also opted for orthodox monetary and fiscal policies based, in many cases, on the gold standard. Mexico was still suffering from the upheavals associated with the Revolution, although political stability at least had begun to improve after the rise to power of General Alvaro Obregón (1920–4), and Brazil was not afraid to intervene in the defense of the all-important coffee sector. However, this was probably the moment that Latin America came closest to the liberal ideal of free markets, minimal state interference, and orthodox macroeconomic policies. Paradoxically, this was not inconsistent with high tariffs designed primarily for revenue purposes that provided a strong stimulus to manufacturing in those countries with a large domestic market. Industry flourished alongside the export sector in a number of countries and no criticism was raised outside the region against policies that – in the case of tariffs – were also being pursued by the United States, the dominions of the Commonwealth, and many European countries.

The Great Depression hit Latin America hard, but belief in the export sector did not waver. However, heterodox policies were needed to protect the export sector, and such policies performed well after 1932 (Chapter 3). They included multiple exchange rates and nontariff barriers, which provided a further stimulus to manufacturing. Industry ended the decade in a much stronger position in many countries. When imports were closed off after the outbreak of World War II, manufacturing in these same countries was well poised to take advantage. By the end of the war, the industrial lobby in the larger countries had become powerful enough to challenge traditional export interests, and government policy began for the first time to give priority to the needs of secondary over primary products.

As a result, the Golden Age of import-substituting industrialization (ISI) began in the 1950s. The work of the ECLAC, based on the assumption of a secular decline in the external terms of trade for primary products, provided the theoretical justification for the policies Latin American governments had already begun to adopt. Tariffs were raised to unheard of levels, this time for protective rather than revenue reasons, and nontariff barriers multiplied. Most countries did not join the General Agreement on Tariffs and Trade (GATT) and even the few that did were not unduly constrained by GATT restrictions on quotas. The industrial lobbies became very forceful (Chapter 13) and were, in large part, responsible for the form that regional integration took in Latin America from 1960 onward. These schemes largely excluded agriculture and services, providing instead reciprocal markets for manufactured goods with very high tariffs against third countries.

The available literature on this period has generated a lively debate over the consequences of the export boom for the growth of the economy. Although there were always concerns about excessive specialization in the export of primary products, after the 1930s crisis, and especially after World War II, criticism became more widespread. On the one hand, there was the problem of single crop production, leading to monoculture that could have catastrophic consequences if market conditions changed. On the other hand, there was the rentier nature of dependence on natural resources, which did not foster investment and capital accumulation. The concentration of activities in big mining companies, large plantations, and vast cattle ranches produced a very uneven income distribution – an obstacle for the creation of an enlarged domestic market. Criticism was also centered on the volatility of the export economies because of shifting demand conditions in foreign markets, the vulnerability of supply to weather conditions, or the rigidity of the gold standard and its negative effect as a conveyor of external shocks.

In time, ISI itself inspired two different reactions. On the left (and sometimes the right as well) nationalism – often combined with macroeconomic populism – resisted the growing weight of foreign capital and the perceived rise in inequality in the ISI model. Instead, nationalists argued for state-owned enterprises, price controls, and a redistribution of resources through social spending rather than progressive taxation. On the right, neoliberals argued for an end to state intervention and an opening of both the trade and capital accounts in the balance of payments. Neither approach was notably successful, as is borne out by the example of Chile, which experimented unsuccessfully with both models in the 1970s. The debt crisis at the beginning of the 1980s marked the final collapse of the ISI model, although it was some years before the new market-friendly export-oriented policies triumphed.

That they did so was attributable not only to the need to extricate the region from the debt crisis through policies that found favor with creditor governments, private foreign banks, and international financial institutions, but also to the rise of globalization. By the end of the 1980s, it was clear that the world economy was undergoing a paradigm shift based on trade liberalization, international capital flows (Chapter 4), and greater integration of the main economies. Countries such as those in Southeast Asia and China, which had adapted their policies to take advantage of the new market opportunities, appeared to flourish. Those that failed to adapt, as in the Middle East or sub-Saharan Africa, appeared to stagnate. This rather simplistic reading of the global policy debate encouraged Latin American governments to jettison the policies that had underpinned ISI and economic nationalism and to fashion a new paradigm that came to be known as the New Economic Model. All of the Latin American republics joined the World Trade Organization (successor to GATT), and liberalization was extended to the financial sector and the capital account of the balance of payments.

The New Economic Model has been no more successful than its predecessor in insulating Latin America against negative external shocks. Although the net barter terms of trade is less of an issue, the volatility of capital flows has become of paramount importance (Chapter 2). Some countries have suffered falls in GDP as sharp as those in the Great Depression as a result of large, unpredictable movements of capital. Long-run growth performance has been much less satisfactory than during the thirty years of ISI, from 1950 to 1980, and income distribution – already the most unequal in the world – has failed to improve (Chapter 14).

Long-run trends are a crucial part of economic history and the editors have devoted several chapters in this volume to their analysis. Agriculture for most of the long twentieth century has been the major source of output and employment in Latin America, as well as the main contributor to foreign exchange (Chapter 12). Education is now recognized as a field in which most Latin American governments have failed to prepare their populations adequately for the rigors of a globalized market place (Chapter 11). Last, but not least, the editors have included a chapter on the environment by Otto Solbrig (Chapter 9), which emphasizes the complexity and fragility of Latin America's ecosystems and the vulnerability of the environment to modern economic growth.

1

GLOBALIZATION IN LATIN AMERICA BEFORE 1940

LUIS BÉRTOLA AND JEFFREY G. WILLIAMSON

GLOBALIZATION AND GROWTH

Some describe the first half of the nineteenth century as decades of lost Latin American economic growth while the region struggled with independence conflicts and their aftermath. Latin America's growth performance in the second half of the twentieth century was also disappointing. By comparison, during the half century between the 1860s and the 1910s, Latin American economies performed fairly well: they kept pace with European growth rates, grew more than other peripheral regions, but grew less than the big winners of the period, the United States and those European countries catching up with Britain.[1] The term "fairly well" may understate Latin American growth given that, after all, it took place during a century that created a truly huge economic gap between the core and the rest of the periphery.[2]

Table 1.1 documents that performance for real per capita income and purchasing-power parity – adjusted real wages of unskilled urban workers, both relative to Great Britain. Using the macroeconomist's rhetoric, there was some Latin American catching up on the hegemonic industrial leader in Europe: per capita income in Latin America rose from 38 to 42 percent of Britain's. Because Britain was losing that leadership to some powerful latecomers, perhaps a better comparison is with a more inclusive

---

[1] Comparisons with the United States are common in the literature, but because *nobody* matched U.S. growth performance in its leap to world industrial dominance over these six decades, such comparisons seem irrelevant.

[2] Lant Pritchett, "Divergence, Big Time," *Journal of Economic Perspectives* 11 (Summer 1997): 3–18.

Table 1.1. *Relative levels of GDP per capita and real wages in Latin America: 1870–1940*

	Latin America	European Core	Latin Europe
1. GDP per capita (UK = 100)			
1870	38	72	39
1890	37	73	39
1900	34	77	38
1913	42	82	40
1929	47	91	48
1940	35	78	40
2. PPP real wages (UK = 100)			
1870	56	87	45
1890	45	86	40
1900	45	84	36
1913	52	88	48
1929	62	93	55
1940	70	83	43

Notes: European Core consists of Britain, France, and Germany. Latin Europe consists of Iberia and Italy. PPP refers to purchasing-power parity.

Sources: GDP per capita from Angus Maddison, *The World Economy: A Millennial Perspective* (Paris, 2001); wages from data underlying Jeffrey G. Williamson, "Real Wages, Inequality, and Globalization in Latin America before 1940," *Revista de Historia Económica* 17 (1999): 101–42.

European industrial core, including Britain, France, and Germany: here, Latin American performance is a little less impressive, with its relative position to that of the fast-growing core falling from 53 to 51 percent. Another relevant comparison is between Latin America and the source of its European immigrants, Iberia and Italy: here, Latin America improved its position from near-parity, with income per capita about 97 or 98 percent of Latin Europe, to a 5 percent advantage. Because it was a relatively labor-scarce and resource-abundant region compared with Europe (especially Latin Europe), real-wage comparisons tend to favor Latin America much more than do per capita income comparisons. Thus, whereas Latin American per capita incomes were about 51 percent of the European core in 1913, real wages were about 59 percent of the core, an 8 percentage point difference. The difference in 1929 was even bigger, 15 percentage points. Finally, not every Latin American country grew "fairly fast." Indeed, economic gaps within the region widened considerably: in 1870, the per capita gross domestic product (GDP) of both Brazil and Mexico was about 55 percent of that of Argentina: by 1913 it was reduced to 22 and 39 percent, respectively.[3]

How much of this economic performance between 1870 and 1913 can be assigned to the forces of globalization? This chapter ponders this question, but it does so only by exploring the impact of international trade. Other chapters in this volume have done the same for the mass migration from Latin Europe (Chapter 10) and for capital inflows from Britain, the United States, and elsewhere (Chapter 2). These three chapters should be read together because capital flows, immigration, trade, and the policies influencing all three cannot really be assessed independently.

The next section explores the important disadvantage associated with isolation from regional and world markets and the transport revolutions that helped liberate so much of Latin America from that isolation. The third section deals with the immense variety in Latin America by focusing on how the distinctly different country resource endowments unfolded during the period, and their impact on export specialization and trade. The fourth section connects with another chapter in this book, asking how independence might have caused massive deglobalization during those decades of lost growth between the 1820s and the 1870s.

Next, we document what happened to the external terms of trade (the ratio of export to import prices) in Latin America between 1820 and 1950. The section replicates the period of deterioration from the 1890s onward, first popularly noted by Raúl Prebisch. It also documents the spectacular improvement in the terms of trade before the 1890s, suggesting that it had something to do with the "fairly fast" Latin American growth during so much of the belle époque. Booming relative prices of exports certainly fostered trade, but trade policy suppressed it: tariff rates were higher in Latin America than almost anywhere else in the world between 1820 and 1929, long before the Great Depression. The sixth section asks why. The answer lies mainly with revenue needs rather than with some precocious import substitution and industrialization policy, but high tariffs still must have had a powerful protective effect. The seventh section pursues these issues further by assessing the connections between export-led growth and weak early industrialization. The penultimate section shows that inequality rose in most of Latin America up to World War I, although it fell thereafter. The correlation between globalization and inequality is likely to have been

---

[3] Angus Maddison, *The World Economy. A Millennial Perspective* (Paris, 2001).

causal, not spurious. The final section offers a research agenda for the future.

DISTANCE, TRANSPORT REVOLUTIONS, AND WORLD MARKETS

In *The Tyranny of Distance*, Geoffrey Blainey showed how isolation shaped Australian history.[4] Early in the nineteenth century, distance isolated both Australia and Asia from Europe, where the industrial revolution was unfolding. Later in the nineteenth century, transport innovations began to erode the disadvantages of geographic isolation, although not completely. The completion of the Suez Canal, cost-reducing innovations on sea-going transport, and railroads penetrating the interior all helped liberate that part of the world from the tyranny of distance.[5]

Should this account regarding economic isolation apply to much of nineteenth-century Latin America as well? Before the completion of the Panama Canal in 1914, the Andean economies – Chile, Peru, and Ecuador – were seriously disadvantaged in European trade. And prior to the introduction of an effective railroad network, the landlocked countries of Bolivia and Paraguay were at an even more serious disadvantage. This was also true of the Mexican interior, the Argentine interior, the Colombian interior, and elsewhere.[6] Thus, the economic distance to the European core varied considerably depending on location in Latin America. A close observer of early nineteenth-century Latin America, Belford Hinton Wilson, reported in 1842 the cost of moving a ton of goods from England to the following capital cities (in pounds sterling): Buenos Aires and Montevideo, 2; Lima, 5.12; Santiago, 6.58; Caracas, 7.76; Mexico City, 17.9; Quito, 21.3; Sucre or

---

[4] Geoffrey Blainey, *The Tyranny of Distance: How Distance Shaped Australia's History* (Melbourne, rev. 1982 ed.)

[5] This focus is certainly consistent with the new economic geography. See Paul Krugman, *Geography and Trade* (Cambridge, 1991); Paul Krugman and Anthony Venables, "Integration and the Competitiveness of Peripheral Industry," in C. Bliss and J. Braga de Macedo, eds., *Unity with Diversity in the European Community* (Cambridge, 1990); John Luke Gallup and Jeffrey Sachs, "Geography and Economic Development," in Boris Pleskovic and Joseph E. Stiglitz, eds., *Annual World Bank Conference on Development Economics, 1998* (Washington, DC, 1999); Damen Acemoglu, Simon Johnson, and James Robinson, "The Colonial Origins of Comparative Development: An Empirical Investigation," *American Economic Review* 91 (December, 2001): 1369–401.

[6] John Coatsworth, *Growth Against Development: The Economic Impact of Railroads in Porfirian Mexico* (Dekalb, IL, 1981); Carlos Newland, "Economic Development and Population Change: Argentina 1810–1870," in John Coatsworth and Alan Taylor, eds., *Latin America and the World Economy Since 1800* (Cambridge, MA, 1998); José Antonio Ocampo, "Una breve historia cafetera de Colombia, 1830–1938," in A. Machado Cartagena, ed., *Miniagricultura 80 años. Transformaciones en la estructura agraria* (Bogotá, 1994), 185–8.

Chuquisaca, 25.6; and Bogotá, 52.9. The range was huge, with the costs to Bogotá, Chuquisaca, Mexico City, Quito, and Sucre nine to twenty-seven times that of Buenos Aires and Montevideo, both well placed on either side of the Rio de la Plata.[7] Furthermore, and as Leandro Prados has pointed out elsewhere in this volume, most of the difference in transport costs from London to Latin American capital cities was the overland freight from the Latin American port to the interior capital.

Distance, geography, and access to foreign markets explained a third of the world's variation in per capita income as late as 1996.[8] Not surprisingly, therefore, geographic isolation helped explain much of the economic ranking of Latin American republics in 1870, too, with poor countries most isolated: Argentina and Uruguay at the top; Cuba and Mexico next; Colombia and southeast Brazil third; and Peru, Ecuador, Bolivia, and Paraguay at the bottom. Of course, there were other factors at work, too, like institutions, demography, slavery, and luck in world commodity markets. After all, Potosí was a very rich colonial enclave in spite of its relative isolation, and the Brazilian Northeast was very poor in spite of its favorable location vis-à-vis European markets. Still, geography played a huge role.

The most populated areas under colonial rule were the highlands. The Andean capital cities and Mexico City were far from accessible harbors, thus increasing transport costs to big foreign markets. This was the case of Bogotá, Quito, Santiago, La Paz, and even Caracas, the latter located near the coast but with difficult harbor access. In contrast, the Latin American regions bordering on the Atlantic, with long coastlines and good navigable river systems, have always been favored (although Spanish colonial policy often served to diminish those natural advantages). These include Argentina, Uruguay, Brazil, Cuba, and the other Caribbean islands. These nations may have failed for other reasons, but geographic isolation certainly wasn't one of them. The harbors were more conveniently located in relation to the lowlands that were suitable for tropical agriculture, as was the case for sugar, coffee, tobacco, cacao, rubber, and other tropical products. The main constraint to expansion facing those land-abundant regions was access to labor, not geography, and access to foreign markets. Slavery was the most common solution to the problem along Colombia's Caribbean

---

[7] David Brading, "Un análisis comparativo del costo de la vida en diversas capitales de hispanoamérica," *Boletín Histórico de la Fundación John Boulton* 20 (March 1969): 229–63.

[8] Stephen Redding and Anthony J. Venables, "Economic Geography and International Inequality" (CEPR Discussion Paper 2568); Henry G. Overman, Stephen Redding, and Anthony J. Venables, "The Economic Geography of Trade, Production, and Income: A Survey of Empirics" (unpublished paper, London School of Economics, August 2001).

coast, in the lowlands of Ecuador near Guayaquil, in the Peruvian coast near El Callao, in the Caribbean, and, of course, in Brazil.

Prior to the railway era, transportation was either by road or water, with water being the cheaper option by far. Thus, investment in river and harbor improvements increased everywhere in the Atlantic economy. Steamships were the most important contribution to nineteenth-century shipping technology, and they increasingly worked the rivers and inland lakes. In addition, a regular trans-Atlantic steam service was inaugurated in 1838, but it must be said that until 1860, steamers mainly carried high-value goods similar to those carried by airplanes today, like passengers, mail, and gourmet food.

The switch from sail to steam may have been gradual, but it accounted for a steady decline in transport costs across the Atlantic.[9] A series of innovations in subsequent decades helped make steamships more efficient: the screw propeller, the compound engine, steel hulls, bigger size, and shorter turn-around time in port. Before 1869, steam tonnage had never exceeded sail tonnage in British shipyards; by 1870, steam tonnage was more than twice as great as sail, and sail tonnage only exceeded steam tonnage in two years after that date.

Refrigeration was another technological innovation with major trade implications. Mechanical refrigeration was developed between 1834 and 1861, and by 1870, chilled beef was being transported from the United States to Europe. In 1876, the first refrigerated ship, the *Frigorifique*, sailed from Argentina to France carrying frozen beef. By the 1880s, South American meat was being exported in large quantities to Europe. Not only did railways and steamships mean that European farmers were faced with overseas competition in the grain market, but refrigeration also deprived them of the natural protection distance had always provided local meat and dairy producers. The consequences for European farmers of this overseas competition were profound.[10]

Transport cost declines from interior to port, and from port to Europe or to the East and Gulf coasts of the United States, ensured that Latin America became more integrated into world markets. The size of the decline around the Atlantic economy can be seen graphically in Figure 1.1. What is labeled the North index accelerates its fall after the 1830s, and what is labeled

---

[9] C. Knick Harley, "Ocean Freight Rates and Productivity, 1740–1913: The Primacy of Mechanical Invention Reaffirmed," *Journal of Economic History* 48 (December 1988): 851–76.

[10] Kevin O'Rourke, "The European Grain Invasion, 1870–1913," *Journal of Economic History* 57 (December 1997): 775–801.

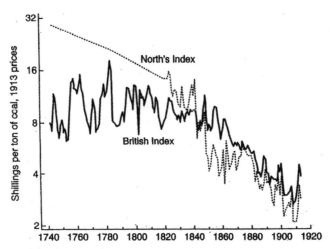

Figure 1.1. Real freight rate indexes: 1741–1913.
Source: C. Knick Harley, "Ocean Freight Rates and Productivity, 1740–1913: The Primacy of Mechanical Invention Reaffirmed," *Journal of Economic History* 48 (December 1988), Figure 1, p. 853.

the British index is fairly stable up to mid-century before undergoing the same, big fall.[11] The North freight rate index among American export routes dropped by more than 41 percent in real terms between 1870 and 1910. The British index fell by about 70 percent, again in real terms, between 1840 and 1910. These two indexes imply a steady decline in Atlantic-economy transport costs of about 1.5 percent per annum, for a total of 45 percentage points up to 1913. One way to get a comparative feel for the magnitude of this decline is to note that tariffs on manufactures entering Organization for Economic Cooperation and Development (OECD) markets fell from 40 percent in the late 1940s to 7 percent in the late 1970s, a 33 percentage point decline over thirty years. This spectacular postwar reclamation of free trade from interwar autarky is still smaller than the 45 percentage point fall in trade barriers between 1870 and 1913 caused by overseas transport improvements. Furthermore, the role of railroads was probably more important. For example, between 1870 and 1913, freight rates in Uruguay fell annually by 0.7 percent on overseas routes but by 3.1 percent along the

[11] Douglass North, "Ocean Freight Rates and Economic Development 1750–1913," *Journal of Economic History* 18 (December 1958): 538–55; C. Knick Harley, "Ocean Freight Rates and Productivity, 1740–1913."

railroads penetrating the interior, four times as much.[12] Railroads were vital in developing exports, but they also served to integrate the domestic market.

Although impressive, it is important to note that the impact of the transport revolution on freight rates was unequal along different routes. As Juan Oribe Stemmer has shown, overseas freight rates fell much less along the southward leg than along the northward leg, and the drop along the latter does not seem to have been as great as that for Asian and North Atlantic routes. The difference may have a great deal to do with the degree of competition among carriers and the role of shipping conferences in setting freight rates. In any case, the northward leg was for the bulky Latin American staple exports – like beef, wheat, and guano, the high-volume, low-value primary products whose trade gained so much by the transport revolution. The southward leg was for Latin American imports – like textiles and machines, the high-value, low-volume manufactures whose trade gained much less from the transport revolution.[13]

Still, these transport innovations significantly lowered the cost of moving goods between markets, an event that should have fostered trade. And trade certainly boomed in Latin America. The share of Latin American exports in GDP was around 10 percent in 1850; in 1912, it was 25 percent. Still, the volume of trade is not, by itself, a very satisfactory index of commodity market integration. It is the cost of moving goods between markets that counts. The cost has two parts, that attributable to transport and that attributable to man-made trade barriers (such as tariffs). The price spread between markets is driven by changes in these costs, and they need not move in the same direction. It turns out that tariffs in the Atlantic economy did not fall from the 1870s to World War I. Instead, it was falling transport costs that provoked globalization. Indeed, rising tariffs in Europe were mainly a defensive response to the competitive winds of market integration as transport costs declined. We shall see subsequently that the rise in tariffs was even greater for Latin America.

It might be well to repeat this fact: although the first global century was certainly more "liberal" than the autarky that followed after 1914, it was still a period of retreat from openness. Yet, the decline in international transport

---

[12] Luis Bértola, *Ensayos de historia económica: Uruguay y la región en la economía mundial, 1870–1990* (Montevideo, 2000), 102.

[13] Juan E. Oribe Stemmer, "Freight Rates in the Trade between Europe and South America," *Journal of Latin American Studies* 21:1 (February 1989): 23–59. On the ensuing trade boom, see Victor Bulmer-Thomas, *The Economic History of Latin America Since Independence*, 2nd ed. (Cambridge, 2003), 394.

costs overwhelmed the retreat from free trade, thus accommodating the trade boom between center and periphery.

RESOURCE ENDOWMENTS, SPECIALIZATION, AND TRADE

ARE ENDOWMENTS FATE?

This question has motivated much of the Latin American historiography in the last four decades. Do factor endowments best explain the per capita income gaps within the region exhibited at the beginning of the first global century? Do they best explain why the gaps increased thereafter?

In his survey for *The Cambridge History of Latin America*, William Glade offered a concise overview of Latin American diversity: between 1870 and 1914, Latin America not only exhibited increasing regional differentiation but also evolved quite a different endowment of factors of production, thanks to the demand-induced (but not solely demand-constrained) development of the period. The resource patterns that underlay the region's economies on the eve of the First World War differed notably from those on which the economic process rested at the outset of the period.[14] Glade adopted an intermediate position between two conflicting approaches to understanding Latin American development. He used the dual-economy approach to describe how the sources of economic transformation were first limited to enclaves exhibiting market-oriented production. As time went on, foreign demand, the transport revolution, and the integration of domestic factor markets made the within-country institutional topography more uniform. Countries where the transformation was incomplete by World War I were ones where the original size of the export sector was small, or where the export sector had limited capacity to replace traditional with capitalist institutions elsewhere in the economy, or both. Thus, incomplete transformation is explained by weak diffusion between sectors.

A group of revisionists argue, on the contrary, that this dual-economy approach fails to give play to important forces that may have suppressed or even reversed diffusion. Instead, these revisionists emphasize that increased market-oriented production often strengthened coercive

---

[14] William Glade, "Latin America and the International Economy, 1870–1914," in Leslie Bethell, ed., *The Cambridge History of Latin America*, vol. 4 (Cambridge, 1986), 46–7.

antimarket relationships rather than weakening them. Exactly how these forces evolved depended on initial endowments and related institutions. Different typologies have been proposed, in which endowments and institutions are assigned varying levels of importance but in which globalization always has a powerful influence on outcomes. There are three camps: those who see the causality as running from institutions to endowments; those who see the causality as running from endowments to institutions; and those eclectics who see a two-way causality.

Among the eclectics, Celso Furtado stands out. He suggested it might be useful to think in terms of three Latin American regions: (1) scarcely populated countries of temperate climate exporting goods similar to those produced in Europe, offering an overseas frontier where high wages attracted free labor; (2) traditional societies specializing in tropical agrarian products that were labor-intensive, the prices of which were relatively low compared with imports, and the wages in which were even lower; and (3) countries exporting minerals, the production of which experienced important productivity improvements that, however, were limited to enclaves controlled by foreign firms. The main institutional aspects considered in this typology are the concentration and nationality of property ownership, the existence of coercive mechanisms for extracting labor, the extent of the market, and the attitudes toward technical change. Osvaldo Sunkel and Pedro Paz added more institutional variables to the typology and Fernando Cardoso and Enzo Faletto extended the approach even further: to them, economic performance was mainly dependent on whether the ownership of natural resources was in the hands of numerous domestic agents – like land in the Río de la Plata area – or in the hands of a few foreign firms – like minerals in the Andean and Mexican regions.[15] For these eclectics, the implications for workers' living standards, economic diversification, and inequality were profound.

Institutional determinists criticized the eclectics from a Marxist point of view. Thus, Augustin Cueva insisted that the persistence of pre-capitalist relations limited the extension of free labor, which, in turn, determined whether high wages, expanding domestic markets, and rapid technical change would emerge.[16] Cardoso and Pérez Brignoli also contributed to this institutional-determinist critique, with a typology very similar to Furtado's: (1) the development of capitalism in new settler economies;

[15] Osvaldo Sunkel and Pedro Paz, *El subdesarrollo latinoamericano y la teoría del desarrollo* (Mexico City, 1970), 321–43; Fernando Cardoso and Enzo Faletto, *Dependency and Development in Latin America* (Berkeley, 1979).
[16] Agustin Cueva, *El desarrollo del capitalismo en América Latina*, 2nd ed. (Mexico City, 1977).

(2) the transition to capitalism in the Andean and Mesoamerican economies that evolved differently because of an initial environment created by the interaction between European feudalism and native institutions; and (3) the transition to capitalism in market-oriented slave economies.[17] The institutional determinists have swollen in numbers with the recent addition of some notable North American scholars. Indeed, Douglass North, William Summerhill, and Barry Weingast,[18] as well as David Landes,[19] have adopted the new institutional economics to explain why Latin American performance differed so much from that of North America. The legacy of colonial institutions, weak property rights, political decentralization, and political instability are the main variables thought to affect growth. Factor endowments play a secondary role for the institutional determinists. Thus, Robinson argues that similar resource endowments, organized in different ways in terms of concentration of wealth and income, have produced very different outcomes in terms of human capital accumulation, technical change, and, thus, economic performance.

Recently, Stanley Engerman and Kenneth Sokoloff have made an important contribution to the endowment determinist literature.[20] They argue that various features of the factor endowments of the three categories of New World economies, including soil, climate, and the size or density of the native population, may have predisposed those colonies toward paths of development associated with different degrees of inequality in wealth, human capital, and political power, as well as with different potentials for economic growth. Even if, later on, institutions may ultimately affect the evolution of factor endowments, the initial conditions with respect to factor endowments had long, lingering effects. The three-economy typology offered by Engerman and Sokoloff is exactly the same as that advanced by Furtado some thirty years before, but the causality is different. Tropical crops, like sugar, are more efficiently cultivated in large estates, thus favoring property concentration. Given scarce native population in those regions, African labor was supplied through slave trade, with a highly unequal income distribution emerging as an outcome. The production of grains in

---

[17] Ciro Flamarion Cardoso and Hector Pérez Brignoli, *Historia económica de américa latina*, vol. 3 (Barcelona, 1979).

[18] Douglass C. North, William Summerhill, and Barry Weingast, "Order, Disorder and Economic Change: Latin America vs. North America," In Bruce Bueno de Mesquita and Hilton Root, eds., *Governing for Prosperity* (New Haven, CT, 2000).

[19] David Landes, *The Wealth and Poverty of Nations* (New York, 1998).

[20] Stanley Engerman and Kenneth Sokoloff, "Factor Endowments, Institutions, and Differential Paths of Growth Among New World Economies: A View from Economic Historians of the United States," in Stephen Haber, ed., *How Latin America Fell Behind* (Stanford, 1997).

new settler societies, on the contrary, never revealed economies of scale, thus favoring a more equal society dominated by small and medium-size holders. The Andean and Mesoamerican regions were characterized by substantial native populations and a privileged few who controlled the services of land, mineral resources, and native labor. These mineral-based regions seem similar to tropical regions, in the sense that both generated an economic structure where large enterprises dominated and substantial inequality resulted. Nevertheless, the explanations for the development of large estates are mainly institutional, and they have their roots in pre-Colombian and colonial experience. In any case, Engerman and Sokoloff's great contribution is to emphasize how different societies with different initial endowments yielded different distributions of income, human capital, and political power, all of which then influenced the extent of the market, the development of institutions conducive to widespread commercialization, technological change, and growth.

Victor Bulmer-Thomas also deserves an important place in this discussion.[21] Like many others, he considers international demand to have been the dynamic force during the belle époque. Differences in performance across Latin America arose mainly from the relation between natural resource endowments, export specialization, and world demand, or what has come to be called the commodity lottery, an idea developed previously by Carlos Díaz-Alejandro. Given the connection between international demand and prices, on the one hand, and natural endowments and export specialization, on the other, economic performance should have been strongly influenced by the luck of the draw in this commodity lottery. Thus, the performance of the export sector depended in large part on demand booms and the price elasticity of demand. Economy-wide performance depended, in turn, on the relative size of the export sector and the extent to which the export boom spilled over into the domestic sector.

The commodity lottery is fine as far as it goes, but labor market institutions also have a profound impact on the export supply response and on the size of any spillover to other sectors. Bulmer-Thomas treats the whole region as labor scarce, and to deal with labor-scarcity issues he believes institutional explanations are essential.[22] For him, highly concentrated natural

---

[21] Victor Bulmer-Thomas, *The Economic History of Latin America Since Independence*, chs. 3–5.

[22] This view is not shared by some scholars, most notably Carlos Díaz-Alejandro, *Essays on the Economic History of the Argentine Republic* (New Haven, CT, 1970); W. Arthur Lewis, *The Evolution of the International Economic Order* (Princeton, NJ, 1978); and Stanley Engerman and Kenneth Sokoloff, "Factor Endowments, Institutions, and Differential Paths of Growth."

resource ownership made it politically possible to impose a labor market solution that relied on nonmarket authoritarian coercion. This strategy implied technological stagnation because there was little incentive to increase labor productivity, and it had a deleterious impact on aggregate economic performance in those parts of Latin America that used it.

DIFFERENT ENDOWMENTS, WORLD MARKETS, AND DIFFERENT PATTERNS OF DEVELOPMENT

Natural Resources

With each export specialization came market characteristics that mattered to performance. Income elasticity of demand mattered, beef offering an example of high income elasticity during the first global century, thus favoring Argentina and Uruguay. The ability of petrochemical technologies to find ways to replace expensive natural resources with cheap synthetics mattered. Chemical fertilizers displacing guano offers a good example, thus disfavoring Peru. Market structure and monopoly power mattered. For most of the nineteenth century, Brazilian coffee had a monopolistic position that allowed the state to impose export taxes and to raise prices (and revenue) by restricting supply. Similarly, Chile had a near monopoly on the mineral production of nitrates, which allowed the state to tax exports without losing its market share. In contrast, Río de la Plata was simply another entrant in the competitive world cattle market, and exporters were price-takers. Most tropical products faced competitive international markets, like cotton (Brazil and Mexico) and tobacco (Cuba). However, sugar cane offers a special tropical product case: not only did it compete with other tropical regions, but it also had to compete with the European beet root production, a situation that provoked a secular decline in the terms of trade facing northeast Brazil and Cuba.

Primary-product export supply depended on many complementary processes. We have already talked about how the transport revolution reduced the cost of moving goods so much that relatively isolated regions suddenly found themselves integrated into the global economy. In some cases, natural resources that had previously lain idle were now exploited as the frontier extended. Northern Mexico, the Río de la Plata, the Amazonia, and several other tropical regions had very low native population densities, and the expansion of the export sector obeyed the general laws of frontier economies unfolding the world around. This frontier case was less common in Latin America where indigenous populations had already extensively

intermediate position (1.8%), and the more temperate lowland settler economies grew fastest (2.8%). As a consequence, the lowlands, mainly those near the Atlantic coast, increased their share in total Latin American population from 44 to 70 percent between 1850 and 1930, with a corresponding contraction of the population share for the highlands. This population shift reveals the dramatic impact of nineteenth- and twentieth-century globalization as it broke down colonial population distributions and pulled population down to the booming export sectors supplying world markets from the lowlands and the Atlantic coast.

From central Chile to central Mexico, there existed huge concentrations of labor that were mobilized through different means in order to meet the demands of the new market-oriented production. Wages were very low in the Andean highlands and, thus, so were European immigration rates. The native population of the tropical lowlands did not easily adapt to plantation work, nor was it large enough to meet the requirements of this kind of export-led production. The population of the Latin American highlands may have been closer to these tropical regions – like Peru, Ecuador, and even Yucatán – but those native populations were not able to survive the climatic conditions of the tropical lowlands. Thus, the tropical regions eased labor scarcity by importing African slaves from the sixteenth to nineteenth centuries. After suppression of the slave trade in the 1840s and eventual abolition of slavery, some countries turned to low-wage Asian workers under labor contracts, often working under conditions of limited personal freedom. Tropical products were produced by low-wage tropical regions throughout the world. Table 1.3 shows that 47 percent came from low-wage tropical Latin America and 70 percent from the low-wage tropical world more generally. Thus, the attraction of free labor to tropical Latin America was not a viable strategy because high labor costs would have priced them out of world product markets. In Brazil, for instance, four million African slaves were introduced in 1531–1855, of which 2.1 million arrived after 1781, and by the mid-nineteenth century, more than half the Brazilian population was black. The labor market liberalized after the abolition of slavery in 1889, but the subsequent low wages and inequality have been long-enduring features of Brazilian society since then.

The labor supply was completely different in the temperate lowlands of the Atlantic coast. These relatively empty areas were flooded by millions of European immigrants producing temperate-climate products that could now reach world markets at competitive prices. According to Nicolás Sánchez-Albornoz, 8.4 million immigrants arrived in Argentina, Brazil, and

Table 1.3. *Structure of world production of exports of primary products between Latin America and high-income or low-income competitors: 1913*

	Latin America	High income	Low income	Total
Settler regions (based on world exports)				
Wool	20	67	12	100
Cattle	30	51	18	100
Linseed	42	34	24	100
Maize	43	53	4	100
Wheat	15	76	10	100
Wheat flour	6	86	6	98
Average	26	61	12	100
Tropical regions (based on world exports)				
Sugar	29	39	27	95
Cacao	42	10	34	86
Rubber	34	39	25	98
Coffee	82	12	5	99
Average	47	25	23	95
Highland regions (based on world production)				
Copper	9	84	7	100
Tin	20	10	70	100
Silver	38	59	3	100
Gold	17	37	46	100
Lead	5	93	2	100
Nitrates	97	3		100
Average	31	48	26	100

Notes: High-income competitors: Europe, United States, Canada, and Australasia. Low-income competitors: Asia and Africa. All averages are unweighted.

Source: Latin America data from Victor Bulmer-Thomas, *The Economic History of Latin America Since Independence*, 2nd ed. (Cambridge, 2003), Table 6.3.

Uruguay between 1881 and 1930, and the foreign born were a very large share of population in these countries.[25] The structure of world markets for these kinds of temperate-climate exports is also shown in Table 1.3. The contrast with tropical-climate exports is striking: 61 percent of the temperate-climate world exports were supplied by high-income countries,

[25] Nicholás Sánchez-Albornoz, "The Population of Latin America, 1850–1930," in Leslie Bethell, ed., *The Cambridge History of Latin America*, vol. 4 (Cambridge, 1986).

and 26 percent by Latin America (mainly the southern cone). Low-wage regions played a marginal role in Latin America and the rest of the world. As the tyranny of distance weakened, the southern cone was offered a way into the core, a process by which the frontier penetrated even more fertile lands, not less. As an outcome, wages in the region were higher than those in the European countries from whence the immigrants came. Thus, the labor market in these regions behaved quite differently from those of the tropical and highland parts of Latin America, both with respect to wage levels and with respect to their institutional features.

COMPARING THE OUTCOMES

When looking at the performance of different Latin American countries, it is useful to keep in mind that the nation-states created after independence often covered more than one region. Brazil offers the best example, but almost all large countries show a huge variety of climates and natural resource endowments within their borders. Still, national-level analysis offers suggestive insights.

One of the more striking facts is that economic differences among Latin America countries were greater near the end of this global era than at the beginning, as we noted in the first section. Both in terms of per capita GDP and real wages, the gap between rich and poor Latin American nations widened. Consistent with those forces of divergence, the settler economy (Argentina, southeast Brazil, and Uruguay) share in total Latin American population rose from 11 to 30 percent between 1870 and 1930 (see Table 1.2). The share of the highlands (Colombia, Mexico, Peru, et al.) fell from 61 to 44 percent over the same period.

What about exports? Latin American export performance was impressive between 1850 and World War I, growing at an annual rate of 3.5 percent. Yet there were huge differences in the level of per capita exports between the settler, tropical, and highland areas (see Table 1.4): per capita exports in the settler countries were twice that of the tropical countries in 1912 and more than four times that of highland countries. Settler countries benefited by having large land areas and small populations, but there are other likely explanations for these huge differences in per capita exports. To repeat one mentioned previously, Latin American settler country exports were competing with those of developed countries and, as marginal producers, they took a relatively high market price as given. In contrast, the price of tropical exports was set in a labor market affected by the after-effects

Table 1.4. *Exports per capita in U.S. dollars: three-year averages*

	1870	1912	Increment
Settler regions	32	56	78
Tropical regions	15	28	90
Highland regions	7	13	81
Latin America	9	20	129
Australia	63	87	37
Canada	20	52	160
New Zealand	97	99	2
United States	10	25	150
Average above four	40	57	42

Source: Estimates on the basis of national data provided by Victor Bulmer-Thomas, *The Economic History of Latin America Since Independence*, 2nd ed. (Cambridge, 2003), Table 3.5.

of slavery, by other forms of coercion, and by an elastic supply of Asian contract labor after abolition (implying a low and fixed reservation wage). Accordingly, W. Arthur Lewis argued that productivity gains were passed on to consumers abroad in the form of low and falling prices.[26] Note, however, that although export levels differed across Latin America, their rates of expansion up to 1912 were remarkably similar.

HOW INDEPENDENCE AND CONFLICT CAUSED DEGLOBALIZATION

In young, recently independent economies with low capacity to tax, few bureaucratic resources to implement efficient collection, and limited access to foreign capital markets, customs revenues are an easy-to-collect source of revenues essential to support central government expenditures on infrastructure and defense. This was certainly true of the newly independent United States. It was even more true for a Latin America beset in the first half of the nineteenth century with the collapse of the colonial fiscal system, civil wars, and violent border disputes. Nor did Latin America have access to European capital markets until later in the century, an event that

[26] W. Arthur Lewis, *The Evolution of the International Economic Order* (Princeton, NJ, 1978).

would have eased the need for tax revenues in the short run. The average share of customs duties in total revenues across eleven of the Latin American republics was 57.8 percent between 1820 and 1890.[27] Customs revenues were even more important for federal governments (65.6%) because local and state governments that form a union typically are reluctant to give up their limited tax weapons. Furthermore, customs revenues are especially important for land-abundant economies because they do not have the population and taxpayer density to make other forms of tax collection efficient. Now, add to this a huge revenue needed to fight wars and we get the high United States civil war tariffs in the early 1860s and the high (and rising) tariffs in a newly independent Latin America that experienced almost continuous war and civil strife between the 1820s and the 1870s.

David Mares reports ten major Latin American wars between 1825 and 1879.[28] Miguel Centeno has counted thirty-three major international and civil wars between 1819 and 1880. Argentina, Brazil, Chile, Cuba, Mexico, Peru, and Uruguay all fought at least two major wars between independence and 1880. Only Brazil and Chile (after 1830) avoided violent military coups. Practically all of Latin America experienced episodes of massive and prolonged civil strife. In six countries, internal civil wars raged more or less continuously for decades after independence.

The universal preoccupation with national defense and internal power struggles pushed the newly independent Latin American countries toward higher revenue-maximizing tariffs. Military expenditures quickly rose to consume over 70 percent and often more than 90 percent of all revenues.[29] Weak governments, under attack from within and without, abandoned internal taxes that required an extensive and loyal bureaucracy and concentrated instead on tax collection at a few ports and mines. The ratio of tariff revenues to imports, a proxy for protection of the import-competing sector, rose in every country for which there are data, as did the customs revenues as a percentage of national government revenues.

In Brazil, the ratio of import duties to imports rose from 15 percent to nearly 30 percent by the 1860s, a rise that was fueled by costly wars with Uruguay, Argentina, and Paraguay as well as by frequent regional and separatist revolts, slave insurrections, and a massive social and racial upheaval in the Amazon region. Between 1821 and 1867, Mexico suffered foreign invasions by Spain, the United States, and France; the secession of

[27] Miguel Centeno, "Blood and Debt: War and Taxation in Nineteenth-Century Latin America," *American Journal of Sociology* 102 (May 1997): 1565–605.
[28] David Mares, *Violent Peace: Militarized Interstate Bargaining In Latin America* (New York, 2001).
[29] Miguel Centeno, "Blood and Debt: War and Taxation in Nineteenth-Century Latin America."

Texas; thirteen major regional revolts; and at least sixty peasant rebellions and indigenous caste wars.[30] Mexico's first tariff law in 1821 imposed a 25 percent ad valorem tariff on all imports. The tariff rate rose still further thereafter: it averaged 36 percent for the 1820s as a whole, then rose to 45 percent in the 1840s, and peaked at 46 percent in the 1870s and 1880s.[31] Argentine tariff policies followed the Brazil/Mexico example. The independence wars (in which Argentine armies invaded Bolivia and Chile), international conflicts, and blockades that followed all served to push tariff rates upward. Colombia offers another good example, where internal military conflicts occurred one fifth of the time between 1820 and 1879. Colombia initially adopted a moderate tariff regime with duties set at their colonial levels of approximately 20 percent. Tariff rates oscillated higher thereafter, rising sharply when trade revenues fell off in 1830–3 and again in 1847, each time followed by modest declines. The Liberal Revolution of 1849–52 raised tariff rates twice: between 1849 and 1905, ad valorem rates on cheap cotton textiles ranged from 43 to 110 percent.

International and internal warfare both appear to have played a major role in pushing the newly independent states toward very high tariffs designed to maximize fiscal revenues. Between 1820 and 1870, the fiscal imperative of Latin America's endemic military conflicts swamped all other preoccupations. We will return to this issue subsequently when we explore the persistence of these tariff policies after 1870, when pax latina americana became the rule.

High tariffs weren't the only way that independence induced deglobalization in the young Latin American republics. Perhaps most important was the collapse of the de facto customs union under colonial rule. To the extent that the colonial umbrella fostered trade and factor mobility within the region, all of those gains were lost after independence created so many small republics, a veritable balkanization of Latin America.[32] We simply do not know how large those losses were, just as we do not know how large the gains were to a United States after its successful revolution, independence, and sustained unification. Probably far less favorable geography would have

---

[30] John Coatsworth, "Patterns of Rural Rebellion in Latin America: Mexico in Comparative Perspective," in Friedrich Katz, ed., *Riot, Rebellion, and Revolution: Rural Social Conflict in Mexico* (Princeton, NJ, 1988).

[31] Edward Beatty, *Institutions and Investment: The Political Basis of Industrialization Before 1911* (Stanford, 2001), 53.

[32] The idea of balkanization has played an important role in the literature on nineteenth-century Latin America. In contrast with some visionary United States of Latin America, there appeared instead many small post-independence nation-states. See, for example, Tulio Halperin Donghi, "Economy and Society in Post-Independence Spanish America," in Leslie Bethell, ed., *The Cambridge History of Latin America*, vol. 3, *From Independence to c. 1870* (Cambridge, 1985).

Of course, country experience varied. Whereas the terms of trade boomed for Argentina, Brazil, and Colombia up to the late 1860s, they rose much more modestly for Mexico and fell dramatically for Cuba. From the 1860s to the 1890s, the terms of trade rose for Brazil, Colombia, Cuba, and the southern cone but fell for Mexico and Peru. After the 1890s, and long before the interwar world economic disaster, the terms of trade fell throughout Latin America. True, the collapse was less pronounced for the southern cone, specializing in temperate-climate primary products, than it was for the others, specializing in mining or tropical primary products.

In short, global market forces were, in general, good for Latin American exports over most of the nineteenth century but bad for Latin American exports over the first half of the twentieth century. What about growth? All economists agree that such terms of trade improvements must have contributed to a rise in income over the short run. We are far less certain about the long run. Indeed, Hans Singer argued that terms of trade improvements for primary-product exporters might, in the long run, contribute to slow growth, and modern development theory usually argues the same.[35] After all, the stimulus to the primary-product-producing export sector is likely to cause deindustrialization or at least industrial slow-down and, to the extent that industry carries modern economic growth, an aggregate growth slow-down is quite possible. The jury is still out on this issue.[36]

WHY WERE TARIFFS SO HIGH DURING THE BELLE ÉPOQUE?

Figure 1.3 plots average world tariffs before World War II, and Figure 1.4 plots them for various world regions. There are six plotted there – the United States, European core, European periphery, European non-Latin offshoots, Asia, and Latin America, and both figures offer some big surprises. Note first the protectionist drift worldwide between 1865 and World War I, a globalization backlash if you will, registering a slow retreat from the liberal and pro-global trade positions in mid-century. The traditional literature written by European economic historians has made much of the tariff

---

[35] Hans Singer, "The Distribution of Gains between Investing and Borrowing Countries."

[36] Although the issue is not yet resolved, recent historical evidence suggests that Singer was right. Christopher Blattman, Jason Hwang, and Jeffrey G. Williamson, "The Impact of the Terms of Trade on Economic Development in the Periphery, 1870–1939: Volatility and Secular Change," NBER Working Paper 10600, National Bureau of Economic Research, Cambridge, MA (June 2004).

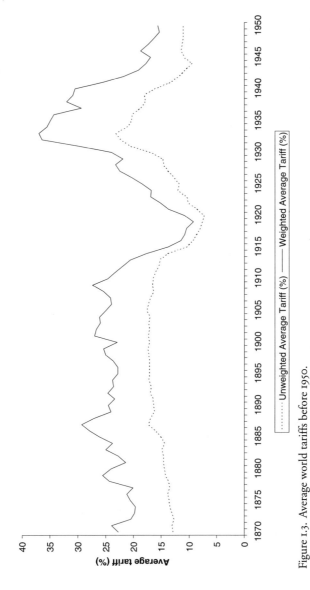

Figure 1.3. Average world tariffs before 1950.

Source: John H. Coatsworth and Jeffrey G. Williamson, "The Roots of Latin American Protectionism: Looking Before the Great Depression" in Antoni Estevadeordal et al., eds., *Integrating the Americas: FTAA and Beyond* (Cambridge, MA, 2004), Figure 2.1, p. 39.

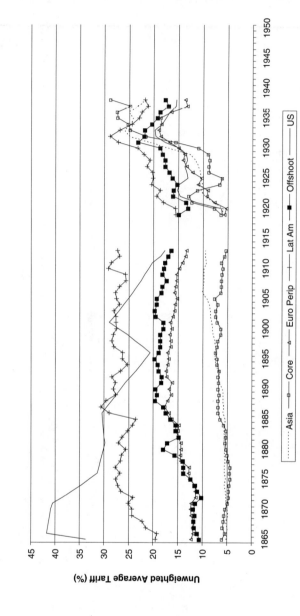

Figure 1.4. Unweighted average of regional tariffs before 1939.
Source: John H. Coatsworth and Jeffrey G. Williamson, "The Roots of Latin American Protectionism: Looking Before the Great Depression" in Antoni Estevadeordal et al., eds., *Integrating the Americas: FTAA and Beyond* (Cambridge, MA, 2004), Figure 2.2, p. 39.

backlash on the continent after the 1870s.[37] Yet this continental move to protection is pretty minor compared with the rise in tariff rates over the same period in Latin America, and this for a region that has been said to have exploited the pre-1914 global boom so well.

The interwar surge to world protection is, of course, better known. The first leap was in the 1920s, which might be interpreted as a policy effort to return to the protection provided before the war. It might also be attributable to postwar deflation. Inflations and deflations seem to have influenced tariff rates in the 1910s, the 1920s, and some other times, a so-called specific-duty effect to which we return later in this section. The second interwar leap in tariff rates was, of course, in the 1930s, with aggressive beggar-my-neighbor policies reinforced by the specific-duty effect. Except for the two that had the highest prewar tariffs, Colombia and Uruguay, tariffs rose everywhere in Latin America. Still, for most Latin American countries, tariff rates rose to levels in the late 1930s that were no higher than they were in the belle époque.[38]

But note the really big fact in Figure 1.4. We are taught that the Latin American reluctance to go open in the late twentieth century was the product of the Great Depression and the delinking import substitution strategies that arose to deal with it.[39] Yet, by 1865, Latin America already had by far the highest tariffs in the world, with the exception of the United States. At the crescendo of the belle époque, Latin American tariffs were at their peak, and still well above the rest of the world.

Apparently, the famous export-led growth spurt in Latin America was consistent with enormous tariffs, even though the spurt might have been even faster without them. Latin American tariffs were still the world's highest in the 1920s, although the gap between Latin America and the rest had shrunk considerably. Oddly enough, it was in the 1930s that the rest of the world finally surpassed Latin America in securing the dubious distinction of being the most protectionist. By the 1950s, and when import-substituting

---

[37] Charles Kindleberger, "Group Behavior and International Trade," *Journal of Political Economy* 59 (February 1951): 30–46; Paul Bairoch, "European Trade Policy, 1815–1914," in Peter Mathias and Sidney Pollard, eds., *The Cambridge Economic History of Europe*, vol. 3 (Cambridge, 1989).

[38] Of course, quotas, exchange rate management, and other nontariff policy instruments served to augment the protectionist impact of tariff barriers far more in the 1930s than in the belle époque, when nontariff barriers were far less common.

[39] Carlos Díaz-Alejandro, "Latin America in the 1930s," in Rosemary Thorp, ed., *Latin America in the 1930s* (New York, 1984); Alan Taylor, "On the Costs of Inward-Looking Development: Price Distortions, Growth, and Divergence in Latin America," *Journal of Economic History* 58 (March 1998): 1–28.

industrialization (ISI) policies were flourishing, Latin American tariffs were actually lower than those in Asia and the European periphery.[40] Thus, whatever explanations are offered for the Latin American commitment to protection, we must search for its origin well before the Great Depression.

So, what was the political economy that determined Latin American tariff policy in the century before the end of the Great Depression? Before we search for answers, we need to confront the tariff-growth debate. About thirty years ago, Paul Bairoch argued that protectionist countries grew faster in the nineteenth century, not slower, as every economist has found for the late twentieth century.[41] Bairoch's pre-1914 evidence was mainly from the European industrial core, and he simply compared growth rates in protectionist and free-trade episodes. More recently, Kevin O'Rourke got the Bairoch finding again, this time using macroeconometric conditional analysis on ten countries in the pre-1914 Atlantic economy.[42]

These pioneering studies suggest that history offers a tariff-growth paradox that took the form of a regime switch somewhere between the start of World War I and the end of World War II: before the switch, high tariffs were associated with fast growth; after the switch, high tariffs were associated with slow growth. Was Latin America part of this paradox, or was it only an attribute of the industrial core? Recent work has shown that although high tariffs were associated with fast growth in the industrial core before World War II, they were not associated with fast growth in most of the periphery, including Latin America. Table 1.5 replicates the tariff-growth paradox. In columns (1) and (2), the estimated coefficient on the log of the tariff rate is 0.36 for 1875–1908 and 1.45 for 1924–34. Thus, and in contrast with late twentieth-century evidence, tariffs were associated with fast growth before 1939. But was this true worldwide, or was there instead an asymmetry between industrial economies in the core and primary producers in the periphery? Presumably, the high-tariff country has to have a big domestic market and has to be ready for industrialization, accumulation, and human capital deepening if the long-run tariff-induced dynamic effects are to offset the short-run gains from trade given up. Table 1.5 tests for asymmetry, and the hypothesis wins, especially in the pre–World War I decades for Latin

---

[40] This finding – higher levels of protection in Asia than in Latin America before the 1970s – is confirmed by Alan Taylor in "On the Costs of Inward-Looking Development," even when more comprehensive measures of protection and openness that include nontariff barriers are employed.

[41] Paul Bairoch, "Free Trade and European Economic Development in the 19th Century," *European Economic Review* 3 (November, 1972): 211–45.

[42] Kevin O'Rourke, "Tariffs and Growth in the Late 19th Century," *Economic Journal* 110 (April 2000): 456–83.

Table 1.5. *Tariff impact on GDP per capita growth by region*

Dependent variable:	Five-year overlapping average growth rate	
	(1) 1875–1908	(2) 1924–1934
ln GDP/capita	0.12	−0.86
	1.23	*−3.03*
ln own tariff	0.36	1.45
	2.28	*2.93*
(European Periphery dummy) × (ln tariff rate)	−0.53	−2.23
	−2.48	*−3.38*
(Latin America dummy) × (ln tariff rate)	−1.04	0.37
	−3.22	*0.33*
(Asia dummy) × (ln tariff rate)	0.20	−2.41
	0.79	*−3.56*
European Periphery dummy	1.12	5.63
	2.05	*3.14*
Latin America dummy	3.36	−2.51
	3.39	*−0.74*
Asia dummy	−0.50	4.18
	−0.95	*2.25*
Constant	−0.43	4.21
	−0.54	*1.41*
Country dummies?	No	No
Time dummies?	No	No
N	1,180	372
R-squared	0.0516	1.1091
Adj. R-squared	0.0451	0.0894

Note: t-statistics are in italics.
Source: John H. Coatsworth and Jeffrey G. Williamson, "The Roots of Latin American Protectionism: Looking Before the Great Depression," in Antoni Estevadeordal et al., eds., *Integrating the Americas: FTAA and Beyond* (Cambridge, MA, 2004), Table 2.1., p. 45.

America (0.36 + [−] 1.04 = −0.68). That is, protection was associated with fast growth in the European core and their English-speaking offshoots, but it was not associated with fast growth in the periphery. Indeed, high tariffs in Latin America were associated with slow growth before World War I.

The moral of the story is that although Latin American policymakers were certainly aware of the pro-protectionist infant-industry argument offered for *zollverein* Germany by Frederich List and for federalist United States by Alexander Hamilton, there is absolutely no evidence after the 1860s that would have supported those arguments for Latin America.[43] We must look elsewhere for plausible explanations for the exceptionally high tariffs in Latin America long before the Great Depression. One of the alternative explanations involves central government revenue needs. As a signal of things to follow, we simply note here that the causation in Table 1.5 could have gone the other way around. That is, Latin American countries achieving rapid GDP per capita growth would also have undergone faster growth in imports and other parts of the tax base, thus reducing the need for high tariff rates. And countries suffering slow growth would have had to keep high tariff rates to ensure adequate revenues.

So what explains those high Latin American tariffs in the belle époque?

REVENUE TARGETS AND OPTIMAL TARIFFS FOR REVENUE MAXIMIZATION

As Douglas Irwin has pointed out for the United States and as Bulmer-Thomas has pointed out for Latin America, the revenue-maximizing tariff hinges crucially on the price elasticity of import demand.[44] Tariff revenue can be expressed as $R = tpM$ where R is revenue, t is the average ad valorem tariff rate, p is the average price of imports, and M is the volume of imports. Assuming for the moment that the typical Latin American country took

[43] Victor Bulmer-Thomas, for example, argues that late nineteenth-century Latin American policy-makers were so aware (*The Economic History of Latin America Since Independence*, 2nd ed., 140). However, it is important to stress "late," because the use of protection specifically and consciously to foster industry does not appear to occur until the 1890s: e.g., Mexico by the early 1890s; Chile with its new tariff in 1897; Brazil in the 1890s; and Colombia in the early 1900s (influenced by the Mexican experience). True, Mexico saw some precocious efforts in the late 1830s and 1840s to promote modern industry, but these lapsed with renewed local and international warfare. So, the qualitative evidence suggests that domestic industry protection becomes a motivation for Latin American tariffs only in the late nineteenth century.

[44] Douglas Irwin, "Higher Tariffs, Lower Revenues? Analyzing the Fiscal Aspects of the Great Tariff Debate of 1888" (NBER Working Paper 6239, National Bureau of Economic Research, October 1997), 8–12; Victor Bulmer-Thomas, *The Economic History of Latin America Since Independence*, 138.

its import and export prices as given, then a little math lets us restate this expression as the change in tariff revenues $dR/dt = pM + (tp)dM/dt$. The revenue-maximizing tariff rate, t^*, is found by setting $dR/dt = 0$ (the peak of some Laffer Curve), in which case $t^* = -1/(1 + \eta)$, where η is the price elasticity of demand for imports. Irwin estimates the price elasticity to have been about -2.6 for the United States between 1869 and 1913.[45] If the price elasticity for Latin America was similar, say about -3, then the average tariff in Latin America would have been very high indeed, 50 percent.

Suppose instead that some Latin American government during the belle époque – riding on an export boom – had in mind some target revenue share in GDP ($R/Y = r$) and could not rely on foreign capital inflows to balance the current account (so $pM = X$), then $r = tpM/Y = tX/Y$. Clearly, if foreign exchange earnings from exports (and thus spent on imports) were booming (an event that could even be caused by a terms of trade boom, denoted here by a fall in p, the relative price of imports), the target revenue share could have been achieved at lower tariff rates. The bigger the export boom and the higher the resulting export share (X/Y), the lower the tariff rate.

So, did Latin American governments act as if they were meeting revenue targets? Holding everything else constant, did they lower tariff rates during world primary-product booms when export shares were high and rising, and did they raise them during world primary-product slumps? They did indeed. Furthermore, those countries that had better access to world capital markets had less short-run need for tariff revenues and had lower tariffs.

The Specific-Duty Effect

It has been argued that inflations and deflations have had a powerful influence on average tariff rates in the past. Import duties were typically specific until modern times, quoted as pesos per bale, yen per yard, or dollars per bag. Under specific duties, abrupt changes in price levels would change import values in the denominator but not the legislated duty in the numerator, thus producing big equivalent ad valorem or percentage rate changes. Thus, tariff rates fell sharply during the wartime inflations between 1914 and 1919 and between 1939 and 1947. Part of the rise in tariffs immediately after World War I was also attributable to postwar deflation and the partial

---

[45] Douglas Irwin, "Higher Tariffs, Lower Revenues? Analyzing the Fiscal Aspects of the Great Tariff Debate of 1888," 14.

attainment of prewar price levels. The price deflation after 1929 was even more spectacular, and it, too, served to raise tariff rates at least on duties that were still specific (import values now declining).

This specific-duty effect has been noted for prerevolutionary Mexico, belle époque Uruguay, and now we know it holds for Latin America as a whole.[46] Still, it cannot explain those relatively high and rising tariff rates in Latin America before World War I.

Strategic Trade Policy, the Terms of Trade and Tariffs

A well-developed theoretical literature on strategic trade policy predicts that nations have an incentive to inflate their own terms of trade with high tariffs, encouraging competitive tariff setting between trading partners. It turns out that most of Latin America faced far higher tariffs than anyone else because they traded with heavily protected countries like the United States and each other. So, did this hostile policy environment abroad trigger a like response at home? The answer is a definite yes, although this was far more important in the interwar years than the belle époque.

Deindustrialization Fears

If Latin American policymakers feared that globalization would induce local deindustrialization, they would have paid close attention to the competitive position of manufacturing at home relative to that abroad. The best indicator of foreign manufacturing's competitiveness would be its ability to drive down the relative price of manufactures in world markets through productivity advance. Thus, deindustrialization fears ought to have been manifested by a rise in Latin American tariff rates when the relative price of manufactures fell in world markets. Figure 1.2 suggests that there was much to fear before the mid-1890s because, relative to the price of Latin America's key primary-product exports, the price of manufactures fell dramatically in world markets. Another way of saying the same thing is that Latin America enjoyed a big improvement in its terms of trade: the price of Latin American primary products rose in world markets relative to manufactures. After 1895, the deindustrialization story changes since there was now nothing to fear: the terms of trade fell and the relative price of manufactures rose. The

---

[46] Graciela Márquez, "The Political Economy of Mexican Protectionism, 1868–1911" (Ph.D. dissertation, Harvard University, 2002), 307; Luis Bértola, *Ensayos de historia económica: Uruguay y la región en la economia mundial, 1870–1990*, chs. 6 and 7.

timing is puzzling because the qualitative literature often identifies a switch about that time in the motivation behind belle époque tariffs from revenue to industrial-protection goals. If deindustrialization fears were all there was to it, we should have seen a switch away from industrial-protection goals after the 1890s (there was less need to protect), not toward them.

The Tariff–Transport Cost Trade-off

Whatever the arguments for protection of manufacturing in the periphery, high transport costs on imports from one's trading partner are just as effective as high tariffs. When transport costs fall dramatically, the winds of competition thus created give powerful incentive to import-competing industries to lobby for more protection. Thus, there must have been plenty of incentive for manufacturing interests in the periphery to lobby for protection as the natural barriers afforded by transport costs melted away in the nineteenth century.

There are two reasons to doubt that the tariff–transport cost trade-off prevailed with the same power in Latin America as in Europe during its "grain invasion." First, and as we noted previously, although overseas freight rates along the northward routes carrying primary products to Europe from the coasts of Latin America followed world trends by collapsing after the 1840s, they fell much less along the southward leg carrying manufactures to Latin America.[47] Second, transport costs into the Latin American interior were much more important protective barriers for local manufacturers than were overseas transport costs. Thus, transport revolutions along the sea lanes connecting Latin America to Europe had far less to do with tariff responses than did investment in railroads at home.[48] Where and when railroads integrated the Latin American interior with the world economy, we see a protectionist response, apparently as import-competing industries successfully lobbied for protection from these new winds of competition.

The Stolper-Samuelson Theorem and Latin American Capitalists

Even if the motivation for Latin American tariffs lay with revenues or some other source, they were still protective. After all, tariffs served to twist relative prices in favor of import-competing sectors, thus suppressing

---

[47] Oribe Stemmer, "Freight Rates," 24.
[48] Luis Bértola, *Ensayos de historia económica*, ch. 4.

growth in the export sector and stimulating urban-based manufacturing. But was protection of manufacturing a central motivation for high tariffs in Latin America, especially after the export-led boom filled treasuries with new revenues that reduced debt service to manageable dimensions?

Ronald Rogowski has used the Stolper-Samuelson theorem to search for an alternative political economy explanation for those extraordinarily high tariffs during the belle époque.[49] Though their economies certainly varied in labor scarcity, every Latin American country faced relative capital scarcity and relative natural resource abundance. Thus, according to Stolper-Samuelson thinking, Latin American capitalists should have been looking to form protectionist coalitions as soon as belle époque peace and growth began to threaten them with freer trade. In most cases, they did not have to look far, either because they managed to dominate oligarchic regimes that excluded other interests, or because they readily found coalition partners willing to help, or both. Capitalists did not, however, look to labor for help. After all, most Latin American countries limited the franchise to a small minority of adult men until well into the twentieth century. Literacy and wealth requirements excluded most potential voters in virtually every country. Of course, nonvoters found other ways to express their interests, but, with few exceptions, restrictions on the adult male franchise did not fall until after 1930, when the votes of scarce labor began to count, just in time for the populists.

Growth, peace, and political stability in the late nineteenth century tended, therefore, to produce oligarchic governments in which urban capitalists – linked to external trade and finance – played a dominant role. In countries that specialized in exporting agricultural products, free-trading landowners formed the second dominant part of the governing oligarchy. Here, the standard view is that something much closer to free trade prevailed where domestic landowners must have dominated politics. Rogowski has argued, for example, that in contrast to the United States, Canada, New Zealand, and other frontier regions, landowners won in Latin America.[50] Rogowski appears to have gotten both the politics and tariff-policy outcome wrong. Four Latin American agricultural exporters – Argentina, Brazil, Colombia, and Uruguay – expanded export production in the late nineteenth century by putting new lands to the plough or modernizing and extending pastoral production (cattle and wool) for export. In backward

---

[49] Ronald Rogowski, *Commerce and Coalitions: How Trade Affects Domestic Political Alignments* (Princeton, NJ, 1989).
[50] Ronald Rogowski, *Commerce and Coalitions*, 47.

economies with high land–labor ratios, Rogowski argued that expanding trade should produce assertive, free-trading, landed interests pitted against defensive populist alliances of capitalists and workers. In all four of these frontier nations, however, tariff rates were substantially higher than in other world regions. Either Latin America's export-producing landowners had less political clout or weaker free-trade preferences than this account suggests. Or both.

Free-trading mineral export interests usually had less direct leverage in governmental decision making. In the case of the three mineral exporters (Mexico, Chile, and Peru), one might have expected mining interests to have allied themselves with powerful regional agricultural interests to lobby against protection. Yet, this did not happen. As we have seen, neither were agricultural exporters very effective in forging free-trade coalitions with other interests. Perhaps one reason why it didn't happen is that free traders might have had their enthusiasm tempered by the knowledge that government revenue had to be raised somehow, and one obvious alternative to the tariff – a tax on land – was abhorrent to the powerful *latifundistas*.[51]

In short, urban capitalists secured explicitly protectionist tariffs for existing and new industries beginning in the 1890s. They did so against weak opposition and in close collaboration with modernizing political elites. They did not yet need the populist coalitions that emerged in the interwar decades.

Policy Packages and Real Exchange Rate Trade-offs

Few policies are decided in isolation from others. Indeed, there were other ways that Latin American governments could have improved the competitive position of import-competing industries, if such protection was their goal, and they explored many of these alternatives in the 1930s and in the ISI years that followed. One powerful tool was manipulating the real exchange rate, something at which Mexico was adept before 1900.[52] When Latin American governments chose to go on the gold standard or to peg to a core currency, they got, in return, more stable real exchange rates and perhaps good advertising for foreign capital. However, they gave up protection via real exchange rate manipulation. The historical facts are consistent with the theory: countries that went on the gold standard raised tariffs.

---

[51] Victor Bulmer-Thomas, *The Economic History of Latin America Since Independence*, 137–8.
[52] Graciela Márquez, "The Political Economy of Mexican Protectionism, 1868–1911"; Victor Bulmer-Thomas, *The Economic History of Latin America Since Independence*, chs. 4 and 5.

Market Size and Density

Big countries, as measured by population size, had lower tariff rates, a result consistent with the view that big domestic markets were more friendly to foreign imports because local firms would have found it easier to carve out regional and product niches, or with the view that large countries are forced to develop alternative revenue sources because they have lower foreign-trade shares in income, or both. Producers in countries with relatively small domestic markets – like Chile, Cuba, and Uruguay – would have found it harder to hide in spatial niches, leading to lobbying for higher tariffs, and governments would have favored this lobbying because tariffs were such a dominant revenue source given high foreign-trade shares.

This section started by pointing out that tariffs in Latin America were far higher than anywhere else in the world from the 1860s to World War I, long before the Great Depression. Indeed, tariff rates in Latin America were even on the rise in the decades before 1914. High tariffs should have favored the domestic import-competing industry, namely, manufacturing. They also should have taken some of the steam out of the export-led boom during the belle époque. But was it protection and deindustrialization fears that motivated those high tariffs? Apparently not. Tariffs in Latin America were viewed mainly as a revenue source, as a strategic policy response to trading partners' tariffs, as a redistributive device for special interests, and as a consequence of other political economy struggles. However, revenue needs were the central motivation behind those exceptionally high tariffs. Although all young countries have revenue needs, they were especially pressing in Latin America, where levels of military conflict were exceptional up to the 1870s when the rest of the world was enjoying pax britannica. Exceptionally high levels of pre-1870 violence led to exceptionally high tariff rates.

EXPORT-LED GROWTH AND INDUSTRIALIZATION

ADVANCING IN CIRCLES: INDUSTRY AND EXPORT-LED GROWTH

By the 1960s and 1970s, regional analysts were obsessed with Latin American underdevelopment in general and the crisis of the ISI model in particular. Whereas colonial heritage and nineteenth-century nation-building were always viewed as central underlying causes of modern underdevelopment, studies of trade policy, almost without exception, started with the 1930s and the ISI model. Typically, industrialization was considered a post–Great Depression phenomenon, evolving as a policy-induced reaction to the interwar crisis of the export-led growth model based on primary-product exports and industrial imports.[53]

A reaction set in during the 1970s, when historians began to stress the importance of what came to be labeled early industry. Many studies explored the features of early industrial growth, dated in some cases from World War I, in others from the 1880s or even earlier, as exemplified by Aurora Gómez's contribution to this volume. By industry, we are not talking about handicraft production embedded in the agrarian–colonial economy; nor are we talking about primary-product processing, activities that added very little value to these primary products before they were exported. We are talking about large industrial enterprises with an advanced division of labor and considerable capital intensity.

Once it had been clearly established that modern industry had existed side by side with export-led growth long before the Great Depression, different scholars offered competing explanations for it. Some thought industrial growth was not possible if export-led growth was truly successful. Thus, the explanation for industrial growth had to be found in various constraints on export-led growth that would have allowed industry to thrive alongside it. One such constraint was protection. As noted in the previous section, a central point of controversy is whether high tariffs emerged to generate revenues for the state or whether they were consciously oriented toward the promotion of industrial growth. This discussion was related to another: were industrial capitalists opposed to export interests and their policies (following some Stolper-Samuelson predictions) or was industrial investment seen as harmonious with export-led growth?[54] Thus, whereas some scholars stress the protection afforded by tariffs and geographic isolation, others view early industrial growth in terms of domestic forces. The latter includes the expansion of local demand, access to cheap raw materials and labor, better output prices, and favorable exchange rates.

Before we can assess this debate, we need to define terms. If by industrialization we mean a process by which manufacturing output grows faster

[53] United Nations. Economic Commission for Latin America (ECLA), *The Process of Industrial Development in Latin America* (New York, 1966).

[54] Colin Lewis, "Industry in Latin America before 1930," in Leslie Bethell, ed., *The Cambridge History of Latin America*, vol. 4 (Cambridge, 1986).

than that of other sectors for a long enough time to significantly alter output mix, then it appears that industrialization was never achieved in Latin America prior to the 1930s. To take the most compelling example, Argentine GDP grew at an annual rate of 5.5 percent between 1875 and 1930, while industry grew at a rate only slightly faster, 6 percent.[55] If we assume that industry represented 12 percent of GDP in 1880, its share, according to these growth rates, should have risen ever so modestly, to 15.2 percent in 1930. In contrast, between 1935 and 1960, the industrial share in Argentina increased from 15 to 21 percent.[56] Uruguay recorded a similar performance between 1870 and 1930, whereas the industrial share increased from 11 to 23 percent between 1930 and 1960. This important part of the southern cone did not undergo significant industrialization before 1930, and it seems unlikely that other Latin American countries underwent a more dramatic industrialization experience. Indeed, manufacturing output shares around World War I were considerably lower elsewhere in Latin America than in Argentina.[57]

Did this result arise from some fault with Latin American industry and its industrialists? Maybe. But it could also have been fostered by what we have come to call the Dutch disease. After all, the relative price of manufactures facing Latin America fell dramatically across the century before the 1890s (see Figure 1.2), a force that gave enormous incentive to primary-product expansion at the expense of import-competing manufactures. Those trends ceased late in the century, after which the relative price of manufactures rose just as dramatically (e.g., Latin America's terms of trade deteriorated). Did this switch in world price trends provoke industrialization throughout Latin America after the 1890s, or did the region have to wait until the 1930s and the introduction of ISI policy?

THE LIMITS OF EXPORT-LED AND INDUSTRY-LED GROWTH

Between 1870 and 1913, the more advanced regions of the world experienced rising industrial shares and associated urbanization. Even world trade was increasingly industrial: while trade in primary products grew more than did that of industrial products in the early nineteenth century, industrial

---

[55] Roberto Cortés Conde and Marcela Harriague, "Estimaciones sobre el PBI en Argentina 1874–1935," (Documento de Trabajo 3, Universidad de San Andrés, Buenos Aires, 1993).

[56] Vázquez Presedo, *Estadísticas Históricas Argentinas. Compendio 1873–1973* (Buenos Aires, 1988).

[57] Brazil 1920, 12.2 percent; Colombia 1925, 6.7 percent; Mexico 1910, 12.3 percent. Victor Bulmer-Thomas, *The Economic History of Latin America Since Independence*, 134.

trade caught up late in the century and forged ahead in the early 1900s. Yet, Latin American exports remained primary products to an overwhelming extent. Were there limits to export-led growth?

First, world demand and prices set one limit. As we have seen, the relative price trend favoring primary products in Latin America turned around after the 1890s, a switch that must have been caused at least partly by a weakened demand for primary products relative to manufactures. However, demand limits cannot be completely isolated from supply limits. If some structural limitation made it difficult for a country to shift resources out of traditional exports and into sectors with fast-growing product demand, its capacity to grow would be diminished.

Second, was Latin America more or less competitive in dynamic products, like those in manufacturing? Were there limits to industrial growth in Latin America? One limit to Latin American industrialization was the domestic market. For most countries in Latin America, domestic markets were far too small, a clear disadvantage resulting from the balkanization of the region two centuries earlier at independence. For example, around the 1850s, the four biggest Latin American countries (Brazil, Colombia, Mexico, and Peru) had, on average, populations one-sixth the size of the four biggest Western European countries (France, Germany, Italy, and the United Kingdom). Alternatively, the next five mid-sized Latin American countries (Argentina, Bolivia, Chile, Cuba, and Venezuela) were, on average, less than one-third the size of the average mid-sized Western European country (Belgium, Netherlands, Portugal, Sweden, and Switzerland). Small populations made for small markets, but poverty, low per capita income, and regional fragmentation made those domestic markets even smaller. In addition, income was unevenly distributed at the start, further shrinking the domestic market for mass-produced goods. And, as shown in the next section, inequality grew even worse during the belle époque as Latin America responded to world demand with export-led growth. None of these factors yielded the kind of local market in which domestic industry could exploit scale economies and improve productivity until it could go it alone in home markets without tariffs, let alone try to penetrate foreign markets.

During the nineteenth century, industrial growth was mainly based on relatively simple technologies, and by 1910 these had spread all over the world. Some Latin American industries did grow during this globalization process, but they did so only behind high tariff walls. Textiles were the leading sector everywhere around the world, but in 1910, Latin America – as illustrated by Mexico – was simply not competitive. As Gregory Clark has shown, compared with England, spindles in Mexico were half again more expensive, and coal was four times more expensive.[58] Yet wages were only half those in England.[59] Was that cheap-labor advantage enough to give Mexico a competitive edge in home and even world markets? Apparently not, because Mexican labor was so inefficient that labor costs per unit of output were higher than in England. Thus, only tariffs ensured the survival of the textile industry in Mexico, and what was true of Mexican textiles was probably true of most industries in Latin America. And, of course, things got even worse over time as tariffs reduced competition and muted the process of innovation.

The timing here is important: Latin America was simply unprepared for the petrochemical industrial wave of the late nineteenth century's second industrial revolution – which embodied more complex technologies, larger scale, and higher skill requirements. International competition in world manufacturing markets depended increasingly on skills, and Latin America, already having lost the battle over old industrial technologies, was hardly well positioned to deal with this new competition. Even in Argentina and Uruguay, the richest part of Latin America, school enrollment rates in the 1910s were very low by North American and European standards: only 42.2 and 33.6 percent of school-aged children attended school in Argentina and Uruguay, respectively, not to mention Brazil, with only 12.3 percent. Overall school attendance in Argentina, Uruguay, and Brazil was 52, 42, and 18 percent, respectively, of that in France, Germany, the United Kingdom, and the United States combined. Illiteracy rates made Latin America look even worse. In 1910, 62 percent of Latin America was illiterate, when the figures for North America were about 8 or 9 percent.[60]

Latin America had to deal with the second industrial revolution before it had undergone the first.

GLOBALIZATION AND INEQUALITY

Looking backward while writing around World War I, two Swedish economists – Eli Heckscher and Bertil Ohlin – argued that the integration of global commodity markets would lead to convergence of international

---

[58] Gregory Clark, "Why Isn't the Whole World Developed? Lessons from the Cotton Mills," *Journal of Economic History* 47 (March 1987): 141–73.

[59] Gregory Clark, "Why Isn't the Whole World Developed?" 146.

[60] Pablo Astorga and Valpy FitzGerald, "Statistical Appendix," in Rosemary Thorp, ed., *Progress, Poverty and Exclusion. An Economic History of Latin America in the Twentieth Century* (Washington, DC, 1998).

Table 1.6. *Wage/rental ratio trends in the resource-abundant periphery: 1870–1939 (1911 = 100)*

Period	Argentina	Uruguay	Burma	Siam	Egypt	Punjab	Australia	United States
1870–1874		1112.5		4699.1		196.7	416.2	233.6
1875–1879		891.3		3908.7	174.3	198.5	253.0	195.0
1880–1884	580.4	728.3		3108.1	276.6	147.2	239.1	188.3
1885–1889	337.1	400.2		2331.6	541.9	150.8	216.3	182.1
1890–1894	364.7	377.2	190.9	1350.8	407.5	108.7	136.2	173.5
1895–1899	311.1	303.6	189.9	301.3	160.1	92.0	147.7	175.0
1900–1904	298.8	233.0	186.8	173.0	166.7	99.8	130.0	172.4
1905–1909	135.2	167.8	139.4	57.2	64.4	92.4	97.9	132.7
1910–1914	84.0	117.9	106.9	109.8	79.8	80.1	100.6	101.1
1915–1919	53.6	120.8	164.7	202.1	83.5	82.5	111.0	124.7
1920–1924	53.1	150.3	113.6	157.9	124.3	81.1	137.2	122.4
1925–1929	51.0	150.2		114.9	120.8	72.6	115.1	160.1
1930–1934	58.4	174.3		113.1	116.2	50.4	98.3	165.2
1935–1939	59.5	213.5		121.6	91.0	33.2	110.5	240.1

Source: Jeffrey G. Williamson, "Land, Labor, and Globalization in the Third World, 1870–1940," *Journal of Economic History* 62 (2002), 73–4.

factor prices, as countries everywhere expanded the production and export of commodities that used their abundant (and cheap) factor intensively. The historical evidence for the southern cone – trends in the ratio of wages to land rents or land values from Argentina and Uruguay – seems to be consistent with the predictions of Heckscher and Ohlin. The ratios appear in Table 1.6.

The trade boom during the half century before World War I led to falling wage–rental ratios in the relatively land-abundant southern cone, just as Heckscher and Ohlin would have predicted. As the exports of land-intensive products boomed, so did the demand for land and therefore rents and land values. As the imports of labor-intensive manufactured products also boomed, the demand for labor fell, at least relative to land, and thus so did the wage–rental or the wage–land-value ratio. Taking 1913 as the base, the wage–rental (or the wage–land-value) ratio plunged from about 6.9 to about 0.6 between 1880–4 and 1915–19 in Argentina, and from 11.1 to 1.2 between 1870–4 and 1915–19 in Uruguay. Alternatively, the ratio of land rents to wages soared by about ten times over these four or five decades. This is a huge change in the relative scarcity of land and labor, with powerful inequality implications. As it turns out, these trends were typical everywhere in the land-abundant periphery that, like Australia and North America or like Thailand and the Punjab, were exporting to the booming industrial core. Exactly the opposite trends were taking place in Europe, especially in those parts of Europe that stuck to their free-trade guns: that is, wage–rental ratios soared in Britain, Ireland, and Scandinavia. To the extent that land holdings were highly concentrated at the top, these trends clearly implied falling inequality in Europe, but rising inequality in the southern cone. Furthermore, when the world economy fell apart after World War I, the steep decline in the wage–rental ratio stopped in Argentina and Uruguay and actually began to rise in the 1930s (see Table 1.6). Presumably, inequality trends reversed as well.

So much for factor demand and globalization. What about factor supply? Sir Arthur Lewis used his famous labor-surplus model to show how early industrialization could create inequality.[61] According to his model, the worker fails to share in GDP per capita growth because elastic labor supplies keep wages and living standards stable. Lewis is quiet about what happens to land rents, but the classical model from which his was derived clearly predicted a rise. Carlos Diaz-Alejandro, on Argentina, and Nathaniel Leff, on Brazil, have both used the labor-surplus model to predict stable real wages in Latin America, appealing to the migration of surplus labor from the Mediterranean.[62] Although the thesis that these parts of Latin America had more elastic labor supplies than the English-speaking New World has been rejected, they did have higher rates of immigration and labor force growth than elsewhere in Latin America. This process of intensification may have suppressed real wage growth relative to other factor prices like land rents. After all, labor supplies were more elastic than land: land–labor ratios fell in the southern cone in spite of new land settlement and expanding frontiers. Meanwhile, rising export prices raised land rents and land values. Note also that the fact that mass migrations into Argentina and Uruguay dropped off sharply after World War I is consistent with the turnaround in the wage–rental ratio drift in Table 1.6.

It follows that the Heckscher-Ohlin globalization model and the Lewis labor-surplus model both predict falling wage–rental ratios and rising inequality in the export-led southern cone prior to World War I, and the

---

[61] Arthur Lewis, "Economic Development with Unlimited Supplies of Labour," *Manchester School of Economic and Social Studies* 22 (May 1954): 139–91.

[62] Carlos Díaz-Alejandro, *Essays on the Economic History of the Argentine Republic*; Nathaniel Leff, "Economic Development and Regional Inequality: Origins of the Brazilian Case," *Quarterly Journal of Economics* 86 (May 1972): 243–62.

opposite thereafter. Regardless of which thesis explains southern cone history best, we need to know whether this experience was ubiquitous across Latin America.

Complete income distributions at various benchmarks from independence to World War II are unavailable for any Latin American country, including Argentina and Uruguay. Still, our interest here is factor prices: unskilled wages, land rents, the premium on skills, and the return to capital. How did the typical unskilled worker, landless laborer, or small-scale farmer near the bottom of the distribution do relative to the typical landowner or capitalist near the top, or even relative to the typical skilled blue-collar worker or educated white-collar employee near the middle?

There are two kinds of evidence available to document inequality trends in belle époque and interwar Latin America: trends in the wage–rental ratio, which we have already explored, but, sad to say, are limited to Argentina and Uruguay; and trends in the ratio of the unskilled wage to GDP per capita, which we have not yet explored, and that are available for seven Latin American regions between 1870 and 1940.

Table 1.7 reports trends in the ratio of the unskilled worker's wage (w) to the returns on all factors per person as measured by Angus Maddison's and Pablo Astorga and Valpy FitzGerald's estimates of GDP per capita (y).[63] These trends in w/y should approximate changes in the economic distance between the working poor near the bottom of the distribution and the average citizen in the middle of the distribution. Argentina, Mexico, and Uruguay document the longest time series, and Table 1.7 shows that all three underwent a long, steep decline in w/y before it flattened out (Mexico) or even rose (Argentina and Uruguay) after World War I. The turning point for all three is 1915–19, a result consistent with wage–rental ratio trends in Table 1.6 documented for just Argentina and Uruguay. Although its time series is shorter, Cuba seemed to obey the same laws of motion and the same turning point. Colombia's time series is even shorter than Cuba's, so we do not know whether or not 1910–14 was a turning point for Colombia. The pre–World War I evidence in Table 1.7 is consistent with either the Heckscher-Ohlin or the Lewis explanations.

But what about after World War I? As the world adopted autarkic policies and as Latin America faced a deterioration in its terms of trade across the

---

[63] Angus Maddison, *Monitoring the World Economy, 1820–1992* (Paris, 1995); Pablo Astorga and Valpy FitzGerald, "The Standard of Living in Latin America During the Twentieth Century" (Development Studies Working Paper 117, Queen Elizabeth House, St. Antony's College, University of Oxford, May 1998).

Table 1.7. *Wage/GDP per capita ratio trends in Latin America: 1870–1939*
(1913 = 1.0)

Period	Argentina	Brazil Southeast	Brazil Northeast	Colombia	Cuba	Mexico	Uruguay
1870–1874	1.6947						
1875–1879	1.3286						
1880–1884	1.4769					1.1881	1.9047
1885–1889	1.5663					1.0899	2.2004
1890–1894	1.5191					1.0387	2.2555
1895–1899	1.4428					1.0503	1.6946
1900–1904	1.4570	1.2209	1.5325			0.9702	1.3658
1905–1909	1.0500	1.1529	1.4431		1.2108	0.8633	1.0966
1910–1914	1.0433	1.0318	1.1451	1.3317	0.9924	0.7738	1.0759
1915–1919	0.9230	0.7899	0.6751	1.5811	0.9329	0.2982	0.8981
1920–1924	1.1298	0.6280	0.5383	1.9191	1.2210	0.3615	1.1346
1925–1929	1.2440	0.5912	0.5361	2.2206	1.4785	0.4613	1.1785
1930–1934	1.4144	0.5760	0.3652	3.0818	1.5704	0.6903	1.4745
1935–1939	1.3032			2.0995	1.4853	0.5129	1.2918

Source: Jeffrey Williamson, "Real Wages, Inequality, and Globalization in Latin America before 1940," *Revisa de Historia Económica* 17, 101 (1999), Table 8.

1920s and 1930s, one would have thought that these deglobalizing forces would have had egalitarian effects. In some cases, that is exactly what we observe in Table 1.7 – a rise in w/y. In Brazil and Mexico, we do not. A continued secular decline in w/y might be expected of Brazil, a huge country with severe regional inequalities, a relatively small trade share in income, and a large domestic labor reservoir with roots in the former slave economy. Mexico may share many of the features of the Brazilian economy, but its development is complicated by the revolution and the reforms that followed.

The regions of new settlement documented in Table 1.7, Argentina and Uruguay, certainly offer the most compelling case for the globalization and inequality connection. These trends of rising inequality during the first great globalization boom and falling inequality during the interwar years of deglobalization are consistent with booms and busts in mass immigration and trade, but we don't know which one mattered most. To the extent that the prewar trade boom (and interwar bust) accounted for the prewar immigration boom (and interwar bust), perhaps we don't care which mattered most given that they would have their origin in the same global forces.

Why did the real wage lag behind GDP per capita in so much of Latin America during the first great globalization boom? Is this evidence of some weaker version of the Lewis model, one without a constant real wage but with sluggish real wage growth and modest trickling down? Is it evidence supporting the factor-price convergence theorem? Or is it both? And why the common turning point for economies with such different attributes? Because it seems unlikely that such dissimilar economies could share the same turning point if the reason was domestic forces at work, the most likely explanation probably lies with world markets. These countries were more likely to have shared similar price shocks that produced similar inequality trends.

Real wages lagged behind GDP per capita growth everywhere in Latin America up to World War I. Real wages outstripped GDP per capita growth in many parts of Latin America thereafter. We interpret these trends as rising inequality during the first great globalization boom and falling inequality during the interwar years of deglobalization. The correlation was probably causal.

AN AGENDA FOR THE FUTURE

In recent decades, we have learned a lot about the impact of globalization forces on pre-1940 Latin America, but much more remains to be done. This survey has raised five major questions that should keep scholars busy over the next few decades.

First: Did export-led growth suppress industrialization enough to account for the fact that although the belle époque achieved a half century of "fairly fast" growth, it did not achieve any significant catching up on the industrial leaders?

Second: Industrialization in Latin America before 1930 was modest at best, but it was fast afterward. How much of that change in performance was attributable to the change in policy from pro-global to anti-global, and how much of it was caused by the dramatic change in the terms of trade drift from steeply rising primary-product prices (relative to manufactured goods) before the 1890s to steeply falling relative primary-product prices after the 1890s? These two forces reinforced each other, but how much because of world markets and how much because of policy?

Third: Independence early in the nineteenth century produced market balkanization and anti-global policies that persisted for a half century or

Latin America, as in the rest of the world, the twentieth-century record of global capital-market integration is famous for its U-shape: high in the early and late decades and low in the middle. But the upswing of the 1980s and 1990s is still more a feature of the developed than the developing countries.

By many measures, Latin America is still much less globalized today than it was 100 years ago in capital markets – and the persistent postwar legacy of controls, interventions, and distortions is largely responsible. This conclusion offers both hope and gloom. If the benefits of tapping into global capital markets can be enjoyed again, the region could experience an era of investment-led growth like that of a century ago. Why it has not done so already suggests significant political and institutional obstacles to that end.

THE COLONIAL BACKDROP

Although this chapter focuses on the nineteenth and twentieth centuries, we should say a word about antecedents. Latin America has experienced four waves of globalization since the European conquest, according to a persuasive chronology of that slippery concept presented by John Coatsworth.[1] We are concerned here only with the economic manifestations of globalization – and in the first two centuries after 1492, economic interaction was limited and confined to trade in a small quantity of goods and the migration of small numbers of peoples.

The extent of economic globalization under the Spanish empire circa 1700 was much smaller than that found under the British Empire two centuries later. Throughout the colonial period, however, capital flows of the type we wish to study were very small in all countries. This is perhaps not too surprising for the sixteenth and seventeenth centuries. The instruments of market-based international investment were not truly established on any scale within a European context until the development of securities markets in Amsterdam and London in the late seventeenth century, and their use did not spread further until much later.

Did it matter that such flows were so small? Did this reflect the institutional failure of the colonizing power (as argued by North) and a failure to see the development potential of the region?[2] Or did the region actually

---

[1] John H. Coatsworth, "Economic and Institutional Trajectories in Pre-Modern Latin America," in John H. Coatsworth and Alan M. Taylor, eds., *Latin America and the World Economy Since 1800* (Cambridge, MA, 1999).

[2] Douglass C. North, *Institutions, Institutional Change, and Economic Performance* (Cambridge, 1990).

prosper quite well all the same? Coatsworth found that the region enjoyed respectably high per capita incomes on the eve of independence – perhaps 66 percent of the U.S. level. Certainly there was no great divergence between the region and the core at that time. To the extent that investment played a role in economic growth (along Solovian lines) we might infer that pre-modern, preindustrial growth in the colonial period was supported by a supply of local saving that was small but ample for the modest demands of the time.

The coming of the modern era, and the economic shocks of the nine-teenth century, changed this equilibrium. In growth terms, Latin America had kept pace with the developed countries in the preceding centuries. The nineteenth century was when Latin America fell behind, with only a hint of convergence at the end of that era. What role did the external capital market play in this new growth environment?

THE FIRST FRENZY

Connections to a wider capital market expanded in the postcolonial era. The countries of an independent Latin America could approach the burgeoning international capital markets of northwestern Europe in search of funds for their fledgling governments seeking to establish security and infrastructure and later for their private sectors in search of development finance. This was a time of potentially fortuitous coincidence of wants. The borrower was capital scarce and needed funds for nation building and economic develop-ment. The lenders were increasingly capital abundant because of modern economic growth that generated higher savings, accumulation, and dimin-ishing returns at home.

Only a mediation of the arbitrage opportunity was needed, but this required a political and institutional foundation, in addition to the technical apparatus of financial markets that had developed over centuries. The most significant early investors in this period were the British, who, in the 1820s, were excited at the prospects for overseas investment in an emerging market expected to enjoy fine economic prospects once freed from the yoke of Iberian imperialism and its restrictive economic practices. The decisive victory at the Battle of Ayacucho in December 1824 coincided with a bull market on the Royal Exchange, and Marichal notes that a "financial fever intensified with the announcement that silver-mining enterprises would be formed to exploit the legendary riches of Mexico, Peru, Colombia, and

Brazil."[3] In 1822, government bond issues were floated by Colombia, Chile, Peru, and the fictitious Poyais with a face value of £3.65 million; in 1824, by Colombia and Peru (again) plus Buenos Aires, Brazil, and Mexico to the tune of £10.4 million; and in 1825, by Peru (yet again) plus Brazil, Mexico, Guadalajara, and Central America for a further £7.1 million. Selling at a moderate discount, these £21 million in government bonds realized a net £16 million for the borrowers. Private parties also joined the frenzy, with mining companies alone raising £3.5 million in capital and gaining authorization for up to £24.1 million. This investment boom dominated activity in London for a couple of years and far exceeded any investment in other regions of the world. Of the 624 new issues on the Royal Exchange in this period, 46 were Latin American, but, being large enterprises, they accounted for almost a third of total investment.

Many of these initial public offerings (IPOs) turned out to be a fraud. Fred Rippy describes the period as a "wild speculation spree" on the part of credulous British investors, who put up their capital for improbable schemes:

Associations were formed to obtain precious metals from the Andean cordilleras, where there were few workers, no fuel for the fires, and no roads for the vehicles; technicians and machinery were hurried off in utmost ignorance of the almost impenetrable mountains and matted jungles that awaited them. There were companies to fish for pearls, to inaugurate steamboat lines, to cut through the American isthmus, to furnish steam engines for mints, to establish colonies of farmers and herdsmen. A churning company was formed to send out milkmaids to the pampas; furs and warming pans were shipped to the tropics![4]

Thus, the new adventure turned sour. When political uncertainties and fiscal burdens escalated because of the wars of independence and subsequent civil wars, the unseasoned sovereign borrowers soon found themselves with no means to service the loans and a wave of defaults ensued. Losses were heavy, and some issues tanked precipitously, as when, reported by Rippy, "the Poyais loan of 1822, the bonanza investment offered by 'King' Gregor McGregor, rose only a point above the issue price of eighty, but soon descended to the appropriate level of zero."[5] All of these government bond

---

[3] Carlos Marichal, *A Century of Debt Crises in Latin America: From Independence to the Great Depression, 1820–1930* (Princeton, NJ, 1989), 12–13.

[4] J. Fred Rippy, *British Investments in Latin America, 1822–1949: A Case Study in the Operations of Private Enterprise in Retarded Regions* (Minneapolis, MN, 1959), 18.

[5] McGregor, a swashbuckling émigré Scots clansman who fought alongside Bolívar, invented the kingdom of Poyais to embellish an area of miasmal swamplands on the Mosquito Coast that had been

issues were in default by 1827, and many remained in arrears, in some cases for decades. The investments in mining, canals, steamboats, butter, and the rest fared no better.

Economies in the region suffered deep macroeconomic instability for decades, bond issues went into default, new lending dried up, and a resort to seigniorage ignited the inflationary fire that has raged or smoldered ever since. The still ongoing pattern of lending booms followed by a default crisis and macroeconomic adjustment was thus inaugurated in the region, a topic to which we shall return later. Suitably chastened, foreign investors held off from investing in the region until political and economic stability seemed more assured, and waited for a resolution of outstanding debts (see Table 2.1).

In subsequent decades, Britain's long-standing involvement in the region was to endure, but not without more of these ups and downs. In addition to being the leading foreign investor in the nineteenth century, Britain was the preeminent foreign investor in Latin America from 1820 to 1914. After the 1820s fiasco, foreign capital beat a retreat from the region. Popular memory of the swindles of 1824–5 faded slowly. Seventy years on, Oscar Wilde made an Argentine canal scam a central part of the plot of *An Ideal Husband*.

The notion that modern capital markets have a weak memory is certainly pervasive and the benefits of reputation can seem hard to detect. Nonetheless, many of these bad debtors paid for their defaults by being excluded for long periods from the financial markets. With some justification, Rippy refers to the initial experience of investment in Latin America as one of "early imprudence and vexation."

THE SECOND SURGE

Despite vexation, the keenest investors were not to be deterred forever. By the 1850s, there was renewed interest in Latin America on the London capital market. Enthusiasm grew in the next two decades, even if the investors were by now savvy enough to avoid the riskier locations and follow the signals given by the few countries that had tried, however sporadically, to maintain

granted to him by an Indian elder. A self-proclaimed prince, McGregor and his bride (Bolívar's niece) were then received at the court of George IV as honored guests. Having fooled the royals and gained celebrity, McGregor was able to sell junk Poyais bonds and real estate in London, Edinburgh, and Paris. He was subsequently jailed in England and France, escaped each time, and returned with his princess to Venezuela as a hero.

Table 2.1. *Default history of Latin American government bonds issued in the 1820s*

Country	Amount owed (£)	Resolution, if any
Brazil	21,129,000	Arrears on interest paid and service resumed in 1829.
Mexico	6,400,000	Refinancing in 1831 to cover principal and arrears on interest. Quickly defaulted on. New refinancing in 1837. More defaults and refunding. Resolved 1864.
Costa Rica	13,608	Inherited share of Central American confederation debt. Principal paid off in 1840, but not arrears on interest.
Chile	1,000,000	Arrears on interest paid and service resumed in 1842.
Peru	1,816,000	Arrears on interest paid and service resumed in 1849. Default in 1876.
Colombia (New Granada)	3,375,000	Inherited 50 percent share of Gran Colombia debt. Principal and arrears paid off by new loan in 1845. Default in 1850. Principal and arrears paid off by new loan in 1861.
Venezuela	1,923,750	Inherited 28.5 percent share of Gran Colombia debt. Principal and arrears paid off by new loan in 1841. Default in 1847. New arrangements and further defaults then follow.
Ecuador	1,451,259	Inherited 21.5 percent share of Gran Colombia debt. Principal paid off by new loan in 1855. Arrears cancelled in exchange for land warrants and Peruvian bonds. Default in 1868.
Guatemala	68,741	Inherited share of Central American confederation debt. Principal and arrears paid off by new loan in 1856.
Buenos Aires	1,000,000	Resumed service in 1857.
El Salvador	27,217	Inherited share of Central American confederation debt. Paid off 90 percent of debt in 1860, but balance not until 1877.
Honduras	27,217	Inherited share of Central American confederation debt. Principal and arrears paid off by new loan in 1867.
Nicaragua	27,717	Inherited share of Central American confederation debt. Paid off 85 percent of debt face value in 1874.

Note: Poyais is omitted.

Source: J. Fred Rippy, *British Investments in Latin America, 1822–1949: A Case Study in the Operations of Private Enterprise in Retarded Regions* (Minneapolis, MN, 1959), 26–8.

some kind of debt service. Of the various 1820s sovereign issues that quickly failed, only the Brazilian default was quickly resolved in 1829, and most remained in default for decades, with refunding attempts frequently subject to failure as well (see Table 2.1). As Rippy noted:

In view of this record, one might have expected British investors to shy away from Latin American government securities. But grandsons seem to profit little from the experience of their grandfathers in the investment field. During the 1860s and early 1870s Englishmen went on another investment spree. It is true that they revealed no enthusiasm for the issues of Colombia, Ecuador, and some of the Central American countries, but they seemed eager to invest in the government paper of most of the others involved in the defaults following the boom of the 1820's.[6]

Despite the checkered debt history of the region, flows did resume and "the trickle of British investments of the 1830's and 1840's became a fairly large stream during the next three decades, branching out into at least seventeen countries."[7] By 1880, these new investments had accumulated into a sizeable stock that dwarfed the cumulative totals of the previous boom in the 1820s, and by then a total of £179 million was outstanding to Britain, £123 million in government bonds (69%) and £56 million in private enterprises (see Table 2.2).

One of the main causes of this new surge in investment was the trade boom experienced by the region, and most of the world, from the 1850s until the onset of the Great Depression of the 1870s. This brought increased economic activity to merchants and landowners, more exports and imports, and, thus, more revenues (principally from customs duties) that governments could use to amortize loans. The continued dominance of the public sector was based on three very different types of loans: loans for rolling over old debts, loans for military purposes, and loans for railway construction, which was heavily supported by the state. Only the latter represented a real net contribution to local capital formation, most of which was supplied by the slow and steady accretion of retained profits in a world of financial underdevelopment. Thus, the significance of these flows should not be overstated for overall economic development. Yet they represented a major increase in leverage for the public sector and a test of the governments' creditworthiness after three decades of financial hibernation. Marichal records that a remarkable total of fifty major foreign loans were

---

[6] Rippy, *British Investments*, 28.
[7] Ibid., 26.

Table 2.2. *British investments in Latin America at the end of 1880 (£)*

Country	Total	Private enterprise	Government bonds	Government bonds in default (year)
Argentina	20,338,709	9,105,009	11,233,700	–
Bolivia	1,654,000	–	1,654,000	1,654,000 (1875)
Brazil	38,869,067	15,808,905	24,060,162	–
Chile	8,466,521	701,417	7,765,104	–
Colombia	3,073,373	973,373	2,100,000	2,100,000 (1879)
Costa Rica	3,304,000	–	3,304,000	3,304,000 (1874)
Cuba	1,231,600	1,231,600	–	–
Dominican Republic	714,300	–	714,300	714,300 (1872)
Ecuador	1,959,380	135,380	1,724,000	1,824,000 (1868)
Guatemala	544,200	–	544,200	544,200 (1876)
Honduras	3,222,000	–	3,222,000	3,222,000 (1872)
Mexico	32,740,916	9,200,116	23,540,800	23,540,800 (1866)
Nicaragua	206,570	206,570	–	–
Paraguay	1,505,400	–	1,505,400	1,505,400 (1874)
Peru	36,177,070	3,488,750	32,688,320	32,688,320 (1876)
Uruguay	7,644,105	4,124,885	3,519,220	–
Venezuela	7,564,390	1,161,590	6,402,800	–
General	10,274,660	10,274,660	–	–
Total	179,490,261	78,773,112	123,078,006	71,097,020

Source: Rippy, *British Investments in Latin America, 1822–1949*, 25, 32.

negotiated from 1850 to 1873, most of them in London and a few in Paris and other European markets.[8]

The impacts of the boom varied by country. Some countries now looked like a good bet. With respect to sovereign loans, Brazil had worked harder than other countries to honor debts and was duly rewarded with the largest share. Rippy notes that "during the sixty years following 1824 Englishmen preferred Brazil as a field of investment to any other Latin American country, largely for the reason that Brazil was politically more stable."[9] One might add that, as a consequence, Brazil could get its act together to service debt.

Other countries did not. For example, not until the Argentines resolved their internecine disputes and settled the national question in the 1860s (and made some attempt to resume service on old debts in 1857) did capital

[8] Marichal, *Century of Debt Crises*, Appendix A.
[9] Rippy, *British Investments*, 28, 150.

again flow, beginning with the national government's loans of 1866 and 1868, the latter critical for the Paraguayan War. Several Argentine provinces also floated loans in 1870–4. Even the defeated Paraguay sold its first bonds in London in 1871. Uruguay and Bolivia could do likewise in 1872 (the first Bolivian issue in 1864 had failed). Chile floated issues in 1858, 1865, 1866, 1867, 1870, and 1873 totaling £8.5 million. Costa Rica, Guatemala, and Honduras all issued nonrefinancing debt (i.e., net inflows) in the peak of the investment boom from 1867 to 1872.

The terms of these loans varied greatly and reflected a high variance in interest rates across debtors worldwide, prior to a great convergence in these rates up to 1914, which we shall discuss shortly. Many of these loans were floated at less than favorable interest rates, reflecting a high assessment of country risk by the creditors, which, we can say with hindsight, was a wise judgment. The country risk also correlated roughly with past bad behavior – both how bad it was and how past. In this period, a good risk like Brazil or Chile could float loans with 5 percent coupons at 80 or 90 (relative to a per value of 100) for a yield of under 6 percent. Peru did about as well. Argentine coupons ran to 6 or 7 percent, and the issues sold at around 90. Costa Rica floated 6s and 7s and sold them for about 70. War-torn Paraguay's coupons paid 8 percent and Honduras as high as 10, but such issues could not sell for more than 80.

As in the 1820s, however, there were intimations again of an overborrowing binge, and questions soon surfaced about the ability of governments, some of them still governing relatively immature and unstable polities, to fulfill their promises to pay on this new mountain of debt. Some loans emerged with a bad smell, most notoriously the Paraguayan fraud: the country was in total disarray after defeat and could never repay – a state of affairs that did not trouble the bankers who had received their commission or the corrupt politicians who had whisked the gold credits off to fund Argentine bank accounts and real estate. The worst abuses tended to be in the smaller republics, often aided and abetted by the European financiers. Their governments' loss of reputation was to have consequences for their access to credit when new lending resumed. But even the genuine loans in the larger republics caused servicing problems as the depression spread. A global macroeconomic and financial crisis was stirring yet again, and a second wave of defaults soon spread over the region in the 1870s. By the end of 1880, of the £123 million of British capital invested in Latin American government bonds, more than £71 million (58%) were in default (see Table 2.2). This was only a small part of a much wider global debt crisis: already as of 1876 fifteen non-European nations had defaulted to the tune of £300 million, including in that very year the large defaults by Peru, Egypt, and Turkey. The capital flows again ground to a halt and irate bondholders chased down the insolvent republics long into the 1880s. The creditors tended to emerge victorious, but the settlements were drawn out and the payoffs were incomplete. Defaulting governments were shut out of new borrowing during negotiations and often for many years beyond.

The crisis cemented in investors' minds the untrustworthiness of Latin American sovereign borrowers, a reputation that was to expand in the years ahead and which persists even to this day. According to Tomz, of the seventy-seven government defaults from 1820 to 1914, fifty-eight involved Latin American countries, and from 1914 to 1931, thirteen of twenty-one. Compared with other periphery countries, the economic potential and sovereign independence of the region obviously encouraged this outcome: the potential for high returns encouraged more borrowing ex ante and the independence from the empire gave more freedom to default ex post. Yet, clearly, the borrowers in the region could not manage their fiscal affairs with anything approaching the prudence of most borrowers in the core countries. Figure 2.1 shows the incidence of sovereign default in the region from 1820 to 1940, and the fraction of years that debtors spent in default status is impressive, 38 percent on average. The better-behaved borrowers like Uruguay (12%) or Brazil (17%) managed to maintain a pretty clean sheet, but the odds of receiving repayment from others like Honduras (79%) or Mexico (57%) were no more favorable than a coin toss.

The 1870s crisis bore some similarities to the events of the 1820s, obviously, but there was one key difference. The poor behavior of the sovereign borrowers was not in any way matched by the private sector, an important divergence. It was not only the sovereign borrowers, but also private enterprises that returned to the capital markets in the 1860s and 1870s. In the frenzy of the 1820s, only a handful of firms had paid a nonzero return on investment, and even then most had failed by 1850. For a while, little private capital had flowed to the region, but this had begun to change.

By 1875, seventy-seven Latin American firms were listed on London's Royal Exchange. In mining, of the eighteen British companies operating in Latin America in 1880, only three dated from before 1850, and nine had been founded in the 1870s. Railway investment got on track in a small way in 1849. But, again, the major construction boom had been in the 1870s, and of the thirty-four railroads with British stakes, twenty-four had been set up in the 1870s. Three tramways, four sanitation projects, and seven

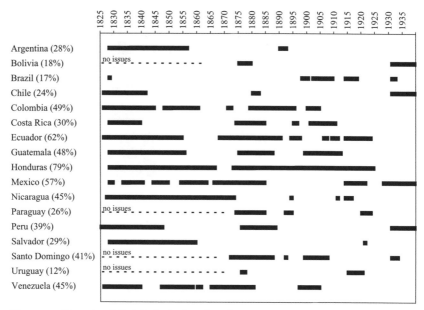

Figure 2.1. Sovereign default in Latin America, 1825–1940.
Note: Fraction of years in default shown in parentheses.
Sources: Default data from Michael Tomz, "How Do Reputations Form? New and Seasoned Borrowers in International Capital Markets," paper presented at the 2001 Annual Meetings of the American Political Science Association, San Francisco. Issue dates from Carlos Marichal, *A Century of Debt Crises in Latin America: From Independence to the Great Depression, 1820–1930* (Princeton, NJ, 1989).

submarine telegraph companies were set up by the British from 1868 to 1880. Of the £56 million total of foreign capital invested in private enterprise, £34 million sat in railways, £11 million in public utilities, and £3 million in mining. These were widely dispersed over a dozen countries (see Table 2.2). Other enterprises supported included shipping, an emerging banking and finance sector, some meat processing and packing on the pampas, and guano in Peru. Real estate investment remained very limited.

In fact, the private enterprises established in Latin America continued to pay handsomely, and an investor widely diversified in the region would have noticed a marked asymmetry between the public and private shares of the portfolio. In 1880, the £56 million of investments in private enterprise, though less than half the size of the sovereign debt, generated a far larger income for investors because the former probably yielded at least 6 percent of par value, but only £52 million of the government loans were actually being serviced, for a yield of perhaps 2 percent of total par value. Most private firms paid good dividends and serviced their debts promptly.

Soon, the usual accusations were flying. Rippy summarized the first sixty years of foreign investment in the region's government bonds as a "decidedly poor investment" and asserted that "British bankers and not a few Latin-American governments alike had been scandalously dishonest. English bankers, brokers, and exporters and grafting Latin-American bureaucrats had profited at the expense of British investors."[10]

TWO GREAT WAVES AND A GREAT CRASH

A new investment boom began in the 1880s, bigger than before, as the global depression receded and economic activity, and especially trade, recovered. Rebuilding a tattered reputation took time for the public borrowers, especially for the defaulting governments. Investment flows changed accordingly. By 1890, more than half the London issues went to the private sector. The overall flows were massive and, by the end of 1890, total British investments were £426 million, more than double the 1880 total. Of this, £194 million sat in government bonds, surpassed by a slightly higher share, £231 million, in private enterprises. After an intervening global depression in the 1890s and a particularly nasty financial and macroeconomic crisis centered on the River Plate, this investment boom was to resume with even greater vigor from 1900 to 1914, at least for the nations lucky enough to have access to the market.

It was soon quite clear that the regional distribution of the investment was to favor only a few countries, namely those that prospered the most in the new trade boom. In the 1880s, capital inflows to the region were concentrated in just five countries: 37 percent in Argentina, 17 percent in Mexico, 14 percent in Brazil, 7 percent in Chile, and 5 percent in Uruguay. Other countries, where trade stagnated, such as Peru and Colombia, received little new investment. Looking at government loan issues, the flows were even more skewed, with 60 percent of all new loans going to Argentina and Uruguay, leading Marichal to term the 1880s a time of "loan frenzy on the Río de la Plata"; more generally, this period seemed to open a new era in Latin American economic history in which "the overall picture is one of a handful of economically dynamic nations that had begun to outstrip the

---

[10] Ibid., 32.

poorer republics of the subcontinent in terms of growth rates."[11] Foreign capital played its part in creating this distinction. There is another way to look at the division: of the big five, four had maintained debt service in the previous crisis; they were rewarded, but defaulters were not.[12]

Capital flows now supported all manner of infrastructure and industry. Railways were always the largest component of these investments, but other important uses included tramways, buses, electricity, canals and docks, finance, and land. Despite the initial promise and the widespread perception (which survives today) that the region's growth would center on the exploitation of its mineral wealth using imported capital, mining and other raw-materials enterprises never constituted more than 4 percent of foreign investment after 1865. Instead, other economic enterprises rose to prominence. Railways accounted for an enormous share, and in 1890 comprised £146 million (93 companies) of the £231 million (289 companies) invested in the private sector. Public utilities came next with £20 million in forty-two enterprises, mining accounted for £13 million in sixty-nine firms, and real estate had grown considerably, with £8 million in twenty-two firms. Nitrates, finance, shipping, and manufacturing each accounted for £4 million to £5 million.

External developments made this surge of foreign investment in the region possible. In the latter half of the nineteenth century, a free-wheeling global capital market, still centered on London, began to boldly supply credit to the developing world within and beyond the empire. The important distinction noted by Stone – a gradually rising share of private sector recipients in total British foreign investment – was not true just of the Latin American share but also of the entire portfolio.[13] One might interpret this as evidence of a tendency over time toward greater depth, integration, and maturity in the London market.

Although impressive in its reach, the universality of this market should not be taken for granted – the country risk perceived by foreign investors remained high and only a handful of Latin American countries had reputation enough regularly to issue external debt. Even as late as 1913, the point

[11] Marichal, *Century of Debt Crises*, 127.
[12] And the Mexicans might have been forgiven after a regime change: they suspended payments in 1867 and only resumed in 1884, but, there, the issue was caught up in a much larger diplomatic dispute over the Maximilian regime, where "spurious" loans had been taken out to finance the French garrison. Ibid., 95, 126.
[13] Irving Stone, "British Direct and Portfolio Investment in Latin America Before 1914," *Journal of Economic History* 37 (1977): 690–722.

of deepest maturation of the global capital market before the 1980s and 1990s, the five countries of Argentina, Brazil, Chile, Mexico, and Uruguay accounted for 90 percent of outstanding Latin American issues in London. Peru and Venezuela made occasional issues, often merely rollovers of earlier defaults. Others were out of the game entirely.

For the major players, an examination of bond yields allows us a crude comparative perspective. Figure 2.2 shows the London bond spread relative to the British Consol on government bond issues for a select group of Latin American countries. It can be seen that before 1890 the spread was much greater than that prevailing on bonds issued by governments in core countries and in the British Empire, though not unusual by the standards of the periphery. The average spread was about 300–500 basis points in Brazil, Chile, and Argentina, around 1,000 in Uruguay and Mexico.

Why were spreads so high, much higher than in the empire? Investors seem to have perceived the risks of default as quite grave in these independent countries, even if gunboat diplomacy and other hardball tactics could, in a desperate moment, be used to enforce some kind of partial repayment. If Latin America was part of some informal empire, it must have been very informal indeed, insufficient to buy it any special preferential access to the capital markets. The spreads are important, however, because, as in all markets, price is likely to affect quantities demanded. The unobserved countries with prohibitively high spreads were effectively priced out of the market. Of those in the market, the economies with lower costs of capital could justify a larger range of investment projects than those more tightly rationed. Only an integrated view of price and quantity data can keep this link in view.

After peace broke out in the region, political stability in the recipient countries was an important stimulus, but institutional conditions were highly favorable to these developments. International capital controls were unknown in this era, and a gradual convergence of national economic policies on the gold standard supplied "common currency" externalities. Besides promoting trade, the gold standard also facilitated capital mobility not just through lowered transaction costs and reduced exchange risk, but also by providing some kind of a commitment mechanism. Evidence shows that countries that adhered to gold in this era benefited from a lower cost of capital, whereas membership in the British Empire had relatively little effect.

Thus, as costs fell, demand rose, and agents from the private and public sector sought funding from foreign markets that appeared better disposed

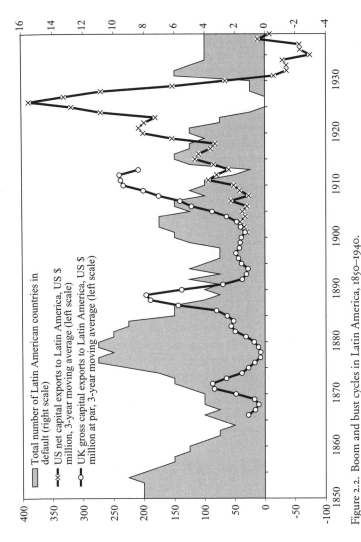

Figure 2.2. Boom and bust cycles in Latin America, 1850–1940.

Sources: Following Christian Suter, "Cyclical Fluctuations in Foreign Investment 1850–1930: The Historical Debate and the Latin American Case," in Carlos Marichal ed., *Proceedings of the Eleventh International Economic History Congress,* vol. B10 (Milan, 1994). Default data from Tomz, "How Do Reputations Form? New and Seasoned Borrowers in International Capital Markets," U.K. flows from Irving Stone, *The Global Export of Capital from Great Britain, 1865–1914: A Statistical Survey* (New York, 1999). U.S. flows from Barbara Stallings, *Banker to the Third World: U.S. Portfolio Investment in Latin America, 1900–1986* (Berkeley, CA, 1987).

than in the past. After a global retrenchment during the 1870s' recession, the first great wave of capital flowing into the region in the 1880s was halted by a crash, with a further wave to follow from the late 1890s until 1913. Moreover, although the principal source was always Britain, several other creditor countries now invested heavily in the region, expanding the supply of capital. The United States' long-term investments in Latin America grew from $308 million in 1897 to $1.6 billion in 1914; French assets grew from $651 million in 1902 to $1.7 billion in 1913. German holdings were estimated at $678 million in 1918. These figures compare to a British total of £1.2 billion ($5.8 billion) in 1913.

Over the course of a few decades, a very significant amount of foreign capital thus entered Latin America, rising from initially almost insignificant levels. By late in the period, around 1900–13, for the largest countries, the ratio of foreign capital to GDP stood at around 2.7, its highest level in history in a developing region. For comparison, in Africa the level was 1.1; in Asia, only 0.4.[14] In this era, scaling appropriately for this perspective by the size of the recipient economy, the most exposed emerging market for foreign investment was Latin America. This was the region in the world economy most assisted by, and yet most at the mercy of, external forces in the capital market (Table 2.3).

Hence, at least for those countries, regions, and industries involved, it can rightly be claimed that "the connection of the industrial centre with Latin America was the driving force behind the capital accumulation process throughout the continent." Whence came this remarkable inflow? The two major investment sources for the entire period 1870–1914 were Europe and the United States. Europe's investments came earlier and were spread more broadly through the region; Britain's investments were most prominent, followed by France and Germany, all three going heavily to the major economies of Argentina, Mexico, and Brazil. U.S. investments came later and were more heavily weighted toward direct investment and geographically more concentrated in Mexico and Cuba. The two major creditors, overall, were Britain and the United States. Britain accounted for around half the foreign investment at this time, the United States for almost 20 percent. Although a sectoral breakdown is not within the scope of a paper directed at long-run macroeconomic trends, we can note that over the entire pre-1914 period, public debt issues absorbed perhaps one quarter of these flows. Private-sector direct investments (including portfolio

---

[14] Michael J. Twomey, *A Century of Foreign Investment in the Third World* (London, 2000).

Table 2.3. *Gross capital flows from Britain, 1865–1914 (£ million)*

	Government	Private	of which: Railways	Total	Distribution World	Periphery
World	–	–	–	3,366	100%	–
Periphery	–	–	–	1,571	47%	–
of which:						
Latin America						
Argentina	78	271	201	349	–	22%
Brazil	79	93	55	173	–	11%
Mexico	16	65	30	82	–	5%
Chile	29	32	15	62	–	4%
Peru	26	11	4	37	–	2%
Uruguay	10	21	16	31	–	2%
Cuba	6	20	13	26	–	2%
Total				760	–	48%
Other periphery						
India	145	172	128	317	–	20%
Russia	70	69	35	139	–	9%
Japan	73	6	2	78	–	5%
China	48	25	15	74	–	5%
Egypt	23	43	1	66	–	4%
Turkey	25	18	9	42	–	3%
Italy	23	18	10	41	–	3%
Spain	8	26	8	34	–	2%
Greece	17	2	0	19	–	1%
Total				812	–	52%

Source: Irving Stone, *The Global Export of Capital from Great Britain, 1865–1914: A Statistical Survey* (New York, 1999).

investment in "free standing companies") accounted for about three quarters. Railroads and public utilities, key infrastructure components, were of particular importance in the latter.

An overview of forty years of inflows, seen as a whole, obscures one important detail of the process, however: its fluctuations and, occasionally, sharp volatility. The bond-yield data hint that the costs of credit were far from smooth, and an examination of the correlations of quantity with these price shocks fills out the picture. As in developing country contexts today, international investment flows were often rudely interrupted by crises, leading to sudden stops and even reversals. In Table 2.4, we can

Table 2.4. *Cumulative gross capital flows from Britain to Latin America, 1880–1913 (£ million)*

Type	Country	1880	Share	1890	Share	1900	Share	1913	Share	Growth rates		
										1880–1890	1890–1900	1900–1913
Private	Argentina	9	3%	78	10%	102	10%	257	12%	24%	3%	7%
	Brazil	10	3%	29	4%	40	4%	90	4%	11%	3%	6%
	Chile	1	0%	12	2%	18	2%	32	2%	28%	4%	4%
	Cuba	1	0%	3	0%	6	1%	20	1%	8%	7%	10%
	Mexico	4	1%	19	2%	27	2%	64	3%	17%	4%	7%
	Peru	2	1%	5	1%	6	1%	11	1%	10%	1%	5%
	Uruguay	5	2%	12	2%	14	1%	20	1%	9%	2%	3%
	These seven	32	11%	157	20%	212	20%	494	24%	17%	3%	7%
	All countries	296	100%	770	100%	1,064	100%	2,065	100%	10%	3%	5%
All	Argentina	21	3%	132	10%	160	9%	332	10%	20%	2%	6%
	Brazil	22	4%	56	4%	74	4%	166	5%	10%	3%	6%
	Chile	8	1%	22	2%	33	2%	60	2%	11%	4%	5%
	Cuba	1	0%	3	0%	6	0%	26	1%	8%	7%	13%
	Mexico	5	1%	26	2%	39	2%	80	3%	18%	4%	6%
	Peru	27	4%	30	2%	30	2%	37	1%	1%	0%	2%
	Uruguay	7	1%	20	1%	23	1%	30	1%	11%	2%	2%
	These seven	90	15%	289	22%	365	20%	732	23%	12%	2%	6%
	All countries	599	100%	1,334	100%	1,812	100%	3,203	100%	8%	3%	4%

Source: Irving Stone, *The Global Export of Capital from Great Britain, 1865–1914.*

follow this process in some detail based on Stone's record of capital calls in the London market (unfortunately, similarly detailed annual data are not available for other source countries).

The 1880s were famously years of "heavy borrowing," to use Williams's description of the country that went to the well more than anyone – Argentina, where British investment grew by a factor of six in the 1880s (24% per annum).[15] Mexico's exposure quintupled, and Brazil's and Uruguay's almost tripled. Peru saw little change. For the region as a whole, British investment swelled at a rate of 8 percent per annum for ten years, more than doubling. The slump in the 1890s is in stark contrast: investments grew at a mere 3 percent per annum, though this decadal rate disguises a period of stagnation from 1890 to 1895. After 1900, investments in the region continued to grow at a respectable rate until 1913, but again only in certain countries, increasing by a factor of four in Cuba, and doubling in Argentina, Brazil, Chile, and Mexico. The patterns are similar for both private and total investment (see Table 2.4).

What benefits did foreign capital bring to the region? Using a rough capital–output ratio of 4, we might guess that during this historical era about one third of the capital stock of Latin America was supplied from external sources, a striking contribution. Certainly, no developing country or region today enjoys such a large boost to its capital stock from overseas, and the positive growth implications can be gleaned from a simple counterfactual that imagines such capital being instantaneously removed: wages and output levels would have plummeted. Table 2.5 explores such a simplified counterfactual using Twomey's data, and the results show what a positive contribution foreign capital might have made to aggregate development circa 1913. In its absence, and *ceteris paribus*, incomes in the region would have been about 17 percent lower on average, with a much greater loss in countries like Argentina, Brazil, and Chile, where foreign capital played a bigger role.

These benefits were significant, but did not come without some offsetting costs, however, given that open capital markets required greater discipline, could quickly punish the guilty for their inconsistent policies, and even hurt innocent bystanders through volatility during the business cycle and contagion during periodic crises. Not every crisis, large and small, warrants mention here. Many defaults were isolated and some simply went on for years. The troubles that beset the region's least creditworthy countries

[15] John H. Williams, *Argentine International Trade Under Inconvertible Paper Currency, 1880–1900* (Cambridge, MA, 1920).

Table 2.5. *Counterfactual: Latin America without foreign capital in 1913–14*

Country	1900 US$ million		FI/GDP	Estimated FI/K (COR = 4)	Counterfactual (capital share = 1/3)	
	GDP	FI			GDP	Change
Argentina	107	279	2.60	0.65	75	−30%
Brazil	23	68	2.96	0.74	15	−36%
Chile	58	122	2.11	0.53	45	−22%
Colombia	38	10	0.27	0.07	37	−2%
Cuba	127	175	1.38	0.35	110	−13%
Guatemala	38	62	1.66	0.42	32	−16%
Honduras	32	50	1.56	0.39	27	−15%
Mexico	49	90	1.83	0.46	40	−18%
Paraguay	41	35	0.86	0.22	38	−8%
Peru	33	40	1.21	0.30	29	−11%
Uruguay	106	172	1.62	0.41	89	−16%
Venezuela	18	17	0.98	0.25	16	−9%
All	670	1120	1.67	0.42	559	−17%

Notes: FI = foreign investment; GDP = gross domestic product; K = capital stock; COR = capital output ratio

Source: Michael J. Twomey, "Patterns of Foreign Investment in Latin America in the Twentieth Century," in John H. Coatsworth and Alan M. Taylor, eds., *Latin America and the World Economy Since 1800* (Cambridge, MA, 1999).

mattered less – capital was flowing at such a dribbling rate into most of these inveterate defaulters, and at such a high cost in risk, that an interruption in its movement was not a major event. These countries struggled along, relying more on domestic saving to finance investment and government finance. This isolated them more from the volatility of the global capital market – but it also restricted their saving supply and choked off growth, a harsh tradeoff. However, the major crises in the 1890s for two major foreign capital recipients deserve mention.

The first crisis was in Argentina, where a calamitous monetary and financial crash, the Baring Crash, brought capital inflows to a sudden halt and plunged the economy into a deep recession for several years. As may be seen from Figure 2.2, country risk exploded not only in Argentina but – in a classic example of contagion – also throughout the region. Neighboring Uruguay was badly affected. Students of the global capital market also see connections to events in Australia and the United States.

This was arguably the world's first example of a modern "emerging market" crisis, combining debt crisis, bank collapse, maturity and currency mismatches, and contagion. As financial development and monetization in Latin American economies grew in the late nineteenth century, government-induced macroeconomic crises were felt more widely. When sovereign risk spreads expanded, the capital market tightened. Domestic banks found themselves in distress and a credit crunch followed, squeezing local borrowers. Whereas government defaults in the 1820s and 1870s could bypass premodern economic modes of production that relied more on retained profits and less on financial intermediation, by the 1890s, the region's more modern economies risked more resounding economic crises after a default.

Argentina's bold development strategy of the 1880s had bubble tendencies from the start, employing as it did a nefarious leveraging system involving the banking sector, which borrowed short in gold and lent long in pesos. When this scheme exploded, the fiscal gap could be covered only by printing money, which predictably broke the exchange rate peg in short order and sent the economy into an inflationary spiral and a generalized financial and banking crisis. For Argentina, stabilization and debt restructuring took the better part of a decade, and in these years foreign capital again bided its time, while a global recession contributed to a delayed recovery. New capital flows began as country risk gradually fell in the mid-1890s.

The other major crisis then hit, in Brazil. It was viewed by commentators at the time almost as a replay of the Baring Crash, and there is evidence to suggest that contagion in country risk from Argentina to Brazil was a contributing factor. Yet there was much else going haywire in Brazil's plan for rapid economic development known as the *Encilhamento*. Political instability was great in the first years of the 1890s, following the proclamation of the Republic, when the country was adjusting to the abolition of slavery, the gold standard had been abandoned, and inconsistent monetary and fiscal policies had the printing presses running at high speed. The money supply almost doubled in the year 1890 alone, and a stock market bubble was underway. The currency steadily devalued by a factor of 3.5 from 1890 to 1898, adding to the domestic costs of debt service. Yet, remarkably, the country maintained debt service and kept issuing new debt to finance ongoing deficits, obtaining new funding from London in 1895–7. It did not default until 1898–1900 and again in 1902–9. However, the real economy was by now in deep recession, having never really recovered from the financial instability of the early 1890s. Matters were made even worse by a severe terms of trade shock caused by a steep decline in coffee prices on world markets. In 1898, the government could no longer meet its obligations. Bonds that had traded at ninety in 1890 were by then trading at fifty.

The two crises did bear one similarity – with each other, as well as with the events of 2001–3. Both Argentina and Brazil had cranked up their government debt levels at a fast pace. There was and is but one cause for this phenomenon – persistent and large deficits and inability of a government to balance its books and set out a sustainable debt path. But, eventually, Argentina and Brazil each hit a debt ceiling and markets were unwilling to roll it over one more time. Both paid a price during messy cleanups that followed. Argentina's national debt service was backstopped by rollovers agreed to by the 1891 Rothschild Committee, but at such a punitive interest rate that the deal had to be renegotiated almost immediately by Romero in 1892–3; the provincial and municipal issues were in disarray for the better part of a decade before being nationalized at a deep discount, a bailout that still appears questionable.[16] Brazil's 1898 Funding Loan, another Rothschild product, had conditions as harsh as any International Monetary Fund (IMF) agreement.

A broader overview of this heyday of international capital markets can give a better sense of the volatility of capital flows and their stop-and-go nature. Figure 2.3 presents annual data on capital flows to the region. The Baring Crash emerges as a major convulsion but by no means the only important capital–market crisis during this period. If the trends are compared with the default and risk data (see Figures 2.1 and 2.2), a more complete picture of the global crises emerges. Booms were typically associated with a convergence in bond spreads; defaults were associated with a sudden stop of capital flows and dramatically increased country risk.

The global capital market quickly recovered from the crisis of the 1890s, although countries badly affected, most notably Argentina, took longer to recover. However, compared with the 1870s boom and bust, this one was not associated with widespread default in the region but rather a more general and global increase in country risk that slowed foreign capital flows for the better part of a decade. Inflows to Argentina and Uruguay were sluggish in the 1890s, but in other countries in the region, the tap was still open, as shown in Table 2.4. Foreign investments had grown at a frenzied 12 percent per annum in the 1880s in the "Big Seven" countries (20% in Argentina!) and this slowed to just 2 percent in the 1890s (and just 2% in Argentina).

---

[16] Juan José Romero became Argentina's finance minister in October 1892.

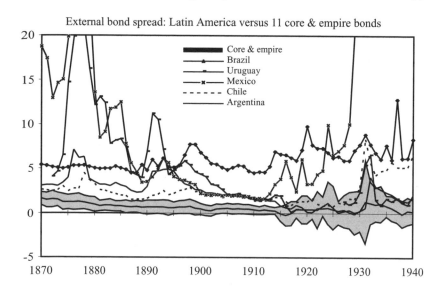

External bond spread: Latin America versus 11 core & empire bonds

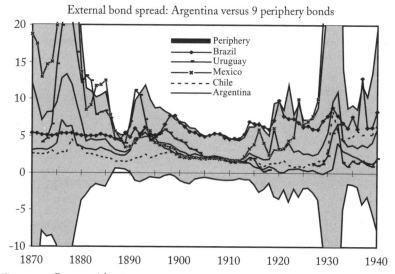

External bond spread: Argentina versus 9 periphery bonds

Figure 2.3. Country risk, 1870–1940.
Source: Global financial data and other sources. Maurice Obstfeld and Alan M. Taylor, *Global Capital Markets: Integration, Crisis, and Growth* (Cambridge, 2004).

When flows resumed, they were brisk and investments grew now at 6 percent per annum in the "Big Seven," as shown in Table 2.4. British private investments in the region doubled from 1900 to 1913 and, overall, increased by about 60 percent, showing the continuing trend toward more private investment. Britain, in 1900, was still the principal investor, with more than half of the investments in the region. Other core countries were joining in quickly. By 1900, France and the United States were becoming major players in the region and, by 1913, they each held about 18 percent of foreign investment in the region. Of the rest, Germany held about 10 percent; Britain, a still large 42 percent; and the remainder was spread among other creditors.

In summation, the period 1870 to 1914 is now rightly regarded as an epoch of economic globalization as great as, or even greater than (by some measures), the one we live in today. Ratios of trade and foreign investment to GDP, and the scale of international migrations, make this period stand out from its predecessors and the period that immediately followed. Whether this phase of globalization was more economic than political will continue to fire debates, but the independent Latin American countries were major players in the process.

Under these conditions, global foreign investments climbed to levels not seen before, and the flows to Latin America surged again in the last great wave of the long nineteenth century from 1900 to 1914. This was one of the smoother booms for the countries of the region. Some had sorted out the worst of their fiscal problems, and the postindependence era with its dysfunctional political economy and endless wars was becoming a distant memory. Many countries now aspired to adopt the gold standard, joining the core countries in establishing a globally stable monetary system that facilitated commercial and financial transactions. There were few warning signs that economic turmoil lay ahead for the countries in the region. Here, and in so many other respects, their fate was rapidly to change once the shocks of the interwar period were unleashed.

THE INTERWAR CRISIS OF WORLD CAPITAL MARKETS

In the space of the next few decades, the integrated global markets for goods, capital, and labor that had been built over the course of the long nineteenth century were effectively destroyed. Their former vigor and sudden disappearance were lamented by contemporaries, but, with the historian's benefit of hindsight and the economist's bent for quantitative measurement, we are better placed now to understand this phase of closure in world markets in a sharper long-run and comparative perspective.

The outbreak of war led to capital controls, and this step, along with subsequent inflationary war finance, marked the effective end of the gold standard regime in the combatant countries until its ill-fated resumption in the late 1920s. Reliant on heavy borrowing from the United States, the European core countries were no longer in any position to export capital to the developing world as they had during the previous golden age. Britain, so essential to the pre-1914 global capital market, emerged from the war quite diminished and, from 1918 through the 1920s, explicit embargoes on foreign investment were occasionally implemented. Britain had supplied the region with £89 million ($431 million) in public loans from 1900 to 1913, but from 1918 to 1931 supplied only £55 million ($250 million); in contrast, from 1918 to 1931 the United States supplied the vast majority of the roughly $2 billion in public loans that were issued, with Britain only accounting for roughly one eighth.

The center of the world capital market gradually shifted from London to New York in these years as a result, but the American capacity to supply funds to the rest of the world did not as rapidly fill the void left by the British. The shift was by no means smooth, but by the late 1920s, capital flows to the region had recovered and in some boom years surpassed the levels seen in the last boom of 1900–14 (see Figure 2.2). There was considerable distress in the region in the wartime years: Brazil defaulted again, for example, as did Uruguay and revolutionary Mexico, but Argentina did not, despite a brutal recession. The 1920s were then a period of marked improvement for Latin American borrowers, notwithstanding the still-uncertain outlook in the world economy. In fact, for a few brief years in the late 1920s, no Latin American government was formally in default, though this was soon to change (see Figures 2.1 and 2.2).

Uncertainty in the global economy reflected the postwar tensions and distrust. Although efforts were undertaken in the 1920s to rebuild the gold standard, free capital markets from wartime controls, and undo the tariffs and quotas imposed on trade, progress was slow, and ended in 1929. The arrival of the world depression brought macroeconomic crisis to the region and its creditors and trading partners. Default became widespread and country risk exploded again in the uncertain environment (see Figure 2.3). The gold standard went into its final death throes. Commodity prices, key to most of the region's export performance, continued a steep downward trend that had begun earlier in the 1920s. To the extent that markets remained open for goods trade or capital export, the channels increasingly turned to favor connections with colonies or with bilateral partners willing to make a deal.

The commitment to an open, multilateral, world economic order would then remain dormant for most of the rest of the twentieth century until reviving recently. This had a predictable impact on the periphery, where markets for their exports dried up and sources of credit failed. The impact was, understandably, felt hardest in the countries that had, up to then, been most dependent on foreign capital and trade and which, by dint of their political independence, could not only rely on anybody's imperial prefer-ences. As we have noted, that region was Latin America. In this region, in these times, force of circumstances demanded new economic thinking and gave birth to new ideologies. The inward turn by the core hurt economically in the short run but in the longer run did more damage by undermining outward-oriented development strategies, creating an understandable iso-lationist backlash that would endure for decades and still haunts us in the present.

Some measures of the impact of closure in global capital markets can be gleaned from data on foreign investments from this period. In all devel-oping countries, foreign investment (FI) as a fraction of gross domestic product (GDP) remained static between 1914 and the 1930s at around 95 percent, although foreign direct investment (FDI) actually rose slightly, from 40 to 51 percent. The latter is intriguing, perhaps a reflection of a need for control in the face of increased economic and political risk and the temptation to "tariff hop" in an age of increased protectionism. However, all of the FDI increase was contained in colonies and none in the inde-pendent countries, which essentially meant Latin America. Although FDI volumes held up, other components did not. The ratio of total FI to GDP fell by almost half in Latin America during this same period, from the level of 2.7 in 1914 to 1.3 in 1929 and 0.87 in 1938. If the FDI component was fairly level in this period, then the remaining investments, debt, and other equity, initially accounting for half of the total, effectively vanished. No other region saw quite so dramatic a retreat of foreign capital from such high levels: in Africa, the FI/GDP ratio fell from 1.3 in 1914 to 0.35 in 1938; in Asia, from 0.4 to 0.26. Evidently, the spike in U.S. capital flows to the region seen in Figure 2.2 was rather brief and, apart from that blip, foreign capital inflows ran mostly dry in this period.

This starvation of investible funds proved very damaging to the economies of the region because a switch to alternative domestic sources of savings was not feasible in the short run. Even by 1914, domestic capital markets in Latin American countries remained weak. Foreign capital, in contrast, came (and also went) embedded in an organizational form, with branch banks and distant stock markets that gave institutional support to the problem of raising finance. Though domestic markets are not the topic of this chapter, it is crucial to recognize their interaction with external finance. Not only did foreign capital bring the resources themselves, it also brought the financial technologies and acumen, the human capital of the financial business enterprise; that is, solutions to the problems of both mobilization and allocation.

When the capital left, so did many of the slowly learned entrepreneurial skills. Problems of misallocation arose. In the country most affected by the withdrawal of foreign capital, Argentina, domestic banks tried to fill the void but only filled their balance sheets with bad loans, with eventually calamitous effects on the whole macroeconomic regime. But even with sound allocation, a deeper problem was how to generate a domestic savings supply equal to the "lost" foreign savings. In some countries, up to half of capital accumulation had been foreign financed, as we have seen. Could domestic savings be doubled overnight to fill the gap? Of course not, because savings are a notoriously slowly evolving component of GDP, determined by many factors, notably expectations for future economic growth and demography, as well as the tax structure, financial frictions, and a host of other influences. Research indicates that, here, Latin America would find no easy solution. Much, if not all, of the inflow of FI to the countries like Argentina, Brazil, Chile, and Mexico before 1914 was, in essence, a response not just to an "investment opportunity gap" (higher return projects on the periphery, so higher demand) but also a "savings supply gap" (higher savings capabilities in the core, so higher supply). The former is often stressed as part of the story of economic development, but the latter can make a huge difference depending on whether the external accounts are open or closed.

The major consequences of this shift in capital markets can be guessed, and in some cases have been measured. The effects were seen from 1914 to 1929 and later. Growth slowed in Latin America, as in the rest of the world, and in the core itself. But the misfortunes of the core during and after the Great War – isolation, hyperinflations, and excessive debts – were not essentially Latin American problems (though they would be later).

Instead, the problems of the core were visited on Latin America through international transmission mechanisms in goods and factor markets. The fall in the terms of trade in the former and the rising scarcity of capital in the latter were fundamental, and intertwined, shocks to the region's growth prospect. In a country such as Argentina, most of the retardation relative to the core during the interwar period is attributable to the sudden collapse in foreign capital supply.

In the 1930s, the situation grew gloomier. The core was mired in its deepest recession yet from 1929 to the bottom in 1933. The gold standard had been patchily rebuilt only to fail again, with Britain suspending in 1931 and the United States in 1933. Capital controls and competitive devaluations were breaking out as macroeconomic policy became activist and uncooperative. Tariff and quota wars, already looming in the 1920s, reached full force with the 1930 Smoot-Hawley Act in the United States and the British imperial preferences adopted in 1932 at Ottawa.

Set this example, and with not much to lose by then, Latin American countries joined in the spirit of these policies, especially the larger countries that adopted a new "reactive" stance in policymaking. In capital markets, the measures began with capital controls and were sometimes followed by attempts to manage multiple exchange-rate regimes, an exercise in trying to apply multiple prices for a single good (money) that led immediately to a black market. According to Bratter's chronology, most of the controls were put in place between 1931 and 1936 (Table 2.6). This represented a serious departure from the principles of sound finance.

The geographical variation in these controls has always invited comment on the political economy of the process. When the Monroe Doctrine is to be invoked as a causal factor, it is noted that the smaller countries of Central America, and also Mexico, stand out among the countries not adopting controls – and these are the same countries with heavy exposure to U.S. investments. Besides the 800-pound gorilla, an alternative or complementary explanation for the pattern might be the internal political economy of each country in the region, where the structure of the polity, measured by representation, autocratic tendencies, and democratic pressure, also partially explains the outcome. The most "reactive" countries also tended to be those most open to democratic or, in the sphere of economics, "populist" pressure. In line with the argument of Eichengreen for the core, drawing on Polanyi, we would expect such countries to feel most acutely the tensions in the classic macroeconomic "trilemma:" that no economy can simultaneously have a fixed exchange rate, free capital mobility, and an activist

Table 2.6. *Latin America's adoption of capital controls as of 1939*

Country	Exchange control, 1930–9			Free market activity			Black market
	None	Begun	Abolished	Tolerated	Controls	None	
Argentina		1931			•		
Bolivia		1931			•		•
Brazil		1931				•	
Chile		1931			•		
Colombia		1931				•	•
Costa Rica		1932			•		
Cuba	•			•			
Dominican Republic	•			•			
Ecuador		1933	1937	•			
El Salvador	•			•			
Guatemala	•			•			
Haiti	•			•			
Honduras		1934				•	
Mexico	•			•			
Nicaragua		1932			•		
Panama	•			•			
Paraguay		1932					
Peru	•			•			
Uruguay		1932				•	
Venezuela		1936		•			

Source: Herbert M. Bratter, "Foreign Exchange Control in Latin America," *Foreign Policy Reports* 14, 23 (1939): 274–88.

monetary policy. Only two out of three are feasible, and pressure for the third inevitably compromises the first two "gold standard rules."[17]

Despite the seeming departures from the principles of sound finance signaled by the abandonment of gold, wholesale default, and widespread controls, many countries in Latin America remained engaged with capital markets as best they could in the 1930s. A small few, notably Argentina, did not default, and they were rewarded with favorable access to the new trickles of capital in the late 1930s. Perhaps hoping for a resumption of normalcy, discussions continued with creditors to renegotiate debts. Soon other

[17] Barry J. Eichengreen, *Globalizing Capital: A History of the International Monetary System* (Princeton, NJ, 1996); Karl Polanyi, *The Great Transformation* (New York, 1944).

governments could borrow once again, partly because recovery in the region was faster than elsewhere in the world, and partly because many governments had shrunk their debt burden through the unsavory and clandestine buyback of their own debt at a deep discount in the secondary market. Through such tricks, or by unilateral offers to creditors, or by renegotiation, several countries achieved substantial debt forgiveness. In this decade, at least, default had little stigma attached – almost every bank, enterprise, or country was afflicted by it. Reputations could be rebuilt, then, but as it would turn out, another war and a global policy response that would seek to contain *haute finance* would soon render these efforts moot, and no significant capital flows would be seen again in the region for three or four decades.

By the end of the 1930s, the stand-off was complete. Investors in the core countries had virtually abandoned the periphery, either by dint of their own domestic controls, controls in the developing countries, or just because of a general increase in economic and political risk in the world as a whole. The Great Depression is a defining moment in world economic history precisely because it was the emergence of these frictions that shaped the greater part of the twentieth-century experience. From the 1940s to the 1980s, the constraints on global capital markets were to fluctuate, but not until the 1990s did notions of globalization surface again, and even then, it could be said, prematurely.

THE POSTWAR PERIOD

Virtually no foreign capital flowed from rich to poor countries for most of the postwar period. A flow picked up in the 1980s and 1990s, but it tended to flow to areas other than Latin America, taking this region that was once highly favored by world investors down a different path. In 1914, and similarly in 1938, the region accounted for about 55 percent of world stock of FI in developing countries, but by 1990, only 37 percent.

Though Latin American postwar economic history labors under the pejorative "inward-looking development" label, it is important to recall that postwar economic isolation was the norm, in both core and periphery, from the start. Trade barriers remained high globally as the General Agreement on Tariffs and Trade (GATT; now the World Trade Organization, WTO) began its task of rebuilding a multilateral trading system. By the 1970s and 1980s, the work of GATT was bearing fruit through the successive

(Tokyo, Kennedy, and Uruguay) rounds of negotiations, although progress was generally slower in developing countries than in the core. In capital markets, however, progress was slow everywhere.

It is crucial to see developing country policies in the larger, global context. Under the articles of the IMF, the new watchdog of international finance, capital mobility was initially repressed. Architects of the Bretton Woods system, like Keynes and White, sought to protect trade and a system of fixed exchange rates, and feared that footloose capital would threaten one or both.[18] In Europe, even current account transactions remained inconvertible in the late 1940s and 1950s, necessitating a cumbersome bilateral payments system to keep trade flowing. The dollar was, for a while, the only freely convertible currency, but other core currencies joined in the 1960s. This was the beginning of the end of the Bretton Woods system, as even limited mobility put strains on the balance of payments of member countries. Exchange rate pressure hit Britain and Germany starting in the late 1960s and then, ultimately, the United States in 1971–2. In March 1973 (after a series of futile adjustments), the dollar floated, taking others with it.

Sitting on the sidelines in this period, most developing countries bided their time and maintained currency controls, even multiple exchange rates, being unwilling to risk their fixed pegs in a truly open capital market. This did not, of course, insulate them from devaluation pressures, as black market rates slid away from official rates, and periodic official depreciations were enacted to maintain some illusion of respectability. In this way, most of the policy innovations of the 1930s, forged during the great economic crisis, eventually persisted and became established components in the postwar policy environment, an era of *dirigisme* and short-lived faith in state planning. Once again, we should stress that in terms of macroeconomic distortions, at this time Latin America did not stand out from other parts of the periphery. Table 2.7 (panel 1) shows that in the 1960s, the black market premium, distortions in relative capital prices, and rates of depreciation were fairly high in both Asia and Latin America.

The comparative picture soon changed. By the 1970s and 1980s, observers started to notice a troubling phenomenon. Notwithstanding the predictions of theory, enough economic data were, by then, being collected to permit serious empirical research on policies and growth in the postwar

---

[18] John Maynard Keynes and Harry Dexter White, representing the United Kingdom and the United States, respectively, were the most influential negotiators at the Bretton Woods Conference.

Table 2.7. *Distortions in Latin America, 1960–90*

	Black market	Tariff	Price of capital	Depreciation	Latin America rank
1960s					
All	0.17	–	0.41	0.03	
Latin America	0.12	–	0.25	0.07	
Southern Cone	0.16	–	0.39	0.21	
Asia-Pacific	0.08	–	0.21	0.08	
NIC4	0.10	–	0.25	0.04	
1970s/80s					
All	0.27	0.17	0.44	0.10	
Latin America	0.26	0.22	0.27	0.37	
Southern Cone	0.32	0.27	0.19	0.60	
Asia-Pacific	0.06	0.13	0.23	0.02	
NIC4	0.03	0.06	0.14	0.00	
Southern Cone	0.32	0.27	0.19	0.60	
Argentina	0.33*	0.29*	0.34*	1.16*	1
Paraguay	0.29*	0.46*	0.46*	0.11	4
Chile	0.52*	0.21*	0.04	0.51*	5
Brazil	0.29*	0.16	0.09	0.83*	8
Uruguay	0.14	0.21*	0.04	0.41*	12
Others	0.24	0.19	0.30	0.28	
Nicaragua	0.62*	0.15	0.48*	0.90*	2
Peru	0.26	0.41*	0.25	0.77*	3
El Salvador	0.56*	0.13	0.68*	0.06	6
Bolivia	0.32*	0.13	0.26*	0.62*	7
Venezuela	0.33*	0.18*	0.21	0.12	9
Costa Rica	0.18	0.16	0.33*	0.13	10
Colombia	0.08	0.31*	0.21	0.17	11
Ecuador	0.18	0.28*	−0.08	0.18	12
Guatemala	0.14	0.08	0.51*	0.08	14
Mexico	0.10	0.08	0.22	0.27*	15
Honduras	0.14	–	0.36*	0.04	–
Panama	0.00	–	0.12	0.00	–

Notes: Annual averages from cross-section data. Black market = black-market premium on the exchange rate; Tariff = own-weight tariff incidence; Price of capital = relative price of capital goods; Depreciation = rate of depreciation of the currency: Southern Cone: Argentina, Brazil, Chile, Paraguay, and Uruguay; NIC4: South Korea, Taiwan, Hong Kong, and Singapore.

Source: Alan M. Taylor, "On the Costs of Inward-Looking Development: Price Distortions, Growth, and Divergence in Latin America," *Journal of Economic History* 58, 1 (1998): 1–28.

period. (This became a major academic industry in the 1990s.) Econometric evidence confirmed what was starting to become obvious to the naked eye: four East Asian Newly Industrialized Countries (NICs) had radically shifted their orientation toward openness and were reaping rewards in fast, export-led growth. Latin American economies, still locked into a more autarkic position, floundered. Table 2.7 (panel 2) also shows this development. Detail in panel 3 shows some surprising policy persistence from the 1930s: still the most reactive countries, where distortions ran highest, were those in the Southern Cone. The extent to which this policy mix retarded Latin American growth is central to policy debates today, and the issue of openness has been extensively discussed. There are few robust correlations in the growth literature, and maybe the only one is between investment and growth; thus, understanding why the region invested so little can explain why growth was so slow.

What then is the importance of this discussion for our understanding of foreign investment? Foreign investment, as noted already, fills the "gap" between domestic saving and domestic investment. But if the latter is repressed, there may be no gap left to fill. This turns out to be a fairly accurate description of postwar Latin America. In econometric exercises, one can show that the distortions in Table 2.7 accounted for almost all of the region's low investment rate and low growth, relative to the NICs. In a counterfactual in which such distortions are removed, what would have happened? Investment rates (and growth) would have surged, pulling in huge amounts of financing from abroad as a side effect. For the region as a whole, investment as a share of GDP would have risen by about five percentage points, something similar in magnitude to the capital flows seen before 1914. Thus, the potential was there for Latin America to reintegrate into a global capital market after World War II, but policy-induced frictions barred the way.

Is this a convincing explanation of why capital did not flow to Latin America and most other developing countries? Another way of looking at this problem proves instructive where, instead of looking at econometric quantity estimates, we look directly at investment prices and expected returns. An exercise of this form was proposed by Robert Lucas, who used the simple uniform technology Cobb-Douglas production function for per capita income, $y = f(k) = Ak^\alpha$, where k is capital per person and α is capital's share of income. Under the critical, but implausible, assumption of identical technologies across countries (A is constant), then the marginal product of capital, $MPK = lf'(k) = \alpha A\, k^{\alpha-1}$ varies inversely with y, such that for two countries $(MPK_1/MPK_2) = (y_1/y_2)^{(\alpha-1)/\alpha}$. In this set up, when $\alpha = 0.4$ and India has a per capita income $1/15$ that of the United States, we predict a marginal product of capital in India fifty-eight times that in the United States. Such arbitrage opportunities seem unlikely, casting doubt on assumptions of perfect capital mobility, uniform technologies, or both.

The mystery soon vanishes once one begins to use auxiliary information on each of these assumptions. Capital prices are heavily distorted upward in many developing countries, as we have seen, so that the returns to investment are pushed down because of the high cost of (physical) capital. Uniform technologies in the United States and India would also imply that the capital output ratio, k/y (a scalar multiple of MPK), would also be fifty-eight times higher in India, yet data on capital stocks can be adduced to falsify this assumption. Correcting for both these problems, an appropriate measure of the differential marginal incentive to invest in two economies is $(MPK_1/MPK_2) = (y_1/p_1 \ k_1)/(y_2/p_2 \ k_2)$, where p is the relative price of capital and k the capital per person.

Compared with the raw measure, this measure shows remarkably little variation across countries in the postwar period, as seen in Table 2.8. Lucas's raw measure of MPK (column 2) implies huge incentives to move capital to all regions, with MPKs at least 10 times the U.S. level, sometimes more than 100 times, except in the NICs: a huge market failure? Not so, once we correct for technology differences (column 3) and price distortions (column 5). The first correction lowers the dispersion of MPKs considerably (column 4), though still with an 80 percent premium in Latin America and more than 100 percent in Africa and South Asia. But those turn out to have been the economies with the most distorted prices, so this correction eliminates all of the excess marginal return in every region, such that in the end, the range of MPKs is from 90 to 130 percent of the U.S. level. Thus, even absent explicit capital controls (which were only lifted fairly recently), unless underlying distortions had changed, there was little incentive for capital to migrate to Latin America.

CONCLUSION

To summarize, only recently have economic reforms begun to undo the price distortions that have been built into the Latin American economies since the generalized interwar autarky and specific policy reactions of the 1930s. Prior to those reforms, the region remained unattractive to foreign

Table 2.8. *Why didn't capital flow to developing countries?*

Region	(1) Income per capita 1985–9 International dollars	(2) Lucas MPK (OECD = 1) (=1/3)	(3) K/Y World prices	(4) MPK (OECD = 1) World prices	(5) PI/PY (World = 1) Local prices	(6) K/Y Local Prices	(7) MPK (OECD = 1) Local prices
OECD	24,077	1.0	1.2	1.0	0.9	1.1	1.0
Middle East	23,851	4.5	0.9	1.3	1.3	1.0	1.1
NICs	14,195	2.3	1.1	1.1	1.1	1.2	0.9
Caribbean	12,047	14.8	0.8	1.4	1.6	1.1	0.9
Latin America	9,806	12.0	1.0	1.8	1.5	1.2	1.3
East Asia	5,285	24.0	0.8	1.4	1.7	1.2	0.9
Africa	3,551	129.5	0.6	3.3	2.7	1.7	1.1
South Asia	2,964	99.1	0.8	2.2	2.2	1.6	1.0

Notes: Omitted are the centrally planned economies and Oceania. MPK = marginal product of capital; K/Y = capital–output ratio; PI/PY = relative price of capital. See text.

Source: Alan M. Taylor, "Argentina and the World Capital Market: Saving, Investment, and International Capital Mobility in the Twentieth Century," *Journal of Development Economics* 57, 1 (1998): 147–84.

Table 2.9. *Foreign investment in Latin America, Asia, and Africa, 1900–90*

Year	1900	1914	1929	1938	1967	1980	1990
A. Foreign Investment							
Total	6.3	15.7	11.0	11.6	16.5	45.5	74.5
Latin America	2.2	8.4	6.5	5.5	9.0	20.7	27.7
Share of total	*.35*	*.54*	*.59*	*.47*	*.55*	*.45*	*.37*
Asia	1.8	5.1	3.7	4.8	4.7	13.7	30.7
Share of total	*.29*	*.32*	*.34*	*.41*	*.28*	*.30*	*.41*
Africa	2.3	2.3	0.7	1.4	2.8	11.0	16.1
Share of total	*.37*	*.15*	*.06*	*.12*	*.17*	*.24*	*.22*
B. Foreign Investment-to-GDP Ratio							
Latin America	1.20	2.71	1.26	0.87	0.33	0.33	0.47
Asia	0.17	0.40	0.23	0.26	0.11	0.15	0.32
Africa	1.33	1.17	0.24	0.35	0.23	0.34	0.74
Total	0.44	0.89	0.45	0.41	0.2	0.24	0.42

Notes: Panel A: Total stock of foreign investment (US$ billion at 1900 U.S. prices). Panel B: For Argentina, the dates are 1900, 1913, 1929, 1938, 1970, 1980, and 1989, and the ratio calculation is at domestic prices.
Source: Twomey, "Patterns of Foreign Investment in Latin America in the Twentieth Century"; and unpublished data.

investors not only because of its low levels of technology (low productivity), but also because price distortions lowered the realizable rate of return on capital. As a result, investment and accumulation were effectively constrained to a lower level, limited by the mobilizing determinants of domestic saving and the allocating capacities of the domestic financial system – and economic growth was held in check. Yet, if the region were to embrace the kinds of policies seen in the late nineteenth century, there is reason to believe that a similar degree of globalization in the capital market would ensue, with positive spillovers for aggregate growth.

Between the past and present eras of globalization, Latin America, like the rest of the world, participated in the dramatic ebb and flow of foreign capital seen everywhere, the only difference being that the retreat was sharper and the resurgence slower. In this, Latin America followed a pattern generally shared throughout the periphery, only more so. A few summary statistics round out this picture. An examination of Twomey's FI data for the entire developing world in Table 2.9 recaps some of the data mentioned so far and presents them in a coherent fashion for the whole twentieth century.

In panel A, total FI (in constant 1900 dollars) rose rapidly to 1914, reaching $15 million; then fell to 1929, and remained at or below its 1914 level until well into the 1960s.

This was roughly half a century of lost progress, given the overall growth of the world economy and the divergence in income levels over this period, factors that would have led one to expect ever-increasing investment flows. Slowly, the flows began again and rose by a factor of three to 1980 and by a factor of five to 1990. This certainly looks like a resumption of globalization, until one considers the normalization more carefully. In panel B, we see that relative to GDP, FI has reached nothing like the levels seen in 1914, and as of 1990 was at roughly one half the peak level, 42 versus 89 percent. The fall in Latin America is greater still, from 270 to 47 percent, with only a small rise from 1967 to 1990. The rather more impressive surge in Asia, a tripling in the ratio of FI to GDP (FI/GDP) since 1967, is indicative of a general shift in the most desired location for FI over the century. An important part of this story would be the "economic miracles" of first Japan and then the East Asian NICs.

However, some countries have experienced an increase in FI/GDP ratios to levels above and beyond those seen in 1914. These are the core countries, and, for this to be consistent with the aforementioned data, it goes without saying that the gross flows from the core countries are now, principally, *to other core countries.* What is going on? The key difference today is that globalization in capital markets, although high in such crude volume terms, has a very different form than 100 years ago. Most gross capital flows are forms of portfolio risk diversification between developed countries and very little takes the form of development finance in the poorer countries.

This is clearly seen in Figure 2.4, using a broader data set for all FI. Here, we see an inverse U-shape, with a different message. As can be seen, Latin America and all developing countries saw their share of world liabilities peak at mid-century. At that point, the periphery stocks of foreign capital accumulated before 1914 were still present and growing, and the core was in disarray. After the war, those stocks began to atrophy: nationalizations, expropriations, capital mobility restrictions, price distortions, devaluations, and defaults took their toll on existing assets and discouraged new flows from coming. Especially after Bretton Woods collapsed (the 1970s) and core countries liberalized the capital account (the 1980s), the core countries found themselves able and willing to invest in each other.

The IMF design succeeded in its own way. Capital flows were repressed for two or three decades. To some degree, so were major developing country

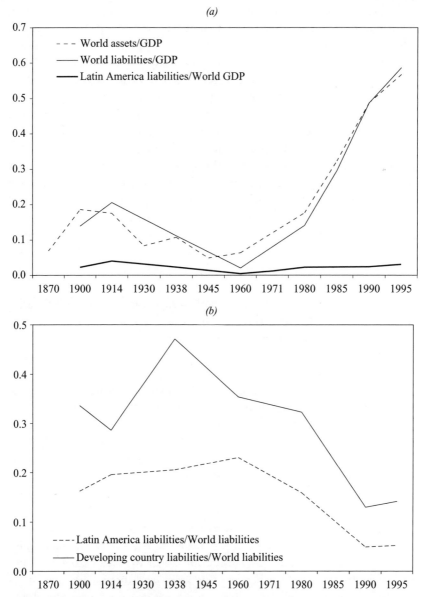

Figure 2.4. World financial liabilities, 1870–1995.
Source: Maurice Obstfeld and Alan M. Taylor, *Global Capital Markets: Integration, Crisis, and Growth* (Cambridge, 2004).

macroeconomic and financial crises. And debt crises were *ipso facto* ruled out because there was so little portfolio investment to speak of. Once capital flows resumed under the less restricted global capital markets of the post–Bretton Woods era, major crises have again swept over the region in a manner eerily reminiscent of the experiences from the 1820s to the 1930s. Sovereign borrowing exploded in the 1970s, especially from banks in core countries eager to find new investments during the growth slowdown of the 1970s and recycle the so-called petrodollars of newly rich Organization of Petroleum Exporting Countries (OPEC) creditors. International bank lending to the "Big Three" – Argentina, Brazil, and Mexico – doubled from 1979 to 1981. In 1982, a default crisis engulfed these countries and many others in the region and elsewhere on the periphery. A recession in the core, high interest rates, weak commodity prices, and overborrowing caused another *déjà vu*. Renegotiations and an orderly work out of this fiasco took almost a decade. The door to global financial markets was temporarily shut once again and the region endured more political and economic turmoil as fiscal adjustments ensued, inflations and hyperinflations were tamed, and political regimes (democratic or otherwise) came and went.

Another boom and bust cycle soon followed, and the two can be seen in Figure 2.5. The emerging-market boom of the early 1990s led some to believe that a new era was about to begin under the sway of so-called "neoliberal" policy reforms, with development finance flowing to the periphery as it had in the distant past, both to public and private recipients this time, and with more and more countries imitating the NICs and experiencing convergence to high levels of income. It has not quite happened yet. The crises and contagions of the late 1990s, not least in the East Asian miracle countries themselves, have disrupted that cozy vision of the future, and we are left with the realization that supposed policy reforms have, in many cases, been adopted weakly, if at all.

Whether there was a convergence of developing countries around a "neoliberal consensus" in the 1990s is a matter of debate. That there was is a popular belief, but widespread evidence remains to be found in the actual data used by political scientists and other researchers to assess changes in economic and political regimes. Overall, measured by the admittedly crude indices of corruption, rule of law, and the like, the institutional gap between rich and poor countries has remained wide. But such characteristics, or deep determinants, do not directly illuminate the recent crises, where the more proximate causes appear to involve an embrace of open capital markets without an adequate understanding of the implications and constraints on

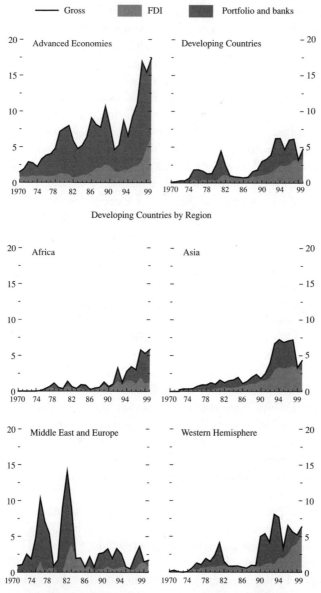

Figure 2.5. Boom and bust cycles, 1970–2000.
Source: International Monetary Fund, *World Economic Outlook* (October 2001), Figure 4.1.

other economic policies. There remains a possible role of contagion and "animal spirits" in the market, though proving the existence of these forces has proved difficult for economic researchers in the 1990s crises. The presence of poor fundamentals has been more robustly identified, as in the crony financial structures and fiscal weakness of the Argentine state.

However, the "Washington consensus" account of the 1990s should not be overemphasized. Although the recent opening of capital markets has been tried here and there with mixed degrees of enthusiasm and mixed results, the overall record for the region as a whole (and the rest of the world) suggests that the opening of developing countries on the capital account has proceeded very slowly indeed, and measures of capital account restrictions show that these countries remain, on the whole, very closed compared with the developed countries, as shown in Figure 2.6. The restrictions measure takes a zero or one value and is averaged across all countries, using the left scale. We see that in 1970, about 80 percent of advanced countries had closed capital markets, falling to 10 percent in 1998. But, in developing countries, the ratio has remained fairly steady at around 80 percent for the entire period. The opening of markets has been unevenly spread across countries and the timing has been spasmodic. The pattern in Latin America shows considerable shifts in policy: a shift to openness in the 1970s coincided with a major capital inflow, but controls were reimposed in several countries in 1978–82 as the debt crisis unfolded. Controls were only later lowered in the early 1990s, when a new influx began.

In the same figure, it is striking also how these measures of restrictions correlate with the extent of FI in each region or country grouping, measured by the ratio of FI (proxied by cumulated capital inflows) to GDP, using the right scale. Note that the scale for developed countries is different: they have witnessed a huge expansion of foreign investment, from about 0.15 to 1.3 on this scale, almost a tenfold increase. The other scales only run up to 0.3 and reflect the much smaller flows of foreign capital to developing countries. There, the ratio has risen from 0.15 to about 0.35, a little more than doubling. The rise was somewhat steeper in Asia but rather flatter in Latin America.

The lessons from these data are clear: for all the talk of the globalization of capital markets in the last few years, two facts have been overlooked. First, the process has been going on for two or three decades. Second, the process has largely bypassed developing countries and, in large part, that reflects their choice: that is, the persistence of autarkic policies in those countries, combined with an institutional environment inimical to

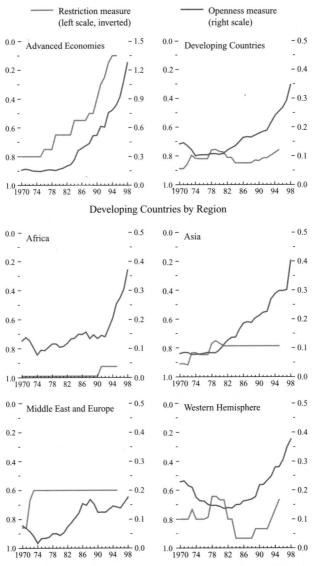

Figure 2.6. Openness and restrictions, 1970–2000.
Notes: The restriction measure is calculated as the "average" value of the on/off measure for the country group. The openness measure is calculated as the average stock of accumulated capital flows (as percent of GDP) in a country group. All respective left and right scales are the same, *except* in the first chart on the right.
Source: International Monetary Fund, *World Economic Outlook* (October 2001), Figure 4.2.

foreign investment. Overall, we might wonder not at how much capital has penetrated developing countries today, but rather how little. As we have already seen in Figure 2.5, capital flows to developing countries are far smaller today than in the first age of globalization.

The contrast with the historical position in 1913 adds greater perspective and only reinforces the impression that the intellectual frenzy over recent symptoms of globalization has been overwrought and misdirected. A century ago, a much greater share of global finance reached poorer countries, and not just under the auspices of empire. The volume of capital flows, although higher to colonies, was not higher to rich countries. Colonies and independent regions like Latin America all had access to the London capital market. From an analytical perspective, the region gave an important test case for historical explanations that rely on the logic of trade (and finance) "following the flag." In the so-called "Age of Empire" here was the first, and at that time only, developing region to have achieved independence. At the same time, it was able to enjoy access to world markets for goods and capital, often to a greater extent than many of the colonies themselves. It made both sovereign issues and private-sector issues, and attracted direct and portfolio investment. Country risk was not significantly higher for non-empire countries, once we control for policy choices and other characteristics. Why is today's globalization so different?

Problems in sequencing reforms have exposed many countries to highly mobile capital flows at a time when their financial systems, regulatory and oversight capacity, and institutional strength have still changed little. This has raised questions as to whether international capital mobility can benefit developing countries without complementary reforms that attack corruption, enhance rule of law, increase transparency, and strengthen property rights. In Latin America, the Argentine debacle of 2001 exposed key weaknesses in all these areas, and left a very bitter taste. Once paraded as a model of emerging market success, Argentina has reverted from poster child to *enfant terrible*.

Without fundamental institutional reforms, the region may not be able to handle foreign investments, but it could benefit from them if it can establish a stable order. In Latin America since 1914, foreign capital has played only a minor role, a parallel of the trend in most developing countries. In contrast to the first era of globalization a century ago, most of the postwar investment successes and failures of the region have been homegrown. Under these conditions, per capita incomes in the region have not fallen behind the core in relative terms. But they did not achieve rapid convergence to the core's level of income per capita, as one might have hoped. Some of this persistent divergence is technological, and can trace its origins to the uneven spread of the industrial revolution and subsequent technological advances since the mid-1800s. But a large share of the gap, perhaps one third to one half, is attributable to capital formation.

For poor countries with low savings, capital formation can only be quickly and significantly augmented through an external supply of capital that is allowed to flow without impediments. This was an option exploited by much of the region from 1870 to 1914 with reasonably favorable results for aggregate growth but under political economy equilibria that were sympathetic to the domestic policy constraints implied by open capital markets. The subsequent historical record shows that most of the world remained closed to foreign capital until the last decade or two, and, in comparative terms, Latin America opted for choices that were deeply autarkic. In the last decade, a greater inclination of developing economies to open capital markets has often collided with political economy constraints that have generated serious crises as policymakers struggle to follow the implied rules of the game.

3

THE EXTERNAL CONTEXT

MARCELO DE PAIVA ABREU

This chapter covers the time span between the great debt crises that began in 1928, when the Wall Street boom and the United States federal contractionary monetary policy started to crowd out new loans to Latin America, and 1982, when the Mexican debt crisis brought an end to the second cycle of voluntary international lending to Latin America that had started about fifteen years before. Between these major balance of payments crises, what happened in Latin America was strongly influenced by events in the world economy, but there was also a long-term trend making these economies much less outward-looking than they had been before the end of the 1920s, and furthermore, before 1914.

Fast recovery from the depression of 1928–33 followed the upturn in the developed economies after 1933. It was interrupted by the recession of 1937 in the United States and then by the effects of the Second World War on the progressive contraction of export markets until 1942. Good export performance and import compression in the remaining war years paved the way for a repayment of old foreign debt. But after the initial postwar period, most of Latin America faced the constraints imposed by the dollar shortage as reserves in dollars were restricted and import prices rocketed. European exports were badly affected by reconstruction demand and the United States was by far the major supplier of imports, even if restricted by the pressures of domestic demand. However, a boom in Latin American export prices in the late 1940s as well as during the Korean War (1950–4), eased the impact of the dollar shortage. World financial markets remained closed for Latin America until the mid-1960s. Foreign finance came mainly from loans by multilateral banks, the World Bank from the late 1940s and the Inter-American Development Bank after 1960, and also from credits extended by suppliers of capital goods.

In the second half of the 1950s, as economic conditions in Europe returned to normalcy, there was a reduction in the importance of U.S. direct investment in Latin America and also of trade links with the United States. Europe recovered some of the ground lost during the 1930s and World War II both in Latin American markets and in relation to foreign direct investment flows toward Latin America. In the early 1960s, the Cuban menace, as seen by the United States, prompted a substantial increase in loans by the U.S. government to Latin America. After 1965, voluntary private bank lending to Latin America was resumed in the wake of the expansion of dollar deposits in Euro-markets as a result of U.S. legislation controlling domestic interest rates and the Soviet Union's interest in holding dollar deposits that were not vulnerable to interference by the United States. Foreign indebtedness was in the form of variable interest rate loans rather than fixed rate bonds as had been the case before 1930. Foreign debt remained low, mainly because of the lack of interest by lenders, but increased rapidly after the mid-1960s.

The 1973–4 oil shock badly affected the position of oil importers as oil prices increased fourfold. However, it was possible for Latin America to finance the transition through further indebtedness as a result of the soft macroeconomic policies adopted in the United States. These allowed nominal interest rates to remain below world inflation until almost the end of the decade. Latin American oil exporters were also unfavorably affected by wrong policies in response to the oil boom that led to heavy capital flight. A second oil shock in the decade led to a further threefold increase in oil prices after 1978. This time, macroeconomic policies in the United States were far from accommodating and monetary restriction led to real interest rates, including country spreads, in excess of 20 percent. For the heavily indebted Latin American economies, this was fatal and the Mexican default of 1982 was rapidly generalized.

The chronological organization of this chapter reflects major changes in the world economy. It is divided into six sections: the impact of the depression on Latin America (1928–33); recovery (1933–7) and further shocks following the 1937 recession in the United States and the beginning of World War II (1937–42); dollar plenty followed by dollar shortage (1942–7); the golden age of import-substituting industrialization (1947 to the early 1960); macroeconomic instability, return of private capital flows, export diversification, and growth (mid-1960s to the early 1970); and two oil shocks and a new debt crisis (1973–82).

In the half century after the end of the 1920s, there was a sharp reduction in the importance of Latin America in the world economy as measured by its importance in global trade and capital flows. Yet it remained, all the same, extremely vulnerable to fluctuations in the world economy. Its importance in world trade had increased since the early 1880s until the early 1950s, but the fall afterward was spectacular: from a peak of 12.4 percent of world exports in 1950, mostly explained by the boom in commodity prices and the slow recovery of Europe, the Latin American share fell below 8 percent in 1960 and to the 5 to 6 percent range in the 1970s and early 1980s, compared with 9.8 percent in 1928. Of the larger economies, only Mexico and Venezuela increased their share of world exports between 1928 and 1982, from 0.74 to 1.13 percent in the former case and from 0.36 to 0.89 percent in the latter. In Brazil, the reduction – from 1.45 to 1.01 percent – was significant, but no large country portrays better the Latin American withdrawal into autarky than Argentina. Its share in world exports decreased by more than 80 percent in the same period: from 3.12 to 0.42 percent of world exports. Chile's record was only slightly better. There was some diversification of Latin American exports. In the late 1920s, only commodities were exported. In the early 1980s, manufactured exports were substantial, not only in some of the bigger non-oil exporting economies (they exceeded 30 percent of total exports in Brazil and 20 percent in Argentina and Colombia), but also in some of the smaller Central American and Caribbean republics (such as Costa Rica, Haiti, and Guatemala).

It can be misleading to compare terms of trade over the long term for Latin America because there was a sharp difference between oil exporting economies and the non-oil exporters. For Latin America as a whole, the terms of trade in the early 1980s were slightly above the 1928 level, after having peaked in the early 1950s almost 30 percent above this initial level. Terms of trade of oil exporters, however, improved almost 200 percent by 1982 in relation to 1928, whereas those of non-oil exporters fell by more than 20 percent.

To a large extent, the history of the foreign debt crisis that followed after the late 1920s, when the first cycle of heavy indebtedness drew to a close, was repeated after 1980. The ratio between total debt and exports for Latin America in 1928, on the eve of the Great Depression, was around 1.5. More than half a century later, in 1980, on the eve of another major balance of payments shock, the ratio was back to almost 2.0. In both cases, in the economies worst hit by the sharp fall in exports and fast rise of debt, the ratio exceeded 5.0 and led inexorably to the temporary reduction of full service, defaults, and the renegotiation of contractual conditions.

The Latin American share of U.S. global foreign direct investment in 1929 was 46.7 percent. Estimates for the geographical distribution of British investment are rather unreliable before 1938, but 21.8 percent, which was the Latin American share in 1938, can be considered as a lower bound estimate for 1929. So Latin America in the late 1920s had attracted at least 37 percent of global foreign direct investment.[1] In 1980, the stock of foreign direct investment in Latin America had decreased to 8.9 percent of the global stock. There was a similar contraction affecting other types of investments. The Latin American share of the stock of dollar and sterling public foreign loans in 1929–30 was no less than 46 percent of the total.[2] In 1981, the Latin American share of world debt had declined to 12 percent.[3]

THE UNEVEN IMPACT OF THE DEPRESSION: 1928–33

Most Latin American economies, and certainly all the bigger ones, faced a major external shock even before 1930. It was the Wall Street boom rather than the 1929 crash that marked the beginning of the depression in Latin America. The massive external shock that hit Latin America affected the balance of payments, first through the capital account and then the current account, as the value of exports fell rapidly because of the contraction of trade volumes and export prices. In many economies, such as Argentina and Brazil, the significant inflow related to foreign loans had come to a total halt by mid-1928. The short-lived recovery of inflows in 1930 was – in some

---

[1] Estimates of European investment from other origins are notoriously unreliable and certainly negligible for Latin America as a whole.

[2] This does not include French or other investments because estimates are of doubtful quality. In any case, French investment in securities was unlikely to have been more than about 13 percent of the combined U.S. dollar and sterling investments.

[3] Data on capital flows from Bank of England, *United Kingdom Overseas Investments 1938 to 1948* (London, 1950); U.S. Department of Commerce, Office of Business Economics, *U.S. Investments in the Latin American Economy* (Washington, DC, 1957); United Nations, Department of Economic and Social Affairs, *External Financing in Latin America* (New York, 1965); United Nations Conference on Trade and Development, *World Investment Report 2000: Cross-border Mergers and Acquisitions and Development* (New York and Geneva, 2000); Robert Devlin, *Debt and Crisis in Latin America: The Supply Side of the Story* (Princeton, NJ, 1989), 14.

cases, such as the large Brazilian coffee realization loan – mainly related to the consolidation of short-term debt.

It is not easy to single out the economy that suffered most from the external shock because the fall in export prices and volumes varied substantially between different economies. Moreover, the capacity to expand export volumes also varied considerably, so that economies with a sharp deterioration in their terms of trade could partly compensate it with a significant increase in export volumes and dampen the reduction in the capacity to import. The reduction of Chile's exports was by far the most significant among the bigger economies: in 1932, the U.S. dollar value of Chilean exports had fallen to the almost unbelievable level of one eighth of its 1929 peak. In most other big economies – Argentina, Brazil, and Mexico – the fall in the value of exports generally started in 1928, reaching a trough in 1932, when the fall was in the 62 to 68 percent range in relation to their peak.[4] In Peru, the reduction was similar but the export peak was reached in 1929. The fall was slightly less significant in Colombia (55 percent in relation to the 1928 peak). In Central America, exports started to fall already in 1926 in countries such as El Salvador and Nicaragua, but in the others, the peak was also in 1928. The trough was generally also in 1932, with the exception of Honduras, where exports remained roughly stable until 1934.

Depending on the specific country, there were sharp contrasts in the behavior of prices and quantities to explain export trends. The volume of Brazil's exports increased by more than 50 percent in 1928–33 and, in Colombia, had also started to rise in 1932. However, in economies such as Mexico and Chile, export volumes fell substantially: by 37 percent in Mexico and by no less than 73 percent in Chile. Export volumes also fell in Argentina but recovered sharply and hovered around 15 to 20 percent below the 1927 peak until the end of the 1930s. Terms of trade fell almost everywhere in Latin America between 1928 and 1932–3: less in Mexico (20.8%), around 35 percent in many economies (Argentina, Brazil, Colombia, and Costa Rica), 45 to 50 percent in Guatemala and Nicaragua, and 60 percent in Chile (1926–33).

All Latin American economies were commodity exporters and remained so at least until the 1960s. Exports were generally concentrated in a small number of commodities. In all Latin America, the leading commodities accounted for more than half of total exports and in ten countries, one

---

[4] All these comments are based on data in U.S. current dollars. The U.S. dollar/gold parity was changed in 1933 from US $20.67 to $35/Troy ounce of gold.

product represented at least fifty percent.[5] Only Brazil was clearly a price maker in the relevant international commodity market and other Latin American coffee exporters were to a very large extent free riders in the unilateral Brazilian coffee valorization policies more or less continuously adopted since 1907.

Exports/gross domestic product (GDP) ratios in 1928 were relatively high in the small Central American economies (56.5% in Costa Rica); mid-range in Argentina (29.8%), Chile (35.1%), Mexico (31.4%), and Peru (33.6%); lower in Colombia (24.8%); and lowest in Brazil (17%).

In the longer term, there was some diversification of Latin American exports, notably the increase in the share of oil in total exports in Venezuela and Mexico. In Brazil, the share of coffee in total exports fell from 71.5 percent in 1928 to 45 percent in the late 1930s because of increased exports of other commodities, especially cotton, but also because coffee prices fell in relation to other export prices. With the recovery of coffee prices in the late 1940s, this apparent export commodity diversification rapidly reversed.

After the seriousness of the external shock was evident, money doctors came to Latin America, still following the traditional division of spheres of influence that had been defined in the 1920s. Experts from the United States and, prominently, Edwin Kemmerer, visited the west coast of South America and the Caribbean, whereas in the east coast, the British remained in control. In the case of Brazil, this was somewhat surprising, given the much more important commercial links with the United States than with the United Kingdom and the rapidly rising inflow of capital from the United States in the 1920s. However, the Hoover administration bungled foreign policy, allowing a politically motivated extension of British financial influence that was to last until the mid-1930s.

In 1930, Kemmerer visited Colombia and recommended many economic policy measures purporting to be improvements on his own former recommendations. Central banking, banking legislation, taxation – almost nothing seemed outside the scope of the mission. In Peru, the gold exchange standard was adopted in April 1931, and a new central bank was created in September 1931. However, by May 1932, it joined the rest of Latin America on the road to inconvertibility and default. There was a remarkable coincidence between the Kemmerer proposals, say in Peru, and what Sir Otto

---

[5] See Victor Bulmer-Thomas, *The Economic History of Latin America Since Independence*, 2nd ed. (Cambridge, 2003), 189. Five of these ten were coffee exporters (Brazil, Colombia, El Salvador, Guatemala, and Nicaragua), two were sugar exporters (Cuba and the Dominican Republic), and the other three were exporters of bananas (Honduras), tin (Bolivia), and oil (Venezuela).

Niemeyer proposed when tendering advice to the new Brazilian government in 1931. The Niemeyer report on Brazilian finances published in July 1931 stressed singularly unrealistic and retrospectively ill-timed proposals that Brazil should raise a sizable loan in the London market so as to make possible a return to the gold standard. Two months after the report was published, the pound sterling went off gold.

In spite of the advice of money doctors, the standard answer by Latin American economies to the external shock ended up being to abandon orthodoxy. The date of Britain's abandonment of the gold standard was crucial. Many countries that had played a waiting game until then decided to shift their policies as it became clear that there was no hope of raising new loans in London. These policies included the abandonment of the gold exchange standard followed by formal devaluation; the introduction of foreign exchange controls, which effectively rationed access to foreign exchange cover; and then some kind of adjustment of payments related to the foreign debt service.

The introduction of controls and sustained overvaluation of the domestic currency were rationalized by two lines of argument. One, valid for all economies, was to make less painful the impact of devaluation on public finances, because there was a lack of symmetry between the strength of the effects of devaluation on expenditures and revenues that transformed external shocks into fiscal shocks. The other argument, valid for those countries with a significant share in specific commodity markets, such as Brazil, dominant in the coffee market, a price maker and not a price taker, was that devaluation could be self-defeating because it would provide incentives to the concentration of sales in the short-term that would depress world prices of such commodities.

However, although most Latin American economies, with the important exception of Central America, ended up abandoning the gold standard before the 1933 devaluation in the United States, the timing of doing so varied considerably. Argentina abandoned the gold standard quite early, closing its *Caja de Conversión* in December 1929. Brazilian foreign reserves vanished by mid-1930, after two years of stubbornly maintaining convertibility while waiting for a favorable change in the international environment. Mexico abandoned the gold standard after a protracted fight to stay on it and a massive monetary contraction in May–July 1931. After a period of flotation, the Mexican peso was pegged to the U.S. dollar in May 1932 and remained so until 1938. Chile went off gold de facto in July 1931, even if this was explicitly recognized only in mid-1932.

Many countries adopted exchange controls as early as 1930. Foreign exchange scarcity was met initially by a mixture of moratoria and ad hoc decisions without a formally defined set of rules. However, after the devaluation of the sterling, formal controls followed. By October 1931, for instance, foreign exchange controls were introduced in Brazil – at the same time as in Argentina and Colombia. This took a form similar to that of many arrangements in Latin America and elsewhere. Foreign exchange was to be compulsorily sold to the government at a fixed rate and, after government demand was met, the residual exchange cover was distributed according to "essentiality" criteria to the private sector. With different formats, some form of exchange control was to remain in place in countries such as Brazil for more than sixty years, if a short period of liberalization after World War II is excluded. Nominal devaluation of the official (overvalued) exchange rate against the U.S. dollar was 66 percent (mil-réis/U.S. dollar) in 1929–32 and real devaluation of 42 percent against the dollar was modest if compared with other Latin American economies. Chile established exchange controls immediately following its foreign debt default in mid-1931. Devaluation reflected the seriousness of the shock: nominal devaluation in the same period was 339 percent against the U.S. dollar, a real devaluation of 60 percent. At the other extreme of the spectrum, real devaluation in Mexico was more modest at 23 percent, very similar to that of Argentina, where the nominal devaluation against the dollar was 62 percent, but domestic deflation was rather modest. Argentina faced pressure to treat British credits preferentially based on the British structural trade deficit with Argentina. This became explicit policy with the Roca-Runciman Anglo-Argentine agreement of 1933.[6] The Colombian peso remained pegged to the dollar until 1933. Only in some economies in Central America and the Caribbean (Cuba, Dominican Republic, Honduras, Panama), where the dollar was de facto or de jure in circulation, was there no exchange control.

In most Latin American economies, the magnitude of the external shock made unavoidable some kind of default or unilateral refinancing of the whole or part of the foreign debt service, especially as it became clear after 1930 for most countries that no new loans could be floated abroad. Mexico was an especially early case, defaulting in 1928. Attempts to renew service at much reduced levels failed and it remained in default until 1942. In mid-1931 Chile also defaulted, and Brazil and Colombia entered into three-year funding loans that provided for automatic refinancing of

[6] See Virgil Salera, *Exchange Control and the Argentine Market* (New York, 1941), chs. 2 and 3.

interest due on at least a part of their foreign loans. As the crisis persisted, Colombia defaulted partially in 1932 and totally in 1933. Argentina's stance on the foreign debt was the most important exception among the bigger Latin American economies because service was maintained in full, with only minor problems affecting provincial loans. Venezuela, by 1930, had redeemed its foreign debt, and some of the smaller Central American and Caribbean economies also avoided default: Honduras, the Dominican Republic, and Haiti.[7] Venezuela is a rather special case among the larger Latin American economies; it adopted a foreign exchange regime based on a floating currency after 1932 in a context of its rising dollar oil revenues. By 1937, the currency had appreciated 50 percent against the U.S. dollar.

The massive external shock suffered by most of Latin America resulted in destabilizing fiscal consequences because there was an imbalance between the impact of foreign exchange devaluation on the revenue side and on the expenditure side. The sharp contraction of imports tended to reduce the contribution of the all-important import duties to total revenue. A significant share of expenditure was indexed to the foreign exchange rate, especially before default and renegotiation of the foreign debt service. Moreover, the interruption of voluntary foreign lending to Latin America restricted deficit financing to domestic sources. In many economies, continuous access to the international financial markets was an essential condition to fully service the foreign debt and even this had frequently required periodical rescheduling of payments in the past. The depression would make explicit the inconsistency between keeping full service flows and the capacity to generate foreign exchange cover.

The crisis implied the interruption of capital flows to most Latin American economies. In some cases, private voluntary lending returned only in the late 1960s, in the middle of the Euro-dollar market boom. Total public foreign debt in Argentina declined after 1914. In the late 1920s, it reached US$745 million, compared with US$1,230 million in Brazil and US$449 million in Chile. Debt–export ratios in these big Latin American debtor countries, which were regularly raising new loans in the late 1920s, varied between 0.9 in Argentina and 2.5 in Brazil. After the external shock, these ratios increased in Argentina to around 2.0 and shot up to 5.5 in Brazil and 11.5 in Chile in 1932 as exports slumped.

In most of Latin America, GDP in the 1920s peaked in 1929. The most important exception among the bigger economies is Mexico, where the

[7] See Bulmer-Thomas, *Economic History*, 214.

peak was in 1926. In some of the smaller economies, the peak GDP was either earlier on, as in Costa Rica in 1928, or later: 1930 (Venezuela and El Salvador) and 1935 (Honduras). The trough was in 1932 for practically all Latin American economies. But in Brazil and Colombia, not only was the fall in GDP limited (5.3% and 2%, respectively), but also recovery started in 1931 as a result of expansionary policies adopted in the wake of the dramatic fall of coffee prices to a third of their peak level in U.S. dollars. By contrast, GDP fell 13.7 percent in Argentina and 21.1 percent in Mexico in 1929–32 (in the latter case, in addition to a fall of 3.7% in 1926–9 from the 1926 peak). Chile had the worst record in Latin America: GDP fell 44.1 percent in the same period. In some Central American republics (Honduras, Guatemala), the fall of GDP from peak to trough exceeded 20 percent, but in Costa Rica it fell only 8.7 percent.[8]

Although the response to the external shock in almost all Latin American economies involved an attempt to shift demand from imports to domestic consumption, the extent to which such policies were successful varied considerably from country to country – among other things, because there was more scope for an effective answer from domestic producers in specific countries than in others. There was, for instance, idle industrial capacity in Brazil after a decade marked by an investment boom followed by recession in the mid-1920s and then by *plata dulce* and a consequent import boom. The effect was much less important in Argentina, where a large share of existing industrial plants in the late 1920s was complementary to exports rather than of the import-substituting kind.

Fast recovery in countries such as Brazil, Colombia, and Mexico was based on expenditure-switching induced by foreign exchange devaluation and the imposition of import controls and also expansionary fiscal and monetary policies. In Brazil, from October 1931, coffee price support based on stockpiling and destruction of coffee production was partly funded by transfers from the central government. This has been claimed as Keynesianism *avant la lettre* but, in fact, was only a recurrent feature of the Brazilian traditional answer to fiscal shocks induced by external shocks through public expenditure financed by printing money. What was peculiar in the policies of the 1930s was the destruction of the equivalent of three world yearly

---

[8] See Juan Braun et al., "Economía chilena 1810–1995: Estadísticas históricas" (*Documento de Trabajo* 187, Pontificia Universidad Católica de Chile, Instituto de Economía, Santiago, 2000), 25; Pablo Gerchunoff and Lucas Llach, *El ciclo de la ilusión del crecimiento: Un siglo de políticas económicas argentinas* (Buenos Aires, 1998), Table 1; Victor Bulmer-Thomas, *The Political Economy of Central America since 1920* (Cambridge, 1987), statistical appendix, Table A.1.

coffee crops between 1931 and the early 1940s. This contributed to support coffee prices because of Brazil's weight as a producer, even if coffee prices fell rapidly to a third of their peak in the late 1920s and remained hovering barely above this level for the rest of the decade. Without such intervention, the fall would have been even more dramatic. In Mexico, a shift in policies occurred in 1932, when expansionary monetary and fiscal policies were adopted. In Colombia, the public deficit rose from 5 percent of central government expenditure in 1928 to nearly 20 percent in 1931. Colombia, as well as other coffee exporters in Latin America, was favored by the artificial recovery of coffee prices prompted by Brazilian policies to support coffee prices.

RECOVERY (1933–1937) AND FURTHER SHOCKS (1937–1942)

As the world economy started to recover after 1933, intervention in the foreign exchange market was made more flexible in many economies of Latin America. The Argentine experiments with different systems of intervention in foreign exchange markets were very influential in other countries. The second stage of exchange control in Argentina involved a segmentation of the foreign exchange markct in official and free-market rates, which allowed the government to have access to cheaper exchange to cover its requirements in foreign currency and to treat imports from Britain more favorably on a discretionary basis by allowing their payment at the official (less devalued) exchange rate. A similar system was adopted in Brazil after 1934, which – although nondiscriminatory – included the possibility of offering a more devalued exchange rate for exporters of nontraditional exports, while coffee exporters were restricted to the official market. This is typically what happened elsewhere in Latin America as exchange controls became looser as a result of the relaxation of external constraints.[9]

In Argentina, Brazil, and Chile, the exchange rate was allowed to revalue against the dollar when the dollar went off gold in 1933. Assessment of real devaluation in 1932–7 is extremely difficult because of the multiplicity of exchange rates, but there is no evidence of major further real devaluation or its reversal. Many Central American and Caribbean republics tried to remain pegged to the dollar in the 1930s. In Central America, only

---

[9] See Salera, *Exchange Control*, 96.

Guatemala and Honduras succeeded. Costa Rica and El Salvador devalued rather early and Nicaragua in 1936, just before the onset of the recession in the United States.

Exports recovered strongly between 1932 and 1937 almost everywhere in Latin America, but still remained considerably below peak predepression levels. In Argentina, rising export prices because of droughts in many agricultural competitors in the world market made possible a recovery of exports to a level 2.3 times above 1932 (but still more than 25% below the 1928 peak). Export growth was lower but still substantial elsewhere: Brazil (1.9 times), Chile (5.3 times, from an extremely low value), Mexico (2.5 times), and Peru (2.4 times). It was still lower in Central America: from Honduras (0.6 times) and Costa Rica (1.3) to Nicaragua and Guatemala (1.5–1.7). Only El Salvador was an exception (2.8 times). Terms of trade improved in most economies, especially in those economies such as Chile with the most significant fall in export prices during the 1928–32 period. But they continued to fall in countries such as Brazil and Costa Rica. In Brazil, this was compensated by a very substantial expansion of export volumes that almost doubled in this period.

The international economic policies of developed economies were a major factor in determining the trade and balance of payments performance and the extent and timing of recovery and growth of different Latin American economies. The effects of such policies depended crucially on the geographical orientation of their trade. Economies that usually generated a surplus in their trade with the United Kingdom were vulnerable to pressure as British foreign economic policy became increasingly less multilateralist. In 1932, the agreements reached in the Ottawa conference reinstated discriminatory access to the British market in the form of imperial preferences, a policy that had been abandoned in the late 1840s. Imperial products would enjoy preferential access to the British market and traditional Argentine exports were consequently diverted.[10] Moreover, the British government was willing to abandon its long-established stance of defending multilateralism, and in countries such as Argentina, where Britain had a structural trade deficit, was prepared to insist on extracting preferred treatment based on discriminatory policies.

British policy in Argentina was based on promotion of the slogan "buy from those who buy from us."[11] It resulted in the Roca-Runciman agreement

---

[10] See Ian M. Drummond, *British Economic Policy and the Empire 1919–1939* (London, 1972), ch. 3.

[11] Famously: "comprar a quien nos compra."

of 1933 and the Eden-Malbrán agreement of 1936 that assured preferential treatment for Britain concerning both the implementation of foreign exchange control regulations and the reduction of import duties on goods of special British interest.[12] The British share of the Argentine market correspondingly increased in the mid-1930s in comparison with those of the United States and Germany. This British policy, however, only applied in those countries where Britain had leverage as a result of its trade deficit. In other Latin American economies, with which the United States had a structural trade deficit, the proposed British slogan was "buy from those who sell you the best."

Those countries that had a traditional surplus in their trade with the United States where in a much better bargaining position than those depending on the British market. Trade policy adopted by the United States in the 1930s evolved from the self-defeating emphasis on "beggar thy neighbor" policies, as implied by the Smoot-Hawley tariff of 1930, to a clear commitment to multilateralism and the promotion of more open trade policies worldwide as a main pillar of the Reciprocal Trade Act of 1934. The United States used its leverage with Latin American countries such as Brazil and Colombia to negotiate new trade agreements and tried with limited success to open up those markets through agreements, including unconditional most-favored-nation clauses. Cuba and Haiti were also included in a second wave of trade agreements.[13] But the United States showed considerable restraint in exerting its bargaining power to gain privileged access to scarce foreign exchange cover, to counter the expansion of compensation trade with European competitors, especially Germany, or to extract preferential treatment for the service of dollar loans.

The introduction of new foreign economic policies in Nazi Germany, following Schacht's New Plan of 1934, resulted in the substantial expansion of trade between some Latin American economies and Germany under compensation agreements through which balanced bilateral trade was conducted in inconvertible marks. Between 1934 and 1938, there were growing frictions between Germany and the United States because of the real or alleged diversion of U.S. exports as a result of the bilateral trade arrangements promoted by the Nazi authorities. In many Latin American economies there was scope for the expansion of German exports through

[12] See Salera, *Exchange Control*, ch. 5; and Jorge Fodor and Arturo O'Connell, "La Argentina y la economia atlántica en la primera mitad del siglo XX," *Desarollo Económico* 13 (1973): 44–55.
[13] See Henry J. Tasca, *The Reciprocal Trade Policy of the United States: A Study in Trade Philosophy* (Philadelphia, PA, 1938), chs. 3 and 5.

bilateral policies, given the traditional German trade deficit, and this, in fact, occurred both in Central America[14] and, to a certain extent, in Brazil. Imports from Germany displaced U.S. products in Central America, but in Brazil it was the British share of the market that shrank. The spectacular increase in Brazilian cotton exports to Germany to about 20 percent of German imports, added to the fact that there was a sharp fall in cotton exports by the United States to Germany, was perhaps the most quoted instance of the alleged distortions related to compensation trade.[15] The standard resource misallocation arguments, however, are of doubtful relevance when there is excessive long-term reliance on a single commodity crop and no full employment.[16]

In many countries, commercial arrears accumulated because, at the fixed exchange rates, the foreign exchange market did not clear and there was excess demand for cheap exchange cover. Negotiations concerning the thawing of commercial arrears were fairly common in Latin America throughout the 1930s. The accumulation of arrears provided leverage for Latin American countries in the process of extracting mid-term financial accommodation, mainly in New York and London, to finance the reduction of arrears.

Recovery in Latin America after 1932 was particularly strong, with GDP growth in the 6 to 7 percent yearly rate range in 1932–9 in Brazil, Chile, Costa Rica, Mexico, and Venezuela, as well as in some of the Caribbean and Central American economies such as Cuba and Guatemala. It was more laggard (3.7–4.8% range) in most other economies, including Argentina (4.4%). It simply did not occur in Honduras and Uruguay. In relation to the peak in the 1920s, growth performance was outstanding in Brazil, Colombia, and Costa Rica and, curiously enough, had nothing to do with the behavior of prices of coffee, their common major commodity export, the prices of which remained very depressed during the whole period.

Taking 1929 as a reference point, the decomposition of GDP growth by sources of growth over the decade indicates that in almost every Latin American country, recovery was linked to a favorable impact of

---

[14] See Bulmer-Thomas, *Political Economy*, 79.

[15] See Howard S. Ellis, *Exchange Control in Central Europe* (Cambridge, MA, 1941), ch. 4, especially the section on exchange control as a "totalitarian institution." Clearing agreements were signed with most major Latin American economies. The German share in total Brazilian imports increased whereas the British share decreased. It is true, however, that U.S. products bore the brunt of direct German competition. Whereas British imports were displaced by German competitors, other U.S. manufactures were displacing British traditional exports.

[16] See Larry Neal, "The Economics and Finance of Bilateral Clearing Agreements: Germany, 1934–8," *Economic History Review* 33, 2 (1979): 398.

home demand and reduced import coefficients. Only in a handful (Brazil, Colombia, El Salvador, Honduras, Venezuela) did export promotion have any importance. If only industrial production is considered, the importance of import substitution is considerably enhanced and import substitution in agriculture was especially important in Central America.

Balance of payments difficulties unfavorably affected both the flow of profit remittances by foreign firms operating in Latin America (because of exchange control) and the capacity to maintain profitability in the face of persistent devaluation. For providers of public services, this was aggravated by the political difficulties involved in seeking readjustment of public prices to compensate for exchange devaluation. British total investment in Latin America, which was heavily concentrated in public utility services and especially in railways, contracted modestly, perhaps about 7 percent, from a total of £876 million between 1928 and 1939.[17] But even U.S. investments in Latin America, which were much less concentrated in public utility services (25.6% of the total in 1929), declined from US$3.462 billion (book value) in 1929 to US$2.705 billion in 1940. U.S. foreign direct investment in 1929 was heavily concentrated in agriculture (23% of the total, mostly in Cuba, Central America, the Dominican Republic, and Haiti), mining (21%, mostly in Chile and Mexico), oil (17%, mostly in Mexico and Venezuela), and utilities (25.6%, mainly in Cuba, but also in most other economies). Most of the reduction was in Cuba (agriculture), Mexico (oil), and Central America and the Caribbean (agriculture and utilities). Only in Argentina, Brazil, and Venezuela did stocks of foreign direct investments of the United States increase modestly (about 20%), but it was only in Brazil that investment in manufacturing rose (by more than 50% to reach US$70 million in 1940).

Improvement in the foreign exchange constraints faced by Latin American economies after 1933 contributed to make possible a revision of the foreign debt policies adopted immediately after the external shock. Yet there was still a wide spectrum of policies implemented by different Latin American countries in their negotiations with the representatives of bondholders. Argentina continued to service the foreign debt. Brazil replaced its funding arrangements with a new arrangement that reduced contractual service by two thirds. There was some interest payment relief,

---

[17] But these estimates by J. Fred Rippy (*British Investments in Latin America, 1822–1949: A Case Study in the Operation of Private Enterprise in Retarded Regions* [Minneapolis, MN, 1959]) are notoriously deficient.

but most of the reduction was attributable to postponement of amortization. For the first time, this included non-federal foreign debt that was not a direct responsibility of the government. Federal involvement in negotiations that included non-federal debt had become unavoidable because of federal intervention in the foreign exchange market. Chile unilaterally decided in early 1935 on a renewal of public foreign debt payments. Debt service was to be related to the country's capacity to pay. Yearly service fell to 10 percent of its contractual level. Between 1935 and 1948, partial payments amounted to about 20 percent of contractual interest. Substantial amounts of the Chilean dollar debt were redeemed in 1935–9 at slightly more than 10 percent of their face value. Peru defaulted in 1931 and paid a small part of the service on the old sterling guano loan until 1937. Only in 1947 would Peru make a comprehensive offer on defaulted foreign debt. The position in other economies was still worse. Mexico remained in default and Colombia defaulted entirely in 1935. External debt default was also the standard answer in most of Central America, where it continued in most countries until after the Second World War, with the exception of Nicaragua and Honduras. Haiti and the Dominican Republic also serviced their foreign debts in full during the 1930s and 1940s.

The sharp 1937 recession in the United States unfavorably affected GDP growth in some Latin American economies. Mainly as a result of a contraction in exports, GDP in the late 1930s fell or was practically stagnant in most of Central America, and also in Argentina and Chile. Argentina had an export boom in the mid-1930s as wheat and maize prices increased with successive crop failures in the United States.[18] But even then, its growth performance, although better than that of stagnant Chile, was considerably poorer than those of Brazil and Mexico. The downturn in the United States served as a pretext for a shift in policies in some Latin American economies, as their balance of payments deteriorated, away from the liberalization that had started in 1934, especially in South America. In Brazil, the federal government defaulted on the public foreign debt, suspending the much-reduced scheduled payments agreed on in 1934. In Argentina, the dual exchange rate regime of 1933, revised to assure preferential treatment to British goods, was discontinued and a universal import licensing system was introduced in late 1938.[19]

---

[18] See Arturo O'Connell, "Argentina into the Depression: Problems of an Open Economy," in Rosemary Thorp, ed., *An Economic History of Twentieth-Century Latin America*, vol. 2, *Latin America in the 1930s: The Role of the Periphery in World Crisis* (Basingstoke, 2000), 199.
[19] See Salera, *Exchange Control*, ch. 8.

The international political crisis in 1938 and the beginning of the Second World War caused an additional external shock in many countries because from September 1939, markets in Germany and Central Europe were practically closed by the British economic blockade. Trade with the United Kingdom and France, as well as with European countries that remained neutral and, increasingly, with other American economies, including the United States, was affected by German submarine activities. By mid-1940, most Western European markets were lost and, after 1941, the Asian markets were lost as well, of which Japan was the most important. The impact was more relevant, of course, on economies that had been relatively less dependent on the U.S. market before the war, such as those in the Southern Cone of South America.

Coffee prices fell substantially after 1937. In 1940, Brazilian terms of trade had decreased a further 30 percent since 1937 (when they were already 45 percent below 1928). There was a strong political motivation in the United States to foster an Inter-American Coffee Agreement that sustained coffee prices and improved balance of payments conditions in Central America, Brazil, and Colombia.

Very early in the war, it was perceived in London that in many neutral countries there would be surplus stocks of commodities available at depressed prices. Neutrals could be persuaded to accept payments into special accounts that could be drawn only to settle claims in sterling. Because of stiff export control in the United Kingdom, drawings were mostly limited to the settlement of financial obligations related to the foreign debt service and foreign direct investment profit remittances. After 1941, Latin American sterling balances accumulated rapidly in London and were a significant share of the relatively large reserves accumulated by Latin America during the war.[20]

The composition of exports increasingly reflected the new demands related to the war effort. Exports to the United States and the United Kingdom were determined by official procurement and preemption of enemy supply. However, it took some time to adjust supply to the new demands. Supply restrictions in the developed economies determined the behavior of imports, sharply restricted in most of Latin America, with the exception of Mexico. The scarcity of imports, together with the relatively strong bargaining power of some Latin American economies, made possible a qualitative change in the import-substitution efforts. In Brazil, a publicly

---

[20] The future convertibility of such balances was not assured, as post-1945 events would show.

owned, relatively small, integrated steel mill was financed by the United States. Similar initiatives in Bolivia and Mexico, where oil was nationalized, and Chile, where a development agency – Corporación de Fomento de la Producción (CORFO) – was established, marked a new era in the direct involvement of the state in the production of goods. Import scarcity was so pressing that it temporarily became the policy of the United States to foster import substitution. As peace approached, this policy would be abandoned.

Some Latin American economies that had been in partial or total default in the late 1930s resumed reduced debt service in the early 1940s. However, the beginning of a general process to reach permanent settlements on outstanding debt, which was made possible by the fast accumulation of foreign reserves, had to wait for the late war period or immediately postwar.[21]

DOLLAR PLENTY AND DOLLAR SHORTAGE: 1942–7

After 1942, there was a rapid growth of foreign reserves in most Latin American economies. This was the combined result of the significant expansion of exports, at a yearly rate above 10 percent between 1939 and 1945, and the contraction of imports because of supply difficulties – including export control – in some of the previous leading suppliers. Expanded exports were often the result of higher export prices rather than of expanded export volumes. Among the larger economies, Venezuela is the main exception because its export volumes expanded by more than 8 percent yearly. The contraction of traditional export markets led to a diversion of Latin American exports, especially manufactures, by the industrially more advanced economies such as Argentina and Brazil, to nontraditional markets in Latin America and even beyond, including, for instance, South Africa. Mexico expanded its exports to the United States dramatically: manufactured exports reached almost 38 percent of total exports in 1945 and external demand was about three times more important than domestic demand as a source of industrial growth during the war. In most Latin American countries, import volumes stagnated or contracted, in some cases sharply, such as in Argentina, where they fell by more than 16 percent. The

---

[21] In some countries, the fast accumulation of reserves acted as a powerful stimulus to prompt negotiations of permanent settlements of the foreign debt.

major exception was, once again, Mexico, where imports expanded at a rate of more than 22 percent on average during the war.

In many economies, the exchange rate regime during the war was based on a fixed nominal exchange rate. In some cases, a multiple exchange rate regime was adopted, maintaining a more appreciated official rate applied to government transactions, and also a more devalued financial rate. Because war inflation was substantial in most of Latin America, there was a sharp erosion of export profits during the war, especially in the case of products that were included in the wartime price controls in the United States. Distortions provoked by exchange rate overvaluation continued after the war. In many economies, fear of inflation rationalized decisions not to devalue, in spite of the high war inflation. Wildly overvalued exchange rates were fixed under the rules of the new International Monetary Fund (IMF) amid optimistic views on structural changes that, it was alleged, had favorably affected the steady-state balance of trade of Latin American economies.[22]

Latin American foreign reserves rose substantially during the war but in certain economies, especially in southern South America, a large share of them were inconvertible. By far, the most important case affected sterling balances because the terms of the United States–United Kingdom loan agreement of 1945 resulted in an implied British commitment to make them inconvertible into scarce dollars. Their reduction was a complex matter and involved massive purchases of British assets by Latin American governments at prices open to controversy. Argentina, moreover, redeemed its substantial non-federal external debt and converted it into internal debt.[23]

The combination of explosive postwar imports – in Latin America as a whole they increased 75 percent in volume in 1945–8 – with a sharp reduction in convertible reserves led, in spite of some improvement in the terms of trade, to balance of payment problems in most Latin American economies. The lack of dollar reserves was combined with trade deficits with the United States because there were no alternative sources of supply for most industrial products. This led to an acute dollar shortage in many

---

[22] Brazil is one of the more extreme examples: the declared parity in 1946 was in line with the average nominal multiple exchange rates of 1939, whereas domestic inflation during the war exceeded 120 percent, compared with 37 percent in the United States.

[23] These uses of foreign reserves are a partial explanation for strongly held views that they had been squandered in the immediate postwar. These harsh criticisms generally failed to take into account the limits to their alternative use imposed by postwar negotiations between Britain and the United States.

parts of Latin America. Peak exports were reached in 1947 in Mexico, in 1948 in Argentina, in 1949 in Chile, and in 1951 in Brazil. In many of these economies, foreign exchange regimes based on the overvaluation of the foreign exchange and import controls continued to be adopted.

The roots of ingrained anti-export bias can be detected here. They are also mixed up with nationalism. For those economies that could consume what they exported, it became tempting to reduce incentives to export to economies that could not pay in cash and to court the masses by increasing real wages and allowing increased domestic consumption of exportables. Postwar payment difficulties in Europe, compounded by the persistent protectionism affecting temperate agriculture, inexorably constrained the exports of those Latin American economies specializing in food and agricultural raw materials. Perón's Argentina is perhaps the best example of such a shift in the direction of autarkical policies.

With the improvement in the foreign reserve position during the war, many Latin American governments became anxious to reach permanent foreign debt settlements with their bondholders in substitution of the sequence of short-term arrangements that had generally marked the 1930s and early 1940s.[24] Some Central American economies such as Nicaragua and Honduras redeemed part of the foreign debt. The Mexican debt agreement of 1942 involved liquidation of principal and interest arrears in the region of US$500 million for only 10 percent of nominal value. The Brazilian agreement of 1943 halved the value of outstanding public foreign debt of almost US$900 million and consolidated it under the guarantee of the federal government. But other economies waited longer to negotiate and extracted still better terms from bondholders. Chile, for instance, only reached agreement with bondholders in 1948, after a long history of default or extremely low service payments combined with debt redemption at low prices. Mexico also settled its pending debt with the foreign oil companies that had been taken over in 1938.

British foreign direct investment practically disappeared from many Latin America economies in the immediate postwar period. Sterling balances were used to buy existing assets. Total foreign direct investment of the United States in Latin America, on the other hand, expanded modestly in the war from US$2.7 billion in 1940 to US$3 billion in 1946. Expansion in Venezuela, Central America, Brazil, Colombia, and Chile was substantial

---

[24] Doubts about the future convertibility of sterling balances were also a strong inducement to open such foreign debt negotiations.

and there was contraction in Argentina and Mexico. About half the investment was in Cuba, Chile, and Venezuela, and was mainly in agricultural activities and mining. Brazil was by far the most important recipient of U.S. foreign direct investment in manufacturing (US$126 million), but the expansion in Mexico was much faster.

THE GOLDEN AGE OF IMPORT-SUBSTITUTING INDUSTRIALIZATION: 1947 TO THE EARLY 1960s

There is some irony in the fact that foreign exchange overvaluation, adopted in some countries, at least partly justified by the fear of inflationary pressures and adverse fiscal consequences, resulted in a powerful inducement to substitute imports under the umbrella of absolute protection provided by stiff import controls.[25] Other arguments in favor of overvaluation in economies with a big share in specific world commodity markets hinged on the intent to maintain high world commodity prices. Such commodity price-support efforts were complemented in some cases by international agreements. The most important of these was for coffee, signed in the early 1960s, given that Brazil found it onerous to continue with its longstanding unilateral price-support policies. In the long term, such policies acted as a powerful inducement to the rise of the coffee output of emerging, higher cost competitors. Import controls were introduced in 1947 in some of the big economies such as Brazil and Mexico. Multiple exchange rate regimes based on a differential treatment of buyers and sellers of foreign exchange eventually became widespread in those economies opting for the import substitution strategy: Argentina, Brazil, and Chile. In contrast, in Mexico, as in Colombia, this strategy was combined with sustained incentives to export, and there was a sequence of devaluations in the early 1940s and mid-1950s.

Export pessimism played an important role in the rationalization of sustained import-substituting policies, especially in the context of inconvertibility in Europe and shrinking markets for the nontraditional exports that had boomed during the war.[26] But as the world economy recovered

---

[25] Temptation to control inflation through foreign exchange overvaluation is a recurring theme in post–World War II Latin America.

[26] With the benefit of hindsight, the widespread fatalism concerning the sharp drop of nontraditional exports seems somewhat surprising. Protests against foreign exchange overvaluation were restricted to exporters of commodities whose prices had not increased spectacularly in the postwar period.

Development, under the Generalized System of Preferences, was of minor importance and subject to discretionary withdrawal.

The international financial markets remained to a large extent closed to Latin America until the mid-1960s. Financial flows were mostly official, such as World Bank and Inter-American Development Bank loans, and suppliers' credits. World Bank loans to Latin America up to 1960 added up to US$1,246 million, about 21.5 percent of total loans approved. This was a lower share of total capital flows than Latin America had been able to attract in the golden pre-1929 years, but in the initial postwar period there was stiff competition from economies in the process of reconstruction in Europe and Asia. The rather modest increase in financing of development projects by the United States during the second Truman administration was reversed by the Republican administration after 1952. A more substantial one occurred with the Alliance for Progress in the early 1960s in reaction to developments in Cuba. Foreign direct investment flows for Latin America as a whole in the 1950s were almost 60 percent of total capital inflows. This would be dramatically reversed in the 1960s and afterwards.

European integration launched by the Treaty of Rome in 1957 had an important demonstration effect in Latin America. Several integration initiatives took place in the early 1960s but, on the whole, they failed to provide the expected stimuli to growth. The emphasis, based on Raúl Prebcish's influence, was on obtaining market sizes compatible with further deepening of import substitution.[29] In 1960, a Latin American Free Trade Association (LAFTA) was created by the Treaty of Montevideo, including all of South America and Mexico with a free trade area as a target for 1972. A Central American Common Market was also created in 1960. Later, at the end of the 1960s, an Andean Common Market and a Caribbean Free Trade Area (CARIFTA, later CARICOM) were formed. There was some reduction of trade barriers in the early 1960s in LAFTA, but opposition by protectionist lobbies managed to freeze trade liberalization afterward and no advance was made on a common tariff. Facilities to finance reciprocal trade were created. The so-called complementary agreements allowed trade liberalization restricted to a subset of members and mainly affected intra-firm trade. In 1968, the time limit to establish a free trade area was extended to 1980. Although not a great success, LAFTA was one of the

---

[29] As opposed to the integration initiatives of the 1990s and 2000s, integration in the 1960s and 1970s was clearly driven by trade diversion of traditional suppliers for the benefit of Latin American alternatives.

factors that explained the expansion of regional trade from 10 to 20 percent of total trade in its first twenty years, together with increased oil prices and the rise of subsidized manufactured exports in some of the big Latin American economies. In 1980, as the Treaty of Montevideo expired, LAFTA was replaced by the Latin American Integration Association (LAIA) and the initial ambitions of full integration were buried.

MACROECONOMIC INSTABILITY, THE RETURN OF CAPITAL FLOWS, EXPORT PROMOTION, AND GROWTH: MID-1960s TO THE EARLY 1970s

From the mid-1960s, export promotion policies became a pillar of foreign economic policy not only in most of the larger Latin American economies – Argentina, Brazil, Colombia, and Mexico – but also in some of the smaller economies, such as Honduras and the Dominican Republic. These policies were based on the provision of massive fiscal and credit incentives. This partial reorientation of the previous strategy based on import-substituting industrialization was much less radical in certain countries than claimed at the time. It is indeed difficult to classify the foreign economic policy strategy of most of the bigger Latin American economies, at least until 1973, as truly outward-looking. It seems more reasonable to think of a cross-eyed strategy, incorporating inertial elements of inwardness and new elements of outwardness geared to export promotion and attraction of foreign direct investment. In economies such as Brazil, reduction of the protection of domestic markets proceeded very slowly, even in the golden years before 1973. Perhaps the more important feature is that government policy remained firmly based on a pick-the-winner framework. The main adjustment in relation to the full-throttle import-substitution strategy, adopted in the past, was that winners now could be selected because of a good hunch concerning their prospects for substituting imports, expanding exports, or both. Subsidiaries of multinationals, previously heavily protected against foreign competition, started to receive substantial subsidies related to export performance.

In many Latin American economies, there was an overhaul of foreign exchange regimes in the 1960s. Explicit multiple exchange rate regimes were abandoned and crawling peg rules adopted – in 1964 in Argentina, in 1967 in Colombia, and in 1968 in Brazil – to assure that the nominal exchange rate was adjusted in line with the difference between domestic inflation and world inflation.[30] Mexico was once again the main exception, having adopted a fixed exchange rate and with a much steadier macroeconomic performance than all other large economies. But the general refurbishment of foreign exchange regimes did not mean that exchange rate overvaluation did not remain widespread and foreign exchange restrictions the rule. It can even be said that the proliferation of export subsidies and import duty rebates, distributed on a discretionary basis, to a large extent replicated the past distortions related to multiple exchange rate regimes.

There was a world trade boom between 1967 and 1973, with an expansion of exports of 17.9 percent yearly. Latin America's performance was not bad, with its exports expanding at a rate only 1.5 percent below the world average. The share of the United States in Latin American exports decreased very little in the decade following 1963, but the Western European recovery in the 1950s was reversed, with its share falling from 35 percent to 29 percent of total exports. This was compensated by a modest increase in the market shares of intra-Latin American trade (from 15% to 18% of total exports), other developing economies (2% to 4%), and the socialist economies (5% to 6%). The share of manufactured exports in total exports increased from 9 percent in 1960 to 21 percent in 1973, and new commodities such as soybeans were added to the traditional list.

In the time span extending from the early 1960s to the first oil crisis of 1973, most big economies in Latin America – Mexico is a major exception – suffered a major macroeconomic slowdown, generally accompanied by a balance of payments crisis and a sharp acceleration of inflation. Argentina led the way in 1962–3, Brazil followed in 1963–7, and Chile went through the very difficult years of the socialist government between 1970 and 1973. Between 1960 and 1973, the GDP of Brazil and Mexico increased by more than 7 percent yearly, significantly above the average of 5.9 percent. But this hides, in the case of Brazil, a rather unstable record: an exceptionally good performance up to 1962 and after 1967, with a recession between. Colombia was the best performer (5.6%) among the large group of below-the-average economies, and the growth of GDP of Venezuela, Peru, and the group of smaller economies was in the 4.7 to 5.4 percent range. The worst performers were Argentina and Chile, where GDP increased 4 percent and

---

[30] In most Latin American economies, however, to the extent that foreign exchange controls remained relevant, the exchange rate was chronically overvalued even after the overhauling of exchange rate regimes in the 1960s.

3.4 percent yearly, respectively, even if, in the former case, the decade after 1963 is known as the *primavera económica*.[31] There was macroeconomic instability in all the southern cone economies: the difference was that the Brazilian average growth was much higher than in Argentina and Chile.

Relations of some of the bigger economies of Latin America with the IMF had been difficult in several episodes between the late 1940s and the early 1960s. Drawings by most Latin American economies were frequent, notably by Argentina (1957, 1959, 1960–3), Brazil (1949, 1951–3, 1958, 1960–1, 1963), Chile (1947, 1953, 1957–9, 1961, 1963), and Mexico (1947, 1954, 1959, 1961). The Latin American share of total drawings from the IMF was high (between 34% and 80.9%) in 1951–4 – even if, in some years, total drawings were rather low – and again in 1957–60 (between 20.9% and 63.8%) as well as in 1963 (69.5%). In 1961, Latin American drawings were substantial, although they were dwarfed by drawings by the United Kingdom. But these were passing problems and renewed access to financial markets from the mid-1960s reduced the importance of access to the IMF until the 1982 crisis. By 1973, inflation and its adverse effects on the balance of payments were under control in most of Latin America, with the exception of Argentina and Chile. In Argentina, for a longer period and in more frequent episodes than in any of the other larger economies, there was high inflation, substantially above the levels reached in other economies in the early 1950s and beyond 100 percent later in the decade. It was, on average, nearly 30 percent a year in the decade ending in 1973.

The foreign debt of many Latin American economies increased rapidly after the late 1960s, even if, at the origin, their level tended to be modest because of the forced abstinence before 1967. Voluntary lending, which had ceased since the late 1920s for most Latin American economies, was again possible after 1965 as the Eurodollar market expanded. The yearly inflows of foreign direct investment into Latin America doubled between the first and the second half of the 1960s, to reach around US$0.5 billion. The rate of inflow increased even more in the early 1970s, when a bubble was in the making: in 1971–3, US$3.4 billion of foreign direct capital entered Latin America, more than in the whole of the 1960s. Much of it was attracted to

---

[31] GDP estimates vary substantially among different sources but this does not affect relative performances in the period. See, for instance, Angus Maddison, *Monitoring the World Economy, 1820–1992* (Paris, 1995); Ricardo Ffrench-Davis, Oscar Muñoz, and José Gabriel Palma, "The Latin American Economies, 1950–1990" in Leslie Bethell, ed., *The Cambridge History of Latin America*, vol. 6, *Latin America since 1930. Economy, Society and Politics*, part 1, *Economy and Society* (Cambridge, 1994); Gerchunoff and Llach, *Ciclo de la ilusión*, statistical appendix.

participate in joint ventures, generally with the involvement of the public sector and domestic firms as part of interventionist public policies. But the share of foreign direct investment in total inflows of foreign capital decreased sharply: in the 1950s it was almost 60 percent, but in 1973–4 it had been reduced to slightly more than 22 percent. Loans raised in the Eurodollar market were concentrated in the larger economies of Latin America and official lending continued to dominate the debt position of the smaller economies.

TWO OIL SHOCKS AND A NEW DEBT CRISIS: 1973–82

Oil prices were multiplied by four in 1973–4 and then again by three in 1978–9. The impact on the balance of payments of Latin American oil importers was severe following the first oil shock and crippling following the second oil shock.[32] This, in the latter case, was because the substantial rise in interest rates was added to the direct impact of oil price increases in the wake of the shift in the economic policies of the United States away from the inflationary accommodation that had followed the first oil shock.

Strategies to face the first shock varied considerably across Latin America. Some economies deepened their commitment to export promotion. Such was the case of the big three Latin American economies – Argentina, Brazil, and Mexico – and also of Colombia and some of the smaller economies such as Haiti and the Dominican Republic. In certain cases, such as that of Brazil, export promotion continued to be combined with a massive import-substituting effort because it was explicit government policy to further reduce dependency on imports as a reaction to the oil shock. This was import substitution in extremis because, with imports representing only 11.9 percent of the supply of industrial products in 1974, it was unlikely that import substitution could serve as a bootstrap to assure growth. Indeed, in 1974–9, the contribution of import substitution to manufacturing output growth in Brazil was only 10.1 percent, similar to that of exports. Protection of the domestic market was again raised through a combination

---

[32] Because of low oil prices in the 1960s, there was little incentive to expand oil production in marginal oil producers. In the early 1980s, the share of oil in the total imports of more dependent economies would peak above 50 percent.

of tariff increases, lists of prohibited imports, national similarity rules, and import deposits. At the same time, approved new projects would enjoy complete exemption from import duties. Residual import substitution mostly affected intermediate and capital goods. High protection of domestic production of capital goods resulted in expensive and non–state-of-the-art import substitution with long-term adverse consequences on the competitiveness of exports.

Fiscal incentives to export in Brazil – including export tax credits, income tax reduction, draw back, and import duty reductions related to export performance – reached a peak average rate in excess of 15 percent in the late 1970s. Average financial incentives were, in the late 1980s, on the order of 11.5 percent. So total subsidies – some legal, others illegal under the rules of the GATT – comfortably exceeded 25 percent of the value of exports.

The return of Latin America to the world financial markets in the second half of the 1960s was possible because of the rapid expansion in the availability of funds in the Eurodollar market and other innovations. This was a borrower's market and almost any developing economy could tap it. After 1973, the increase in oil prices further stimulated the increase in foreign indebtedness as the main element in the adjustment policies of many economies in Latin America. Expansionary macroeconomic policies in the United States made this possible because the resulting low nominal interest rates cum high inflation made some economists underline the rationality of borrowing at negative real interest rates, but they failed to mention that, in contrast with pre-1930 foreign debt, interest rates were now linked to short-term rates in the market.[33] Bonds were only a small proportion of the total debt of Latin American economies. So, an eventual default would hit commercial banks and not bondholders, as had been the case in the debt crisis of the end of the 1920s. Even oil exporters resorted to a perverse combination of foreign exchange overvaluation, new foreign loans, and capital flight. Debt crises would require the bailout of banks in lender economies rather than result in losses by "widows and orphans."

Export promotion policies were often combined with a rather risky strategy concerning the rate of expansion of foreign debt that can be described as an attempted *fuite en avant*. The idea was that it made sense to avoid a recessive adjustment and use access to foreign finance, at negative real interest rates, to foster another spurt of import substitution. Open or potentially

---

[33] Different country risks are reflected in different spreads that needed to be added to a basic rate such as the London Interbank Offer Rate (LIBOR).

high inflation made it tempting to toy with foreign exchange overvaluation, and public finances deteriorated with a sharp fall in public savings.
Bad macroeconomic policies were closely linked to dependence on continued access to world financial markets and, in consequence, a rapidly rising
foreign debt.

There was a sharp deterioration of the international environment in
the wake of the second oil shock of the 1970s because the United States
adopted a totally different macroeconomic stance compared with the soft
post-1973 policies. A stringent monetary policy led to a sharp increase in
nominal interest rates coupled with low inflation. This increase in nominal
interest rates after 1978 led to a soaring increase in foreign debt service as a
proportion of exports for Latin America as a whole, from 26.6 percent in
1975 to 59 percent in 1982. Foreign direct investment flows were dwarfed
by flows related to loans: the share of loans in total flows continued to
increase and remained close to 85 percent in 1974–81. The contribution
of foreign direct investment and official capital flows, which had made up
three quarters of the total inflows of foreign capital into Latin America in
the 1960s, fell to only a third by 1980. Interest of the banks was concentrated
in the bigger economies. In the smaller Latin American economies, official
debt remained more important than private flows even after these *plata
dulce* years.

Starting in 1980, it became increasingly difficult for some countries to
continue with their massive borrowing from private banks. The restrictions
were partly explained by the impact of prudential limits on bank exposure
to specific risks and affected Brazil first, then Argentina, and finally Mexico,
more suddenly, in August 1982.

Propped by import substitution and export promotion, Brazil's GDP
increased at 5.7 percent yearly between 1973 and 1981, extending a very
long period of high growth since the early 1940s with only relatively minor
reversals such as that of 1963–5. Yet, by 1981, recession arrived as policies
became contractionary in an attempt to fight inflation that was accelerating
to more than 100 percent yearly and to cope with balance of payments
difficulties.

The other above-average performer among the larger Latin American
economies in the 1973–81 period besides Brazil was Mexico, which also
started the 1970s with a strategy based on export promotion. Mexico's
adherence to a standard export promotion strategy was, however, brought
to a close by the discovery of large oil fields in 1976, when its economic
strategy was narrowed to the promotion of oil exports. The deterioration

of Mexico's macroeconomic performance was more or less in line with that of Brazil. Between 1971 and 1976, the foreign debt quadrupled to reach US$27.9 billion. Incentives to capital flight increased with the overvaluation of the peso and persistently low domestic interest rates. At the end of 1976, inflation surged to 60 percent a year and a stabilization program was agreed on with the IMF, with the usual mix of monetary and fiscal austerity and trade liberalization. But good intentions were dropped when the possibilities opened by the new oil riches became clear. Economic policy was deeply affected. Public expenditures soared and the nominal deficit rose to 17.6 percent of GDP in 1981. Imports of inputs and capital goods more than doubled in 1978–80; those of consumption goods trebled. By 1981, the foreign debt had risen to US$81 billion. It has been estimated that capital flight represented between 38 and 53 percent of the debt accumulated in 1977–82. Oil prices peaked in 1981 and started to fall. There is some irony in the fact that the balance of payments crisis of 1982 affected both oil importers and oil exporters in Latin America with more or less the same intensity.

Smaller economies that had reacted to the new environment in the 1970s by trying to promote exports, especially exports of manufactures, included Colombia, the Dominican Republic, and Haiti, all of which had growth performances above the Latin American average. Colombia was also favorably affected by the sharp rise in coffee prices that trebled in 1975–7 because of a big Brazilian frost.

Another group of Latin American economies avoided import substitution, export promotion of manufactures, and the outward-looking policies adopted in Argentina, Chile, and Uruguay. They concentrated efforts on policies to promote nonindustrial exports. This included economies specializing in primary commodities and those concentrating efforts on services, such as Paraguay and Panama. In Paraguay, activity was boosted, with GDP growing at more than 8 percent yearly in the 1970s, by the building of the two big bi-national hydroelectric plants of Itaipú and Yaciretá, and by increased soy exports. Panama, with much less success in terms of sustained growth, established an offshore financial center whose activities peaked in 1982. Of the Latin American oil and gas producers – Venezuela, Ecuador, and Bolivia – only Ecuador had a good performance in the wake of the rise in oil and gas prices, with GDP increasing 9.7 percent yearly in the 1970s. In all these economies, the oil sector came to be controlled by state-owned enterprises, including Venezuela, where the oil industry was nationalized in 1975. Some of the Central American economies were favorably affected by the coffee price boom after 1975: GDP increased 5.7 percent yearly in the 1970s in Costa Rica and Guatemala. However, political instability became widespread, particularly affecting Nicaragua after 1979.

Three southern cone economies – Argentina, Chile, and Uruguay – adopted policies that gave absolute priority to price stabilization. These policies emphasized the need to reduce traditional anti-export bias, to open up the protected domestic markets, and to remove foreign exchange controls, including the capital account. They were generally adopted after political coups by military regimes, starting with the overthrow of Allende's government in Chile in 1973 and following the demise of Peronism in 1976 in Argentina. Policies were based on a monetary approach to the balance of payments. But in every episode, initial real foreign exchange devaluations coupled with trade liberalization, generally starting at extremely high levels of protection, ended up in exchange-rate overvaluation attributable to the failure of experiments to break inflationary expectations by preannouncing future exchange-rate devaluations below the rate of inflation. This discouraged exports, promoted import booms, and led to a rapid rise in foreign indebtedness and capital flight. Peru abandoned its experiment rather early, following balance of payments problems created by an import boom. But experiences in the Southern Cone were more sustained and deeply affected the level of activity. The growth performance of these economies in 1973–81 was far below the Latin American average, with GDP growing in Argentina and Chile barely above 2 percent and in Uruguay at 3.5 percent yearly.

Multilateral trade negotiations in the 1970s brought no especially favorable developments to the Latin American economies. The Tokyo Round of GATT did not significantly improve market access for agricultural or textile and apparel products.[34] The United States shifted away from its traditional postwar defense of nondiscrimination to an emphasis on reciprocity. The new GATT codes covered issues of specific interest to the developed economies, such as subsidies. The more industrialized Latin American economies became targets of the new policy of the United States that sought to bring subsidies favoring exports of manufactures under stricter control. Generous fiscal rebates that were illegal under the GATT rules had been adopted in countries such as Brazil, but were discontinued under pressure by the United States.

---

[34] See Gilbert R. Winham, *International Trade and the Tokyo Round Negotiation* (Princeton, NJ, 1986) for the negotiations on the codes and on special and differential treatment in favor of developing countries.

Exports of manufactures by Latin America continued to increase in the 1970s. In some of the big economies such as Brazil, they exceeded 30 percent of total exports. They also increased in some of the smaller successful exporters of industrial products such as Guatemala and Haiti. The United States absorbed around 36 percent of Latin American total exports and the European share continued to decline, to reach 21 percent. Exports to Latin America itself increased from 18 to 21 percent and to the other developing countries from 4 to 7 percent. This was a reflection of the increased share of manufactured exports in total exports because they were mainly directed to Latin America, and also of the proliferation of countertrade deals involving Latin American countries and suppliers of oil, mainly in the Middle East.

CONCLUSIONS

The second oil shock of the 1970s, and the consequent steep increase in interest rates and the interruption of capital flows, made rescheduling of payments in foreign currency in the heavily indebted Latin American economies inevitable in 1982. This marked the end of the second long period of foreign indebtedness since independence. After slightly more than half a century, a new shock, similar to that of the late 1920s, affected Latin America and was to have, at least in the case of some of its economies, even more significant and persistent consequences on the level of economic activity.

There are many similarities between the crisis at the end of the 1920s and that of the early 1980s, but also some sharp contrasts. Perhaps the most important contrast is that the 1982 crisis originated with difficulties specifically related to indebtedness of Latin American economies and was much more intense there than elsewhere. The worldwide Great Depression was relatively mild in Latin America and was rapidly followed by a period of high growth in many of its economies. Also in contrast with the 1930s, the Latin American debt crisis of 1982 would place the international banks under strain. It was not a question of hurting "widows and orphans," as in the 1930s; there was now the systemic danger of a domino effect driving banks in developed economies into bankruptcy. In the 1930s, the banking system in developed economies, especially in the United States and Central Europe, had been under severe strain but this had nothing to do with the crisis in developing economies.

The weight of Latin America in the world economy dramatically decreased in the slightly more than half a century after the late 1920s:

its shares in world trade, bank/bond debt, and foreign direct investment all fell heavily, as mentioned in the introduction. This was because of a combination of factors that included protectionism in developed economies, but also, most important, inward-looking policies in Latin American economies that were only modestly, or partially, reversed after the 1960s. Latin America did not fare badly in terms of growth during this slightly extended half a century, but it marginally lost ground to the developed economies, even if it was not directly affected by major turmoils such as World War II.[35] Although much more closed than in earlier years, Latin America was still as vulnerable to external shocks as in the old days of greater integration to the world economy.

One can speak of 1928 as the end of the era of laissez faire. Argentina and Uruguay perhaps fit this interpretation much better than other economies in Latin America. But even if it was not an era of clear laissez faire for all countries, it certainly was an era of less protection and less state intervention than after the Great Depression and the post–World War II days. The year 1928 was the beginning of an era that ended in 1982, the era of import substitution and much more state intervention in the economy. To the traditional conflict between the level of indebtedness and the capacity to generate foreign exchange earnings – now in an environment of variable interest rates – were added significant structural weaknesses such as a profound financial crisis of the state and the need to dismantle a web of interventionist instruments that had outlived their usefulness. These difficulties were to make recovery in many economies of Latin America a much slower and more painful process in the 1980s than it had been in the 1930s.

---

[35] GDP per capita in Latin America increased 1.95 percent yearly in 1928–1982, compared with 2.38 percent in the OECD and 1.09 percent in Asia. Weighted rates computed using the data of Maddison, *Monitoring*.

4

GLOBALIZATION AND THE NEW ECONOMIC MODEL IN LATIN AMERICA

VICTOR BULMER-THOMAS

The import-substituting industrialization (ISI) model of development reached maturity in the 1950s. It began to show signs of decadence in the 1960s when timid reforms were attempted in several countries to address its major weaknesses. In the Southern Cone (Argentina, Chile, and Uruguay), economic reforms became more radical in the 1970s,[1] but elsewhere in Latin America the reform movement stalled and the distortions attributable to the ISI model became more apparent. By 1982, when the debt crisis struck Latin America, the ISI model was almost completely discredited and there were few voices left to defend it.

The debt crisis in Latin America at the beginning of the 1980s had many causes.[2] The export sector was too small and insufficiently dynamic to finance the increase in debt service payments; the rise in world interest rates pushed up the cost of servicing the debt; and the growth in world liquidity in the 1970s meant that banks started to look for new business in the larger developing countries. The latter would now come to be known as "emerging" countries to emphasize the shallowness of their financial markets and their potential for absorbing new inflows of capital.

Extricating Latin America from the debt crisis would prove to be a long and costly affair. The term "lost decade" has rightly been used to describe the stagnation in real gross domestic product (GDP) per head that resulted in the 1980s from the adjustment programs adopted throughout the

---

[1] See, in particular, J. Ramos, *Neoconservative Economics in the Southern Cone of Latin America, 1973–83* (Baltimore, MD, 1986).
[2] There are many good studies of the debt crisis in Latin America. See, for example, R. Devlin, *Debt and Crisis in Latin America: The Supply Side of the Story* (Princeton, NJ, 1989).

region.[3] These programs were designed to ensure that Latin American countries did not default on their debt and, to that extent, they were largely successful. However, a high price was paid in terms of the reduction in social spending and the deterioration in infrastructure.

Latin America was in the middle of this adjustment process when the world economy entered a new phase known as globalization.[4] Whereas product and factor markets had become increasingly integrated after the Second World War, there was a qualitative change in this process starting in the 1980s. Thus, Latin America's efforts to extricate itself from the debt crisis took place just as the rate of growth of world trade and international capital flows started to accelerate.

These new external conditions heavily influenced the nature of Latin America's adjustment process. ISI now looked completely inappropriate. Hostility to direct foreign investment (DFI), so powerful in the 1970s, now appeared reactionary. Latin America, it was argued by the new elite trained in the United States, needed to adjust in a way that allowed the region to participate fully in this new phase of global capitalism through the adoption of neoliberal policies. The new mood was captured by the phrase "The Washington Consensus," which listed a series of reforms supported not only by the international financial institutions in Washington, DC, but also by the elites in Latin America.[5]

The first stage of reforms, concentrating on trade and financial market liberalization, was relatively easy to implement and coincided with the return of economic growth to Latin America in the first half of the 1990s. The second stage, concentrating on the rule of law, the quality of institutions, and microeconomic reforms, proved much more difficult.[6] The second stage coincided with the end of economic growth and a modest decline in GDP per head in the five years after 1997.[7] This led to a deep sense of pessimism in Latin America by the beginning of the new millennium, with opinion divided on whether the region should abandon the

---

[3] The phrase "lost decade" was first used by the Economic Commission for Latin America and the Caribbean (ECLAC). It quickly gained acceptance as an accurate short-hand account of economic performance in the 1980s.

[4] The word "globalization" is widely attributed to an article in *The Economist* in the mid-1980s, although the phenomenon itself is much older.

[5] See Jeffrey Williamson, ed., *Latin American Adjustment: How Much has Happened?* (Washington, DC, 1990).

[6] See P. Kuczynski and J. Williamson, eds., *After the Washington Consensus: Restarting Growth and Reform in Latin America* (Washington, DC, 2003).

[7] See ECLAC, *Preliminary Overview of the Economies of Latin America and the Caribbean* (Santiago, 2002), 108.

neoliberal model altogether and experiment instead with heterodox policies or persevere with the New Economic Model, as it had come to be called, through widening and deepening the reform process.

This chapter is divided into four parts. The first part looks at the new external context after 1980 and examines the main trends of relevance to Latin America. The second explores the Latin American response to globalization from the mid-1980s to the present. The third part examines the outcome of the Latin American response in terms of economic welfare. The conclusions are presented in the final part.

THE EXTERNAL CONTEXT

Before the First World War, the world economy had been relatively open. Tariff rates were modest, nontariff barriers were not as yet a major problem, there were few restrictions on capital flows, and even labor was free to migrate to many countries. As a result, in this earlier phase of "globalization," trade was often a very high proportion of GDP, foreign capital flows represented a significant share of gross capital formation, and the foreign-born often represented a large minority of the labor force.[8]

The openness of the global economic system ended in 1914 and was only partially restored in the 1920s. New restrictions on trade and factor movements were applied in the 1930s. By the time of the Second World War, despite the efforts of the United States to restore trade liberalization through bilateral treaties, the world economy was probably less integrated than at any time in the previous century.

The Bretton Woods conference in 1944, leading to the foundation of the International Monetary Fund (IMF) and the International Bank for Reconstruction and Development (universally known as the World Bank), provided part of the institutional framework for lifting restrictions on trade and capital movements (labor movement was no longer on the agenda as a result of the fear of high unemployment in advanced capitalist countries). However, Bretton Woods postponed detailed consideration of the establishment of an International Trade Organization (ITO) that would have had direct responsibility for lowering restrictions on imports.

Frustration at the lack of progress toward an ITO led a small number of countries to hold a conference in Geneva in 1947. This led to the General

---

[8] See the chapter by Alan Taylor in this volume.

Agreement on Tariffs and Trade (GATT), which was strictly limited in scope (it had no responsibility for agriculture or services), had no judicial powers (its decisions were nonbinding), and failed to win the support of developing countries (only three Latin American countries joined). Even by its most enthusiastic supporters it was seen as little more than a stop-gap pending the creation of an ITO.[9]

The conference to launch an ITO was held in Havana in 1948 and appeared to have achieved its purpose, with fifty-six countries (almost all the members of the United Nations) signing the treaty. However, it was not ratified by the U.S. Congress and never came into force. For almost fifty years, the world was left with GATT to oversee the liberalization of trade despite the fact that GATT had never been intended to have more than a temporary role.

Despite its institutional weaknesses, GATT was remarkably successful from the standpoint of its advanced country members.[10] Most of their trade was in manufactured goods with each other and GATT helped to liberalize such trade through a series of negotiations culminating in the Uruguay Round launched in 1986. GATT restricted the use of nontariff barriers among its members and oversaw the reduction of tariffs.

These changes led to a rapid growth in world trade. Its volume rose faster than real global GDP in almost every year after GATT was created. As a result, trade as a proportion of GDP rose in many countries. This was true of all developed countries, which accounted for some two-thirds of world trade throughout this period, and also of some developing countries – notably the tiger economies of East Asia.[11] It did not, however, happen in the larger Latin American countries as a result of the continued support for ISI and the resulting bias against exports.

The global recession at the beginning of the 1980s, which contributed substantially to the Latin American debt crisis, took its toll on world trade. However, after a period of stagnation, world exports began to grow rapidly (see Figure 4.1). They doubled in dollar terms between 1986 and 1994 and continued to rise rapidly thereafter.[12] This spectacular growth was only

---

[9] On the evolution of GATT from such unpromising beginnings, see A. Winters, "The Road to Uruguay," *Economic Journal* 100, 403 (1990).

[10] See W. M. Scammell, *The International Economy since 1945* (Basingstoke, 1980).

[11] On the emergence of one of these tigers (South Korea), see Alice Amsden, *Asia's Next Giant: South Korea and Late Industrialization* (London, 1989).

[12] Developed countries continued to account for most of this trade. Even in 2000, their share of world exports was two thirds. See IMF, *Direction of Trade Statistics Yearbook 2002* (Washington, DC, 2002), 2.

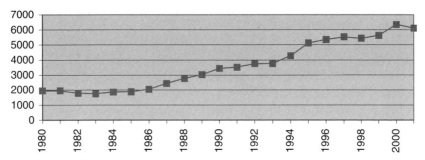

Figure 4.1. World exports in US$ billions, 1980–2001.
Source: IMF, International Financial Statistics, August 2002.

brought to an end by the United States recession in 2001 that marked the end of the information technology boom.

The rapid growth in world trade meant that trade as a share of GDP rose significantly. For the world as a whole, the ratio rose from 32.5 percent in 1990 to 40 percent in 2001.[13] In the high income countries, the ratio jumped from 32.3 to 37.9 percent, and the euro-zone saw the ratio increase from 44.9 to 56.3 percent.[14] In the developing countries, the ratio of trade to GDP jumped from 33.8 to 48.9 percent, a huge increase that was heavily influenced by the emergence of China as a global exporter of the first rank.

If the world economy was more open to trade at the end of the twentieth century than fifty years before, it was not necessarily more open than in 1900. There are some countries, notably the United Kingdom and Japan, where trade is a lower proportion of GDP today than a century ago. However, GDP is now dominated by services – not goods – and many of these services are nontraded. When the comparison is made between trade in goods and goods GDP, the evidence suggests strongly that the world is now more integrated in trade terms than ever before. This ratio increased from 82.3 percent in 1990 to 112.3 percent in 2001 for high income countries and, even in low and middle income countries, it rose from 74.4 to 93.7 percent.[15]

The greater integration of world product markets is a result of many forces. A major part has been played by GATT, culminating in the Uruguay

---

[13] See World Bank, *World Development Indicators* (Washington, DC, 2003), 312.

[14] The euro only came into existence as a physical currency in 2001, when it was adopted by all the members of the European Union except Denmark, Sweden, and the United Kingdom. However, "euro-zone" is often used to describe these same countries before the euro was officially adopted.

[15] See World Bank, *World Development Indicators*, 312.

Round. The latter, the most ambitious of all the GATT rounds, was concluded in 1993 and led to the creation of the World Trade Organization
(WTO) in 1995. This institution has many of the features expected of the
ITO fifty years before. It has responsibility for agriculture and services as
well as manufactures, it includes most developing countries, and it has
binding powers in the case of disputes.[16]

Under GATT/WTO, tariff rates have tumbled. The weighted mean tariff
in the United States in 2001 stood at 1.8 percent. In the European Union, it
fell from 3.7 percent in 1988 to 2.6 percent in 2001. Even in Japan, despite
its alleged proclivity for protectionism, it had fallen to 2.1 percent by the
beginning of the twenty-first century.[17] Just as important, the scourge of
nontariff barriers began to be tackled with the WTO authorized to take
whatever steps were necessary to outlaw them. With the exception of trade
in agricultural products, where developed country protection for the home
market and subsidies for exports remained rife, the trend toward greater
global trade liberalization was very marked.

The success of GATT in liberalizing trade in goods and of the WTO
in doing the same for services begs the question, "Why have these efforts
succeeded where previously they failed?" The answer is provided by the
dominant role played by multinational corporations (MNCs), whose subsidiaries account for some 60 percent of world trade. There are now some
60,000 MNCs in the world and they are no longer confined to developed
countries. Each MNC has an average of eight subsidiaries and these subsidiaries trade with each other so intensively that intra-MNC trade alone
represents around 40 percent of world trade.[18]

MNCs and their subsidiaries exchange an array of goods and services that
has undermined traditional theories of international trade. The Heckscher-
Ohlin theorem, with its emphasis on intersectoral trade, no longer holds
for much of foreign commerce.[19] Instead of selling each other goods from
different industries, countries are selling each other goods and services
from the same sectors. This intra-industry trade, in which the subsidiaries
of MNCs play a key role, now dominates trade patterns among developed
countries and is increasingly important in trade between developed and

---

[16] See J. Jackson, *The World Trade Organization: Constitution and Jurisprudence* (London, 1998).

[17] See World Bank, *World Development Indicators*, 326–7.

[18] See United Nations, *World Investment Report* (New York, 2000).

[19] The Heckscher-Ohlin theorem states that countries will specialize in those products that use intensively the factor of production in relative abundance. This implies that international trade between
countries will take place in different products and not in the same products.

developing countries. It is even emerging as an important factor in trade among developing countries.[20]

Without the impulse to trade liberalization from the MNCs, it is doubtful whether the government negotiators at GATT rounds would have been able to make so much progress. The removal of trade barriers has been a vital part of these companies' strategy as their production processes have become more spatially diffuse. Competition in developed country markets has led to a constant search for greater efficiency and lower costs of production. With a large gap in wage rates between rich and poor countries, a decision by one MNC to shift part of the production process to developing countries was bound to be followed by others.

The integration of the world economy through trade may be driven primarily by MNCs, but the trade networks now embrace the developing countries. Within the developing world, a special role has been played by East Asia. Beginning with the four dragons (Hong Kong, Singapore, South Korea, and Taiwan), the Newly Industrialized Countries (NICs) of East Asia now include Malaysia, Indonesia, Philippines, and China. These eight countries have become key locations in global production chains that stretch around the world, making possible rates of growth of real GDP that, until the 1997 Asian financial crisis, were the highest in the world.

This is the world that Latin America faced as it sought to extricate itself from the debt crisis. Although some Asian NICs may have increased indebtedness as fast as in Latin America, they had large and dynamic export sectors that could generate the foreign exchange to service the debt. Their role in the global division of labor meant that current account deficits could be financed through DFI when portfolio capital was scarce. And their geographical proximity to Japan, the fastest growing advanced economy until the 1990s, provided them with a powerful engine of growth.

The integration of the product markets is an important part of globalization. However, it is not the only part and may not even be the most important. The driving force in modern capitalism is the flow of international capital. These flows dried up almost completely in the 1930s and restrictions on capital were only slowly lifted after the Second World War. Unlike the case of trade, there was no gradual process of capital account liberalization and there were also serious reversals as countries faced balance

---

[20] For the Latin American case, see Victor Bulmer-Thomas, "Regional Integration and Intra-Industry Trade," in Victor Bulmer-Thomas, ed., *Regional Integration in Latin America and the Caribbean: The Political Economy of Open Regionalism* (London, 2001).

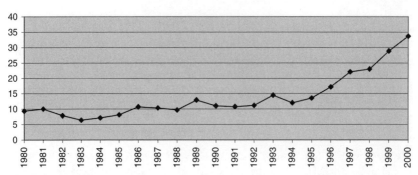

Figure 4.2. High income countries: gross private capital flows (% of GDP), 1980–2000.
Source: World Bank, *World Development Indicators 2002.*

of payments problems. The United States, for example, extended its restrictions on outflows of capital in the 1960s and the United Kingdom did the same in the 1970s.

The Reagan–Thatcher revolution in the 1980s had many characteristics, but one of the most striking was the bonfire of capital account and currency restrictions. Ironically, this took place after the boom in bank lending to Latin America that led to the debt crisis. Yet there can be no doubting the qualitative change that took place in the scale of capital flows in the mid-1980s. Because high income countries are both exporters and importers of capital, the best way to capture this change is by summing the inflows and outflows of all private capital (direct, portfolio, and other) and normalizing by expressing the result as a percentage of GDP.

The result is given in Figure 4.2, where the structural break in the mid-1980s for the high income countries is immediately apparent. From a low of 7.1 percent in 1985, the ratio had jumped to nearly 15 percent by 1995 and nearly 35 percent by 2000. For the countries making up the euro-zone, perhaps the most integrated bloc in the world, the ratio had reached 32.2 percent by the end of the twentieth century. By contrast, the ratio for low income countries remained depressed throughout the period. It was 0.7 percent in 1988 and only 2.0 percent a decade later. Most of these private gross capital flows went from developed countries to developed countries.

The acceleration in private capital flows was not only attributable to the lifting of restrictions on the capital account of the balance of payments. It was also caused by the new international division of labor and the need for MNCs to expand their operations around the world. DFI,

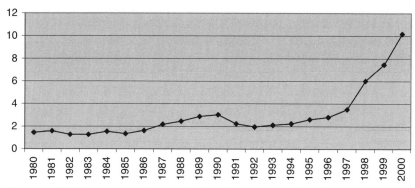

Figure 4.3. High income countries: gross foreign direct investment (% of GDP), 1980–2000.
Source: World Bank, *World Development Indicators 2002.*

also measured as the sum of outflows and inflows, shows a similar trend (Figure 4.3), rising for high income countries from below 2 percent of GDP in 1985 to 10 percent in 2000. In the United States, where the size of the domestic economy reduces the relative importance of gross capital flows, gross DFI flows represented almost half of all private capital flows by the end of the 1990s.

These DFI flows increased in importance in all regions of the world after the mid-1980s. In middle income countries, they quadrupled as a share of GDP between 1988 and 1998, reaching 1.6 percent. In upper middle income countries, they rose even faster, to 2.2 percent. Even in low income countries, they had risen to nearly 1 percent in 2001 from 0.2 a decade earlier.[21] No country that was serious about meeting the challenge of globalization could afford to ignore this trend, and governments all over the world reformed their legislation on DFI in order to increase their chances of benefiting from the increased mobility of capital.

Despite the growing importance of DFI, portfolio capital continued to dominate gross capital flows. Restrictions on the financial sector were lifted in advanced countries. Mergers and acquisitions within the financial sectors accelerated. Local institutions became regional and regional institutions became global. New financial instruments were pioneered and the bond markets were especially dynamic. Developing countries were redefined as

[21] See World Bank, *World Development Indicators*, 16 and 332.

"emerging," "pre-emerging," or "frontier," and pressure built up inside and outside to make the equity markets more liquid and accessible.

The elimination of restrictions on capital movements in developed countries in the 1980s was followed by their elimination in developing countries in the 1990s. The IMF and the World Bank put pressure on borrowing countries to liberalize the capital account of the balance of payments. In many cases this was premature,[22] as Southern Cone countries in Latin America had discovered to their cost at the beginning of the 1980s. Yet these lessons were not heeded and the speed of liberalization was one of the main reasons for the financial crisis that hit Asia in 1997.

The other reason for the Asian financial crisis was the pegging of local currencies to the dollar at a time when the dollar was exceptionally strong. Unlike trade and capital account liberalization, there was no consensus on exchange rate management and the debate has continued to rage in favor of fixed or floating currencies. However, globalization introduced a new element into the debate because closer integration of trade and factor markets raises the possibility of currency substitution. A number of developing countries have therefore experimented with new exchange rate arrangements ranging from currency boards (e.g., Hong Kong) to adoption of foreign currencies (e.g., Montenegro).

Latin America's efforts to exit from the debt crisis had to take these new circumstances into account. The short-run need to adjust the external sector to free up resources with which to service the foreign debt was over-shadowed by the medium-term requirement of adapting to the challenge of globalization. How this twin challenge was met is the subject of the second part of this chapter.

THE LATIN AMERICAN RESPONSE

The need to save foreign exchange in order to meet the rising costs of debt service led Latin American countries at first to increase – not decrease – the restrictions on imports. After the Mexican government threatened to default in August 1982, tariffs were raised in many countries and nontariff barriers (NTBs) increased sharply. In addition, output was falling as a result

---

[22] The Asian financial crisis in 1997 and subsequent financial crises in other parts of the developing world led to a reconsideration of the merits of capital account liberalization. For a severe critique, see Joseph Stiglitz, *Globalization and its Discontents* (New York, 2002).

of the decline in the terms of trade, the global recession, and the tightening of fiscal policy.[23]

Imports did indeed fall, but so did the value of exports. The resulting small trade surplus was insufficient to service the debt and Latin American countries were dependent on inflows of capital from official sources coupled with creative accounting by the international private creditors in order to avoid falling into default. The net transfer of resources turned negative because debt service payments far exceeded the net inflow of capital.[24]

The United States, as might have been expected, took the lead in coordinating the response of the creditors (private and official) to the Latin American debt crisis. The first public recognition that the position of the debtors was unsustainable came in 1985 with the announcement of the Baker Plan. Named after the U.S. Secretary of the Treasury at the time, the Baker Plan identified the crisis as one of liquidity rather than solvency, but the additional resources provided under the scheme were quite inadequate. By February 1987, Brazil had declared a moratorium and international banks rushed to declare their Latin American loans as value-impaired. This forced them to make loan-loss provisions, but these were cushioned by permission from the fiscal authorities in their countries to write them off against tax.

The Baker Plan was followed by the Brady Plan in 1989, named after Nicholas Brady, who succeeded James Baker as U.S. Treasury Secretary. This scheme was more radical in that it offered private creditors a menu from which they could choose provided they had met the conditions for adjustment stabilization agreed with the IMF. The most popular choice was to exchange the nominal value of bank debt for bonds with a lower face value with collateral provided by zero-coupon Treasury bills. These Brady bonds, as they were immediately dubbed, allowed banks to exit from their exposure to Latin America and therefore brought to an end the 1980s debt crisis.

It did not, of course, end the problem of indebtedness. The debt now took the form of bonds rather than bank loans, but the export sector in most countries was still very small in relation to both the size of the economy and the debt itself. Indeed, many commentators at the time argued that the Brady Plan, like the Baker Plan, was too little and too late.

[23] See Victor Bulmer-Thomas, *The Economic History of Latin America since Independence*, 2nd ed. (Cambridge, 2003), ch. 11.

[24] The net transfer of resources is defined as net capital inflows less payments of interest and profit remittances.

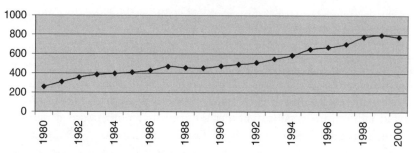

Figure 4.4. Latin American external debt, 1980–2000 (US$ billion).
Source: World Bank, *World Development Indicators 2002.*

We shall never know whether the critics were right or wrong because the Brady Plan was soon overtaken by events. For reasons discussed subsequently, the main Latin American countries were suddenly the beneficiary of new capital inflows starting in 1990 that reversed the negative net transfer of resources. Instead of foreign currency scarcity, there was foreign exchange abundance. Some governments even issued new bonds in order to retire the Brady bonds.

The result was a surge in external indebtedness just after the Brady Plan was supposed to have ended the debt crisis (see Figure 4.4). The main Latin American countries experienced a build-up of debt that was even greater than in the period before 1982. This time, the creditors were largely anonymous because they were bondholders rather than banks, making a coordinated creditor response extremely difficult.

The capital inflows in the first half of the 1990s were mainly portfolio. Only one third consisted of DFI. A few countries, notably Chile, adopted restrictions on short-term capital inflows, but most were only too happy to capture whatever foreign resources were available.[25] The result was a dangerous increase in speculative capital and an excessive dependence on foreign capital for financing domestic investment.

The first evidence that the increase in debt was unsustainable came with the Mexican financial crisis in 1994. Dubbed the first such crisis of the twenty-first century by Michel Camdessus (the IMF's Director at the time), the Mexican crisis led to an unprecedented rescue package mounted by the IMF and coordinated by the United States. Mexico avoided default

[25] See Ricardo Ffrench-Davis and S. Griffith-Jones, eds., *Coping with Capital Surges: The Return of Finance to Latin America* (Boulder, CO, 1995).

and the spreads on Latin American bonds returned to their previous levels, but it was an ominous warning of the difficulties that lay ahead.

The *tequila* crisis, as it was known, only temporarily reversed the net inflow of capital to Latin America. This continued almost unabated until the end of 1998. At this point, the Asian financial crisis, coupled with the Russian default in August 1998, led to a reassessment by creditors of Latin American risk. Thus, the ability of governments and companies in Latin America to borrow their way out of difficulty came to an end as the century closed.[26]

There have been three circumstances under which Latin American countries have been able to cope with the new debt reality. First, some countries (discussed later) have been able to increase the size of their export sectors in relation to GDP. Just as South Korea escaped the 1980s debt crisis because it was able to export its way out of trouble, so a handful of Latin American countries has been able to bring down the ratio of debt and debt servicing to exports through rapid growth of the export sector.

Second, some countries – for reasons explored subsequently – have been able to finance a growing proportion of their current account deficits through DFI rather than debt. The inflows of DFI were linked to the process of privatization in Latin America, reaching a peak in 1998. They declined rapidly thereafter, however, as the opportunities for privatization came to an end in most countries.

Third, many Latin American countries are too small to be attractive to foreign private creditors. Portfolio investors will not invest in equity markets with small turnover and little liquidity. Governments of such countries find it difficult to issue bonds. As a result, smaller Latin American countries have been dependent on official sources of capital, which is subject to conditions as well as being rationed.

The generalized debt crisis of the 1980s did not, therefore, repeat itself in the 1990s, even if some countries had very serious debt problems. Brazil came close to a moratorium in 1998 before the devaluation of the *real* in January 1999 and again in 2002 in the run-up to the presidential elections. Ecuador defaulted on its Brady bonds in 2000 and Argentina defaulted on most of its foreign debt at the end of 2001. And Cuba's debt problems have been so severe that it has been in arrears with almost all its creditors since the early 1980s.

---

[26] The net transfer of resources had once again turned negative by 2002.

The policies to tackle the debt crisis were being adopted at the same time as globalization was advancing in the rest of the world. This made it particularly difficult to meet the challenge of globalization and raised the possibility of contradictory policies. Tariffs, for example, needed to be raised to create a trade surplus to meet debt service payments, but needed to be lowered to promote the trade liberalization favored by globalization.

The Southern Cone countries had experimented with neoliberal policies in the 1970s, but these had been overwhelmed by the debt crisis and went into reverse. It was not until 1984 that Chile once again felt confident enough to return to the trade liberalization policies it had adopted so aggressively after 1975. Ecuador flirted briefly with tariff reductions in 1984, but Congress – not for the first time in recent Ecuadorian history – stymied the neoliberal instincts of the executive.

The most important shift away from ISI, however, came in Mexico in 1985, with the decision by the de la Madrid administration (1982–8) to join GATT. At a stroke, the quantitative restrictions that had underpinned Mexican industry for decades came under fire and a program of tariff reductions was also agreed. Those other Latin American countries that had not yet applied to GATT all did so in the following years so that by the end of the century, every Latin American and Caribbean country except the Bahamas was a member of the WTO (GATT's successor).

The Mexican government's decision had less to do with globalization, a word that had only just been coined, and more to do with the need to expand the export sector. Paradoxical though it may seem, reducing tariffs and NTBs is often the first step toward promoting exports. The reason is the impact of import restrictions on the exchange rate, which tends to become overvalued, and the increase in costs of export production from high tariffs on imported inputs.

Mexico's trade liberalization policies led to a deepening of its trade links with the United States. The non-oil share of exports, most of which goes to the United States, went from 20 percent in the early 1980s to 80 percent in the early 1990s. At that point, Mexico began to negotiate its entry into the free trade agreement launched by the United States and Canada in 1989. The result was the North American Free Trade Agreement or NAFTA, which came into force on January 1, 1994.[27] This has led to a further deepening

---

[27] On NAFTA, see G. Grayson, *The North American Free Trade Agreement: Regional Community and the New World Order* (Lanham, MD, 1995).

of the trade ties between Mexico and the United States, to the point where Mexico now accounts for half of all trade between the United States and Latin America.[28]

This bilateral trade is not, however, typical of trade between the United States and Latin America. Mexico's trade with the United States consists mainly of manufactured goods and is largely intra-industry. Indeed, eight of the top eleven Mexican imports from the United States now feature in the top eleven Mexican exports to the United States.[29] And Mexico has become very dependent on exports to the United States, which accounted for 31 percent of GDP in 2000.[30] Not surprisingly, Mexico went into recession in 2001 as a result of the economic slowdown in its northern neighbor.

Elsewhere in Latin America, trade liberalization has been less successful. Tariffs have been reduced everywhere and some countries such as Bolivia and Chile have adopted a uniform tariff. However, export performance has been overwhelmingly affected by the value of the real exchange rate. This has often moved in the "wrong" direction. Thus, when trade barriers are reduced, the real exchange rate should depreciate, providing an additional incentive to exporters.

Why was the movement in the real exchange rate so perverse? In many countries, trade liberalization occurred just as capital returned to Latin America. The net inflows pushed up the value of the real exchange rate and encouraged imports, but not exports. This was the problem in Mexico from 1990 to 1994, in Argentina after 1991, and in Brazil from 1994 to 1998. As a result, export performance in many countries has been modest and Latin America's increasing share of world exports is mainly attributable to Mexico.

The disappointing performance of the export sector was one of the reasons for the re-evaluation of regional integration. The schemes established in the 1960s had been discredited by the debt crisis because they were so strongly associated with ISI – albeit at the regional level. However, a new attempt was made in the 1990s to launch integration schemes that would promote exports without encouraging protection against third countries. The Central American Common Market was relaunched in 1990,

---

[28] See Victor Bulmer-Thomas and S. Page, "Trade Relations in the Americas: MERCOSUR, the Free Trade Area of the Americas and the European Union," in Victor Bulmer-Thomas and James Dunkerley, eds., *The United States and Latin America: The New Agenda* (Cambridge, MA, 1999).
[29] See Bulmer-Thomas, *Regional Integration in Latin America*, 85.
[30] See ECLAC, *Statistical Yearbook for Latin America and the Caribbean* (Santiago, 2002), 341.

the Caribbean Community (CARICOM) in 1992, and the Andean Pact (renamed the Andean Community) in 1995.[31]

The most innovative new integration scheme was the Mercado Común del Sur (MERCOSUR), formally adopted in 1991. Linking Argentina, Brazil, Paraguay, and Uruguay (Bolivia and Chile became associate members in 1996), it had a clear political purpose as well as economic objectives. When the Clinton administration announced in 1994 United States support for a Free Trade Area of the Americas (FTAA), MERCOSUR was quick to negotiate as a bloc to prevent the United States from dominating the hemispheric agenda on regional integration. However, MERCOSUR's early promise was not fulfilled. The common external tariff was never adopted in full and the scheme suffered from the economic instability brought about both by external shocks and the absence of macroeconomic coordination.[32]

Trade liberalization is only one of the ways in which Latin America has adjusted to globalization. Just as important has been the liberalization of the capital account of the balance of payments and a new approach to foreign capital. The old hostility to DFI, so strong in the 1970s, has gone and country after country has introduced new legislation to promote DFI, with very few sectors or activities reserved for domestic capital.

As part of this new approach to DFI, all Latin American governments have divested themselves of state-owned enterprises (SOEs). A few of these behemoths still exist, particularly in the oil industry, but they are now the exception rather than the rule. Even Cuba has participated in this process of privatization, with the added twist that the purchase of the assets is restricted to foreigners. Elsewhere, domestic private groups have been active in the purchase of SOEs, but so have foreigners. As a result, the stock of DFI has surged in public utilities, airlines, railways, and steel companies and other sectors where SOEs were previously common.

It is perhaps in the mining sector that the transformation has been most marked. Latin America has a long history of discrimination against DFI in mining, going back to the formation of YPF (an oil monopoly) by the Argentine state in 1922, if not before. The rationale for this was complex and included resentment at foreign company practices, rent-seeking by cash-strapped governments, and nationalism. Yet, nearly two centuries after the end of colonialism in most of Latin America, it is still the mineral resources

---

[31] On all these regional integration schemes, see Bulmer-Thomas, *Regional Integration in Latin America*.
[32] Intraregional trade in MERCOSUR was particularly badly hit by the Argentine financial crisis in 2001/2, when imports were reduced by 60 percent.

that most attract foreign companies. Thus, Latin America had little choice but to liberalize access of foreign capital into the mining sector if it wanted to receive DFI.

The liberalization of the capital account has not been limited to DFI. On the contrary, for most of the 1990s, the foreign investment coming to Latin America has been private portfolio capital. This has not been in the form of bank lending, the dominant form of foreign capital in the 1970s, but bonds and, to a lesser extent, equity. Trade credits from banks and other short-term loans have continued but, in general, the international banks were only too quick to seize the opportunity for exit offered by the Brady bonds. The growth of the international bond market has been dramatic and the main Latin American governments and companies tapped into it with relative ease. They were given a head start by the issuance of Brady bonds that transformed what had become almost an exotic form of Latin American debt into one with broad appeal. Furthermore, this foreign currency market was open to nationals (both companies and individuals), providing a welcome hedge against devaluation and an opportunity for portfolio diversification.

The international bond markets offered Latin America an opportunity to issue debt at lower real interest rates than in the shallow domestic financial markets. This was so even after making allowance for expected exchange rate movements, provided that the country risk premium could be held to a moderate level. Governments therefore put a huge effort into reducing the risk premium through sophisticated "road shows" in New York and London and greater transparency on the fiscal accounts and rules on company disclosures.

These efforts did not go unrewarded by the ratings agencies. By the beginning of 2003, Chile had been given A- on its long-term foreign currency debt; Colombia – despite the high levels of domestic violence – received BB; and El Salvador, which had been embroiled in civil war as late as the early 1990s, was awarded BB+.[33] The ratings agencies were more circumspect about the big three (Argentina, Brazil, and Mexico), although Mexico was rewarded with investment grade status during 2000 as the era of the one-party state finally came to an end.

The ratings, modest country risk premiums, and low international interest rates all encouraged Latin American governments, as well as larger

---

[33] See World Bank, *World Development Indicators*, 262–4. The ratings quoted are those awarded by Standard and Poor.

companies, to switch out of domestic currency debt into foreign bonds. The result was an unhealthy expansion of external indebtedness in many countries, particularly Argentina and Brazil, which were vulnerable to a widening of the risk premium and any unwillingness of the bond markets to refinance. When Argentine difficulties finally surfaced in 2001, the country was found to account for 25 percent of all emerging market fixed interest debt.

If Latin America's attempts to tap into the international bond market were too successful, the opposite was true of its efforts to attract equity capital. All attempts to broaden the appeal of the local stock markets failed. Only a small number of stocks were listed, most domestic companies preferring to remain 100 percent controlled by their family shareholders. Most of the listed stocks were not actively traded, so liquidity was a serious problem. The larger firms sought a listing as American Depositary Receipts (ADRs)[34] on the New York exchange and mergers and acquisitions by foreign companies led some of the most important companies to delist. By 2000, only two markets – São Paulo and Mexico City – had any appeal for foreign investors, and stocks in these markets accounted for 80 to 90 percent of the typical Latin American fund.

Latin America's liberalization of the capital account was therefore less satisfactory than its liberalization of the current account. Many of the smaller countries remained unattractive to foreign capital regardless of what they did, and DFI flowed primarily to mineral extraction and former SOEs. Assembly plants set up by foreign companies flourished in parts of the Caribbean Basin, but this was a reflection of temporary tax breaks in the United States more than anything else.[35] The larger countries, on the other hand, became too dependent on the foreign currency bond market. Mexico was the first to suffer (in 1994) but was rescued by its international creditors and was able to use currency depreciation to build up a massive export capacity. Argentina and Brazil were not so fortunate.

Latin America's efforts to adjust to globalization through liberalization of the current and capital accounts were matched by reforms to the domestic economy. Indeed, to a large extent, the external adjustment required a domestic response. This was particularly true of monetary and fiscal policy

---

[34] These ADRs were deemed to be much more liquid and were therefore popular with foreign investors. For U.S. investors, they had the additional advantage of avoiding exchange rate risk.

[35] The most important of these tax breaks was the Caribbean Basin Initiative (CBI), first introduced in 1984. This led to a boom in assembly plants in many countries, but a number of factories transferred production to Mexico after the adoption of NAFTA.

where irresponsible behavior was now much more likely to be punished. Thus, high rates of inflation could not be tolerated when tariffs were falling (trade liberalization) and real exchange rates rising (capital inflows).

Monetary policy has been transformed in Latin America in the last twenty years. Central banks have become much more autonomous (e.g., Brazil) and some have been given complete independence (e.g., Mexico). Regulation of the banking systems has been improved and the entry of foreign banks has increased efficiency, even if competition is still limited. The ability of the public sector to monetize fiscal deficits has been severely curtailed. The outcome, as we will see in the next section, has been a big fall in inflation in Latin America to rates that have not been seen for decades. Indeed, such has been the improvement in the quality and credibility of monetary policy that nominal exchange rate devaluation is no longer necessarily a guide to the rate of inflation.[36]

The most serious weakness in monetary policy has been the failure to lower the real cost of borrowing. This is partly because of the shallowness of the financial markets, but also because of the huge spread between borrowing and lending rates. Indeed, it is not unknown for the real lending rate to be close to zero while the real borrowing rate is above 10 percent. Lack of competition in the financial markets is primarily to blame, and this has not yet been overcome through liberalization of the capital account of the balance of payments. In practice, only the largest Latin American companies have access to the international capital market so that small and medium-sized enterprises (SMEs) are restricted to borrowing in the domestic market and are crippled by high rates.

This unsatisfactory state of affairs arises in part because financial institutions have become major creditors to the public sector and are not so dependent on private sector business. As mentioned previously, the foreign-currency bonds are often held by domestic agents and these are principally the banks. Thus, the banks benefit from the country risk premium and the banks are also the most likely to hold the domestic currency debt issued by governments.

It might appear from the aforementioned that fiscal policy did not improve after the debt crisis. In fact, it did, but it is necessary to distinguish between the primary balance (net of interest payments) and the nominal balance. The primary balance has moved into surplus in most countries,

---

[36] This has been particularly true of Argentina and Brazil, where large devaluations in 2001/2 did not lead to a permanent increase in inflation as had originally been feared.

as taxes have been increased, defense spending cut, and subsidies to SOEs eliminated. Equity considerations have been largely sacrificed in the search for increased revenues with an emphasis on broad-based sales taxes, particularly value-added tax. And federal countries have made serious efforts to control spending by provincial governments. However, interest payments on the public debt – both domestic and foreign – have remained a major drain on state finances, leading to nominal deficits that were sometimes large even when the primary balance was in surplus.

The tightness of fiscal policy, in terms of macroeconomic stability, is more closely approximated by the primary than the nominal balance. Thus, fiscal policy has been restrictive in many countries at the cost of lower investment and also at the expense of social spending. Targeting of social spending on lower income groups, promoted by the World Bank in particular, became more popular and enjoyed some success – notably in Chile. However, the impact of social spending has not in general improved the secondary distribution of income.[37]

The reasons for this have been complex, but two stand out. First, educational spending on universities – a large part of the total – has favored the middle and upper deciles of the income distribution. Second, state spending on pensions in Latin America goes overwhelmingly to the middle classes rather than the poor. Although most governments have privatized – in whole or in part – their pension systems, there is a long lag before state liabilities cease. The reason is that older workers remain in the state system and continue to benefit until they die.[38]

Although something approaching a consensus has developed in relation to fiscal and monetary policy in Latin America since the debt crisis, the same cannot be said about exchange rate policy. All Latin American countries, except dollarized Panama, devalued in the 1980s and early 1990s in an effort to adjust the external sector, both to create resources to service the debt and to promote exports. However, the similarity ends there. One group, led by Argentina, marched resolutely toward fixed currencies and *de facto* dollarization. Another group, led by Chile, adopted a crawling peg with a real exchange rate target. The third group, led by Mexico after 1994 and joined by Brazil in 1999, opted for exchange rate flexibility.

---

[37] On the impact of social spending on income distribution, see the chapter by Miguel Székely and Andrés Montes in this volume.

[38] For a case study of Chile, see C. Scott, "The Distributive Impact of the New Economic Model in Chile," in Victor Bulmer-Thomas, ed., *The New Economic Model in Latin America and its Impact on Income Distribution and Poverty* (New York, 1996).

The first group initially enjoyed great success. Inflation came down to international levels and was accompanied by financial deepening. However, the risk premium did not disappear and a spread remained between domestic and foreign interest rates. Thus, the logic of this group has been to move toward *de jure* dollarization with Ecuador and El Salvador joining Panama. Argentina appeared to be moving in this direction, with nearly 70 percent of bank deposits denominated in dollars by the fourth quarter of 2001. However, default on the external debt at the end of 2001 triggered a devaluation of the currency and a difficult period of *pesoification* as the authorities struggled to reverse the dollarization of the 1990s.

The second group also enjoyed initial success in achieving the target. However, the difficulty of attracting foreign capital after the Asian financial crisis led to a dismantling of restrictions on foreign capital inflows and a move toward full currency flexibility. Only the smaller countries, such as Costa Rica, were able to persevere with real exchange rate targeting. Other countries, including Chile and Colombia, effectively joined the third group at the end of the 1990s.

Thus, Latin America found itself divided into two camps on exchange rate policy. In the fixed exchange rate group, dollarization appeared to be the logical step or at least a monetary union based on a regional currency. In the other group, formal dollarization looked increasingly unlikely, although the dollar was often used in pricing assets. Both groups claimed to be adjusting to globalization, so that at least with respect to exchange rate policy, the implications of world economic integration appear to have been ambiguous.

THE OUTCOME

It is not easy at this distance to judge Latin America's economic performance since the debt crisis. Two decades is a short time in economic history and there is a sharp contrast between the adjustment of the 1980s and the recovery of the 1990s. Nevertheless, certain patterns emerge with clarity. In what follows, I concentrate on growth, trade, capital flows, and inflation. The equity performance is analyzed in Chapter 14 and the impact on the environment in Chapter 9.

The rate of growth of GDP per head in the two decades since the debt crisis is shown in Table 4.1. Although there was a modest improvement between the 1980s and the 1990s, the result is not impressive. It can be

Table 4.1. *Growth of GDP per head (US$ at 1995 prices), 1981–2001*

	1981–90	1991–2001
Argentina	−2.1	2.1
Bolivia	−1.9	1.0
Brazil	−0.4	1.1
Chile	1.4	4.2
Colombia	1.6	0.6
Costa Rica	−0.7	1.8
Cuba	2.8	−1.6
Dominican Republic	0.2	3.8
Ecuador	−0.9	−0.1
El Salvador	−1.5	2.0
Guatemala	−1.6	1.2
Haiti	−2.9	−2.8
Honduras	−0.8	0.3
Mexico	−0.2	1.5
Nicaragua	−4.1	0.5
Panama	−0.7	2.4
Paraguay	0.0	−0.9
Peru	−3.3	1.8
Uruguay	−0.6	1.8
Venezuela	−3.2	0.3
Latin America	−0.9	1.2

Source: Victor Bulmer-Thomas, *The Economic History of Latin America since Independence*, 2nd ed. (Cambridge, 2003), 383, Table 11.4.

argued that the long-run performance should not be judged by the 1980s because this was a period of adjustment to the excesses of ISI and the debt crisis. However, even if the analysis is confined to the period since 1990, the results are still disappointing, with a low average rate of growth of GDP per head (1.2 percent) and a high variance. Furthermore, the five years after 1997 were marked by virtual stagnation in GDP per head in Latin America, leading to it being described as the "lost half-decade."

Since the mid-1980s, only one country (Chile) has been able unambiguously to exceed its performance during the inward-looking phase of development from 1950 to 1980, although the Dominican Republic achieved a very credible annual growth rate in GDP per head in the 1990s (see Table 4.1).[39] Argentina initially improved its long-run rate of growth of real GDP per head, but this was undermined by a deep recession after 1998.[40] The other cases of superior growth are all rather unusual. El Salvador, for example, grew rapidly in the 1990s, but this was after a long civil war, and the rate of growth is heavily influenced by the remittances sent by all those who had left the country for the United States.

Mexico's performance has been an illustration of the costs and benefits of globalization. One of the first to adjust, Mexico was also quick to liberalize its current and capital accounts and to integrate its economy into the North American economic space. Although performance could be damaged by domestic mistakes, as in the excessive build-up of debt in the early 1990s, the long-run trend toward a greater dependence on the U.S. market has become clear.

When the U.S. economy performed well, Mexico benefited handsomely. Growth was export-led and export expansion generated a boom in other parts of the economy despite the weak backward linkages from the maquila industry on the northern border. The economy became less dependent on oil and manufactured exports became less dependent on the assembly industry. However, Mexico went into recession as soon as the U.S. economy slowed down. With some 30 percent of its GDP in exports and nearly 90 percent of its exports going to the United States, this was perhaps inevitable. Mexico's economic fortunes are now increasingly bound up with those of the United States.[41]

Argentina's performance has been a case study in the dangers of inconsistent policies. On many criteria, Argentina in the 1990s was the most neoliberal economy in Latin America, with widespread privatization, complete capital account liberalization, and a large measure of trade liberalization. Yet the exchange rate policy, under which the local currency was pegged to the U.S. dollar under a virtual currency board regime, imposed fiscal obligations on the government that were never fully respected. The result was a lack of fiscal discipline, leading to a massive increase in external debt. As long as the economy grew rapidly, the debt problem could be contained. It

---

[39] The Dominican Republic, however, suffered a major banking crisis in 2003, leading to a collapse of the exchange rate and a fall in real GDP.

[40] The collapse of Argentine GDP in 2002 (it fell by 11 percent) wiped out the long-run improvement in GDP per head that had been achieved in the first half of the 1990s.

[41] Mexico has made a big effort to diversify its trading links, signing free trade agreements with other Latin American countries as well as with the European Union. However, the gravitational pull of the United States has proved irresistible and the links with the United States have, if anything, grown stronger.

became unsustainable, however, when growth stopped after 1998 and the authorities had no instruments at their disposal with which to stimulate the economy.[42]

The other big disappointment has been Brazil. The largest economy in the region, Brazil has consistently failed to achieve its potential. Adjustment and liberalization were delayed until the 1990s, so this harsh judgment may prove premature. However, greater fiscal and monetary responsibility, low inflation, trade and financial liberalization, and the promotion of DFI have not yet enabled Brazil to shift to a higher long-run sustainable growth rate.[43]

The obstacles in Brazil are numerous. The rate of investment is held back by low domestic savings, as in so many parts of Latin America and unlike in Asia; foreign capital cannot be relied on to close the gap. High real interest rates discourage borrowing by the private sector for productive purposes. Exports responded only modestly to devaluation and remained less than 10 percent of GDP until 2004 (compared with more than 20 percent in China at the end of the 1990s). Brazil's income inequality, one of the worst in the world, also acts as a brake on its economic performance, although this is more controversial. At the very least, Brazil does not enjoy the benefits such as high savings rates that are supposed to accompany an unequal distribution of income.

The transition from ISI would have required greater attention to foreign trade, with or without globalization. The reason is that Latin America saw its share of world trade decline steadily after 1950 to the point where it had reached a mere 3.5 percent in 1980 (much lower than its share of world population). Although some of this decline could be attributed to a specialization in primary products at a time when primary products trade was growing less fast than total trade, it was also attributable to the relentless anti-export bias associated with the inward-looking model of development.

The strategy to reverse the decline in world market share has had two components. First has been the greater attention to the export sector through policies designed to favor traded over nontraded goods and within tradeables to favor exportables over importables. Second has been the desire to diversify exports away from primary products toward manufactured goods and even services.

---

[42] See M. Mussa, *Argentina and the Fund: From Triumph to Tragedy* (Washington, DC, 2002).

[43] The difficulties facing Brazil were compounded by the 1988 constitution creating state obligations in the area of social security that were increasingly onerous. These could only be tackled through constitutional reform, which became a priority for the government of President Lula (2003–).

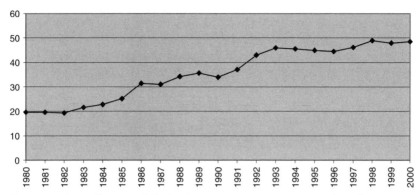

Figure 4.5. Diversification of Latin American exports, 1980–2000 (% of exports in manufacturing).
Source: World Bank, *World Development Indicators 2002.*

The results for Latin America as a whole have been impressive, although they are heavily influenced by Mexico. Thus, the share of world exports has indeed increased since the mid-1980s, but this is mainly because of Mexico's export boom. By 2000, Mexico accounted for half of all Latin America's exports. Excluding Mexico, the Latin American performance has been much less satisfactory. However, some smaller countries – notably Chile, but also Costa Rica – also increased world market share rapidly.

Aggregate figures for Latin America are always heavily influenced by Brazil and trade is no exception. Thus, the poor performance of Latin America (excluding Mexico) reflected the Brazilian export sector's lack of dynamism. This has been all the more puzzling in view of the increase in export competitiveness after the devaluation in January 1999. The Brazilian authorities tended to blame agricultural protectionism in rich countries for this sad state of affairs, but in truth it has been much more complex.

The diversification of Latin America's exports has been much more satisfactory (see Figure 4.5). Once again, the results have been heavily influenced by Mexico, but this time they are reinforced by Brazil. Yet in most countries, the contribution of primary products to total exports has been in decline and it must be borne in mind that the statistics in Figure 4.5 do not include service exports.

Diversification has had several causes. In smaller countries, it has been helped by the growth of the maquila industry. Haiti, for example, has one of the lowest ratios of primary products to total exports and this is entirely attributable to the assembly plants exporting light manufactures to the

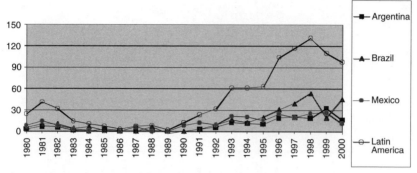

Figure 4.6. Net private capital flows, 1980–2000 (US$ billion).
Source: World Bank, *World Development Indicators 2002.*

United States. In Costa Rica, the establishment by Intel of a computer-chip factory at the end of the 1990s doubled the gross value of exports within two years. In larger countries, it also reflects investments by MNCs as part of the production chain linking subsidiaries across the world.

Regional integration has also been an important cause of diversification. The new phase of integration has encouraged the export of manufactured goods to neighboring countries. Indeed, despite the absence of formal discrimination against agricultural products, almost all intraregional trade in Latin America is in manufactures and a growing proportion of this is intra-industry trade as well. However, the impact of regional integration would appear to be quite limited because each scheme – with the notable exception of NAFTA – has found it difficult to increase the share of total trade that is intraregional. This peaked at 20 percent in MERCOSUR, 15 percent in the CACM, and 10 percent in the Andean Community and CARICOM.

Capital account liberalization and other measures have helped to bring foreign investment to Latin America. There has been a big increase in net private capital flows to the region (see Figure 4.6), which once again reflects the size and importance of the main economies (not only Brazil and Mexico, but this time also Argentina). These annual flows help explain the big increase in total external debt, which, by 2000, had reached nearly $800 billion (see Figure 4.4). Considering that the stock of debt had been "only" $258 billion in 1980, shortly before the debt crisis was triggered, and that the economic performance after 1980 was far from stellar, it is clear that the increase in debt was neither justified nor sustainable.

DFI was not attracted to Latin America in the 1980s. However, that changed in the 1990s and by the end of the decade, the annual flow had increased significantly and accounted for two thirds of the inflow of net private capital. As a result, DFI raised its contribution to domestic investment from less than 5 percent in 1980 to nearly 20 percent in 2000.[44] This ratio, similar to what is found in Southeast Asia, has been welcomed by governments in the region, but it came too late to prevent the build-up of the external debt. This now hangs like an albatross around the Latin American neck. Only a handful of countries (Bolivia, Haiti, Honduras, and Nicaragua) qualify for the relief developed for highly indebted poor countries (HIPC) by the international creditors; for the larger countries, HIPC is irrelevant because it does not apply to debt owed to the private sector.

The most impressive Latin American performance has been in terms of inflation stabilization. This has been a success story with only minor qualifications,[45] as Table 4.2 makes clear. Given the long history of chronic inflation in many countries before 1980, this is all the more remarkable. Furthermore, the impact of adjustment programs in the 1980s at first exacerbated inflationary pressures through the impact of currency depreciation, increases in sales taxes, and ending of subsidies on the price level.

The fall in inflation rates at the beginning of the 1990s was mainly attributable to real exchange rate appreciation. The inflows of capital led to currency overvaluation that reduced inflation, but undermined external competitiveness at the same time. The classic example is provided by Argentina, where the rate of inflation fell from more than 50 percent a month at the beginning of 1991 to an annual rate of less than 1 percent by 1996.[46] However, the cost in terms of lost competitiveness was high. The real exchange rate appreciated by anything from 30 to 50 percent depending on which domestic price deflator is used.

A fall in inflation caused by currency overvaluation is not sustainable. Yet, inflation rates remained low even when real exchange rates depreciated. The reasons were both economic and psychological. Tight fiscal and monetary policies allowed the authorities to compensate for the impact of currency falls, and trade liberalization lowered tariffs and increased competition in the tradeable goods sector at the same time. However, inflation reduction also had a psychological component. Inflationary expectations were broken

---

[44] This ratio fell again, however, at the start of the new century, as a result of the decline in DFI to Latin America.

[45] The most important exception has been Venezuela, where inflation remained in double digits for almost all of the period since the debt crisis.

[46] Argentina even had price deflation between 1999 and 2001. See ECLAC, *Statistical Yearbook*, 741.

Victor Bulmer-Thomas

Table 4.2. *Latin America: consumer prices (Dec–Dec variations)*

				Latin America: Consumer prices (Dec–Dec variations)						
	1993	1994	1995	1996	1997	1998	1999	2000	2001	2002
Argentina	7.4	3.9	1.6	0.1	0.3	0.7	−1.8	−0.7	−1.5	40.6
Bolivia	9.3	8.5	12.6	7.9	6.7	4.4	3.1	3.4	0.9	2.3
Brazil	2,477.2	916.5	22.4	9.6	5.2	1.7	8.9	6.0	7.7	10.9
Chile	12.2	8.9	8.2	6.6	6.0	4.7	2.3	4.5	2.6	3.0
Colombia	22.6	22.6	19.5	21.6	17.7	16.7	9.2	8.8	7.6	7.1
Costa Rica	9.0	19.9	22.6	13.9	11.2	12.4	10.1	10.2	11.0	10.0
Cuba	0.0	0.0	−11.5	−4.9	1.9	2.9	−2.9	−3.0	−0.5	5.0
Dominican Republic	2.8	14.3	9.2	4.0	8.4	7.8	5.1	9.0	4.4	8.8
Ecuador	31.0	25.3	22.8	25.5	30.7	43.4	60.7	91.0	22.4	9.7
El Salvador	12.1	8.9	11.4	7.4	1.9	4.2	−1.0	4.3	1.4	1.4
Guatemala	11.6	11.6	8.6	10.9	7.1	7.5	4.9	5.1	8.9	6.3
Haiti	44.3	32.2	24.8	14.5	15.7	7.4	9.7	19.0	8.1	10.1
Honduras	13.0	28.9	26.8	25.3	12.8	15.7	10.9	10.1	8.8	7.7
Mexico	8.0	7.1	52.0	27.7	15.7	18.6	12.3	9.0	4.4	5.4
Nicaragua	19.5	12.4	11.1	12.1	7.2	18.5	7.2	9.9	4.7	4.2
Panama	0.9	1.4	0.8	2.3	−0.5	1.4	1.5	0.7	0.0	1.6
Paraguay	20.4	18.3	10.5	8.2	6.2	14.6	5.4	8.6	8.4	14.6
Peru	39.5	15.4	10.2	11.8	6.5	6.0	3.7	3.7	−0.1	1.5
Uruguay	52.9	44.1	35.4	24.3	15.2	8.6	4.2	5.1	3.6	24.7
Venezuela	45.9	70.8	56.6	103.2	37.6	29.9	20.0	13.4	12.3	30.7
Latin America	872.4	328.7	26.0	18.6	10.7	10.0	9.7	9.0	6.1	11.4

Source: Economic Commission for Latin America and the Caribbean, *Preliminary Overview of the Economics of Latin America and the Caribbean* (Santiago, 2002), 110.

in the first half of the 1990s, allowing governments to phase out indexation and making it less likely inflation would return.

This section has concentrated on the traditional measures of macroeconomic performance: growth, trade, capital flows, and inflation. However, the two decades after 1980 witnessed an important change in Latin America that consolidated a trend beginning even earlier. This was the demographic transition, under which the fall in death rates beginning in the 1920s was finally matched by a fall in birth rates. Thus, the main Latin American countries faced a more manageable annual increase in population, although a number of the smaller countries such as Honduras and Nicaragua remained stuck in the first phase of the demographic transition (i.e., high birth rates and low death rates).

In the 1980s, the annual rate of growth of the population fell to an annual average of 2.1 percent and in the 1990s it fell again to 1.6 percent.[47] At the start of the new millennium, it was still falling. Given that the population had been growing at nearly 3 percent per year in the 1960s, Latin America has achieved a big reduction in the rate of demographic expansion. The full implications of this on the environment, social spending, labor market, and pensions will take many years – if not decades – to be worked out, but it does offer some comfort in the light of the disappointing macroeconomic performance.

CONCLUSIONS

Latin America began the process of adjustment to globalization in the mid-1980s. The objectives were not only to counter the negative impact of the debt crisis but also to reverse the disengagement of the region from the world's product and factor markets. This reversal had been a consequence of several decades of inward-looking development coupled with a growing hostility to DFI.

The goal of countering the negative impact of the debt crisis has been partially successful. Latin America did succeed in extricating itself from the debt overhang represented by commercial bank loans, but at the expense of a huge increase in bond indebtedness. In part, this was attributable to the exchange of bank loans for bonds under the Brady Plan, but it was also caused by the ease of tapping the international bond market in the 1990s.

The bond markets proved just as fickle as commercial creditors. Capital flowed to Latin America in abundance when global liquidity was strong, but the inflow proved vulnerable to events over which Latin America had no control. The Mexican financial crisis in 1994 affected all of Latin America, although the circumstances in other countries were very different. The Asian financial crisis in 1997 and the Russian default the following year proved to be the catalyst for a rise in the country risk premiums in Latin America despite the lack of synchronization in the real economies of emerging markets. Last, but not least, the terrorist attack on the United States in

---

[47] See Bulmer-Thomas, *The Economic History of Latin America*, 7, Table 1.2.

September 2001 led to an increase in risk aversion and a flight to quality from which Latin America inevitably suffered.

Adjustment to globalization has therefore not ended Latin America's debt problems, although they now take new forms. Debt in the 1990s increased faster than nominal GDP, leading to a rise in the debt/GDP ratio. Similarly, the increase in the dollar value of exports was in many cases insufficient to reduce the debt service ratio (interest plus amortization as a share of exports). The rate of domestic saving rose, but capital formation needed to rise as well as a result of the neglect of investment in the 1980s. Thus, the gap between domestic savings and investment remained, leading to a need for foreign resources.

The second objective – integration into global product and factor markets – was also only partially successful. The share of trade (exports plus imports) in GDP rose, but this only meant that trade was growing faster than GDP. Given the bias against exports and imports under ISI, this rising trade ratio was hardly surprising. More relevant is Latin America's share of world exports.

This share increased after 1990, but the rise is entirely explained by Mexico. Indeed, when Mexico is excluded from the Latin American figure, the ratio is virtually unchanged. Just as disturbing is the failure of all the Latin American integration schemes excluding NAFTA to increase world market share of exports in the 1990s. Latin America's export performance may have been superior to what had gone before, but it still did not measure up against the competition from outside.

Mexico's outstanding export performance has many explanations. On the supply side, competitiveness was increased through tax reform (including tariff reductions) and the adoption (after 1994) of a flexible exchange rate. Yet these measures were common to almost all countries in the region. What was different in Mexico's case was the demand side. Even before NAFTA was launched, Mexico had become increasingly integrated into the North American economic space, with many firms taking investment decisions on a regional rather than a national basis. DFI linked Mexico to its northern neighbor and Mexican firms began to acquire a presence in the United States.[48]

---

[48] Mexico's privileged position could not prevent increased competition from China. The entry of the People's Republic into the World Trade Organization at the start of the new millennium led to some investment diversion from Mexico to China and much greater competition for Mexican exports in the United States.

Mexico's trading links with the United States proved so strong that they dominate all of Latin America's trade links. In the decade from 1988 to 1998, Latin America's exports to the United States grew at 14 percent a year, compared with U.S. imports from all sources of 7.8 percent. By contrast, Latin America's exports to the European Union, Japan, and other industrial countries grew more slowly than their imports from all sources. Thus, Latin America's share of U.S. imports increased – mainly because of Mexico – while its share of other markets declined. These other markets were of little importance to Mexico but of much greater significance for the rest of Latin America.

Latin America's integration into world product markets was therefore disappointing. However, there was one notable exception – the drugs trade. Despite all efforts at interdiction, including crop spraying, financial support for substitutes, and draconian measures against money laundering, the export of narcotics from Latin America continued unabated. A decline in production in one country simply led to an increase in another; a clampdown on distribution through one channel always led to the emergence of other conduits.[49] A few voices were heard calling for legalization of the drugs trade, but the importing countries were not yet ready for such drastic steps.

Latin America's integration into global factor markets was more successful than its integration into product markets. By the end of the 1990s, the region's share of global DFI had risen to about 10 percent – more than double what it had been a decade before – and DFI was spread around the region, attracted not just to Mexico but to other countries as well. The region was also well represented – perhaps too well – in the global bond market.

The other global factor market (labor) remained subject to major restrictions, although this had not prevented wide-scale migration from Latin America to other parts of the world – notably the United States.[50] Migratory movements were also important within Latin America; Bolivians and Paraguayans, for example, formed a large part of the Argentine labor force by the end of the century, and Nicaraguans represented at least 10 percent

---

[49] An example is *Plan Colombia*, adopted with the support of the United States in Colombia. By 2003, it was clearly succeeding in its aim of reducing coca cultivation and shipments of cocaine to the United States, but total coca production in Latin America was largely unaffected.

[50] Remittances to Latin America by migrants living abroad were estimated at more than US$30 billion by the beginning of the twenty-first century. In some countries, they reached nearly 10 percent of GDP.

of the Costa Rican population. These labor movements led to a massive flow of remittances to relatives in Latin America and to a modest transfer of technology.

Where Latin America still lags far behind is in the knowledge economy. Its educational deficit remains severe despite high-level recognition in the 1990s of the need for accelerated investment.[51] The use of the Internet is at very low levels compared with developed countries. By 2001, there were only 59 personal computers per 1,000 people, compared with 286 in the euro-zone and 625 in the United States.[52] Signs of a productivity revolution inspired by the New Economy, as in North America, were conspicuous by their absence.

Thus, the long march toward globalization has not brought the benefits many expected. Growth rates have been disappointing and remain below those before 1980 in most countries. The region has opened up to foreign trade, but the basis for Latin America's renewed integration into the world economy remains unclear. Labor is abundant, but it is not cheap compared with many countries in Asia.[53] Capital is scarce domestically and can only be obtained from abroad at high cost. The region is still rich in natural resources, but the pattern of world demand and residual protectionism does not favor agricultural exports. That leaves mining exports and it is a sad comment on 500 years of economic history that Latin America's comparative advantage is still seen by many to lie with precious metals and other minerals.

[51] See the chapter by Fernando Reimers in this volume.
[52] See World Bank, *World Development Indicators*, 300.
[53] This point is made in some detail in the chapter by Miguel Székely and Andrés Montes in this volume.

Part II

ONSET OF MODERNIZATION

5

THE INSTITUTIONAL FRAMEWORK

ALAN DYE

Conventional explanatory frameworks often depict Latin America's institutional structures as static and inflexible. Some conclude that the economic successes of Western Europe were not transferable to Latin America. Others shun potentially misleading international comparisons outside the region, especially with North America. Institutional rigidities are perceived as derivative of cultural traits fixed by traditional ideologies or mindsets; anchored by colonial institutional structures; and labeled as semifeudal, neoscholastic, patrimonialist, absolutist, corporatist, and so on. Although it identified the proximate causes with external factors, even dependency thinking found the root causes of dependency in deficiencies of the Iberian institutional legacy – in concentrations of power, transnationalism, or entrepreneurial inadequacies among the elite.

This tendency toward cultural determinism in Latin America's institutions falls in sharp contrast to the predominant narratives of North American institutional history. Contrast, for example, William Parker with Stanley and Barbara Stein. Parker tells how colonial settlers in North America almost immediately broke apart the mercantilist and corporate forms of organization that founded their colonies, whereas the Steins tell how rigid Iberian mercantilist institutions debilitated Latin America and subordinated it to peripheral status. Or compare Richard Morse with Alexis de Tocqueville. Morse characterizes Iberian emigrants to Latin America as encumbered by the moral obligations of the Old World social hierarchy, which they carried with them and used to create a New World social order that mirrored the Old World's organic social hierarchy of race, birthplace, and nobility. This perception of inflexibility in institutional transmission differs from Tocqueville's description of European migrants to North America carrying both the seeds of liberalism and the moral obligations of social hierarchy. He saw them as free to choose and cast off ideas that encumbered them.[1] One cannot help but ask why the two worlds were so inconsistent. Why would immigrants to North America be free to select from among the ideas and institutions of the Old World but not immigrants to Latin America? Why would the peoples who settled British North America become empowered then to imitate the economic success of Western Europe, but not those who settled Latin America?

A resurgence of interest in the historical study of institutions has brought new vigor to these large questions of institutional foundations and their long-run economic consequences. Against prior convention, the new work takes inspiration from international comparisons, especially from the evolutionary dynamics of transatlantic New World colonization. It adopts a perspective that aims at a consistent understanding of the long-run divergence or distinctiveness of New World paths of institutional change. It rejects as inconsistent the notion of rigid exogenous institutional transmission, and significantly, it pursues explicit counterfactual reasoning to conceptualize a greater range of possibilities for institutional change in Latin America.

NEW WORLD INSTITUTIONAL DIVERGENCE

The progress of recent decades could not have been made without the precise definitions of institutions and formal approaches developed under the rubric of the New Institutional Economics. After three decades of refinement, the theory now combines two complementary approaches. The first approach emphasizes the function of institutions as humanly devised *constraints*. This approach was pioneered by Douglass North, who characterized institutions as the "rules of the game" that shape human interaction. Such rules may be embodied formally, as in laws, regulations, and procedural codes, or constituted informally, as in social norms, conventions, or customs. A second approach conceptualizes institutions as rules or social norms that produce *sustained or equilibrium behavior*. This approach came out of game-theoretic research seeking to explain the emergence and

---

[1] Richard M. Morse, "The Heritage of Latin America," in Louis Hartz, ed., *The Founding of New Societies* (New York, 1964); William N. Parker, "Political Controls on a National Economy," in *Europe, America, and the Wider World: Essays on the Economic History of Western Capitalism*, vol. 2 (New York, 1991); Barbara and Stanley Stein, *The Colonial Heritage of Latin America* (New York, 1970); Alexis de Tocqueville, *Democracy in America*, trans. George Lawrence (New York, 1966).

sustainability of social norms, conventions, and other apparently unselfish cooperative behavior not underpinned by third-party enforcement.[2] The critical insights in the second approach are that, in many social interactions, people make decisions based on what they expect others to do. Significantly, some cooperative behavior appears to be sustainable only when it is *self-enforcing*; that is, only when multiple individuals' actions, based on their expectations about others' actions, are all mutually consistent with the joint outcome.

Institutional innovations are feasible through the endogenous decisions of individuals in collective settings. However, formal institutional changes are often impeded without complementary and compatible changes of a complex array of informal rules or social norms. In postindependence Latin America, there was a proliferation of liberal institutional innovations – new constitutions and legal codes, reorganizations of judiciaries, modernization of monetary and fiscal institutions, and liberalization of sectoral economic policies. A prominent question in the literature has been whether Western European liberal ideas were or could be reshaped to fit these different political environments. New institutional theory says it may not be straightforward. For example, it may not be possible to achieve the intended effects from introducing Western European ideas of the individual right of property or the U.S. institution of federalism without complementary and consistent changes in social expectations. Furthermore, introducing foreign institutions into Latin America's distinct social environments could have unintended consequences. Embedded social norms or other institutional rigidities often prevent institutions from deviating far from preexisting ideas and practices, thus making them path dependent and highly sensitive to the critical historical moments of institutional formation. According to the theory, institutional frameworks with radically different formative histories might never converge, even if one is observed to be superior to another.

Stanley Engerman and Kenneth Sokoloff, using this theoretical concept, offer an alternative endogenous explanation for the persistent institutional divergence of Latin America and the United States – one that departs from conventional culturally deterministic explanations.[3] Their main insight is that the institutional divergence was associated with key

---

[2] Douglass C. North, *Institutions, Institutional Change and Economic Performance* (Cambridge, 1990), 3–4, 7. The main contributions to the second approach are surveyed in Masahiko Aoki, *Toward a Comparative Institutional Analysis* (Cambridge, MA, 2001).

[3] Stanley L. Engerman and Kenneth L. Sokoloff, "Factor Endowments, Institutions, and Differential Paths of Growth Among New World Economies: A View from Economic Historians of the United States," in Stephen Haber, ed., *How Latin America Fell Behind* (Stanford, CA, 1997), 260–304.

economic decisions, at the time of the original European occupation of a region, which produced persistent regional differences in the use of coercive labor institutions. This idea emerged from an observation in comparative Atlantic history: though New World colonies were founded and governed by people of European origin, until into the nineteenth century, the Amerindian and African inhabitants were more populous. Engerman and Sokoloff propose that geographical variation in the use of coercive labor institutions explains the observed differences in the long-run paths of institutional development. The colonies that were most successful at extracting labor with coercive institutions, though initially the most prosperous, were, after centuries of institutional development, the least prosperous. Meanwhile, the growth trajectories of colonies that were least successful with coercive labor institutions – in British North America – diverged upward in the long run.

The key social force, in their analysis, is the inequality of wealth that coercive labor institutions produced. In coercive colonies where initial wealth disparities were large, a small wealthy elite wielded disproportionate control of political decisions. They colluded politically to write laws, occupy government offices, use the coercive powers of the state to their own benefit, and exclude access by the lower classes and ethnic minorities to resources and wealth. Even after the most brutal coercive practices were abolished, elites in control of governments continued to erect institutional barriers to social mobility and wealth accumulation. By contrast, in colonies where economic opportunity and access to wealth were more evenly distributed, the early colonizing authorities, in the interests of revenue collection, established rule of law, made property in land and credit widely accessible, and created formal institutions that enforced contracts with fewer class-related barriers. Markets developed more autonomously and stimulated entrepreneurial activity in a wider range of social classes, who invested in physical, human, and social capital. Where laborers were free to pursue independent opportunities and had access to land, the dispersion of wealth was greater, and political and economic rights were extended more broadly. Freedoms gave common people economic and social mobility and amplified the rates of participation and the network density of local markets.

The conditions that determined the initial use of institutions of coercion in the Engerman-Sokoloff model were factor endowments at the time of colonization, which determined locally optimal crop or mining specializations, labor demands and supplies, and the institutions to exploit them. Although this component of the model has been criticized as oversimplified, a comprehensive explanation of the origins of the initial institutional conditions would not overturn the model's principal implication: it explains how the basic institutional frameworks in divergent New World colonial settings could persist indefinitely without assuming they were fixed exogenously. Although the institutions have not remained static, their distributional outcomes emerged from different formative conditions and were self-reinforcing through endogenous decision making in path-dependent political and legal institutions.

The main strength of their analysis is its effective challenge to old, inconsistent habits of thinking of the Latin American institutional framework as exogenous and fixed by rigid cultural bedrock. For example, it offers an alternative, less culturally deterministic way of understanding the colonial legacy in Latin America, including some of the most prominent ideas of social embeddedness, such as Claudio Véliz's proposition that Spanish America has been constrained economically by a centralist bureaucratic tradition, or Morse's notion that it mysteriously remain shackled to preindustrial Hapsburg institutions.[4] But although offering an alternative explanation of long-run institutional rigidities, the self-reinforcement model does not capture the complexity of institutional evolution in Latin America. For example, it does not account well for the diversity of possible political outcomes (multiple equilibria) or the inherent political instability that we observe in the national histories. Though it gives a convincing explanation of persistent wealth disparities, its predictions of political outcomes are too deterministic. It oversimplifies the political bargain among the elite, overstates the elite's political cohesiveness, and overlooks factors that caused bitter political divisions and revolutionary political changes. Though long-run institutional changes have characteristically followed slow, incremental paths, they have also, at critical moments, taken surprising turns with unexpected consequences. This point stands out in the problems of national reconstruction at independence.

INDEPENDENCE

Independence was a critical moment that opened up the future path of institutional change to many possibilities. When Latin American revolutionaries

---

[4] Claudio Véliz, *The Centralist Tradition in Latin America* (Princeton, NJ, 1980); Robert M. Morse, "Heritage."

seized power, there was a real opportunity for national unification and governments based on liberal institutions, to which some leaders aspired; but it did not materialize. As John Coatsworth writes, the opportunity for modernization was "squandered."[5] While trying to build the fundamental institutions of government, liberals and conservatives collided into civil war and led their countries into persistent political instability. The consequence was a devastating economic collapse, which showed no recovery before the reemergence of liberal reforms after mid-century.

The opportunity that independence offered for embarking upon a different growth trajectory reflects a larger principle – crisis often provides a window of opportunity for altering the path of institutional change. Yet discontinuous or revolutionary change does entail risk. The path of institutional change in Latin America at independence could have taken many directions. To understand the process of institutional change, one need ask: What directions, other than the observed one, were reasonably plausible? How feasible was a smooth transition to liberal government, and what shapes could it have taken? The elite leadership reflected both competing political objectives and fundamental uncertainty about the best strategies for achieving them. One strategy called for cooperation, as in the self-reinforcement model of political collusion. Another called for the dismantling and replacement of the costly mercantilist institutions of the old regime. Those hurt by imperial policies collided with those who feared the social consequences of a radical deviation from known institutions. Political demands for a liberal–conservative compromise did not materialize because grounds for it were not found or were considered too costly. Political bargaining to supply formal institutional changes was obstructed by the break with former political institutions. Independence, which transferred the seat of political authority to the colonies, coincided with the collapse of the state, in effect leaving Latin American elites without functioning institutions for making collective decisions. The first task of recovery was to reestablish formal political institutions to give orderly governance to collective decisions – a necessary condition for an orderly political answer to demands for economic reforms. But the implementation and enforcement of reforms of economic policy depended on institutions higher up in the legal and political hierarchy. Functioning constitutional, statutory, and

---

[5] John H. Coatsworth, "Notes on the Comparative Economic History of Latin America and the United States," in Walter L. Bernecker and Hans Werner Tobler, eds., *Development and Underdevelopment in America: Contrasts of Economic Growth in North and Latin America in Historical Perspective* (New York, 1993).

procedural laws, and the organizational capacity to enforce them, were a necessary underpinning to effective policy reforms.

We are only beginning to understand the effects of postrevolutionary political disorder on long-run economic growth. Most conventional interpretations acknowledge that it introduced delays, but otherwise ignore it. Latin America's chronic economic disappointments are explained, instead, by late entry into the world system or by the colonial legacy. But one cannot properly assess alleged causes of underperformance without clearly specifying feasible counterfactual alternatives that might have given superior performance, and it is improper to gauge actual outcomes against unrealistic alternatives. To comprehend the economic consequences of the institutional choices that led to political breakdown after independence, we need to identify, describe, and examine how an alternative superior set of institutions might have been implemented. The next sections look into this question, beginning with the institutional foundations that created the platform for supplying other institutional changes.

CONSTITUTIONAL FOUNDATIONS

Why did elites have so much trouble coming to an agreement over fundamental political institutions? Disagreement began with the question of how to frame the new constitutions. Jeremy Adelman, in *Republic of Capital*, gives an illuminating account of how this controversy played out in the birth of the Argentine nation.[6] Yet, generally, scholarly treatment of the historical significance of constitutions shows an inconsistency. Many dismiss poorly enforced constitutions as meaningless and do not factor in the consequences of constitutional ineffectiveness on the implementation and enforcement of economic policy. Studies that focus on policy-level institutional changes often inconsistently assume an underlying stable and functional constitutional order.

Despite the inconsistencies, the conceptual link between political institutions and economic performance is straightforward. The appropriability of private returns to investment was the main channel through which constitutions and other political institutions affected private economic activity. Individual decisions about how to hold and use assets were sensitive to the

---

[6] Jeremy Adelman, *Republic of Capital. Buenos Aires and the Legal Transformation of the Atlantic World* (Stanford, CA, 1999).

existence of stable, predictable rules governing property rights, enforcement of contracts, and other regulations. One can distinguish three different ways that property-rights infringements discouraged investment. First, weak governments sometimes failed to defend property rights from intrusion or seizures by other private individuals. To compensate, investors spent larger sums on private security. Second, property holders had to confront the "dilemma of the sovereign." Governments sometimes confiscated private wealth or selectively enforced the property rights of political supporters or allies but not those of opponents. Third, investors had to consider the political risks of both current and future governments. Even if current property rights were enforced, investors had to factor in the political risks of future governments. Without effective long-term constraints, such as constitutional limits, a successor government could adversely change the rules and alter the returns to an investment. Constitutions were the most fundamental layer of institutions provided to enforce property rights and private contracts because they determined the rules for shaping the institutions of enforcement in the hierarchy below them. However, if constitutional rules were too variable or unpredictable, those uncertainties were also transmitted to the lower-order institutions.

How stable have constitutional rules been in Latin American history? Table 5.1, which displays the constitutions written between 1810 and 2000, gives a striking image of the high frequency with which constitutional rules have been altered and reflects a record of uncertainty about constitutional rules and their expected longevity. Before reading too much into the table, caution is warranted that the political charters called "constitutions" were heterogeneous in character and intent. How or whether they were ratified varied, and many were contested as invalid by political opponents. Others were honored more in breach than in fact. But even ignoring the question of enforcement, historians trying to count them must make judgments about questionable cases; consequently, lists have varied depending on how these judgments were made. Table 5.1 follows a predetermined set of guidelines. It lists the dates of promulgation of newly framed constitutions, provisional or incomplete charters that aimed to define bases of fundamental law or governmental structure, and restorations of previous constitutions. It does not include formal suspensions of constitutions. Though some dictatorial regimes formally suspended the incumbent constitution, counting formal suspensions would not capture most constitutional breaches. It was more common for a dictatorial regime to ratify or decree its own constitution, engage in selective violation of an existing constitution, or make liberal use of constitutional emergency powers, known as "states of siege." The list in

Table 5.1 also understates the extent to which constitutional rules changed by ignoring constitutional amendments and reforms, which, though relevant, would be more difficult to enumerate.

Granted these qualifications, two observations stand out. First, even ignoring formal and de facto suspensions, the average duration of constitutional documents was about fifteen years. Omitting the 1810–29 period of revolution and postrevolutionary transition to eliminate the bias of postrevolutionary provisional constitutions, the average duration was still only twenty years. Yet, there was considerable variation in the degree of instability. Between 1830 and 2000, the country with the longest average duration was Chile, at seventy-four years, and the country with the shortest average duration was the Dominican Republic, at six years.

THE COMMITMENT PROBLEM

Liberal constitutional framers warned that their nations were at a crossroads and that history offered two possible outcomes. They could follow the path of the United States into a peaceful, prosperous transition to independent rule, or they could follow the road of France, of failed constitutionalism and political disorder. Peaceful and orderly transition depended on the cooperation of rival political factions. They, like scholars after them, adopted a contractarian interpretation – the constitution was a multilateral pact or contract, and the framers' central problem was to negotiate a set of rules that political contenders could universally accept. This was the function of the constitutional congresses.

Recent analyses question the completeness of the contractarian interpretation, noting that third-party enforcement could not ensure that the new constitutions would be honored. Constitutional stability depended on whether the ruling party or faction could credibly commit to honor the constitution. This required that the ruling faction and its rivals each had to perceive compliance as in their self-interest. But why would any rival strongman have surrendered his private militia and submitted to constitutional limits if he perceived them as against his interests? Why would a faction that ruled by force submit to a constitutional requirement that it step down to allow an elected rival assume power? Rivals seeking to control the government had incentives to comply with a constitution only if they expected to benefit in the long run from the orderly political process it would create. In turn, those expected long-run benefits depended on whether they believed future ruling factions would also willingly accept the same limits. Few countries had histories that offered any expectation that the constitution would not be violated, overturned, or opportunistically altered within a few

Table 5.1. *Constitutions of Latin America*

	Number of new constitutions				Years of most durable const.	Dates of promulgation of constitutions
	All	1810–1829	1830–1916	1917–2000		
Cuba	8		3	5	32	1897, 1898, 1902, 1934, 1940, 1952, 1959, 1976
Brazil	8	1	1	6	67	**1824**, 1891, 1934, 1937, 1946, **1967**, 1969, 1988
Uruguay	6	0	1	5	88	**1830**, 1918, 1934, 1942, 1952, 1967
Chile	9	6	1	2	92	*1812*, *1814*, *1818*, *1822*, *1823*, *1828*, **1833, 1925**, 1980
Argentina	9	6	1	2	96	*1815*, *1816*, *1817*, *1819*, *1825*, *1826*, **1853**, 1949, 1955*
Mexico	9	3	5	1	83	1812, *1814*, 1824, *1835*, 1836, 1843, 1847, **1857, 1917**
Paraguay	6	1	2	3	70	1813, 1844, **1870**, 1940, 1967, 1992
Colombia	14	4	9	1	105	1811, *1819*†, *1821*†, 1828, 1830, 1831, 1832, 1843, 1853, 1858, *1861*, *1863*, **1886**, 1991
Costa Rica	12	2	8	2	61	*1821*, *1824*†, 1841, 1844, 1847, 1848, 1859, 1869, 1871, **1882**, **1943**, 1949
Bolivia	15	1	9	6	60	1826, 1831, 1834, 1839, 1843, 1851, *1861*, 1868, 1871, **1878**, **1938**, 1945, 1947, 1967, 1995
El Salvador	15	1	8	6	53	*1824*†, 1841, 1864, 1871, 1872, 1880, 1883, 1885, **1886**, **1939**, 1945*, 1950, 1962, 1982, 1983
Peru	17	3	10	4	46	1823, 1826, 1828, 1834, 1837, 1839, *1855*, 1856, 1860, 1867, 1868*, *1879*, 1881*, 1920, 1933, 1979, 1993
Guatemala	9	1	3	5	42	*1824*†, *1839*, 1851, 1879, 1921, 1945, **1956**, 1965, 1985

Country						Constitution dates
Venezuela	26	3	12	11	38	1811, *1819†*, 1821†, 1830, 1857, 1858, 1864, *1874*, 1881, 1891, 1893, 1901, 1904, 1909, *1914*, 1922, 1925, 1928, 1929, 1931, 1936, 1946, 1947, 1953, 1961, 1999
Nicaragua	12	1	6	5	35	1824*, 1838, **1854**, 1858, 1893, **1905**, 1911, **1939**, 1948, 1950, 1974, 1987
Dominican Republic	26		17	9	28	1844, **1854**, 1858, 1866, 1868, 1872, 1874, 1875, 1877, 1878, 1879, 1880, 1881, 1887, 1896, 1907, 1908, 1924, 1927, 1934, 1942, 1947, 1961, 1963, 1966, 1994
Ecuador	21	2	12	7	23	1812, 1821†, 1830, 1835, 1843, 1845, 1851, 1852, 1861, 1869, **1878**, 1884, **1897**, 1906, 1929, 1945, 1946, **1967**, 1978, 1979, 1998
Honduras	17	1	10	6	21	1824†, 1839, 1848, 1865, 1873, 1874, 1880, 1894, 1904, 1906, 1908*, 1921, 1924, 1936, **1957**, 1965, 1982
Average	13.3	2.0	6.6	4.7	57.8	
Std Deviation	6.2	1.8	4.7	2.7	26.7	

Notes: Scholarly lists of Latin American constitutions, though similar, generally do not agree in all details. The table lists promulgation dates of constitutions, including federations and restorations of former constitutions. Amendments to and reforms of an existing constitution are not included. Dictatorial pronouncements of new constitutional documents are included, but acts of suspension without replacement of the existing constitution are excluded.

Legend: Shaded areas indicate constitutions that lasted no more than 10 years. Bold fonts indicate constitutions that lasted 50 years or more. Italics indicate constitutions designated as provisional.

* indicates a restoration of a previous constitution.

† indicates a constitution of a subsequently unsuccessful confederation.

Sources: See bibliographical essay.

years of its ratification. The credibility of commitment thus broke down with distrust or doubts about its survivability.

The chronic difficulties of establishing effective constitutional constraints in Latin America thus reflect the general problem of creating a credible commitment to limited government. Independence was a critical time because the collective decisions made then determined whether subsequent governments encountered the commitment problem from a prior condition of political instability or of constitutional order. The latter could be maintained by the cooperation of rival political factions, but the former would have to alter the historically determined distrust in the self-enforcement of formal political rules. In a recent study, Douglass North, William Summerhill, and Barry Weingast argue that the problem of establishing constitutional limits in Latin America was rooted in the institutional discontinuities the newly created nations faced trying to reestablish formal political institutions. Comparison with the former British North American colonies brings the point into greater relief. Unlike the latter, where the former colonies drafted their first constitutions out of experience with representative colonial assemblies, Latin America had more limited experience with representative government (especially the Spanish colonies), and it was at too narrow a scope to serve as an effective precedent for smooth transition to representative national governments. Furthermore, whereas the states that emerged from British colonial America reduced the negotiation costs of framing commitments to the federal constitution by deferring most constitutional powers to the states, in Latin America, no comparable formula was available to reduce the costs of negotiating a national constitution that was acceptable to both liberal and conservative factions.[7]

The ethnic and socioeconomic heterogeneity of Latin American populations seems to have been a critical factor. North, Summerhill, and Weingast argue that the credible commitments to the state and federal constitutions of the United States were underpinned by an ideology of constitutional inviolability – a shared popular belief that a serious constitutional transgression must be and would be met with popular resistance, if necessary. If these were the underpinnings of limited government in the early United States, then relative wealth disparities may be key to explain the difference between the United States and Latin American experiences. Greater wealth

---

[7] Douglass C. North, William Summerhill, and Barry R. Weingast, "Order, Disorder and Economic Change: Latin American versus North America," in Bruce Bueno de Mesquita and Hilton L. Root, eds., *Governing for Prosperity* (New Haven, CT, 2000), 59–84.

disparities in Latin America created sharp class distinctions, which caused ideologies about constitutional inviolability to diverge. Uprisings against perceived transgressions of government occurred, but elite and popular, and liberal and conservative, views differed over what constituted a serious transgression or which transgressions merited resistance. Elites perceived a trade-off between two political risks – threats to property by government predation or by social disturbance and popular invasions. A popular uprising could result in a demand for redistribution rather than a defense of the constitutional protections of property or political rights.

Historians have shown that leading spokespersons in the Latin American constitutional assemblies were aware of these trade-offs but differed about which threat weighed heaviest. Many conservatives and liberals feared popular uprisings more than tyranny and called for order and stability more than political freedoms.[8] In the first series of constitutional assemblies, distrust of popular representation prevailed over cries for political openness and resulted in suffrage rights that severely restricted popular political participation. Although the evidence collected to date is sketchy, it shows that around the middle of the nineteenth century, suffrage restrictions limited voting rights to about 2 percent or less of the male population, compared with about 24 percent in the United States (or 28% of white males). By 1880, qualified voters in Latin American countries represented no more than 4 to 6 percent of the male population, compared with 37 percent (or 43% of white males) in the United States.[9] Even so, the low rates of suffrage actually overstate the effective political openness because electoral fraud was widespread.

Early constitutional formulas showed concerns for civil protections against tyranny but, over time, those concerns were given less weight and constitutions were revised to strengthen presidents and reduce constitutional checks to their power. An important device, included in almost all constitutions, was the state of siege, which extended to presidents' extraordinary powers to suspend constitutional rights in the event of a social disturbance or similar threat. These powers contributed to a lack of moderation in political competition. States of siege were used liberally to suppress political opposition, rig electoral outcomes, and justify opportunistic violations

---

[8] See especially Jeremy Adelman, *Republic of Capital*; Charles A. Hale, *Mexican Liberalism in the Age of Mora, 1821–1853* (New Haven, CT, 1968); and Tortcuato S. Di Tella, *National Popular Politics in Early Independent Mexico, 1820–1847* (Albuquerque, NM, 1996).

[9] Stanley L. Engerman and Kenneth L. Sokoloff, "The Evolution of Suffrage Institutions in the New World" (National Bureau of Economic Research Working Paper 8512, October 2001).

of constitutional rights. Therefore, they raised the stakes of losing power or the costs of submitting to electoral defeat. In repeated instances, they gave a constitutional mechanism for the seizure of dictatorial powers.

Commitment problems explain persistent constitutional cycling. If a party entering into power expected future ruling parties to suspend or revise the constitution, it had incentives to reject the incumbent constitution and promulgate a new one designed to benefit its constituency. Nonincumbent political parties expected to do the same if they took office. Historical patterns of constitutional revision reflected this incentive. In Venezuela – where its twenty-six constitutions make it one of the most prolific – entering political regimes promulgated new constitutions as manifestos of political agendas. Some historians suggest that an entering Venezuelan government that failed to promulgate its own constitution risked losing its political credibility. Consistent with this, though most constitutions included procedures for their replacement, most new constitutions did not comply with the incumbent constitution's rules. Unrepresentative or corrupt ratification procedures are often offered as a proximate cause to explain why one constitution was replaced with another. The implication of the commitment problem is that the integrity of the ratification test was endogenous to the expected longevity of the constitution. When countries had histories of constitutional cycling, a current government was less likely to perceive any benefit from keeping the incumbent constitution sufficient to offset the advantages of installing its preferred constitutional rules. Cycling was self-reinforcing.

What were the economic consequences? Oscillating constitutional rules increased perceived political risks. Governments that could change rules midstream could and did alter rules for financing or possessing private claims to income streams opportunistically to reward supporters and punish opponents. This does not imply that one should see a drop in investment in the event of a military takeover or revolution. Investors anticipated the probabilities of such events and incorporated them into their long-term risk calculations. It has been shown, for example, that Mexican investment behavior did not change much before and after the Mexican Revolution, which can be taken as evidence that investment rates in Mexico were dampened by perceptions of political risk, anticipating property-rights insecurity, well before the actual threats materialized.[10]

---

[10] Stephen Haber, Noel Maurer, and Armando Razo, "When the Law Does Not Matter: The Rise and Decline of the Mexican Oil Industry," *Journal of Economic History* 63, 1 (2003): 1–32.

THE ALTERNATIVE OF VERTICAL COMMITMENTS

Conventional histories of Latin America in the nineteenth century describe a period of political disorder after independence, followed eventually by national political consolidation, in most cases, decades later. By contrast, Table 5.1 suggests various patterns and degrees of political consolidation. One interesting pattern is observed by grouping constitutions by length of duration. Table 5.1 highlights three groups: those that endured fifty years or more (identified with bold font), those that endured ten years or less (identified by shaded areas), and an intermediate group. Most countries had significant periods of constitutional cycling, with few lasting more than ten years. Periods of one or more consecutive constitutions, each enduring at least fifty years, might be interpreted as a significant degree of constitutional stability. Ten out of eighteen countries experienced such stability, at least for one period of time. This suggests that most Latin American countries achieved some political cooperation at least temporarily, but the timing and duration of those periods varied considerably. We also observe a pattern in which half the countries that achieved some stability did so during the period of export-led growth and saw it end with the collapse of export-led growth around 1930. The diversity-cum-regularity points to the need for better theory about political institutions that fall into the intermediate space between political disorder and limited government. What alternative models, besides self-enforcing formal constitutions, were available to governments seeking to internalize political contests within a set of stable rules?

Mexico is one country for which the study of institutional alternatives has advanced significantly. Research shows that innovative political leaders used alternative configurations of credible commitments to formulate stable political rules. The Mexican Constitution of 1857, which has been called one of the most liberal constitutions of Latin America, initially faced violent opposition from conservatives. The stability that was achieved after the overthrow of the French emperor, Maximilian, depended on frequent states of siege during the presidency of Benito Juárez. The political stability tenuously achieved under Juárez was strengthened by political innovations after the rise to power of Porfirio Díaz (1876–1911), which finally brought an end to the political cycling, disorder, and unconstitutionality that had plagued Mexico during its first half-century of independence. After the long political struggle, the liberals were fully victorious, but political stability was not founded on the credible commitments of limited government.

Díaz and a narrow political support base had to reform Mexico's political institutions to solve the problem of credible commitments if the regime was to survive. The chronic inability of the government to finance itself, build a tax base, exert political control over national territorial claims, and enforce its decrees had to be resolved. Stephen Haber, Armando Razo, and Noel Maurer show how the Díaz government adopted a "cronyist" strategy to the commitment problem. Central to the strategy was the regime's vertical relational commitments to a select group of "cronies" – nascent banking and industrialist interests with whom it made reciprocal relational commitments. Through concessions of corporate charters, government contracts, and informal arrangements, extending exclusive rights and regulatory exemptions, the government handed out monopoly rights to streams of rents in exchange for a reciprocal obligation to finance the state, generally through soft lines of credit. The exchange of government and private services was credible to both parties because both parties were made better off. This stimulated private investment and gave the government a reliable source of credit, which strengthened the government's enforcement of select property rights and contributed to the development of modern transportation and industrial establishments.[11]

Despite extreme industrial concentration, this strategy notably achieved high rates of industrialization and average growth in incomes per capita exceeding 2 percent per year, in contrast to little or no growth in previous decades. This success rested on the stimulus provided to insiders, who perceived lower political risk, higher expected rates of return, and relative durability of their entitlements. The contemporaneous rise of trading opportunities in the United States complemented the prosperity; but realizing those trading opportunities depended on the government's provision of public goods – especially railroad concessions – and perceptions of creditworthiness among foreign lenders, which the Díaz regime cultivated. But the economic achievements of cronyism were strictly limited and planted the seeds of the regime's destruction. Whereas it stimulated higher rates of investment, a growing economy, and growing private returns to entrepreneurship, the government could not meet mounting private demands for outsiders to be integrated into the system because they competed with, and would have constituted a breach of, previously assigned exclusive entitlements to insiders. Elites on the outside, blocked from mobilizing economically,

---

[11] Stephen Haber, Armando Razo, and Noel Maurer, *The Politics of Property Rights: Political Instability, Credible Commitments, and Economic Growth in Mexico, 1876–1929* (Cambridge, 2003).

mobilized politically. Disaffected, they leveraged the growing skewness in the distribution of wealth to build a revolutionary coalition with labor and peasants that brought the collapse of the regime in 1910–11.

Despite the political discontinuity of revolution, the institutional formula of the *Pax Porfiriana* was path dependent – the logic of vertical commitment between the state and key private sectors survived the revolution. Chronologically, it was interrupted by an interim of political chaos, but as the revolutionary government reconsolidated, Haber, Razo, and Mauer show that its stability was based on a restoration of vertical relational commitments with key private interests. Through the years of political turmoil, successive presidents – Carranza, Obregón, and Calles – each took steps toward rebuilding the network of private interests that had financed the Porfirian regime. The new constitutional order combined many of the same private interests, but it also strategically incorporated some formerly excluded constituencies, especially organized labor and the peasantry. These two groups had organized during the Revolution, and they could not be completely repressed after Díaz was defeated. Popularization of the new order was necessary to restore political stability. Labor, which had begun to organize effectively in 1910, had obtained collective contracts by 1912 and its first pro-labor legislation in 1915. It then obtained one of the most revolutionary innovations of the Constitution of 1917. Article 123 constituted an extensive list of guarantees to organized labor, many of which were inscriptions into fundamental law of legislative achievements won since 1912.

These concessions achieved their goal of pacifying labor and promoting the recovery and growth of the Mexican industrial sector. However, like the arrangements that preceded them, the economic benefits were bounded. Concessions were implemented formally by creating corporate entities that served as semipublic governance bodies, comprising representatives from industry, organized labor, and mediators from the government. The institutions that evolved combined modern regulatory forms with bureaucratic formulas reminiscent of Spanish centralism. First, the state brought labor and owners together to supervise the collective bargaining of labor contracts, which resulted in the institutionalization of annual industrywide conventions to write uniform contracts. Second, it created joint commissions to adjudicate disputes, effectively seizing the authority to mediate negotiations and disputes between factory owners and organized labor. State-coordinated labor boards were then set up to decide on labor contracts that were standardized across industries annually.

These boards, at municipal and state levels, were corporatist entities, composed of representatives of both interest groups and a government mediator and vested with powers to approve internal factory rules and settle disputes.

The centralization of political power, especially to control the banking system, subordinate the labor movement, and later, to contain agrarian movements, was key to the success of both the Porfirian and Revolutionary regimes. Consistent with Véliz, the vertical formula for building credible commitments created a centralist configuration of power. Its adhesives included a system of formal and informal agreements that aimed first to strengthen the state to achieve political stability. Political contests were internalized and the recourse to violence suppressed by handing out entitlements to streams of monopoly rents to concentrated economic and political interests, with dampening effects on long-run economic performance.

Looking again at Table 5.1, we know that the historical narratives of other countries that achieved some degree of constitutional stability differed considerably from Mexico's. For example, the creation of the Argentine Republic, under the Constitution of 1853, established several decades of political stability, but not without regular electoral fraud and states of siege that maintained conservative elite control of the government until 1912. Scholars argue that Argentina had entered a phase of transition to limited constitutional government that was interrupted by a military takeover in 1930. As another case, Chile's Constitution of 1833 met with compliance for nearly all of the ninety-two years it was in effect. Nonetheless, its formal rules limited political competition and preserved oligarchic control. If relatively respected and admired, it was also one of the most aristocratic of Latin American constitutions. The Central American and Andean countries that achieved some constitutional stability did so under widely different social conditions. Apart from the earlier stability depicted for Chile, Uruguay, Argentina, and Mexico, the timing shown in Table 5.1 suggests the significance of the late nineteenth-century export-led growth as a factor in the rise of political cooperation. Similarly, its collapse in 1930 is correlated with a subsequent increase in instability.

INCOMPATIBILITY OF FOREIGN CONSTITUTIONS

An alternative explanation of instability holds that Latin American constitutions were unstable because they were too closely patterned after the

U.S. constitution, and thus incompatible with local political needs. If Latin American constitutional framers tried to lift the U.S. Constitution out of its context and place it in their own, it could not be expected to perform with the same effects. Its enforceability depended on social or cultural factors embedded in country-specific informal institutions. But, however valid theoretically, the argument is not supported with evidence. Constitutional rules may not have been socially optimal, but they were also not copies of the U.S. or other foreign constitutions. Moreover, to the extent that they borrowed articles from them, frequent revisions made Latin American constitutions more Latin American. Their framers studied all the major constitutions at their disposal and often preferred European models, except in a few articles. In the first few years, the Spanish Constitution of 1812 and the French Constitution of 1814 were influential. Subsequent European and Latin American influences included the Bolivarian, Argentine, and Chilean constitutions, as well as the Weimar Constitution of 1919. Furthermore, though constitutional framers studied the existing models, they did so with a critical eye and modified articles to suit the special needs of their countries as they saw them.

Their choices often revealed preferences for designs that preserved cultural, ideological, or institutional continuity. Notably, most set up unitary governments, often with governance structures resembling Spanish or French administrative designs. Though most early states experimented with federalist schemes, federations fragmented, and fragmented states set up unitary (centralist) governments. The few nations that eventually adopted federalist institutions – Argentina, Brazil, Mexico, and Venezuela – each adopted different federalist designs, but all were more centralist than the U.S. model. The growth-enhancing consequences of sound fiscal federalism or "market-preserving federalism," thought to have unintended positive economic consequences in the U.S. case, were generally not reproduced by the Latin American federalist states.

Finally, the choice of the presidential over the parliamentary form of government, which all Latin American countries adopted, seems to have been adopted from the U.S. model. However, it can be argued that the presidential model with strong executive powers would have been the preferred one anyway. Even in the first constitutions, presidential powers were assigned differently than in the United States. Presidents had more powers to legislate by decree, greater unilateral powers to declare emergencies or suspend constitutional rights, and fewer checks caused by the separation of powers. As for federalist governments, presidents were usually granted powers to intervene in states' affairs and even to replace governors with appointees when "necessary." This amounted to presidential vetoes over state autonomy. If the concept of the president in Latin America was initially adapted from the U.S. model, it was not an imitation, and thereafter it followed a separate evolutionary path.

LEGAL AND JUDICIAL REFORMS

In the 1820s, political demands for replacement of the cumbersome bodies of colonial laws with modern criminal, civil, commercial, and other specialized legal codes surfaced immediately. One pressing area was the commercial code. The body of commercial law in force in the Spanish colonies at independence was the *Ordenanzas de Bilbao*, originally written for that port city in northern Spain. The *Ordenanzas* had not been revised since 1737 and were known to be obsolete in a commercial world of increasing transactional complexity. Reforms of the civil codes, to modernize laws on property, contracting, debt, and other personal obligations, were also intensely in demand. The body of private contract law was encumbered by paternalistic impediments to individual contracting rights that originated in medieval law. It included such doctrines as lesion, just price, restrictions on resale of purchased goods, and paternalistic vendor obligations to buyers. The liberal agenda called for modern doctrines of freedom of contract (restricted only in special circumstances), the doctrine of individual will, and caveat emptor, which simplified rule of law in impersonalized exchange and facilitated market integration.

Despite demands for reform, the first republican governments uniformly opted to retain Spanish colonial law among their first legislative acts. This was necessary to avoid anarchy, pending new legislation to enact legal reforms. At independence, the republics had no substitute body of law ready for adoption, and it would take time to develop one. In the meantime, in most cases, as the first republican governments collapsed, efforts to rebuild the institutions of the state consumed attention and new codifications were generally delayed until after mid-century. Table 5.2 shows the dates of promulgation of civil, commercial, and mining codes for selected countries.

In the face of rising demand, the supply of institutional changes confronted several kinds of constraints. First, the provision of government

Table 5.2. *Dates of first reformed civil, commercial, and mining codes*

Country	Civil	Commercial	Mining
Argentina	1871	1862	1885
Chile	1855	1865	1874
Colombia	1858–1860	1858–1869	1867, 1873*
Venezuela	1862	1862	1854
Peru	1836*, 1852	1853*, 1902	1900
Bolivia	1831	1834*	1838*, 1852
Mexico	1871	1854*, 1884	1884
Brazil	1916	1850	1891*
Uruguay	1869	1865	1884

Notes: Codification in Colombia began in the provinces. The most significant codes were written during the range of dates shown. The first mining codes were in Antioquia and Cauca. Peru's first civil code was promulgated under the Bolivian autocratic rule of Andrés Santa Cruz. It was revoked in 1839, when the Spanish colonial code was reinstated. Resolution to write a new commercial code emerged in 1834, but it was not adopted. Bolivia's first commercial and mining codes promulgated in 1834 under Santa Cruz, but the mining code was found inadequate and suspended in 1836, and the Spanish *Ordenanzas de Nueva España* were reinstated in 1839. The commercial code fell into disuse and the *Ordenanzas de Bilbao* were reinstated in 1843. In Mexico, a new code (*Código de Lares*) was promulgated in 1854 under Santa Anna, but it was revoked in 1855, after he lost power. The Brazilian Constitution of 1891 granted subsoil rights to the surface owner. *Sources:* See bibliographical essay.

services, including the proposed legal reforms, required investments of real resources. Among the requisite resources, the specialized human capital needed was especially scarce. Legal scholars or jurists with the expertise to systemize legal codes were few in postrevolutionary Latin America. Bourbon policy in prerevolutionary colonial Spain had excluded most creoles from high office, and many loyalists with training and experience had returned to Spain. Many of the best legal minds were diverted into framing constitutional law or into political or military occupations. Meanwhile, jurists with formal training in the application of the law were in short supply. It was not uncommon for clergy, with training only in ecclesiastical law, or prominent persons with no legal training to fill judges' posts. One 1839 observer noted that in one state in Mexico, only two judges were trained as lawyers; the rest were clergy.[12]

Second, the formal political institutions needed to make these decisions did not exist until constitutions were written to organize and provide a governance structure for the political system. Unstable political systems did not always halt progress on drafting legal reforms, but instability lowered the incentives that politicians, administrators, and jurists had to work on them. The value of the work to the jurist or politician was a function of its expected longevity. Political instability increased the risk that the effort to frame a proposed code might not be rewarded, either from never being promulgated or from nullification by a successor regime. For example, Peru's first civil code was decreed by the Bolivian dictator, Andrés Santa Cruz, in 1836, during the brief confederation with Bolivia, and revoked in 1839. A code of Peruvian authorship was drawn up in 1847, but it was held up in Congress until it was approved in 1852. The process of establishing Venezuela's civil code was even more disrupted. Four commissions were appointed between 1830 and 1857, yet the first civil code was not promulgated until 1862. A decree by an incoming dictator revoked it and reinstated the Spanish colonial law less than four months later. From 1862 to 1930, nine different civil codes were brought into force by alternating regimes, each borrowing from different sources – Spanish, French, and Italian.

Third, Latin American legislative organizations were procedurally under-developed and inefficient at debating and approving legal changes. Without traditions of representative government, political transaction costs of approving legislation were higher. Effective rules or norms governing committee assignments and other legislative procedures would have improved the efficiency and predictability of legislative activity, but we have little specific knowledge of the norms that governed legislative proceedings, on or off the floors, in early Latin American legislatures. Evidence exists, however, of both failed proposals and the use of procedural rules to facilitate their success. As one example, Brazilian jurist Teixeira de Freitas composed a highly respected *Esboço de código civil* in 1859. It was used heavily by other jurists, Dalmacio Vélez Sarsfield and Eduardo Acevedo, when they drafted the Argentine and Uruguayan civil codes of 1871 and 1869. Notwithstanding its success abroad, Teixeira's proposed code ran into repeated political

---

[12] Cyrus Vance and Helen L. Clagett, *Guide to the Law and Legal Literature of Mexico* (Washington, DC, 1945), 105, citing Aurelio Campillo Camarillo, *Apuntamientos de derecho procesal civil* (Jalapa, 1939), xlvii.

roadblocks at home and was never approved. A series of other proposals ran into similar legislative roadblocks. Although efforts began in the 1850s, Brazil had no modern civil code until 1916. On the other hand, Argentina's 1862 commercial code benefited from a procedural rule. To prevent endless haggling, the legislature introduced a closed rule, disallowing debate and amendments on specific articles.

CIVIL V. COMMON LAW

It is sometimes suggested that the Iberian legal tradition's basis in Roman civil law, instead of in the English common law tradition, had significant long-run economic consequences. The main distinction between the two, most scholars agree, is the importance of precedent to common law and codification to civil law. Both traditions aim at a common principle: ex ante predictability in the enforcement of law discourages individuals from violating it. But the two legal systems pursue predictability with different strategies: the common law establishes predictability by the accumulation of legal precedents and interpretive decisions by a politically independent, objective judiciary. The civil law tradition attempts to rationalize bodies of laws as comprehensive systems of consistent, transparent codes. Ideally, legal codes give complete, consistent, and transparent bodies of law that jurists apply without gaps or ambiguities and, in principle, without need for judicial discretion. A formal rule of *stare decisis*, by which rulings are to be guided by prior decisions, does not exist in the civil law tradition. According to civil law principle, any incompleteness in the legal code should be submitted to the legislature for perfection but not subjected to mutation by individual judicial decisions.

The usual economic argument is that the English common law system is more supportive of market-based economic growth because it is more adaptable and more responsive to decentralized private interest. However, empirical evidence for this proposition in cross-country studies is mixed, and economic historians of Latin America have not investigated it sufficiently.[13] Regardless, the civil law tradition in Latin America had an important effect on the rate and timing of postrevolutionary legal reforms. Spanish colonial law was criticized as obscure, complicated, and in conflict

---

[13] As examples, Rafael La Porta et al., "Law and Finance," *Journal of Political Economy* 106 (1998): 1113–55, find statistical support for it; but John Londregan, "Common Law vs. the Civil Code: Precedent and Predictability" (working paper, January 2002) does not.

with national aspirations. Political pressure to reform it had been building since before independence. But the response lag was greater in the civil law tradition than would have occurred under a common law system. In the latter, demands for legal changes were met with incremental, decentralized responses. Where statutory law lagged, judge-made law filled in gaps. By contrast, the civil law tradition resisted incremental adaptation. The proper response under the civil law system was to undertake systematic reforms of the codes, which required comprehensive reviews by legal scholars followed by legislative action.

The elaboration and adaptation of systemic legal doctrine was a grand undertaking, and the costs of achieving it were particularly high in nineteenth-century Latin America because of the lumpy requirement of designing original legal codes and the shortage of legal experts. The authors of new legal codes were individuals or committees of experts, but their approval required legislative action; therefore, authors assembled documents with an eye to political approval. The writing process involved debates at universities and law schools, polling for opinions, and formal reviews and votes in legislatures. Attempts to economize on those costs could result in failure. For example, Bolivia was the first country to enact its own commercial code, in 1834, yet it proved a hastily written, inefficient document. The country reinstated the *Ordenanzas* of Bilbao in 1843. In another instance, the Dominican Republic operated first under Spanish law, then the Haitian code, then, in 1845, adopted the French code by decree, but no official translation into Spanish was made until 1875.

Codification reinforced other centralist tendencies. As an intellectual endeavor, it followed centralist philosophical traditions of legal rationalization exemplified in the Code Napoléon. Codifiers frequently used French, Spanish, Italian, and German codes. The Chilean codes were also used as models where political centralism was strong. Coatsworth and Tortella emphasize the prerogatives of the Crown in the Spanish version of civil law tradition in the Bourbon era. Adelman emphasizes the influence, in the latter European civil law tradition, of the notion of legislative supremacy as the sole source of rational law, against the notion of judicial autonomy and judge-made law in the common law tradition. In the civil law tradition, judges were not given formal autonomy to interpret statutes; their roles as functionaries were to apply the law but, in principle, not to make or interpret it. Although strict denial of any interpretative function to the courts was not feasible in practice, its refusal as a formal principle affected the normal procedures for correcting defective law. Adelman finds, for example, that in the debates over founding the judiciary in Argentina, "for the most part lawmakers self-consciously opted to deplete judges of any discretionary authority."[14] Legislative supremacy was intended to protect the state from judicial tyranny, but in Latin American political systems where presidential powers vis-à-vis the legislature were strengthened, it often seems to have weakened the courts and contributed to the concentration of power in the executive.

A formal principle of judicial independence is often included in constitutions, but legal guarantees of independence and constitutional tenures were not always respected. Adelman proposes that the civil law tradition guided or "informed [constitutional] framers' views of checks and balances on state authority," leading them to deemphasize characteristically North American concerns to curb state powers and strengthen the powers of the state to confront destabilizing political forces.

Finally, not only the legal tradition but also the process of framing legal codes had a centralizing effect. Codification was conducted at the national level, in part, because there were economies of scale in the production of legal codes, and the pool of requisite human capital was concentrated in the capital cities. In addition, unlike in common law systems, codification was intended to destroy prior law, however derived, and replace it with centrally produced law. Even in federalist systems, economies of scale in codification caused provincial governments to adopt codes authored in the capital cities. In some cases, such as Mexico and Colombia, provincial capitals contributed to what eventually became the national codes. Nevertheless, the centralizing tendencies eventually dominated. Mexico first experimented with a national commercial code under Emperor Maximillian by using a provincial model, the *Codigo Larges*, but dropped it (along with the emperor) until the victorious republicans could make one of their own. In Colombia, the national government abandoned federalism in 1886, consolidated its formerly decentralized system of legal and administrative codes, and set up unitary judicial and administrative institutions after 1886.

JUDICIAL REFORMS

The economic consequences of legal reforms depended on enforcement and thus on the organization of the judicial system. Constitutions provided outlines for reorganizing and modernizing judiciaries, but reforms

---

[14] Adelman, *Republic of Capital*, 201–2; Coatsworth and Tortella, "Institutions."

of procedural law were required to complete the task. If the courts were uncertain about procedure, then judicial action to enforce contracts and property rights was more uncertain.

Judicial reforms were delayed along with other legislative reforms but, more important, uncertainties about constitutional durability spilled over to destabilize the organization of judicial systems. In Mexico, for example, the federalist Constitution of 1824 established a two-level system of state and federal courts, resembling the U.S. system. When General Santa Anna seized power, he abolished federalism and, in 1837, centralized the federal judiciary. He reorganized it again in 1843. The successor federalist government restored the federalist structure to the judiciary in 1845, but a subsequent *coup d'état* recentralized the judiciary in 1853. The federalist structure was restored again in 1855 and written into the Constitution of 1857, but it was dismantled again in 1859 because of civil war, then suppressed under Maximilian, and restored gradually after 1863. The first organic law for the federal court system was promulgated in 1880 under Díaz. Similar histories of repeated reorganizations of the judiciaries in Peru and Venezuela give further evidence that political cycling halted judicial reorganizations and made them unstable. The economic consequences are difficult to measure but straightforward to describe. Political instability disrupted efforts to establish regular procedures and professional ethical standards, authoritarian governments controlled appointees to the bench, and coercive threats sometimes swayed their decisions.

Despite liberal demands to abolish the system of specialized tribunals, inherited from the complex colonial system of courts, the most important *fueros* (of the church, military, commercial, and mining guilds) generally remained intact until mid-century. Even after legal reforms, interest groups retained some corporate rights through official trade associations and commissions. Mexico, for example, initially abolished special commercial tribunals in 1823 and 1827 only to restore them later, pressured by special interests. Their jurisdictions were handed to the ordinary courts, but merchants were so critical of the inefficiencies of the ordinary courts that, in the late 1820s and 1830s, several states created chambers of commerce with special mercantile courts. When Santa Anna consolidated the federal courts into a centralist system in 1837, he abolished all other state courts but preserved the state commercial tribunals, and eventually expanded the system of special courts by authorizing the creation of chambers of commerce and mercantile tribunals in all major port cities. Chambers of commerce and their tribunals revived some of the monopoly rights enjoyed by the dominant merchant groups by controlling the number of merchants in their communities. To engage in business as a merchant required a special patent, or license, issued by the local chamber of commerce. The consequences included higher prices, reduced competition, and discouragement of commercial innovations.

Reforms that may be superior in principle were not superior in practice if they introduced greater unpredictability. Disrupted by repeated reorganizations, political interference, and insufficient staffing, ordinary courts were often notoriously unpredictable. Though sometimes motivated by rent-seeking, evidence shows that many demands to continue specialized tribunals came from common people who saw them as more efficient or predictable than the ordinary courts. A study of the military tribunal in Mexico shows that much of the political pressure to preserve the military *fuero* came from widows and children of military officers afraid to be exposed to the arbitrariness of the ordinary court system. Merchants and mining entrepreneurs expressed the same criticisms. The later creation of corporatist bureaucracies, as in mining, merchant, and labor boards, similarly targeted improved predictability in specialized contexts. They did so, however, in ways that increased the vertical integration of public and private sectors and invited more rent-seeking behavior. Although the long-run effect is debated, evidence shows that judicial and other bureaucratic continuity delayed, attenuated, or eased some of the revolutionary impact of the liberal reforms.

PROPERTY RIGHTS AND REFORMS

If political instability and the uncertain duration of constitutional rules spilled over into judicial systems, that unpredictability spilled over again into entrepreneurs' perceptions of the enforcement of property rights. Policy-level reforms encountered two kinds of enforcement problems. First, current enforcement was often uncertain or partial. Second, even if currently enforced, the long-run enforcement of a reform was uncertain if successor governments were unconstrained by constitutional limits. Through the mechanisms of enforcement, uncertainty about the effectiveness of constitutional limits on government was transmitted into more specific institutional reforms. Enforcement problems were encountered in the reforms of land, labor, and capital markets in domestic, import, and export markets. Space does not permit discussion of them all, so I focus on property rights in land, from which extensions to the enforceability of holding or exchanging other kinds of property or assets may be inferred.

At the end of the colonial period, the institutions of land ownership were in disarray. For several reasons, maintaining formal property rights in land, especially in rural areas, had come to involve high transaction costs, including private guards and frequent litigation. The original royal land grants had only vaguely specified property boundaries. Property limits were defined, for example, using potentially ambiguous natural landmarks (e.g., streams, hills), by declaring their adjacency to an existing (also poorly defined) grant, or even as a vague circular perimeter around a geographical point. These methods clearly were rationally chosen at original colonization to minimize the transaction costs of transferring land rights when the low value of the land did not justify the higher transaction costs of precise measurement. But the method was not updated with need. Boundary disputes thus became endemic as further population growth increased the demand for lands.

Spanish American institutions for making claims created overlapping formal claims and introduced ambiguities about rightful possession. First, original land grants were made on the condition that the lands would be occupied and used. The condition was often neglected by grantees; and yet, except in rare cases, the Crown did not revoke land grants for noncompliance. The institution of *composición*, established later, allowed parties to purchase rights to unoccupied lands on the legal principle that they were part of the royal patrimony. When competing claims emerged, conflicting jurisprudence found *composiciones*, original land grants, and historical claims of village communities to be valid. As time passed, most of the original *cédulas* documenting the grants had deteriorated or were lost. Typically, if any documentary evidence for land claims existed, it was ad hoc. There were no central registries; therefore, competing documentary "proofs" were issued by notaries and local officials. Use of sales receipts was common (but whereas they might name the property, they usually did not specify its boundaries). These kinds of evidence were easily forged and, therefore, in principle, unverifiable. In colonial courts, the Crown was the final arbiter, but independence eliminated the royal prerogative and introduced greater uncertainty into the legal standards for settling disputes. By the nineteenth century, endless legal disputes were a normal cost of formal land ownership.

At local levels, claims were often secured by local informal institutions; therefore, informal markets for land existed parallel to formal markets.

Problems with formal claims drove more property in land into informal markets. There were not one but many sets of informal institutions. We know little about them, but we know that they were less integrated than modern land markets, segmented by the social networks in which they existed – in local elite, ethnic, and poor communities. They facilitated exchange, but informal land markets were not perfect substitutes for formal land markets because they were geographically limited and, except within elite social networks, could not serve as security for credit. Therefore, formalization of titles offered substantial private and public-good benefits. More secure titles meant fewer resources would be dissipated in unnecessary court expenses, bribes, and maintaining private guards to police claims. Lower risks of owning property in land would increase its market value and encourage more active rural land and credit markets. Yet despite potential economic benefits, reforms of land laws to improve titling institutions were slow to be approved, did not go the heart of the problem, and were often derailed.

Why were reforms slow to emerge? Governments encountered constraints that limited the credibility and legitimacy of their policies. Legitimacy is a subtle, but essential, concept for understanding the enforcement of policy reforms. A policy may be described as legitimate when compliance was reinforced by a socially accepted norm or shared belief that it should be respected or obeyed. If most people willingly complied, formal rules worked well and required limited exercise of the state's coercive powers; but, if a critical mass refused to comply, formal rules were too costly to enforce. Governments' legitimacy to implement land reforms depended on their ability to obtain self-enforcing compliance of local *hacendados*, squatters, or villagers. The liberal rules adopted to formalize titles often conflicted with rights established in informal institutions. Generally, they were unsuccessful unless land claimants perceived net private gains from formalizing their titles. Historians have often thought that the main source of political demand for formal titles came from wealthy landowners (assuming they had a comparative advantage in legal institutions), yet that is not what the record shows.

There were several related issues. First, formalizing titles required expenses to survey land, set up registry offices, and provide local judicial and police forces to enforce titles. These costs were covered at the owners' expense or indirectly through local payment of taxes, processing fees, or bribes. With low population densities, many lands were used for subsistence, forage, or grazing and did not generate incomes per hectare high enough to justify the private cost of surveying. The legislative initiative, therefore, usually came instead from governments seeking to establish effective property rights over public lands. With private property rights in dispute, governments were unable to sell or lease public lands for revenue because the titles they issued were subject to subsequent legal challenges. An investigation in Mexico under Juárez found that much of the land considered as public land was disputed by private land claimants, yet most disputants had documentation for only a fraction of their claims.

Second, many land claimants expected the existing informal institutions to work better than titles to enforce their property rights. If formal titles were not enforced by the government, there was little reason to have one. There were reasons to doubt the effectiveness of government enforcement of property rights. Even though legal reforms required it, surveying was often dispensed with because of the high cost and dangers of conducting them. The inadequacy of police protection was also a factor. Prior to reform, landowners employed private security forces or relied on local informal institutions to enforce their claims. Without major changes in police protection, most expected to continue to incur private security expenses. For similar reasons, peasants and indigenous communities were reluctant to abandon traditional institutions of enforcement.

Third, title reforms imposed risks of adverse rulings. The uncertainty of courts' rulings was factored into landowners' expectations as risks of losing their land, or a portion of it. Formalization required making one's claims, and one's imperfect documentation, public. Uncertainty about the legal outcomes of disputes depended on the validity of competing claims, the arbitrariness or unpredictability of judicial rulings, and expected biases of the court.

The policies enacted varied significantly with context, so it is useful to focus on an example. In Mexico, the liberal *Ley Lerdo* of 1856 provided for the disentailment and conversion of all corporate (inalienable) lands into fee-simple property, targeting in particular ecclesiastical and village communal lands. For the latter, the law established low-cost procedures by which indigenous peasants could receive title for the lands they tilled. Although the law is generally regarded as a sincere effort to transfer modern property rights to the peasants, outcomes varied considerably. Peasants' private rights to property in village communities were relatively secure, allocated and enforced according to local custom. The security of titles promised by the national government, under Juárez, was less certain. Enforcement depended in part on local authorities within the villages, who often opposed the reform because it undermined their authority. Jurisdiction over land rights passed from village officials to the courts, which had been destabilized by political instability and repeated reorganizations. Peasants correctly attached perceptions of enforcement risk to the liberal land reform. The courts were known to be unpredictable, arbitrary, and swayed by local government and *hacendado* interests.

System effects complicated the impact of land reform laws. Their expected effectiveness depended on their compatibility with other formal and informal rules. Under traditional communal institutions, peasants held various kinds of rights to different parts of each village's communal lands, including exclusive private usufruct rights to till a specified plot and common grazing and forage rights in the marginal areas claimed by the community. Even though the *Ley Lerdo* aimed to preserve some of these rights, it put others at risk. The boundaries of communal claims were not well specified, and claims were often disputed by adjacent village communities or *hacendados*. Moreover, the land reform laws proposed to accommodate peasant property rights only in a narrow doctrinaire way, which, if implemented, threatened to disrupt local economies. The rights offered did not allow a continuation of some customary agrarian technologies. The more complex governance systems, to which peasants were accustomed, functioned in part to diversify agricultural risks. The reform law proposed to modernize land laws without complementing them with alternative institutions for diversifying risk.

A final problem was that, no matter how sincere its policy was, the Juárez government had no means of ensuring that future governments would enforce it. The case can be made by looking at what happened in successive regimes. The Juárez government's inability to implement the reforms on communal lands was characteristic of repeated failed attempts by a number of the Mexican states to implement similar reforms. That pattern changed under the more stable Porfirian regime, both in its objectives and effectiveness. Among the first measures the Díaz regime undertook to build its credibility was the granting of a large number of concessions to railroad companies. As soon as these concessions were made, private seizures of lands (especially village lands) along projected railway routes escalated, usurped by speculators. Occasionally, villages challenged the seizures in the courts. Coatsworth finds that, although in previous periods the courts were perhaps less biased, during this period they usually favored the *hacendado* usurpers.[15] In effect, the reform laws were corrupted by courts bending to political demands and used, not as the Juárez government had intended, but rather to invalidate peasants' claims. The legal act was not reversed, but its intended effect was. The dismantling of communal land rights and the vast expansion of the *latifundios* in Mexico are believed to have occurred largely during this period, in this institutional environment.

An early accomplishment of the Díaz government was the implementation of a general survey of public lands. A study by Robert Holden examines the complex set of political and economic factors that had to be balanced to implement the policy. The Díaz regime contracted with private companies to complete the survey, compensating them with one-third of all public lands they documented and surveyed. This resulted in the survey of approximately one-third of the nation's land, and according to one estimate, land prices rose by 50 percent as a consequence.[16] The survey was itself a remarkable feat. Similar efforts by other Latin American governments were unsuccessful because of landowner opposition. Nevertheless, as a title reform policy, it was not comprehensive. To avoid confrontation with landowners, it did not target private lands, except for those adjacent to or overlapping with public lands. Consequently, most established landowner areas were left unsurveyed.

The continued murkiness of land titles had negative spillover effects onto national economic development. Among the most significant, it impeded not only the supply but also the demand for modern mortgage credit. A modern mortgage market could have improved the efficiency of credit by facilitating regional rural credit-market integration. However, the modern mortgage instrument required perfected titles. Wherever titles remained defective, landowners continued to use and to prefer informal credit markets based on locally specific kinship-based or other social networks. Continued reliance on locally specific informal credit markets limited landowners' access to credit and wealth holders' ability to diversify their portfolios using national assets, possibly encouraging them to use foreign capital markets more frequently to manage risk.

Insight into the problems of clearing up property rights may be obtained by contrasting the U.S. federal government's approach to the same problems. The 930,000 square miles of Mexican land transferred to the United

[15] John H. Coatsworth, "Railroads, Landholding, and Agrarian Protest in the Early Porfiriato," *Hispanic American Historical Review* 54, 1 (1974): 48–71.

[16] Robert Holden, *Mexico and the Survey of Public Lands: The Management of Modernization 1876–1911* (DeKalb, IL, 1994).

States in 1848 as a result of the Mexican–American War embodied the same endemic disarray of property rights in land as elsewhere in Mexico. A potentially explosive political situation was brewing in California during the post-1848 provisional military government. Under the Treaty of Guadalupe-Hidalgo, the U.S. federal government was obligated to honor the property rights of owners of Spanish and Mexican land grants or titles (which would be costly to renege because many owners were by then American citizens). Competing against that obligation were hordes of squatters who had settled in California after the discovery of gold there in 1848. (The news spread about the same time as the transfer took place.) The squatting issue was explosive because many settlers had squatted on land that was claimed under Spanish or Mexican land grants. Following Hispanic tradition, the land grants were made on the condition of occupation and use. If interpreted by the letter, failure to meet that condition made the lands available for squatters to claim under U.S. federal laws of preemption. The United States had a history of accommodating squatters' claims on federal lands, and squatters' shared expectations had led them to act as if that tradition would be honored in California. Landowners opposed squatters' demands, arguing that adjudicating the rights to land grants by the letter would be unjust and inconsistent with preestablished practices, which, under the common law tradition in the United States, should be upheld. It created considerable uncertainty as to how the prior land claims would be validated.

The United States moved quickly to establish firm titles, with boundaries fixed by survey, undisputed and in public registry. U.S. federal authorities had observed in previous phases of territorial expansion that failure to provide strong incentives for claimants to bring their claims forward led to slow resolution of claims and occasional violence. Therefore, in contrast with Mexico, Congress made formal declaration of all land claims mandatory. Claimants were required to file their claims, along with documentation, by a certain deadline; failure to do so resulted in automatic forfeiture of the land to the public domain. If the courts validated the claim, the land then had to be surveyed and all boundary disputes resolved. In contrast with Mexico, landowners generally accepted the legitimacy of the government to mandate the presentation of claims and complied with it, though claimants of Mexican land grants (of both Mexican and U.S. nationality) complained that the process discriminated against them. Californian landowners' acceptance of mandatory formalization of titles was coupled with an expectation that government policies would facilitate the development of a competitive mortgage market that would increase the value of the title. In fact, formalization of titles was complemented by long-run expectations of a full range of complementary institutions and policies.

The Brazilian interior offers a contrasting example of landowner skepticism and resistance to titling reform. Like the western United States, issues of squatters' rights had strong political salience. For centuries, settlers migrating inland from coastal settlements claimed lands (*posses*) by squatting. Initially, the interior was very sparsely inhabited; squatters' vast claims often encompassed several square leagues. Informal institutions grew up locally that identified owners and supported local land transfers; but though these practices were self-enforcing among locals, they were opaque to outsiders. As westward migration continued, and particularly as coffee exports from Brazil took off before mid-century, competition for interior lands intensified. Newcomer squatters, unaware or unwilling to respect prior claims, encroached upon lands that were already occupied. As the demand for land increased, violent conflicts over disputed lands became a serious social and political problem. At the root of the problem was legal uncertainty. The main colonial law governing transfers of Crown lands created the institution of the *sesmaria*, by which property rights to Crown lands were purchased on the condition that they were put into "beneficial use." Yet, prior to the coffee boom, land values were so low that enforcement of the law was neglected. The *sesmaria*, which fell into disuse because of the superiority of the squatting option, was abolished in 1823. For more than twenty-five years, squatting was the only institution in effect for acquiring unoccupied Crown lands, and no formal law governed it.

In the 1840s, the Brazilian government tried to address the legal issue. The Council of State submitted a proposal for legal reform to the Chamber of Deputies in 1843. It had three main objectives. First, it proposed to settle land disputes by conducting surveys and formalizing titles after undertaking a judicial review to verify the validity of claims. Second, to generate government revenues, squatting on the remaining unoccupied public lands would be abolished, and Crown lands would be sold. On claimed lands, titles issued to preexisting *posses* were to have size limits, and portions of *posses* exceeding those limits would be reclaimed as public domain. Third, Crown lands were to be priced sufficiently high to slow the rate of new land acquisition.

The proposed reform law, however, met with such outrage and opposition from squatters that all efforts toward reform were blocked for years. A land law was finally approved in 1850 only by accommodating squatters' demands and compromising its effectiveness. The new law required registry of claims but no survey or judicial review; as a consequence, it did not provide a mechanism for resolving disputes. Though nominally it abolished squatting and required purchase of public lands, the provision was not enforced. Squatters in effect continued to have de facto free access to public lands, and claim sizes remained unconstrained. The law was ineffective at settling disputes and generating government revenues. The federalist constitution of 1891 surrendered jurisdiction of public land policy to the states where regional landowners dominated land policies. Recent work by Alston, Libecap, and Mueller shows that uncertainty over the application of the beneficial use principle continues to invite violence in land disputes in the Amazon region today.

Central to the land problems in Brazil and Mexico were the government's poor credibility and doubtful ability to enforce formal property rights in sparsely populated rural areas where land values were low but rising. Examination of settlement in other countries shows that the outcomes, either in the security of titles or in their distributive effects, were not always the same. Colombia's settlement history is known for the nineteenth-century Antioqueño migration of smallholder settlers from Medellín along the central cordillera into Caldas and Quindío. The lands into which these settlers went were also claimed by heirs of large land grantees, who had long abandoned the rugged lands as worthless. As squatters (called *colonos* in Colombian folklore) settled the mountainous slopes and planted food crops and coffee, grant holders tried to reclaim their lands. In the meantime, new towns had proliferated, where courts in the new *municipios* ruled most often in favor of the settlers' claims, consistent with the perceived local public interest, though usually requiring moderate compensation to grant holders. Elsewhere in Colombia, land claims were concentrated, and property rights were "murky" and unverifiable. Nevertheless, the political demands of a large rural middle class occupying some of the best coffee lands, proud of its *colono* heritage, appears to have had an effect on the enforcement of the "occupation and use" provision of traditional Hispanic land law. A 1926 ruling by the Supreme Court permitted squatting on private, unused land unless the claimant could produce the original *cédula* or title by which the land had left the national patrimony. The impossibility of this requirement led to widespread evictions and rural unrest for years, but eventually it led to the Land Law of 1936, which enforced squatters' rights and set the standard of documentary proof of land claims so as to favor squatters. As a mechanism to increase the predictability of enforcement, to prevent it from being discarded by local judiciaries, the law created a special land court, with circuit judges on horseback, to adjudicate disputes between landowners and squatters. In the long run, however, the law had the unintended consequence of encouraging large land claimants to firm up their property claims by eliminating tenancies in their best lands (which invited squatting) and converting them to cattle-raising. This was responsible for a land use pattern that a 1949 World Bank mission declared "unusual," in which the rich, flat lands in the high Andean plateaus were underutilized as pasturage whereas the neighboring steep rocky slopes were occupied by smallholders planting maize, causing serious erosion.

The frontier settlement of Argentina brings these issues into greater relief. Unlike Brazil or Colombia, both public and private claims to new lands on the expanding frontier in the Argentine pampas were made more effective by an initially unambiguous definition of formal property rights. In the province of Buenos Aires, the process of frontier expansion was in the first instance a military operation that preceded settlement. Private settlers did not wander out into the frontier in advance of government because of the threat of hostile indigenous tribes. Instead, private interests pressured for military campaigns to pacify the frontier to convert it into grazing land. This was the principal reason for the rise of the *caudillo* dictator, Juan Manuel de Rosas. Military successes added vast tracts to the public domain, for which formal property rights were quickly defined and transferred to private hands, either by lease or sale, to raise government revenues and defray military and other government costs. Like Brazil, population on the frontier was sparse so that public lands were privatized in vast tracts. But, unlike Brazil, formalization of private property rights proceeded with greater regularity from the outset. The credibility of the government to make its claims to the public domain effective was a function of the public goods it provided in military services to pacify and defend frontier lands. Despite confiscations by Rosas that were nullified later, most property rights in land were well defined. Over time, this facilitated development of active land and mortgage markets. Mortgage credit, in turn, was instrumental in, though not solely responsible for, the extraordinary expansion of the Argentine economy during its belle époque of export-led growth prior to World War I.

The thesis that *latifundismo*, or the holding of vast expanses of land in economically unproductive "semifeudal" institutional arrangements, has been the main cause of Latin American underdevelopment has been largely abandoned by scholars who have examined the economic behavior of the landed classes and the institutional underpinnings of land markets. In Mexico, for example, research on the *hacienda* has revealed that landowners did not possess semifeudal, precapitalist mentalities, as convention once depicted them. Rather, they operated their enterprises as rational businessmen. The *hacienda* economy in Mexico expanded and receded with export demand and the development of the modern transportation network. When it receded, land markets facilitated the transfer of land use to villages and peasants. Similarly, the thesis of *latifundismo* in the plantation economies has been shown to be inaccurate. The rise of the "colossal" Cuban sugar *centrales* in the early twentieth century, which had been portrayed as a product of onerous semifeudal cane growers' contracts imposed by foreign capitalists, were, instead, the product of modernization – the adoption of new large-scale processing technology and managerial techniques. The cane growers' contracts that were criticized were indeed burdensome – they unloaded considerable risk onto cane growers who were less capable than mill owners of absorbing it. However, the terms of the contracts were fully explained by the transaction costs of supplying cane to the mill using the new milling technologies. Furthermore, the legal environment did not prevent cane growers from abandoning their contracts if the terms were too harsh. Yet, despite the terms, cane growers' contracts were coveted and contributed income streams responsible for the growth of a rural middle class in Cuba.

This new understanding of the functioning of property rights in land and markets in Latin America may displace, but it does not undo, the proposition that the unequal wealth distribution is central to chronic social, economic, and political problems in Latin American countries. For example, in Buenos Aires, as land-intensive ranching gave way to the expansion of the wheat economy after 1890, wheat farmers characteristically leased land from *estancias*. As leaseholders, they had no access to mortgages and no alternative means to secure long-term credit. Adelman contrasts the extent of agricultural mechanization in the wheat economies of Buenos Aires and western Canada. In the latter region, most farmers owned their land and mortgaged it to obtain long-term credit for improvements, including high rates of mechanization. He offers some evidence showing a relationship between low rates of farm ownership and low rates of investment in mechanical technology. Taylor, who has explored the relationship econometrically, finds evidence that is not inconsistent with this relationship, although statistically it is difficult to verify or refute.[17]

---

[17] Jeremy Adelman, *Frontier Development: Land, Labour, and Capital on the Wheatlands of Argentina and Canada, 1890–1914* (Oxford, 1994); Alan M. Taylor, "*Latifundia* as Malefactor in Economic Development? Scale, Tenancy, and Agriculture on the Pampas, 1880–1914," *Research in Economic History* 17 (1997): 261–300.

The prevalence of farm ownership is traced to the slow privatization of public lands in western Canada under a Jeffersonian-style homestead policy with size limits of 160 to 320 acres. By contrast, Buenos Aires had disposed of virtually all of its public domain in sales campaigns without effective size limits prior to the rise of the wheat economy. In Canada, the preservation of public domain and the continued option of home-steading put an opportunity-cost cap on market prices for acquiring new farmland, making farm ownership for new settlers a continued possibility. However, in Buenos Aires, with no remaining public domain, land prices were driven up by speculation over future export-led expansion, and farm-ers found the costs of leasing land more attractive. Meanwhile, research has shown that the landed and commercial elite, operating through their control of political institutions, produced legislation that loosened mort-gage credit so as to fuel the wave of land speculation. Related to this, the Argentine government's chronic struggle since independence to estab-lish solid fiscal institutions underlay both the rapid disposal of the public domain – to raise revenues – and the inflationary finance that fueled land speculation.

CONCLUSIONS

The post-1930 political crises and the postwar cycling of populism and military takeovers have sometimes been associated with the rise of a new era of statism in Latin America. Yet the political instability, constitutional revisionism, and centralist corporatism of the first era reflect persistent insti-tutional patterns that can be traced far back to the colonial institutional legacy, persistent inequality, elite control of government, unpredictable or biased judiciaries, uncertain property-rights enforcement, high political risk, and economic barriers that have blocked the participation of poten-tial entrepreneurs. The root causes of these problems are difficult to sort through. The long view of history points to the existence of a self-reinforcing institutional process that repeatedly restored political power to a conserva-tive elite determined to preserve a preexisting and highly skewed distribu-tion of property rights. But doubts may be raised about the simplicity and deterministic predictions of the Engerman-Sokoloff reinforcement mecha-nism. The problems described here in enforcing property rights in land are paralleled in other studies of credit markets, fiscal institutions, and other key sectors or policy areas.[18] Government's ability to act depended on the credibility and expected longevity of enforcement. The instability of political regimes damaged credibility because individuals expected wide policy swings and reversals and unpredictable or inequitable rulings on property rights. Investors, trying to anticipate long-run effects, were deterred by political risk. When reformers tried genuinely to attack these problems, they ran up against unanticipated barriers as systems of interactive formal and informal institutions persisted, each constrained by its functional relationship with others. Institutions have had powerful influence, yet, by definition, they are humanly devised and humanly alterable. Alterability suggests manipulability for policy aims. This fact lends hope to the prospect of positive reform. However, if those efforts are to be undertaken with greater confidence about the outcomes, scholars need to obtain a better understanding of the complexity, uniqueness, and latent crises in each national system.

[18] As examples, with regard to banking, see Noel Maurer, *The Power and The Money: The Mexican Financial System, 1876–1932* (Stanford, CA, 2003); in regard to monetary and fiscal institutions, see several contributions from Michael D. Bordo and Roberto Cortés Conde, eds., *Transferring Wealth and Power from the Old to the New World: Monetary and Fiscal Institutions in the 17th Through the 19th Centuries* (Cambridge, 2001); and Gerardo della Paolera and Alan M. Taylor, *Straining at the Anchor: The Argentine Currency Board and the Search for Macroeconomic Stability, 1880–1935* (Chicago, 2001).

6

FISCAL AND MONETARY REGIMES

ROBERTO CORTÉS CONDE

MODERNIZATION FROM THE END OF THE NINETEENTH CENTURY TO WORLD WAR I

Throughout Latin America, the formation of national states in the last decades of the nineteenth century went together with the growth of their economies. Wars and political conflicts ended, isolation was mostly overcome thanks to new transportation technologies, and central governments became stronger. This process coincided with the modernization of political and economic institutions and included the creation of new fiscal and monetary institutions. Public finances and tax administration were reordered. Anachronistic taxes on production and local trade were dropped, and states financed themselves increasingly through indirect taxes such as duties on foreign trade (especially on imported consumer goods). This became possible because Latin American economies were oriented toward foreign markets. Enjoying control of rising customs revenues, central governments consolidated their power. In years when peace prevailed, the role of the armed forces diminished and war expenditures declined. Thus, expenditures grew on items related to economic development, such as subsidies, public works investment, railways, and education. Administrations still suffered the consequences of prior wars in the form of high debt burdens. There were efforts to tap foreign capital markets and to create domestic ones although those efforts suffered from widespread suspicion about the governments'

This article was part of a research project supported by a grant from the Inter-American Development Bank (BID-UdeSA ATN/SF-6885 – RG) with the collaboration of Marcela Harriague as researcher and Marcelo Barbieri as research assistant.

arbitrary procedures. Governments proceeded to monetize their debts through private or mixed banks established during the economic boom. In other cases, treasuries issued money directly.

By the last decades of the nineteenth century, silver coins were used as a means of payment (the peso of eight *reales* of colonial days, a silver ounce of twenty-seven grams), together with notes convertible into metallic coins issued by banks and, sometimes, government forced-circulation paper money. When issues of convertible bank notes exceeded money demand, specie outflows occurred, which finally led to inconvertibility generally followed by larger money issues and depreciation. In several countries, and at different times, this led to periods of high inflation. In response, countries strove to reach monetary and fiscal stability in order to go back to convertibility and, by the end of the century and because of silver depreciation, to adopt the gold standard.

This chapter is organized in the following way: The first section examines the period from 1880 to World War I and is divided in two subsections, "Consolidation of Nation-States: (1880–1900)" and "The Great Expansion: (1900–1914)." The second section analyzes the period "Between the Wars: (1914–1945)," which is also subdivided in two subperiods, "the 1914–1930 period" and the "1930–1945 period." The last section of the chapter "From World War II to the 1980s" studies "Growth with Inflationary Financing: 1945–1960" and "Growth and Stabilization Efforts: 1960–1980." The final section draws conclusions.

THE CONSOLIDATION OF NATION-STATES: 1880–1900

After about 1850, efforts were made to eliminate customs duties and taxes on the circulation of domestic goods (*alcabalas*), which had kept markets segmented. External customs had already become the primary source of revenue. Tax-collecting powers were granted at various governmental levels, with more decentralized (federalist) systems prevailing in the larger countries (Argentina, Brazil, and Mexico).

Although the currency regime inherited from Spain was bimetallic (gold and silver), silver coins were the main currency. In some countries, banks that issued convertible notes were created, and laws aimed at organizing the financial system passed. In others, the treasury issued money directly. After 1870, silver depreciation affected mainly producing countries such as Mexico, Bolivia, and Chile. Unlike the Hispanic American countries, Brazil adopted the gold standard early on, in 1846, establishing a gold/silver rate of 1:15.625.[1] Because gold was not used for everyday transactions, banks issued notes that circulated among the public. The Bank of Brazil, founded in 1853, enjoyed a monopoly on issuing money. In Chile, because of the fall in copper prices that affected government income in 1878, the forced circulation of paper money was decreed. This lasted until 1925. In Colombia, by 1860, treasury notes had forced circulation. In 1881, the National Bank was founded with the right to emit bank notes and the privileges of a state bank. In Bolivia, the silver peso had been the general currency since colonial times; it was the old peso of eight *reales*, coined in Potosí and eventually known as the *boliviano*. In Peru, silver pesos predominated initially, although the *boliviano* also circulated. The 1863 monetary law established the *sol*, divided into 100 cents, with a weight of twenty-five grams of silver. Peru also changed from the bimetallic to the silver standard (gold remaining as commodity currency). In the interior of Argentina, silver coins circulated, while in the province of Buenos Aires, government paper money was common.

The consolidation of the central government took place in Mexico during the presidencies of Porfirio Díaz, who governed the country autocratically from 1876 to 1910 (with just one cosmetic interruption in 1880–4). Revenue rose in nominal terms, but expenditure increased even more. There were two reasons for this imbalance. The most important was silver depreciation. The state received revenues from taxes paid in silver exports, the price of which fell sharply beginning in the 1880s. Meanwhile, the foreign debt had to be paid in gold. The second factor feeding the fiscal imbalance was the Díaz government's ambitious public works and railroad-building programs, which facilitated its political consolidation.

In Brazil, with the establishment of the republican regime in 1889, a federalist decentralization took place that led to an increase in the power of states to collect export taxes. The 1891 Constitution introduced a more decentralized fiscal system. This was important during the coffee export boom. Because Brazil had an almost monopolistic position in the international market, it could transfer the burden of export taxes to foreign consumers, thus avoiding internal political resistance. Coffee taxes, furthermore, became the main fiscal resource for the state of São Paulo. By 1907, central government outlays had dropped by 66 percent, whereas those of the states had risen by 25 percent and municipal expenses by 9 percent. Another important change had to do with the monetary and

---

[1] Carlos Manuel Peláez and Wilson Suzigan, *Historia monetaria do Brasil* (Rio de Janeiro, 1976), 67.

banking reform. Because of currency depreciation, taxes were collected in gold. Customs duties represented half of the revenue of the federal government, and exports were the main source of revenue of some states. Toward the end of the century, a sales tax was added.

In Chile, the expansion of the modern state was aided by the incorporation of the northern nitrate provinces after the War of the Pacific (1879–83). By imposing duties on exports, the state seized almost half of the operating profits of the rich fields. The share of state royalties and taxes on the extraction of natural resources in fiscal revenue increased from 5 percent in 1830 to 25 percent in 1880, 47 percent in 1890, 56 percent in 1900, and 53 percent in 1910. Between 1869 and 1879, foreign-trade revenues rose by 1 percent a year and thereafter at a rate of 7 percent. Before the war, the Chilean government collected trade revenues of about one million pounds. In 1890, it received more than two million pounds, and in 1910, five and a half million pounds. Between 1879 and 1895, state income rose tenfold and, according to Gabriel Palma, this growth influenced the entire economy by means of a fiscal multiplier.[2] The state avoided the difficult political question of burdening other taxpayers by taking its revenues from mining rents. Although nitrate export revenues were high, Chile raised tariffs on imports in response to protectionist interests. The alliance between industrialists seeking protection from imports of manufactures and farmers who feared an invasion of Argentine goods to the mining zones was a decisive factor in raising some tariffs, although Chile's tariff levels were moderate in comparison to the rest of the region.

In Colombia, the conservatives returned to power in 1884, one year after the outbreak of the civil war. In 1886, the Constitution was reformed and Colombia turned to a centralized system of government. One of the main resources of local states, the big cattle slaughter revenue (*degüello*), returned to the central government. In 1892, domestic taxes were levied on cigarettes and others were allotted to the central government. The return to the central government's monopolistic control caused great dissatisfaction. Between 1890 and 1893, the national government's income equaled 62 percent of the overall income and those of the departments equaled 28 percent, whereas municipalities hardly reached 10 percent. The customs system was modified to avoid multiple exemptions and to increase protection. In

[2] Gabriel Palma, "Trying to 'tax and spend' oneself out of the 'Dutch Disease': The Chilean Economy from the War of the Pacific to the Great Depression," in Enrique Cárdenas, José Ocampo, and Rosemary Thorp, eds., *An Economic History of Twentieth-Century Latin America* (London, 2000), 234–56.

1897, the states recovered the slaughter revenue without offering additional services in return, as the national police had been founded in 1891 and the central government took over high school education.[3] Customs duties continued to be the main revenue, followed by salt mine leases.

In Argentina, during the 1880s, resources originated from customs increased thanks to the continuous expansion of foreign trade. The national government was the main beneficiary of this expansion and left the until-then quite powerful provinces far behind. Between 1880 and 1890, income rose by approximately 300 percent. The population increased from 2.5 million to 3.4 million and gross domestic product (GDP) grew at an average annual rate of 12 percent.[4] Import duties were the main source of income (more than 60 percent of total national revenues). Land sales were not taxed. In 1891, after the Baring crisis and the fall in import-tax collections, a law was passed that allotted a major share of domestic taxes to the national government at the expense of the provinces.

For Peru, the War of the Pacific was a watershed event because the country not only had to face a rise in military expenses but also the loss of its nitrate provinces. The province of Tarapacá was relinquished to Chile, and those of Arica and Tacna fell under Chile's control, pending a plebiscite that took place ten years later.[5] Once the war was over, Peru found itself in an extremely complicated situation. The country had to obtain funds to avoid bankruptcy. The foreign debt itself was the greatest problem. Railways did not produce as much as expected to stimulate the economy. The income originating from guano dropped because of an international fall in prices. The nitrate lands, which served as a guarantee for foreign loans, were relinquished to Chile. In 1886, a group of British interests took charge of the foreign debt in exchange for the right to exploit guano and mineral deposits and the South and Central railways. Gradually, Peru started to recover from the War of the Pacific shock.[6]

Access to foreign capital coincided with a widespread and gradual shift to a monetary regime in which government paper currency became generalized. The share of bank notes in the money supply increased (except in Mexico, Bolivia, and Peru, all silver-producing countries). The governments' needs for financing and the frustrating experiences with private

[3] Luís Fernando López Garavito, *Historia de la hacienda y el tesoro en Colombia, 1821–1900* (Santafé de Bogotá, 1992), 337.

[4] Roberto Cortés Conde, *La economía Argentina en el largo plazo* (Buenos Aires, 1997).

[5] Richard Nyrop, *Perú: A Country Study* (Washington, DC, 1981), 24.

[6] Ibid., 25.

banks of issue ended in inflationary episodes followed by more orthodox restrictive policies, and efforts began for the adoption of the gold standard. Convertibility–inconvertibility episodes were recurrent, though some countries maintained legal tender (fiat money) paper currency for a long time (e.g., Chile).

In Brazil, a monetary and banking reform, the so-called Ouro Preto reform implemented by Minister Ruy Barbosa, authorized free banks of issue, which printed a great amount of money of legal tender, unleashing inflation. The creation of free banks coincided with the suppression of slavery. The metallic currency system was not flexible enough to pay wages within a free labor system. The great expansion of banking money caused the huge inflation known as the *encilhamento* between 1889 and 1891. To stop the rise in costs that continued until 1892, hard contraction policies were implemented in the latter years of the decade, which ended in deep recession and deflation between 1900 and 1902. A banking crisis occurred in September 1901, when banks were forced to have a legal reserve of 100 percent over deposits.[7]

Argentina had a mixed monetary system. Metallic coins that circulated in the interior (the silver *boliviano*) coexisted with the government of Buenos Aires' inconvertible paper currency and banknotes. From 1867, "metallic notes" and notes from the Bank of the Province of Buenos Aires' Foreign Exchange Office also served as currency. Up to 1881, the official monetary unit was the old Spanish silver peso. In 1881, a law established a new monetary unit, the gold peso with twenty-five grams of 900/000 silver instead of twenty-seven grams. However, in 1885, the system returned to inconvertibility.[8] A law passed in 1887 authorized free banking business with guaranteed banks, with gold deposited as guarantee. The government intervened by means of the National Bank, trying to sustain the value of the paper peso. During the years 1887 and 1888, the premium for gold was stabilized at about 30 percent. Nevertheless, that dirty flotation implied an important loss of reserves. This caused an extraordinary capital outflow, much greater than the amount required to pay the debt service or the balance of trade deficit.[9] The huge note issues by guaranteed banks led to the 1890 Baring crisis and, finally, to the liquidation of the banks. Consequently, the central

---

[7] Peláez and Suzigan, *Historia monetaria*, 141.

[8] Roberto Cortés Conde, *Dinero, deuda y crisis, evolución monetaria y fiscal argentina:1862–90* (Buenos Aires, 1989).

[9] Roberto Cortés Conde, "Finanzas Públicas, Moneda y Bancos (1810–1899)," in M.A. De Marco, ed., *Nueva Historia de la Nación Argentina*, vol. V, (Buenos Aires, 2000).

government took control of all monetary issues. From 1890, money issue became an exclusive right of the national government.

Between 1890 and 1900, however, no more currency was issued. This brought about a big monetary contraction taking into account that population and the economy grew significantly. In April 1891, the monetary contraction deepened because a great banking panic reached its highest peak when the National and Provincial Banks closed, starting a liquidation phase that extended to other banks, with the consequent impossibility for savers to use their deposits as currency. The 1899 monetary reform established that the conversion fund founded in 1890 would issue notes in a new currency unit (the national peso, equivalent to 0.44 cents of the gold peso), upon delivery of gold equivalent, and would return gold to those who requested it at the same exchange rate. A Currency Board was organized, following the Bank of England's Issue Department, leaving the discount and deposit functions to commercial banks. It thus distinguished itself from other European and American models, which granted their banks of issue (as central banks) rediscount facilities and the possibility of creating money by means of credit to the government or to the financial sector.

In the last decades of the century, Bolivia faced the consequences of the devaluation of silver, its main source of income and circulating currency. In 1895, in order to provide stability, limited legal tender was granted to the gold sovereign (Great Britain) and the Peruvian gold pound. In Peru, at the start of the War of the Pacific (1879) and during the following years, the government sought financing from the banks, which issued notes accepted for payment of fiscal liabilities. In 1875, these notes had been declared inconvertible, and the issue of them increased extraordinarily, triggering hyperinflation in 1883 and their demonetization in 1889. There was a huge capital flight because of the war, and only fiscal notes – and the "boliviano" in the South of the country – remained in circulation.[10] Because of the fall in foreign-trade revenues during Piérola's second presidential term (1895–9), a tax on salt consumption was levied and, when printed notes lost all their value, silver coins came back to circulation. In 1897, their coinage was discontinued in order to increase their value, and that same year – in a process that would end up pegging the currency to the gold standard – the decision was taken to collect customs duties in gold.

[10] Laura Randall, "A *Comparative Economic History of Latin America: Argentina, Brazil, Mexico, and Perú, 1500–1914*" (Ann Arbor, University Microfilms International, 1977), 120.

THE GREAT EXPANSION, 1900–1914

In the first decade of the twentieth century, foreign trade grew rapidly in Latin America and, consequently, fiscal revenues increased. The fiscal balance also improved because revenues were collected in a nondepreciating currency. In those countries that adopted the gold standard, foreign debts were consolidated, except in Mexico, where there was a general turmoil during the revolution starting in 1910. Outlays went mainly to infrastructure, also with the exception of Mexico.

In 1903, Mexico established that customs duties should be paid in gold, which helped balance its budget, because most debt was payable in gold. In 1905, a monetary reform put the country on the gold standard, but the outbreak of the Mexican Revolution led to a long period of political and economic instability.

In Colombia, the One Thousand Days War (1899–1902) caused a severe drop in tax collections, while war outlays gave rise to huge deficits. Inflation affected customs revenues because they were collected in paper money. Even after the civil war ended, defense outlays remained at a high level because of Panama's secession.[11] The wartime inflation led to a long-lasting reaction: the adoption of conservative monetary and fiscal policies aimed at avoiding similar situations in the future. After that, there came a period of stability lasting until the 1920s. In 1905, taxes on liquor, furs, tobacco, cigarettes, and matches were allocated to the national government, but in 1909, a decentralized system was reestablished and taxes on liquor and tobacco went back to the provinces.

In Argentina, expenditures went mainly to public works, railways, and education. An impressive growth of exports allowed increasing imports, the main source of fiscal revenue. Between 1900 and 1910, the burden of debt payment shrank from 35 percent to 10 percent of the total income. Another operation was the launching of a widely placed bond – the 5 percent Argentine internal credit, by which the government began financing itself in the domestic capital market.

Up to 1902, there were deficits in Brazil, but during the next five years the situation changed. In fact, during those years, there was a slight surplus attributable to orthodox measures. The service of the debt increased in *milreis* because of devaluation and reached 25 percent of total expenses. A similar percentage of the budget went to military expenditures. Transfers

---

[11] Panama was part of Colombia until it became independent in 1903.

and subsidies remained low, amounting to less than 4 percent of total government outlays. Increasing capital expenditures should be mentioned because they reached almost 20 percent between 1910 and 1913, after falling to 4 percent between 1897 and 1902. The three administrations prior to World War I implemented large public-works programs (railways, canals, or ports).[12]

Several countries – such as Argentina, Brazil, Mexico, Peru, and Uruguay – adopted the gold standard (under a Currency Board with 100% gold reserves, or government banks of issue and mixed systems with different levels of reserves). Colombia and Chile remained under a regime of forced circulation. There was general use of paper money.

In Colombia, money issue, which grew more than 100 percent per year during the One Thousand Days War, was the only source of financing, producing huge inflation. During the following period, Colombia kept a forced circulation system, mainly of treasury notes and notes issued by banks. Metal coins also circulated, though with a smaller share in the circulation. Paper money was slowly written off, and it was possible to return to convertibility in 1923. With the 1905 reform, it was possible to reduce the debt attributable to fiduciary currency circulation by devaluing it according to the market exchange rate (100 paper money pesos = 1 gold peso) and making conversion easier. Also in 1905, the Central Bank of Colombia began operating. In 1907, fiscal revenues earmarked to paper money amortization were not enough, and the nonissuing commitment was violated.[13]

In Argentina, after some early hesitations, the Currency Board had a remarkable success. The gold inflow guaranteed currency supply expansion, which increased more than 11 percent annually between 1903 and 1913. The Currency Board regime stressed the seasonal and procyclical nature of money expansion and contraction. During harvest season, there was gold inflow and credit expanded additionally because banks wanted to place their surpluses. During the winter season, banks were concerned with the amount of their reserves and contracted credit. The National Bank took some measures to reduce its impact, such as lending without taking account of its reserve fluctuations. After a long expansion period, the first problems appeared in 1912 because of the crisis in the Balkans,

[12] Raymond W. Goldsmith, *Brazil 1850–1984: Desenvolvimento financiero sob un século de inflação* (São Paulo, 1986), 123–4.
[13] Jorge Enrique Ibáñez Nájar, "Antecedentes legales de la creación del Banco de la República," in *Banco de la República: Antecedentes, evolución y estructura* (Bogotá, 1990), 58–65.

with an important reserve outflow. The start of World War I in 1914 and the immediate suspension of convertibility in belligerent countries caused a high gold outflow, which led the Argentine administration to suspend convertibility.

In Bolivia, although silver coins circulated, there were already banks issuing notes convertible into silver. In 1904, British gold coins and *peruanos* (Peruvian gold pounds) were granted legal tender status, and in 1908 they were granted unlimited legal tender status (gold standard). Banks had to convert bank notes into gold, and 50 percent of customs duties were collected in gold. The government stopped silver circulation, which was then used just for some fractional currency and exported as a commodity. In 1904, the "*peso boliviano*" was pegged to the gold standard, at a rate of 12.5 *bolivianos* per British pound.[14] The National Bank of Bolivia was founded as a semi-official agency, with the exclusive right to issue money after 1911.

In 1901, Peru adopted the gold standard, establishing the convertibility of notes and silver coins into gold at a rate of one Peruvian pound to ten *soles*. The gold standard regime coincided with a number of monetary disturbances caused by external factors, the most important of which was the 1907 U.S. crisis. In 1914, because of the war, convertibility was suspended and gold exports forbidden; money issue and expenditures increased and inflation began.

BETWEEN THE WARS: 1914–1945

THE 1914–1930 PERIOD

World War I and the subsequent protectionist policies adopted by the developed countries caused a sharp reduction in international trade, leading to fiscal crises in regimes based on taxes on foreign trade. The crisis showed the need to reform the fiscal system to avoid its high level of dependence on foreign trade, emphasized by the effect of foreign currency inflows (outflows) on monetary expansion (contraction). In countries with a federal political regime, reforms had to redefine the relationship between federal and state (or provincial) governments because central governments depended mainly on customs revenues (even in countries such as Brazil, where export taxes also went to the states).

---

[14] Eduardo López Rivas, *Esquema de la Historia Económica de Bolivia* (Oruro, 1955), 20.

At first, the need to implement reforms rose as a response to the international emergency, although things were expected to go back to normal once it was over. Although this did not happen, governments were still convinced that they could return to the old system. Still, some countries started collecting income and sales taxes. It was only after 1930, however, that major fiscal reforms were implemented, when the expectation of going back to "normalcy" finally disappeared.

Mexico's fiscal system was undermined by the revolution that went on until 1917. The centralized tax administration disappeared. Each revolutionary chief collected taxes within the territories under his control and issued paper money as the main source of revenue. During the World War I years, the price of oil and industrial minerals substantially increased but not so much as to cover the costs of the general disorder and the foreign companies' reluctance to pay royalties. When the civil war was over and Venustiano Carranza became President, the tax administration was put in order and taxes were imposed on oil companies (the 1917 Constitution declared the subsoil to be the nation's property).

During the postwar period, the international demand for food and raw materials declined, affecting most Latin American countries. The resulting fall in revenues called for a reduction of expenditures, which was never successful, and fiscal deficits were recurrent. Expenditure composition changed: first, economic outlays went up because of public works and, in the 1920s, social expenditures also increased.

Since the turn of the century, Chile had made huge investments in infrastructure, health, and education (reaching one of the highest levels in Latin America) by using resources derived from the government's share in mining rents. In Brazil's coffee-producing states, especially São Paulo, expenditures included financing, purchase, and storage of coffee stocks to stabilize world prices. In Argentina, expenditure fell during the first postwar years.[15] In the 1920s, during the expansion phase, outlays went up again and there was a substantial increase in real wages and in the number of public servants, public works being the main expenditure item.[16]

In Bolivia, most of the expenditure went to the army, public education, and the police. There were also substantial investment expenses not included in the budget, such as those for public works. In Peru, under

---

[15] Pablo Gerchunoff and Lucas Llach, *El ciclo de la ilusión y el desencanto: un siglo de políticas económicas en Argentina* (Buenos Aires, 1998), 71.
[16] Ibid., 98.

Leguía's (1919–30) second presidency, large public works programs were undertaken and many schools created.[17] In Mexico, during the revolution and the civil war, most of the expenditure went to the military. After the 1920s, it was expenditure on infrastructure that grew. In Colombia, there were considerable investments in railways and roads during a period called "growth through debt," coincident with substantial capital inflows and foreign financing mainly from the United States.

The fall in revenues during World War I led to recurring deficits, domestically financed either by local banks, by money issue (as in Chile until 1925, when the Central Bank was created), or by increasing floating debt (as in Argentina and Brazil). Colombia faced tax-revenue declines and resorted to tapping Currency Board funds. In Mexico, during the revolution, the government resorted first to foreign bank credits (afterwards repudiated); later, the contending factions paid for their war expenses by issuing money.

In the 1920s, those countries that had serviced their debts or made new arrangements with their creditors reentered the international capital market. Up to 1923, Brazil had substantial deficits, but between then and the beginning of the 1930s, budgets were more balanced, and the country's financial needs were covered by foreign credits. In Chile, during the 1920s, domestic reforms stemming from the Kemmerer mission and easier terms of payment in the international capital market made foreign loans available.[18] That determined an increase in expenditure, which went on until the beginning of the 1930s and increased the foreign debt. A fall in fiscal revenues because of the 1930 economic crisis led the country to default. Lacking access to foreign credit and depending only on direct taxes on internal revenue, Mexico cut down expenditure and tried to balance its accounts.

When World War I broke out, convertibility was suspended. In the postwar period, several countries made efforts to go back to the gold standard, this time with new central banks. In the Andean countries, central banks were mostly founded during the 1920s. Peru, which had changed from silver to the gold standard at the beginning of the twentieth century, admitted an unlimited mintage of gold coins, whereas silver and copper coins could only be minted upon authorization by special laws. In Bolivia, though silver coins were commonly used, three banks were issuing notes convertible

---

[17] Nyrop, *Perú*, 28.
[18] Paul W. Drake, "La Creación de los Bancos Centrales en los Países Andinos," in Pedro Tedde and Carlos Marichal, eds., *La Formación de los Bancos Centrales en España y América Latina (siglos XIX y XX)*, (Madrid, 1989), 107–9.

into silver coins, among other commercial activities. In the countries with currency boards, money issue was limited by the inflows to reserves. In others, money was issued against commercial credit or government debt. Only a part of the reserves were in gold.

After several frustrated efforts to adopt the gold standard, Chile continued until 1925 under a paper-money forced circulation. In other countries, such as Colombia, the forced circulation (mainly treasury notes and notes from banks of issue) went on until 1923, when the country went back to convertibility.

In Mexico, in July 1913, convertibility was suspended, and between June 1913 and August 1914, the peso depreciated by 40 percent. From August 1914 to June 1916, paper money predominated. The amount of different notes in circulation was huge (a 1916 decree refers to twenty-one different types of paper money, all of them of legal tender, to which illegal issues – many of them not strictly counterfeit – were added). Paper money quickly depreciated. By the middle of 1915, acknowledging the problems that counterfeit money entailed, and in spite of the fact that accepting *constitucionalista* notes was considered a debt of honor, it was decided to exchange them for a new currency, giving the other notes no value at all. The new currency, though difficult to counterfeit, also suffered a large depreciation because of over-issuing.

As in Europe, World War I entailed the suspension of convertibility in most Latin American countries with high gold outflows, such as Argentina, Brazil, and Peru. The latter declared a four-day legal holiday in August 1914, followed by the passage of a law that forbade free gold exports; commercial banks were authorized to issue banknotes called "circular cashier's checks," backed by the assets of the banks of issue and guaranteed by metallic gold.

During the inconvertibility period, currencies floated. In some cases (e.g., Argentina), the money issue was still backed by gold reserves. At first, the peso suffered a slight depreciation; then, between 1915 and 1918, it appreciated 2 percent with regard to the dollar and 3 percent to the pound sterling. From 1920 on, the peso floated, showing a small depreciation during the first half of the 1920s and going back to prewar values with reference to the gold peso, the dollar, and sterling in the second half of the decade.[19] In other cases, the money issue answered to the government's credit needs.

In the 1920s, with the different Kemmerer missions to Andean countries, the first Latin American central banks were founded. The first was

---

[19] Rafael Olarra Jiménez, *Evolución Monetaria Argentina* (Buenos Aires, 1968), 183.

created in Peru in 1922. In Colombia, the Bank of the Republic, founded in 1923, was the second of its type in Latin America. In Chile, in 1925, during the Kemmerer mission, a mixed bank was created, with the participation of national and foreign banks. In Mexico, the 1917 Constitution had acknowledged the need to have a monetary authority and reserved the money-issue monopoly for the state. In 1925, after implementing a fiscal austerity program, Secretary of Finance Alberto Pani founded the Bank of Mexico. Nevertheless, the right to issue money had to be postponed until the next decade because people were reluctant to accept paper money. In its earliest years, up to 1931, the Bank of Mexico operated like a commercial bank with monopoly of issue. Central banks were also created in Guatemala (1925), Ecuador (1927), Bolivia (1929), El Salvador (1934), Argentina (1935), Costa Rica (1936), and Venezuela (1939). By the 1950s, central banks had been created in nearly every Latin American country.

Latin American central banks were closer to the U.S. Federal Reserve model (Banking School) than to the Currency Board model. They could issue money backed not only by reserves but also by commercial credit. In Chile, in the 1920s, the Central Bank had a conservative policy, accumulating reserves equal to 100 percent of the currency and deposits. It could not lend the public sector more than 20 percent of its paid capital and reserves.[20] Regulations were established for the banking system, and minimum bank reserves were increased from 10 percent to 20 percent. By the end of the 1920s, additional credit institutions with Central Bank backing were created, such as the Agrarian Credit Bank, the Mining Credit Bank, and the Industrial Credit Institute.

In the first half of the 1920s, Colombia reestablished its earlier monetary and exchange rate policy: money issued was convertible (at an exchange rate of 1 peso = 0.96 dollars that lasted until 1932). That meant its Central Bank was closer to the Federal Reserve than to the Bank of England because money issues were backed not only by reserves but also by credits to the government and the private sector. Between 1923 and 1931, the country returned to the gold standard and the correlation between currency and reserves was remarkably high (0.98). In fact, it was a gold exchange standard that allowed the country to have its reserves in foreign currency (as, in fact, happened, because it had most of its reserves in the United States).

Several other countries, in order to converge domestic prices to international levels, also returned to the gold standard. By the middle of the 1920s, Mexico and Chile had done so. Brazil reentered the gold standard in 1926

---

[20] Drake, "La Creación de Bancos Centrales," 96–8.

with a new currency unit, the *cruceiro*, equivalent to one *milreis*, at a new exchange rate of sixpence. Until 1930, there was a fixed exchange rate backed by the *Caixa de Estabilização* (CE), an institution similar to a Currency Board. The CE had a monopoly of issuing money backed by gold – after the *Banco do Brasil* lost that right – and used it to increase the monetary supply by around 30 percent over the next three years. However, in 1929, when exports went down and capital flight began, the system showed its weakness and convertibility was suspended.[21] In Argentina, the Currency Board reopened in 1927, and the country reentered the gold standard at the same prewar parity: 0.44 gold peso per each national paper money peso. That entailed a substantial price deflation.

THE 1930–1945 PERIOD

The decline in foreign trade during the 1930s crisis was greater than during World War I and was no longer perceived as temporary. This provoked a not-always-successful implementation of more thoughtful tax reforms. Greater importance was now given to income taxes and taxes on domestic consumption. In several countries, especially Argentina, Brazil, and Colombia, a new and increasingly substantial source of nontax resources became available from the moment exchange controls were established: the gap between the exchange rate paid to exporters and the one paid by importers. Because of the need to depart from the gold standard and the subsequent devaluation, this gap allowed government to take a share of exporters' excess profits (mainly in the case of natural resource-intensive exports). This so-called exchange rate differential was a substantial source of foreign currency that could be assigned to pay the foreign debt (a practice that Argentine administrations followed). In Colombia, the Special Exchange Account (including the gaps for foreign bills of exchange and those for gold revaluation cashed in 1938) was used to service the debts incurred by the government during the war with Peru. It also served to create a Stabilization Fund, designed to keep the prices of government bonds stable and to regulate monetary policy.

Compared with taxes, this mechanism had some advantages because no parliamentary approval was required, which spared the government hard negotiations with politicians to pass taxes. In federal countries, this provided an income that national governments did not have to share with states or provinces.

[21] Steven Topik, *The Political Economy of the Brazilian State, 1889–1930* (Austin, TX, 1987), 50.

Another nonfiscal income source was money issue. Although the powers of the new central banks followed the Federal Reserve model (designed to promote private credit), the crisis forced them to become a main source of government financing. Probably the most important feature of this period – because of its impact on economies and subsequent economic policies – was the fact that the 1930s crisis and World War II put an end to international capital markets. When that source was lost, governments resorted to financing through money issue, which appeared as a convenient response mainly because, attributable to the deflation of the 1930s, there was a high money demand and people apparently accepted the new issues. As a source of revenue not dependent on parliamentary approval, it had an enormous political appeal for governments because they could make a better impression on voters without having to negotiate approval. In addition, nobody felt deprived of anything; finally, in federal countries, money issuing was a resource that fell under the jurisdiction of the central authority.

There was a general fall in revenues because of the decrease in foreign trade, in spite of the new taxes created to make up for the loss. In Argentina, 55 percent of the tax system relied on foreign trade, so when it shrank, customs duties decreased between 1930 and 1932 by more than 20 percent. As substitutes, an income tax (a short-lived turnover tax) and a tax on sales were created.

In Mexico, the situation was similar: taxes on foreign trade, which represented 50 percent of the fiscal revenue in 1930, went down to less than 30 percent in 1935. This was compensated, to some extent, by an increase in export taxes (oil), especially during World War II. From then on, direct taxes experienced a substantial increase, especially those levied on income, which, after 1943, represented on average 25 percent of fiscal revenue.

The impact of World War II varied according to the country with which trade was mainly conducted. Those countries having a closer commercial relationship with Great Britain, such as Argentina, suffered a substantial decline in import and customs revenues. Those with a closer relationship to the United States, such as Brazil and especially Mexico, went through a commercial reactivation that improved their import capacity and produced fiscal revenue increases. In Colombia, a tax reform in 1935 was aimed at a fairer distribution of the fiscal burden, levying higher taxes on higher incomes by imposing a gradual increase in income tax rates up to a maximum 17 percent as well as a capital levy and an excess profits tax. By the end of the 1930s, taxes were producing more fiscal income than were customs revenues.

In Chile, copper replaced nitrates as the main source of mining revenues but suffered a 40 percent decline between 1930 and 1935. Mining's share in fiscal revenues went down to 10 percent in those same years. In Mexico, when foreign companies were finally forced to pay royalties, those on mineral extraction, especially oil, became substantial, going from 16 million pesos in 1930 to 33 million pesos in 1935.

The consensus that made import taxes the main source of revenue, which had been the basis for the consolidation of the nation-states during the export boom, broke down. Changes implemented in nonmining countries were unable to enjoy a similar consensus because they resorted to taxing income or wealth; those countries with mining-derived revenues had fewer problems. In the search for alternatives, several governments relied increasingly on new sources of nontax revenue, such as exchange rate differentials (a rent on natural resources) and on the inflationary tax (in fact, a tax on labor). As time went by, exporters realized how damaging the exchange rate gap was for them and in many cases, such as in Argentina, exports stagnated even after the war, when international trade recovered and exceeded its previous volume.

In the face of the deep fall in revenues, the initial response consisted of cutting expenses. From 1929, Mexico adopted orthodox policies[22] and, from 1930, Brazil and Argentina did the same. Governments found themselves facing a complicated problem. They had to pay the bureaucracies they had enlarged and the huge payments – mostly in foreign currency – due on their debts, which had grown rapidly during the 1920s almost everywhere. In Mexico, administrative expenses grew after 1930 until they reached 63 percent of expenditure in 1933–4. In Argentina, this share was about 58 percent for the same period. Argentina's payments on the public debt amounted to 29 percent of the outlays of the national government.[23]

Between 1932 and 1937, a substantial change took place in expenditure policies. Although at first in a mild way, governments started spending beyond revenues. The resulting deficits were financed by the central banks. In addition, the composition of expenditures changed: there were increases in expenses related to public works (Argentina, Brazil, and Chile), agriculture and irrigation (Chile and Colombia), and social policies (Chile). Subsidies, financing of private business projects, and outlays for companies

[22] Enrique Cárdenas, *La hacienda pública y la política económica, 1929–1958* (Mexico City, 1994).
[23] Gerchunoff and Llach, *El ciclo de la ilusión y el desencanto*, 134.

managed by the state also grew. In Mexico, agricultural (irrigation) and infrastructure projects were implemented, in many cases financed by the national development banks. During 1938, oil companies were expropriated, but they were not included in the budget and were only incorporated after the budgetary reform of 1966. State intervention grew not only in the form of exchange and price controls during the war but also through subsidies granted via credit agencies (e.g., Crédito Agrícola in Chile and the regulatory boards in Argentina).

The departure from the gold standard and the resulting devaluation made payments owed in strong currencies more difficult. In the face of this problem, which implied that a much stronger effort would be needed to comply with foreign obligations, most countries decided to suspend payments abroad and found immediate relief. The rarefied international situation, the almost complete closure of international capital markets, the long world war, and the postwar controls on capital movements made the consequences of default less serious than in normal conditions. In Latin America, all the major countries except Argentina defaulted.

Governments deliberately ran up deficits. It is true that, unlike the United States, the historical experience in most countries during the nineteenth century had been of generalized deficits. But, during the 1930s, the idea that deficits could contribute to the expansion of the economy took root. Formerly considered taboo, deficits turned into a recommended practice to foster economic activity.

As a consequence of the 1930 crisis, convertibility was suspended and the gold standard abandoned. By departing from the gold standard, governments could resort to the central banks for the finance previously supplied by capital markets. The domestic debt started decreasing as a consequence of the inflation that had caused an increase in prices during wartime. In turn, the foreign debt increased, but in most cases it ceased to be paid until later, when new payments were agreed upon.

Chile had returned to the gold standard in 1926, but the 1930 crisis hit the mining sector and led to a rapid loss of reserves (about 50%). In spite of Kemmerer's recommendation to maintain the gold standard by applying restrictive monetary policies and high interest rates, exchange controls were implemented in July 1931 and payments on foreign debt suspended. The gold standard was only maintained for six years (until April 1932), when it was formally abandoned and followed by a big devaluation and the creation of an Exchange Control Committee. In 1932, the Central Bank's reserves fell to 25 percent. Afterward, gold was revalued to double its value in pesos.

Credit institutions were created and, during the war, gold inflows were sterilized.

In Argentina, the Currency Board was closed in 1929. In April 1931, the fall in economic activity was such that the country had to resort to two laws passed in 1914 to allow the Currency Board, for the first time in the twentieth century, to issue money with no gold backing. As Britain unexpectedly announced its departure from the gold standard and let the pound devalue in September 1931, Argentina attempted to improvise exchange controls in October. A new administration allowed the peso to depreciate in 1932, by applying a contractionary fiscal policy together with an expansionary monetary one. In May, the Currency Board was allowed to issue money backed by public bonds. Thus, for the first time since the Convertibility Act of 1899, the government could obtain financing by issuing money, and for the second time, money issue took place without an increase in reserves. In 1935, the Central Bank was created and granted faculties to stabilize the currency and smooth the economic cycle, for which it was allowed to resort to rediscounts and open market interventions.

In Brazil during 1929, after the first evidences of the crisis, there was an outflow of reserves, and in 1930, convertibility was suspended and devaluation followed. In 1931, Brazil established exchange controls. At the beginning of the 1930s, after being excluded from international capital markets, the government did not resort to the Bank of Brazil for financing. However, from 1937 on, the Bank financed fiscal deficits through money issues (between 1939 and 1945, it provided 2 billion *milreis* to the treasury).

In Colombia, as in other countries, the initial reaction to the crisis consisted of lowering expenditures and contracting the monetary supply. As the crisis deepened, pressure increased for the Bank of the Republic to depart from the gold standard and ease credit to the government. On September 24, 1931, following the British steps, convertibility was abandoned and exchange controls introduced. Despite the lack of reserves, the Bank of the Republic granted credits to the government. One year before, in 1930, the Congress had authorized the Bank of the Republic to take a share of the bonds issued and issue money in exchange. The Bank's legal reserves requirement was lowered from 60 percent to 50 percent of the total circulating notes and demand deposits. Monetary policy became more flexible and had a more active role.[24] The peso was devalued, and in 1933 it was 50 percent under its 1931 level; in 1936, the exchange was 1 dollar = 1.7 peso.

---

[24] Adolfo Meisel Roca, "La segunda misión Kemmerer," in *Banco de la República* (Bogotá, 1990), 343–5.

FROM WORLD WAR II TO THE 1980s

GROWTH WITH INFLATIONARY FINANCING: 1945–1960

The war years had made clearer the changes that had occurred since the 1930 crisis and the long depression. A growing autarky produced a fall in fiscal revenues coming from foreign trade, which had to be compensated with other sources. Fiscal reforms attempted earlier but never completed were now implemented. The changes included taxes on wealth and domestic consumption (sales taxes), aimed at obtaining a more stable source of revenue.

In Argentina, the tax regime had already changed in the 1930s with the establishment of an income tax and the transformation of the excise tax into a sales tax. The Brazilian tax structure did not experience major changes either. The taxes on consumption, income, and imports continually decreased because inflation eroded tariff revenues based on specific duties. In 1953, customs revenues did not exceed 4 percent of overall fiscal income. The situation changed when the 1957 reform established a different tax structure. States started financing themselves through sales taxes.

In Mexico, the tax ratio to GDP was low and the tax system was underdeveloped. With the purpose of increasing tax collection, the Income Tax Law was reformed in 1951, and new taxes (commonly called internal taxes) were levied on the sale of certain products such as beer, cigarettes, spirits, cars, and trucks. Partly because of this, and because of the great increase in foreign trade, tax revenues grew by 25.1 percent between 1949 and 1951, generating a surplus beyond the expenditure increase.[25] In 1948,[26] a tax on commercial income was created (ISIM, *Impuestos Sobre Ingresos Mercantiles*). It was very much criticized because it was a "cascade" tax. It lasted until the end of the 1970s, when it was replaced by a Value Added Tax (VAT). Since the 1920s, there had been three unsuccessful attempts to amend the Constitution with the aim of providing a more solid institutional framework for the Mexican tax system. It was necessary for the states to adhere to the regime, but by 1957, only seventeen of them had joined. The remaining fourteen did not do so until 1971–2.[27]

---

[25] Cárdenas, *La hacienda pública*, 146.
[26] Luis Aboites Aguilar, "Imposición Directa, Combate a la 'Anarquía' y Cambio en la Relación Federación-Estados" (Mexico City, 2001), 48.
[27] Ibid., 18.

During the postwar years, resources not derived from taxation (already in use since the 1930s) became the most relevant source of revenue. They consisted of exchange differentials and the appropriation of bank deposits by means of increases in legal bank reserves or the nationalization of deposits in the financial system.

In Argentina, significant nontax resources were raised through the establishment of a multiple-rate exchange control system. In fact, this became the main source of payments on the external debt. When the gold standard was abandoned in the 1930s and depreciations occurred, export prices in local currency significantly increased, and the government decided it should share in the exporters' extraordinary profits. This could happen as long as local prices (wages) did not increase to catch up with devaluation. When wages finally went up, the exporters' benefits vanished because the peso had become overvalued. The income of thousands of producers was affected. For this reason, producers covertly opposed this tax by diminishing production and, consequently, exports.

In 1946, with Perón in office, fiscal and monetary instruments were put at the disposal of the administration's goals. Public expenditure increased, taking the government's share in the GDP from about 20 percent in 1945 to more than 30 percent in 1955. This was the result of several factors: among them, construction of infrastructure, purchase of companies that became part of the public sector, and a rise in public-sector wages. The financing of foreign trade transactions was done directly through Central Bank rediscounts. Also, there were rediscounts given for credits provided to companies and mortgage loans to help private building construction.[28]

The Brazilian case was different. For a long time, the country enjoyed a de facto monopoly in international coffee markets and was able to transfer the cost of devaluation to foreign consumers.[29] Since 1950, exchange rate manipulation had been the main tool of economic policy. Nontax financing mechanisms appeared (exchange differentials, compulsory deposits, and the inflationary tax). The exchange policy was different with regard to coffee: sometimes a negative differential rate was applied (*agio*), as happened in 1954, when the exchange rate for exports of all products was 28.36 Cr./ US$, and the one applied to coffee exports was 23.36.[30] At other times, coffee

[28] Raúl Prebisch, "Plan 1955," Memoria anual del Banco Central (Buenos Aires, 1955).
[29] Sérgio Besserman Viana, "Duas tentativas de estabilização: 1951–1954," in Marcelo de Paiva Abreu, *A Ordem do Progresso. Cem anos de política econômica republicana 1889–1989* (Río de Janeiro, 1990), 140.
[30] Ibid., 140.

received subsidies, as happened in the second half of 1954, when – in the face of a drop in coffee production because of adverse weather conditions – the government established by decree a minimum price for coffee with the aim of optimizing the exchange profit.

During the Kubitschek administration (1956–60), it was decided to promote economic development through increased government intervention. The *Plan de Metas* aimed at making Brazil advance in five years a distance it would have taken fifty years to cover otherwise. The economy grew, between 1957 and 1961, at 8.2 percent per annum; between 1945 and 1964, public expenditure rose from 14.6 percent to 18.9 percent of GDP. The share of the federal government was about 50 percent, but there was greater decentralization between 1950 and 1960. Until 1953, revenues and expenditures grew at comparable rates, with minor deficits. Between 1955 and 1964, the deficit increased, together with inflation. The investment rate was high, and the state had an active share in it (almost 20% of overall national capital formation). The corresponding expenses were not completely covered by tax revenues, which translated into the need for deficit financing.

In Mexico, the state had always played an important role in the economy, but after the Constitution of 1917 its participation grew. The government fostered the "stabilizing development" program by means of public investment, subsidies, and protection of domestic production. Initially, all these measures had no inflationary effects.[31] Between 1959 and 1967, public expenditure rose to 9.2 percent of GDP, while in the 1950–1958 period, it amounted to 7.4 percent.

The postwar era also witnessed the widespread development of public enterprise. When a high level of investment was required or a sector was considered strategic, Latin American governments assumed direct control over the production of those goods and services. This was done by buying enterprises (nationalization) or by creating new ones. These companies, in many cases, had the highest volume of personnel and sales. They included oil and other mineral extracting companies, public utilities, and companies devoted to direct production of goods such as steel and petrochemicals.

The administration of state-owned companies often escaped strict accounting controls and suffered from a double managerial problem. On the one hand, for the political parties in power, they became "booty" where they could give employment to their people without being subject to budget limitations. On the other hand, as happened with public utilities, tariffs

---

[31] Because they did not resort to money issuing but to deposits from the private sector.

were subsidized in order to maintain real wages (Argentina, Mexico, Brazil, and Chile), contributing to the deficit. To cover these deficits, state-owned companies obtained loans abroad, increasing the overall public debt, or received treasury contributions or loans through rediscounts by the Central Bank, widening the deficit and feeding inflation.

In Brazil, by the mid-1950s, the state started to take control of many basic resources, such as water (through the three most important water plants: CSN, *Cosipa and Usiminas*); oil production and refining (*Petrobras*); iron ore production and exportation (*Companhia Vale do Rio Doce*); and caustic soda production (*Companhia Nacional de Alcalis*). The Brazilian state also increased its share in the production of electricity.[32]

In Chile, the government created CORFO (*Corporación de Fomento de la Producción*) in 1939 and used it to create public utilities such as ENDESA (*Empresa Nacional de Electricidad,* 1944), CAP (*Compañía de Acero del Pacífico,* 1946), ENAP (*Empresa Nacional del Petróleo,* 1950), and IANSA (*Industria Azucarera Nacional,* 1952). Between 1939 and 1973, CORFO played a significant role in the economic life of the country by direct investment and through credit allocation to foster new industries.[33]

In Argentina after 1945, the state's direct participation in the economy also became stronger. Nationalizations focused on public utilities: *Gas del Estado* was created in 1945 and *Empresa Nacional de Telecomunicaciones* (ENTEL) in 1946. During the years 1947–50, state investment concentrated in public transportation: mainly trains, ships, and planes.[34]

Policy goals in this period were different from those of the previous period. On the one hand, state intervention aimed at sustaining economic development by promoting domestic industry. On the other hand, governments attempted to improve income distribution by means of transfers, more marked in the case of Chile and Argentina than in Brazil and Mexico, with programs ending up in persistent inflation. Precisely for this reason, in Argentina and Chile – where social pressure was stronger – growth stagnated in the 1950s, much earlier than in Brazil and Mexico.

The state understood that, wherever natural resources or idle private savings existed, it had the power to mobilize them. Then it could provide economic rents for those sectors it wanted to promote and, by sharing

---

[32] Luiz Orenstein et al., "Democracia com Desenvolvimento: 1956–1961" in Marcelo de Paiva Abreu, *A Ordem do Progresso, Cem anos de política econômica republicana 1889–1989* (Río de Janeiro, 1990), 182.

[33] Patricio Meller, *Un Siglo de Economía Política Chilena: 1890–1990* (Santiago, 1996).

[34] Marie-Ange Véganzonès and Carlos Winograd, *Argentina en el Siglo XX: Crónica de un Crecimiento Anunciado* (Paris, 1997), 164.

those rents, also help them through externalities (infrastructure) or subsidies. The assumption was that capital formation would result from the reinvestment of these extraordinary profits (economic rents), allowing sustained economic development. However, these goals were not attained because those who received the rents did not reinvest them, especially in countries where such privileges were thought not to last long (because of the growing and sustained struggle over income distribution caused by the government-induced changes in relative prices).

Difficulties in obtaining financing and large fiscal deficits led to repeated crises, followed by devaluations and reforms aimed at balancing fiscal accounts and the external sector and at stabilizing currencies. By the end of the 1950s and the early 1960s (toward the end of the 1960s in Mexico), it was no longer possible to obtain financing from the appropriation of savings by means of monetary and exchange mechanisms, which now had serious inflationary consequences. Appropriation of the natural resources' rents through controls with multiple exchange rates also led to crises in the balance of payments, which interrupted growth, and depreciations, which contributed to a marked monetary instability. In turn, all this led to the implementation of reforms aimed at recovering fiscal and monetary balance, as well as an improvement in the external accounts.

In Argentina, imbalances had a strong impact on the foreign sector, where a first payment crisis occurred in 1949, to be followed by a more serious one in 1951–2, complicated by the weather conditions that produced two crop failures. The government was forced to implement a stabilization plan.

Until 1964, the Brazilian government was able to collect the inflation tax, keeping inflation over 20 percent in the second half of the 1950s. Serious fiscal imbalances led to a second episode of high inflation at the beginning of the 1960s. High inflation caused a demonetization of the economy – that is, a drop in the actual amount of money, both monetary base and deposits. In 1945, the monetary base was more than 20 percent of the GDP, but had fallen to 10.5 percent in 1964.

In 1958, under President Kubitschek, a Plan of Monetary Stabilization was implemented as an answer to inflationary pressures in the foreign and public sectors. The reforms failed to replace the tax structure based on foreign trade that had existed up to the 1930s. It proved impossible to come to an agreement on a new tax regime and the resulting imbalances were large.

Although state intervention in the industrialization and growth process was not abandoned, it became necessary to find other sources of capital formation. This meant opening the economies to capital inflows and, consequently, to foreign trade. To do this, the Latin American governments had to achieve a modicum of fiscal and monetary stability, a goal that remained unfulfilled for two more decades.

Powerful vested interests had developed that were reluctant to embrace changes that implied a loss of the privileges they had acquired through changes in relative prices, protection, and subsidies. Simultaneously, a social transformation had taken place that resulted in huge urban concentrations (in Mexico City, Rio de Janeiro, São Paulo, and Buenos Aires, the population was more than 10 million), implying greater political participation and popular pressure on governments, a phenomenon unknown to prewar Latin America. The new tax structure had to be adapted in the middle of extremely complex conditions. For this reason, during the 1960s and 1970s, ambition was limited to reducing the imbalances and to handling expenditures more carefully with the aim of avoiding an excessive closing of the economy.

To the powers of the Central Bank to preserve monetary stability, the 1946 reform in Argentina added other objectives such as to expand the economy and to maintain employment. It also decreed that private banks' deposits should be nationalized and that these banks should operate from then on as agents of the Central Bank. The latter was to remunerate private banks for the deposits it received from them; it would in turn grant rediscounts so that banks could give credits and would collect interest from them. The Central Bank recycled private savings to favored banks – mainly official ones – with the peculiarity that it lent this money at nominal rates below inflation, which meant an assignment of income from creditors to debtors. Rediscounts surpassed deposits systematically, turning themselves into a significant money creation, and feeding the inflation of those years. Rediscounts, which surpassed deposits by 17 percent in 1947, exceeded them by 70 percent in 1956.[35]

In Brazil, throughout the whole period (1945–60), money emission was huge. A nonconvertible paper-money system ruled, and the *Banco do Brasil* enjoyed the issuing monopoly. The local currency devalued by 9,700 percent. Prices rose 7,000 percent in this fifteen-year period (in contrast to 80% in the United States).[36] At first, under an exchange control regime and with a significant gap between the official and the black-market exchange rates,

---

[35] Aldo Arnaudo, *Cincuenta Años de Política Financiera Argentina* (Buenos Aires, 1987), 56.
[36] Goldsmith, *Desenvolvimento Financiero*, 250.

the government maintained an overvalued currency, affecting imports and the balance of payments. The money supply increased by 26 percent per year between 1946 and 1964, although at a varying pace. During the first half of the period (1946–56), it grew at a yearly 16 percent; in the second half, at 49 percent; and in the last three years, at 75 percent. The increase was mainly caused by a rise in the monetary base. This was lower at first, but grew enormously during the 1960s.

In Mexico, the economy underwent a monetization process after the end of the revolutionary period. Money supply was boosted after 1925, when the Bank of Mexico was created, and again from 1932, when wages started to be paid in paper money. Checks against bank deposits became a more usual means of payment. The budgetary balance, reached after the 1954 devaluation, limited the internal causes of monetary expansion until 1959, with deficits below 1 percent of the GDP.[37] The reserves' fluctuations were the most significant factor in money creation, followed by credits to the private sector.

The economy became more and more monetized. The stock market did not play a significant role and most of the transactions were related to government bonds. The share of floating interest bonds was low, at least until 1960. Between 1955 and 1960, the Bank of Mexico reduced its bond holdings, as a way to contract the money supply, whereas private banks and individuals increased theirs.[38] The Bank of Mexico resorted to the legal reserves' mechanism in order to route credit and to compel other institutions to finance the fiscal deficit through the purchase of public bonds. During this period, financing institutions appeared and gradually came under the Bank of Mexico's regulations. Private credit also began to flourish. During the 1950s, financing institutions grew more than deposit and savings banks (which had had their golden age during the 1940s), because they could offer more profitable and liquid instruments, which became popular among savers. Moreover, these institutions were less affected by the limitations imposed by the Bank of Mexico on the use of funds than most private credit institutions.

After 1954, a sharp devaluation in exchange rate stability (1 dollar = 12.5 pesos) contributed to a significant capital inflow that came to finance the private sector, relieving the state from such tasks. Mexico also had an

---

[37] Cárdenas, *La hacienda pública.*
[38] Dwight Brothers and Leopoldo Solís, *Evolución Financiera de México* (Mexico City, 1967), 60–5 and 90–2.

important source of reserves derived from transactions in the U.S. border area, and from tourism.

In Mexico, the main public credit institution was the *Nacional Financiera*, which managed (and guaranteed) international loans and a great number of funds and special trusts for different sectors.[39] Most resources from the national credit institutions were devoted to financing industrial and agricultural activities, although loans granted to small companies, foreign trade, construction, and public utilities were also significant. The *Banco Nacional de Crédito Ejidal*, the *Banco Nacional de Crédito Agrícola*, and the *Banco Nacional Agropecuario* were aimed at the agricultural sector, which received special support.[40]

In Brazil, the *Superintendencia de Moneda y Crédito* (SUMOC) was created in 1945 and added to two monetary agencies: the *Carteira de Redescuento* (CARED) and the *Caixa de Mobilização Bancaria* (CAMOB), already existing in the *Banco do Brasil*. The new agency, linked to the Secretary of Finance, was created to implement monetary policy and check inflation. It was granted powers to establish the requirements for opening new banks and set legal banking reserves. CAMOB assisted commercial banks by granting liquidity. It did so by discounting the short- and medium-term bonds banks had in their portfolios. CARED assisted them in the short run, contributing to increased means of payment and speeding up inflation.[41]

GROWTH AND STABILIZATION EFFORTS: 1960–1980

As deficits, imbalances, and crises accumulated, even the least inclined Latin American governments were forced to adopt measures to restore balance: reduction of expenditures (mainly investments) and credit restriction. These measures had recessive consequences and forced changes in relative prices, which raised strong opposition. Mexico, with its long period of "stabilizing development," was a different case, because it avoided the inflation that destabilized other countries.

Confrontations over who had to pay for industrialization and a more equal income distribution were stronger in those countries where social development was more advanced and industrializing processes had culminated in huge urban concentrations. Distributive conflicts leading to the

[39] Ibid., 41–2.
[40] Antonio Ortiz Mena, "El desarrollo estabilizador: Reflexiones sobre una época," E.T.E Nro°146, (México City, 1970), 431.
[41] Peláez and Suzigan, *História Monetaria*, 238.

outbreak of a war of attrition between opposing sectors – similar to the one Europe had gone through in the 1920s – developed during the Cold War. Rulers with populist tendencies became suspect as potential allies of those that threatened the stability of the hemispheric coalition headed by the United States. That led, in different moments, to military interventions (in Brazil in 1964 and Argentina in 1966), very often marked by the need to adopt adjustment measures backed by some sectors and resisted by others, creating deeply conflictive situations that were arbitrated by the military in Argentina, Brazil, Chile, Peru, Bolivia, and Uruguay, among others.

In Brazil, several anti-inflation stabilization programs were adopted in the decade after 1953, but none worked for more than a short time.[42] In the early 1960s, problems caused by growth based on financing through inflationary taxes led to a severe crisis in the balance of payments. In 1964, a unilateral default on foreign liabilities was declared. The economic situation was worsened by a political crisis and by the confrontation between the left and the right, all in the middle of the tense Cold War climate that had reached the South American continent. To avoid the victory of the left and reorganize an increasingly chaotic economy, in March 1964, the military seized power. The new regime, headed by General Humberto de Alencar Castello Branco, set out to fight inflation and reach balance of payments equilibrium, considered necessary conditions for sustained growth. Inflation was deemed to be the result of demand pressures caused by the fiscal deficit, the huge private sector debt, and excessive wage rises (public sector included). It was decided to contain expenditure, curb private sector credit, and reduce wages. The International Monetary Fund (IMF) suggested a shock strategy, but Finance Minister Roberto Campos chose a more gradual approach that reached some of the same goals by reforming the inefficient tax system, centralizing and increasing the federal share, and avoiding the erosion imposed by inflation on tax collection. To that effect, a 1964 law applied a monetary correction factor to taxes. This, together with a better organized tax collection, allowed an increase in revenues of 3.4 percent at all levels of government, from 15.2 percent of GDP in 1964 to 18.6 percent in 1966.[43] The budget deficit fell because of both a decrease in expenditure, which went from 12.4 percent of GDP in 1964 to 11.2 percent in 1967, and the reduction of public sector wages.

---

[42] Thomas Skidmore, *The Politics of Military Rule in Brazil 1964–85* (New York, 1988), 33.
[43] Goldsmith, *Desenvolvimento Financiero*, 486.

Nonetheless, during its first years, the military regime's efforts to contain expenditure were unsuccessful. The budget was finally balanced, but this was misleading, because the public sector now included not only the government but also a large number of public enterprises, and an important quasifiscal cost generated by the Central Bank.[44] The deficit did fall from more than 4 percent of GDP in 1963 to approximately 1 percent in 1966. Even so, the government, which had seen its liabilities eroded by inflation (which beyond a certain level substantially reduced the inflation tax), had to resort to another instrument: indexed debt issues. At first, this widened the debt market (because it eliminated the fear of capital loss through inflation) but, unlike the inflation tax, it imposed a heavy interest burden at constant prices. Thus, the deficit was no longer financed by money emission but by selling debt securities.[45]

In Brazil, in 1967, a new customs system was established with a big tariff reduction, though industries continued to be highly protected.[46] Monetary correction clauses were applied to public debt issues, with which the government tried to replace inflationary financing. From 1964 on, national treasury liabilities, or ORTN (National Treasury Adjustable Bonds), were issued with indexation clauses and became the basis of government financing in this period.

From 1967 on, with a healthier fiscal situation, fiscal incentives in Brazil were introduced as a part of the government's industrial policy, with an emphasis on exports. In 1973, subsidies represented 21 percent of the effectively collected income.[47] These policies would have consequences for the fiscal deficit and public debt.[48] Indexation mechanisms reduced the inflation tax collected by the public sector (or by the finance system on deposits at sight). The inflation tax, representing more than 4 percent of GDP in the first part of the 1960s, went down to 1 percent and 2 percent.[49] The total financial transfers went down from levels higher than 7 percent of GDP to around 3 percent.

---

[44] Goldsmith, *Desenvolvimento Financiero*, 483

[45] André Lara Resende, "Establização e Reforma: 1964–67," in *A Ordem do Progresso*, 218.

[46] Luiz Correa do Lago, "A retomada do crescimento e as distorcoes do milagre: 1967–1973," in *A Ordem do Progresso*, 274

[47] Ibid., 264.

[48] Dionisio Dias Carneiro, "Crise e Esperanca: 1974–1980," in *A Ordem do Progresso*, 313.

[49] Marcelo de Paiva Abreu and Dorte Verner, *Long-Term Brazilian Economic Growth, 1930–94* (Paris, 1997), 113.

In Argentina, the most populist period came to an end with the 1952 crisis that forced adjustments to balance the external sector. The limits to expansion with inflationary financing were visible by the mid-1950s, but it was President Frondizi, in 1959, who took a decisive turn. His government intensified industrialization, extending it to capital and intermediate goods – this time not with the compulsory capture of savings but by appealing to private foreign capital. The government saw the possibility of mobilizing investment provided it offered to the largely foreign private sector the exploitation of natural resources and captive markets for a demand that in some items (e.g., motor vehicles) had been repressed for years. The government was conscious that it had to tackle the imbalances, aggravated after it came to office in 1958. Therefore, a tough adjustment program agreed to with the IMF was adopted at the end of that year. The program implied a reduction in expenditure by cutting salaries of public employees and a decrease in the railways' operating deficit by closing branches. It also implied eliminating subsidies, reducing the money supply, contracting credit, and keeping a stable exchange rate (abandoning controls and allowing free convertibility). These measures caused harsh political and social resistance during 1959 and a severe recession that preceded strong growth in 1961 and 1962, when the exchange was kept fixed at eighty-two pesos per U.S. dollar.

In Mexico, "growth with stability" had not solved the problems generated by population expansion and the need to give employment to the increasing number of persons who were entering the labor market. Industrial development goals had promoted rapid urban population growth that created infrastructure, transportation, and housing problems. In addition, wider communication and, consequently, greater participation and rising social demands added to the potential for conflicts, which erupted in 1968.

The Echeverría administration (1970–6) inherited a difficult situation with an overvalued currency resulting from keeping the exchange rate fixed at 12.5 pesos per dollar from 1954, in spite of the differential evolution of domestic prices compared with international ones. The current account deficit widened 3.4 times between 1958 and the mid-1970s, going from US$385 million to US$1,318 million, on account of large public projects and the incapacity of industries to finance their own expansion. In 1971, the government instituted restrictive monetary and fiscal policies. Then, faced with the need to reverse the effects of contractionary policies, it sought to continue with economic expansion by placing more emphasis on social expenditure and a better income distribution to popular sectors.

However, in view of the persistence of imbalances, that decision ended up aggravating the problems it intended to solve. The state took yet a more active stance in the economy, as the public sector's total expenses rose from 17 percent to around 26 percent of GDP between 1970 and 1976. Expenditures went from almost 15 percent to 21 percent of GDP; private investment was stagnant; and public investment went from 7 percent to 9.7 percent of the GDP. Social expenditure rose from 4.3 percent to 7 percent of the GDP. Expenditure was oriented mainly to financing urban sectors, water, large transportation and housing programs, and the development of agriculture, which practically tripled its share of government support during the period, going from 0.9 percent to 2.6 percent of the GDP.

Tax collection did not match expenditure increases. The federal government's tax revenues went from 7 percent to 9.5 percent of GDP. Although the income tax was the main source of public resources, its contribution was unchanged. The state-owned companies' contribution to the federal government's tax revenues declined from 24.6 percent to 19.1 percent. Tax collection on consumption and production went from 12.6 percent to an overall 20.8 percent. The price policy adopted by state enterprises, consisting of subsidizing popular consumption, was one of the great deficit generators. The deficit went from 3 percent to 8.2 percent of GDP, financed by money creation and domestic debt. The foreign debt was increased nominally by 300 percent during the six years of Echeverría's presidency (equivalent to 20% of the GDP).[50]

Already in 1975, the situation appeared untenable in terms of public finances, the external deficit, and exchange rate overvaluation. Fiscal problems accelerated in 1975 because of massive capital flights and were fueled by the government–business confrontation that ended with the devaluation of the peso. In 1976, in the middle of a fiscal and payments crisis, the government called upon the IMF for assistance and applied adjustment measures to control the fiscal deficit. The new administration of President José López Portillo, which took office in December, reduced expenditures and contracted the monetary supply, reformed the tax system, and created the VAT, although the latter was implemented only in 1980. At first, VAT had a 10 percent rate and 6 percent for border zones. Some goods and services were exempted. With time, this tax would become the second in importance, although the income tax continued to be first. A

---

[50] Marcos Chávez, "Las Finanzas Públicas de México, 1970–2000. Crónica del Fracaso de la Política Fiscal," Programa de Ciencia, Tecnología y Desarrollo (Procientec), (México City, 2001).

National System of Fiscal Coordination was established, which attempted to introduce greater efficiency in fiscal administration.

What passed largely unnoticed in the 1960s and 1970s, and in the end frustrated most policy makers, was that generating the necessary macroeconomic balances to attract private investment and a state with huge expenditures in subsidies and an overextended bureaucracy were difficult to reconcile. In most cases, efforts to restore macroeconomic equilibrium were meant not to affect the industrializing process but to deepen it, making it more efficient by strengthening import substitution in both intermediate and capital goods (in Brazil, 1964–80; in Argentina, 1967–9; and in Mexico, 1972–80) and extending it to exports (a field in which Brazil was more successful). Fixed exchange rates acted as an anchor for monetary stability and a requirement for capital inflows, the assets of which in local currencies were thus protected from local currency depreciation. On the other hand, fixed exchange rates produced serious problems of currency appreciation (Dutch disease) or overvaluation when domestic prices rose faster than international ones.

Government expenditure began to be financed by debt in the 1960s. The external debt had almost disappeared during the isolation of the 1930s depression and the War World II years. Because financing instruments had been reestablished with international public agencies, the Latin American countries tried to secure loans for big public works (dams, roads, energy in Brazil) and, to a lesser extent, private enterprises (aluminum and steel in Argentina), which required state endorsement. When private companies failed to pay their private debts, government guarantees turned them into national debt.

In Mexico there was an important change in the sources of external financing from multilateral organizations to private banks. Interest rates were variable. Between 1974 and 1976, the foreign debt practically doubled and went largely to finance deficits and maintain the fixed exchange rate, which caused a huge capital flight.[51]

Neither the Mexican federal government nor the public enterprises could create enough savings to finance their investments. As a result, they depended increasingly on debt, both domestic and foreign. By 1975, nearly all investment was debt-financed. External debt increased significantly from 1973 to 1976. Even though the flow of credits from abroad dropped in 1977–9

[51] Carlos Bazdresch and Santiago Levy, "Populism and Economic Policy in México 1970–1982," in Rudiger Dornbusch and Sebastian Edwards, eds., *The Macroeconomics of Populism in Latin America* (Chicago, 1991), 246.

as a share of GDP, the high level of investment, especially that of PEMEX (*Petróleos Mexicanos*) and the federal government, required even greater reliance on external debt than in the early 1970s. To finance the mounting fiscal deficits, the government resorted more and more to foreign borrowing. The external debt of the public sector increased, from US$4 billion in 1970 to US$19.6 billion in 1976 and US$33.1 billion in 1979.[52]

In Brazil, as debt payments became a larger item in public expenditure, the government decided to take them out of the treasury register and make the Central Bank pay them directly with money creation. In 1973, the fiscal accounts had a slight surplus. However, a substantial part of expenditure was not included in the budget, as happened with subsidized interest rates and public-debt monetary corrections, which were part of the so-called monetary budget.[53] From 1967, subsidized credit policies were implemented, which included credits for consumption, agriculture, exporting sectors, and housing, in some cases accompanied by fiscal exemptions.[54] Indexation and subsidized credits (to agriculture and export producers) determined the existence of different exchange rates.[55]

The increasing vulnerability resulting from an ever-growing debt was further complicated by two factors: the 1973 oil price shock and the change in U.S. monetary policies. In 1973, oil prices went up three times because of an Organization of Petroleum Exporting Countries (OPEC) cartel agreement. Brazil had developed an integration strategy for its huge territory, choosing road-building as the least expensive one, its domestic trade becoming deeply dependent on automobile transportation. Because 80 percent of its oil supply was imported, the price shock affected imports, and the government was forced to reduce the least critical ones, reducing growth in important consuming sectors.

In 1972, Brazil entered the international capital markets. At first it placed securities in Germany and deposits in the United States, thus reaching a previously nonaccessible market where there was a plentiful eurodollar supply because of capital outflows from the United States caused by large deficits and rising inflation.[56] Brazil decided to keep its high level of growth (the 1975–1979 National Development Plan aimed at a 10 percent annual growth) and financed imports by debt. Substantial expenditure

---

[52] Jorge Hierro and Allen Sanginés, "Public Sector Behavior in Mexico," in Felipe Larraín and Marcelo Selowsky, eds., *The Public Sector and the Latin American Crisis* (San Francisco, 1991), 157.
[53] Ibid., 265.
[54] Ibid., 237.
[55] Ibid., 256.
[56] Ibid., 278.

went to investment in *Petrobrás*, to the construction of the Itaipú dam, and to subsidizing production of fuel from alcohol. By 1974, the Brazilian debt had jumped from 6.2 percent to 11.9 percent of GDP. Foreign debt was mainly medium and short term, and it was mostly placed in commercial banks, especially after 1973. By this time, the debt represented a substantial accumulation that became Brazil's main problem for the next decade. Interest rates were not only higher than those applied by multilateral agencies, but also fluctuating, which would also have a negative bearing on the future. Inflation, after going down until 1973, went up again to more than 20 percent.

In Argentina, during the first part of the period, the government financed the deficit mainly with domestic debt (1960–4). Subsequently, note issues became the main tool to finance excess expenditures and only from 1976 on did the external debt start to play a very important role in closing the gap between revenues and expenditures. In the 1976–86 period, gross foreign debt rose to 80 percent of the GDP. In fact, these ten years can be divided into a first period (1976–82), during which the foreign debt increased US$35 billion, and a second one (1982–6), during which it was difficult to obtain new funds, and the increase of US$12 billion was mainly explained by the refinancing of the interest payment.[57]

The alternative was to resort to the domestic capital market. Previously, governments had imposed forced savings by increasing bank reserves, by nationalizing deposits, and by inflation. In the 1990s, instead, they issued bonds for the public to purchase, but because the obligations sold through the banking system paid interest rates lower than the inflation rate, to make them attractive to buyers, they had to be protected from inflation by means of indexation. This opened up a new and important source of financing for the state, but it had an explosive effect for the future because of its huge accumulation. Governments had been used to eroding their liabilities through inflation and devaluation. From this time on, that would not happen.

Regarding monetary policy in Brazil, the most important event was the foundation of the Central Bank in 1964. Up to that moment, Brazil lacked a bank with money control and money-issuing powers. Previously, monetary-policy control powers were assigned to the SUMOC, founded in 1945, whereas the Bank of Brazil acted both as a bank of issue and a commercial bank, having rediscount authorization through the CARED (Rediscount Portfolio) (1945) and the CAMOB (1931). Roberto Campos had designed an independent Central Bank but in spite of that, in 1967, after a strong confrontation with the government, the bank lost its autonomy. In spite of the fact that the 1964 stabilization program was not completely successful, it allowed institutional changes that had a bearing on the economic results of the 1960s. It reduced the fiscal deficit, reordered the tax system, restructured the financial system (Central Bank, Mortgage National Bank), and introduced indexation mechanisms, unifying and simplifying the foreign exchange system.

For Finance Minister Delfim Netto, cost pressures, not demand ones, determined inflation (during the Castelo Branco administration, Roberto Campos had assumed that inflation was caused by demand-pull factors). Consequently, he adopted an expansionary monetary policy, substantially increasing credit. Expenditure grew directly because of subsidies given by the federal government and indirectly through money creation by the Central Bank. Expenditure was also influenced by the enlarged government entrepreneurial activity (several new state enterprises were created), especially when the treasury had to finance its losses.

Between 1964 and 1973, money supply fluctuated between 15 percent and 18 percent of GDP, though circulation velocity remained stable; after 1973, the relationship went down to 12 percent and in 1980 it represented 8.3 percent. This was the result of the effect of inflationary acceleration and indexation mechanisms on financial assets (other than currency), causing economic demonetization.

In Argentina, after 1976, the Central Bank, which had been financing the treasury, began to spend directly by creating money to subsidize foreign currency purchases and foreign reserves, but above all, in the 1980s, by remunerating bank deposits in the Central Bank (*encajes*). When the government had more limited access to financing, it raised bank reserves and remained with a substantial part of commercial banking deposits, which were remunerated. This was called quasifiscal expenditure and was a significant source of deficit. Until 1974, changes in the Central Bank reserves practically compensated rediscounts and subsidies granted. Consequently, the Central Bank's quasifiscal expense was almost insignificant. In 1974, on the contrary, the fall in reserves reflected a negative quasifiscal expenditure equivalent to almost 4 percent of GDP. The fall in currency reserves continued in 1975, resulting in a quasifiscal expenditure of 3.4 percent of GDP. In 1976, there was a substantial change, to positive quasifiscal expenses of about 2.25 percent of GDP as a result of the 180-day swap granted in 1975, so as to induce private capital inflow. The subsidy for currency futures sales, at preferential prices, was about 5 percent of GDP.[58]

In Mexico, during the stabilizing development period, the main source of financing for the deficit had come from the banking system through high reserve requirements. Because the financial markets were still underdeveloped, the government did not float any bonds. The Central Bank lent funds acquired from the banks to the Treasury. From 1970 to 1976, total credit from the Central Bank to the public sector grew 12 percent a year on average in real terms. Because external borrowing was restricted, internal debt with the Central Bank was adjusted in keeping with the government's budget constraint.

After 1973, inflation occurred and expectations of devaluation appeared, causing capital outflows. To secure additional funds for the government, the Bank of Mexico increased the reserve ratio, from 34.8 percent in 1971 to 51.1 percent in 1976. Even this measure proved insufficient to meet the needs of the public sector. The response was to boost the currency issue at an annual real rate of growth of 11 percent. The increase in the monetary base more than matched the fall in the money multiplier. For this reason, the average annual rate of growth of M1 in nominal terms was almost 20 percent. This expansion fueled inflation and increased the balance of payments problem that culminated in the 1976 devaluation.

In contrast, total credit to the public sector from the Central Bank grew at a moderate pace from 1977 to 1979. With the fiscal deficit still within reasonable proportions and the wide availability of foreign credit, the authorities were able to control the expansion of domestic credit and the monetary aggregates.[59]

In 1981, there was a sharp reduction in oil prices, fiscal revenues shrank, and the fiscal deficit soared to 13 percent of GDP. As a consequence of public finance imbalance, the debt reached 58 percent of GDP and debt payments were more than 30 percent of total expenditures. Economic growth was a negative 1 percent and there was a huge outflow of capital. After a currency depreciation of 479 percent, the state nationalized the banks and transformed dollar deposits into peso deposits. In August 1982, the state defaulted on the foreign debt and began making the efforts needed to balance the situation.

---

[58] Schenone, "Public Sector Behavior in Argentina," 21–2.
[59] Hierro and Sanginés, "Public Sector Behavior in Mexico," 159.

CONCLUSIONS

The period of the formation of nation-states coincided with the constitution of a tax state, where national finances were modernized, jurisdictions established, and tax revenues more efficiently managed. The nature of taxes changed. In the past, they had mainly consisted of monopoly contributions and taxes on domestic trade or the indigenous population. From then on, the tax system centered on foreign trade. The unification of nation-states was financed by customs duties, which increased substantially as exports expanded. In those countries whose exports enjoyed a dominant position in the market, export taxes – a way in which government participated in natural resources' rents – were the main source of their income (mainly Brazilian coffee and Chilean copper). That was not the case with other exports, where taxes would have negatively affected a huge number of producers; there, taxes were mainly levied on imported consumer goods. As a rule, the increase in tax collections made it possible to put an end to civil wars and to consolidate the nation-state, which, during most of the nineteenth century, survived precariously within a framework of poverty and war. Although military expenditures declined, those destined to pay off earlier debts increased. In spite of this constraint, governments became more accountable and public works were built, making the export boom possible.

In colonial times, only silver coins were used as a means of payment, to which convertible bank notes, treasury notes, or government inconvertible paper money were added. For long periods, notes had a forced circulation. In several countries, private or mixed banks of issue were founded, acting as government financing agents. By the early twentieth century, there were several efforts to adopt the gold standard with a pure Currency Board system or some variation of it.

The sharp drop in imports during World War I led to a general crisis. However, the hardest constraints were imposed by the long-lasting depression of the 1930s, with its catastrophic reduction in international trade and capital flows. That meant important institutional changes. Up to this point, most governments had relied on taxes that were easy to collect, such as mineral royalties or import taxes collected at ports. The latter were generally transferred to prices (and, therefore, not felt as a government exaction, especially if of moderate weight). To replace this system, new taxes on profits, income, or wealth were adopted, raising stronger opposition. Latin American governments tried several reforms, but none was successful in raising sufficient revenues to cover the vastly expanded list of government social and economic responsibilities. From then on, and until the end of the century, various fiscal reforms were attempted, all of which proved unsuitable as foundations for the Leviathan state created in the 1930s.

Prompted by the sharp reduction in revenues from foreign trade, governments sought new revenue sources of easy collection. On the one hand, governments sought to increase their share of rents from the export of natural resources. On the other hand, departing from the gold standard entailed substantial devaluations, which represented excess profits for exporters who were earning in foreign currency and spending in local depreciated currency. Resorting to exchange controls, Brazil and Argentina established multiple exchange rates and collected an exchange differential, which represented for certain periods of time a share in the revenue they had created with the devaluations.

During the 1920s and 1930s, central banks were founded throughout Latin America. Formerly, governments had used banks of issue to place short- or long-term debt, but in the new world order, where international capital markets had disappeared, central banks monopolized money issue and were under government control, becoming the main source of financing. In some cases, financing was obtained by appropriating private savings, through a rise in bank reserves (Mexico), which were remunerated. In others, financing was directly obtained by issuing money (Argentina, Chile, and Brazil), though this had an inflationary impact. Although, at first, this mechanism was used to solve problems created by the depression through raising revenues, providing liquidity to banking systems, and financing public works, in the following decades, it would be deliberately used to foster industrial growth.

In the postwar period, the new methods of state finance pioneered in the 1930s were improved and deepened by several Latin American governments to implement their new industrial policies. At the same time, big social changes took place, such as rural migrations, urbanization, increased number of industrial workers, and unionization. Those social changes meant new demands and pressures to develop new activities. Nonetheless, the Latin American governments were unable to adopt substantial reforms that might have provided sufficient taxes. Instead, governments preferred to finance their activities through the appropriation of the natural resources' rents (whenever prices were favorable) or taxes on labor (social security system contributions and inflation). Rent generation was supposed to encourage investment and provide income to be reinvested, promoting growth and a more equitable income distribution. However, the results of these mechanisms were different than expected: inflation, fall in exports, crisis in the balance of payments that limited the development process, and a worsening of income distribution.

The scheme of growth and equity with inflationary financing had already showed its weaknesses in the 1950s. The following decades were spent in the search for more reliable sources of revenue. A more favorable international framework, where international trade recovered and limitations to capital movement were gradually dropped, made it possible to obtain capital abroad and, for certain key sectors such as infrastructure and transportation, direct investments were made. Without abandoning the state's dominant role in the process, investment was encouraged via exchange incentives or captive markets.

However, more was required for external capital to flow in sufficient quantities. It was necessary to ensure macroeconomic stability in order to guarantee the currency in which profits would be made and the availability of remittances. This posed an extremely difficult task. Procedures used in the postwar era had created remarkable imbalances in the currency, public finance, and the foreign sector. Coming back to balance implied tough adjustments, with expenditure and credit reduction, which affected those sectors that had grown under the protectionist scheme (and had eroded their debts and subsidized their capital formation). Numerous stabilization programs were attempted, with varied results. Most created recessions, generating extremely strong opposition, which made those programs fail, unleashing new devaluations and inflationary processes. In some cases, reforms showed some positive results in the long run because a more ordered state came out of them (Argentina and Brazil during the 1960s), and a more modern economy. Attracting foreign capital required guaranteeing that no capital losses would result from inflation. This implied that debt should be issued with monetary correction indexes or floating interest rates. Within the new international financial context, this widened the debt market but implied a heavy burden for the future. The situation became more difficult because the foreign debt had been taken at low interest rates, something that changed when the United States raised rates to unprecedented levels at the end of the 1970s. This made debts more burdensome and called into question the region's capacity to pay. Massive capital flight took place, leading to new devaluations and inflation.

7

EXPORT-LED INDUSTRIALIZATION

RICHARD SALVUCCI

INTRODUCTION

The title of this chapter requires, perhaps, some explanation. Accounts of trade and production in Latin America between 1870 and 1930 typically focus on the development of export economies; describe commodity cycles, their causes, and consequences; and attend, to a lesser degree, to the beginnings or acceleration of industrialization. Although I accept this scheme and, to an extent, follow it, the rationale for this chapter is different. For one thing, accounts of the commodity cycle are numerous, and the best ones can scarcely be bettered. For another, the emphasis on export economies, although by no means incorrect, is nevertheless somewhat misleading. Industrialization in Argentina, Brazil, Chile, Colombia, Mexico, and Peru was not independent of international trade, much less opposed to it, but complementary to, consistent with, or even consequent upon the expansion of the external sector. Even the advent of the railroad in Latin America, once understood primarily as a means of facilitating the production of exportable goods, is now known to have had a powerful impact on the domestic market in some places, such as Argentina, and was less associated with international trade in others, such as Mexico, than commonly supposed. Marco Palacios (the reader may consult the bibliographical essay for the literature mentioned in the text) has questioned the validity of the export-led model of growth in Colombia. Export-led growth did not begin in the 1870s but rather commenced in the twentieth century: only a small share of Colombian agricultural output – perhaps 10 percent – was exported. And although there were places, like Cuba, in which a conventional model in which a large part of infrastructure and industrial value added was the result of the spread of sugarcane, the welfare consequences of this development seem more debatable than they once were.

In this sense, the decline of the dependency model, so influential and fruitful to a previous generation of scholars, has proved liberating. It is not simply a matter of new findings but, more important, of new questions and novel explanations. The finding that open economies following comparative advantage enjoyed high and, indeed, sometimes surprising levels of domestic income comes as no surprise to students of conventional theories of economic development. But by implication, such studies locate poor domestic economic performance squarely in the configuration of domestic policies, politics, and institutions. They must shift the research program of scholars to aspects of constitutional and political organization; public finance and financial architecture; the definition and assignment of property rights; and even to education, all of which are more promising explanations for "underdevelopment" than the simple distributional consequences of international trade. And the literature on economic "convergence," broadly defined as the tendency of low-income economies to grow more quickly than their high-income counterparts, necessarily raises interesting but disturbing questions for Latin America. Why did the successful economies, such as Argentina, Cuba, and perhaps Chile, poised for integration into the world's upper-income ranks, "diverge" or fizzle out after promising beginnings? Was it luck, poor policies, changes in the world economy, or "weak foundations"? The intellectual framework of export economies does not easily accommodate all of these issues, many of quite recent vintage.

The final reason for departing from the framework of export economies is heuristic. In recent years, international economic historians have demonstrated intense interest in the workings of the gold standard. Although much of the research is driven by new techniques of time-series analysis or concerned with drawing policy lessons about currency regimes, its implications for Latin America are intriguing. Older studies of the gold standard in Argentina and Chile have now been updated, and there is new work on Brazil and Mexico as well. The attraction of these studies lies in their intellectual coherence, for they provide a systematic study of the difficulties inherent in maintaining a balance between domestic and external performance under fixed exchange rates. At the same time, for those economies that went to gold later, the silver standard was profoundly affected by international economic trends that altered the rough equilibrium that prevailed between gold and silver in the post-Napoleonic world. Concretely, the rapid and deep depreciation of silver against gold after 1872 that persisted into the middle 1890s effectively placed Mexico, Peru, and Central America on continuing exchange devaluation, a development that affected export performance and the strength of the export-oriented elites. Moreover, in the face of unstable or persistently deteriorating terms of trade, fixing the exchange rate in terms of gold had consequences, such as substantial swings in output, that have been insufficiently understood. So, this approach makes for a somewhat different account of a field that has changed dramatically in the past thirty years.

A BRIEF OVERVIEW OF TRENDS IN PRODUCTION AND TRADE

First, a few figures. According to the British statistician, Michael Mulhall (1829–1900), in his *The Progress of the World*, "the states of South America are little more than half a century old, and yet they have made considerable progress, especially in the last twenty years."[1] Argentina, where he resided for some time, was an especial example of material advance, but Brazil and Chile, too, Mulhall observed, "[have] left the others far behind." In his *History of Prices Since the Year 1850*, he argued that Argentine wealth per head, £130, exceeded the European average (£123) given the low levels of southern Europe and Russia.[2] Even Mexico (£90 per head) had attained the levels of Spain and Portugal, although it lagged far behind that of the neighboring United States (£190). If anything, tiny Uruguay (£152) was still more impressive. The point of citing Mulhall is not to argue that his figures were strictly accurate, even if modern research supports his conclusions about the relative affluence of Argentina. Instead, it was the dynamic of growth in the mid to late Victorian era that impressed him. At the aggregate level, at least, there were places that shared in the "progress" of the Victorian boom of which Mulhall was an avatar.

Still, the devil is in the details, and the details of growth and trade are not easy to come by. Later, we assemble a number of statistics, some more reliable than others, to document the pace and pattern of growth for many countries over a long period. Here, coverage is somewhat limited, but

---

[1] Michael Mulhall, *The Progress of the World* (Shannon, Ireland, 1971; orig. publ. London, 1880), 471.
[2] Michael Mulhall, *History of Prices Since the Year 1850* (London, 1885), 112.

uses ostensibly homogeneous and comparable data to provide a frame of reference. The two sources I employ, André A. Hofman, *The Economic Development of Latin America in the Twentieth Century*, and Angus Maddison, *The World Economy: A Millennial Perspective*, have common roots at the University of Groningen and share both methodology and sources.[3] Inevitably, data on population and production in Latin America before 1870 are apt to induce a good deal of skepticism. Maddison's reliance on the work of Angel Rosenblat for population data is particularly problematic for the specialist. But this has nothing to do with the period *after* 1870, where we can proceed with more confidence.

As to Mulhall's claim that rapid economic progress dated from the 1860s, it is impossible to demonstrate, at least to judge from Hofman and Maddison. The earliest data for which we have standardized estimates are for 1870. Tables 7.1 and 7.2 provide estimates of the average annual compound growth of merchandise exports and real gross domestic product (GDP) for some seven countries. The median growth rate of merchandise exports in 1870–1913 was 3.4 percent in this, the Augustan age of the "export economies." But, perhaps surprisingly, the median rate in 1913–29 is even higher, 3.8 percent, which suggests (imperfectly, to be sure) that it is possible to exaggerate the long-run consequences of World War I. Argentina, Mexico, and Venezuela all experienced lower rates in 1913–29 than previously, and in Argentina, the decline was grievous, some 2.5 percentage points per year. But Mexico surely reflects the impact of the revolution that lasted from 1910 through 1920 as well as the precipitous decline in oil production and export in the 1920s. Surprisingly, the substitution of Venezuelan for Mexican production that occurred at this point (Venezuela succeeded Mexico as the world's largest exporter because of discoveries in the Maracaibo basin) did not arrest the fall in the rate of Venezuelan export growth, which was 0.3 percentage points per year higher in 1870–1913 than in 1913–29. Whereas Brazilian export growth remained steady at 1.9 percent in 1870–1929, and Brazil came to be the largest coffee producer in the world, Chile, Colombia, and Peru all experienced increases in exports in 1913–29, ranging from the merely noticeable to absolutely staggering. In Chile, the increase reflected the substitution of copper for nitrates after the war and substantial exchange depreciation as well, although the Great Depression brought the growth of the 1920s to a decisive end. Peru's exports

[3] André A. Hofman, *The Economic Development of Latin America in the Twentieth Century* (Cheltenham, UK, 2000); Angus Maddison, *The World Economy: A Millennial Perspective* (Paris, 2001).

Table 7.1. *Merchandise export growth average annual compound rate (1990 prices)*

	1870–1913	1913–1929
Argentina	5.2	2.7
Brazil	1.9	1.9
Chile	3.4	3.9
Colombia	2.0	6.8
Mexico	5.4	2.7
Peru	1.7	6.2
Venezuela	4.1	3.8
Median	3.4	3.8

Sources: André Hofman, *The Economic Development of Latin America in the 20th Century* (Cheltenham, UK, 2000), 23; and Angus Maddison, *The World Economy: A Millienial Perspective* (Paris, 2001), 361. Hofman draws on an earlier publication of Maddison's, *Monitoring the World Economy, 1820–1992* (Paris, 1995) for 1870–1913, p. 236. The base year, 1990, is consistent throughout.

were driven by a sharp change in their composition away from sugar and cotton toward more rapidly growing petroleum, particularly in the 1920s. In Colombia, the expansion was led by coffee, the exports of which doubled in volume in the 1920s, according to José Antonio Ocampo and María Mercedes Botero.

Table 7.2. *Real GDP average annual compound growth (1980 international dollars)*

	1870–1913	1913–1929	1900–1931
Argentina	6.02	3.5	6.4
Brazil	2.38	4.7	4.5
Chile		2.9	3.7
Colombia		4.7	4.2
Mexico	3.38	0.8	2.6
Venezuela	2.8	8.2	3.3

Source: Hofman, *The Economic Development of Latin America in the 20th Century*, pp. 30 and 167.

As to the geographical composition of trade, Victor Bulmer-Thomas has put the matter well, writing that "Britain and Latin America appeared to be made for each other in the nineteenth century." Britain, of course, supplied manufactured goods such as cottons in which it had strong comparative advantage, and Britain could finance its exports as well. Latin America, for its part, met a growing demand for food and raw materials in Great Britain. But by World War I, Britain had been overtaken as a trade partner by the United States in most countries, although Argentina remained a crucial British market down to the 1930s.

Finding comparable growth rates of GDP in 1870–1930 is not easy. Drawing on Maddison's data, which are expressed in terms of 1990 international dollars, for 1870–1913, Argentina, the fastest grower, registered an average annual compound rate of 6 percent. Mexico was slower, but still substantial, at 3.4 percent. Venezuela managed a quite respectable 2.8 percent. Brazil was the laggard at about 2.4 percent.

Comparing this same group from World War I through the Great Depression is instructive. The substantial reduction in Argentine exports paralleled a sharp decline in output growth of 2.5 percentage points per year, or about 40 percent, confirming that World War I was a caesura in the country's economic history. The war's effect on other "export economies" was by no means uniform. Brazilian output increased even as exports stagnated. Venezuelan output rose by 5.4 percentage points, which is to say, nearly doubled, even as the rate of export growth declined. Growth in Mexico collapsed, of course, but distinguishing between the international costs of World War I and the loss in output exacted by civil war and revolution in Mexico is not straightforward. By the outbreak of World War I, a strict correspondence between movements in exports and total output no longer held, another reason for regarding facile characterizations of the "age of the export economies" with a grain of salt.

THE GOLD STANDARD AND THE LATIN AMERICAN PERIPHERY

This is not the place for an exhaustive treatment of the history, theory, or practice of the gold standard and its variants. The reader may consult the bibliographical essay for a representative selection of items that do so. Here, perhaps, all that is needed is a basic sketch.

Basically, the gold standard was a monetary regime in which the value of the home currency was defined in terms of gold. What this meant, in effect, was that the value of the currency was defined not only in terms of domestic circulation but also in terms of foreign currencies fixed to gold. Because the price of gold was broadly stable, a prerequisite for defining any currency in terms of a commodity, this meant, in essence, that countries "on the gold standard" were linked by a system of fixed exchange rates. Crucially, because the home currency was defined in gold, one could imagine it circulating beyond a country's frontiers and within the boundaries of other countries linked to gold, which was, indeed, sometimes the case. In the simplest model, fluctuations in a country's international position, which, by assumption, are limited to merchandise trade alone, would produce variations in the domestic money supply: namely, an export surplus gained money; an import surplus lost it. Because the domestic price level depended in part on the supply of money, and because prices are inversely related to scarcity, a rise in the domestic money supply (reduced scarcity) raised prices; a fall in the money supply (increased scarcity) reduced them, assuming an unchanged demand for money in either case. Again, in the simplest case, famously associated with the Scottish philosopher David Hume (1711–76), export and import surpluses would be self-correcting because the rise or fall of domestic prices would reduce or improve the competitiveness of home goods relative to substitutes produced abroad. Thus, an export surplus would induce an inflow of cheaper substitutes produced abroad, whereas an import surplus would lower prices and spur exports. For this reason, the Humean model of the gold standard was said to be self-regulating or self-adjusting, although it is important to realize that the export- and import-competing sectors would experience real variations in their production. Thus, even under the simplest account of the gold standard, domestic economic performance and a country's international position are inextricably linked.

The system becomes somewhat more complicated when borrowing and long-term lending between countries takes place because the balance of payments must now reflect capital as well as merchandise movements. The adjustment to disturbances in the balance of trade may change as well. Strictly speaking, it would be difficult to find any international financial historian who would agree that the gold standard operated in the simple Humean way or by following what have been traditionally called "the rules of the game." From the standpoint of the major European powers that participated in the gold standard, namely Great Britain, France, and Germany, and from that of the United States as well, the operational details of the gold standard, not to mention its much vaunted "automatic" adjustment process, have been largely relegated to the status of one of the foundation myths of international financial history.

But if the view from the center has gradually moved to a somewhat less orthodox consensus on how the gold standard (or, increasingly after 1880, the gold exchange standard, in which currencies convertible into gold could also be held as reserves) worked, the view from the periphery has always been a skeptical one. Perhaps Alec Ford presented the most eloquent and influential criticism of the operation of the gold standard in Latin America in his book, *The Gold Standard 1880–1914. Britain and Argentina.*[4] Fundamentally, Ford argued that the automatic and smooth adjustment of macroeconomies under the gold standard was, if not wholly illusory, more properly attributed to its operation in and impact on Great Britain. Moreover, for a peripheral economy engaged in exporting primary commodities, the operation of the gold standard amplified booms and busts rather than mitigating them, so that domestic adjustment to international imbalances was anything but smooth. In other words, the gold standard operated procyclically in the periphery.

For example, Ford argued that a country whose growth was driven by exports of primary commodities would experience large inflows of specie under the gold standard. Thus, growth would be accompanied by a monetary expansion, rather than by the automatic tightening the Humean mechanism contemplated. For Ford, such tightening was more likely to occur in countries in which growth followed an autonomous increase in domestic investment to which no monetary accommodation necessarily occurred – in other words, in Great Britain rather than in Argentina. Moreover, Ford believed that the Bank of England could stem an outflow of gold by raising interest rates, the so-called Bank Rate. Countries with primitive financial systems and no central bank could do no such thing, which meant that Latin America under the gold standard lacked a policy instrument available to the center countries and was thus unable to moderate the effects of a gold outflow consequent on a trade deficit. Further, because countries like Argentina (the argument has been made for Colombia by William McGreevey as well) did not produce substitutes for the goods they imported from Great Britain (capital goods), their demand for imports

[4] Alec Ford, *The Gold Standard 1880–1914. Britain and Argentina* (London, 1962).

would tend to be relatively inelastic. As a result, trade deficits would persist unless home demand fell dramatically. So the adjustment process in Latin America would be subject to busts, or deep recessions – an awkward accompaniment to the monetarily induced booms that occurred during expansions. The system, in Ford's view, was far from stabilizing in Latin America and, in fact, could be viewed as inherently destabilizing or, in the jargon, "procyclical."

As if all this were not enough, several other unpleasant facts about the gold standard in Latin America followed. Because export-oriented elites in Argentina (and the argument has been made for Brazil and Chile as well) were paid in gold, they had a natural bias in favor of currency depreciation. Where domestic monetary systems included a paper component that fluctuated in terms of gold, export elites naturally favored depreciation, for their export receipts could then purchase more domestic goods, or non-tradables, such as land. In the event of an appreciation, or increase in value of the currency, elites were likely to favor suspension of gold convertibility: abandoning the gold standard, in other words.

Another unpleasant fact was that commodity and capital shocks in Latin America would tend to go hand-in-hand. What Ford termed the "cushion" available to Great Britain of attracting capital when gold flowed out was not likely to be available to Latin America because lenders would be highly unlikely to advance funds to countries whose primary source of repayment, receipts from commodity exports, had fallen.

A third unpleasant fact for Latin America was the very instability of commodity prices relative to the price of manufactures. This is not so much an example of the "declining terms of trade" thesis as it is the simple recognition that agricultural prices will inevitably be more variable than the price of industrial goods because of the inherently greater instability of supply. This meant, in essence, that export receipts would tend to be more variable than a country's import bill, particularly given the structure of international trade in the nineteenth century, when Latin America exchanged a variety of commodities for wage goods such as cotton cloth or for capital goods as domestic industrialization there got underway.

These unpleasant facts about the gold standard meant that countries in the periphery would not necessarily find the operation of the gold standard beneficial, and that even if they did, their ability to adhere to the gold standard in the long run would be highly doubtful. And, in fact, the record of Latin America in this period is one of spotty, imperfect, and variable adherence to the gold standard, an interesting commentary on the instability of

Table 7.3. *Latin America and the gold standard, 1870–1930*

Argentina		
	1876–1881	inconvertible paper standard
	1881–1885	gold standard
	1885–1903	inconvertible paper standard
	1903–1914	gold standard
	1914–1927	inconvertible paper standard
	1927–1929	gold standard
Bolivia		
	1825–1914	silver standard
	1914–1928	inconvertible paper standard
	1928–1931	gold exchange standard
Brazil		
	1822–1906	inconvertible paper standard
	1906–1914	gold standard
	1914–1927	inconvertible paper standard
	1927–1930	gold standard
Chile		
	1875–1895	inconvertible paper standard
	1895–1898	gold standard
	1898–1926	inconvertible paper standard
	1926–1932	gold exchange standard
Colombia		
	1871–1885	gold standard
	1885–1903	inconvertible paper standard
	1903–1914	gold standard
	1914–1923	mixed standard
	1923–1931	gold exchange standard
Costa Rica		
	1871–1900	bimetallic standard
	1900–1914	gold standard
	1914–1924	inconvertible paper standard
	1924–1932	gold exchange standard
Ecuador		
	1875–1884	inconvertible paper standard
	1884–1900	bimetallic standard
	1900–1914	gold standard
	1914–1926	inconvertible paper standard
	1926–1932	gold exchange standard
El Salvador		
	1883–1892	bimetallic standard
	1892–1894	gold standard
	1894–1914	silver standard
	1914–1919	inconvertible paper standard
	1919–1931	gold exchange standard

Table 7.3. *(cont.)*

Guatemala		
	1870–1897	bimetallic standard
	1897–1925	inconvertible paper standard
	1925–1933	gold exchange standard
Honduras		
	1879–1931	silver standard
	1931–1934	gold exchange standard
Mexico		
	1867–1905	silver standard
	1905–1913	gold exchange standard
	1913–1925	mixed standard
	1925–1931	gold exchange standard
Paraguay		
	1885–1923	Inconvertible paper standard
	1923–1932	Argentine peso standard
Peru		
	1875–1898	inconvertible paper standard
	1898–1914	gold standard
	1914–1930	inconvertible paper standard
Uruguay		
	1865–1914	gold standard
	1914–1931	inconvertible paper standard
Venezuela		
	1879–1931	gold standard

Notes and Sources: The institutional arrangements and monetary regimes under which Latin American operated between 1870 and 1930 are fraught with confusion. Few authors provide precisely the same chronology and detail. The authoritative attempt to sort these matters out is of David George Cowen, "A World of Difference: Exchange Rate Regime Choice and Economic Performance in the Interwar Years" (Ph.D. dissertation, The University of Texas at Austin, 1995), Appendix 3.

monetary regimes during the period. The definitions and dating of being "on the gold standard" vary widely, but Table 7.3 provides some details of the adherence of Latin America to the gold standard.

On the whole, then, it suggests that adherence to the gold standard in Latin America between 1870 and 1930 was difficult, and that the advantages of maintaining some form of gold convertibility may have been illusory. In fact, Albert Fishlow has suggested that the merits of remaining on a floating exchange rate there were substantial, and that these advantages, rather than the preference of export elites for currency depreciation – not a consideration that should be underestimated – explain why Latin America under the gold standard might as fairly be termed Latin America "on and off" the gold standard. For, if nothing, else, as Keynes pointed out, the system of fixed exchange rates efficiently transmitted economic crises between countries, a dubious benefit for peripheral economies rendered more, rather than less, stable by the monetary regime.

The principal implication of this discussion is the difficulty of consistent long-term growth from peripheral countries under the gold standard. If, in fact, macroeconomic stability were not a strong point of the system, the ability of the Latin American economies to provide adequate levels of income and satisfactory rates of growth would be quite questionable. As Victor Bulmer-Thomas has pointed out, the main reason why income levels there in the twentieth century are well behind those of the developed countries in general, not to mention the Organization for Economic Cooperation and Development (OECD) members (Mexico excluded, of course), is because consistent, long-term performance is virtually impossible to find. Volatility, in other words, is as much a cause as a consequence of "underdevelopment," and it is difficult to see how the currency regime described by Alec Ford and others could have done anything other than amplify domestic volatility, the intrinsic variability of commodity prices aside. In this regard, as we shall see, the growth experienced by Colombia, Mexico, and Peru, and by Central America on silver through the mid-1890s, may well suggest merit to the continuing depreciation of the exchange rate that the international fall in silver prices brought after 1872.

Recent studies of Brazil and Chile have amplified, augmented, and extended these findings. Brazil, for instance, was able to adopt the gold standard when ample capital imports allowed it to do so, but remaining there proved difficult. The domestic fluctuations in macroeconomic activity described by Ford occurred with an appreciating exchange rate (which raised opposition from coffee exporters); rising imports; a deteriorating balance of payments; and, inevitably, pressure to suspend convertibility altogether. The gold standard brought price rather than macroeconomic stability to Brazil, historians of its operation have concluded. Chile was able to remain on the gold standard only for brief periods of time (1870–8, 1895–8), buffeted as it was by large fluctuations in copper and nitrate exports. Moreover, wages and prices in Chile proved highly inflexible, which made the country an unlikely candidate for a fixed exchange rate, given that a decline in external demand required deflation, which was difficult to achieve. Chile benefited from a floating exchange rate between

1880 and 1894, so avoiding financial panics and balance of payment crises.

In light of this discussion, it is important to notice that opposition to the gold standard has not been unanimous and that there has been particularly eloquent dissent from Argentine economic historians, whose acquaintance with the gold standard, macroeconomic performance, and price stability has found such recent echo under the "convertibility" system introduced by Carlos Menem in 1991 to put an end to hyperinflation, and abandoned under excruciating deflationary pressures in the beginning of 2002. One of the principal criticisms of Ford, offered by Roberto Cortés Conde, is twofold. First, Cortés Conde argues that Ford's statistical evidence was based to some degree on John Williams's classic study, *Argentine International Trade Under Inconvertible Paper Money,*[5] the calculations of the trade balance and capital flows in which Cortés Conde judged seriously deficient, and, therefore, likely to exaggerate the degree of adjustment (driven by changes in the money supply) to unfavorable imbalances demanded under a fixed exchange rate. Yet, perhaps more important, Cortés Conde argued that the benefits of proceeding under the gold standard, and, particularly, under the monetary discipline that strict convertibility imposed, more than outweighed the costs of lost output. In a country with weak financial institutions or a political environment prone to inflationary finance, Cortés Conde suggests, it is the benefit of a flexible exchange rate (such as that offered by depreciating silver) that is questionable, for which Cortés Conde offered the experience of Argentina with price inflation before 1870, or at the time of the Baring Crisis (1890), as an object lesson.

Gerardo della Paolera and Alan Taylor have made a similar criticism, trenchant and sophisticated, in their study of the Currency Board in Argentina. It is important to understand that part of the novelty of the argument made by della Paolera and Taylor is that it relies on the monetary approach to the balance of payments to make its case. The monetary approach to the balance of payments regards all adjustment, both in the short and in the long run, as a monetary phenomenon, because people are free to trade financial assets across countries. So a change in the wealth of a country's citizens leads them to buy or sell financial assets rather than goods internationally, and money moves between countries immediately rather than as a result of changes in the balance of trade. By implication, then, the large

[5] John H. Williams, *Argentine International Trade Under Inconvertible Paper Money, 1880–1900* (Cambridge, MA, 1920).

fluctuations emphasized by Ford in his study play little or no role in this model of balance of payments adjustment under the gold standard. In fact, della Paolera and Taylor argue that macroeconomic performance under the gold standard in Argentina was especially good, with average annual real growth of 5.8 percent and annual inflation of 2.6 percent between 1899 and 1914. They nevertheless, however, suggest that the system was extremely vulnerable to external shocks that came with World War I and the collapse of the gold standard, and to a weak financial system that could not maintain the fixed exchange rate when international pressures intervened.

The strongest arguments made in favor of silver or, in effect, against the gold standard, have been advanced by Rosemary Thorp and Geoffrey Bertram in their work on Peru, with concurrence from Alfonso Quiroz. It is important to understand that the price of silver in terms of gold fell dramatically after 1872, from roughly \$1.32 (measured in United States gold coin of an ounce, 1,000 fine, taken at an average price in London) to \$0.59 in 1898, or a fall of more than 55 percent. This amounted to a very substantial devaluation for those countries on silver, and its importance is recognized by Thorpe and Bertram as a cause of the growth of Peruvian exports. Conversely, the devaluation of silver raised the price of import-competing goods, such as textiles, which provided a distinct impetus to import substitution. By the same token, Thorp and Bertram attribute something of the slowdown in Peruvian growth to Peru's move to the gold standard after 1897, which was explicitly opposed by agro-exporters, miners, and business interests associated with them but supported by financial interests concerned with the preservation of their capital. However, even in this case, Quiroz has observed that exchange volatility created uncertainty, and that uncertainty, in turn, was transmitted to the real economy.

One can make similar arguments for Colombia, Central America, and Mexico. Héctor Pérez-Brignoli notices that a rapid upswing in exports from the region, where all five countries remained on silver into the twentieth century, ended in 1897, followed thereafter by relative stagnation. The available statistical evidence, crude to be sure, is consistent with the hypothesis that the depreciation of the exchange rate stimulated exports, although the rate of export growth in Costa Rica appears to have been significantly higher than elsewhere. Colombia was effectively on the silver standard from 1850 through 1885. Because of intervening political difficulties and monetary complexities, the evidence relating depreciation to export growth is not unambiguous, but the volume of exports in Colombia (measured in terms of gold pesos) doubled between the mid-1870s and the late 1890s, a rate of growth of about 3 percent per year.

A similar upswing in Mexico is evident after 1877 as well, although the explanation for the export boom there must go beyond the depreciation of the exchange rate alone. The effects of the depreciation of silver in Mexico were particularly complex because of the country's status as a major international producer and exporter of the metal. Falling silver prices meant a major deterioration in the barter terms of trade for exports of silver, approximately half of all Mexican exports. But for other commodities priced in gold, domestic receipts in silver increased. At the same time, service on the foreign debt, which had been frequently suspended from 1827 through 1887, rose because of the depreciation of the peso, placing further pressure on the Díaz government, which was deeply concerned with access to foreign capital markets. The issue in Mexico was, therefore, politically divisive, and the move to the gold standard came in 1905 only after considerable debate both within and outside the government. Ironically, this carefully managed transition was to be overturned in the general upheaval that accompanied the outbreak of the Mexican Revolution in 1910, when convertibility was suspended.

By and large, then, the great bulk of the scholarly literature sustains the skepticism that Alec Ford brought to the operation of the gold standard in Latin America down to World War I. Historians of Argentina, influenced by a history of inflation under inconvertible currency, have been the greatest dissenters, arguing in favor of the stabilizing effects of the gold standard on prices and production. But a significant body of work contends otherwise, not only in Latin America but elsewhere. In the European periphery, in Italy and Spain, stability was more a function of prudent fiscal management and a healthy balance of payments than it was the result of maintaining a fixed exchange rate and a domestic money supply linked rigidly, even mechanically, to gold.

After World War I, there was a general return to gold in Latin America, although resumption of convertibility was generally delayed until well into the 1920s, as it was in Brazil (1926), Argentina (1927), or Mexico (1927). Of the countries for which we have adequate studies, only one, Argentina, resumed convertibility at the prewar parity. When the Great Depression hit, Argentina and Brazil abandoned the gold standard first, followed by Mexico. All would undergo significant exchange-rate depreciation after 1930, and by 1933, their currencies had fallen to between 30 and 60 percent of their gold parities in 1929. As Carlos Díaz Alejandro, Jeffrey Sachs, and Barry Eichengreen have all emphasized, those countries that abandoned gold most quickly avoided deflation and were able to recover from the Great Depression expeditiously.

What conclusion can we draw from a review of the literature on monetary regimes in Latin America in this period? The basic lesson, it seems, is that there were no easy choices, let alone "good" choices to be had, at least in terms of their macroeconomic implications. As for the gold standard, Michael Bordo and Barry Eichengreen have concluded that it was "intrinsically fragile, prone to confidence problems, and a transmission belt for policy mistakes."[6]

SOURCES, RATES, AND PATTERNS OF ECONOMIC GROWTH

In the long run, economic growth depends on increasing aggregate supply. In the short run, variations in growth are largely the result of changes in aggregate demand. Aggregate supply, in turn, depends on the availability of productive factors, labor and capital broadly defined, and the efficiency with which those factors are used – which is to say, on technology, the evolution of which is commonly measured by the change in what is termed total factor productivity. Aggregate demand, in the short run, is affected by a variety of real and monetary factors, including disturbances in the money supply, changes in the terms of trade and the outlook of consumers and investors, and political factors, all of which can be conventionally measured by the components of aggregate demand.

For our purposes, the developments that had the greatest impact on aggregate supply were innovations in domestic transportation and immigration. Innovations in domestic transportation of particular interest were railways, whose impact on potential output were substantial in Argentina, Brazil, and Mexico, but somewhat less so in Colombia. Immigration matters because of the expansion of the labor force it implied because natural rates of population increase were low. Although it is true that innovations in ocean transportation and transportation technology ultimately made export expansion possible, their impact on Latin America has been less well studied. There are also a few subtle points about the role of immigration in economic growth that must be considered.

John Coatsworth, Sandra Kuntz, Colin Lewis, Rory Miller, Paolo Riguzzi, and William Summerhill have done the principal work on the

[6] Barry Eichengreen and Michael Bordo, "The Rise and Fall of a Barbarous Relic: The Role of Gold in the International Monetary System," in Guillermo H. Calvo, Rudiger Dornbusch, and Maurice Obstfeld, eds., *Money, Capital Mobility, and Trade: Essays in Honor of Robert A. Mundell* (Cambridge, MA, 2001), 85.

impact of railroads on the Latin American economies in the nineteenth century. Coatsworth and Summerhill concluded that the "social savings" generated by railroads carrying freight and passengers in Argentina, Mexico, and Brazil was substantial, although, inevitably, issues of measurement pose some challenge. A recent study embodying estimates of social savings now exists for Colombia as well, although its findings are at a variance with those of Coatsworth and Summerhill. There has also been some discussion of the importance of railroad development in Bolivia, Chile, Cuba, Central America, and Peru, although the evidence is less systematic. The idea behind "social savings" is closely related to that of opportunity cost, the difference between what resources are earning relative to their next best use. Hence, the social savings produced by railroads (or any other transportation innovation that economizes on resources) are a measure of the value of resources freed up from employment in less productive means of conveyance of people or freight. For our purposes, they are a measure of the increase in a society's potential output or income.

Viewed from this perspective, it is difficult to imagine another innovation whose potential impact on economic growth was greater. The costs of overland transportation under colonial conditions were notoriously high and, in the early nineteenth century, were frequently elevated by military activities that drew heavily on the supply of draft animals. So it was that the repeated political upheavals experienced after independence magnified the importance of innovations that reduced the physical costs of domestic trade.

Although the impact of railroads on transportation costs is crucial, there are other dimensions to the issue as well. The effect of the railroads on supply was greatest where they formed an integrated network, as they did in Argentina, Chile, and Mexico, even if, as in Mexico, not all sections of the country were equally well served. Maps 7.1, 7.2, and 7.3 show the density of the railroad systems of these three countries. Moreover, it is clear that the effectiveness of railroad development was not independent of state activity. Like the gold standard, railroads were a token of modernity and a symbol of progress and, therefore, highly attractive to the politicians of the countries in which they operated. Policies designed to integrate markets and promote regional development had a substantial effect on economic growth, and when lines ran through populated areas, as they sometimes did in Mexico, careful government negotiation with popular interests could be crucial to ensuring successful operation and profitable results. Theresa van Hoy has analyzed this theme with particular care in her study of railroad development in southern Mexico, where she speaks of "authoritarian policies" but "democratic implementations."

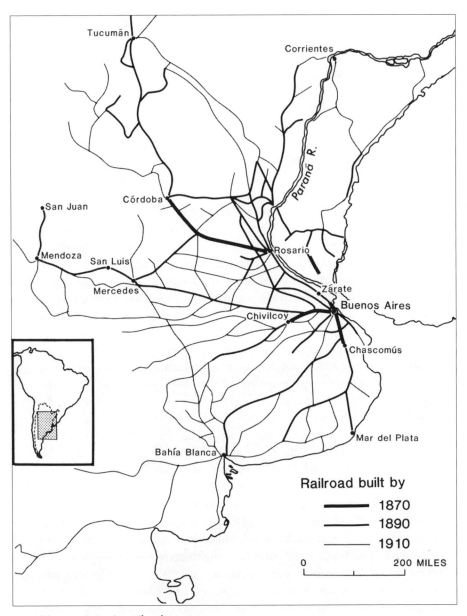

Map 7.1. Argentine railroads, 1910.
Source: David Rock, *Argentina, 1516–1987: From Spanish Colonization to Alfonsín,* revised and expanded ed., (Berkeley, 1987), 170.

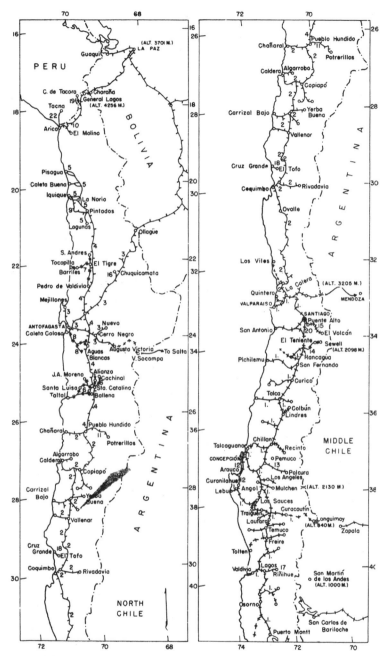

Map 7.2. Chilean railroads, 1942.
Source: U.S. Department of Commerce, Board of Economic Warfare, Geography Division, "Railways of Chile" (Washington, DC: August 31, 1942).

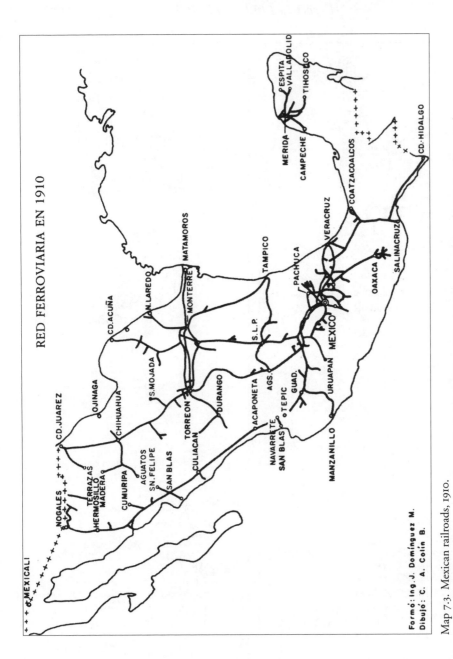

RED FERROVIARIA EN 1910

Formó: Ing. J. Domínguez M.
Dibujó: C. A. Colín B.

Map 7.3. Mexican railroads, 1910.
Source: Sergio Ortiz Hernán, *Los ferrocarriles de México: Una visión social y económica* (2 vols., Mexico City, 1987). 245.

Railroad development in Latin America began early in Cuba, in 1837, but it was not, generally speaking, until the latter half of the nineteenth century, and more specifically, until the 1880s and 1890s, that major expansions in Argentina, Brazil, and Mexico got underway. Railroad construction began in Colombia in the 1870s and 1880s as well, but because of political turmoil and war (1899–1902), many of the roads built were confiscated or destroyed. For this and other reasons, the railroad boom in Colombia was delayed until well into the 1920s. In general, the period between 1870 and 1930 witnessed the greatest expansion of the rail network in the history of Latin America and much less was constructed thereafter. In 1870, there were roughly 4,000 kilometers of railroads in Latin America. By 1930, the total had reached 117,000 kilometers. In a broad sense, activity in four countries – Argentina, Brazil, Mexico, and Chile – led the way.

The estimated contributions to potential GDP, the social savings generated by the railroads, were, by and large, substantial, except in Colombia. These estimates, provided by Coatsworth, Ramírez, and Summerhill, are consistent in that all, other than Colombia, are large by virtually any standard of measurement. For example, Summerhill calculates that the direct social savings from railroads in Argentina, based on freight carriage, were somewhere between 12 and 26 percent of Argentine GDP in 1913, a figure that sounds surprisingly large in view of Argentina's largely tractable terrain. But an ample share of Argentine output was transported, which, in turn, implied that the contribution of railroads would be significant. So, for instance, by 1890, 84 percent of all wheat and 53 percent of all corn produced in Argentina was transported by rail. Even as early as 1892, at a time when the Argentina *belle époque* was just beginning, the railroads produced a social saving of between 6 and 10 percent of GDP, which is still very substantial. Perhaps more important, Summerhill's analysis implies that much of Argentina's overall productivity growth can be explained by the expansion of the rail network, suggesting that economies of scale, a more efficient allocation of resources, and even changes in crop mix as the acreage devoted to linseed, oats, and barley came to rival that sowed in corn, if not in wheat (which, in its turn, had revolutionized exports), were all associated with an increasing density of rail transport. Moreover, an astonishing increase in commercialization occurred in Argentina under the stimulus of railroad extension. In the late 1880s, for instance, approximately two million acres in Argentina were sown in wheat, much of which was exported. By 1930, the figure had risen to twenty-one million acres. In Argentina, Summerhill concludes, the contribution of the railroads to productive potential was as great as immigration's.

Table 7.4. *Some railroad freight social savings estimates*

Country (Author)	Year	Social savings (percent GDP)
Argentina (Summerhill)	1913	12–26
Colombia (Ramírez)	1927	2.25–4.11
Mexico (Coatsworth)	1910	14.9–16.6
Mexico (Summerhill)	1910	8–17

Sources: After María Teresa Ramírez, "Los ferrocarriles y su impacto sobre la economía colombiana," *Revista de Historia Económica* 19, 1 (2001); William Summerhill, "Transport Improvements and Economic Growth in Brazil and Mexico," in Stephen Haber, ed., *How Latin America Fell Behind: Essays on the Economic Histories of Brazil and Mexico (1800–1914)* (Stanford, CA, 1997), 93–117; and "Profit and Productivity on Argentine Railroads, 1857–1913" (unpublished).

The results that Coatsworth, Summerhill, Kuntz, and Riguzzi have produced for Mexico are broadly consistent with the evidence on Argentina. In terms of sheer size, Coatsworth's estimate of the social savings for Mexican railroad was on the order of Summerhill's for Argentina, but Summerhill has reduced the Mexican figure somewhat to account for differences in the assumed responsiveness of demand for freight transport to changes in relative prices. Summerhill's figure for Mexico in 1910 (for freight) is between 8 and 17 percent of GDP – again, a very large number. Because railroad building in Mexico got off to a very late start, some twenty years later than in Argentina, this effectively means that its stimulative impact was largest at the very end of the nineteenth century. Although there is no question that railroad development was linked to the expansion of exports (especially in Bolivia, Cuba, Peru, and Central America) and, hence, to a multiplier effect in terms of total output, there is also considerable evidence that their impact on purely domestic output was large as well. Sandra Kuntz has shown that items such as coal, coke, construction materials, firewood, and maize formed a large, and sometimes overwhelming, proportion of the physical volumes carried by Mexican rail lines at the end of the nineteenth century.

The implications of this change were several. On the one hand, opening the coalfields of northern Mexico to exploitation and transportation facilitated the beginnings of heavy industry, if not precisely of a capital-goods sector linked directly to the railway. On the other hand, the impact on domestic agricultural productivity, historically quite low, was vital. A careful study by Simon Miller of the regional economy of Querétaro shows that the arrival of the railroads there in 1882 opened new markets to hitherto purely local production; augmented land values; and provided a spur to mechanization – withal a development perceived in the region as nearly revolutionary and associated with commercial and financial modernization *tout court*. More evidence for this was the increasing presence of corn from the United States in Mexican markets, some five million bushels between 1883 and 1885 alone. These developments were literally unprecedented and lend substance to the social savings for Mexico calculated by Coatsworth and Summerhill. Nor are these results limited to Mexico alone. In his account of railroad building in the Peruvian central highlands, Rory Miller finds that railroad construction drove down transportation costs 20 to 30 percent between 1890 and 1930, exercising a major impact on the location and productivity of copper mining.

There are, finally, results for Brazilian railroads calculated by Summerhill and augmented by Nathaniel Leff. For Brazil, the putative impact of railroads on both domestic and exportable production was not unlike what occurred in Argentina and Mexico. In Brazil, too, railroads came late, the large upswing in their growth occurring first in the 1890s. As in Mexico, railroads had a dramatic impact on the transportation of domestic goods, with Leff estimating that, even on Brazil's "coffee railroads," the share of noncoffee freight carried on the eve of the outbreak of World War I ranged anywhere from 60 to more than 80 percent by volume. In Brazil, too, this development was at least in part by design because the structure of railroad rates discriminated in favor of the domestic agricultural sector (foodstuffs, livestock, and timber), which was now linked more efficiently to urban markets. In some areas, such as the northeast, Leff estimates that transportation costs fell by 50 percent, with a consequent impact on relative prices. At the same time, the "coffee lines" experienced annual increases in coffee shipments on the order of 7 percent per year, which implies a doubling of shipments in a decade. For this reason, then, Leff argues that Brazil was now launched on a path of long-term economic development. Scholars agree that even though the Brazilian railroad network was concentrated mostly along the coast and in the southeast (there was effectively little or no development in the interior), it brought a larger degree of internal integration to the economy than was hitherto prevalent.

Summerhill's social savings calculations are a piece of this argument, ranging from 6 to 11 percent of GDP in 1913 on freight, and a surprisingly large 4 percent for passenger service (versus, say, something on the order of 1.5 percent for Mexico). Summerhill's conclusions, although cautious, point to an obvious fact. In Latin America, railroads mattered for growth and, in some places, they mattered a great deal. That this finding emerges should perhaps not surprise, for the tradition of structuralist economic thinking so long current in the region has always emphasized sluggish adjustments in supply as a primary obstacle to economic development, and public, as opposed to private enterprise as its agent. These putatively large returns to railroad construction in the presence of insecure property rights, political upheavals, and undeveloped capital markets go some way to explaining why railroads as, so to speak, engines of economic growth, went nowhere for many years: the divergence between private and social rates of return was simply too great. Domestic investors, capital-constrained, and, perhaps, alert to the true risks of investing, were unable or unwilling to seize the opportunities offered. Foreign investors, inevitably cautious, regarded some of these markets with great trepidation. For most of the nineteenth century, or at least after default in 1827, the risk premium on Mexican bonds was rarely less than 10 percentage points above the yield on British consols, and when the yield on Mexican bonds did converge to the consol rate in 1887, it was for the first time in nearly a quarter century. For Argentina, significantly, the perceived risk was considerably lower, and, according to calculations by Cortés Conde, country risk was usually less than 10 percentage points after 1864, except in moments of severe strain. Hence, Argentina's earlier start in railroad construction, and a larger network in 1877 than Brazil, Chile, Peru, and, of course, Mexico, which had almost nothing. Because the bulk of railroad construction that occurred after 1870 depended on capital from Great Britain, the United States, and France, the attitude of foreign investors toward the principal railroad-building countries was, essentially, a decisive consideration.

Colombia was somewhat different. Here, recent estimates by María Teresa Ramírez for 1927 place the social savings for Colombia between 2 and 4 percent of GDP, by far the smallest estimate thus far for Latin America. Perhaps the simplest explanation is that the measure of social savings depends on the existence and cost of alternative means of transportation. Because railroads were constructed with some delay in Colombia, road and highway transport was already available, reducing the share of coffee transported by railways and raising the responsiveness of shippers to fluctuations in the price of rail transportation. And finally, the railroad in Colombia did not form a true network, as it did in Argentina, or to a lesser extent, in Brazil, Chile, and Mexico. Most were built to link up to the Magdalena River, and the effect they had in knitting together markets across the country – one with very difficult geography – was blunted. For this reason, then, railroads in Colombia highlight the conditions under which rail development was important for economic growth in Latin America. In Central America, too, the railroad has been considered less important from the standpoint of social savings than elsewhere, even if the region was said to have experienced a "transportation revolution" in the second half of the nineteenth century. Other places, such as Ecuador, had little or no railroad development, and in Venezuela, most railroad building took place between 1880 and 1900, with little occurring thereafter.

An issue that is closely related to the impact of railroads on economic development, but perhaps requiring separate comment, is the transfer of public or communal lands to private control that often occurred in response to or in conjunction with the extension of railways. In Bolivia, Mexico, and Peru, at various times from the 1870s and 1880s (in Mexico) to the late nineteenth and first decade of the twentieth century (Bolivia and Peru), the economic growth experienced by regions first linked by rail to new markets provided both the incentive and the means to expropriate the lands of free villages. In Mexico, the spread of the rail network and the privatization of public lands by survey companies were clearly related, if only as two expressions of a general policy, the goal of which was to promote Mexico's commercial development. More concretely, there is visually compelling correspondence between those parts of the country (in the north) where the survey companies were very active and the construction of rail trunk lines. The figures are striking. During the Porfiriato, nearly 11 percent of Mexican territory was given over to the land-survey companies in compensation.

In Central America, the history of the expropriation of village lands after 1870 is well known, and in Guatemala, for instance, the wholesale transfer of "unproductive" lands given over to maize being switched to the increasingly profitable cash crop of coffee has been studied in great detail. Yet, whatever one makes of these developments, it is very difficult to credit them with the character of an ostensibly commercial phenomenon – that resources and output that were previously mobilized and allocated outside a market framework were now more "efficiently" employed. A persuasive analysis by Héctor Lindo Fuentes of price dispersion among subsistence commodities such as maize shows substantial uniformity in prices across villages in El Salvador, which Lindo Fuentes takes to be evidence of the market embeddedness of transactions. The same held true in Colombia, where peasant producers brought tobacco, sugarcane, cotton, and cacao to markets throughout the countryside. Whatever else elites accomplished during this burst of entrepreneurial energies, they did not bring the discipline or efficiency of the market to bear on these agricultural economies for the first time. Thus, it seems that a simple equation of the spread of private property in land with material progress confuses changes in distribution with changes in output, or at the very least, overstates the growth in product, and obscures the deterioration in the distribution of wealth. Generalization is difficult because the impact of these policies on vast expanses of largely empty land on the northern Mexican steppes would be very different from what occurred, in, say, the coffee plantations of the densely populated regions in highland Guatemala, or in Santander and Antioquia in Colombia. Yet even in Mexico, pressure on village lands became increasingly powerful as the commercial potential of crops such as sugarcane came to bear on village lands in Morelos during the Porfiriato.

Nor was the phenomenon restricted solely to the indigenous heartlands of Mesoamerica. McGreevey, although fixing no dimensions on the process, concludes that the collective appropriation of village, public, and church lands in the second half of the nineteenth century in Colombia was extremely significant. Here, the transfer of such lands was linked to the rise of an export commodity, tobacco, in the lowlands and to the expansion of cattle ranching in the highlands for the domestic market. Moreover, because the scale requirements of tobacco production were large, the spread of tobacco cultivation raised income and land values dramatically, but concentrated them as well. Catharine LeGrand emphasizes that much of Colombia's national territory was, strictly speaking, not titled until well into the nineteenth century and that the dimensions of the transfer of public lands into private hands was enormous, something like 2.4 million hectares of land between 1870 and 1930. In Argentina, too, as Carl Solberg has written, much new land came on to the market in the 1860s and 1870s, when the provinces rolled back the Indian frontier and acquired vast new expanses of public land, much of which ended up in the hands of the cattlemen who comprised the backbone of the rural oligarchy, the whole undertaking perhaps symbolized by General Julio Roca's "conquest of the wilderness" in 1879, and substantial sales of public land would continue well after that date.

Although these pressures (and usurpations) reflected changing valuations that producers placed on land, they also highlight the importance of population for economic growth. Historically, efforts to dispossess villages of land in Colombia, Mexico, and Central America were also efforts to drive their populations into a labor market by rupturing the ancient nexus between Indians and peasants, and their lands. There was nothing new about these efforts in the period after 1870 save, perhaps, the aggressiveness with which they were undertaken under the stimulus of increased international commodity demand. Labor rather than land had, by and large, become the scarce factor of production in the massive depopulation that followed what Alfred Crosby termed the "Columbian Exchange." Where attachment to village life made peasants reluctant to enter the rhythms of commercial production, or where population centers lay distant from the demands of highland mines or lowland plantations – as they did, for example, in Peru (in cotton growing) and Central America (in bananas) – extra-market devices featuring a variety of names had become common means of acquiring labor. In an economic sense, these were structural problems, a mismatch between labor supply and demand. In the period after 1870, as commercial opportunities and pressures intensified, new means of acquiring or enlarging labor forces became widespread. Because African slavery faced extinction in the Spanish Caribbean in 1870 by the Moret Law, or in Brazil by abolition in 1888, the response was essentially limited to the use of free labor, although freedom in this context must be interpreted circumspectly. By the same token, because the natural rate of population growth in Latin America was relatively slow, immigration frequently became a crucial source of labor, especially in Argentina, where inexpensive labor was a critical element in the success of pampean agriculture. It is, therefore, necessary to spend some time considering the importance of population for economic development in this period.

In theory, all changes in production could be attributed to changes in the size of the labor force (an increase in total output), or in productivity per member of the labor force (an increase in per capita output), or both. Practically speaking, population increase is a way of estimating growth in the labor force because, as things stand, the data from this period are not likely to yield much more. It is also, perhaps, useful to consider the quality of labor and, particularly, the extent to which education did or did not augment productivity. Recent findings suggest that Latin America, in this regard, had also fallen well behind more advanced nations of the Atlantic economy by the late nineteenth century. Finally, where it is possible to

Table 7.5. *Population growth rates (percent per year)*

Argentina, 1889–1930	3.1
Brazil, 1890–1929	2.1
Chile, 1870–1930	1.6
Colombia, 1843–1912	1.5
Mexico, 1895–1930	0.75
Peru, 1896–1928	2.2
Venezuela, 1870–1930	1.1

Source: Based on author's calculations.

identify them, changes in demographic structure may also shed light on larger patterns of economic growth, as they crucially do in Argentina.

As the data in Table 7.5 suggest, population growth in Latin America in this period was highly uneven. For purposes of discussion, it is possible to distinguish between those countries whose populations grew quite slowly, those that increased at a more typical rate, and those whose demographic growth was truly rapid. The median rate of growth, given the uncertainties in the data, seems to be about 2 percent or so, with Mexico and Colombia at the lower end of the scale, Argentina at the upper, and Brazil, Chile, Peru, and Uruguay at various intermediate levels. There is naturally a reasonably strong association between the rate of population growth and GDP growth in this period (see Figure 7.1). The scatter

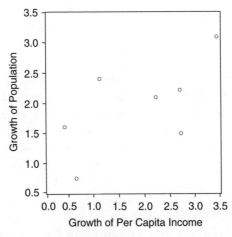

Figure 7.1. Growth of population and per capita income.

diagram displays the association for those countries for which we have data, and it is strongly positive, with a simple correlation between population and output growth of 0.92. Perhaps more important, there is also a positive association between population growth (in logs) and per capita income growth (the difference between the logs of output and population growth), with a simple correlation of 0.78. Countries with more rapidly growing populations also had higher income growth per head. The result is not as unusual as it might seem. In the long run, with the extension of rail networks and, hence, the frontiers of commercial agriculture, more people had more, rather than less, land and capital with which to work, so diminishing returns did not occur. Juan Bautista Alberdi's (1810–84) celebrated aphorism, "to govern is to populate," makes perfect sense in this context. Nor is the result dependent strictly on the data we have collected. A similar exercise linking per capita GDP in 1913 to the growth rate of population between 1870 and 1913 for eight countries (Argentina, Brazil, Chile, Colombia, Mexico, Peru, Uruguay, and Venezuela) in 1990 international dollars drawn from Angus Maddison's *The World Economy* produces similar results (see Figure 7.2). Population growth raised rather than lowered per capita income in the period between 1870 and 1930.

Where natural increase substantially comprised the bulk of population increase, as it did in Mexico, demographic change was painfully small. Robert McCaa has estimated that the annual growth rate of the population

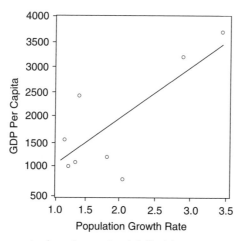

Figure 7.2. GDP per capita (1990 international dollars) in 1930 versus population growth rate 1870–1913.
Source: Maddison, *The World Economy*, 193, 195.

there between 1876 and 1910 was no more than 1.71 percent, and after 1900, the rate slowed to 1.09 percent. The Revolution, according to McCaa, produced a demographic disaster, perhaps the worst since the sixteenth century, with population falling by one million (total population in 1910 was about fifteen million). Total growth from 1910 through 1930 was no more than 1.4 million, or less than the increase for 1900–10. Demographic growth per se could have therefore done little or nothing to raise total output, and Mexico was not, and had never been, a magnet for foreign immigration. So in some portions of Mexico, such as the Yucatán peninsula, which were remote from major population centers or from poles of economic growth to which workers could migrate (the proximity of northern Mexico to the United States is the usual example), relative labor scarcity in the face of growing commercial demands produced a history of repression on the henequen plantations. Yet what was true for henequen was not invariably the case for other commodities. Sugarcane planters in Morelos may have despoiled villages of their lands, but they also substituted capital for labor in producing and processing sugar. Over time, this industry actually required not more but *relatively less* labor, a fact reflected in both census data and in the nature of agrarian protest during the Mexican Revolution. Still, Mexico's overall record of growth between 1895 and 1930 suggests that slow population increase was an obstacle to economic growth.

Colombia, too, experienced relatively slow population growth, with an overall average between 1870 and 1930 of something just over 1 percent per year. Catharine LeGrand suggests that immigration into Colombia was not large, and that the creation of an adequate labor force under the pressure of export expansion was inevitably difficult, particularly when it involved peasants who migrated into frontier regions. Hacendados from western Cundinamarca and Tolima imported workers from the eastern highlands through a system of labor contracting called *enganche*. But there were also widespread conflicts in the interior, in western Colombia, and along the Caribbean coast between peasants settled on public lands, known collectively as *colonos*, and land entrepreneurs interested in developing lands for cattle ranching, the production of forest products, or coffee plantations. Again, there is no reason to assume that an increase in the export surplus measures the increase in domestic output because it is clear that the peasant population was not entirely outside the market economy to begin with. Rather, the effort to appropriate previously untitled (but hardly vacant) lands was designed to mobilize a labor force adequate to the needs of an export economy in which a rural proletariat was absent and population growth was slow. Thus, LeGrand concludes, "in order to generate a *labor force* (italics mine) . . . entrepreneurs logically sought to turn the public lands into private properties . . . The fact that the population of Colombia was much smaller . . . accounts in part for the difficulties large proprietors had in acquiring labor."[7]

Chile, too, experienced slow population growth, at a rate of about 1.6 percent per year. Nevertheless, Arnold Bauer has suggested that economic expansion under the stimulus of external demand, first in wheat and later in the export mining sector of nitrates and copper, was not significantly hindered by labor shortages experienced elsewhere in Latin America because "Central Chile . . . was an area with plentiful if idle hands." Indeed, Patricio Meller estimates that nitrate exports grew at something over 6 percent per year between 1880 and 1930, and Carmen Cariola and Oswaldo Sunkel point to the "spectacular" population growth in the Norte Grande that facilitated the growth of nitrate exports.

Peru experienced somewhat more rapid demographic increase. The annual rate of population growth between 1876 and 1940 was in the neighborhood of 2 percent yearly, and after the termination of Chinese indentured immigration in 1874, immigration did not figure importantly. In Peru, too, the rise of sugar plantations on the north coast in the valleys of Lambayeque, Jequetepeque, Chicama, and Santa Catalina presented major problems of labor recruitment, a difficulty addressed to some extent by the rise of the infamous *enganchadores*, or labor contractors, who facilitated migration from the Sierra to the coast. Peter Klarén refers to the "critical shortage of labor" in the emerging sugar industry, concluding that an adequate supply of labor had long been a major problem for the region's sugar planters.

Like Peru, Brazil's population grew at roughly 2 percent between 1872 and 1940, or from about 9.9 million to 41.2 million people. But a few distinct features of demographic change require comment. Unlike Mexico and Peru, Brazil experienced substantial immigration, with the total flow between 1870 and 1920 amounting to about 3.3 million persons, of whom 1.4 million, or some 42 percent, were of Italian origin, followed by lesser but still significant numbers of Spaniards, Japanese, and Arabs. There was a pronounced tendency for immigration to increase in the wake of the abolition of African slavery. Immigration exceeded 100,000 for the first time in 1888,

---

[7] Catherine LeGrand, *Frontier Expansion and Peasant Protest in Colombia, 1830–1936* (Albuquerque, NM, 1986), 38, 40.

and something in excess of a million immigrants were to follow in the 1890s, with more than 200,000 in 1891 alone. As Nathaniel Leff observes, the connection between the abolition of slavery and the rise of immigration was not circumstantial but purposeful because the coffee planters of São Paulo pressured the central government and the province of São Paulo to subsidize European immigration and to ensure an elastic supply of labor in the face of abolition. Thus, in Leff's view, the abolition of slavery in Brazil did not have the same effects on the labor supply that it did in the U.S. South after the Civil War. As Leff put the matter, labor markets in Brazil differed because "shifts in the demand curve for labor determined shifts in the supply schedule of workers," something that seems quite different from what occurred in Mexico and Peru. As a result, Brazilian income growth in 1890–1929 was a respectable 4.3 percent per year. Still, the emergence of large estates on the Brazilian coffee frontier was accompanied by the expropriation of settlers who were expelled onto public lands farther in the interior in a process that LeGrand explicitly compares with Colombia.

THE IMPACT OF DEMAND

Variations in production, prices, and employment in the short run are typically attributed to fluctuations in demand because its determinants can change relatively quickly. Political upheavals and monetary disturbances can occur suddenly and with little warning, the result of the vagaries of regime changes, an untoward mining discovery (e.g., gold in California and Australia in 1849), or legislation affecting the supply and demand of precious metals under the gold and silver standards (e.g., that undertaken by the Latin Monetary Union between 1865 and 1878). At the same time, variations in international commodity prices, which could to some extent be taken as given (the major exception, of course, would be Brazilian coffee and the valorization schemes, wherein Brazil, with its large share of the global market, sought to support the price of coffee by reducing its supply), could vary rapidly and unexpectedly from year to year as well, presenting producers with a rapidly evolving picture of demand. Indeed, to an extent, the leitmotiv of discussions of the commodity cycle is the variability of prices, something that Bulmer-Thomas has termed the "commodity lottery." Yet a composite picture of these forces, by definition, would be difficult to provide because they are as varied as the countries whose history we have chosen to analyze. But some attempt at generalization is necessary to make the story intelligible and coherent rather than episodic, disjointed, and anecdotal.

One of the best-known discussions in the literature of economic development is the question of the terms of trade, or the relative prices of exports. In essence, the net barter terms of trade is the measure most commonly computed because it is the one for which data are most readily available, and, hence, the framework within which comparisons are routinely, if sometimes facilely, made. The subject is of particular relevance to the history of Latin America because the terms of trade literature is traditionally associated with the work of the distinguished Argentine economist, Raúl Prebisch (1901–85). At a basic level, an "improvement" in the terms of trade – that is, an increase in the price of exports relative to imports – represents an increase in real income for the exporting country because the relative price of exports improves. "Deterioration," on the other hand, implies that real income has fallen. In the history of Latin America, the notion of deteriorating terms of trade has sometimes served as a justification for the rejection of liberal economic prescriptions that rely on free trade as an engine of growth because under such conditions, trade could ostensibly become impoverishing. By extension, attempts to alter comparative advantage, such as import substitution industrialization, seem logical if demand for a commodity – and hence its relative price – is falling. This explains the historical importance so often ascribed to the analysis of the net barter terms of trade.

Whereas accounts of the terms of trade are frequently carried out at a high level of aggregation, it makes some sense to proceed at the country level when the commodity composition of exports differs, as it did in Latin America, even if variations in income in the developed (importing) countries imposed some measure of correlation on export price movements in Latin America. And, given the limits of the data, a striking heterogeneity in country experience in the period 1870 through 1930 is apparent. There was no overall tendency for the net barter terms of trade to deteriorate, even if each country did experience episodes of deterioration, and even if some countries, most notably Mexico and Peru, did experience falling terms of trade after 1870. This is especially important when one considers that studies of the period before 1870 reveal much the same thing. In other words, for roughly the first century of their independence, the nations of Latin America, considered on the whole and individually, experienced growing rather than declining demand for their tradables if the relevant metric is the net barter terms of trade.

Obviously, some countries, especially those with similar export baskets, display some correlation in the net barter terms of trade. Argentina and Uruguay (r = .53), Brazil and Colombia (r = .57), and Mexico and Peru (r = .53) exhibit this sort of behavior, although for time series, the correlations do not seem to be extremely high. But many more of the pairs of correlations are low or even negative, pointing instead to a diversity of experiences. Moreover, examining the degree to which the terms of trade cointegrate or trend together suggests little common behavior, even where Brazil and Colombia, Argentina and Uruguay, or Peru and Mexico are concerned. In other words, the national experiences of the export economies remain, at some level, irreducibly distinct, a point Daniel Díaz Fuentes emphasized in an account of the operation of the gold standard in Latin America in the interwar period, or which, for purposes of comparison, Angus Deaton had made for export economies in Africa. At best, it seems, pairs of countries display common behavior, but that is all.

Nevertheless, there are patterns in the data that call for some comment, particularly because they apparently represent the reversal of trends that characterized the half-century between 1820 and 1870. Although it is not true that there was a uniform deterioration in the net barter terms of trade across Latin America, there was some tendency for a decline to occur in many of the major economies if, by decline, we mean a lower average in the terminal decade than in the initial one (see Table 7.6). Thus, in this sense, Argentina, Brazil, Mexico, Peru, and Venezuela experienced some deterioration in the terms of trade, and in Mexico, the deterioration was pronounced because the terms of trade had fallen by 60 percent over the period. But Colombia, Chile, Cuba, and Uruguay all experienced improving terms of trade, and for Cuba, the reversal was all the more dramatic considering the sharp fall in the relative price of Cuban exports earlier in the nineteenth century. Moreover, if we look instead at the time trend fit to each series, we see a slightly different result. We may regard Argentina, Cuba, and Colombia as essentially trendless because their positive coefficients do not differ significantly from zero. Chile and Uruguay each present, to a greater or lesser extent, a positive trend. Brazil, Mexico, Peru, and Venezuela all present a negative trend and, in the case of Mexico and Peru, the deterioration ranges from 1.6 to 2.4 percent per year. Thus, the "commodity lottery" favored some countries, worked decidedly against the interests of still others, or was irrelevant to a few more. A common pattern, much less a generalized, secular deterioration in the terms of trade, is difficult to find. Indeed, there seems to be little apparent connection between the growth of output

Table 7.6. *Net barter terms of trade. By decades, 1870–1930, and time trend in percent per year*

	Brazil	Mexico	Colombia	Cuba	Chile	Argentina	Uruguay	Peru	Venezuela
1870–79	116	177	102	85			65		127
1880–89	123	140	129	88	70	98	83		136
1890–99	128	119	151	94	64	82	102	108	171
1900–09	100	100	100	100	100	100	100	100	100
1910–19	91	94	107	105	110	101	119	84	97
1920–29	93	73	120	92	91	77		61	

Country	Trend (percent per year)	R^2
Argentina	−0.19	−0.003
Brazil*	−0.76	−0.193
Chile*	1.15	0.330
Colombia	0.08	0.004
Cuba	0.07	−0.011
Mexico*	−1.61	0.809
Peru*	−2.43	0.663
Venezuela*	−1.10	0.236
Uruguay*	1.45	0.785

*Significant at the 99 percent level. R^2 is adjusted for degrees of freedom.
Notes and Sources: All series have been rebased to 1900–09. In a few instances, it has been necessary to interpolate a missing year or two to complete the series. Most of the data employed has been published. I include here only the principal sources. For Argentina, I am indebted to Alan Taylor. For Brazil, see Reinaldo Gonçalves and Amir Coelho Barros, "Tendências dos termos de troca: a tese de Prebisch e a economia brasiliera – 1850/1879," *Pesquisa e planejamento econômico*, 12, 1 (1982), 109–31; for Chile, Thomas B. Birnberg and Stephen A. Resnick, *Colonial Development. An Econometric Study* (New Haven, CT, 1975), 267; for Colombia, José Antonio Ocampo, *Colombia y la economía mundial*, 95–97; for Cuba, Birmberg and Resnick, *Colonial Development*, 273, and Linda K. Salvucci and Richard J. Salvucci, "Cuba and the Latin American Terms of Trade: Old Theories, New Evidence," *Journal of Interdisciplinary History*, 31, 2 (2000), 197–222; for Mexico, Edward Beatty, "The Impact of Foreign Trade on the Mexican Economy: Terms of Trade and the Rise of Industry, 1880–1923," *Journal of Latin American Studies*, 32 (2000), 399–433; for Peru, Seminario and Beltrán, *Crecimiento económico en el Perú*, 301–302; for Uruguay, Luis Bertola, "An Overview of the Economic History of Uruguay since the 1870s," EH.Net Encyclopedia, edited by Robert Whaples, July 6, 2004, http://eh.net/encyclopedia/?article=Bertola.Uruguay.final; for Venezuela, Baptista, *Bases cuantitativas*, 311, 313.

and changes in the terms of trade given that both improvements and deteriorations are observed, whereas GDP increases.

The difficulty, to repeat, is that such questions can be handled convincingly only at a disaggregated and, here specifically, national level. Consider, for instance, Mexico and Peru. Here, as Edward Beatty explains, the deteriorating terms of trade reflected not an *overall* decline in the demand for Mexican exports but rather the fate of silver, of which Mexico was a relatively large exporter and producer. Although it is true that demand for silver was relatively inelastic, a reflection of the increasing demonetization of the metal internationally after 1870, Mexican production and export actually increased, which, in turn, depressed its market price. The same held true for Peru, at least in the early years of the series, because Peruvian production and export of silver expanded as well. Silver comprised a quarter of Peruvian exports by value in the mid-1890s, and as late as 1910, still represented 10 percent of Peruvian exports. Later, Beatty proposes, the deterioration in the Mexican terms of trade was driven by the rise in the price of its import basket, especially during World War I and its aftermath. According to Thorp and Bertram, the same held true for Peru, whose import prices after 1915 rose dramatically, much more so than, say, Brazil's and Chile's, whose terms of trade did not decline by proportionally as much. But Beatty emphasizes that the purchasing power of Mexican exports, the so-called income terms of trade (export revenues deflated by an import price index), strongly increased over the period, especially when the barter terms of trade were falling, at an overall rate (1880–1923) of 4.8 percent per year. The rate of increase of the purchasing power of Peruvian exports (calculated from data compiled from Seminario and Beltrán) (1896–1929) is an almost identical 4.6 percent. Thus, for both Mexico and Peru, the deterioration in the net barter terms of trade was offset by an increase in the purchasing power of exports. And, in both Mexico and Peru, the export base diversified, with Mexico producing and exporting henequen, gold, cattle hides, and nonferrous metals. Peru, argue Thorp and Bertram, had an unusually diverse export base for Latin America, with sugar, copper, cotton, rubber, and petroleum successively driving export performance. Whatever the vicissitudes of international demand, both Mexico and Peru experienced sufficiently rapid productivity increases in the export sector to maintain, if not increase, their share of international commodity markets.

The situation for Venezuela was somewhat similar in that its net barter terms of trade deteriorated, but its income terms of trade nevertheless rose.

The overall change in the income terms of trade between 1870 and 1920, using data supplied by Asdrúbal Baptista, was positive, at somewhat less than 1 percent per year. But this is deceptive. The purchasing power of Venezuelan exports is more accurately described by a nonlinear trend in which the income terms of trade *rose* at about 4.4 percent per year between 1870 and 1895 and then fell at somewhat less than 1 percent per year between 1895 and 1920. The explanation for this pattern appears to be tied to changes in the price of coffee, which accounted for a major share of exports before petroleum took hold in the 1920s, as well as generally sharp import price increases in the latter part of the period. Still, simply describing the pattern of the Venezuelan terms of trade as deteriorating would be quite misleading. Like Mexico and Peru, the purchasing power of its exports rose.

For Brazil, Leff indicates that both the net barter and income terms of trade rose after 1870, but his analysis is limited to the years down to World War I. If we look instead at the more comprehensive analysis by Reinaldo Gonçalves and Amir Coelho Barros, they find that the net barter terms of trade fell between 1870 and 1939 at a yearly rate of 0.98 percent and, indeed, between 1870 and 1913 as well, albeit at a very low (0.09 percent) rate. This series, in turn, has been used by the Instituto Brasileiro de Geografia e Estatística to calculate the income terms of trade. Between 1870 and 1930, the purchasing power of Brazil's exports rose at a rate of 2.1 percent per year and, indeed, did so predictably except during the years between 1914 and 1922.

Thus, even where the net barter terms of trade declined – which is to say, even where relative price trends did not favor Latin America – the purchasing power of exports rose between 2.1 and 4.6 percent per year, doubling roughly every ten to thirty years. This finding is entirely consistent with the argument made by Enzo Grilli and Maw Cheng Yang in their highly influential study of the terms of trade of the developed countries between 1900 and 1986: the fall that occurred in the net barter terms of trade of the primary commodity exporters after World War II may have been more than compensated by an improvement in their income terms of trade. Their conclusion is worth quoting:

In the presence of a strong improvement in the purchasing power of commodities and in the income terms of trade of non-oil-exporting developing countries, the negative welfare significance of falling relative prices of non-fuel primary commodities should not be overstated . . . The presumption . . . is that the negative effects of declining real export prices may have been at least in part mitigated by productivity growth.

In other words, in Brazil, Peru, Mexico, and Venezuela, it was productivity growth in agriculture, mining, and extractive industries that drove down prices, not a lack of demand.

This analysis could also be extended to countries whose terms of trade were positive or essentially trendless. For example, from 1902 through 1930, Cuba's income terms of trade grew at a rate of 3.4 percent per year. When we consider that other research has concluded that the purchasing power of Cuban exports grew throughout the nineteenth century as well, we may reasonably conclude that, whatever happened to the relative price of Cuban exports, their purchasing power grew over the century from 1830 through 1930. Similarly, the Chilean income terms of trade grew at a very rapid rate between 1888 and 1930, around 6.1 percent yearly. More precisely, they grew at this rate until 1919, when a clear structural break marking the end of World War I occurred, at which point the trend rate of growth fell by 65 percent! The explanation for this break was the impact of the end of the war (and the invention of synthetic substitutes by German scientists) on nitrate production in Chile, which accounted for a quarter of GDP. José Antonio Ocampo also argues that the purchasing power of Colombian exports rose dramatically between 1870 and 1898.

Although it is true that an argument concerning the deterioration in the net barter terms of trade appears less than persuasive, it would be premature to conclude that the terms of trade were therefore not an issue. Although the literature is not conclusive, and perhaps cannot be, there is some indication that volatility in the terms of trade is associated with slower growth and structural change. This makes intuitive sense because a string of good years (or bad) in the export sector sends an unambiguous signal to domestic markets. The problem, among others, is what counts for evidence of volatility, or what would be considered an unacceptably high (or desirably low) level of price instability. One conventional measure is to divide the standard error of the regression (a measure of the difference between fitted and observed measures of the terms of trade) by their mean value. This asks, in essence, whether a time trend is a useful predictor: do they grow (or decline) steadily or not? As a rule of thumb, the standard error of the regression should not be more than 10 to 15 percent of the mean of the dependent variable. As the data in Table 7.7 show, the trend regressions are all reasonably good models, with the relevant statistic ranging from 2 percent (Uruguay) to 6 percent (Venezuela) and a median value of 4.1. By this standard, Cuba, Mexico, Peru, and Uruguay were relatively less volatile in their net barter terms of trade than were Argentina, Colombia, Chile, Brazil, and Venezuela. One suspects that there is a connection

Table 7.7. *Stability of the terms of trade*

	Percent
Argentina	4.3
Brazil	5.6
Chile	4.6
Colombia	4.3
Cuba	3.9
Mexico	2.7
Peru	3.6
Venezuela	6.0
Uruguay	2.0
Median	4.1

Note: Defined at the standard error of the regression of the terms of trade divided by the mean of the dependent variable.
Source: Based on author's data in Table 7.6. Higher numbers mean greater instability.

between relatively higher volatility in the terms of trade (susceptibility to external shocks, in other words) and the difficulties that Argentina, Brazil, and Chile had with adherence to the gold standard. In other words, it was the intrinsic and growing unpredictability of the external environment rather than a transfer of resources from the periphery to the center that made satisfactory macroeconomic performance difficult for Latin America between 1870 and 1930. To put it simply, a fixed exchange rate (the gold standard, in this case) will magnify the effect that fluctuations in the terms of trade have on domestic output. Flexible exchange rates insulate a country's economy from changes in the terms of trade. A fixed exchange rate and deteriorating terms of trade, such as Mexico experienced after moving to gold in 1905, was unfortunate and may well have contributed to the outbreak of revolutionary violence in 1910.

STRUCTURAL TRANSFORMATION: THE ORIGINS OF INDUSTRIALIZATION

As Edward Beatty has argued, historians' views of the link between export growth and industrialization have undergone a substantial change in recent decades. For one thing, as Beatty points out, by 1930, a substantial amount

of industrialization was already underway. What happened beginning with
the Great Depression in Mexico, as Enrique Cárdenas has suggested, for
instance, or after World War II elsewhere in Latin America, was not a
dramatic new departure but a continuation of changes that had begun
well before. In some cases, and Mexico has been well studied by Stephen
Haber, there can be no doubt that the true origins of modern industrialization can be traced back to the 1880s, if not before. Also, as Beatty
has noted, the export economies provided a foundation of physical infrastructure (e.g., rail networks and port facilities) or state capacity that was
to be crucial in activating and directing later efforts at import-substitution
industrialization. Still, the degree of industrialization that occurred between
1870 and 1930 should not be exaggerated. The share of agricultural output in national product remained substantial, especially when measured
by employment. The data in Table 7.8 suggest this quite convincingly,
even when due allowance is made for uncertainties in their provenance,
calculation, and interpretation. From the standpoint of economic development, most of Latin America remained poor and sparsely populated
as late as 1900. Neither condition is consistent with a high degree of
domestic industrialization, and in the absence of restrictions on imports
or deliberate attempts to foster industrialization, the result of an export
boom was more likely an expansion of the market for imported manufactures rather than an expansion of domestic production. This was especially
true of resource-rich economies that had a strong comparative advantage
in foodstuffs, fibers, minerals, and other raw materials. There, the problem of Dutch disease or the chronic overvaluation of the exchange rate
driven by the rapid generation of foreign exchange made industrialization especially difficult. This was an old problem for the Latin American
export economies reaching well back into the silver booms of the colonial period in Mexico and there had been other episodes in Brazil, Chile,
Costa Rica, Cuba, and Peru as well in the intervening years. By and large,
the degree of structural transformation that had occurred in Latin America by 1900 was about typical for the relative level of per capita income
in the countries for which we have data. Argentina, perhaps, is the one
example of a relatively wealthy country that had less industrialization than
one might expect – notice, in particular, the contrast with Uruguay, where
Luis Bértola finds that the products of the modern meat industry, cattle-
breeding industry, the wheat flour complex, and the production of wine
led to a particularly rapid increase in the share of manufactures in GDP in
the 1920s.

Table 7.8. *Sectoral composition of output, 1870–1930 (percentages rounded)*

	Primary	Secondary	Tertiary
Argentina			
1900	49	22	29
1935	33	30	37
Brazil			
1910	36	14	50
1920	32	17	51
1930	31	17	52
Chile			
1930	34	16	50
Mexico			
1900	29	12	59
1910	29	12	60
1920	35	15	50
1930	28	15	53
Peru			
1900	40	15	45
1910	39	18	43
1920	40	17	43
1930	43	15	42
Uruguay			
1870	47	36	18
1910	44	37	19
1930	40	44	16
Venezuela			
1920	35	8	57
1930	37	14	49

Notes: Argentina is measured over 1875–1900 and 1900–35. Chile is 1907–30. For Mexico, 1920 is 1921. Uruguay is 1872 (1870) and 1912 (1910).

Primary includes agriculture and ranching in Argentina and Uruguay, agriculture and mining in Mexico, and agriculture and petroleum in Venezuela. Secondary includes industry and construction in Argentina and Venezuela, and manufacturing and construction in Mexico and Venezuela. Tertiary includes services variously defined: for example, transportation, commerce, and government in Argentina; distribution and services in Peru; and in Mexico, commerce, transportation, communications, electricity, and services.

Sources: Argentina: Ana María Cerro, "La conducta cíclica de la actividad económica de Argentina en el período 1820–1970." Brazil: Marcelo de P. Abreu and Afonso S. Bevilacqua, "Brazil as an Export Economy, 1880–1930," in Enrique Cárdenas et al., *An Economic History of Latin America*, 1, 33. Chile: Markos J. Mamalakis, *The Growth and Structure of the Chilean Economy*, 15. Mexico: calculated from *La economía mexicana en cifras, 1990*, 11th ed. (Mexico City, 1990), 121–2. Peru: Bruno Seminario and Arlette Beltrán, *Crecimiento económico en el Perú: 1896–1995*, 285–6. Venezuela: calculated from Asdrúbal Baptista, *Bases cuantitativas de la economía venezolana*, 59. Uruguay: Luis Bértola et al., *El PBI de Uruguay, 1870–1936*, 30.

There was, nevertheless, more than a casual association between export booms and industrialization. In Colombia, for instance, the cotton textile industry got underway in Antioquia and was a product of the region's coffee boom. Santiago Montenegro emphasizes that the capital that financed cotton textiles in the early twentieth century came from a variety of sources in Colombia, including merchants' trading profits. In Chile, Cariola and Sunkel suggest that the expansion of nitrate exports contributed to the formation of a national market, especially in consumer goods such as footwear and bottled beer, and to the building of a transportation network. Of course, these examples pale in importance to developments that occurred in Brazil and Mexico. Here, industrialization seems to have been more extensive and subject to a host of institutional, financial, political, and economic influences that conditioned its subsequent evolution in important ways.

In Brazil, the rapid growth of coffee production and export at the end of the nineteenth and during the first quarter of the twentieth century coincided with the consolidation of republicanism and the beginning of industrialization. Brazilian scholars and historians agree that income generated by coffee exports was a proximate source of industrialization. As Marcelo de Paiva Abreu has observed, Brazil's large share of international coffee production implied considerable control over pricing and rendered growers less resistant to protective tariffs that promoted domestic industrialization even though they raised costs. The contrast with Argentina was striking, for here the country was a price-taker and hence wedded more closely to free trade and laissez faire with, as we have noticed, a correspondingly reduced share of industrialization outside of meat processing and packing.

In Mexico, both Stephen Haber and Edward Beatty have demonstrated that the output of light industry and, in particular, cotton textiles, beer, and cigarettes began to increase substantially in the 1890s. Haber, in particular, has emphasized the importance of developing capital markets in Mexico for mobilizing finance, something that, in his view, was more important in Mexico than in Brazil, where the basic infrastructure for internal exchange was not yet in place. Beatty shows that the Díaz government relied on a regime of high tariffs (especially high effective protection, which increased value added, or national product). Beatty also finds that Mexico engaged in a kind of industrial policy as well as in patent reform, all with an eye toward encouraging manufacturing. Nevertheless, as Haber has argued, small markets and protection tended to produce high costs and inefficiencies. These were disguised by the sharp depreciation of silver to which we have already alluded because the fall in silver raised the relative prices of tradables, such as manufactures, and increased their production. Other tradables, such as mineral resources, would have benefited as well, which again suggests the complementarity between primary export expansion and industrialization in the later nineteenth century.

An indirect way of judging the progress of industrialization is by measuring the extent of import substitution. Domestic production of textiles would displace imports to an extent, whereas industrialization would increase the share of capital goods imported to produce consumer goods. In Brazil, the relation was very clear. Data assembled by Richard Graham show that the share of textiles in British imports fell from around 60 percent in 1870 to about 36 percent in 1910. At the same time, the share of capital goods in imports rose from 26 to 42 percent, a pattern consistent with the use of imported machinery to produce textiles that formerly had been imported.

In Mexico, Beatty has demonstrated a similar phenomenon. Coarse cloth imports fell by 4.3 percent per year between 1895 and 1908, tobacco products at the rate of 5.5 percent, and beer at 4 percent. All were objects of import substitution. At the same time, imports of producer goods rose at nearly 11 percent per year.

Finally, we might contrast the situation in Mexico or Brazil with Argentina, whose industrialization was limited. As Carlos Díaz Alejandro observed, the Argentine government provided limited support for industrialization before 1930, perhaps fearful of limiting the market for its own agricultural exports. Nevertheless, Díaz Alejandro emphasizes that much pre-1930 manufacturing growth can be attributed to export expansion: meat packing and dairy processing, milling, wool washing, and so forth. Between 15 and 20 percent of the gross value of manufacturing before 1930 was exported.

CONCLUSIONS

When London caught a cold, it was once said, Buenos Aires contracted pneumonia – the consequence of tight links between Britain and Argentina, and of the ability of the gold standard to transmit macroeconomic shocks. In recent years, Argentine economic historians have judged pneumonia preferable to systemic collapse. Our conclusion might follow macroeconomic historian Bradford deLong, who argues that the choice of an exchange rate regime, fixed or flexible, depends on a country's individual circumstances. Certainly, during 1870 through 1930, it appears that Latin America had no ideal choice. Flexible exchange rates did have their advantages, particularly for those countries whose exports and industrialization were aided by the depreciation of silver. But, as Casasus complained in Mexico, the price in volatility was very high and it may well be, following contemporary thinking, that the volatility of the international environment created sufficient uncertainty to act as a significant constraint on economic growth. In any event, price stability and macroeconomic stability are not the same thing, and macroeconomic stability became increasingly difficult to come by between 1870 and 1930.

Certainly, we find only limited evidence that factors affecting aggregate supply and demand ultimately acted as obstacles to growth. The railroad had truly massive effects on supply, and not only of exportables. In country after country, a revaluation of resources to reflect changed productivities followed in the wake of railroad building. The railroad was not merely a highway to external dependency. And the construction of such infrastructure also made a decisive beginning possible for industrialization, especially in Mexico and Brazil, although the true bulk of industrial modernization would await the end of the Great Depression and World War II. But a start toward structural transformation had been made, export age or no.

As far as demand goes, we find no real evidence that there was a generalized deterioration in the terms of trade, although deterioration in the net barter terms of trade did occur in some instances. More impressive was the response of the export sector in bringing larger volumes of exportables to market and, hence, raising the income terms of trade, which points in the direction of productivity increase. As was Bulmer-Thomas, we are left with an impression that it was the speed or generality through which productivity gains were transferred to the rest of the economy that was the critical issue – the mechanism that equalized productivity across sectors that proved sluggish. Again, this may have stemmed from uncertainties in the international environment, especially those that impeded the formation of or interfered with consistent market signals. Slow population growth may well have acted as an obstacle to economic growth in some regions, but the study of the connection between demographic change and economic growth in Latin America is still in its very early stages.

8

THE DEVELOPMENT OF
INFRASTRUCTURE

WILLIAM R. SUMMERHILL

Between 1870 and 1930, Latin American nations experienced an unprecedented expansion of physical infrastructure. The economies of Latin America, most of them laggards by the standards of North Atlantic economic performance, began to grow with a new-found rapidity, as investment in modern transportation increased during the late nineteenth century. For many nations of the region, this era became one of genuine economic transformation. Increasing exports of primary commodities, rising imports of capital goods, the expansion of activities drawing directly and indirectly on overseas investment, the rising share of modern manufacturing in output, and a generalized increase in the pace and scope of economic activity were all tied closely to the timing and character of the region's infrastructural development. The causation in this process ran both ways. Infrastructure development fostered economic growth, as marketing and transaction costs fell. Economic growth led to new sequences of infrastructure investment, as the demand for improvements increased, the costs of provision fell, and new bottlenecks emerged, creating commercial and political pressures for follow-on investment. In 1850, no major country in Latin America possessed any of the trappings of modern transport technology. Half a century later, most of them did, and had experienced considerable economic change as a result.

This chapter draws on the findings of studies over the last several decades that have sought to isolate, with increasing empirical and analytical rigor, the implications of infrastructure development for Latin American economic growth. The core component of infrastructure in this era necessarily involved the transportation revolution. Transport investment raised incomes and output by integrating markets and providing new opportunities for specialization in agriculture and manufacturing. Railway construction, port improvements, and the eventual spread of motor roads collectively propelled economic growth across much of the region by the early twentieth century. Sequences of increasing infrastructural development and higher levels of economic activity fed back into each other, accelerating, in several cases quite dramatically, the rate of material progress.

Infrastructure that facilitates the production and exchange of private goods occupies a strategic position in the capital stock of modern economies. By infrastructure, economists usually mean transportation facilities, though the term at times is employed to encompass publicly owned capital in the energy sector. The transformative potential of investments in infrastructure is widely recognized by economic analysts and stems from infrastructure's ability to raise the productivity of existing resources, expand the supply of new resources, and foster both extensive and intensive economic growth. Empirical estimates of the economic returns to the formation of infrastructure capital, even in the late twentieth century, are astoundingly high.[1] Investments in the Latin American infrastructure in an earlier period, the critical decades of transformation before 1930, turn out to be no less important to the process of economic growth.

Beyond highlighting the principal characteristics of infrastructure in Latin America and sketching its development, this chapter argues that the accelerated pace of infrastructure investment after 1870, particularly in steam locomotion, provided the chief impetus to the transition to modern rates of economic growth in much of the region. Two qualifications are in order from the outset. First, assertions about the primacy of one factor necessarily collide with a number of problems, including one of endogeneity. Latin America's export earnings paid for imported railroad capital, yet the railroad was required to break through the barriers of geography that restricted export growth, and the availability of export earnings did not necessarily ensure that railroads would be built or were built where they were most needed. The resolution of this causal puzzle depends on the circumstances of each particular case. Second, the particular impact of any single infrastructure project is an empirical question that requires

---

[1] Alicia Munnell, "Infrastructure Investment and Economic Growth," *Journal of Economic Perspectives* 6:4 (Autumn 1992): 189–98; Peter J. Wylie, "Infrastructure and Canadian Economic Growth 1946–1991," *Canadian Journal of Economics*, 29: Special Issue: Part 1 (April 1996): 350–5; and Edward M. Gramlich, "Infrastructure Investment: A Review Essay," *Journal of Economic Literature* 32 (September 1994): 1176–96 provide summaries of the main empirical results of assessments of infrastructural development in the high-income North American economies in the latter decades of the twentieth century.

careful, theoretically informed investigation. A railway extension, the construction of a feeder roadway, or the financing of a port improvement are all actions that involve an investment of resources with implications for both allocative efficiency and the distribution of wealth. These effects can vary considerably across specific projects, regions, decades, and countries, and accurately documenting them for all of Latin America requires far more research among primary sources than has been done to date. The assertions in this chapter about the impact of infrastructure are thus necessarily incomplete, yet they provide a set of useful characterizations against which the findings of future work will have to be compared. Although durable economic expansion cannot be attributed to a single cause alone, it now seems unlikely that any other technological or institutional innovation was more important in the transition to economic growth in Latin America before 1930.

Moreover, the history of internal improvements in Latin American nations has a very strong policy component that is not yet adequately studied. Political factors reigned supreme in the processes of infrastructure concession, subsidy, and regulation. Yet these remain poorly understood. By the late nineteenth century, transport improvements became a central feature of the political-economic landscape throughout Latin America. That infrastructure policies interacted with other features of the polity is not surprising and did not necessarily work the same way from country to country. Because policy is a product of political preferences and the institutions that aggregate those preferences into political outcomes, the formal institutions governing decisions on transport subsidy and regulation were important. Even in economies where a pure price system exists, the large minimum-efficient scale of infrastructure investment, uncertainty over the current or future level of demand for infrastructure services, and worries on the part of investors over the prospect of excessive regulation or expropriation mean that infrastructure investment may languish at levels much lower than are warranted by prevailing conditions, and less than necessary for future growth. In short, because of the public-goods character of much infrastructure, well-functioning markets may get things wrong, resulting in a poor allocation of infrastructure projects. Perceptions of the public interest, even in Latin American polities where the politically relevant public was limited by a highly restricted franchise or semi-authoritarian government, created heavy pressure for intervention to remedy market failures and better serve the particular pecuniary interests of politically influential groups. Market interventions by the state often succeeded in ameliorating such failures but typically did so in a way skewed to suit particular interests stemming from the thirst for profits. Unfortunately, chronicles and narrative descriptions of infrastructural successes and failures in Latin America, although informative, cannot substitute for careful analysis of the institutions governing the choice of economic policies. Dissecting the politics of infrastructure requires a much greater understanding of actual policy making – including both the political incentives of policy makers and the institutions in which they operate – than presently exists for most of nineteenth-century Latin America.[2]

The upshot of the experience with infrastructure development between 1870 and 1930 is best summarized along the following lines. Many of the areas in Latin America with strong economic potential did not possess extensive arrays of roads, networks of canals, or even interlocking systems of natural inland waterways on the eve of the railway age. Freely navigable rivers were abundant in some regions, such as portions of the Southern Cone, but virtually absent from others, as in the case of interior Mexico and northern South America. There was, of course, no mechanism that guaranteed that the waterways that were navigable would be located where human populations could make best use of them commercially. Regions that suffered from backward pre-rail transport systems, limited inland navigation, and thus often extraordinarily high long-distance transport costs stood to gain considerably from infrastructure investment.

In these areas, railroads were truly necessary for both the export sector and domestic markets. By the late nineteenth century, railway construction provided a specific form of infrastructure capital that offered greater efficiency and affordability of overland transportation for goods and passengers alike in Latin America. By providing for low-cost inland movement, steam locomotion effected a tremendous increase in the supply of transport services to Latin American economies before 1930. This increase was complemented by innovations in ocean shipping and the associated creation of port facilities. Infrastructure investment embodied in transport improvements freed up capital and labor previously employed in producing transport services, permitting these factors of production to be used in other activities, raising the productivity with which they were employed, bolstering the growth of both agriculture and industry, and thereby raising

[2] One effort in this direction is William Summerhill, "Institutional Determinants of Railroad Subsidy and Regulation in Imperial Brazil," in Stephen Haber, ed., *Political Institutions and Economic Growth in Latin America: Essays in Policy, History, and Political Economy* (Stanford, CA, 2000).

national income. Where the demand for transport services was sufficient to compensate the cost of infrastructure investment, the net benefits were substantial. In this way, railways served as an important stimulus to economic growth in Latin America. Indeed, the sheer magnitude of the aggregate economic gains several Latin American countries derived from railway capital was unprecedented by international standards. By 1930, when the pace of railway expansion had already slowed, transport services along nascent motor roadways built on the higher levels of economic performance provided by the previous generations of infrastructural investment and, in many areas, served to sustain the process of intensive economic growth that was underway.

This chapter proceeds by providing an overview of four categories of infrastructure investment in Latin America before 1930. It first discusses the relatively limited development of terrestrial transportation before the advent of the steam-powered locomotion. It then traces the course of railway expansion and provides a summary of the main findings on the railway's impact. In reviewing the consequences of railway development, it focuses on the cases of Argentina, Mexico, Brazil, and Colombia. Three factors motivate this restricted examination. First, it is impossible to do justice to even the basic details of all Latin American countries in a single chapter. Second, these countries include the most important cases in terms of the extent of their infrastructure investments. Indeed, by 1900, the first three of these countries accounted for fully 75 percent of all railway track in Latin America. Finally, to date, rigorous econometric assessment of the railway's impact remains limited to these four cases.

Although railway expansion was by far the most important component of infrastructural development, it did not proceed in isolation from advances in other forms of infrastructure. The third section of the chapter, therefore, takes up the topic of port improvements in the age of export growth and mass migration. The rise of motor roads in the early twentieth century briefly occupies the conclusion.

ROADWAYS BEFORE STEAM

Large-scale investments in infrastructure came to Latin America relatively late. In partaking of the transportation revolution in a late-comer fashion, Latin America in effect largely skipped the turnpike era of internal improvements. Even in the best of cases, only very limited improvements to inland roads preceded railway development. Descriptions of transport conditions in Latin America by contemporaries in the first part of the nineteenth century provide historians with a sense of the strength of the brake on economic growth arising from backward pre-rail transport systems. Early roads throughout Latin America reflected in varying degrees the combination of two features: pre-contact indigenous routes of movement and the location of commercial centers that appeared during the colonial era. In a good many cases, colonial roads had their origins in indigenous trails when the latter proved useful to the evolution of commerce and trade.[3] In northeastern Brazil, trails from coastal ports evolved into crude, unpaved roads for animal traffic and carts that carried sugar for export. Elsewhere, roads, at times paved with stone, were constructed to facilitate the movement and monitoring of gold shipments from Minas Gerais to the coasts of Rio de Janeiro and São Paulo.[4] In Mexico, cart roads connected the capital both to the port of Veracruz and to the silver-mining regions, and in Central America, much of the colonial trade in indigo moved along simple trails. Throughout the Andes, footpaths frequently proved resistant to any transformation into roads, given the difficult terrain. In all too many areas, the costs of shipping goods were wildly exorbitant, and only those products with relatively high value-to-weight ratios were worth moving over any appreciable distance. An additional part of the challenge posed by slow, inefficient transportation in nineteenth-century Latin America was a frequent lack of physical security and the dissipation of public funds that could have been used to maintain and improve the highways. In much of mainland Spanish America, the factionalized struggles to capture control of the state made it difficult to consistently pursue and support policies designed to enhance communications. Moreover, warfare, brigandage, and hostile indigenous populations further increased the risk and thereby exacerbated the costs of overland movement.[5]

A geography highly unfavorable to inland movement was the chief culprit in the high costs of transport that plagued nineteenth-century Latin America. The steep mountain ranges of Mexico, Brazil, Colombia, and the other Andean regions physically partitioned large expanses, providing

---

[3] John H. Coatsworth, *Growth Against Development: The Economic Impact of Railroads in Porfirian Mexico* (DeKalb, IL, 1981), 17–18.

[4] Richard Momsen, *Rates Over the Serra do Mar* (Rio de Janeiro, 1964).

[5] Stephen Haber, *Industry and Underdevelopment: The Industrialization of Mexico, 1890–1930* (Stanford, CA, 1989), 13–15, 24–5; Bert J. Barickman, "'Tame Indians,' 'Wild Heathens,' and Settlers in Southern Bahia in the Late Eighteenth and Early Nineteenth Centuries," *The Americas* 51:3 (1995): 325–68.

natural barriers that were extremely difficult to breach and leaving markets geographically fragmented. Lacking navigable rivers, mid-nineteenth-century Mexico had long relied on a combination of wagons, animals, and human porters to move freight through the country. The Spanish colonial government, seeking to improve basic transport conditions, had grafted a road network on top of the pre-contact indigenous transport routes in order to link the major population centers, mines, and ports. Yet, by the end of the eighteenth century, Mexico's colonial transport system had fallen into disrepair, and there were not many stretches of road that would permit the passage of wheeled vehicle traffic. Wagons continued to carry freight wherever possible, but the bulk of the goods shipped in the nineteenth century was hauled over Mexico's steep terrain by mule.[6] In Colombia, the backbone of the limited transport system in the nineteenth century was the Magdalena River. Seasonal variations of water level and the presence of rapids impeded through passage. The cost of movement was elevated by the requirement of portage for a full twenty kilometers along one stretch of the river.[7] The introduction of steamboats later in the century helped reduce costs, but the river route did not otherwise enjoy any improvements in navigability. Nor was there much relief provided by turnpikes. Colombia's roads at independence were the paths inherited from colonial era, and no new roads were built before 1850. The steep mountains of the interior at many points did not even permit mules to pass, so that human porters were an especially important means of moving freight. Shipment by porter cost six times that by mule.[8] The little road building that did occur after 1850 was limited to linking the lowlands with the coast and did not involve the interior.[9]

In Brazil, few rivers were navigable in any commercially significant sense, and many were of limited relevance to all but the most local versions of trade. The absence of cheap, long-haul waterborne transport in inland areas with rich agronomic endowments and the virtual lack of an active colonial road-building scheme conditioned early settlement patterns. Unsurprisingly, at the start of the nineteenth century, much of Brazil's population lived within a few days travel of the coast. Interior settlement was limited to areas that were relatively accessible and to regions possessing readily marketable, high value-to-weight goods, such as the gold and diamond

---

[6] Coatsworth, *Growth Against Development*, 17–24.
[7] William Paul McGreevey, *An Economic History of Colombia, 1845–1930* (Cambridge, 1971), 42.
[8] Ibid., 42–8.
[9] Ibid., 162.

fields of Minas Gerais. Hilly and mountainous terrain, especially along the coast, extended from the northeast to the south, presenting an obstacle to overland communication with the interior that was just as imposing as inland mountain ranges elsewhere in the hemisphere. Even with its natural endowment of rivers, Brazil's pre-rail transport system was likely more rudimentary as that of Mexico. Argentina in particular, and the Rio de la Plata region in general, did not suffer to the same degree the topographic conditions that impeded overland communications in Mexico, Colombia, and Brazil. Up-country terrain grew more hilly than what was found on the littoral, and as one approached Andean ranges, the physical impediments to movement became quite obvious. Yet the major inland water routes did suffer barriers that could not be easily remedied by nineteenth-century channeling and canal-building techniques. The Paraná-Paraguay river system that connected the Rio de la Plata to the Mato Grosso region north of Asunción was far too shallow in some spots to allow for year-round movement.[10] Both the Uruguay and Paraná rivers had fall barriers that made unimpeded through passage impossible. Although the region did not have the mountainous terrain that complicated road building in other places, overland movement on roadways still suffered the normal vagaries of poor maintenance, washout, and minimal improvements in the half-century following independence. No figures exist to indicate the extent of road mileage or investment in roadways by public authorities in either the late colonial or early national period. In general, Latin America as a whole suffered from limited road capacity, and the capacity that did exist was crude, often little more than ruts, and barely suitable. In a few cases, turnpike companies were granted concessions, licenses, and even public subsidy by the mid-nineteenth century, though these improved roads were exceptional.[11] Although case studies of road companies are almost completely absent from the literature, it is a fair assessment that such roads, while improving the conditions of transit, did not offer much of a cost advantage for shippers. From the colonial Spanish Caribbean to the mainland republics, complaints by public officials and commercial interests alike commonly attributed economic stagnation to the lack of internal improvements. Given the physical location of productive possibilities, overland shipment became

---

[10] Thomas Whigham, *The Politics of River Trade: Tradition and Development in the Upper Plata, 1780–1870* (Albuquerque, NM, 1991), 4–7.
[11] Domingos Giroletti, "A Companhia e a Rodovia União e Indústria e o Desenvolvimento de Juiz de Fora, 1850 a 1900" (typescript, Belo Horizonte, 1980).

the predominant means of inland freight transportation in many regions of Latin America that had the brightest economic prospects. Yet road building, debilitated by the factors sketched previously, did not provide much in terms of new infrastructure at any time in the nineteenth century, did not in the aggregate contribute much to the transition to modern rates of economic growth, and never captured much tangible interest from policymakers until after the implantation of railways.

THE EXPANSION OF RAILWAY INFRASTRUCTURE

Railways were the most palpable of all of the infrastructure investments that characterized the economic modernization of Latin America in the nineteenth century.[12] They were widely heralded throughout the region even before their construction as the superlative solution to the problems posed by the high cost of overland interior transportation in the region. In many cases, that promise was realized, as proposed projects gradually came to fruition and brought major reductions in transport costs. The limited public and private resources of the newly independent Latin American countries made it difficult to improve the quality or capacity of the transport sector in the first half of the nineteenth century. Concessions in countries such as Brazil and Mexico were first made in the 1830s, but only Cuba executed its plans to build lines before mid-century. By and large, it was not until the second half of the century that Latin American nations began to construct rail networks in earnest. In Colombia, railways first traversed the Isthmus of Panama in 1855, but the country did not place another line in operation until 1871.[13] Until then, freight was carried by river wherever possible, but most of it was shipped overland across steep terrain on the backs of humans and mules.[14] Mexico had no significant railway until the completion of the line between Veracruz and Mexico City in 1873.[15] Brazil enjoyed its first railway in 1854, but the early major lines were not in place until the 1860s.[16]

---

[12] Roberto Cortés Conde, *The First Stages of Modernization in Spanish America* (New York, 1974).
[13] McGreevey, *Economic History of Colombia*, 253.   [14] Ibid., 43–5.
[15] Arthur P. Schmidt Jr., *Social and Economic Effect of the Railroad in Puebla and Veracruz, Mexico, 1867–1911* (New York, 1987), 1–11.
[16] Manoel da Cunha Galvão, *Notícia sobre as Estradas de Ferro do Brasil* (Rio de Janeiro, 1869).

Table 8.1. *Length of railway track in service by country, 1870–1930*

Year	Argentina	Bolivia	Brazil	Colombia	Costa Rica	Cuba	Chile	Ecuador	Guatemala	Honduras	Mexico
1870	732		744	80		1,295	797				417
1880	2,516		3,398	131		1,418	1,777	68			1,074
1890	9,432	238	9,973	282		1,646	2,747	82	190		9,544
1900	16,563	525	15,316	636	282	1,792	4,354	501	567		13,615
1910	27,994	823	21,326	875	654	3,281	5,945	750	662		19,280
1920	33,884	1,597	28,535	1,445	727	3,853	8,211	1,000	741	671	20,800
1930	38,120	1,953	32,478	2,843	669	4,381	8,937	1,132	819	1,109	23,345

Year	Nicaragua	Panama	Paraguay	Peru	Puerto Rico	Dominican Republic	El Salvador	Uruguay	Venezuela	Total
1870			72	669				23		4,065
1880	21		72	1,770				371		10,382
1890	175		217	1,599		127	87	1,133		34,134
1900	225		251	1,790	220	187	105	1,729	851	54,151
1910	235	81	251	1,962	290	233	121	2,373	879	81,590
1920	257	180	467	2,116	545	236	283	2,668	885	101,463
1930	235	349	497	3,056	545		623	2,746	885	115,786

Note: Length expressed in kilometers.
Source: Jesús Sanz Fernández, ed., *Historia de Los Ferrocarriles de Iberoamérica, 1837–1995* (Madrid, 1988).

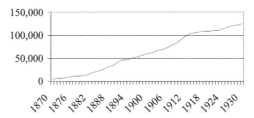

Figure 8.1. Kilometers of railway track in service in Latin America, 1870–1930
Note: Time series is based on continuous series of trackage for five countries (Argentina, Brazil, Chile, Cuba, and Mexico) and interpolated series for the other countries of the region.
Source: Jesús Sanz Fernández, ed., *Historia de los ferrocarriles de Iberoamérica, 1837–1995* (Madrid, 1998).

In 1850, few Latin American countries yet possessed a single kilometer of railway track. Table 8.1 shows that Latin America as a whole still had fewer than 5,000 kilometers of track by 1870. However, in the ensuing six decades, the capacity of the sector expanded rapidly. By 1930, 125,000 kilometers of railways were in operation. Figure 8.1 charts the expansion of track in service in Latin America from 1870 to 1930. During the 1870s, growth was weak, though the 1880s brought a considerable upswing. Growing political stability, improved financial intermediation, the spillover of savings from high-income economies abroad, and especially innovations in metals production (including the introduction of the Bessemer process, which reduced the cost of steel rails and rolling stock) account for the accelerated increase in the 1880s.[17] Expansion continued, albeit at a reduced pace, in the 1890s, slowed in particular by financial crises in Argentina and Brazil, both of which had accounted for a major share of the overall growth in Latin American railroad capacity up to that point. A sharp acceleration in the amount of new track placed in service during the first decade of the twentieth century stalled with the disruptions of the First World War, and railway expansion never again attained the earlier pace of growth. Interwar financial problems were followed by the Great Depression of the 1930s, while at the same time, motor roads gradually began to offer substitutes for the railroad for both passenger services and numerous classes of freight.

The geographic distribution of railways across Latin America generally followed, for much of the period, the imperatives of size, taking into

---

[17] B. R. Mitchell, *British Historical Statistics* (Cambridge, 1988), 273; U.S. Bureau of the Census, *Historical Statistics of the United States* (New York, 1976), 208–9.

account both territory and population, though several exceptions are noteworthy. Table 8.2 reveals the distribution of railway capacity by country, with capacity imperfectly indicated by the proportion of all Latin American railway track in service. Unsurprisingly, Argentina, Mexico, Brazil, and Chile accounted for the vast bulk of the region's rail capacity. Cuba, with its early head start, still possessed in 1870 more track in service than anyplace else in Latin America, though it is no surprise that it did not keep up through the end of the century and did not maintain its lead. Southern South America quickly emerged to dominate the rest of Latin America in terms of track per nation. By 1890, Argentina and Brazil together accounted for more than half of all railways in Latin America. In 1900, these two countries, together with Mexico, had 75 percent of the region's track. At the other extreme, the smaller nations, especially those of Central America, never held more than a miniscule share of the region's lines. Yet railway development was not exclusively a large-country phenomenon. Irrespective of their relative shares of the region's total rail capacity, nearly all of the Latin American countries enjoyed impressive increases in the extension of their respective railway systems between 1870 and 1930. Table 8.3 presents the trend rates of the expansion of railway track in service, by country. No pattern can be readily discerned in the rates of growth. Small and large countries alike were among the fastest growers in proportional terms. Honduras, starting of course from a very low base level of track, witnessed a quicker rate of railway expansion after 1870 than Argentina, Brazil, or Mexico. For most countries, the rate of increase in railway capacity likely outstripped the rate of growth of national income, as the railway substituted for preexisting modes of shipment and simultaneously created income effects that generated new demands for its own services. Of all the countries listed, only the Dominican Republic, Peru, and Venezuela stand out as truly laggard in terms of the expansion of their railway systems. In general terms, the rapid growth of railways throughout the region is testimony to the broader process of extensive economic growth underway between 1870 and 1930.

The length of track in service is a simple but useful indicator of capacity, though alone it does not take into account differences in relative intensity, either in terms of the population served or in utilization. Here there were significant differences across Latin America. Additional insights can be readily gleaned by considering the amount of track in terms of population. Table 8.4 provides such evidence for 1913, at the peak of railway growth and

Table 8.2. Share of total Latin American railway track by country (1870–1930)

Year	Argentina	Brazil	Cuba	Chile	Mexico	Peru	Uruguay	Bolivia	Colombia	Venezuela
1870	15.2%	15.4%	26.8%	16.5%	8.6%	13.9%	0.5%	0.0%	1.7%	0.0%
1880	19.9%	26.9%	11.2%	14.1%	8.5%	14.0%	2.9%	0.0%	1.0%	0.0%
1890	25.2%	26.6%	4.4%	7.3%	25.5%	4.3%	3.0%	0.6%	0.8%	0.0%
1900	27.8%	25.7%	3.0%	7.3%	22.9%	3.0%	2.9%	0.9%	1.1%	1.4%
1910	31.8%	24.2%	3.7%	6.8%	21.9%	2.2%	2.7%	0.9%	1.0%	1.0%
1920	31.1%	26.2%	3.5%	7.5%	19.1%	1.9%	2.4%	1.5%	1.3%	0.8%
1930	30.6%	26.0%	3.5%	7.2%	18.7%	2.5%	2.2%	1.6%	2.3%	0.7%

Year	Costa Rica	Ecuador	Guatemala	Honduras	Nicaragua	Panama	Paraguay	Puerto Rico	Dominican Republic	El Salvador
1870	0.0%	0.0%	0.0%	0.0%	0.0%	0.0%	1.5%	0.0%	0.0%	0.0%
1880	0.0%	0.5%	0.0%	0.0%	0.2%	0.0%	0.6%	0.0%	0.0%	0.0%
1890	0.0%	0.2%	0.5%	0.0%	0.5%	0.0%	0.6%	0.0%	0.3%	0.2%
1900	0.5%	0.8%	1.0%	0.0%	0.4%	0.0%	0.4%	0.4%	0.3%	0.2%
1910	0.7%	0.9%	0.8%	0.0%	0.3%	0.1%	0.3%	0.3%	0.3%	0.1%
1920	0.7%	0.9%	0.7%	0.6%	0.2%	0.2%	0.4%	0.5%	0.2%	0.3%
1930	0.5%	0.9%	0.7%	0.9%	0.2%	0.3%	0.4%	0.4%	0.0%	0.5%

Source: Sanz Fernández, *Historia de los ferrocarriles de Iberoamérica, 1837–1995*.

Table 8.3. *Trend rate of growth of railway track by country,*
1870–1930

Country	Trend rate of growth (% per year)
Honduras	6.5
Panama	6.5
Ecuador	6.4
Argentina	6.3
Mexico	6.3
Colombia	5.8
Uruguay	5.6
Brazil	5.5
Bolivia	5.4
Puerto Rico	4.7
Chile	3.9
Paraguay	3.9
Costa Rica	3.3
Guatemala	2.6
Cuba	2.5
Nicaragua	2.5
Dominican Republic	1.7
Peru	1
Venezuela	1

Note: In percent per annum. Trend rate of growth calculated by regressing the natural logarithm of track in service against a time trend.
Source: Sanz Fernández, *Historia de los ferrocarriles de Iberoamérica, 1837–1995.*

on the eve of the dramatic slowdown of the expansion of railway capacity throughout Latin America. Argentina had by far the greatest intensity of capacity in the region, with nearly four kilometers of track for every one thousand people. Neighboring Uruguay had only half that ratio. The Argentine ratio of track per capita was actually on par with that of the United States at the turn of the century. Chile, Brazil, and Mexico register a notch lower than Argentina but rank high by hemispheric standards. Colombia, Ecuador, and Panama, despite the late-breaking and impressively rapid growth rates of their railways, still had, by 1913, very low levels of track per capita. Panama, with its extensive coastlines and, ultimately, its canal, was not likely in great need of railway transport, to be sure. But the mountainous inland regions of Colombia and Ecuador would have benefited

Table 8.4. *Normalized extension of railways in service in Latin America, 1913*

Country	Track in service (Km)	Population (1,000s)	Km of track per 1,000 people
Argentina	31,186	7,917	3.94
Chile	8,147	3,509	2.32
Uruguay	2,592	1,316	1.97
Costa Rica	619	387	1.60
Cuba	3,846	2,507	1.53
Mexico	20,447	14,855	1.38
Brazil	26,062	24,161	1.08
Guatemala	987	1,180	0.84
Peru	3,317	4,347	0.76
Bolivia	1,440	2,025	0.71
Paraguay	373	657	0.57
Nicaragua	322	581	0.55
Honduras	241	588	0.41
Ecuador	587	1,469	0.40
Venezuela	858	2,633	0.33
El Salvador	328	1,058	0.31
Colombia	1,166	5,318	0.22
Panama	76	378	0.20

Source: Victor Bulmer-Thomas, *The Economic History of Latin America Since Independence* (Cambridge, 1994)

considerably from higher levels of railway services. Similar variation appears across the larger Latin American economies when rough measures of capacity utilization are taken into consideration for the countries in which such information is available. Reliable measures of railway output are not yet available for all of the countries, preventing a systematic comparison of rates of utilization. Argentina was by far the most railway-intensive of the Latin American economies, exhibiting far greater density of freight service per kilometer of track in 1913 than any other case for which freight-density measures are available. The level of freight service per capita in Argentina was staggering by regional standards, more than seven times that for Brazil and nearly three times that for Mexico.[18]

[18] William R. Summerhill, "Economic Consequences of Argentine Railroad Development" (mimeograph, 2000).

FINANCING RAILWAYS

Finance proved to be a serious hurdle for all infrastructure investments in the nineteenth century. In spite of the overwhelming advantages in most regions offered by railways, so obvious to many contemporary observers, the curious fact is that the new technology was adopted relatively late in most of Latin America. Little of this tardiness was attributable to a shortage of earnings from exports. Because the capital equipment, and even technical expertise, required for railway construction and operation came from abroad, it is a tautology that export earnings necessarily were required to pay for railways. Thus, the possibility of creating infrastructure with a foreign technology necessarily hinged, in an aggregate accounting sense, on the ability to successfully establish export activities. As Bulmer-Thomas has aptly noted, the fate of individual Latin American countries in the nineteenth-century commodity lottery could matter deeply.[19] Yet export earnings were available in most Latin American countries, even in the 1840s, in amounts large enough to begin to create some railways, although railways were not built outside of colonial Cuba. Although export earnings were necessary to import the capital goods needed for railways, their existence proved in no way a sufficient condition for the finance of infrastructure. Other factors were more important in attracting railway investment, and the abilities of individual nations to tap domestic and foreign savings for infrastructure varied considerably in this regard. Much of Spanish America had defaulted on sovereign debt after independence, complicating dramatically the ability of government to secure funds for internal improvements.[20] In a region with badly underdeveloped capital markets, the resources to finance huge investments required for the construction of railways were few and far between. With their high fixed costs and uncertain future profits, railways required large initial outlays, and a large dose of investor confidence, to construct and operate. In countries lacking the financial institutions capable of mobilizing a large volume of private savings and converting them into loanable funds, financing railway construction proved to be a major obstacle to infrastructural development. Indeed, the early railway history of Latin America is marked by government railway concessions that never

---

[19] Victor Bulmer-Thomas, *The Economic History of Latin America Since Independence*, 2nd ed. (Cambridge, 2003).
[20] Carlos Marichal, *A Century of Debt Crisis in Latin America* (Princeton, NJ, 1989).

bore fruit.[21] Capital drawn from a variety of domestic sources, including governments, helped finance the construction of the earliest lines. In light of the institutional constraints on the domestic financial intermediation and low savings rates, the countries of the region soon turned to the far more advanced capital markets of the industrializing North Atlantic economies. These they tapped for funds that were not forthcoming domestically. Given the great uncertainty over the profits to be generated by the railways, central and provincial governments in Argentina, Mexico, and Brazil offered investors blandishments in the form of subsidies and profit guarantees to attract railway investors. The various financial arrangements employed in constructing the early railway systems meant that, by the turn of the century, countries had railway sectors that combined multiple mechanisms of finance, drawing funds from the personal savings of single owners, local stock and bond issues, foreign stock and bond issues, and state coffers. In most countries, the single largest source of initial investment in infrastructure was the overseas capital markets.[22]

In Mexico, some early regional lines were financed by local entrepreneurs using sundry mechanisms to raise funds, including a lottery in one case. However, it was U.S. firms that ultimately garnered concessions to build the major trunk lines of the country in the late nineteenth century, and U.S. investors ultimately financed much of Mexico's railway construction. "Mexicanization" of the nation's railways by the government after the turn of the century also drew on foreign capital markets to raise loans, enabling the government to buy controlling shares of the major lines and better control rates and service.[23] In Argentina and Brazil, the early lines were similarly built using funds drawn from local and foreign markets, but also relied heavily on government involvement. Brazil's second railway, the Dom Pedro II, bogged down financially in its first decade of operation. The Brazilian government interceded, buying out the shareholders and becoming the

---

[21] Coatsworth, *Growth Against Development*, 33–8. For Brazil, one need only compare the list of hundreds of concessions granted as of the early 1890s with the much smaller number of lines actually in operation in the early twentieth century; João Chrockatt Pereira de Castro, *Brazilian Railways: Their History, Legislation, and Development* (Rio de Janeiro, 1893), and Brazil, Ministério da Viação e Obras Públicas, Inspectoria Federal das Estradas, *Estatística das Estradas de Ferro da União Relativo ao Anno 1898* (Rio de Janeiro, 1899).

[22] The role of the British capital market in Latin America is addressed in Lance E. Davis and Robert A. Huttenback, *Mammon and the Pursuit of Empire* (Cambridge, 1988); Michael Edelstein, *Overseas Investment in the Age of High Imperialism: The United Kingdom 1850–1914* (New York, 1982); and Irving Stone, *The Composition and Distribution of British Investment in Latin America, 1865 to 1913* (New York, 1987).

[23] Coatsworth, *Growth Against Development*, 37–8, 44–6.

sole owner of the line, which it thereafter extended, ultimately making it the largest and most important railway in the country.[24] An ensuing wave of railway construction, built in the late 1850s and the 1860s in the northeast and in São Paulo, was undertaken by British companies, financed initially by stock issues, and later by bonds, in London.[25] Brazilians also financed railways through local stock and bond issues, as was the case of the Companhia Paulista and the Companhia Mogiana in São Paulo, and the early phase of the Leopoldina, in Minas Gerais. In all of these cases, local funds could not alone sustain additional investment, and to finance expansion, Brazilian-owned lines regularly turned to London to obtain loans.[26] Argentina financed its early lines with local private funds, government construction, and British capital that enjoyed dividend guarantees, though here the pattern involved a reversal of the Brazilian and Mexican experiences near the end of the century. In the wake of the Baring Crisis in the 1890s, some of the government-owned lines were actually turned over to private hands.[27]

Governments sought to satisfy regional interests by adopting a liberal concession scheme. In Mexico, the central government passed concessions down to state governments, whereas in Brazil, provinces could concede routes within their borders but the central government granted concessions to both intra- and interprovincial lines. Railroad routing and location in Latin America were sometimes a function of economic prospects but were also heavily influenced by the political and financial strength of local interests. *Fazendeiros, estancieros*, and *hacendados* seeking to add to their wealth lobbied to ensure that a railway would pass near their properties in order to raise the value of their land. The fact that all landowners desired access to the cheapest transport possible meant that disputes over the trace of proposed rail line were frequent, at times slowing construction.[28] The result for each country was a rail system whose layout was closely tied to extant areas of settlement and within regions where immediate prospects for

[24] Almir Chaiban El-Kareh, *Filha branca de mãe preta: A Companhia da Estrada de Ferro D. Pedro II, 1855–1865* (Petrópolis, 1982), 117–28.

[25] Richard Graham, *Britain and the Onset of Modernization in Brazil* (Cambridge, 1968), 51–72.

[26] Flávio Azevedo Marques de Saes, *As ferrovias de São Paulo, 1870–1940* (São Paulo, 1981), 165–7; Colin M. Lewis, *Public Policy and Private Initiative: Railway Building in São Paulo, 1860–1889* (London, 1991), 35–51.

[27] Colin M. Lewis, *British Railways in Argentina, 1857–1914* (London, 1983), 124–45.

[28] Competing traces of the Companhia Paulista in São Paulo, for example, were disputed by various parties; see Robert Mattoon, "The Companhia Paulista de Estradas de Ferro, 1868–1900: Local Railway Enterprise in São Paulo, Brazil" (Ph.D. dissertation, Yale University, 1972), 50–60.

commercial profit (though not necessarily the profitability of the railways) were considerable. Mexico possessed a well-integrated rail grid by 1910, linking the major population centers to the coasts and to the United States. Argentine rail lines fanned out from Buenos Aires, with an impressive degree of cross-cutting articulation by 1900. By the turn of the century, Brazil had two large regional concentrations of connected railways: one in the northeast, which tied the interior to major ports, and a separate network linking the cities, farming areas, and ports of the south and south center.

Latin American societies and economies were predominantly rural for much of the period, and landowners played a central role in shaping the course of public transport policies. In particular, landowners lobbied government to reduce railway freight charges. By way of comparison, in the United States, agrarian populists complaining about rail rates had to await relief from state-level regulation and the passage of the Interstate Commerce Act in 1887. Most Latin Americans had recourse to central government intervention in rate-setting from the outset. Although much of Latin America was made up of high-tariff countries, to further boost construction railway equipment was typically imported at reduced rates or altogether duty-free. The policies regarding concessions, guarantees, and subsidy were one reason that despite their late start, Latin American rail systems grew at a relatively fast rate. Indeed, without such preferential policies, the pace at which cheap transport services diffused through the countryside would have been far slower.

Accompanying the deceleration of railway construction after 1914 was a reduced supply of investible funds from abroad.[29] Domestic capital markets in Latin America, which had developed considerably since the 1870s, remained too small, and savings rates too low, to carry alone the burden of finance going forward from the Great War.[30] Demands for capital, not exclusive to infrastructure, remained high after 1914, but the supply conditions were altered dramatically. As finance stagnated, so did the expansion of Latin American rail systems.

Treating capital, whether foreign or domestic in origin, as a single factor, even in infrastructure, is a far too general formulation to provide satisfactory

[29] See the contribution by Alan Taylor in this volume.
[30] On the financial disruptions in Brazil generally, see Winston Fritsch, *External Constraints on Economic Policy in Brazil* (Pittsburgh, PA, 1988); for Argentina, see Gerardo della Paolera and Alan M. Taylor, *Straining at the Anchor: The Argentine Currency Board and the Search for Macroeconomic Stability, 1880–1935* (Chicago, 2001). In Mexico, this coincided with the most violent and financially disruptive phase of the Revolution; see Stephen Haber et al., *The Politics of Property Rights* (Cambridge, 2003), 80–123.

analytical insights. To assess its economic impact, capital must be disaggregated into its component parts because the contribution of investment varied considerably across individual sectors and even specific investment projects. On average, railways absorbed far more capital than any other activity in this era. The consequences of railway capital formation have warranted focused investigation.

IMPACTS OF RAILWAY INVESTMENT

The extent to which transport improvements promoted longer-term economic growth in Latin America depended on several interrelated effects. Railways altered existing production relationships, sometimes profoundly. The lower costs of transport they offered influenced the decisions of consumers of transport services, who were often agricultural producers. The leading examples involve regions such as the Argentine pampa and the fertile interior regions of south-central Brazil, which had been beyond feasible exploitation before the introduction of the railroad. These experienced a wave of new settlement, investment, and commercial activity once infrastructure made them accessible. Transportation cost reductions widened the area of profitable cultivation, stimulating the rise of new agricultural enterprises, new settlement, new crops, and new investments in farming. Rapidly rising agricultural production and incomes were typically the result.

Assessing the impact of the transport infrastructure that was implanted in Latin America in the late nineteenth century requires the consideration of an array of benefits and costs and not just private profits to infrastructure investment. Conventionally, there were four channels by which transport infrastructure registered its impact on the economy. First was the direct cost savings on transporting goods and people by rail, or the "social saving." Reductions in transport costs freed up resources for other uses, creating a net savings to the economy as a whole. The second channel was the "forward linkage" from railways to other sectors of the economy. Railways provided an impetus to new activities and often fostered increases in the stock of resources available to firms and sectors that relied on transport services. When such forward linkages transpired, they usually took the form of new investment in agriculture, mining, and industry and, sometimes, new settlement. The third channel involved the demand for inputs necessary for the construction and operation of railways ("backward linkages"), stimulating industries that in turn further raised output per capita. The fourth channel is a residual category encompassing various consequences fostered in an indirect fashion by the interaction of railway development with legal structures, government, and the like ("institutional externalities"). In Latin America, the impulse to growth via these different channels was highly unbalanced. The social savings and the forward linkages were generally of much greater magnitude, and greater importance, than the other categories of linkage.

The first and most obvious impact of investments in railways in Latin America was the direct effect of the reduction of transport costs. Cost reductions per unit of freight or per passenger trip included lower fares and charges, savings on time, and reductions in travel hazards that the railroad provided. Railroads reduced the resource requirements for producing a given amount of transport services. The magnitude of these direct gains depended on the availability of affordable substitutes for the railroad and the share of the economy's output that required transportation. Where either substitutes were affordable or the share of total output carried by rail was small, the income gain from railway infrastructure was modest. Even where gains were large, they must still be considered in terms of the cost of securing them – that is, relative to the cost of providing the infrastructure. A railway that was too costly, in terms of the capital required to establish it, might not have been economical at all.

The poor pre-rail conditions in Brazil, Colombia, Argentina, and Mexico meant that the cost of carrying freight and moving passengers was quite high, and the unit cost savings provided by the railway were large. When added to the costs of other inputs to production, transport costs were high enough in many regions to eliminate any chance of profit for potential producers of a wide variety of crops and manufactures over very large areas of Latin America. Goods that were otherwise affordable at the farm or factory gate became prohibitively expensive once the transport bill was tacked on. This transport-cost wedge between producers and final users limited large portions of the population to purchasing only the most basic of necessities. When confronted with long, arduous journeys by foot, animal, or expensive trips by coach, many persons never ventured far from their immediate locale. Such features sharply limited the opportunities for material progress. Economies marked by high transport costs had vastly lower levels of economic activity, and thus lower levels of income, than those that enjoyed easy access to navigable waterways or manmade forms of infrastructure. With the relative price of shipment so high in so much of Latin America, it is little wonder that farmers, mine owners, nascent industrialists, and governments sought to improve transport conditions and lower costs by implanting a more efficient technology from abroad. Railways, by providing low-cost shipment, directly improved allocative efficiency and raised the level of output and income. In the case of the labor market, railways could enhance the geographic mobility of free workers, making it possible for them to go to jobs over distances previously considered unbridgeable.

The estimation of the magnitude of these direct effects is an exercise in applied benefit–cost analysis. The direct impact of the railway can be partitioned into the resource savings produced by the two main categories of transport services: the savings on freight shipment and the benefits of passenger travel. The freight social saving of railways is conventionally defined as the difference between the actual cost of shipping goods in one year by rail and the cost of shipping the same goods over the same distances by an alternative means of transport in the absence of railways. Passenger social savings are analogous, being the difference between the costs of passenger rail travel and the cost of traveling by nonrail modes of transport.

Including the cost of passenger travel time, the cost savings that railways created on these two types of service comprised an addition to the economy's total output. Because total output in the economy with railways was equal to the final output of the transport sector and the output of the sectors that produced all other goods and services, dependence on wagon or mule transport to produce the output of the transport sector meant that labor and capital involved in transport services could not be used in the production of other goods. Producing freight transport service with railways would release labor and capital involved in transport to other activities in the economy. The freight social saving achieved by shifting from costly nonrail modes of shipment to railways is equivalent to the loss in national income incurred by hypothetically switching from railroads to the next-best mode of transport. Passenger social savings arise in a very similar fashion and are equal to the total amount of resources saved by transporting people by rail rather than the alternatives (walking, riding, coaching).

Throughout Latin America, railway expansion resulted in large unit savings on freight services. The unit cost of shipping merchandise fell considerably in the decades following the opening of the first railways. The decline in the unit-cost in Mexico between 1878 and 1910 was at least an order of magnitude and was nearly that much in Argentina from the 1860s to 1913.[31]

---

[31] Coatsworth, *Growth Against Development*, 96–104; Summerhill, "Economic Consequences of Argentine Railroad Development."

Brazil's decline in the real transport charges over the same interval of time was similarly on the order of tenfold.[32] With the growth of each nation's rail system during the second half of the nineteenth century accompanied by a growing volume of freight services, social savings became quite large by the end of the nineteenth century. In 1900, freight social savings accounted for as much as one third of Brazilian and Mexican national income, and in Argentina they were around one quarter of the economy's total output. Colombian freight social savings were less than in these cases. For the late 1920s, an upper-bound measure runs between 3.4 and 7.9 percent of gross domestic product (GDP). That the social savings for Colombia were smaller than these other cases can be attributed to two features: Colombia's relatively low share of railroad transport output in GDP (which is also indicated by its relatively low level of track per capita), and the availability of some water substitutes for a portion of railroad traffic.[33] Passenger benefits were much less than freight savings in these countries, which contrasts with the results found in more advanced economies, where passenger benefits comprised a large share of the total direct impact of railroads.[34] Passenger benefits were, in part, proportional to the value of travel time that railroads saved, which differed a good deal between backward and advanced economies because of the higher wages of the latter.

The historical and economic significance of the social savings can be better understood in a broader comparative context. Table 8.5 presents direct savings estimates on railways in a variety of cases at various points in time. Direct comparisons across countries are more difficult to make than implied by the table, because of the differing assumptions underpinning the estimates in each case. Note, however, that in contrast to the results derived from studies of railways in North Atlantic economies, and even from some backward economies in which pre-rail transport was relatively efficient, the freight social savings from railways in Latin America were often large by global standards.

Even with large social savings, infrastructure investments could be uneconomical if the returns to the economy that they generated were not large enough to justify the capital dedicated to the railroad sectors. Yet, based on

[32] William Summerhill, *Order Against Progress: Government, Foreign Investment, and Railroads in Brazil, 1854–1913* (Stanford, CA, 2003), 74–83.

[33] María Teresa Ramírez, "Los ferrocarriles y su impacto sobre la economía colombiana," *Revista de Historia Económica* 15:1 (2001): 81–91.

[34] Gary Hawke, *Railways and Economic Growth in England and Wales, 1840–1870* (London, 1970), 40–54; Albert Fishlow, *American Railroads and the Transformation of the Antebellum Economy* (Cambridge, 1966), 90–2; J. Hayden Boyd and Gary M. Walton, "The Social Saving from Nineteenth-Century Rail Passenger Services," *Explorations in Economic History* 9 (Spring 1972): 233–54.

Table 8.5. *Estimates of railway freight social savings for various countries*

Country	Year	Social saving as a share of GDP (percent)
England and Wales	1865	4.1
England and Wales	1890	11.0
France	1872	5.8
Germany	1890s	5.0
Spain	1912	23.7
Belgium	1865	2.5
Belgium	1912	4.5
Russia	1907	4.6
China	1933	0.5
United States	1859	3.7
United States	1890	8.9
Argentina	1913	26.0
Colombia	1927	7.9
Mexico	1910	38.5
Brazil	1913	22.0

Source: Summerhill, *Order Against Progress*, 98.

what is known about the social rate of return for at least three Latin America cases, it is clear that investment in railway infrastructure was a wise one in the aggregate (though such investments could still be considerably unfruitful in specific instances). For several major lines (including the largest and most heavily traveled) in Mexico, Argentina, and Brazil, the social rates of return to railroad infrastructure were quite large, easily high enough to justify investment, and even subsidy. The social return to investment in the Mexican Central railway system exceeded 20 percent per year by the 1890s, the social returns implied by the benefit–cost ratios on Colombia's larger railroads in the 1920s were impressive, and a conservative estimate for the social rate of return for the railway sector in Brazil in 1913 ranged between 18 and 23 percent.[35] In terms of their direct benefits, outlays on railway systems were an investment in Latin American infrastructure with handsome aggregate returns.

[35] Coatsworth, "Impact of Railroads on the Economic Development of Mexico" (Ph.D. dissertation, University of Wisconsin, Madison, 1972), 140–2; McGreevey, *Economic History of Colombia*, 264–9; Summerhill, *Order Against Progress*, 99–105.

LINKAGE EFFECTS

The notion of linkages serves to categorize the various potential ties between one economic activity and others. In the case of railroads, there were many possible channels of such effects. Conventionally, historians have focused heavily on forward and backward linkages from railroad development, along with other externalities that do not fit cleanly into any single category. Forward linkages from Latin American railways were of the conventional type, in the sense that they created incentives for crop expansion, new investment, and, in the relatively more labor-scarce regions, immigration. As the railway networks grew, cheap transport became available on an increasingly broader scale, pushing beyond the boundaries of cultivation that prevailed at the moment of the railway's first appearance. Moreover, railways themselves became more efficient over time, producing output at a lower unit cost as they operated at higher levels of capacity utilization. Hence, the forward linkages were dynamic in nature.

The main elements comprising the forward linkage generally reduce to the increase in the stocks of factors of production. Railways in some areas reinforced traditional patterns of commerce; in others, they rearranged things completely. These linkages varied from nation to nation and even across regions within nations. The rather dramatic reduction in transport charges created marked regional realignments in crop specialization and the output mix. In the settler economies of Argentina and southern Brazil, it was railways that fostered heavy flows of immigrants from abroad to the interior. They may well have encouraged higher savings and new investments, though the evidence on such points is so scant as to justify excluding any detailed discussion of them. By bringing more land, and frequently higher-productivity lands, into use, railway extensions raised the average products of labor and capital in the affected areas. And by shifting out the demand curve of labor, immigrants were attracted by higher wages, leading to a mutually reinforcing process of capital and labor importation. The strength of these effects depended on the conditions in each setting. In Mexico, railways revitalized the mining industry, which generated large capital inflows but led to virtually no immigration. In Argentina, by way of contrast, huge quantities of capital and labor poured into the country as the railroad opened highly fertile farmland to new cultivation.

In short, forward linkages generated a unique boost in the level of output per capita, beyond that registered by the direct social savings, though to date there are few quantitative measures of their size. Instead, the more

qualitative effects have occupied historians' discussions of the railway forward linkage in Latin America. Railways have long been viewed as having
played a pivotal role in Latin America, less through their role in raising
incomes and more in terms of increasing the export orientation of the
region's economies. In virtually all of Latin America, railroads boosted
export activities and, in Mexico and Argentina, the effect was so strong
that the export sectors grew faster than the economy as a whole. In Mexico,
market conditions, mineral endowments, and railway transport rate policies
favored rapid export-sector growth during the Porfiriato. By one estimate,
in 1910 more than 50 percent of the tonnage on Mexico's most important rail line was export-sector produce, more than double the ratio that
obtained in 1885.[36] Mexico's exports were especially railway-intensive, using
a large share of rail transport capacity. The consequences of this for altering the output mix of the economy were dramatic. In 1910, the share of
exports in GDP had nearly doubled over their share in 1877, rising to 17.5
percent.[37] In Argentina, the overall output mix similarly responded to railway development, accelerating the shift from pastoral activities to intensive
agriculture and making for rapid increases in the volume of exports. Probably even more so than in the case of Mexico, the surge of late-nineteenth
century export growth in Argentina rested almost entirely on the arrival of
railways.

In an interesting departure from the Argentine and Mexican pattern of
a railway-induced growth, Brazilian railways differed with regard to their
forward linkage effects and their impact on the output mix of the economy.
Railway expansion in Brazil was actually accompanied by a declining share
of export-sector freight and a slowly declining ratio of exports to GDP.
The share of exports in Brazilian GDP declined at an annual rate of somewhere around 1 percent from 1870 to 1913.[38] Though Brazilian railways were
intended to foster export growth from the outset, they, in fact, generated
even more rapid growth in the domestic-use sector of the economy. In
Colombia, the rise of the coffee sector in the late nineteenth century owed

[36] Coatsworth, *Growth Against Development*, 130–4. However, the intensity of the railroads' effect on
   Mexico's export sector has been disputed; compare Coatsworth, *Growth Against Development*, 122–33,
   and Kuntz Ficker, *Empresa extranjera y mercado interno: el Ferrocarril Central Mexicano, 1880–1907*
   (Mexico City, 1995), 211–348.
[37] John H. Coatsworth, "The Decline of the Mexican Economy, 1800–1860," in Reinhard Liehr, ed.,
   *America Latina en la época de Simón Bolívar: La formación de las economías nacionales y los intereses
   económicos europeos, 1800–1850* (Berlin, 1989).
[38] Summerhill, *Order Against Progress*, 135–47.

much to railway development, and most of the lines built there before 1914 were established with an eye to boosting the coffee trade. But even there, the export linkage turned out to be weaker than one might have expected.[39]

Railways in Latin America did not have powerful domestic backward linkages, despite the fact that railway construction and operation required large quantities of iron and steel, coal, and sophisticated capital equipment. Absolute weakness was apparent in the very limited demands for domestic manufactures, minerals, and financial inputs derived from railway construction in the region. Backward linkages from Latin American railways were not especially weak in comparison with the advanced economies of the North Atlantic. That Latin American railways do not appear to have been uniquely deficient in this regard can be gleaned from a careful examination of the nature of backward linkages in the industrializing economies. The advanced economies of the North Atlantic enjoyed their ascendance because of changes across a broad front of activities that collectively comprised sustained economic growth. There, the successful articulation of even modest backward linkages depended on a process of industrial advance that predated the diffusion of steam locomotion.[40]

Though Latin American nations did not come to provision the bulk of their own railway needs before 1930, there was, in a number of cases, a modest magnification of industries that supplied the railways. Nearly everywhere in Latin America, domestic railway shops over time came to provide repair services and basic fabrication of rolling stock in the form of passenger cars and freight wagons. Assembly activities still required a high portion of imported content in many nations because domestic manufacturing was not able to provide basic components. Porfirian Mexico succeeded in manufacturing some of its own rails and also provided some of its own fuel coal. But there were strong limits to these possibilities for most of the period under study; by the turn of the century, Mexico possessed only a single modern steel mill.[41] In Brazil, no domestic iron and steel manufacture developed in response to railways, coal mining in the south received little stimulus from railway operation, and only items of basic rolling stock came to be manufactured domestically during this period. Chile, like most

---

[39] Ramírez, "Ferrocarilles y su Impacto," 102–8.
[40] Germany stands out as the principal exception in this regard; see Rainer Fremdling, "Railroads and German Economic Growth: A Leading Sector Analysis with a Comparison to the United States and Great Britain," *Journal of Economic History* 37:3 (1977): 583–604.
[41] Haber, *Industry and Underdevelopment*, 30–7.

other nations, provided some of the inputs for railroads and established assembly and maintenance facilities for rolling stock. But it did not enjoy an industrial boom as a result of railway development.[42]

In the absence of domestic backward linkages, Latin American railways created leakages from the income stream that Latin America would not have had if it had been able to tap its own derived demands for railway inputs. In Mexico, it is estimated that around 60 percent of railway revenues in 1910 were spent abroad on imported railway inputs.[43] In Brazil, the ratio was even higher and the leakage from foreign provisioning ran to as much as 3 percent of GDP.[44] By importing its railroad inputs, the region exported potentially significant employment and income effects overseas. That so many inputs came from abroad may be interpreted to mean that railways somehow caused the Latin American economies to miss out on a critical opportunity to develop a manufacturing base and industrialize. Yet there is little reason to expect railways in Latin America to have created around them an entire manufacturing sector because they did not typically do this elsewhere. In advanced industrializing economies, the backward linkages from railways to industry were of limited importance because domestic iron, steel, and coal activities were already large and well developed, as part of a generalized process of industrialization predating the construction of railways.[45]

By contrast, such linkages were unimportant in countries like Brazil because the domestic iron sector was so backward and domestic coal was woefully inadequate in terms of quantity and quality. Identifying the specific reasons for the absence of stronger backward linkages from railways in Latin America requires an analysis looking beyond railways to the conditions of industry itself in the pre-railroad era.[46] Beyond their industrial potential, railways also registered some – though often modest – impact on domestic capital markets via lines that issued debt and equity at home.

Future research will, no doubt, better illuminate the full array of benefits and costs that railway infrastructure investment created. Studies that explicitly consider the relative merits and pitfalls of the rapid increase in foreign

---

[42] Guillermo Guajardo, "Nuevos datos para un viejo debate: los vínculos entre ferrocarriles e industrialización en Chile y México, 1860–1950," *El Trimestre Económico* 65:258 (1998): 213–61.

[43] Coatsworth, *Growth Against Development*, 143–4.

[44] Summerhill, *Order Against Progress*, 133.

[45] Robert W. Fogel, *Railroads and American Economic Growth* (Baltimore, MD, 1964), 190–210; Fishlow, *American Railroads*, 141–3.

[46] William Callaghan, "Obstacles to Industrialization: The Iron and Steel Industry in Brazil During the Old Republic" (Ph.D. dissertation, University of Texas, Austin, 1981).

investment, the differential transport cost reductions resulting from the pattern of regulation, and the opportunity costs of subsidy policy, will aid in refining the characterizations historians establish with respect to infrastructure. The results to date for Mexico, Brazil, Colombia, and Argentina suggest that these countries, like other economies that had especially backward pre-rail transport systems, captured benefits from infrastructure in the form of railways that outstripped any other sources of material progress in terms of their impact. Railway expansion in Latin America removed one of the most important impediments to the process of economic growth – high internal transport costs. By integrating markets and creating gains from regional specialization and improved interregional terms of trade, infrastructure embodied in railways spurred per capita income growth in the Latin American economies and laid the groundwork for the formation of national markets that were required to initiate and sustain modern industrialization.

PORT IMPROVEMENTS

The importance of steam in the transportation revolution was, of course, not limited to locomotives on land. Even before railways began to rapidly expand in Latin America, steam-powered shipping had already registered an impact. The application of steam to freighters, and the creation of steel-hulled ships, reduced the costs of shipping exports from Latin American ports to overseas markets and the costs of importing key inputs, including the very materials needed to construct railways. But these cost reductions were, in fact, modest in comparison to the impact of the railroad on inland transport costs. Real overseas shipping rates to South America fell by as much as one half between 1870 and 1930, but with considerable fluctuation around the trend.[47] The shipping component was but a small fraction of the overall transport costs incurred by Latin American foreign trade. Indeed, the development of new areas of settlement and production depended far less on shipping than it did on the decline in inland transport costs, which proved to be indispensable to the integration of markets for agriculture and manufacturing.

---

[47] Saif I. Shah Mohammed and Jeffrey Williamson, "Freight Rates and Productivity Gains in British Tramp Shipping, 1869–1950" (National Bureau of Economic Research, Working Paper no. 9531, 2003), Appendix 2, 7–8.

Table 8.6. *Merchant shipping registered in selected Latin American countries, 1920 (1,000s of registered tons)*

Country	Merchant shipping capacity steam	Merchant shipping capacity sail
Argentina	140	20
Brazil	475	22
Chile	52	20
Cuba	44	–
Honduras	31	–
Mexico	42	–
Peru	33	22
Uruguay	52	18
Venezuela	4.9	–

Source: B. R. Mitchell, *International Historical Statistics, the Americas, 1750–1988* (New York, 1993).

As trade expanded in Latin America, ships with a larger displacement, and the large number of ships visiting Latin American ports, required port expansion and improvements. Domestic merchant marine fleets emerged to augment foreign-owned shipping lines serving the region. Partial figures on the volume of shipping registered in selected Latin American nations in 1920 are presented in Table 8.6. Unsurprisingly, the largest economies in the aggregate possessed the most significant commercial shipping fleets. By 1920, Latin America had long enjoyed access to modern shipping services. Steam vessels appeared with growing frequency in the Rio de la Plata already in the 1850s.[48] But by the 1870s and 1880s, with railways hauling larger volumes of freight, much of it bound for export, countries confronted bottlenecks at ports throughout the region. Facilities that were barely adequate for the volume of trade in the first half of the nineteenth century proved wholly inadequate for the export booms of the last third of the century. Infrastructure expansion in railways thus created derived demands for port investments to handle larger volumes of commodity output. Historians have not yet supplied for ports the detailed empirical analog to the literature on railways. It is known that port improvements appeared broadly across Latin America. The simplest version of such improvements involved

[48] Clifton B. Kroeber, *The Growth of the Shipping Industry in the Rio de la Plata Region, 1794–1860* (Madison, WI, 1957), 129.

expanding the amount of dock space available. More complex versions of upgrades were common and included not just dock construction but also the dredging of channels, landfills to provide more frontage, establishment of dry docks and other repair facilities, and the creation of large warehouse complexes.

Even still, the high-throughput requirements of modern trade outstripped the capacity that was available in many of Latin America's traditional ports. This, combined with localized regional shifts in production, led to secondary ports picking up an important share of commerce in the larger countries. Competition between port cities further helped spur the necessary increases in capacity for docking, loading, and discharging freight. In Argentina, despite Buenos Aires's early position as the country's principal port, by 1910, a large increment of basic commodity trade went through secondary port facilities rather than the capital city.[49] Puerto Madero's inauguration in the late 1880s was a response to the stunning export expansion underway in Argentina.[50] It brought a significant increase in the port capacity for Buenos Aires. Puerto Madero's opening in 1897 also bit into the trade that had been growing at Rosário and other ports along the Rio de la Plata, as the expanding rail network and the multitude of port facilities provided shippers with new options for routing.[51]

No estimate exists of the capital invested in port improvements or even measures of the overall increase in the handling capacity for the period 1870–1930. Some broad features are apparent from the descriptive literature. As in the case of railroads, a mixed public and private effort underpinned Latin American port projects. Some port operations and upgrades were done by private concessionaires; others were executed directly by governments.[52] For instance, up until the 1860s, the port facilities along the Rio de la Plata were mainly privately owned. With expansion of trade toward the end of the century, government began to take on a broader scope of direct responsibilities in many ports.[53]

In Chile, bottlenecks appeared as nitrate extraction grew, and the trade soon became limited by inadequate port facilities. Capacity increases

[49] Lewis, *British Railways*, 210; Silvia B. Lázzaro, *Estado, capital extranjero y sistema portuario argentino, 1880–1914* (Buenos Aires, 1992), 112.
[50] Edgardo J. Rocca, *El Puerto de Buenos Aires en la historia* (Buenos Aires, 1996), 155–62.
[51] Luis Dodero, *La navegación en la Cuenca del Plata y sus propulsores* (Buenos Aires, 1961), 52–4.
[52] Lázzaro, *Estado, Capital extranjero*; Joanne Fox Przeworski, *The Decline of the Copper Industry in Chile and the Entrance of North American Capital, 1870–1916* (New York, 1980), 137.
[53] Kroeber, *Growth of the Shipping Industry*, 41–2.

between 1870 and 1912 allowed total shipping per year in Chilean ports to jump from five million tons to more than fifty million tons, a full order-of-magnitude increase.[54] As was done in Brazilian shipping, on certain routes, the Chilean government subsidized commercial rates to guarantee service into ports in areas of secondary importance in commerce. In Brazil, the extensive coastline meant that most regions of the country enjoyed relatively good access to basic port facilities.[55] As the capacity of individual ships increased and trade increased as a result of coffee cultivation, first in Rio de Janeiro and then later in São Paulo, most shipping activity concentrated in ports along the country's southern coastline. Late nineteenth-century port modernization and expansion concentrated in this region, and the ports of Rio de Janeiro and Santos in particular underwent a series of major expansions. Although publicly supervised, major ports like that of Rio were privately administered. Contracts awarded for the administration of the port changed hands at several points, suggesting that public authorities fostered a competitive environment as a way of securing better port services.[56]

Through public and private investments, Latin America's ports increased their capacity in the era of export-led growth. Demand-driven improvements in shipping infrastructure made it possible for the region's economies to realize their comparative advantage in the trade in primary products. In combination with the massive increase in inland transport services, port modernization proved to be a central element in the transition to economic growth throughout the region.

CONCLUSION: THE RISE OF MOTOR ROADS AND THE ECLIPSE OF THE RAILWAY

The financial difficulties that appeared in Latin America with the onset of the First World War, which slowed railway expansion, came at a critical historical moment in the development of modern transport technology. The successful and cost-effective innovation of the internal combustion engine, in combination with affordable petroleum fuel, provided a highly flexible mode of transport that both complemented and substituted railway

---

[54] Przeworski, *Decline of the Copper Industry*, 148.
[55] Brazil, *Portos do Brasil* (Rio de Janeiro, 1926), passim.
[56] Sergio Lamarão, *Dos trapiches ao porto* (Rio de Janeiro, 1991), 128–52.

Table 8.7. *Motor vehicles in use in Latin America, 1930 (1,000s)*

Country	Passenger cars	Commercial vehicles
Argentina	344	92
Bolivia	1.2	1
Brazil	133	67
Chile	28	15
Colombia	8.8	5
Costa Rica	1.4	0.5
Cuba	27	15
Ecuador	1.4	1
El Salvador	1.8	0.4
Guatemala	2	0.8
Honduras	0.7	0.4
Mexico	63	25
Nicaragua	1	0.2
Panama	6.3	1.7
Paraguay	0.7	1
Peru	8.7	5.2
Uruguay	37	10
Venezuela	11	6.8

Source: Mitchell, *International Historical Statistics, the Americas, 1750–1988.*

services. Cars and trucks were not only competitive means of movement for both passengers and certain classes of freight but also had the advantage of point-to-point delivery, which could never be emulated by railways. The appearance of motor vehicles in Latin America thus opened a new chapter in the transportation revolution in the region.

Yet the successful diffusion of automobiles in Latin America depended on the existence of trafficable routes, which was the very same issue that bedeviled early nineteenth-century transport improvements. Exploiting the advantages of motor vehicles thus required attention to the question of roads and required a level of investment in them that had never previously existed in Latin America. Table 8.7 provides indicators of the numbers of motor vehicles in use throughout the region at the end of the period under consideration by. No measures of aggregate road mileage or public investments in highways are available for Latin America as a whole. The figures in Table 8.7 reveal expected tendencies. Economies that were larger, in the aggregate, had greater numbers of motor vehicles in service. All indications are that these countries undertook considerable investments in public highway infrastructure following the First World War. In postrevolutionary Mexico during a rapidly expanding public investment effort, the share of government investments directed to roadways increased from 7.3 percent in 1925 to more than 30 percent in 1937.[57] In Brazil, by 1915, the federal budget provided funds for road construction, and additional subsidies soon followed. State governments in the Old Republic independently pursued their own road construction programs energetically in the 1920s, providing both feeder roads to existing rail lines and new highways that permitted direct movement over longer distances by truck.[58]

For many categories of goods, shipment by road even today remains less viable than shipment by rail, especially with respect to the products of mining and forestry. Yet for most other goods, and for passengers, trucks, cars, and buses provided a powerful competitive force against railways. In the six decades since 1870, Latin American countries had come full circle with their infrastructure requirements, from crude highways whose need for improvement was obviated by the iron horse, through the complete cycle of railway expansion, then back to roads in order to accommodate the new means of locomotion. By 1930, there was much about the mobility of people and commerce in Latin America that had changed and, along with it, both the level and structure of economic activity. Yet, by that point, the railways, which still did most of the heavy lifting in providing transport services, were no longer seen as the central component of future infrastructure expansion. The way forward for large sectors of many Latin American economies and, for both exports and the domestic economy, became the highway.

---

[57] Enrique Cárdenas, *La industrialización mexicana durante la gran depresión* (Mexico City, 1987), 155.
[58] Richard Downes, "Autos over Rails: How U.S. Business Supplanted the British in Brazil, 1910–1928," *Journal of Latin American Studies* 24, 3 (October 1992): 551–83.

Part III

FACTOR ENDOWMENTS

9

ECONOMIC GROWTH
AND ENVIRONMENTAL CHANGE

OTTO T. SOLBRIG

INTRODUCTION

Economic activity inevitably alters the natural environment. Lately, there has been a great deal of concern that increased human activity is having effects on the natural environment that may be irreversible, with possibly negative effects on human societies, such as the loss of the ozone layer or global warming. But what is the environment?

Environment is not an easy concept to define. In a fundamental and very general sense, the environment is the surroundings of an object. However, to distinguish between an object and its environment is an abstraction because in nature nothing stands alone and all objects are linked through material and energy flows.

The environment is then an abstraction, a human construct. For most persons, the environment is the physical and biological surroundings: land (lithosphere), water (hydrosphere), air (atmosphere), and wildlife (biosphere) in their different manifestations. There is less agreement as to whether aspects of human societies – such as poverty or income inequality – can also be considered part of the environment of an activity. Increasingly, the tendency is to consider them part of the environment, the so-called social environment. An economic history of the environment is consequently a history of the modifications effected by humans on their physical and biological surroundings and, to a lesser extent, on society.

The use of the term environment in the aforementioned sense is relatively new. The older literature speaks of nature. Yet nature is a more restricted term because it refers only to the physical and biological aspects of the surroundings of an object. Furthermore, it implies an existence independent from the object being studied. The term environment is also related conceptually to that of development.[1] Until the middle of the twentieth century, humans conquered nature in quest of economic gain. With the implantation of the development paradigm, the approach is that development is limited by environmental constraints.[2] This represents an important conceptual shift.

The physical and biological environment provides the resources that sustain human existence: food and water, fibers and skins for clothing, materials for shelter and tools, and fuel. Given its importance for human existence, from ancient time, nature has been provided with religious, ethical, and esthetical value. These estimations determine how human societies perceive the environment and condition the methods they employ to extract resources from their surroundings. Yet human societies, regardless of their religious or ethical values, have modified the environment by gathering, hunting, cultivating, logging, mining, and building. Otherwise people could not survive. As human societies have grown in numbers and their economic activities multiplied, the rate of extraction of resources from the environment has increased by several orders of magnitude. When most of the population was rural, the role of nature was clearly understood. Today, with a mostly urban population, the connection between economic growth and environmental change is not always clearly comprehended.

We call the physical and biological elements of an area and their mutual interactions the ecosystem of such an area. This can refer to a small area, as small as a drop of water, or it can encompass the entire Earth. Ecologists are very aware that the world's natural ecosystem is a thermodynamically open system, which depends on the capture by green plants of solar energy. This energy then circulates through the ecosystem, fueling the work undertaken by all organisms in their daily life. Humans are no exception. It has been calculated that humans utilize at present 7 percent of the world's photosynthetic energy to feed themselves and their domestic animals, but affect indirectly around 40 percent of the solar energy captured by plants. In addition, human societies are utilizing fossil energy, which is the solar energy captured by plants in the past. Consequently, over half the energy that circulates through the Earth at present flows through a system that

---

[1] W. Sachs, "Global Ecology and the Shadow of 'Development,'" in W. Sachs, ed., *Global Ecology* (Halifax, 1993).

[2] D. H. Meadows et al., *The Limits to Growth: A Report to the Club of Rome's Project on the Predicament of Mankind* (New York, 1972).

is either entirely human made, or is influenced in its behavior by human societies. This is an unprecedented situation in the Earth's history.

But although open thermodynamically, the Earth is a closed system in relation to material flows. In nature, all materials cycle, albeit at different rates. People depend on the natural processes that cycle nitrogen, carbon, water, phosphorous, and other essential elements. Humans make use of these processes that have been called ecosystem services when they dump wastes into rivers, oceans, landfills, and the atmosphere, which nature eventually turns first into harmless compounds and then reduces to its basic elements, which are then recycled.

Until now, this process of relying on the natural ecosystem to capture solar energy and circulate wastes has worked very well and human societies have adapted to it. Yet there are many signs that point out that, as the human economic system has grown and the natural ecosystem has shrunk, the system is beginning to fail. The accumulation of carbon dioxide and other greenhouse gases in the atmosphere is a clear sign that the natural system cannot cycle carbon out of the atmosphere at the same rate that it is inputted. Likewise, the accumulation of oxides of nitrogen (NO_x) in the atmosphere, in water, and on land is a sign of the inability of the ecosystem to cycle nitrogen compounds at the same rate as human societies eject them.

The consumption of energy and materials and the production of wastes are not evenly distributed among nations and regions. Europe, the United States, and Japan have clearly exceeded the capacity of their remaining natural ecosystems to provide the needed ecological services. A clear indication of this is their need to import fossil energy, minerals, and, in the case of Europe and Japan, also food. Other regions of the world are net exporters of these products, hastening the disintegration of their own natural ecosystems' capacity as they export natural capital. Historically, Latin America has been such a region.

With industrialization and globalization,[3] the environmental impact of humans has changed in intensity and scope. Before the industrial era, most human activities had only a local impact and very occasionally a regional impact. Increasingly, the scale of the imprint has enlarged and today we deal with truly global effects such as the thinning of the ozone layer, the increase in atmospheric carbon dioxide, and global warming. The enlarged scale of

[3] John Coatsworth, "Cycles of Globalization, Economic Growth and Human Welfare in Latin America," in Otto Solbrig, R. Paarlberg, and F. di Castri, eds., *Globalization and the Rural Environment* (Cambridge, MA, 2001), 23–48.

the environmental impact of human activities is of universal concern. There is fear that it may affect the very survival of human societies or, as is more likely in the short term, that it may have a very negative economic impact.[4]

Latin America and the Caribbean are an agglomeration of different countries, landscapes, and ecosystems. They share a common cultural tradition that justifies our consideration of the environmental impact of people in this region. The diversity of landscapes and physical settings, nonetheless, means that there will be a great diversity of human impacts that will have to be considered independently.

The imprint of humans on the environment in Latin America is of ancient origin. Early hunter-gatherers who invaded the continent thirty thousand years ago were responsible for the disappearance of many animal species, such as woolly mammoths and giant sloths, and the modification of local landscapes. The environmental impact was considerably increased with the advent of native agriculture six thousand years ago. A further impact was the introduction of the plow, livestock, and intensive mining by Europeans after Columbus's voyages; and once again in the nineteenth century with the introduction of new methodologies for resource extraction as a result of the development of the Atlantic economy following European industrialization. Finally, the intensification of agriculture and extractive activities in the last fifty years brought a further increase in the rate of environmental modification.

The use of natural resources by people and their effect on the environment are predominantly a function of human density, the level of economic activity, and the technologies employed. Environmental impact is also a function of the physical and biological characteristics of an area. The negative consequences of a given activity such as mining or agriculture, under similar conditions, will be much greater in a mountainous area than in a flat region; greater in the tropics or the arctic than in temperate regions, and so on. In discussing the history of the environment, great attention has to be paid to geographical characteristics. In the debates regarding environmental impact, there is a tendency to emphasize one or the other (geography, population, culture) factor. Yet all three are intimately connected and cannot be easily separated.

The environmental impact can also be considered as a question of land use (Figure 9.1). Every human activity affects land use. The social, cultural, political, demographic, and economic characteristics of each society

---

[4] H. E. Daly, *Beyond Growth* (Boston, 1996).

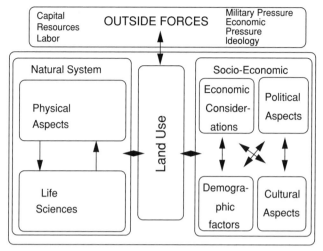

Figure 9.1. Determinants of land use.
Note: To the right are the principal social determinants and, to the left, the natural constraints. Above are some external forces that increasingly affect land use.

condition its impact on land use. In turn, the kind and intensity of land use govern the degree to which the natural ecosystem is modified. Yet, as these modifications affect the characteristics of the ecosystem, they in turn feed back on land use and eventually on human society. Human communities, in turn, are not isolated but interact with other nations through commerce, capital and technological flows, ideological exchanges, and military and power relations. Those interactions affect how a given society uses its land and treats its environment. Increasingly, land use depends on decisions taken to meet the needs of the global economy, with local needs playing a minor role. This often leads to land degradation, the costs of which are borne mostly at the local level.

Most writing regarding environmental impacts tends to focus on only certain aspects, be they the impact of economic growth on the natural environment, the cost of extraction of goods from the land, or the influence of exterior forces on society. Seldom do investigations take all aspects into consideration. Yet environmental problems are intimately connected with food and fiber production, wealth creation, demographic control, and income distribution, and cannot be fully understood if each force impacting the environment is taken in isolation.

In this chapter, I am primarily concerned with the environmental impact of economic activities and land use on the Latin American environment. I first briefly describe the Latin American geography because this knowledge is necessary to understand the diversity of landscapes and their susceptibility to human impact. I then describe three selected land uses: henequen, coffee, and cattle, which exemplify the commercial and development patterns that evolved early in the long twentieth century and would determine the way land was used in Latin America for the rest of the century. I follow this with an evaluation of the current principal types of land use and economic activities, and their impact on the landscape. I try to include demographic, economic, political, and ideological aspects where possible. I emphasize the changes that took place in the last fifty years. I conclude with a personal assessment of this history.

An important technical problem is how to measure the environmental impact of people in Latin America. Ideally we would like to have a precise quantitative measure of ecosystem service modification. Such measures do not exist. Instead, we have isolated measures such as soil erosion, nutrient flows, changes in hydrology, and climate change, from which modification of ecosystem services can be inferred. But even these measures tend to be plagued by technical problems.

INTRODUCTION AND CLASSIFICATION OF THE PRINCIPAL ENVIRONMENTAL CHARACTERISTICS OF LATIN AMERICA AND THE CARIBBEAN

Any ecosystem can be divided into two subsystems: the natural subsystem consisting of an assemblage of physical components (geology, hydrology, climate) and biological components, and a human subsystem (Figure 9.1). The two subsystems are connected through land use. The natural subsystem processes the energy that comes from the sun through both the physical assemblage (atmosphere, geology, climate) and the biological subsystem (primary producers, consumers, decomposers). There exists a dynamic balance between these two natural subassemblages. Natural events of a physical nature such as earthquakes, landslides, devastating floods, hurricanes, tornadoes, and destructive storms denude an area of vegetation and soil cover and increase the fragility of the landscape by removing the soil cover and increasing erosion. Materials are removed from high laying areas and moved to lower plains or into the sea. On the other hand, through the slow process of biological succession, vegetation consolidates the ground, creates soil, accumulates nutrients, and increases the resilience of an area to erosion. The meteorological conditions and the topographical characteristics of an area tilt the balance toward stability and resilience (e.g., forests) or toward instability and fragility (e.g., steep slopes that denude land of vegetation).

Humans, through their economic activities, increase instability by removing vegetation and plowing in agriculture, changing drainage patterns through road construction and other infrastructure, affecting slopes when mining, and in general acting as the equivalent of another source of physical disturbance. Humans do not degrade the landscape as much as they create situations that favor the action of degrading natural physical forces. Lately, modern technology has added an entirely new source of environmental degradation – chemical degradation – through the use of agro-chemicals and production of industrial wastes.

To use the land for economic gain while avoiding or at least mitigating some of the negative consequences of human use requires the expenditure of energy and materials. Terraces can be built on mountain slopes to reduce the effects of water erosion; roads can be built respecting contour lines rather than cutting across drainage patterns; barriers can be built to keep sediments from silting rivers and lakes; fertilizer can be applied to reduce the loss of soil nutrients; factories can be designed so as to reduce or eliminate waste. However, these works will increase costs in the short term, while prolonging the useful life of the economic operations. The impacts of economic activities on the land and the cost of their mitigation depend on the geographical characteristics of a region. Therefore, to understand the environmental impact of economic activities, we must first ascertain the geological history and the geographical features of the American continent and determine the distribution of its natural resources.

The North and South American landmasses have been separate for most of the geological history of the Earth. Only recently – in geological terms – have they become connected. South America, with a surface of about 18 million square kilometers, is about twice the size of Europe, but is smaller than Asia, Africa, or North America.[5] It has roughly a triangular shape, with a southern apex and its widest point close to the equator at latitude five degrees south.

One hundred eighty million years ago, during the Jurassic period, South America, together with Africa, Australia, Antarctica, and India, formed part of a southern continent known as Gondwanaland. This landmass broke

[5] Jorge Morello, *Perfil ecológico de Sudamérica* (Madrid, 1984).

apart during the late Jurassic period and each section drifted in different directions until they reached their present position.[6] These movements are still continuing. As South America drifted westward, a series of parallel mountain chains in a north-south direction formed in its western border. The Andean chain is the latest manifestation of this ongoing process, whereas the Sierras Pampeanas (e.g., Aconquija, Ambato, Sierras de Comechingones) in Argentina are older evidences of the process of mountain building. In geological terms, the eastern part of South America contains the oldest rocks and the western part, the newest. The natural ecosystems of South America took shape during the last rising of the Andean Cordillera some five million years ago.

Three geomorphologic features characterize the continent. On its western flank we find the huge massif of the Cordillera of the Andes, the second largest mountain range in the world, and the only one that is continuous from the northern to the southern hemisphere. This area is narrowest in Ecuador (100 kilometers) and widest in Bolivia (700 kilometers). On the eastern bulge of the continent, we find the oldest rocks, the Guyana and Brazilian shields of Precambrian origin. These have been highly weathered and eroded. Finally, between them and extending also from the northern to the southern hemisphere, sediments eroded from the Cordillera de los Andes by wind and water form a very large sedimentary basin (Figure 9.2). This sedimentary area can be subdivided into three very large river basins: the Orinoco River basin in the north, the Amazonas River basin in the center, and the La Plata River basin in the south. All three basins are connected, and an adventurous person could paddle in a shallow canoe from the mouth of the Orinoco River to the mouth of the La Plata River.

The Cordillera de los Andes is the controlling element in the geography of South America. It divides the subcontinent into a narrow Pacific watershed, and a much more extensive Atlantic one. The rivers in the Pacific basin are short and flow rapidly; those on the Atlantic watershed are long and lazy. They are among the largest and with the greatest flow of water in the world. The Cordillera also is a determinant of the climate of the region.[7]

All along the Pacific coast, from Chile to Colombia, the horizontal distance between the ocean and permanent snowfields is only forty to fifty

[6] R. S. Dietz and J. C. Holden, "The Breakup of Pangaea," in *Continents Adrift* (San Francisco, 1971), 102–13.
[7] Morello, *Perfil ecológico de Sudamérica.*

Figure 9.2. Map of South America.
Notes: Principal ecological areas of South America: 1. Brazilian shield, 2. Guyana shield, 3. Patagonia, 4. Sierras Pampeanas, 5. Andean Cordillera, 6. The sedimentary basin extending from Venezuela to the Argentine pampas.
Source: Jorge Morello, *Perfil ecológico de Sudamérica* (Madrid, 1984).

kilometers, though it entails a vertical distance of around five to six kilometers, crossing in many cases lowland tropical evergreen forest, montane
forests, and páramo vegetation. The enormous variety of microclimates,
attributable to differences in altitude and exposure, condition also an enormous array of agro-ecological situations. Cacao might be grown at the foot
of the mountain, coffee in middle elevations, and corn and wheat at higher
altitudes.

On the eastern flank of the continent, a diversity of eco-climatic regimes
is also found, determined by latitude and rainfall, from evergreen moist
forest, such as the Serra do Mar in Brazil, to semideserts in Patagonia.
However, here the areas occupied by a given ecoregion[8] are much greater
in extent than in the western flank or the mountain areas.

Soils in the Andean regions are high in nutrients, whereas lowland tropical soils are weathered, acid, and infertile. Temperate soils in the southern
temperate region are among the best in the world. Much of South America
is either very dry or very wet. This affects the vegetation. In certain areas –
the Amazon basin, the coastal areas of Brazil, the Guyanas, the Chocó region
of western Colombia, and the region of southern Chile and southwestern
Argentina flanking the Andes – the land was originally covered with magnificent forests very rich in species. Other regions – the northern Venezuela
coast in Falcón state, the coastal regions of Peru and northern Chile, interior
Argentina and Patagonia, and much of the Bolivian altiplano – are deserts
or semideserts where only scattered xerophytic shrubs and succulents grow
(Figure 9.2).

From an ecological viewpoint, the Andean mountain slopes are the most
fragile because of the steepness of the slopes. They are followed by the
tropical Amazonas River basin, and other tropical rainforest regions such
as the Chocó in Colombia or the Guyanas area, because of the effect of
torrential tropical rains on the soil. Most resilient are temperate grasslands
such as the pampas.

During the Cretaceous period, some 200 million years ago, when South
America was separating from Africa and initiating its westward march that
would create the South Atlantic Ocean, North America existed as two isolated islands, separated by a broad but shallow sea, called the Bearpaw Sea.[9]
The westernmost of these extended southward to include Baja California

---

[8] E. Dinnerstein et al., "Conservation Assessment of the Terrestrial Ecoregions of Latin America and
the Caribbean" (Washington, DC, 1995).
[9] T. Flannery, *The Eternal Frontier* (New York, 2001).

and most of northern Mexico. This period also marks the beginning of the formation of the great mountain chains of the northern continent, the Sierra Madre in Mexico, the Rocky Mountains and the Sierra Nevada and coastal mountains of California in North America, and the Antillean Arc in the Caribbean. Their growth was gradual, with the appearance of first isolated chains that nevertheless had a strong impact on the climate. During the Upper Tertiary, approximately 20 million years ago, these mountains acquired their present dimensions.[10]

The geological configuration of Mexico, Central America, and the Caribbean is more complex than that of South America.[11] The Sierra Madre in Mexico encloses between its two chains a series of plateaus where some of the original inhabitants settled and established their cultures. Between the nineteenth and twentieth degrees of latitude, a sequence of large volcanoes unites the two chains of the Sierra Madre. South of there, we find a series of older volcanoes and, on the eastern flank, the coastal plain that extends to Guatemala and Honduras. The Antillean Arc is the result of continental drift of the Antillean plate and volcanic activity, particularly in the larger and western islands, and marine activity in the eastern islands.

Latin America can be divided into four principal ecological regions: the lowland tropics, the mountain areas, the temperate zone, and the desert areas. Each shows distinct climate, soil, vegetation, and ecological characteristics. Each region shows unique agricultural potentials and different degrees of fragility, and each of them has a different history of land use and abuse.

In the first place, we find the lowland humid tropics, the domain of tropical forests and savannas. This is a very fragile area ecologically and the one that presents the most daunting environmental problems. It extends from southern Mexico to Peru, Bolivia, Paraguay, and southern Brazil (Figure 9.2). During the first half of the twentieth century, it was thinly occupied by Europeans and their descendants, and then primarily along river courses. Today, however, whenever access is granted to this region through the construction of roads, thousands of landless peasants and miners stream to occupy it. This is what has been happening in the Amazon basin, the Chocó region of Colombia, Central America, and southern Mexico. The resulting impacts – deforestation followed by erosion and soil

[10] J. Aubouin et al., "Esquisse paléo- géographique et structurale des Andes méridionales," *Revue de Géographie Physique et Géologie Dynamique* 15 (1973): 11–72.
[11] C. W. Stearn, R. L. Carroll, and T. H. Clark, *Geological Evolution of North America*, 3rd ed. (New York, 1979), 566.

degradation, and mercury poisoning and silting of streams by gold miners – are of great concern.

The tropical savannas have been areas of low human density dedicated, until recently, mostly to extensive cattle raising. This is now changing, especially in Brazil. But the advance of the agricultural frontier in the savannas is not driven primarily by peasants in search of land, as it is in the rainforest regions, but is the result of a process of well-financed modernization, supported and encouraged by government policies aimed at increasing agricultural exports. The environmental impact of agricultural intensification in the savannas has depended on the technologies employed but has generally been negative, resulting in increased soil erosion and loss of biodiversity.

The mountain regions are very heterogeneous and – depending on exposure, latitude, and altitude – can have very different characteristics. The eastern slope of the northern Andes (Colombia, Venezuela, Ecuador, Peru) was originally the home of subtropical forests of a different character and specific composition than the lowland jungles. Here, since the last century, a process of human occupation based on the growing of coffee (and, in some regions, cacao) has prevailed. Lately, this area has seen an agricultural frontier of sorts, based on the illegal growing of coca, with all the negative environmental impacts associated with it.

The high plateau of Peru and Bolivia known as the Puna configures still another tropical mountain landscape, one of ancient occupation. Mining has been an activity of great local environmental impact in this region, whereas agriculture has been confined to local valleys. Aside from the impact of mining, environmental impact has been limited because of the nature of traditional agriculture that prevails.

The temperate and subtropical regions found in central and northern Mexico, Chile, Argentina, Uruguay, and southern Brazil present a diversity of landscapes and vegetation types, including conifer and broadleaved forests, shrub-lands, and grasslands. This was where Europeans first settled, and these were the regions they first impacted. They are the most productive and ecologically most resilient of the Latin American landscapes. The original vegetation such as the *Araucaria* forests in Brazil or the grasslands of southern Brazil, Uruguay, and the pampas region of Argentina have been almost completely eradicated and replaced by fields and pastures.

The last major landscape type is the deserts and semideserts, both north and south: the northern subdeserts of Mexico, primarily in the states of Sonora and Chihuahua; the extreme deserts of coastal northern Chile and southern Peru; the interior semideserts known as the Monte and Patagonia in Argentina; the coastal regions of the state of Falcón in Venezuela; and the area of northeastern Brazil known as the Caatinga. These are fragile systems, and although human activity tends to be low except in mining enclaves, human impact on the environment has been generally severe.

Each of these regions has a unique environmental history and present land use that, together with their innate characteristics, determines the impact that humans are having on the environment.

EVOLUTION OF RESOURCE EXTRACTION AND ENVIRONMENTAL CONDITIONS DURING THE LONG TWENTIETH CENTURY

The principal uses to which land can be put are for food and fiber production, grazing of domestic animals, growing of trees, mining, housing, and urban services, industry, infrastructure, or recreation. In this chapter, I consider four categories of land use: *arable land*, which is used in agriculture; *pastures*, land used to grow domestic animals; *forests*, both natural and human made; and *nonagricultural land*, which includes all other uses.

The nonagricultural use of land (urban, infrastructure, industry) has the greatest impact on the environment, but it occupies only about 3 percent of the land surface worldwide.[12] Arable land is the second most important source of environmental modification. Its importance is far greater than urban use, given that agriculture accounted for some 7.4 percent of the land surface of Latin America in 1990 (12.7% in Mexico, Central America, and the Caribbean; 6.5% in South America).[13] Pastures can involve a great deal of alteration when they are sown pastures, or they may involve minimum change in the case of lightly grazed natural pastures. They occupy about 28.7 percent of the land of the region (31.7% in Central America and the Caribbean, 28.2% in South America). Forests, both plantation and natural forest, occupy about 43.5 percent of the land surface (21.2% in Central America and the Caribbean, 47.3% in South America). Natural forests are among the least modified landscapes. The remaining 20 percent of the land surface of Latin America and the Caribbean is presently nonusable: high

---

[12] M. G. Wolman and F. G. A. Fournier, *Land Transformation in Agriculture* (Chichester, 1987).
[13] World Bank, *World Development Indicators 2001*.

mountain areas, areas covered by ice, extreme deserts, and flooded areas. Yet these are capable of being affected by humans when used as dumping grounds, for military exercises, or for indiscriminate harvesting of natural vegetation. We do not consider ocean and coastal waters that also have seen enormous alterations in this century because of human activity.

Compared with other parts of the world, Latin America, particularly South America, still has a large area in forests. Cropland is about 50 percent below the worldwide average; pastures are slightly higher. The relative importance of each of these land-use categories varies from country to country and in each of the four major ecosystem types. Yet, the average environmental impact should be slightly less than in other parts of the world.

The colonial and early independence period in Latin America created its share of environmental alteration (see Volume I) and landscape modification. However, technologies used in agriculture and mining during the colonial period utilized limited exterior power and were of low impact compared with the technologies that were introduced in the twentieth century. Geographically, they were concentrated in coastal regions or around mining enclaves.

The Industrial Revolution produced a more specialized world economy than its eighteenth-century predecessor. As the countries of Europe, particularly England, began to specialize in manufactures for export, they came to require large imports of foodstuffs and industrial raw materials. Latin America became an important supplier of these needs. The rise in income of the European population also greatly expanded the demand for a number of tropical agricultural products, such as sugar, coffee, and cocoa, which had previously been high-priced luxuries.

At the end of the nineteenth century, most Latin American countries were emerging from a long period of civil wars and internal conflict. In each country, the victorious landed elite, in order to insert their country's economy into those of Europe and the United States, adopted a policy of export-oriented development based on the sale of natural products.[14] A period of economic growth based on the adoption of modern technologies in mining and agriculture began around 1880. It would last, with many ups and downs, until the world depression of the 1930s.

Because there was virtually no other source of income and employment than agriculture and mining throughout the colonial period and the first

[14] B. Albert, *South America and the First World War* (1988); Victor Bulmer-Thomas, *The Economic History of Latin America since Independence*, 2nd ed. (Cambridge, 2003).

century of independence – the small industrial and commercial sector being incapable of absorbing much labor – growth could occur only by an increase in the primary export sector. There were, however, significant regional differences. These activities increased land use and had a direct impact on the natural environment.

With the end of the civil wars, political and economic power in the new countries passed firmly into the hands of the primary producers, the landowning and mining classes. Mining and agriculture accounted for nearly all of the region's exports. Landowners benefited from free trade by acquiring wider markets for raw materials and also by being able to satisfy their consumption needs through imports. As demand for Latin American products increased, production costs were reduced for many primary products through shifts in the location of production or through technical advances.

The decision to adopt a development model based on exports had the effect of creating two economic sectors: an expanding sector oriented toward exports, based on the exploitation of natural resources, mainly minerals and agricultural products (both foodstuffs and nonfood items), and a sector oriented toward the internal market, which was primarily a producer of foodstuffs and some traditional manufactures. Capital and know-how flowed to the export sector, whereas the labor-intensive domestic sector grew only slowly. There were, however, significant differences in these two sectors from country to country (see the chapter on agriculture).

The insertion of Latin America into the Atlantic economy brought with it an increase in trade. Between 1700 and 1820, the volume of total trade increased about threefold, or at less than 1 percent a year. Between 1820 and 1870, trade expanded fivefold, and fivefold again between 1870 and the First World War, or at a rate of 3 percent annually.[15] During the nineteenth century, nearly all the expansion took place in agricultural products. Industrial metals and petroleum did not become important exports until the 1920s or later, and the precious metals had lost most of their significance by the late eighteenth century.

The landed elite was able to appropriate the best and most productive land, where it established large estates known with different names – *haciendas, hatos, fundos, estancias* – where semifeudal labor relations often existed.[16] This contrasted with the sector that produced for the local market.

[15] J. Grunwald and P. Musgrove, *Natural Resources in Latin American Development* (Baltimore, 1970); D. Goodman and M. Redclift, *Environment and Development in Latin America* (Manchester, 1991).

[16] Arnold Bauer, *Chilean Rural Society from the Spanish Conquest to 1930* (Cambridge, 1975), 265.

Here, small parcels – *minifundia* – prevailed, capital investments were very low, technologies traditional, and labor investments high. Because the best lands were taken over by the export sector, either by purchase or by coercion, the small producers were pushed into increasingly marginal areas. In general the level of productivity in the primary export sector, whether agricultural or mineral, was much higher than in subsistence agriculture.

A question that has been asked repeatedly but which we do not discuss here is why the growth of the export sector was not followed by industrialization. In some cases – such as the state of São Paulo in Brazil – such was the case, but in most cases it was not.

THREE EARLY TYPES OF LAND USE

Land use is the best indicator of environmental impact. Space does not permit a detailed analysis of land use in Latin America (but see the chapter on agriculture in this volume for further uses), so I discuss some selected land uses, their evolution and their environmental impact during the long twentieth century. I divide the presentation into two parts. First I discuss three early economic land uses representative of the export sector: henequen in Mexico, coffee in tropical South America, and cattle raising in Mexico and Argentina. These activities had different environmental impacts. In the second part of my exposition, I discuss some of the major types of land use prevalent in the last fifty years. It will be seen that, contrary to what some authors have affirmed, intensified land use does not necessarily have a greater environmental impact.

EARLY EXPANSION OF TROPICAL PERENNIAL CROPS: HENEQUEN

Mexico is probably the paradigmatic case of the early growth of the export sector. After a long period of instability following independence, Mexico's landed elite united behind the dictatorial government of Porfirio Díaz (1876–1911). His government pursued internal stability and economic growth. This was accomplished through an alliance between the government and the landed elite and through important concessions to foreign entrepreneurs, especially in mining and ranching. The landed elite took advantage of the political climate to appropriate the best agricultural and grazing land, through coercion and semilegal means. The expansion of production was especially notable at the two opposite ends of the country: the henequen plantations in the Yucatán peninsula and the cattle ranches in northern Mexico.

Henequen (*Agave fourcroydes*) was domesticated by the ancient Maya and used by them and the Aztecs for making cordage and rough garments. It is a cactus-like plant that grows best in dry and rocky environments such as the dry northeastern area of the Yucatán peninsula. Until the middle of the nineteenth century, the growing of henequen was a cottage industry. Two technological developments, one external and the other internal, brought henequen growing to prominence.

In 1840, Cyrus McCormick brought to market in the United States a mechanical wheat reaper that soon evolved into an automatic reaper-binder. To tie the sheaves, this machine used twine that originally came from the Philippines (Manila hemp) or Europe (Russian hemp). The invention of a mechanical knotting device in 1878 by John Appleby for the McCormick binder increased the demand for twine exponentially. Henequen at the beginning was not competitive because of the high costs of production (the fibers were extracted from the leaves by hand) and the low quality of the product. The invention in Mexico of a machine to extract the fibers (the Molina wheel) and an effort by Mexican producers to improve the quality of their product led henequen to become, by the end of the nineteenth century, the preferred fiber for the elaboration of twine. This totally changed land use and labor relations in Yucatán.

The Yucatán haciendas in the nineteenth century were primarily cattle and corn haciendas, with some garden planting of henequen for the local market. Sugar was the principal crop during most of the century, grown in the deeper soils and more humid climate along the southeastern frontier of the state. The development of sugar haciendas brought with it an encroachment by the landowners into communal lands held for centuries in usufruct by Mayan communities. To ensure a source of cheap labor, debt peonage proliferated, institutionalized by a series of government decrees. This set a precedent for the growth of the henequen hacienda.

When an international market developed for henequen, buoyed by initial high prices, it displaced sugar, tobacco, and forest products, and the Yucatán region quickly became a monocrop economy with all the ecological and social drawbacks that this entails.[17] Whereas in 1845 henequen production

---

[17] Gilbert Joseph, *Revolution from Without: Yucatán, Mexico and the United States 1880–1924* (Cambridge, 1982).

in Yucatán occupied only some 600 hectares and accounted for only 6 percent of total agricultural production, by 1890, some 100 thousand hectares produced 45 thousand tons of fibers. The peak of production was reached in 1914 with 150 thousand tons. Remaining communal lands were taken over by henequen haciendas and the local Indian population was forced to work there through a system of debt peonage and physical coercion.[18]

The virtual monopoly that Yucatán interests had on henequen production shaped the business interests of the United States users, who wished to assure a dependable supply at a low price. Because land was entirely in the hands of local hacendados, it was almost impossible to establish a competing production in Mexico. Attempts to grow Russian hemp in the United States or abroad did not prosper because of high production costs. In the end, the local need for capital and the lack of a native capital market allowed U.S. interests to indirectly control the Mexican henequen production. Through a series of arrangements between New York cordage interests and local export brokers, the Americans were able to reduce the price. The best known of these deals is the one between the International Harvester Corporation (the successor firm to the McCormick Company) and Olegario Molina y Compañia. International Harvester, which controlled the henequen market in the United States, agreed to buy exclusively from the Molina Company at a fixed price. This created a three-tier social structure in Yucatán. At the top, some thirty families controlled the export market. Below them were the local hacendados or henequeros, perennially in debt and forced to sell their fibers at low prices to the exporters who controlled the credit market. These market manipulations lowered the price of henequen and squeezed the profits of the hacienda owners. They reacted by reducing the wages and working conditions of their workers, who became little more than slaves, and by increasing production, which only contributed to further reduce prices.

It is difficult to assess the environmental impact of henequen production at the turn of the century. The increased acreage clearly affected the native vegetation and fauna. Yet henequen is a perennial plant growing on rocky soils in an area of low rainfall. The technology employed involved little input. The impact on the physical environment probably was limited. The principal effect was on the social fabric of the region. Another impact was the growth of transport infrastructure, both roads and railroads.

---

[18] A. Wells, *Yucatán's Gilded Age. Haciendas, Henequen, and International Harvester, 1860–1915* (Albuquerque, NM, 1985).

After the Mexican revolution, the government took over the commercial-ization of henequen and tried to control its price by limiting sales (a scheme known as valorization). It also eliminated debt patronage, though it did not return communal lands until the government of Lázaro Cardenas in the 1930s. The increase in price made other fibers more competitive. Principal among them was another species of Mexican *Agave*, sisal (*A. sisilana*). This spineless species, grown in Kenya and Brazil, has more tensil strength than henequen but requires better soil and more humidity. But it was the inven-tion of the harvester combine and its diffusion in the 1920s and 1930s and the corresponding reduction in the demand for hard fibers that destroyed the henequen industry. The final blow was the appearance of synthetic fibers such as nylon and dacron for the construction of ropes. Henequen serves today a very limited market and production. The area dedicated to henequen in Yucatán in 2000 was 10 thousand hectares,[19] down from its peak of 630 thousand hectares in 1915.

EARLY EXPANSION OF TROPICAL PERENNIAL CROPS: COFFEE

Coffee was introduced into Haiti from France in 1723.[20] From there, it slowly diffused to other Latin American countries. Aided by the spread of coffee leaf blight in Indonesia and Ceylon, by the middle of the nineteenth century Latin America had become the principal producer of coffee in the world, a distinction it still holds. Brazil was and is the principal producer. The coffee story is similar to that of henequen, with some variations. How-ever, the environmental impact of coffee production has been much greater than that of henequen plantations.

Coffee is a tropical shrub that grows as an understory plant in the montane forests of Kenya and Ethiopia. The French introduced coffee on an experimental basis into Haiti and Martinique, while the Dutch sub-sequently introduced it into Suriname.[21] From here it diffused gradually into Brazil and Venezuela. It spread from there to the mountain slopes of Mexico, Central America, the Antilles, and the Andes, from Venezuela and Colombia to Ecuador and Peru. Coffee can be grown as an under-story shrub in the forest, in which case we call it shade-coffee, or in open fields, so-called sun-coffee. When grown in open fields, its yields are higher

[19] United Nations Food and Agriculture Organization (FAO), FAOSTAT Database, Rome.
[20] Otto Solbrig and D. J. Solbrig, *So Shall You Reap* (Washington, DC, 1996).
[21] Ibid.

but the quality is lower. Coffee is very demanding in nutrients, which shade-coffee receives from the litter of shade trees. Sun-coffee must be fertilized heavily or it exhausts soil resources quickly.

Coffee growing started in Brazil in the second half of the eighteenth century in the states of Espiritu Santo and Rio do Janeiro. From its very beginning it was grown in open fields. It became an important export staple only after independence. It spread first to the Paraiba Valley[22] and later to the highlands of central and western São Paulo state, which became the biggest coffee-producing area of the world early in the twentieth century.

The spread of coffee had the effect of significantly reducing the extent of the rich coastal forests of Brazil and creating serious problems of erosion. Coffee, especially in the Paraiba Valley, was grown on mountain slopes that were denuded of trees, and then planted in rows at right angles to contour lines. This form of agriculture soon exhausted the soil (much of which was washed down the slopes). Farmers then moved on and repeated the process in a new virgin plot. The environmental impact was manifold: loss of forests and their biodiversity, soil erosion, and silting of watercourses.

In Central America, coffee growing started in Costa Rica in the 1830s, soon occupying the central plateau of the country. From there, coffee growing spread north to El Salvador and Guatemala and, eventually, Nicaragua.[23] By the middle of the nineteenth century, coffee was the major export product of Central America. By the end of the century, railroads were built that joined the central plateau of Costa Rica and Guatemala with the Atlantic coast in order to expedite the export of coffee. The railroads in turn served as ways of penetration into the interior.

In Colombia, the coffee at the beginning was also an itinerant crop, as it was in Brazil, moving from Cúcuta to Santander to Cundinamarca. From 1870 on, coffee expanded along both slopes of the valley of the river Cauca, south of Medellín. By the end of the nineteenth century, coffee production in Colombia reached 270 thousand metric tons. In Colombia, coffee was grown as an understory plant, its environmental impact being less pronounced than in Brazil.

As with the case of henequen, we find that coffee production in Colombia also involved a three-tier system. At the top were large commission houses mostly owned by foreigners, although there were also some Colombian

---

[22] Stanley Stein, *Vassouras, a Brazilian Coffee County 1850–1890* (New York, 1976).
[23] C. F. S. Cardoso, "La formación de la hacienda cafetalera costarricense en el Siglo XIX," in Enrique Florescano, ed., *Haciendas, latifundios y plantaciones en américa latina*, 2nd ed. (Mexico City, 1978), 635–67; H. Pérez Brignoli, *Breve historia de Centroamérica*, 3rd ed. (Madrid, 1988), 205.

interests involved. Large coffee producers, which were price takers, shipped directly abroad to these commission houses and often were in debt to them for monetary advances on the crop. Small producers sold to agents of the foreign houses or to local exporters. In turn, owners put pressure on labor. Independent laborers were given a plot of land on which to plant coffee. For this they had to deposit a sum of money that was returned with interest after the bushes began to bear (some three to five years). Landowners could thereby obtain the services of labor as well as the use of capital, and see their land turned into productive coffee haciendas.[24] From there on, the arrangement was usually one of "half and half." The sharecropper was in charge of the shrubs, their harvest, and the labor-consuming task of drying the coffee, and paying all expenses, for which he got to keep half the production.[25]

CATTLE RAISING IN TEMPERATE REGIONS: THE SOUTHERN CONE AND MEXICO

The pampas region of Argentina and Uruguay were used during the nineteenth century to raise cattle and sheep for export of salted meat and wool. The cattle were of low quality, raised on open ranges. With the invention of refrigerated transport, a lucrative fresh-meat market opened up in Europe, especially England, that was one of the linchpins in the rapid development of Argentina and Uruguay.

The English market demanded good-quality beef. Argentine ranchers imported bulls of English breeds, especially Shorthorn (Durhams) and Hereford (white face) to improve the herds. The mild climate of the pampas and their natural grasses allowed raising cattle without stabulation. The simultaneous spread of agriculture created an opportunity for a dual land use that the local *estancieros* (ranchers) were quick to exploit. Part of the ranch was rented to immigrant farmers, mostly Italians, for periods of three to five years, with the proviso that the land had to be left planted in alfalfa at the end of the lease period. Cattle were fattened on these fields, and when, after a period of years, the alfalfa declined, the cycle was repeated. The alfalfa and the cattle manure increased the fertility of the soil, a very good solution from the point of view of the soil. This was a technology that was economically profitable and environmentally advantageous. It prevailed

[24] Charles Berquist, *Coffee and Conflict in Colombia, 1886–1910* (Durham, NC, 1978).
[25] M. Palacios, *Coffee in Colombia, 1850–1970* (Cambridge, 1980).

with few changes until the middle of the twentieth century and in a much-diminished way until today.[26]

Two types of ranches developed: breeders, found in the more marginal areas of the pampa, and fatteners, who occupied a more central geographical area and were intimately connected with the exporters. These were highly concentrated in the hands of one U.S. and two British firms. Because chilled beef could be kept only for four weeks and ships took approximately three to reach British ports, processing plants were situated next to harbors. It took only twenty-four hours to process beef and load a ship.

On account of their oligopolistic position, exporters controlled the price of beef, which they tried to keep down. In turn, fatteners who sold to the meatpacking companies passed price changes down to breeders. They, in turn, lowered the salaries of ranch hands, whose working conditions were very precarious. Breeders also supplied the national market, where the price indirectly was set by how much fatteners were willing to pay for a steer. Because that price was low by international standards, the Argentine public got access to meat at a low price, which explains in part the addiction to a high meat diet in the country. Fatteners controlled the Cattlemen's Association (*Sociedad Rural Argentina*), a very influential lobby. The situation was basically not dissimilar to that in the henequen industry: a concentrated market where foreign buyers keep prices down by negotiating with a local elite, which, in turn, takes advantage of a dispersed set of producers who carry the brunt of the costs of such a system. And, as in Mexico, working conditions and pay of ranch hands were substandard but not nearly as bad as in Mexico because in the pampas there tended to be a labor shortage.

In northern Mexico at the beginning of the long twentieth century, the picture was different from that in the southern henequen-growing region. It was also different from the pampas. In Mexico, huge cattle ranches were developed to produce heifers to be fattened in the United States. Some of these ranches – the best known is Babicora of the Hearst family – were owned and operated by U.S. citizens, whereas others were in the hands of the local landed elite, such as the Terraza and the Madero families. Yet the labor relations did not differ very much from those in the Yucatán peninsula.

Two factors triggered the growth of ranching in northern Mexico: the pacification of the frontier and the end of Apache Indian raids, and the

---

[26] Otto Solbrig, *Una solución argentina al problema de la erosión de los suelos* (Buenos Aires, 1995); Otto T. Solbrig and E. Viglizzo, *Sustainable Farming in the Argentine Pampas: History, Society, Economy and Ecology* (The David Rockefeller Center for Latin American Studies, Harvard University, Working Papers on Latin America No. 99/00-1, 1999).

building of a network of railroads. In the 1880s, a railroad was built with U.S. capital in northern Mexico, linking Brownsville, Laredo, and El Paso with Torreón and points farther south. Cattle raising north of the border was becoming expensive as more and more land was used to cultivate crops. Raising cattle in northern Mexico was relatively inexpensive. After two years, animals were shipped north to be fattened for the U.S. market. Profits were sizable for both the U.S. and Mexican ranchers.

It is difficult to assess the environmental impact of the Mexican ranching operations at the turn of the century. Cattle were raised on the open range. There are indications that there was overgrazing that would be detrimental to the vegetation and lead to erosion. As in Yucatán, the rights of many communities were not respected and this led to several uprisings, best known of which are the Yaqui wars and the uprisings in Chihuahua that led to the Tomochi massacre.

These three examples illustrate the pattern of land use that developed early in the century: a market controlled by concentrated foreign interests, such as International Harvester, which controlled the market for henequen fibers, or the Anglo, Swift, and Armour meatpacking plants that controlled the English meat market. These interacted with a small local elite to keep commodity prices down. The local elite, in turn, was capable of passing the cost of the lower prices down to producers, whose profits were severely affected and who harshly squeezed labor. Similar systems existed in relation to other export commodities such as bananas, sugar, salitre, and rubber, although each case has its own unique characteristics. Because the systems of resource extraction were extensive, the effect on the physical and biological environment was moderate, but the effect on the native social fabric was high.

The world depression of the 1930s severely disrupted this pattern of production. Some countries, such as Argentina, tried to maintain market share by making special concessions; others, such as Brazil, defaulted on their debts. Mexico nationalized its oil industry and embarked on a strategy of import substitution, as happened also in most of the other countries.

THE ENVIRONMENT IN THE SECOND HALF
OF THE CENTURY

Landscape transformation in the first half of the twentieth century was confined mostly to areas near the coast where the population was concentrated.

An exception to this was the Andes, home to a large indigenous population that was experiencing a demographic increase after the disastrous decline of the sixteenth and seventeenth centuries. Agricultural activities, mostly of an extensive nature, had only a reduced environmental impact and although mining enclaves such as salitre exploitation in northern Chile had important impacts, they were confined to a few sites. This was to change dramatically in the second half of the century, a result of demographic and economic growth. Intensification of agriculture and a massive move of population toward hitherto unoccupied areas, especially tropical forests and savanna regions, took place.

The end of the Second World War ushered in a new economic order. The United States became the hegemonic power and replaced Great Britain as the main market and principal source of financing for Latin America. At the start of the 1950s, most countries in the area decided to pursue a more isolationist policy of import substitution. Although successful in its early stages, when many countries experienced fast economic growth, most notably Mexico and Brazil, it soon ran out of steam. For the most part, the highly protected industries turned out to be technically backward and non-competitive. They also were – and still are – highly polluting. Eventually, in order to obtain the necessary foreign exchange, most countries returned to the early policy of exporting natural products, primarily agricultural and mineral. Forest products became an important export as well as fish and other marine resources. With it came a high degree of landscape transformation of a scope and intensity that had not been witnessed before and that has alarmed national and foreign governments, environmentalists, and international institutions. Attention has been focused on the Amazon basin, but landscape transformation and degradation has occurred throughout Latin America in the last fifty years and still continues unabated.

Some indicators of the environmental transformation and degradation of Latin America's environment are a higher rate of deforestation, greater use of fossil fuels, increased water pollution, and loss of biodiversity. Other indicators are a very high rate of population growth, now in decline, and increased social and economic inequality.

The growth of population and the moves toward the intensification of agriculture were paramount in the territorial expansion of agriculture and livestock growing and the concomitant deforestation. During the second half of the century Latin America experienced the highest population growth in its history: a 216 percent increase between 1950 and 2000. This varied considerably, ranging from some Caribbean islands with less than a

Table 9.1. *Rural environment and land use*

| | Rural population | | | | Land area (million hectares) | Percent of land area | | | | | |
| | Percent of | Total | Annual growth | People per sq. km | | Arable land | | Permanent crops | | Other | |
	1980	1999	1980–99	1998	1998	1980	1998	1980	1998	1980	1998
Argentina	17	10	-1.2	15	2,737	9.1	9.1	0.8	0.8	90.1	90.1
Bolivia	55	38	0.3	156	1,084	1.7	1.8	0.2	0.2	98.1	98.0
Brazil	34	19	-1.3	62	8,457	4.6	6.3	1.2	1.4	94.2	92.3
Chile	19	15	0.2	111	749	5.1	2.6	0.3	0.4	94.6	96.9
Colombia	36	27	0.4	529	1,039	3.6	2.0	1.4	2.0	95.0	96.0
Costa Rica	57	52	1.9	824	51	5.5	4.4	4.4	5.5	90.1	90.1
Cuba	32	25	-0.6	77	110	23.9	33.1	6.4	7.6	69.7	59.3
Dominican Republic	50	36	0.3	280	48	22.1	22.1	7.2	9.9	70.6	68.0
Ecuador	53	36	0.3	284	277	5.6	5.7	3.3	5.2	91.1	89.2
El Salvador	58	54	1.1	582	21	26.9	27.0	11.7	12.1	61.4	60.9
Guatemala	63	61	2.4	482	108	11.7	12.5	4.4	5.0	83.9	82.4
Haiti	76	65	1.1	895	28	19.8	20.3	12.5	12.7	67.7	67.0
Honduras	65	48	1.4	179	112	13.9	15.1	1.8	3.1	84.3	81.7
Mexico	34	26	0.5	98	1,909	12.1	13.2	0.8	1.1	87.1	85.7
Nicaragua	50	44	2.1	87	121	9.5	20.2	1.5	2.4	89.1	77.4
Panama	50	44	1.3	244	74	5.8	6.7	1.6	2.1	92.5	91.2
Paraguay	58	45	1.5	108	397	4.1	5.5	0.3	0.2	95.6	94.2
Peru	35	28	0.7	189	1,280	2.5	2.9	0.3	0.4	97.2	96.7
Puerto Rico	33	25	-0.4	2,990	9	8.3	3.7	7.3	5.1	84.3	91.2
Uruguay	15	9	-2.0	24	175	8.0	7.2	0.3	0.3	91.7	92.5
Venezuela	21	13	0.1	120	882	3.2	3.0	0.9	1.0	95.9	96.0
Latin America	35	25	0.0	252	20,062	5.8	6.7	1.1	1.3	93.1	92.1

Source: World Bank (Washington, DC).

50 percent population growth rate to increases of more than 300 percent in some mainland countries (Nicaragua, Costa Rica, Honduras, and Venezuela). Such a dramatic increase in a population that was 59 percent rural in 1950 had a significant effect on Latin American societies. One effect was a massive movement of people to cities, with the consequence that by the year 2000, the rural population was reduced to only 24.3 percent of the total. That is, although in absolute numbers the total population doubled, the rural population increased by only a third. Averages hide, however, significant and very important differences among countries in the size and growth of the rural population.

One group of countries, formed by a mixture of some Caribbean islands (Puerto Rico, Cuba), the Southern Cone countries (Uruguay, Argentina, Chile), and Brazil, actually saw an absolute decrease in their rural population. At the other end of the spectrum, we find all the Central American countries, whose rural population more than doubled: Panama (126%), Honduras (167%), El Salvador (171%), Nicaragua (201%), Guatemala (228%), and Costa Rica (266%). Paraguay (148%) is the only South American country with a similar increase in the rural population. Not surprisingly, these countries also have the highest rate of deforestation in Latin America.

The enormous growth of the population had a very negative environmental impact. The combination of very high demographic growth and rural–urban migration produced some of the largest cities in the world; many of them, such as Mexico City and Santiago de Chile, are notorious for their unhealthy air, unreliable water supply, and serious social problems. It also led to the creation of very polluting industries such as the *maquilladoras* along the Mexico–U.S. border, or the notorious industrial city of Cubatão near the port city of Santos in Brazil, nicknamed the "valley of death."[27] But it was in the rural areas where the greatest landscape transformations took place, with concomitant serious environmental problems.

SOME TYPES OF LAND USE SINCE 1950

In the last fifty years, Latin America has experienced enormous land-use changes. In the lowland tropics, land hitherto unused has been occupied and transformed mostly into extensive cattle-ranching operations or

[27] But now fortunately restored to health. "Cubatão: Brazil's Ecological Success," *The Financial Times*, June 10, 1988.

agriculture. In temperate regions, agriculture has intensified significantly. New crops, mainly oil-crops, fruits, and vegetables for export, are supplanting traditional food staples. Fossil fuel energy production and use is up, as is the use of hydroelectric power, indicators of a much more intensive use of land. These developments all indicate an accelerating environmental transformation with both negative and positive implications, as we will see.

TRANSFORMATION OF TROPICAL LOWLAND FORESTS

We lack reliable appraisals of the original extent of forests and woodlands in Latin America. It is estimated[28] that forest originally occupied slightly above half (55%) of the South American landmass and two thirds of Mexico, Central America, and the Caribbean (67%). By 1997, it was judged that only 63 percent of the original forests were still extant in Mexico, 55 percent in Central America and the Caribbean, and 69 percent in South America. The first serious forest inventory for the entire region was made in 1980 by the Food and Agriculture Organization (FAO).[29] In 1990 and 2000, other inventories allowed estimates of the rate of deforestation for the 1980–90 and 1990–2000 decades. It was found that although the largest surface decrease in forested area in that period was in Brazil – not surprising given that in 1980, almost six million square kilometers of the more than ten million square kilometers of forest and woodland in Latin America were there – the greatest rate of deforestation in Latin America has been in Central America and the Caribbean. In South America, Paraguay and Ecuador are the countries with the greatest rate of deforestation.

Brazil lost in the 1980–90 decade a little more than 6 percent of its forests, which is probably an underestimate. This figure is dwarfed by what happened in Haiti (38.7%), Costa Rica (25.8%), Dominican Republic (24.6%), Paraguay (23.8%), and El Salvador (20.2%). Also, Honduras, Panama, Nicaragua, Ecuador, and Guatemala all had forest losses between 15 and 20 percent in this decade, whereas Mexico, Venezuela, and Bolivia lost more than 10 percent of their forests in only ten years. Overall, deforestation in the 1980–90 decade in Latin America reduced native forests by more than 7 percent. This pattern has continued, with Guatemala showing a decrease

---

[28] D. Bryant, D. Nielsen, and L. Tangley, *The Last Frontier Forest: Ecosystems and Economy at the Edge* (Washington, DC, 1997).
[29] FAO, FAOSTAT database, Rome.

of almost 17 percent of its forests in the 1990–2000 period and Central America and the Caribbean showing a 10.8 percent loss of forest in that period. The loss of tropical forests in South America was considerably less, at 4 percent for the last ten years (representing an annual loss of 0.4%). Yet some countries such as Ecuador (12%), Bolivia (5.7%), Venezuela (5.4%), and Mexico (4.4%) had losses well above the average. Brazil's loss, at 2.3 percent in the last ten years, was slightly below the South American average. These figures, as bad as they are, indicate a slight decreasing tendency in deforestation rates, but not very much.

There is a great deal of uncertainty and inconsistency in the figures regarding deforestation presented by different agencies. In part this has to do with the definition of undisturbed forests and with the technical difficulties involved in estimating deforestation over such vast areas. Satellite images can be used but they cannot ascertain how much of an extant forest is modified or partially logged. Yet regardless of the accuracy of the figures, it is clear that the problem is serious. According to FAO, South American forests that account for 25 percent of the world's forests, in the 1990–2000 period, accounted for 50 percent of the lands that were deforested.

The reasons for this high rate of deforestation are manifold. They vary, as is to be expected, from one region to another. Commercial logging is an important factor, but not the most important in every region. Demand for tropical woods has increased worldwide and the enormous reduction in the forests of the Far East has put enormous pressure on American forests. Commercial logging is most intense in areas with good communications. Commercial logging does not normally deforest an area because only a few species are of commercial value. The construction of logging roads, however, allows the penetration of squatters and settlers into logged areas.

Transformation of forested land for agriculture and particularly cattle raising is probably the principal cause of deforestation. The advance of the agricultural frontier, in turn, is related to the demographic growth of Latin America, to agricultural modernization in the better lands, and to government policy (see the next section). Cattle raising has been attributed to the demand of the United States market for cheap meat, especially by fast-food restaurants (the "hamburger connection"). Although there is a connection, especially in Central America, this reason has been much exaggerated. Extensive cattle raising for the domestic market in frontier regions with poor communications is the most popular economic activity, especially when there are government incentives, such as in Brazil.

THE IMPACT OF THE EXPANDING AGRICULTURAL FRONTIER IN
THE LOWLAND TROPICS

One of the salient characteristics of Latin America, especially tropical South America, in the last fifty years has been the move toward the interior of the continent. This movement has been spearheaded by the construction of roads by governments eager to open new territories to colonization and funded by international agencies hoping to encourage economic development. The principal activities at these new frontiers have been peasant agriculture, growing both food and illegal crops; extensive ranching; logging; forest-product extraction; and mining. The unregulated nature of many of these activities has created serious social and environmental problems.

The changes have been quite dramatic. The overall agricultural area in Latin America increased by 15 percent between 1965 and 1992. However, many countries saw much higher increases. Between 1965 and 1992, agricultural land in Costa Rica expanded by 84.6 percent, in Ecuador by 68.1 percent, in Paraguay by 60.9 percent, in Brazil by 47 percent, and in Cuba by 38.7 percent. Furthermore, Panama, Nicaragua, Chile, Honduras, and Guatemala experienced increases of more than 20 percent in land dedicated to agriculture. Agriculture expanded for the most part into areas previously occupied by forests. Much of the new agriculture is characterized by low technology, low capital, and high labor inputs, and much of what it produces is for self-consumption. Yet there also was an increase in the growing of export crops in these countries. Many countries, most notably Chile, Argentina, and Brazil, saw enormous increases in productivity.

Brazil presents a paradigmatic case. Two different types of agricultural expansion took place in Brazil. One is the expansion of high-input, commercial agriculture that took place mainly in the old agricultural areas of the southern states of São Paulo, Paraná, Santa Catarina, and Rio Grande do Sul, as well as in newly opened savanna lands in the states of Goias, Mato Grosso, and Mato Grosso do Sul. The other type of agriculture is small-holder agriculture in frontier regions in the Amazon basin, especially in the states of Rondonia, Acre, and Pará.

The process had its start with the intensification and modernization of agriculture in the southern states of São Paulo, Paraná, Santa Catarina, and Rio Grande do Sul in the 1960s. One result of this process was that the larger and better capitalized farms started displacing the small, traditional farmers, most of whom went bankrupt and were forced to sell their land. These displaced farmers then moved to the newly opened areas on the frontier, especially in the states of Rondonia, Acre, and Goias. The government of Brazil, at the time, encouraged this. Fearing an influx of landless peasants into the cities, it embarked on an ambitious program of road construction and rural colonization of the Amazon region. The first project was the Transamazonian highway,[30] built in the early 1970s. This project was a dismal failure because fewer than ten thousand families were relocated. The next project, however, the paving of Br 360 from Cuiaba to Porto Velho in Rondonia and its prolongation to Rio Branco in the state of Acre, and the associated colonization project, unleashed a massive movement of small farmers into the forest margin areas of these two territories that were soon to become states. These projects were financed by loans from the World Bank.[31] In spite of well-intentioned plans to protect the forest and set aside Indian reserves, the population pressure at the frontier produced significant landscape transformation, deforestation, the destruction of native Indian lands, and, in some cases, the virtual destruction of certain native ethnic groups.

The dynamics of this process are worth describing. INCRA, the colonization agency of the Brazilian government, allots eighty to one hundered hectare plots of forest in designated areas. Pioneer settlers clear, on the average, one to three hectares a year and plant beans, corn, and rice, the Brazilian food staples, mostly for home consumption. The ashes of the burned trees serve as fertilizer, but given the extreme poverty of the soils, within two to three years, crop yields are too low to justify the labor of cultivating the exhausted land. The *colono* then deforests a new agricultural parcel, and transforms the old parcels into pasture and begins to build a herd of cattle. Although the law only allows him to deforest half of the plot, such strictures are seldom enforced. After a few years, the now "improved" plot (no forest, some pasture) is sold to either new settlers or local ranchers. The colono then moves on to open a new plot farther down the road. In this manner, a wave of pioneer settlers deforests the forest border, leaving behind a tropical grassland for the ranchers. According to the intensity of the management, these grasslands have a lifetime of twenty years or more. Very persistent weeds of difficult and costly control then invade the fields, at which point they are abandoned.

[30] N. J. H. Smith, *Rainforest Corridors* (Berkeley, CA, 1982).
[31] B. Rich, *Mortgaging the Earth* (Boston, 1994).

THE GROWTH OF AGRICULTURE AND CATTLE RANCHING IN
SAVANNA AREAS

Not all tropical lowlands are covered with forests in Latin America. A significant area in Venezuela, Colombia, Brazil, Paraguay, and Bolivia is the domain of savannas known as *llanos, campos, chaco,* or *cerrado*. By definition, savannas are areas with a continuous cover of grasses and a discontinuous layer of woody vegetation that can be shrubby and very sparse or formed by sizable trees and fairly dense, and every conceivable intermediate condition. Although the transformation of savannas is not covered under the rubric of deforestation, they have been affected by the advancing agricultural frontier as much or more than forested areas.

Latin American tropical savannas have experienced a very aggressive agricultural frontier in the second half of the twentieth century, particularly in the Brazilian cerrados but also in Bolivia, Colombia, and Venezuela. Contrary to the somewhat disorganized and traditional agriculture in frontier forest regions, in savannas regions of Latin America, agriculture has been technically advanced and capital intensive for agronomic reasons.

Latin American savanna soils are among the worst for agriculture anywhere. For the most part, they are highly acidic, with a pH below 5; very low nutrient content, especially phosphorous, calcium, and nitrogen; and a high concentration of heavy metals – chiefly iron and aluminum. Only the very specialized flora of the region can naturally grow in these soils. Agriculture is not possible without expensive intervention. Fields must be limed in order to change the acidity and neutralize the negative effect of aluminum, and heavy doses of phosphorous and nitrogen must be applied. Only then is agriculture possible. Such interventions are expensive, with costs in the order of 800 to 1,000 dollars per hectare.[32] It is clear that only well-financed farmers can operate here. The case of the Brazilian savannas known as *cerrado* is a good example.

Until the late 1960s, agriculture in the cerrado was restricted to floodplains along watercourses where pockets of good soil are found. Corn, beans, rice, and cotton were the principal crops in these enclaves, occupied for the most part by small family farms and producing for the internal market. The rest of the area was dedicated to extensive cattle raising, also

[32] E. Wagner, "Desenvolvimento da região dos Cerrados," in W. Goedert, ed., *Solos dos Cerrados. Tecnologias e estratégias de manejo* (São Paulo, 1985) 19–31.

for domestic consumption. This changed with the arrival of the military governments in 1964.

One of the goals of the military governments was to increase agricultural production so as to increase and diversify exports and create the savings needed for industrialization.[33] Credits on very favorable terms were offered to farmers. It was this policy that modernized the agriculture of the southern states and started the migration of small farmers to the forest edges described previously. Some displaced farmers from the south, those technologically best prepared and who knew how to obtain credit, also moved into the cerrado area. In a short time, the cerrado became a major producer of soybeans and helped Brazil become the principal exporter of this oilseed in the world.

In 1970, only 43 percent of the total area of the states of Goias, Mato Grosso, and Mato Grosso do Sul, approximately 63.5 million hectares, was used – mostly for a very extensive cattle-raising operation. By 1985, already 30.6 million additional hectares had been transformed. The expansion of world demand for soybeans, especially from Europe, has been one of the principal factors for the development of agriculture in the Brazilian cerrado. In 1975, the cerrado area already produced approximately 6 percent of the soybean production of Brazil. By the 1990s, there were about 1.4 million hectares of soybeans in the cerrado, representing more than 25 percent of Brazil's production. The cerrado also produced 13 percent of the rice crop of Brazil and approximately 16 percent in the case of maize.[34] In fewer than fifty years, some fifty million hectares of savannas have been replaced by either crops or artificial pastures, about the same surface that has been deforested in the entire country in that same period.[35]

Cattle raising in the cerrado, which used to be very extensive, has also been modernized and production intensified. Until recently, the only form of management used to be the burning of the range toward the end of the dry period. One of the changes that has taken place, especially in the southern and central portions (states of Goias, Mato Grosso do Norte, and Mato Grosso) has been the replacement of the native grasses with planted pastures of introduced African grasses of the genera *Bracchiaria, Panicum, Hyparhenia,* and *Melinis.* Burning is still part of range management, with

[33] C. A. Klink, A. G. Moreira, and Otto Solbrig, "Ecological Impact of Agricultural Development in the Brazilian Cerrados," in M. D. Young and O. T. Solbrig, eds., *The World's Savannas* (New York, 1993), 93–120.

[34] C. J. R. Alho and E. Souza Martins, *De grão em grão, o Cerrado perde espaço* (Brasilia, 1995).

[35] G. Sarmiento, *La transformación de los ecosistemas de la América Latina* (Buenos Aires, 2000).

negative environmental consequences, but yields are up and so is the animal carrying capacity.

Burning has the effect of reducing the regeneration of the rich woody vegetation. Slowly the region is becoming a grassy savanna – that is, a landscape of grasses with scattered trees. Fires also spread into adjacent forests where they can burn enormous surfaces and are another contributor to the reduction of the rainforests.

One effect of this intensive ranching operation, as well as intensive agriculture, is to reduce the need for labor. Furthermore, export prices have been dropping steadily, cutting into profit margins. In this context, small operators cannot compete because their costs are higher. It all results in a decrease of the rural population that migrates either to the cities (the majority) or to the forest margins. It also has engendered a strong protest movement in Brazil of landless peasants (*Sem Terra*) that advocates land reform.

Similar processes are taking place in savanna areas in Bolivia, in the dry Chaco area of Argentina and Paraguay, and to a lesser extent in Venezuela. It is estimated that in another ten to twenty years, most of the savanna areas of Latin America will have been transformed for agriculture or ranching.

INTENSIFICATION OF COMMERCIAL AGRICULTURE OUTSIDE OF
THE SAVANNAS

Commercial agriculture has expanded on the better lands from Mexico to Argentina and Chile (Table 9.2). The sector serves principally the export markets of Europe, Asia, and the United States with a variety of products: Colombian and Central American coffee, soybeans from Brazil and Argentina (but also Paraguay and Bolivia), and vegetables and fruits from Chile, Argentina, Brazil, and Mexico.

Agriculture the world over has become transformed in the last fifty years from a family enterprise serving mostly local urban centers to a vast commercial activity serving the world market through food conglomerates. Most family farms have become incorporated as businesses and become larger to reap the benefits of scale. In the process, capital has replaced labor, and a number of regional businesses that used to serve the farmer – suppliers, banks, insurance agents, etc. – located in small rural towns have tended to be replaced by big businesses operating out of large cities. Small towns increasingly are becoming ghost towns. This change is most

Table 9.2. *Total agricultural area 1965–2000 (in hectares)*

Country	1965	2000	Percent of change
Argentina	1,681,210	1,692,000	0.6
Bolivia	296,150	360,370	21.7
Brazil	1,672,000	2,508,200	50.0
Chile	140,690	152,320	8.3
Colombia	390,980	454,650	16.3
Costa Rica	15,550	28,450	83.0
Cuba	45,480	66,650	46.5
Dominican Republic	31,420	36,960	17.6
Ecuador	47,300	81,080	71.4
El Salvador	12,750	16,040	25.8
Guatemala	26,940	45,070	67.3
Haiti	13,400	14,000	4.5
Honduras	35,950	29,350	−18.4
Mexico	979,790	1,073,000	9.5
Nicaragua	52,880	75,610	43.0
Panama	16,580	21,320	28.6
Paraguay	148,950	240,780	61.7
Peru	298,200	313,100	5.0
Puerto Rico	5,850	2,910	−50.25
Uruguay	151,000	148,830	−1.4
Venezuela	195,140	216,450	10.9
Latin America	6,258,210	7,577,140	21.1

Sources: CIAT (Environmental Indicators) and FAO (FAOSTAT Database).

advanced in the United States but is also noticeable in the most productive lands of Latin America, from Chile and Argentina to central Mexico. One important factor in the rural–urban migration has been the growth of agribusiness.

This change has profound environmental implications. The intensification of production can increase soil erosion, reduce biodiversity, and lead to the local extinction of most wildlife. An added problem is chemical pollution of air and water, with serious concomitant health problems for farm workers.

The expansion of production in Latin America in the last forty years, the result of more cultivated surface and higher yields, is remarkable. This varied with the product, with the traditional crops not faring nearly as well as cereals, fruits, and especially oil crops. The production of fiber crops (mainly cotton) fell in the last forty years by 12 percent whereas the surface harvested decreased by 50 percent, in spite of yield increases of almost 80 percent. Coffee-harvested area also was reduced by 17 percent, but production increased by 19 percent because of an increase of 45 percent in yields. Roots and tubers (yucca, potatoes, and sweet potatoes), a staple of the Latin American diet, saw a modest 12 percent increase in surface and 60 percent in production because of an increase in yields of 30 percent. Considering that the population doubled in this period, a 60 percent increase indicates a change in the local diet. Another traditional crop in Latin America, sugar cane, saw a greater participation. Its harvested surface increased by 92 percent and its production by almost 150 percent because of an increase in yields of 32 percent. This reflects mainly the increase in sugar production in Brazil to produce alcohol for use as fuel in automobiles. Cereals (principally maize, wheat, and rice) saw a minor increase in cultivated surface (34%) but an increase in production of 214 percent because yields more than doubled (134%), attributable to better seeds and more fertilizer use.

Yet it was the new export crops – fruits and vegetables and oil crops – that had truly spectacular increases. The surface dedicated to growing fruits has increased in Latin America and the Caribbean from 2,257,714 hectares to 6,966,115 hectares, a 209 percent increase, whereas production went from 5,503,911 metric tons to 37,370,237 metric tons, a 239 percent increase. Citrus contributed significantly. The surface harvested with citrus (primarily in Brazil and Argentina) increased by 484 percent and production increased by 579 percent! But the most spectacular increase was in oil crops, the harvested surface of which went from 8,643,005 hectares to 32,488,029 hectares, an increase of 275 percent and production of which increased by 715 percent. Soybeans, a new crop in Latin America, introduced in the 1970s, was the principal oil crop. Argentina and Brazil were the two principal producers and exporters of soybeans. In Argentina, production went from 59,000 tons in 1970 to 25,700,000 tons in 2000, and in Brazil it went from 271,488 in 1970 to 36,814,676 tons in 2000.

Low air-transport costs and new methods of cultivation and harvesting allowed the growth of fruits and especially perishable vegetables for exports. Four Latin American countries were the major players in this market: Argentina, Brazil, Chile, and Mexico. Argentina has exported fruits, especially apples and pears, since the 1930s, primarily to Europe. Its production went from 234,263 metric tons in 1960 to 1,657,637 metric tons in 2000, a 700 percent increase. The value of its fruit and vegetable exports went from 27 million dollars to 1,072 million dollars, an almost 4,000 percent increase. Yet, its performance is not as spectacular as that of Mexico and especially Chile. Chile's export production went from 109,364 metric tons in 1960 to 1,840,673 in 2000, a 1,600 percent increase, and the value of its exports went from 16 million to 1,787 million dollars in that same period. The performances of Brazil and Mexico were in between those of Argentina and Chile, although the quantities they exported were higher.

Such intensification of agriculture increases the risks of environmental degradation. Soil erosion and loss of soil organic matter are two of the problems. Others are increased production of carbon dioxide, nitric oxide, and methane, three powerful greenhouse gases associated with poor soil management and increased livestock herds. Intensification led to increased use of industrial inputs, especially machinery and tractors, as well as fertilizers, herbicides, and pesticides. Chemical inputs are now in common use in Latin America and their employment is increasing. If not applied carefully, they can be dangerous to human health and that of wildlife, and they can seep into drinking water and lakes and streams.

Chemical fertilizer use increased massively in Latin America between 1960 and 2000 (from 1,787,423 to 10,448,089 metric tons), especially in South America, where there was 1,400 percent increase. Fertilizers are used principally in areas where agriculture has intensified, and particularly for high-value products such as fruits and vegetables, flowers, and greenhouse-grown crops. In itself, the use of fertilizer is highly recommended in order not to exhaust the soil. However, when used in high doses, and especially in areas of high rainfall, it can lead to serious problems of contamination.

Agricultural intensification does not necessarily mean environmental degradation because measures can be taken to mitigate or eliminate some of the harmful effects. One such technical development with beneficial effects that is spreading in Argentina and Brazil, but also in Paraguay, Bolivia, and Chile, is No-Till agriculture. This technology, which forgoes plowing in favor of sowing directly into the stubble, has turned out to be not only profitable but has also had enormous beneficial effects on the soil, reducing erosion by an order of magnitude or more, and increasing wildlife. Likewise, the trend among agrochemicals is for the use of less powerful toxic compounds, easily destroyed by soil microorganisms and with no residual effects. Nevertheless, the inevitable trend toward intensification is worrisome.

PEASANT FARMING AND ILLEGAL CROPS

One effect of the spread of agribusiness has been to reduce peasant farming and to push it into increasingly more marginal areas. By peasant farming we refer to farming that is done primarily to feed the household, with no or little surplus. One consequence, already mentioned, is deforestation in the Amazon basin. Another effect has been the turning to the growing of illegal drugs by marginal farmers, especially in the Andean mountains of Bolivia, Peru, and Colombia and, increasingly, also in Mexico. Coca (*Erythroxylon coca*), a plant native to South America and of ancient cultivation and use, is the principal drug grown in the Andean countries, whereas marijuana (*Cannabis sativa*) is grown principally in Mexico.

Illegal crops present a double environmental threat. The need to avoid detection of these crops means that they are grown as itinerant crops, leading to much more deforestation and environmental change than would otherwise be necessary. The interest in eradication leads the authorities to use defoliants and powerful herbicides that affect many more species and surface than that occupied by the illegal crop. Coca has traditionally been grown on mountain slopes at intermediate altitudes on terraces. When it is grown illegally and as an itinerant crop, farmers do not build terraces, which increases erosion by producing landslides.

FORESTRY

Four economic activities have had an inordinate environmental impact: forestry, energy production, use of water resources, and mining and oil exploration.

The demand for wood in general and for tropical woods in particular has increased very significantly in the world. As the forests of the Far East have become logged to extinction, the attention of the market has increasingly shifted to Africa and Latin America (Table 9.3).

Close to 50 percent of the land surface of South America is covered with forests, mostly natural but increasingly planted with an average wood density of 20 metric tons per hectare – which is twice the world's average. We already have mentioned how these forests are being transformed for agro-pastoral uses. The extraction of wood is also increasing at a fast pace (Table 9.4). Roundwood extraction in South America increased from 13 million cubic meters in 1961 to 30 million cubic meters in 1998, a

Table 9.3. *Surface area in forest and woodlands (in order of rate of change)*

Country	1980 (Km²)	1990 (Km²)	Percent change
Argentina	600,500	592,000	1.4
Bolivia	556,592	493,170	11.4
Brazil	5,978,159	5,611,066	6.1
Chile	86,800	88,000	−1.4
Colombia	577,338	540,637	6.4
Costa Rica	19,233	14,276	25.8
Cuba	18,877	17,147	9.2
Dominican Republic	14,279	10,773	24.6
Ecuador	143,422	119,622	16.6
El Salvador	1,546	1,233	20.3
Guatemala	50,379	42,251	16.2
Haiti	380	233	38.7
Honduras	57,204	46,046	19.5
Mexico	553,657	485,856	12.3
Nicaragua	72,535	60,133	17.1
Panama	37,623	31,157	17.2
Paraguay	168,840	128,585	23.8
Peru	706,182	679,057	3.8
Puerto Rico	2,995	2,995	0.00
Uruguay	6,270	6,690	−6.7
Venezuela	516,810	456,910	11.6
Latin America	10,169,621	9,427,837	7.9

Source: CIAT (Cali).

126 percent increase. The situation was worse in Central America, where extraction volumes were higher and went from 28.8 million to 70.2 million, almost a 150 percent increase. The countries that have been most affected in Central America are Guatemala (253%), Costa Rica (216%), and Honduras (152%). In South America, roundwood extraction was highest in Paraguay (370%), Ecuador (344%), Venezuela (226%), and Bolivia (198%). Brazil had an increased roundwood extraction of 114 percent in the last forty years, slightly below the average in South America. Yet, at 105,733,000 cubic meters, it was the largest producer of roundwood in Latin America. Two interesting cases are represented by Uruguay and Chile. Uruguay showed an increase of 389 percent in roundwood production (from a very small

Table 9.4. *Total roundwood production (thousand cubic meters)*

Country	1961	1966	1971	1976	1981	1986	1991	1996	2001
Argentina	11,343	5,617	6,743	7,598	7,191	9,524	9,924	11,428	9,970
Bolivia	666	788	969	1,130	1,253	1,358	1,608	2,185	2,722
Brazil	92,083	105,081	123,308	144,895	185,660	207,696	205,556	198,653	236,422
Chile	6,785	8,342	9,284	10,046	13,304	16,978	24,013	29,831	37,790
Colombia	9,856	10,797	11,843	12,953	14,049	15,983	18,232	18,487	12,501
Costa Rica	1,677	1,984	2,568	3,329	3,384	3,490	3,907	5,119	5,161
Cuba	1,875	1,284	1,997	2,075	2,968	2,994	2,756	2,756	1,696
Dominican Rep.	685	517	411	462	516	562	562	562	562
Ecuador	2,550	2,915	3,734	4,081	5,636	5,588	6,258	10,562	10,920
El Salvador	3,103	3,595	4,257	4,812	5,300	5,401	4,683	4,330	5,200
Guatemala	3,687	4,357	5,051	5,545	9,134	10,195	11,263	13,087	15,337
Haiti	3,230	3,505	3,800	4,113	4,456	4,867	5,703	6,193	6,397
Honduras	2,845	3,356	3,700	4,322	4,894	5,294	5,928	6,684	9,552
Mexico	8,932	11,159	13,546	16,993	17,758	19,836	21,300	21,962	45,156
Nicaragua	1,697	1,791	2,424	2,936	3,251	3,005	3,547	4,026	5,884
Panama	539	595	662	824	920	936	974	1,059	1,337
Paraguay	1,720	2,865	3,416	4,129	5,814	7,112	7,640	8,097	9,690
Peru	4,532	2,823	6,011	7,581	7,773	8,328	7,657	7,914	8,370
Uruguay	1,260	1,880	1,891	2,174	2,321	3,165	3,320	4,041	5,812
Venezuela	624	891	949	1,144	1,118	1,395	1,637	2,119	4,620
Latin America	159,689	174,142	206,564	241,142	296,700	333,707	346,468	359,095	435,099

Source: FAO, FAOSTAT Database.

base), all of it from plantations, and Chile showed a 366 percent increase, in great part (but not all) from plantations.

Logging is not necessarily negative. It is an important source of income for a country and, if done sustainably, it can actually be a source of employment and of recreation, as is the case in the United States and Europe. Unfortunately, logging in Latin America is very predatory with little attention paid to the long term. Although many laws and regulations have been enacted, they usually are not enforced. Both temperate and tropical forests have been affected.

Tropical forests are notorious for their great diversity and the low density of component species. Only a few species – usually not more than three to five, and at most ten – are of commercial value, and logging is therefore very selective. However, in order to get to the trees, logging concerns open roads that are avenues of entry for landless peasants that squat on forest lands and destroy the remaining trees in preparing their agricultural plots. Furthermore, heavy tractors and other equipment required for the extraction of the logs destroy seedlings and saplings, compact the soil, and are a source of disturbance. Loggers also hunt wild fauna, including rare and endangered species, which is another source of concern.

ENERGY USE

Energy use is an indicator of economic activity and is considered also as a good indicator of human intervention in the environment.[36] Energy use, especially fossil fuels, also has a direct effect on the environment, affecting atmosphere and water as well as human health.

Total energy consumption in Latin America doubled between 1971 and 1997 (106%), which correlates with the changes in land use, the rates of deforestation, and increases in agricultural area and intensification observed (Table 9.5). There were, as expected, great differences among countries, from a huge increase in Ecuador (1,598%) to a decrease in Haiti (−6%). A more meaningful statistic is consumption per person. The average per person consumption in Central America and the Caribbean was 1.2 thousand metric tons of oil or equivalent, and in South America, 1.1 thousand. This

---

[36] M. Winograd, *Environmental Indicators for Latin American and the Caribbean: Toward Land-Use Sustainability* (Cali, 1995); M. Winograd, A. Farrow, and J. Eade, *Atlas de indicadores para América Latina y el Caribe* (Cali, 1998).

Table 9.5. *Total energy consumption from all energy sources (in thousand metric tons of oil equivalent)*

Country	1971	1976	1981	1986	1991	1996	1997
Argentina	33,651.8	37,187.5	40,872.1	43,141.9	45,464.5	58,920.5	61,709.6
Bolivia	989.3	1,620.5	2,487.4	2,755.4	3,073.5	3,633.1	4,254.4
Brazil	70,420.9	94,478.8	104,694.6	127,477.8	137,972.4	163,334.1	172,030.2
Chile	8,237.9	8,083.5	9,701.8	10,086.4	14,214.8	20,456.2	23,011.7
Colombia	14,095.4	16,641.8	19,914.5	23,002.1	26,889.3	31,392.5	30,480.6
Costa Rica	1,134.1	1,315.2	1,446.3	1,700.8	2,097.2	2,601.4	2,662.7
Cuba	10,623.1	13,443.1	15,146.3	14,343.5	14,096.3	13,251.1	14,272.7
Dominican Rep.	2,372.7	3,190.2	3,593.8	3,858.8	4,042.1	5,183.1	5,453.4
Ecuador	2,346.6	3,712.5	5,409.9	5,876.8	6,705.3	8,565.6	8,513.4
El Salvador	1,762.8	2,630.3	2,739.0	2,480.0	3,124.8	4,055.5	4,094.6
Guatemala	2,798.5	3,613.0	3,569.2	3,640.6	4,523.2	5,402.4	5,632.5
Haiti	1,510.8	1,827.1	1,747.9	1,484.3	1,579.8	1,965.8	1,778.5
Honduras	1,394.8	1,611.6	1,871.3	2,024.3	2,455.7	2,946.0	3,181.9
Mexico	45,586.6	66,193.2	105,678.1	108,731.3	129,334.8	136,813.0	141,520.3
Nicaragua	1,288.6	1,670.3	1,615.4	2,044.4	2,204.5	2,421.0	2,572.8
Panama	1,729.7	1,809.8	1,363.3	1,551.8	1,643.1	2,192.1	2,327.7
Paraguay	1,382.6	1,625.5	2,095.4	2,441.9	3,183.3	3,988.9	4,191.4
Peru	9,490.0	10,989.4	11,780.1	12,092.7	11,626.4	14,009.2	15,127.1
Uruguay	2,414.8	2,475.2	2,530.6	2,088.9	2,414.4	2,830.6	2,883.5
Venezuela	23,383.5	26,434.2	37,152.3	38,774.3	49,659.1	54,961.7	57,530.3
Latin America	236,614.5	300,552.7	375,409.3	409,598	466,304.5	538,923.8	563,229.3

Notes: Total energy consumption is the amount of energy from all sources used by each country in the year specified. It is important to note that, unlike IEA, WRI includes losses through transportation, friction, heat loss, and other inefficiencies as energy consumption; consumption equals indigenous production plus imports minus exports plus stock changes minus international marine bunkers.

Sources: International Energy Agency (IEA), *Energy Balances of Organization for Economic Cooperation and Development (OECD) Countries, 1960–1997* (Paris, 1999), and *Energy Balances on OECD Countries, 1960–1996* on diskette (Paris, 1998).

represents an increase of 41 and 36 percent, respectively, since 1971. The countries in Latin America with the highest per person consumption of commercial energy were Venezuela (2.5), Argentina (1.7), Chile (1.6), Mexico (1.5), Cuba (1.3), and Brazil (1.1). Chile and Mexico had the greatest individual increases (84% and 72%), whereas Haiti (−30%), Panama (−23%), Peru (−11%), and Nicaragua (−6%) saw the individual consumption of commercial energy go down in this period.

The energy consumption picture indicates that it increased at a rate very similar to population growth but that there were significant shifts in energy consumption between countries. The figures are somewhat distorted given that in some oil-producing countries such as Venezuela, domestic energy prices are below world market valuations, whereas in others, such as Chile and Brazil, which have to import most of their energy, prices tend to be higher.

Latin America has a great hydroelectric potential, as yet mostly untapped (Table 9.6). Nevertheless, there was a great increase in the use of this source of energy. Overall, hydroelectric energy production in the continent rose by more than 500 percent (700% in South America, 250% in Central America and the Caribbean) – that is, five times higher than overall use of energy. Brazil – an oil-poor country – leads the continent in hydroelectric production, followed by Venezuela, Paraguay, Colombia, Argentina, and Mexico. The laggards are Nicaragua, Haiti, and Cuba, with minuscule hydroelectric production.

Dam construction presents serious problems for local populations, wildlife, and vegetation. Improper planning and inattention to deforestation in the watershed serving a dam can result in serious silting of reservoirs that reduce the life of the dam. The efficiency of a dam as a source of electricity is measured by the kilowatts (Kw) of electricity produced per hectares of land (Ha) that are inundated. Dams situated in mountainous areas with steep falls are much more efficient than those in relatively flat land. The three most efficient dams in Latin America are the Paulo Alfonso in Brazil (2,490 Kw/Ha), the Pehuenche (1,250 Kw/Ha) in Chile, and the Guavio (1,067 Kw/Ha) in Colombia. Itaipú, the largest dam in Latin America, situated on the Paraná River at the Brazil–Paraguay border, has an efficiency of only 93 Kw/Ha. Even less efficient are the huge dams of Tucururi in northern Brazil, with an efficiency of 30 Kw/Ha; the Salto Grande on the Uruguay River at the Argentine–Uruguay border, with an efficiency of 24 Kw/Ha; and the Chocón on the Limay River in Argentina, with only a 15 Kw/Ha efficiency. These last three projects have flooded large areas,

Table 9.6. *Hydro-electricity production (thousand metric tons oil equivalent)*

Country	1971	1976	1981	1986	1991	1997
Argentina	132.8	431.1	1,262.9	1,807.3	1,375.5	2,421.5
Bolivia	77.2	96.8	99.4	95.8	108.0	198.3
Brazil	3,715.1	7,130.5	11,245.7	15,688.0	18,729.2	23,999.5
Chile	378.1	536.2	652.6	969.5	1,129.0	1,629.2
Colombia	573.0	875.8	1,239.1	1,858.3	2,373.1	2,820.7
Costa Rica	88.4	124.6	196.5	248.6	314.4	413.5
Cuba	9.5	4.6	5.2	5.1	9.0	8.0
Dominican Republic	50.7	73.9	129.3	131.2	48.0	115.1
Ecuador	37.8	52.0	67.0	345.0	440.1	582.7
El Salvador	44.9	16.9	47.0	88.4	72.7	102.7
Guatemala	22.4	26.3	24.8	148.1	196.8	323.4
Haiti	2.3	14.6	21.4	27.4	28.6	17.2
Honduras	20.8	37.2	71.6	123.7	199.3	279.2
Mexico	1,236.8	1,479.1	2,115.4	1,721.4	1,879.4	2,273.1
Nicaragua	17.5	37.8	45.0	34.9	29.0	35.0
Panama	7.1	11.9	114.7	180.3	163.9	237.9
Paraguay	13.2	42.1	55.5	1,018.4	2,520.2	4,338.9
Peru	368.3	498.6	687.7	865.0	965.9	1,136.5
Uruguay	126.3	105.1	331.7	627.3	525.7	557.8
Venezuela	463.5	909.7	1,297.6	2,163.7	3,829.8	4,915.1
Latin America	7,396.8	12,514.5	19,720.8	28,160.0	34,947.8	46,415.4

Sources: IEA, *Energy Balances of Organization for Economic Cooperation and Development (OECD) Countries, 1960–1997,* and *Energy Balances of Non-OECD Countries, 1971–1997* (Paris, 1999). International Energy Agency (IEA) 1971–1997 in five-year intervals (WRI).

which, in the case of Tucururi, involved rich tropical forests, their wildlife, and ancestral Indian lands. Furthermore, hunting by the high numbers of construction workers in these projects usually depletes the local wildlife.

WATER AND COASTAL RESOURCES

Coastal resources are a significant economic asset, but a very fragile one. For some Latin American countries – primarily Caribbean island states – tourism attracted by magnificent beaches is the principal source of income. Yet the construction of hotel infrastructure is threatening the resource on which they depend, creating water pollution, beach erosion, and destruction of mangrove vegetation.

Coastal resources are also being endangered by the development of the shrimp-breeding industry, especially in Ecuador. For this purpose, inlets are enclosed and fertilized, thereby altering nutrient relations and endangering coastal vegetation, especially the very unique and fragile coastal mangrove thickets. Mangroves are not only biologically unique, they also play a very important role as protectors of coastal areas from sea encroachment and erosion, and are breeding grounds for many important commercial fish species. It is estimated that half of the mangrove areas are threatened by human activities.[37]

Latin America is singularly well provided in freshwater resources. At a time when shortages of fresh water are a serious threat to many developing and some developed countries, all Latin American countries, with the exception of some Caribbean islands, have enormous reserves. Mexico is the Latin American mainland country that uses the largest percentage (19%) of its freshwater resources. Yet, although there is no real threat of overall shortages, there are problems in distribution, and many watercourses are seriously polluted.

Indiscriminate commercial fishing on some of the large rivers such as the Amazonas and the Paraná and pollution are threatening the rich ictiological fauna of many of these rivers. So, for example, in the lower Paraná sixty thousand tons of fish were extracted in 2000, half of them of one species, the sábalo, which is exported mostly to Brazil. The lower Paraná has more than three hundred species, some of which, like the dorado, attract sport fishermen from all over the world, an important economic activity.

THE ENVIRONMENTAL IMPACT OF MINING AND OIL EXPLORATION

Latin America is an important producer and exporter of minerals. It is also a major producer of petroleum and contains the largest reserves outside of the Middle East. It furnishes about one-fifth of the world's supply of copper and holds about one-third of the world's reserves of this mineral. In addition, it has about 15 percent of the world's reserves of tin, 34 percent of molybdenum, 60 percent of lithium, 23 percent of silver, 20 percent of

---

[37] H. Hamilton and S. Snedaker, *Handbook for Mangrove Area Management* (1984).

Table 9.7. *Total indigenous energy production (thousand metric tons of oil equivalent)*

Country	1971	1976	1981	1986	1991	1997
Argentina	30,557.9	31,039.8	39,452.0	41,748.6	48,584.4	80,133.5
Bolivia	2,119.3	4,123.2	4,456.5	4,751.3	4,989.0	5,953.1
Brazil	49,445.4	54,218.2	63,931.1	96,569.4	98,880.5	120,235.8
Chile	4,730.7	5,051.4	6,073.9	6,878.4	7,867.2	8,167.9
Colombia	19,370.2	16,922.3	19,114.5	33,344.8	49,404.5	67,524.5
Costa Rica	663.1	718.5	784.1	987.3	1,055.9	1,157.1
Cuba	3,428.7	3,474.5	4,214.3	4,859.7	5,959.8	7,254.7
Dominican Republic	1,217.4	1,340.9	1,568.4	1,393.8	1,064.0	1,423.3
Ecuador	1,342.1	10,887.2	12,051.1	16,383.3	17,221.1	22,791.8
El Salvador	1,254.9	1,900.6	2,147.9	1,825.9	2,100.1	2,648.9
Guatemala	1,934.5	2,595.5	2,510.5	2,992.5	3,366.5	4,433.1
Haiti	1,378.0	1,623.2	1,569.0	1,222.6	1,267.9	1,298.3
Honduras	1,012.2	1,135.7	1,334.3	1,478.7	1,702.2	2,003.4
Mexico	45,500.0	69,863.5	173,859.0	183,630.6	201,923.4	223,132.3
Nicaragua	736.4	888.3	923.5	1,267.7	1,541.3	1,528.5
Panama	344.3	403.8	558.1	603.7	573.0	807.7
Paraguay	1,171.1	1,312.7	1,623.4	2,780.4	4,857.5	6,959.5
Peru	7,608.7	8,576.2	14,763.1	15,039.7	11,590.9	12,225.0
Uruguay	519.0	534.5	835.5	1,262.6	1,112.0	1,085.7
Venezuela	198,855.8	136,550.7	130,511.8	119,146.5	146,291.1	203,978.6
Latin America	373,189.7	353,160.7	482,282	538,167.5	611,352.3	774,742.7

Sources: IEA, *Energy Balances of Organization for Economic Cooperation and Development (OECD) Countries, 1960–1997,* and *Energy Balances of Non-OECD Countries, 1971–1997* (IEA, 1971–1997) in five-year intervals (WRI).

iron ore, and lesser amounts of other minerals, such as lead (9%), uranium (9%), zinc (7.5%), nickel (6.1%), and gold (5.8%).[38]

Energy, principally liquid fuels and gas, is one of Latin America's principal exports and source of foreign exchange (Table 9.7). From Venezuela to Argentina, the foot of the Andes is a large geosincline that contains vast reserves of petroleum. In 1996, Latin America produced 508,093,000 million tons of petroleum. Mexico and Venezuela were the largest producers, followed by Brazil, Argentina, Colombia, Ecuador, Peru, Cuba, and Chile,

[38] U.N. Economic Commission for Latin America and the Caribbean, *The Environmental Dimension in Development Planning* (Santiago, 1985).

in that order. Oil exploration and extraction that used to be a major environmental disruption is done today with minimum environmental impact. Nevertheless, building roads into remote areas can open them up for colonization, as has been the case in the Ecuadorian Amazon. Furthermore, spills attributable to pipeline and tanker accidents can create serious local environmental problems, particularly in times of civil violence. Both Venezuela and Colombia have had their pipelines blown up repeatedly by guerrillas, creating serious oil spills.

Exports of copper provide some 5 percent of the region's foreign exchange, a share surpassed only by the exports of petroleum, coffee, and sugar. Copper is mined in ten Latin American countries, but only in three – Chile, Mexico, and Peru – is copper mining of importance. In Chile, the copper industry is a major element in the economy, accounting for some 60 percent of exports, 13 percent of government revenues, and 4 percent of GNP.

The open-pit iron mine in Carajas, Brazil, is the largest one of its kind. The mineral is exported largely to Japan. Brazil uses charcoal to produce pig iron and steel. The Carajas mine is a model of providing for minimum environmental impact. However, the pig-iron industries that have grown up along the Carajas-San Luis railroad are a major source of deforestation because they convert native forests into charcoal[39] used in smelting.

Mining can be very contaminating, especially if there are no good environmental controls. The environmental problems associated with mining involve all stages from the extraction of mineral ores from the ground to their final processing. One of the most serious problems is the release into watercourses of untreated or only partially treated effluents, from the discharge of solid residues, and especially from the discharge of chemical wastes resulting from the oxidation of ores containing sulfur. Most of the metals mined in Latin America are extracted as sulfur salts (copper, zinc, lead, silver, mercury, and arsenic). The release of these wastes is a principal reason for the contamination of rivers, some of which serve as sources of drinking water for large populations, such as the Rimac that provides the drinking water to the city of Lima.

A very serious problem in many areas, but especially in the Amazon basin, is the contamination of watercourses by mercury, a byproduct of gold

[39] A. B. Anderson, "Deforestation in Amazonia: Dynamics, Causes, and Alternatives," in A. B. Anderson, ed., *Alternatives to Deforestation: Steps Towards Sustainable Use of Amazon Rain Forest* (New York, 1990), 3–23.

extraction from auriferous sands. Some of this is produced by thousands of very poor individual miners who pan gold in Amazonian rivers, but a significant part comes from organized dredging by larger enterprises. The mercury in these waters is a cause of fish kills and mercury poisoning of an undetermined number of local inhabitants, especially Indians.

CONCLUSIONS

Latin America possesses some of the most enchanting landscapes in the world. Beautiful tropical beaches with sand like sugar compete in magnificence with splendid snow-capped mountain peaks from Cerro Bolívar in Venezuela to Cerro Fitzroy in Patagonia. The majesty of the Beagle Canal in Tierra del Fuego, with imposing glaciers reaching to the very sea, can only be compared with the sublime beauty of the Cataratas de Iguazú on the Argentine–Brazilian border, Salto del Angel in Venezuela, or the towers of Torres del Paine National Park in Chile. The tropical jungles of the Amazon basin are unique, but so is the vegetation of the dry Quebrada de Humahuaca in Argentina or the Sonoran desert in Mexico.

That these and all the other witnesses to the vigor of nature in Latin America must be preserved for coming generations should be obvious to everyone. It is also obvious that natural resources must be developed to improve the welfare of the population, and that this must be done so as to be sustainable. Yet the growth of the population, their undisciplined quest for economic betterment, and the greed of some and the incompetence of many are endangering these objectives. Tourists, developers, erroneous government policies, greedy and incompetent politicians, and negligence all combine to create environmental disasters.

Yet the history of the environment in Latin America in the twentieth century is not only one of deterioration; it also shows a growing awareness that the path of development pursued at present is nonsustainable. If the patterns described in this chapter were to continue as in the past, not only does it threaten the beauty of the area, it also seriously puts in question the ability of the ecosystem to deliver the services on which humanity relies. To change course means a change in perception and in development strategy, not only by Latin Americans, but also by the entire economic system, especially the developed world that has been sucking natural capital from Latin America for more than a century.

More environmentally friendly technologies, such a No-Till agriculture, integrated pest management, sustainable logging practices, and more careful attention to dam location, must be adopted. For this to happen, attention must be paid to the profitability of the new technologies. Governments must adopt policies that encourage sustainable use of the rich trove of natural resources that Latin America possesses. We see some of this starting to happen, but the rate of adoption of sustainable practices must increase considerably if further environmental deterioration is to be reduced significantly.

10

LABOR AND IMMIGRATION

BLANCA SÁNCHEZ-ALONSO

The role of Latin America in the international economy has changed in many ways when we compare the late nineteenth century and the late twentieth century, but in no other aspect has Latin America changed more that in its position in the international labor market. Around 1900, Latin America was the destination of millions of immigrants, particularly for millions of Europeans, and some Latin American countries were competing for labor in the international market. By the end of the twentieth century, Latin America had experienced a "population explosion" in the 1960s and the 1970s and today the region is no longer a destination for immigration. On the contrary, one of the main features of almost all Latin American countries nowadays is the high volume of emigration to the United States and Europe.

This chapter concentrates on the period in which Latin America was a major receiving area of European immigration – that is, the so-called age of mass migration between the years of 1880 and 1930. Needless to say, immigration was not a new phenomenon in the 1880s. Scattered immigrants had been arriving in the region since the 1830s and in the middle decades of the nineteenth century there were a substantial number of immigrant colonies in Brazil, Chile, Argentina, Paraguay, and Mexico. The slave trade had also been a traditional source of foreign population, particularly in Brazil and the Caribbean, and Latin America had been well integrated into the international labor market through the Atlantic slave

I would like to thank the editors for their comments and suggestions. I am also grateful to Alejandro Vázquez and Bruce Sacerdote for their data on passage fares and to all participants in the London and Buenos Aires meetings for their suggestions, particularly to Carlos Marichal for his very insightful comments. Tim Dore gave me very useful references.

trade. Chinese immigrants were also relatively important in Peru and Cuba. But it was not until the 1870s and the 1880s that immigration, mainly from Europe, reached massive proportions and changed the social and economic evolution of several major Latin American countries.

Although many countries in the region tried to attract immigrants, foreign labor concentrated in a few destinations: Argentina, Brazil, Cuba, and Uruguay. Over the period 1880–1914, only a few countries in Latin America were integrated into the free international labor market. The chapter focuses mainly on the River Plate countries, Brazil, and Cuba, although brief overviews of other countries such as Chile and Mexico are included. It deals with national units, though some migration scholars have argued that the regional approach is more appropriate because immigrants concentrated in specific regions and cities. This chapter considers Latin America in the international labor market from a global perspective. The general aim of the chapter is to survey existing knowledge and to open possible new lines for future research.

The first section surveys migration trends in the main receiving countries. It focuses on the national origins of the flows and discusses the evolution of real wages. The section makes comparisons among Latin American countries and other areas receiving immigrants in the same period, particularly the United States. The second section deals with policy issues. An explicit comparison between Brazil and Argentina, the two big competitors for foreign labor, is carried out with references to immigration policies in other countries, such as Australia and Canada. The third section concentrates on the immigrants as laborers: the selectivity of the migration process, where the immigrants concentrated, and their contribution to the labor force in the receiving countries. The section also deals with the issue of the human capital brought in by immigrants (proxied by literacy and occupations) and also with immigrants' contributions to social capital in the receiving countries. The fourth section explores the consequences of immigration in the long run for some Latin American countries. The focus is mainly on changes in the composition of the labor force and long-run impacts on demographic structure, paying special attention to age distribution. A final section concludes.

1. MIGRATION TRENDS

The nineteenth century's improvements in transport and communication and the progressive elimination of institutional barriers to commerce induced an impressive increase in commodity and factor mobility. The opening of economic relations affected both sides of the Atlantic economy, promoting a rise in international commerce and an extraordinary increase in factor mobility as some 60 million Europeans emigrated to the New World in the century following 1820. In broad terms, the economies of the New World were characterized by dual scarcity – capital and labor – and by cheap and abundant land. Latin American countries needed to augment the supply of labor and capital to exploit natural resources. However, not all countries shared this labor scarcity. Mexico had a relatively large native population, and Brazil had both a large slave labor force and a large native population. In 1870, the Argentine population was less than 2 million, the Cuban population stood at 1.3 million, and Uruguay had a little more than 350,000 inhabitants. In contrast, the Brazilian population was nearly 10 million and Mexico had around 9 million. Resource abundance and scarcity of labor was characteristic of the River Plate area and the Brazilian hinterland.

Nevertheless, almost all Latin American governments tried to attract foreign labor after independence. Some countries needed to increase the labor force because of the scarcity of the native population. Others tried to prevent labor shortages in certain sectors. Some governments thought that the immigration of a culturally "superior" European population would contribute to economic and social modernization.

From 1850 onward, Europe was the main supplier of both capital and labor to the world, but European countries were not the only sources of immigration into Latin America. Chinese "coolies" were employed in the Peruvian guano, sugar, and cotton industries (around 75,000 Chinese contract laborers were transported to Peru before 1880 and the inflow continued afterward), in the sugar plantations of Cuba and the Caribbean, and in railway construction in Mexico and some Central American countries.

The influx of Asian and other indentured laborers was particularly important in the Caribbean. The British, French, and Dutch plantation economies in the region found their supply of labor in British India or in the Dutch colonies in Asia. It is interesting to note that at the same time that the indenture system was finally disappearing from the United States, the abolition of slavery in the British West Indies produced a renewed demand for indentured labor. The arrival of Asians and Chinese bound to servitude to the Caribbean had very different implications from the arrival of Europeans free to choose their jobs and places of residence, but the explanation of this migratory flow can be found in the same powerful economic forces (to enlarge the labor supply and lower labor costs) as the arrival of

Europeans to the Brazilian plantations. Servitude remained legal in the British Caribbean until its abolition in 1917. These migratory flows from China and Asia were not massive compared with the European stream, but in the century up to 1916, more than 700,000 indentured laborers from Asia were transported to the region. In addition, after 1907, the state of São Paulo became a major destination for Japanese immigration.

African slaves were also part of the world supply of labor to Latin America. In terms of immigration alone, America was an extension of Africa rather than Europe until late in the nineteenth century. Eltis calculates that it was not until 1840 that arrivals from Europe surpassed those from Africa. In the course of the nineteenth century, 600,000 to 700,000 African slaves reached Spanish America and almost twice that number were transported to Brazil up to 1870, when the slave trade was finally suppressed. Despite the rising cost of slaves and the increasing risks of the trade because of British pressure, in the first half of the nineteenth century, the volume of forced African slave migrations to Latin America tended to follow the pattern of growth and decline in labor demand. This labor demand was, in turn, related to the European demand for sugar, coffee, and cotton, which increased throughout the nineteenth century. The African slave population concentrated mainly in Brazil and the Caribbean.

According to the invaluable work of Ferenczi and Willcox,[1] the main trends in international migration are well documented. The majority of European immigrants went to the United States (Table 10.1). Until the last quarter of the nineteenth century, Latin America remained almost out of the free international labor market. Various colonization projects had brought more or less numerous European groups to some countries in the central decades of the nineteenth century, but most plans failed miserably. The German colonies were the most successful in southern Brazil and Chile; the Welsh in Patagonia are another example, as are some French colonies in the Southern Cone. Italians contributed to various successful colonies in Argentina. But it was not until the 1880s that Argentina, Brazil, and Uruguay started receiving a massive inflow of European immigrants.

There are various reasons for this delay: the political instability in the new republics, for example, in Argentina and Uruguay; the low demand for labor in the majority of the Latin American countries either because of a large native population, as in Mexico, or because of the use of slave labor, as in Brazil or Cuba; the high cost of the passage and the duration

---

[1] See the bibliographical essay corresponding to this chapter for works mentioned in the text.

Table 10.1. *Gross intercontinental immigration into selected areas, 1871–1940 (in thousands)*

	United States	Canada	Argentina	Brazil	Cuba	Uruguay
1871–80	2,433	220	261	219		112
1881–90	4,852	359	841	525		140
1891–1900	3,684	231	648	1,129		90
1901–10	8,666	947	1,764	671	243	21
1911–20	4,775	1,154	1,205	798	367	57
1921–30	2,723	987	1,397	840		21
1931–40	443	82	310	239		57

Sources: William Woodruff, *Impact of Western Man. A Study of Europe's Role in the World Economy, 1750–1960* (London, 1966), 108; and Imre Ferenczi and Walter F. Willcox, *International Migrations*, vol. 1 (New York, 1929).

of the trip to those countries where labor was scarce, wages high, and natural resources abundant, such as Argentina or Uruguay; natural disadvantages attributable to geography and climate in the Latin American hinterland; and "some political and cultural characteristics not attractive for immigrants of different ethnic origins" as the United Nations reported in explaining why Latin America lagged behind the United States in attracting immigrants.[2]

The situation changed for many countries after the 1870s. Political stability and a firm political will to attract foreign immigration that had been growing in the 1850s and 1860s led Latin American governments to look for foreign immigrants mainly from Europe. Institutional factors such as religious freedom, the right of private ownership, respect for civil rights, and a friendly atmosphere toward foreigners also played a role. The 1853 Argentinean constitution even gave foreigners some advantages over nationals such as exemption from military service.

From an economic perspective, the most powerful force for change was that Latin America experienced a boom in its traditional role as a supplier of primary goods. Exports rose, capital flows from Europe began to arrive, and investment in the transport system (railways) allowed the exploitation of the abundant natural resources to become a real possibility. The combination of declining transport costs, rising exports and capital inflows, new

---

[2] United Nations, *The Determinants and Consequences of Population Trends* (New York, 1953).

agricultural frontiers, high wages, and urban development contributed decisively to the integration of Latin America into the international economy. Geographic and economic isolation continued, however, to be a reality for many countries in the region, particularly those on the Pacific coast or in Central America, that remained poorly integrated into the world market.

Argentina, Brazil after the abolition of slavery, Uruguay, and Cuba were the main winners in the competition for foreign labor: more than 90 percent of the 13 million European immigrants who went to Latin America between 1870 and 1930 chose these four destinations. There were relatively modest immigration flows to countries such as Chile, Venezuela, and Mexico, but others, like Paraguay, failed almost completely in the goal of establishing colonies with European immigrants.[3]

Gross immigration figures differ considerably from net immigration. It has been argued that one of the main features of European immigration to Latin America was the high rate of return migration. However, return migration increased all over the world from the 1880s onward. By the 1890s, an increasing fraction of those who emigrated to the United States never intended to remain permanently and returned to their home country. Temporary movement in search of wage jobs, often over long distances and crossing national boundaries, was common in many of the European regions from which the "new" immigrants were drawn. Estimation of net immigration is particularly difficult for some countries like Brazil, where departure records are of dubious reliability because of serious underestimation. Sánchez-Albornoz estimates that between 1892 and 1930, only 46 percent of immigrants remained permanently in the state of São Paulo and the same rate is found in Cuba (47%) between 1902 and 1930. For Argentina, it has been calculated that the rate of return was around 53 percent.

Net immigration in Argentina over the period 1881–1930 reached 3.8 million. Uruguay attracted during the same period nearly 600,000 immigrants; more or less the same number remained in Cuba between 1902 and 1930, whereas Chile hardly reached 200,000 individuals. In contrast, only 25,000 immigrants entered Paraguay in the same years and Mexico received fewer than 18,000 net immigrants in 1911–24.

European immigration to Latin America presents clear fluctuations similar to the general trend of immigration in other destination countries

---

[3] With the exception of some isolated German colonies in Asunción and Alto Paraguay, all the attempts to encourage more northern European immigrants failed.

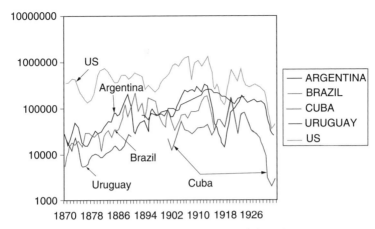

Figure 10.1. Immigration to Latin American countries and the U.S., 1870–1933.
Source: Imre Ferenczi and Walter F. Willcox, *International Migrations*, vol. 1 (New York, 1929).

(Figure 10.1). During the nineteenth century, migratory flows took a clear upward trend in the 1880s, led by Brazil and Argentina, then fell in the 1890s, more rapidly in Argentina than in other countries because of the effects of the Baring crisis. Actually, arrivals to Brazil surpassed those to Argentina in the 1890s. It was not until the turn of the century that immigration to Latin America reached really massive proportions. The period 1904–13 saw the highest concentration of arrivals in Argentina, Uruguay, and Cuba, whereas Brazil showed a more moderate increase. Latin America, then, only entered the age of mass migration in the first years of the twentieth century just prior to World War I. The mass migration era was short-lived because after the war the rate of immigration was no longer as high as before 1914, although there was a peak in the migratory flows in the years immediately after the conflict. Cuba is the main exception to the downward trend of the 1920s because of the extraordinary demand for labor during the sugar boom.

In the international labor market, the European sources of emigration also changed over time and it is important to relate the chronological profile of European emigration to the Latin American delay in attracting immigrants. In the central decades of the nineteenth century, the dominant migratory streams were from the British Isles, Germany, and the Scandinavian countries; southern and eastern Europeans followed in the 1880s. The diffusion of industrialization across Europe and the "Malthusian devil"

crossing Europe from north to south and from west to east, together with
the agrarian crisis of the late nineteenth century, have often been invoked as
explanations for this change in emigration origins. An emigration life cycle
has been identified for many countries and it can be related to demographic
transition, industrialization, and the influence of a growing stock of previous emigrants abroad. Southern and eastern European countries were on
the upswing of their emigration cycle in the decades prior to World War I.

European emigrants from the so-called new emigration countries had
a wider array of destination options than those who traveled in the middle
of the nineteenth century. Emigrants could opt for the United States, as
many in fact did, but Canada and Australia were also attractive destinations.
The Latin American countries started their efforts to attract European
immigrants more or less at the same time.

Late nineteenth-century European emigrants had also an extraordinary
advantage in transportation: trips were shorter, safer, and cheaper. Long-
term series on an annual basis for transatlantic passage fares are not available
for many European countries, particularly for southern Europe. On the
basis of the scattered available evidence, Table 10.2 presents data on passage
fares for Spanish emigrants to their three main destinations. It also includes,
for comparison, the fares paid by British emigrants for passage to the United
States.[4] There is a clear downward trend after the mid-nineteenth century
for fares to Brazil, Argentina, and Cuba. The cheapest fares from Spain
were for travel to Cuba, which remained quite stable over time.[5] Fares to
Brazil and Argentina were much more expensive than to Cuba in the 1870s
and 1880s, but both experienced a sharp decline in the years of massive
emigration. In the 1880s, according to Cortés Conde, an Italian worker
could finance his transatlantic trip with only 20 percent of his income.
In contrast, Spanish emigrants had to face the cost of the passage from
lower levels of income. For an agricultural worker in the north of Spain,
the cost of the trip in the 1880s was around 153 working days in a working
year of around 250 days. However, this income constraint was relieved
by the sending of remittances and prepaid tickets to finance the moves of
relatives and friends. The same situation developed in Italy and presumably
in Portugal, thus explaining the massive emigration in the first decade of

---

[4] The British data in Bruce I. Sacerdote, "On Transport Cost From Europe to the New World"
(unpublished manuscript, Harvard University, 1995). I am grateful to Tim Dore for this reference
and to Bruce Sacerdote for allowing me to use his unpublished data.
[5] It should be borne in mind that Spanish data refer to prices from Galician ports. The trip from the
Canary Islands to Cuba was cheaper.

Table 10.2. *Transatlantic passage fares, 1850–1914 (in current $)*

	Spain–Brazil	Spain–Argentina	Spain–Cuba	Britain–USA
1850–1860	n.a.	$45.18	$33.32	$44.00[a]
1870–1880*	$50.71	$52.30	$36.70	$26.55
1881–1890**	$45.54	$46.60	$32.10	$20.40
1904–1914***	$31.20	$35.19	$34.21	$33.00

Notes:
* For Latin American countries, 1872–1880.
** For Spain–Cuba, 1881–1886.
*** For Spain–Brazil, 1906–1914; for Britain–USA, 1904–1912.
[a] Fares were exceptionally high for the years 1850–1851. Average fare for 1852–1862 were $36.90.
Sources: Spanish data refer to passages from Galician ports: Alejandro Vázquez Gonzalez, *La emigración gallega a América, 1830–1930* (Ph.D. dissertation, Universidad de Santiago de Compostela, 1999). Britain–USA data refer to passages from Liverpool to New York: Bruce I. Sacerdote, "On Transport Cost from Europe to the New World" (unpublished manuscript, Harvard University, 1995). I thank Tim Dore for this reference.

the twentieth century. Table 10.2 also documents a convergence trend of Spanish fares with British fares: in the first decade of the twentieth century, a period of massive emigration from Spain, fares to Latin America were quite similar to those from Britain to the United States. We have also scattered evidence for passenger fares from Spanish ports to the United States in the years 1911–14: for Spanish emigrants, the trip to the United States cost $40, compared with $38 to Brazil, $33 to Argentina, and $39 to Cuba. British emigrants to the United States had to pay $34 to travel to the United States in those years. The role of migratory networks, the diffusion of information (or the lack of it regarding the United States), culture, language, and the existence of old colonial links in the case of Cuba seem to explain the Spanish preference for Latin American countries better than the cost of the passage.

However, the significance of the transport revolution for emigration traffic lay not so much in the declining price of the ticket shown in Table 10.2 as in the increasing speed, comfort, safety, regularity, and accessibility of passenger services. The average time for the travel from northern Spain to Cuba in the 1850s was thirty-eight days by sailing vessels. By the early 1900s, steamers could do the trip in about nine to twelve days. The same trend is found in the River Plate route, where steamers cut the trip from around fifty-five days in the mid-nineteenth century to twelve days in the

1910s. This dramatic reduction in the duration of the Atlantic crossing was important in two different ways: one, it reduced effectively the cost of migration when the opportunity cost of the earning time wasted on board is added to the monetary cost of the trip; and two, it was particularly important for temporary migrants and contributed decisively to raise their rate of return. For seasonal migrants, such as the *golondrinas* (swallows) between Italy and Argentina at different harvest times, it is quite obvious that this kind of migration would have been impossible in the days of the sailing ships.

Spanish and Portuguese emigration was largely concentrated into selected destinations in Latin America, in contrast to Italian emigration. Iberian emigrants did not head to North America in large numbers, although Italians, particularly from the south, did so. It has been said that from the 1880s onward, international labor markets were segmented along a Latin versus non-Latin divide.[6] However, although it is true that Latin America gained its European immigrants mainly from southern Europe, there was also a considerable flow of migrants from central Europe and from east and southeast European countries in the years prior to World War I. All of these European regions of departure were, to a far greater degree than Portugal or Spain, also countries of origin for the migrations to the United States. In the late nineteenth century, northern European emigrants had long and well-established migratory traditions toward the United States, which was a country that showed the greatest ability to absorb relatively large numbers of immigrants because of its own size: in the 1860s, the United States population was around 30 million, compared with 1.5 million in Argentina. Therefore, the ability of Argentina to attract large numbers of immigrants relative to its own population is striking not only in the Latin American context but also compared with Australia or Canada (Table 10.3).

The "new immigrants" from southern and eastern Europe, who joined the flow since the 1880s, were different from those who crossed the Atlantic in the earlier waves. Early and mid-nineteenth-century immigrants often traveled in family groups, they intended to acquire land and settle permanently in the New World, and their occupational backgrounds were

---

[6] Alan M. Taylor, "Mass Migration to Distant Southern Shores. Argentina and Australia, 1870–1939," in Timothy J. Hatton and Jeffrey G. Williamson, eds., *Migration and the International Labor Market, 1850–1939* (New York, 1994), 5–71; Hatton and Williamson, *The Age of Mass Migration. Causes and Economic Impact*, ch. 6 (New York, 1998).

Table 10.3. *New World immigration rates by decade (per thousand population)*

	1861–70	1871–80	1881–90	1891–1900	1901–10
Argentina	9.9	11.7	22.2	13.7	29.2
Brazil		2.0	4.1	7.2	3.4
Cuba					118.4
Australia	12.2	10.0	14.7	0.7	0.9
Canada	8.3	5.5	7.8	4.9	16.7
United States	6.5	5.5	8.6	5.3	10.2

Source: Jeffrey G. Williamson, "Real Wages Inequality and Globalization in Latin America before 1940," in Pablo Martín Aceña, Adolfo Meisel, and Carlos Newland, eds., *La historia económica en américa latina. Revista de Historia Económica* Special Issue (1999), 101–42.

those of semiskilled artisans displaced by industrialization. In contrast, late nineteenth-century immigrants traveled alone in higher numbers (except those who went to Brazil), they entered urban unskilled occupations, and, to a lesser extent, became agricultural tenants. The majority of them were common laborers, with a high proportion of illiterates. They also exhibited high rates of returns. The high return-migration rate among immigrants from southern Europe, the so-called birds of passage, is often explained by two reasons: the transport revolution that made the return trip easier, with shorter and cheaper trips, as mentioned earlier, and the intention of returning before departure of the immigrants themselves as a different migratory strategy from those pioneers who settled in the land. It has also been argued that access to land ownership was more difficult in Latin American countries than in the United States, but there is a growing consensus in the literature that these "new immigrants" were really looking for temporary migration to maximize the wage differential between the sending and receiving countries. It also must be remembered that when massive immigration arrived in countries like Argentina, there was no empty land because the land had been effectively distributed among natives and a few pioneer immigrants. Gallo and Cortés Conde have argued that the agricultural tenancy system that prevailed in the Argentinean pampa was an efficient institution both for immigrants with hardly any capital and for landowners with large extensions of land to cultivate. In contrast, the plantation system in Brazil and the Caribbean was never the best environment for immigrants to gain access to land ownership, although some immigrants became small landowners in southeast Brazil.

Traditional studies on international migration focused on income per capita differentials between sending and receiving regions in order to explain why people migrated. According to Maddison's figures, gross domestic product (GDP) per capita grew at an annual rate of 2.5 percent in Argentina, 0.3 percent in Brazil, 2.2 percent in Mexico, and 1.2 percent in Uruguay during the period 1870–1913. Between 1913 and 1950, Argentine, Mexican, and Uruguayan growth rates decreased to 0.7, 0.8, and 0.9 percent, respectively, whereas Brazil had a better performance (GDP per capita grew at 2%).

In recent years, it has been forcibly argued that the relevant variable for studying international migrations is not per capita income but real wage differentials. People made their calculations based on future earnings and not on a statistical variable such as GDP per capita. The pioneering research done by Cortés Conde in relation to Italian and Argentine wages was the first step in that direction. Thanks to the work done by Williamson, we can now document real wages on a yearly basis in Latin America for Argentina, Brazil, Colombia, Mexico, and Uruguay from 1870 onward, and for Cuba since 1905. Data refer to purchasing power–adjusted real wages for urban unskilled labor. Some might argue that rural wages could be more relevant to future immigrants in Europe if they were thinking of working on the land. Although many immigrants might have originally had that intention, the immigrant population in Latin America mainly concentrated in the urban sector. Seasonal migrants, such as the *golondrinas* in the Argentine pampa, were surely more affected by agricultural wages in the host country. The same can be said for immigrants in the sugar plantations in Cuba in the 1920s, but *golondrinas* were only a tiny minority of the total flow of immigrants to Argentina and many of the immigrants to Cuban agriculture ended up being employed in the urban sector. The same happened to immigrants in the Brazilian plantations who moved to the industrial sector in the city of São Paulo.

From an aggregate point of view, Williamson's real wage series provides a general picture of the evolution of wages in Latin America, which is homogeneous and comparable to those in the countries of origin. Moreover, the Latin American real wage hierarchy and evolution seem to be consistent with other qualitative and quantitative accounts.[7] Argentina and Uruguay

---

[7] This is hardly surprising because Williamson's data relies heavily on independent studies carried out at national levels, such as those of Robert Cortés Conde, Luis Bertola, and Alan Dye, among others.

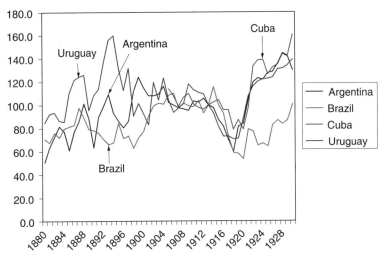

Figure 10.2. Latin American real wages, 1880–1940: immigration countries (1913 = 100). *Source:* Jeffrey G. Williamson, "Real Wages Inequality and Globalization in Latin America before 1940," in Pablo Martín Aceña, Adolfo Meisel, and Carlos Newland, eds., *La historia Económica de América Latina, Revista de Historia Económica* Special Issue (1999), 101–42.

show the highest wages up to 1914. The Cuban sugar boom in the 1920s explains the high wages in that period (Figure 10.2). In the 1870s, real wages in Argentina were around 76 percent relative to Great Britain. In the first decade of the twentieth century, Argentinean wages were 96 percent those of Britain, whereas Uruguayan wages were almost 88 percent relative to Great Britain. The rest of the six countries sampled in the Williamson study did not show wages as high as those in the River Plate. Brazilian wages in the southeast, where immigrants concentrated, were just 42 percent relative to British wages in the first decade of the twentieth century and Mexico attained a relative level of 42 percent. Cuba only reached wages around 90 percent of the British in the 1920s. These data can partly explain why the British did not migrate in great numbers to the Latin American countries, but the relevant comparisons are with those countries in Latin Europe that did send workers to Latin American countries: Italy, Portugal, and Spain (Table 10.4 and Figure 10.3). Wages in Argentina and Uruguay were systematically more than 200 percent higher relative to a weighted average of Italy, Portugal, and Spain. They were over 160 percent higher in Cuba in the years prior to World War I, but were also much higher in Mexico than in the Mediterranean countries, though Mexico never experienced mass immigration from Europe.

Table 10.4. *Real wage performance by decade relative to the Mediterranean countries (weighted average of Italy, Portugal, and Spain)*

	Argentina	Brazil SE	Brazil NE	Colombia	Cuba	Mexico	Uruguay
1850s		35.8					
1870s	207.7	48.9	15.5	53.1			
1890s	267.8	47.5	10.1	79.1		173.2	324.8
1909–1913	212.1	47.8	16.8	53.1	160.5	140.9	211.5
1930s	201.1			94.4	152.2	63	187

Source: Jeffrey Williamson, "Real Wages and Relative Factor Prices in the Third World, 1820–1940: Latin America" (Discussion Paper no. 1853, Harvard Institute of Economic Research, October 1998).

Because in the United States real wages were higher than in Britain, it is quite obvious why Latin American countries could not compete with the United States. Within Latin America, hardly any country could compete with Argentina. Consequently, migratory flows were higher in Argentina than in Brazil, Cuba, or Uruguay. Subsidies and contract labor in the coffee sector allowed Brazil to compete to a certain extent with Cuba and the River Plate. Brazilian data pose a challenge for the classic interpretation of migration because of wage differentials: Italians, Portuguese, and Spaniards immigrated to Brazil in large numbers, but real wages in Brazil were less than 50 percent higher than wage levels in the Mediterranean countries. The fact that the Brazilian government paid for travel expenses in an extensive immigration subsidy program can explain why southern Europeans went to Brazil in spite of a not very high wage gap: subsidized immigration allowed potential emigrants to Brazil to overcome the income constraint that would have prevented many of them from long-distance immigration. However, in the Brazilian case, neither real wages in the coffee sector nor urban wages, such as those in Williamson's study, can satisfactorily explain the migratory flows. Focusing only on real wages does not suffice to explain Brazil's immigration.

Money wages in the coffee plantations of southeast Brazil, where the majority of immigrants settled, came from three separate sources. First, there was the payment established in the *colono* contract for the care of the coffee trees through the annual production cycle. According to Holloway, this salary accounted roughly for one half to two thirds of the income of the

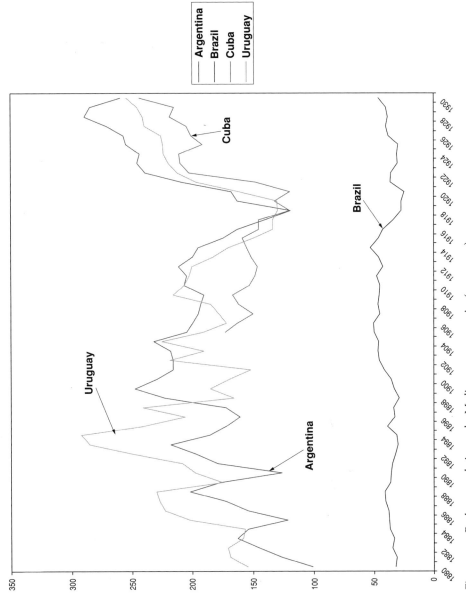

Figure 10.3. Real wages relative to the Mediterranean countries (1913 = 100).

Source: Williamson, "Real Wages, Inequality and Globalization in Latin America before 1940," 101–42.

colono family. The second important source of money wages came from the coffee harvest. As in the first case, the family contracted its labor as a unit. The harvest portion of the *colono's* family income fluctuated considerably from year to year because of wide variations in yield per coffee tree. The third source of money income, which was much less important than the other two, came from occasional day labor. Money wages were also different in the frontier, the intermediate areas, and the older zones of southeast Brazil. Moreover, any analysis of the standard of living of the coffee workers in Brazil is incomplete without considering the nonmonetary income workers received, which was a crucial part of the system. Free housing was a standard provision of *colonos'* work contracts. They were also provided with land to grow their own food and with pasture for livestock. *Colonos* were also allowed to sell their produce to rural stores.

Because the coffee worker paid no rent, either in money, products, or labor, in return for these nonmonetary provisions, generalizations about the *colono's* real wages are difficult to make. Food and rent are always an important part of a worker's budget, and Holloway estimates that perhaps 70 percent of a *colono* family's total income came in the form of free housing, food crops, or pasture lands. Thus, advantages that the *colono* contract offered to the immigrant workers are not captured by Williamson's real wages. The system included the security of a minimum annual income, low expenses, and, consequently, the possibility of accumulating savings through free housing and cheap food, and finally the possibility of maximizing family income by fully using the labor of all members of the family. Obviously, the larger the number of dependents in the family, the smaller this advantage would be.

The huge wage gap between the sending regions in Europe and the Latin American countries has led scholars to argue that the Latin American destination countries experienced an unlimited supply of labor. The similarities between Brazil's experience and Arthur Lewis's model of economic development with "unlimited supplies of labor" because of immigration from Europe were discussed at length by Leff. Lewis himself thought it was the case for Latin America in the late nineteenth century, and Cortés Conde and Díaz Alejandro strongly argued the same for Argentina: without European immigration, the elastic supply of labor in the Argentinean labor market would have been impossible to achieve on the basis of the native labor force alone. After the abolition of slavery in Brazil, which had provided the coffee planters in São Paulo with an elastic supply of labor, a new labor market institution was developed to maintain that elastic supply of low-cost labor from overseas: subsidized immigration. By bringing immigrant workers from Europe, Brazilian planters were able to keep wage levels low. Output and employment in the export sector of the economy could expand over the long run with minimal upward pressure on real wages: between 1880 and 1914, real wages in the coffee sector do not seem to have increased. The interest of the planters in securing a large supply of low-wage labor is clear, but the native Brazilian population, particularly laborers in the northeast, might well have benefited from a reduction in the supply of unskilled labor from overseas. The question then is why coffee planters preferred to subsidize immigration from overseas instead of hiring native workers from the low-wage areas of northeast Brazil. Brazil lacked an integrated national labor market, but political interests of the planters also played a role.

The hypothesis concerning the elastic supply of labor from the Mediterranean countries has been put to an econometric test recently by Hatton and Williamson, who show that for the three Latin countries in Europe, the wage gap between sending and receiving countries certainly influenced emigration, but the elasticities are relatively small. In all three cases, a 10 percent increase in the wage ratio raised emigration by less than one per thousand in the long run, compared with Britain and Ireland, where long-run responses of 2.2 and 2.3 per thousand are observed. This result provides strong evidence to support the view that the supply of Latin European labor to the New World was not relatively elastic, as assumed in the literature. According to them, late nineteenth-century emigration from southern Europe was not income constrained and the supply of labor from Latin countries in Europe was not more elastic than the rest of Europe. However, more detailed research has shown that emigration was indeed income constrained in Spain and Italy.[8] The unlimited-supply-of-labor hypothesis still awaits further testing, particularly for Brazil, the most challenging case.

Real wage gaps between sending regions in Europe and the New World do not explain the choice of destination of emigrants from southern Europe. Italian wages in 1870 were 44 percent of those in Argentina and 22 percent of those in the United States. In the 1870s and 1880s, the majority of Italian emigrants went to Argentina and not to the United States. Spanish

---

[8] Sánchez-Alonso, "Those Who Left and Those Who Stayed Behind: Explaining Emigration from the Regions of Spain, 1880–1914," *Journal of Economic History* 60 (2000), 730–55, and Faini and Venturini, "Italian Emigration in the Pre-War Period" in Hatton and Williamson, *Migration and the International Labor Market, 1850–1939*, 72–90.

wages in 1870s were 57 percent of those in Argentina but only 30 percent of those in the United States. Between 1900 and 1913, less than fifty thousand Spaniards emigrated to the United States and the numbers were lower in the nineteenth century. One of the most distinctive features of Spanish emigration and, to a certain extent, of Portuguese as well, is a constant and persistent orientation toward the Latin American countries. Languages or the similarity of language in the Italian case, religion, and cultural identity have often been invoked as an explanation for the Mediterranean preference for Latin America. Unlike Italians and Portuguese emigrants from the Azores, who gradually broke down the cultural and language barriers and headed to North America, Spaniards did not. Cuba, where Spaniards enjoyed a privileged position until 1898, may have acted as a substitute for the United States. Spanish emigrants obviously preferred a Spanish colony to the American market; consequently, they never developed migratory chains or acquired sufficient knowledge of employment opportunities in the United States. After Cuban independence, they continued emigrating to Cuba in even larger numbers than before. Destination-country policy might also have been a powerful explanation of the destination choices of emigrants from southern Europe, particularly in the case of subsidized immigration to Brazil.

The Italian case stands in sharp contrast to Portugal and Spain. Italians shifted destinations from Latin America to the United States. In the period 1886–95, more than 38 percent of Italian emigrants chose Argentina and Brazil as destinations, whereas only fewer than 16 percent went to the United States. The trend was reversed in 1906–15, when only 15 percent of Italians went to the two Latin American countries in contrast to nearly 40 percent to the United States. In the north of Italy, Argentina and Brazil were the favored destinations for 75 percent of the emigrants between 1881 and 1911; in the same period, 65 percent of southern Italians chose the United States. Econometric exercises carried out to explain these differences in Italian emigrants' overseas destinations have come to no conclusive results. It seems that path dependency and the diffusion of information across immigrant networks played an important role, or it could be that different labor markets in Argentina and the United States attracted different Italian emigrants.

Latin America was late entering the age of free mass migration. Massive inflows were limited from the last decade of the nineteenth century (downturn years for intercontinental migration) to 1914. Prior to World War I,

Latin America had to compete for labor in the international market with the United States and, to a lesser extent, with other destination countries. After World War I, economic development in the European countries of origin was faster than before, whereas migration flows from southern Europe went to European countries such as France or Germany in higher numbers.

The Latin American real wage hierarchy explains why the River Plate countries attracted the largest inflow of migrants. But other forces mattered as well, as the Brazilian case shows. International labor markets were segmented, but segmentation existed long before the mass immigration era. Italians were already quite numerous in some Latin American countries in the 1860s, and the Portuguese and the Spaniards enjoyed a relatively privileged position in colonies and ex-colonies. Culture, language, and the diffusion of information through early migrants networks were powerful forces directing southern Europeans toward Latin American countries. Immigration policies could have also played a role, but it seems that policies reinforced the already existing trend.

2. IMMIGRATION POLICIES

After independence and particularly in the central decades of the nineteenth century, many Latin American governments tried to attract foreign immigrants for colonization projects. Nevertheless, only a few countries adopted a mass immigration policy. Mass immigration was not popular with all governments. Foreigners, particularly Europeans, were considered as potentially dangerous to the established social and political order and many governments thought that systems such as contract or indentured labor were only suitable for alleviating labor shortages in specific sectors.[9]

Some countries failed to attract large numbers of immigrants in spite of favorable policies. Others, like Peru and the Caribbean countries, opted for indentured immigrants for particular sectors. Policies encouraging mass immigration were implemented in Argentina, Uruguay, Brazil, and Cuba, but with different aims and consequences. The open door policy was

---

[9] Virtually all immigration legislation excluded sick and handicapped individuals as well as people with criminal records in the country of origin, anarchists, and other political groups considered dangerous.

a reality, however, only for European immigration. In this respect, the migration policies of the Latin American countries of massive immigration were not much different from those followed by other receiving countries. Chinese workers and, in general, contract laborers were largely excluded in late nineteenth-century United States and Canada. The Chinese were also charged a special poll tax in Australia and New Zealand. Moreover, Australian attempts to specifically restrict Indian immigration were vetoed by the British government on the grounds that India was part of the Empire. Chinese immigrants were also considered undesirable in Argentina, Uruguay, and in the first years of the Cuban republic, but Brazil did receive Japanese immigrants.

Although Argentina and Brazil aimed to attract large numbers of European immigrants and both opted for an open door policy, the means employed to reach the same end were entirely different. Argentina has been considered a textbook case of a liberal immigration policy after the 1853 Constitution and the legislation passed in 1876. Some have argued that the most powerful element in the Argentine immigration policy was the liberal Constitution of 1853 that gave foreigners basic civil rights such as freedom of association, movement, profession, and religion, among others. Only two criteria for exclusion appeared in the Immigration Law of 1876: health and age (people older than sixty were excluded). On the eve of World War I, administrative controls on arrivals, particularly for those considered politically dangerous, were more strict than before but a free immigration policy was applied all through the period. In 1923, some minor modifications imposing certain bureaucratic requirements were introduced into Argentine legislation in order to control more carefully the suitability of immigrants. It was not until 1932 that Argentina established, for the first time, the requirement of a labor contract prior to arrival or proof of financial means. Close relatives of already-resident immigrants were freely admitted.

Immigration policy was designed not only to people the pampa and give value to the abundant natural resources, but also to serve the original goal of bringing culturally "superior" immigrants from northern Europe to eliminate the hostile-to-development colonial mentality and to "civilize" the country. Spaniards were not particularly welcome in the central decades of the nineteenth century, and they were described by a prominent Argentinean, Sarmiento, as a "race of atrophied minds." In the early years of colonization (the 1870s), Argentina tried to attract Protestants from northern Europe, particularly Germans, but when it became a reality that Italians and Spaniards were actually arriving in massive numbers, the Argentines made virtue out of necessity by inventing the concept of "Latinity" and interpreting the result as a culturally praiseworthy achievement. It is also worth noticing that because the Argentine Immigration Law of 1876 defined an immigrant as a second- and third-class passenger from overseas, people from the neighboring Latin American countries of Paraguay and Bolivia were excluded. Both have large indigenous populations.

With no other immigrant group did the Argentine attitude change so dramatically as with the Spaniards. Spaniards were the hated enemy in 1810 during the struggle for independence, but in the centennial celebration years Argentinean elites were proud to claim colonial ancestors to distinguish themselves from the new urban lower and middle classes made up of immigrants from eastern Europe and the Middle East. Moya has recorded the subtleties of Argentine ruling class mentality that considered that having a Basque family name was a sign of distinction while popular jokes on *gallegos* (Spanish immigrants in general) were, and still are, common. In Argentina, the native population from the interior region was less appreciated as workers than southern Europeans, not to mention the British or the French, who never found any hostility.

The fact that Argentina, in spite of initial preferences, had a de facto open door policy that pulled masses of immigrants from southern Europe has led to the conclusion that Argentine policy did not select immigrants, in contrast to other countries of immigration. Despite somewhat similar endowments, Canadian policies were less favorable to massive immigration than those of Argentina because of a different income distribution and franchise, according to Solberg. Exclusion criteria in Canada moved from a general and vague definition of "undesirables" to the specification, after 1910, of those "immigrants belonging to any race deemed unsuited to the climate or requirements of Canada."[10] Taylor has stressed the fact that Australia's selective policy excluded poor immigrants from southern Europe. Australia did select immigrants from high-wage white northern European labor markets (namely Britain). In contrast, the nonselective immigration policy of Argentina drew immigrants from low-wage, Latin (although white, one must add) southern European labor markets (Italy and

---

[10] Quoted in Donald Avery, *Reluctant Host: Canada's Response to Immigrant Workers, 1896–1994* (Toronto, 1995), 124.

Spain). According to Taylor different migratory policies attracted, therefore, different types of immigrants and this had long-run economic and
demographic consequences (see Section 4).

Australian immigration policy had in common with Argentina's the
need to increase population to exploit the abundant natural resources, but
Australian policy also had a very different goal: defense against possible
aggression (from Asians, it was made clear). Still, in the early years of the
twentieth century, Australians felt isolated and vulnerable whereas Argen-
tineans felt absolutely integrated into the Atlantic economy. The main
difference between Australian and Argentine immigration policies was,
however, that Australia had an assisted immigration program over the entire
period, more or less generous according to its own economic conditions:
50 percent of arrivals in the 1870s were assisted but only 10 percent in
the crisis years of the 1890s. By contrast, in the entire period of massive
immigration to Argentina, 1880–1930, the government paid for immigrants'
travel expenses in only three years, 1887–9.

It might be that the right comparison of migration policies should not
be between Australia and Argentina but between Australia and Brazil.
Although the Brazilian policy that subsidized immigration was not exactly
the same as the Australian assisted immigration scheme, both governments
took a much more active role in selecting immigrants than did Argentina.
It has been argued that in the absence of the assisted passage scheme, a
significant proportion of migrants who came to Australia would not have
been able to travel.[11] The same argument can be applied to Brazil, with
its lower wages and harsher plantation working conditions than in rural
Argentina or Uruguay. Contrary to Brazil, assisted immigration became
highly unpopular in Australia after the 1890s crisis, in which it contributed
to high levels of unemployment. In Brazil, subsidized immigration might
have been unpopular among native workers and ex-slaves, but it had the
strong support of Brazilian planters. The explicit goal of Brazilian immigration policy was to maintain a constant supply of labor to keep wages low.
In Australia, the general objective of labor growth was subject to the constraint that living standards were maintained. Whereas in Brazil immigrants
were effectively selected to work on the land, in Australia (in Victoria and
New South Wales), the nomination system was geared to introduce those

---

[11] This appears quite clear comparing the cost of the trip from Britain to Australia and the United
States. In the 1860s, traveling to Australia cost almost double traveling to the United States ($77
compared with $39.50).

"classes, and those alone who can readily assimilate in the industrial life."[12] In contrast, immigrants who could pay their own passage to Brazil were considered relatively undesirable because they were believed likely to enter nonagricultural occupations, "thus bringing in consumers instead of elements of production."[13] Another major difference is that, in Australia, the assisted immigration policy had an evident pro-British bias and the whole system was established in cooperation with the British government. Brazilian policy had also a bias but in favor of the most destitute emigrants from Europe. However, subsidized immigration for poor people was sometimes hardly feasible in the countries of origin without local organized support, and this was more or less easily neutralized by big landowners (*latifundistas*) in southern Europe.

The Australian policy seems to be more consistent with a relative shortage of skilled labor caused by technical progress than with discrimination according to national origins. The root of the problem in Brazil and in other Latin American countries was the unwillingness of employers to use wages to clear the market. According to Bulmer-Thomas, this reluctance to raise real wages concentrated income in the export sector and in the owners of the land, and it also undermined the search for labor-saving technological innovations in response to rising real wages.

Whereas it is clear that Australia actively looked for the exclusion of Asian immigrants, it is not so clear that southern European migrants, namely Italians, were also considered undesirable and effectively discouraged from entering the country as a matter of policy. Italians were most welcome in Australia after 1945 and they were not excluded from Canada, another British Dominion. On the contrary, after 1895, Canada initiated intensive recruiting campaigns in Italy and in rural districts of Austro-Hungary and Russia. We simply do not know how many Mediterranean emigrants were discouraged from traveling to Australia.

Segmentation of the international labor markets by culture, lack of information, and distance costs in the case of Australia were apparently more effective than immigration policies. The international labor market was segmented long before massive immigration started. Pioneer immigrants in Argentina in the 1860s were pulled by others along the chain of migration.

---

[12] New South Wales Parliamentary Papers, 1913. Quoted in David Pope, "Population and Australian Economic Development, 1900–1930," in Rodney Maddock and Ian W. McLean, eds., *The Australian Economy in the Long Run* (Cambridge, 1987), 48.

[13] São Paulo. Secretaria de Agricultura, 1896. Quoted in Thomas Holloway, *Immigrants on the Land. Coffee and Society in São Paulo, 1886–1934* (Chapel Hill, NC, 1980), 44.

British emigrants who chose Canada or Australia did so as subjects in an imperial framework that offered them various advantages. Something similar happened to the Spaniards in Cuba before 1898. Potential emigrants from southern Europe had, by the 1880s, well-established connections and numerous shipping companies traveling to Brazil and the River Plate. In the first decade of the twentieth century, these companies were competing in prices and traveling conditions to get more passengers. Emigrants willing to go to Australia would have presumably had to travel first to British ports. At least in the Spanish case, there was not a single shipping company traveling directly to Australia. There was not a large pool of emigrants willing to go to Australia and those who considered it were discouraged by Australian immigration policy. Australia and Argentina were never competing destinations in the Southern Hemisphere.

The main competitor for Argentina was Brazil, and the country to imitate in immigration policies was the United States. When Brazil started its subsidized program in 1888, Argentines thought that they would not be able to compete. It was not by chance that Argentina started paying travel expenses from Europe in the same year. This is a clear example of how one country's immigration policy may have been influenced by the immigration policy of another country. The Argentine program was short-lived – it was abandoned in 1890 because of the Baring crisis. For partly accidental and partly unknown reasons, the majority of the Argentine subsidized passages were distributed in Spain and Italy, thereby reinforcing the already existing trend. After 1890, Argentine politicians decided, in a kind of Darwinistic turn of mind, that spontaneous immigration was better than organized or assisted immigration because only the best would emigrate.

The most outstanding immigration policy in Latin America was that of Brazil. The early beginnings of immigration to São Paulo were not primarily the result of conditions in Europe or a strong pull from Brazil. Rather, the impending end of slavery forced the coffee planters to look elsewhere for workers. Slavery and free labor coexisted for some years. In the period before slavery ended – that is, up to 1886 – more than half a million free and subsidized European immigrants arrived in Brazil to work on the coffee plantations, according to Klein. Constant strikes and revolts of these free coffee workers convinced planters that the two groups should never work in the same units. Thus, when total emancipation occurred and the ex-slaves abandoned the coffee states, the planters of São Paulo, Minas Gerais, and Rio de Janeiro resorted to free immigrant workers. With the cessation of overseas arrivals of slaves and the downward pressure that they exerted on wages, subsidizing European immigration appeared as the best solution for maintaining a constant supply of labor. The transition went more smoothly than might have been expected because, although labor costs rose, emancipation took place at the height of the coffee boom.

Brazil, like the rest of the Latin American countries, could not compete with the United States, but neither could it compete for mass immigration by offering high wages, as Argentina did. Therefore, the flow was expected to be low if the country relied solely on an open-door immigration policy. In fact, the inflow was smaller than in Argentina but still enough to secure a supply of labor for the coffee plantations. It was perfectly rational from the planters' point of view to use subsidies to shift their labor supply schedule downward, saving on both their current and future marginal labor costs. Between 1890 and 1913, the stock of coffee trees in São Paulo state (used as a proxy for the demand for labor) increased at a rate of approximately 6.5 percent per year. The interest of the planters in securing a large supply of low-cost labor was clear. The subsidized immigration program was an extraordinary success. From 1889 to the Great Depression, nearly 2.25 million immigrants came in, compared with the population of São Paulo in 1886 of 1.25 million. Around 58 percent of all immigrants in that period were subsidized by the state of São Paulo. Italians predominated, supplying 73 percent of all arrivals from 1887 through 1900. Spain and Portugal were also major beneficiaries of the Brazilian system. From 1900 to 1930, the nationality distribution was more diverse. In the 1920s, Romanians, Lithuanians, Poles, and Syrio-Lebanese (the *turcos* as they were popularly called both in Brazil and Argentina because they came from the former Ottoman Empire) also entered São Paulo. Among the new arrivals, the most important single group was the Japanese. Brazilian immigration policy did not discriminate by national origin although southern Europeans were considered superior workers.

Immigrants were not drawn to Brazil simply by high wages but by a combination of transport subsidies, which raised the net private returns to immigrants; labor contracts, which offered them a secure job; and nonmonetary provisions such as free housing, which allowed them to reduce their expenses and consequently increase their savings. By making the subsidy a grant rather than a loan, the planters avoided having workers with a heavy debt burden on arrival, and by channeling it through the government of

São Paulo, planters were able to share costs because everyone who paid state taxes contributed to the program. From 1886, the beginning of its policy of actively promoting immigration, up to 1930, the government of São Paulo spent the equivalent of nearly US$ 37 million. Funds came from tax revenues on coffee exports, which averaged just over 5 percent of total tax revenues for the entire 1892–1930 period. Almost at the same time that the United States experienced a growing pressure for restrictions on immigration, the Brazilian government was spending millions to attract immigrants.

Holloway provides an excellent description of Brazilian propaganda, the construction of infrastructure (railways and a hostel for immigrants), and the activities of the society created in 1886 to transport immigrants: the *Sociedade Promotora da Imigraçao*. Going to Brazil was perceived in southern Europe as a good investment. The Italian government tried briefly to ban subsidized immigration to Brazil in 1890–1, but the flow continued afterward and reached the highest levels ever recorded. Literary sources, official propaganda in Italy, and even immigrants' letters stressed the miserable conditions of work on the Brazilian plantations, but Italians kept traveling to Brazil.

To qualify for a subsidized passage, immigrants had to meet well-defined criteria of gender, age, and family structure. In that sense, the Brazilian immigration policy was quite selective. Immigrants had to be European agricultural workers. Nearly all subsidized immigrants listed their profession as farmer (*agricultor*). All those who entered under contract were to be in family units carefully defined: (a) married couples under age forty-five with no children, (b) married couples with children with at least one working-age male per family, and (c) widows or widowers with children, again with at least one working-age male per family. The state paid full passage for persons age twelve and older but only half passage for children in the seven-to-eleven age group and one quarter passage for those aged three though six. Because the shipping companies had to repatriate nonsuitable immigrants, they were strictly selected. The system gave the authorities considerable control not only over which immigrants entered but also over immigrants' occupations after their arrival. Not a single country in the age of mass migration and for such a long period of time had as detailed and selective an immigration policy as Brazil.

After 1900, the subsidy program was changed. The program shifted to a system of partial subsidies. Instead of the current price of the passage, the state paid a set fee of fifty francs for each qualified immigrant and an annual limit was established on the number of immigrants subsidized each year. The flat fee system was sometimes less than the full price of the passage, but it meant a considerable reduction in travel costs, just as in the Australian assisted immigration scheme. Internal migration and unsubsidized immigration from abroad increased in the 1920s, and this led to growing support for an end to the subsidy policy in official circles. In late 1927, it was finally declared that the government would no longer pay transportation subsidies from foreign countries to São Paulo. The general policy of prepaid ocean passages ended in 1928. São Paulo planters criticized the ending of subsidies, but the collapse of the international economy in the 1930s made it clear that the system had ended forever. According to the immigration policy model developed by Timmer and Williamson, labor market forces account for the greater part of this major policy switch from an open immigration policy with generous subsidies to a restrictive policy in 1928.

The general belief is that the growth of São Paulo's coffee industry and exports in the last decade of the nineteenth century would have been impossible without the influx of immigrants from overseas. But Brazil had a relatively large native population that might have provided a pool of coffee workers. The Brazilian natives, particularly in the northeast, might well have benefited from a reduction in the supply of unskilled labor from overseas, but were excluded from the coffee plantations in the southeast by the segmentation of the Brazilian national labor market and as a matter of policy choice. The large distances between Brazil's regions meant high transportation costs. Free internal labor migration from the northeast to the booming southeast was precluded by the absence of capital-market institutions to finance native workers' investment in internal migration. The question, then, is why planters did not subsidize the internal migration of native workers. Was it cheaper to pay transport subsidies to cross the Atlantic? Was it the lack of transport infrastructure (railways) between the north and south of Brazil that prevented migration to the southeast? It seems unlikely that the transportation costs of bringing workers from the northeast to the southeast of the country exceeded the cost of transporting workers from southern Europe to Brazil. In fact, the planters experimented with efforts to stimulate internal migration in the two decades after 1850, when slaves where shipped from the less remunerative sugar zones of the northeastern regions to Santos and Rio de Janeiro. However, these slaves, many of whom were not field hands, could not fill the enormous demand for agricultural workers in the coffee region. Thus, internal migration proved too costly to supply cheap labor on a large scale.[14] It may be that northern native workers had low levels of mobility because of political restrictions or had a special attachment to the land because of sociocultural reasons. But between 1872 and 1910, hundreds of thousands of workers from the northeast emigrated to the Amazon region. Beginning during World War I, because of the shortage of overseas immigrants because of the war, the flow of working people from other parts of Brazil to the coffee area grew relative to overseas sources. From 1914 through 1929, a quarter of a million internal migrants passed through the São Paulo government's labor system, and many others entered the state without official assistance. Therefore, paying subsidies to European workers represents a deliberate decision to give them preference. For the planters, bringing subsistence-oriented peasants from northeast Brazil to the coffee plantations was not as desirable as persuading masses of Europeans to come quickly through the immigration program. Part of the reason for this, according to Leff, lies in the racial attitudes of the coffee planters, which led them to prefer European laborers to mulatto workers. However, because the interest of the planters was primarily in securing a large supply of workers, it is not so clear why they should have preferred European immigrants. It does not seem that they were trying to stimulate future economic growth and social change with white immigration of European origin as the Argentines did, and the fact that they willingly accepted Japanese workers in the early decades of the twentieth century casts some doubt on the idea that the planters absolutely preferred European immigrants because of their cultural superiority over the Brazilian native population.

Cuba had also to face the problem of transition to free labor. The British planters in the Caribbean had adapted to the end of slavery by importing indentured Asian workers. Spain could provide no such help from elsewhere in its small empire. There was insuperable opposition in Cuba to free African labor, and the Chinese had ended contract labor in Cuba by the 1880s. The Spanish government also rejected the idea of heavily subsidized immigration as expensive and unfair to small holders who would have to be taxed to support immigration for the benefit of large planters. So the Spanish government tried, quite unsuccessfully, to encourage immigration from Spain and to "whiten" the island through Spanish immigrants,

[14] According to Klein, high transport costs, increasingly severe export taxes, and provincial government restrictions seem to have seriously curtailed this internal slave trade by the late 1870s and early 1880s. It might be the case that this experience led planters to reject the idea of bringing native workers from the northeast.

particularly after the abolition of slavery, to aid the planters who had lost their slave labor force. But whereas in Britain both the government and a wide array of organizations encouraged emigration to Canada and Australia, nothing similar existed in the Spanish case. British imperial discourse led to specific assisted migration plans and recruiting schemes supported from both sides of the migratory flow. Neither before Cuban independence nor after 1900 did the Spanish authorities effectively support emigration to Latin America. During the first years of independence, under U.S. control, highly restrictive immigration laws forbade the importation of agricultural laborers (especially Chinese) to Cuba. In 1906, when sugar production had already regained prewar levels, Cuban immigration policy encouraged the arrival of workers from Europe, in general, and from Spain, in particular. Because Spanish laborers moved quite rapidly to the industrial and urban sectors, hence raising white agricultural workers' wages, the immigration of hired black Haitians and Jamaicans was eventually authorized in 1912. From this time on, as the sugar industry continued to expand, West Indians dominated the labor force on many sugar plantations. West Indians' immigration was further facilitated by the Immigration Act of 1917, which even countenanced the immigration of Chinese, hitherto prohibited. Immigration policy in Cuba was determined chiefly by the needs of the economy and hence by the international demand for Cuban sugar. On the whole, Latin American immigration policies were driven by labor market conditions rather than by ethnic concerns.

In order to understand the different migratory policies adopted during the period by Latin American governments, future research should ask who gained and who lost from massive immigration (Were the immigrants complementary or substitute workers compared with native labor?) and who was in a position to do something about it. The research agenda should go beyond the analysis of well-known facts – for example, that losers are always unskilled labor and winners are the owners of other factors of production, land, capital, and perhaps even skills. Where land ownership and political control were highly concentrated, an increase in the scarcity of labor relative to land created both a demand for and a supply from the landowner-controlled governments of policies encouraging immigration, either through indenture contract systems or by subsidizing immigrants to travel to the plantations or large estates.

The issue of unemployment and how it affected the perception of immigration in Latin America has not been fully examined in the context of immigration policies. High rates of return migration in periods of crisis and relatively high unemployment, such as Argentina in the 1890s, might be understood as similar in outcome to what a policy of immigrant restriction would have achieved. Research has not yet established whether the skill premium on wages was further increased by more unskilled immigrants. Studies of electoral participation and the franchise struggles could yield some clues about who was in a position to do something in the political arena.

3. DID LATIN AMERICA RECEIVE "LOW QUALITY" IMMIGRATION?

In spite of the intentions of the Latin American governments to attract immigrants from northern Europe, the arrival flow was mainly from southern Europe: Italy, Spain, and Portugal. These immigrants are often alleged to have been more illiterate, poorer, and more backward than those who went to the United States. As far back as the Dillingham Commission in the United States, the general belief in the low quality of immigrants from southern Europe has been repeated in almost all accounts of transatlantic migration. The idea that Latin America received immigrants poorer than those who went to the United States comes from the comparisons made, in macroeconomic terms, of the countries of origin. It is true that Italy, Spain, and Portugal were poor and backward nations compared with Great Britain or Germany in terms of per capita income, but were Italian immigrants themselves poorer than Swedish or Irish immigrants? Were northern Italians emigrating to Argentina in the 1880s more backward than the Irish traveling to the United States in the 1860s? This section explores the issue of the "low quality" of southern European immigrants by analyzing their occupation and literacy rates and their potential contribution to economic development in the Latin American countries via the creation of social capital.

As elsewhere, immigrants to Latin America were typically young adults who carried very high labor participation rates to the receiving countries. The benefits of emigrating were greater for single, unskilled, young adults than for the population at large. Being unskilled might also have been an advantage because the immigrants had little technology or country-specific human capital and, therefore, would have had less to lose in future rents in the host country. Sometimes unskilled occupations, particularly in the case of women, such as seamstresses, washerwomen, or cooks, were readily transferable to a new urban labor market.

Two different aggregate sources can be used to analyze occupational distribution among immigrants: migration statistics and population censuses in the countries of destination. Immigration statistics in the receiving countries always recorded the immigrant's profession. Apart from broad classifications such as agricultural worker or commerce employee, the problem with these data is that immigrants usually declared the profession they believed was going to be better received in the host country. In Cuba, the strong pull from the sugar sector explains why around 80 to 90 percent of immigrants arriving to the country in the first decade of the twentieth century declared themselves to be hired hands or agricultural workers. Sometimes immigration officials carelessly compiled the lists writing quotation marks after the most frequently cited professions: farmers or agricultural workers. The same problems can be found in the emigration statistics in Europe.

Passenger ship lists are also useful for analyzing the personal characteristics of immigrants. Up until now, this possibility has hardly been explored for the Latin American countries, in contrast to research done for the United States and Australia. Because passenger lists are normally nominative, data linkage with censuses, municipal registers, or other nominative sources allows tracing mobility in occupation across time.

The broad picture that emerges from aggregate statistics is one of a migratory flow overwhelmingly composed of unskilled labor from rural origins. Even in Argentina, the most diversified economy, the majority of arrivals were agricultural workers and day laborers (*jornaleros*), although there are interesting differences between the two largest immigrant groups. Italians had a higher proportion of farmers, whereas Spaniards were much more often classified as day laborers. The "Various Professions" group is more numerous in the Italian case than for the Spaniards. A careful examination of arrival statistics shows that in 1913, Italian masons and carpenters were more than double the Spanish percentage. It might be that the better knowledge Italians had of the Argentine labor market explains this greater professional diversification, particularly in the early decades of the twentieth century when the diffusion of information about opportunities in the destination countries was widespread across Italian regions.

The low quality of immigrants has also been a common feature of almost all accounts of Brazilian immigration. Because they arrived with subsidized passages, it is generally assumed that people who went to São Paulo were from the lowest economic levels of the groups that emigrated to the New World. It has been argued that the whole subsidizing program had the explicit goal of importing workers so destitute that they would have no choice but to work on the plantations, so Brazil got "the poorest of the poor" bringing in the painful spectacle of their illiteracy and poverty. Argentine immigration officials frequently complained of the low quality and extreme backwardness of European immigrants reemigrating to Buenos Aires from Brazilian ports. Brazilian records of arrivals show that 79 percent of Spanish immigrants through the port of Santos were classified as agricultural workers, in contrast to only 48 percent of the Portuguese and half of the Italian immigrants. The second most numerous group were individuals with no profession, presumably women and children. The majority of immigrants to Brazil arrived in family units and were agricultural workers, a pattern influenced by the eligibility requirements for transportation subsidies. However, the fact that emigrants to Brazil from Portugal, Spain, and Italy came from the relatively less backward areas of the north and not from the poorer south, where masses of agricultural day laborers were allegedly living in miserable conditions, casts some doubt on the expression "the poorest of the poor."

The distinction between occupational sectors such as agriculture, commerce, or industry drawn from the aggregate statistics may have been meaningless for two main reasons. First, in the European countries of origin, the majority of the active population was employed in agriculture. In 1911, 60 percent of the male labor force in Italy was still engaged in the primary sector and the majority of the unskilled laborers, no matter what their designation in the statistics, in fact, came from the rural population. Higher percentages of employment in agriculture and lower rates of urbanization are found in Spain, Portugal, and other countries of origin of immigrants to Latin America. It would have been surprising had European emigrants to Latin America from southern and eastern Europe had lower percentages of agricultural workers than their countries of origin. The second reason is that because immigrants often changed country and occupation at the same time, especially when they were young, it is not clear whether the information about immigrants on their arrival is a useful indicator of their subsequent labor market performance.

What all these immigrant groups brought was not wealth but the ability to create wealth, whether on a modest scale or a grand scale, through specific skills or just hard work. What is clear is that they did not share the disdain for work of the original Spanish and Portuguese settlers' in Latin America (or the British in India). Census information provides a better picture of the adjustment of immigrants to the host labor market.

Not all Latin American censuses differentiate foreigners by nationality or country of origin, and most of the time it is impossible to get information about second-generation immigrants from official censuses. By definition, a census records population at one time. Therefore, it is impossible to distinguish between permanent and temporary immigrants and to know about their length of stay in the country. The length of stay is a crucial variable for tracing immigrant cohorts and analyzing patterns of social mobility. Spanish families living in the city of Buenos Aires in 1895, when a national census was done, presented a low occupational profile in general terms, but their average length of stay in the country was five years or less, presumably because the majority of them arrived in the late 1880s when the Argentine government paid for their travel expenses. Over time, immigrants were better able to match their skills with opportunities in the local labor market. That is why research with nominative data, such as that by Moya for the city of Buenos Aires, has proved so useful.

The broad picture that emerges from population censuses is that immigration to Latin America contributed decisively to the urban labor force in commerce, industry, construction, domestic service, and the general unskilled labor force. In some countries, immigrants were particularly successful in becoming owners of industries or commercial enterprises. Even if the goal of many immigrants was to work on the land, the fact is that for a majority of them migration was rural–urban migration, although this transition was accomplished by crossing the Atlantic. The highest concentration of immigrants in urban populations was found in the River Plate countries. Foreigners made up 35 percent of the total urban population in Argentina in 1895 and 37 percent in 1914. The proportion is much higher in Buenos Aires, where almost half the population of the city in 1914 was composed of immigrants. Montevideo was also a city made up with foreigners – 30 percent of the population in 1908.

Immigration, then, contributed decisively to the rate of urbanization in Latin America. In 1910, those countries with the most immigrants had the highest percentage of their populations living in towns with 20,000 or more inhabitants: Argentina 28.4 percent, Uruguay 30.3, and Cuba 28 percent, compared with the 10.3 percent of urban population in Mexico. The exceptions to this general trend were Brazil, with a low rate of urbanization (12%), and Chile, with a higher percentage of urban population (23%). Actually, the Southern Cone countries' rates of urbanization were higher than those in the countries of origin of immigrants (27%, 12.3%, and 17% in Italy, Portugal, and Spain, respectively) and similar to the United States (30.9%).

This concentration of immigrants in urban activities has often been explained as a result of the existence of a wealthy native oligarchy who prevented immigrants from settling on the land and becoming landowners, in sharp contrast with what happened in the United States. This traditional stereotype has been partially rejected for some countries. In Argentina, Cortés Conde and Miguez, among others, have shown that the agricultural land market was open and that many more immigrants than is generally believed became landowners. A different matter is the fact that many immigrants in the pampa region opted for tenancy or sharecropping, particularly the Italians. The advantages of being a tenant farmer, given lack of capital and knowledge of the new environment and cultivation system, have been forcibly argued by Gallo. In 1914, foreigners owned 37 percent of rural properties in Argentina (medium and small) and made up 60 percent of tenant farmers. Data for Brazil also show that immigrants acquired rural properties in a higher proportion than the literature suggests. Destitute and backward immigrants in Brazil, as the literature has described them, were able to accumulate savings and to buy plots of land. Although immigrants were, in general, underrepresented among rural proprietors, 14.3 percent of owners in São Paulo in 1905 were Italians. Only fewer than 4 percent were Portuguese, the largest urban group among immigrants in Brazil. Portuguese properties had, however, a higher average value and size than those of Italians. In 1934, according to Holloway, the picture was more or less the same for the Portuguese regarding the average value of their properties, but the Italian properties had a much higher value than in 1905.

The timing of arrival and the existence or nonexistence of colonial links can explain differences in access to land for different immigrant groups. Italians were the most successful in acquiring land in Argentina because they were the pioneer group in the era of mass migration. In the 1880s, the ratio of Italian arrivals to Argentina compared with Spaniards was fourteen to one. When massive Spanish immigration to the country reached its peak in the years prior to World War I, Argentina was much more urban than in the 1880s. Some early immigrants to Argentina, such as the Welsh or the Basques, were also extremely successful in becoming landowners. The colonial links of the Portuguese with Brazil and the Spaniards with all the rest, particularly with Cuba until 1898, explain why the population from the ex-metropolis concentrated in the urban and commercial cities like Rio de Janeiro and Havana and not in the rural sector. The high proportion of Spanish-born bank employees in Cuba in 1907 (56.9%) reflects the weight of Spanish banks in Cuba in the years before independence. The advantage of the language and established connections with local commercial networks contributed to reinforce this trend. The experience of the Spaniards in Mexico illustrates this point clearly. Spanish immigration flow to Mexico hardly reached 0.2 percent of the Mexican population in 1910 (29,500 individuals). However, their influence in the creation of Mexican industries, businesses, and commercial enterprises has led Mexican historians to define these immigrants as a "privileged immigration." Urban orientation was clear among Spanish immigrants; during the *Porfiriato*, Spaniards belonged to the high middle class in the main cities of the country. In 1930, only 3 percent of the Spaniards living in Mexico were engaged in agriculture; many were influential in the Mexican business sector.

In Cuba, after independence, even though one in three Spanish-born males was employed in agriculture, Spaniards were responsible for 56 percent of all commercial activities. In the 1920s, with the arrival of massive immigration from the West Indies to the sugar industry, Spaniards were progressively displaced out of the agricultural sector. The predominance of Spaniards in the commercial sector is also noticeable in Argentina, not so much as owners, where they competed with other immigrant groups like the Italians, the British, or the French, but as employees because of the language advantage. In 1909, Italians, who made up 22 percent of the population of the city, owned 38 percent of the commercial establishments in Buenos Aires. According to Moya, Spaniards were more successful than native workers in Buenos Aires in securing skilled occupations and entering into commerce, but less successful in securing white-collar jobs. Compared with their Italian competitors, Spaniards showed an advantage in language skills and literacy rates but were unable to translate this into a clear dominance in the labor market.

Southern European immigrants to the Latin American countries were generally overrepresented in commercial activities in the urban centers. Given the high rates of return migration and considering that many might never have had the intention of settling permanently in the receiving country, it is not clear why low access to landownership should be considered an indicator of immigrant failure or low quality. Research done in the southern European emigration countries shows that the main goal of emigrants was to buy land not in the immigration country but in their country of origin with savings accumulated during the migration years.

The general picture found in the literature about the "low quality" of the immigrants to Latin America comes from the comparison within the United States labor market between "old" immigrants coming from northern Europe and "new" immigrants from the southern and eastern European countries. This picture, however, is entirely reversed, for a particular case: the Italians in Argentina compared with Italians in the United States. Italian integration, success (whatever the definition of success), and mobility differed markedly between the two societies. The United States received a larger group of unskilled and illiterate day laborers from the south of Italy whereas Argentina received the more qualified and literate immigrants from the north. Baily makes clear that those Italians who chose Buenos Aires as their destination were better received by the host society and generally achieved greater economic and social success than those who went to New York. Regarding the rate of property ownership, Italians did far better in Argentina than in the United States, and a comparative analysis carried out by Klein concludes that Italians were the most successful immigrant group in Argentina, even more than the Spaniards, who were almost as numerous and had the advantage of the language. Moya's research has also revised the idea of the relative success of Spanish immigrants in Buenos Aires, although his work is confined to the city of Buenos Aires.

It has been argued that it was primarily the differences between the U.S. and Argentine labor markets that explain why the two countries attracted distinct types of Italian immigrants. The timing of arrival, competition with other immigrant groups, and a different attitude in the host society also had an influence in selecting different types of emigrants. In the United States, Italians were not among the first arrivals – they had to compete with older and well-established immigrant groups and with masses of other immigrants arriving at the same time. They lacked the language advantage and cultural affinity. Therefore, in the United States, Italians were at the bottom of the scale among European immigrants. In Argentina, there was an important Italian community even before Italian Unification. In 1869, Italians were already 23 percent of the population of Buenos Aires. At that time, however, there was no Italian community to speak of in the United States. Positive selection of immigrants occurred in the case of Argentina whereas the contrary occurred for the United States.

Low levels of literacy have been a frequently used indicator of the low quality of the immigrants in Latin America. Because, in their countries of origin, literacy rates were lower than in source countries of immigrants to the United States, particularly Scandinavia, the general view that emerges from the comparison with Australia, Canada, and the United States is that of a highly illiterate migratory flow to Latin America. Although this picture is true from a broad perspective, some qualifications can be made on the human capital brought by immigrants to Latin America. We can gather information on literacy either from the aggregate immigration statistics or from population censuses. The latter can be biased, particularly for children, if immigrants acquired literacy in the host country. This was often true for immigrants, such as the Portuguese in Brazil or the Spaniards in the whole of Latin America, because of the advantage of the language for children attending school in the receiving countries. But the formation of human capital requires society's resources and the cost of educating a large number of immigrants can be substantial.

According to Argentine statistics, 40 percent of immigrants arriving in the peak years of the 1880s were illiterate. In 1914, a year of massive arrivals, the percentage had slightly increased to 41.7, whereas after World War I, it was much lower: 18 percent. It can be assumed that Argentina, which had the most diversified and urban economy of all the massive immigration countries, would have attracted more literate immigrants. On the contrary, it might also be that because Argentina had open mass immigration, the literacy level would have been lower than in more selective flows. Surprisingly, only 34 percent of immigrants older than seven who arrived in the port of Santos in Brazil between 1908 and 1936 were illiterate, but there are sharp differences among national groups. Lower levels of literacy corresponded to Spaniards (65% illiterate), whereas the Japanese showed the highest levels of human capital, with only 10 percent illiterate. Among the European groups, 32 percent of the Italians and 52 percent of the Portuguese were illiterate. The 1920 census showed an illiteracy rate of 56 percent for immigrants compared with 73 percent for the native-born population of the state of São Paulo.

The argument that subsidized immigration attracted more ignorant immigrants to Brazil is only confirmed for the Spanish flow. However, Spaniards seemed to have chosen their destination according to their literacy levels. It is understandable that the more literate Spanish immigrants were to be found in Cuba before 1898 because of the colonial status of the island. But surprisingly, Spanish immigrants were still highly literate after independence. The proportion of literate Spanish immigrants arriving on the island ranged from 62.6 percent in 1912 to 94.1 in 1924. This trend suggests that even when the demand rose for unskilled labor on the sugar plantations, the percentage of literates among Spanish immigrants increased. This trend might also reflect the general upward trend in Spanish literacy in the 1920s. Of the few Spanish emigrants who went to the United States in the 1890s, 90 percent were literate, a proportion that contradicts the stress sometimes placed on the huge literacy gaps between Scandinavians and "new" immigrants in the United States. Although some historians have expressed doubts about the Cuban data on immigrants' literacy, population censuses show the same picture. Almost 74 percent of the male Spanish-born population aged twenty-one and older living in Cuba in 1899 were literate, and the proportion increased to 77 percent in 1919. Including women and younger population groups would undoubtedly raise the illiteracy levels, but the general picture that emerges from these data conflicts with the traditional image of Spanish emigrants as generally illiterate. With the exception of Brazil and some special cases, such as the Spaniards employed in the construction of the Panama Canal and on plantations in remote places such as Hawaii, Spaniards were always among the most literate group in the countries of destination of massive immigration.

The important issue to consider in analyzing immigrants' human capital is whether they were positively selected according to the literacy levels of their countries of origin and whether they contributed to raise levels of human capital in the countries of destination.

According to the Argentine population census, only 26 percent of Spaniards over the age of seven living in Argentina were illiterate in 1914, compared with 50 percent of the total Spanish population in 1910. Illiteracy rates in Italy were 38 percent in 1911, a percentage similar to that of the Italians living in Argentina. In Portugal, nearly 70 percent of the population was illiterate in 1910 compared with only 52 percent of Portuguese immigrants to São Paulo. It seems, then, that the Latin American countries received a more literate migratory flow, at least from the Iberian Peninsula, than the populations of origin.

However, given the selectivity of the emigration process by age and the concentration of southern European emigrants from a few regions, the comparison of immigrants' literacy rates with the overall literacy rates of residents is inadequate. In the three main European countries of origin, the northern areas from which the majority of immigrants were drawn tended to be more literate than other parts of the countries, particularly in the Italian case. But in Italy, the selectivity of the transatlantic migratory flow seems to have been lower than in other countries: the larger the migratory flow, the closer the typical emigrant was to the average population of origin. When immigrants' literacy is compared with the literacy rates of potential emigrants, from regions of high emigration, the selectivity of the process appears quite clear for Spain and Portugal. In Spain in 1910, 66 percent of

Galician males aged sixteen to twenty were literate and the corresponding figure for the population of Asturias, where the majority of emigrants went to Cuba, was more than 80 percent. The Canary Islands, with low literacy rates and high emigration rates to Cuba and Venezuela, are the exception to the general conclusion that Spanish emigrants were highly selected by literacy levels. In Portugal, in the years 1890–3, comparing male illiteracy rates among immigrants with those of the population from which the emigrants were selected shows that 68 percent of males in the emigrant's age group were illiterate compared with 52 percent of actual Portuguese emigrants. Because 1890–3 was a period of extraordinarily high emigration to Brazil that tended to increase the share of illiterate emigrants, the general conclusion is that Portuguese emigrants were, as a rule, more literate than the Portuguese population.

The literacy rates of immigrants can also be compared to those of the populations in the receiving countries. That the European immigrants had higher levels of literacy than the host population in the countries of destination appears quite clear for those countries with large native populations, like Mexico and Brazil. Brazil and Cuba also had large populations of slave origin with low levels of literacy. It is difficult to make the same assertion about literacy rates of the receiving population in countries like Argentina and Uruguay. Native populations in the River Plate at the turn of the century were already composed largely of immigrants' descendants, impossible to distinguish in population censuses. Leaving aside the fact that not all governments made the same effort to raise the levels of education of their populations, aggregate data show that those countries that had the smallest native population around 1850 and the largest inflow of European population showed the lowest illiteracy rates around 1910. The Latin American ranking is led by Uruguay (25% illiterates in 1908). Uruguay was the country where the ratio of immigrants to native population was highest. Argentina had 38 percent illiterates, whereas Chile, with much lower immigration rates than the River Plate, still had 50 percent of its population illiterate in the 1910s. Mexico's illiteracy rate was 72 percent of the population, higher than Brazil (65%) and Cuba (45%), where the proportion of population of African origin was the largest in this group of Latin American countries. These data are certainly discouraging when compared to literacy rates in the same period in other countries of immigration like the United States (7.7% illiterates), Canada (10%), and Australia (4.5%). Therefore, although immigrants might have contributed to raise literacy levels in some Latin American countries, other forces mattered more, particularly public support and political commitment to increase the educational levels of the population.

This does not deny the fact that those countries that received the largest number of immigrants could have had an overall better-educated labor force had immigrants been positively selected. Did immigration add special skills or entrepreneurial abilities to the labor force? It has already been mentioned that immigrants were generally overrepresented among industrial and commercial proprietors. Immigrants also contributed importantly to the industrial labor force and urban low and middle classes. In Argentina, Germani was among the first to stress the modernizing role of immigrants and their exceptional contribution to the development of an entrepreneurial class. For Brazil, Dean has argued that in the southeast, immigrants and their children were to play an important role in the supply of entrepreneurship for industrialization in São Paulo and for modernization of the rural sector. Immigrants in Argentina and Brazil came to account for a disproportionately large share of the workers in the São Paulo and Buenos Aires manufacturing systems, but although in the first country there is a wide consensus in the historiography about the positive role immigrants played, there is not a unanimous view for the Brazilian case. After the end of their contracts to work in the coffee plantations, many immigrants moved to the city of São Paulo. Some historians have argued that this inflow was important in increasing the labor supply for local industries. The immigrants' heavy participation in the local industrial labor force did not occur because they constituted a well-trained and disciplined labor force. Moreover, according to Leff, immigration was neither a necessary nor a sufficient condition for provoking the developmental effects that have been credited to it. Industrial growth would probably have occurred in a similar fashion in the absence of immigration. If overseas immigrants had not been available, the supply of labor to fill the growing demand for industrial workers in São Paulo would have had to come from domestic sources. This suggestive counterfactual has never been tested. European workers had, nevertheless, a good reputation as workers both on the land and in the industrial and urban labor force. All reports from Brazil, Argentina, and Cuba concerning the quality at the work place of Italian, Spaniard, and Portuguese immigrants stressed that they were hard-working, sober, enduring, and well-behaved. It was not uncommon for them to work even harder abroad than at home, a fact also noted for immigrant textile factory workers in the United States.

It has also been argued that immigration contributed to the creation and expansion of an internal market for manufactured goods. The role of immigrants as consumers allowed some industries to benefit from economies of scale, particularly consumption industries such as textiles. Argentine historiography has frequently stressed immigration's contribution to population growth that increased demand for Argentine industries producing for the internal market. A skeptical view is found in the Brazilian case. High income levels because of revenues from coffee exports would probably have been enough to raise the demand for manufactured goods anyway. Given the size of the Brazilian population, increasing demand might well have occurred without European immigration just from raising the wages of the large native population. Immigrants' contribution to the growth of an internal market for manufactured goods in Brazil and elsewhere might have been influenced by the austere consumption standards that many immigrants adopted in their effort to accumulate savings for remission abroad. Born in relatively poor rural areas in Europe, they were used to an extreme frugality. In the long run, however, second-generation immigrants might have had different consumption patterns.

There is no a general conclusion to be drawn about the role of immigrants in supplying entrepreneurial skills or about their contribution to the growth of internal demand. For Argentina and Uruguay, a positive answer seems to be part of the general consensus. Immigrants did contribute to the business class in countries with low immigration rates such as Mexico or Chile, but neither in Cuba nor in Brazil can immigration be credited for such an impact.

Finally, immigrants might have also contributed in the host societies to the creation of social capital. Although it is difficult to give a precise definition, social capital is associated with good economic performance, and a growing body of research documents significant correlations between social capital variables, such as membership in civic organizations, and positive economic outcomes. Trust and cooperation are the key words in social capital. Societies work best, and have always worked best, where citizens trust their fellow citizens, work cooperatively with them for common goals, and thus share a civic culture. Because immigrants contributed to the creation of associations, it is worthwhile to see this associational growth in some Latin American countries in the light of the concept of social capital. It is fair to say, however, that although theory and research have tended to confirm the effects of social capital, the underlying mechanisms that create social capital have yet to be fully understood.

In immigration studies, the relatively new concept of social capital might lead to new perspectives on immigrants' associational activities and could be particularly useful in the study of immigrants' contribution to economic development in the long run. Cultural affinity also makes a contribution to the creation of social capital. Southern Europeans in Latin America brought cultural capital that included language, manners, religion, and shared values that were readily accepted in the receiving countries. A lot of research effort has been devoted by historians to analyzing immigrants' associations, mutual-aid societies, newspapers, clubs, and the like in the receiving countries. The Italians, in particular, have received preferential attention, with research done by Baily, Devoto, and others for the Argentine case. High levels of social capital have been found in northern Italy as compared to the south. Because social capital is assumed to be transferable, it may be that the Latin American countries received not only more literate and skilled Italian immigrants but also more immigrants with the ability to contribute to the growth of social capital. In other words, countries like Argentina that received the largest inflow of northern Italians imported social capital from Europe. A successful group, like the Italians all over Latin America, might have succeeded because it had higher levels of social capital than the native population or other immigrant groups.

As in Argentina and the other Latin American countries in the late nineteenth and early twentieth centuries, immigrants from eastern and southern Europe organized mutual-aid societies, social and recreational clubs, newspapers, and the like in the United States. Research similar to what Gamm and Putman have carried out for the growth of voluntary associations in the United States between 1840 and 1940 using city directories might be illuminating for analyzing the contribution of immigrants to associational life in the Latin America immigration countries.

4. IMMIGRATION AND POPULATION GROWTH: DEMOGRAPHIC GIFT OR DEMOGRAPHIC BURDEN?

Contrary to what happened in the second half of the twentieth century, when high population growth was one of the main worries of the Latin American countries, in the nineteenth and early twentieth centuries, population growth was not the main concern of Latin American governments. For some countries like Argentina, Uruguay, or Chile, the problem was rather the opposite and the solution was to increase population by immigration.

The large numbers of immigrants who settled permanently in Latin America contributed to the growth of the population in the long run. This was especially true for countries like Argentina, Uruguay, and Brazil. In the 1880s, almost 26 percent of total population growth in Argentina was attributable to immigration. Over the next period, 1891–1910, the share attributable to immigration decreased to 14 percent and, in the 1920s, it was only 9 percent. Lower percentages are found in Brazil. In 1901–20, immigration was responsible for only 7 percent of Brazilian population growth, whereas in the high immigration years of 1891–1900, the share was a spectacular 30.2 percent.

Throughout the age of mass migration, those countries that received the largest number of immigrants had the highest rates of population growth. According to Maddison's data, in the years 1870 through 1913, the highest rates corresponded to Argentina (3.4%) and then Uruguay (2.7%). Brazil and Cuba had lower rates of population growth (2.1% and 1.5%, respectively). These rates were much higher than those found in countries with low immigration, like Chile (1.4%) and Mexico (1.1%). High rates of population growth were also found, however, in Latin American countries with extremely low figures of overseas immigration: Costa Rica (2.1%), Dominican Republic (2.7%), and Colombia (1.8%).

Immigration not only affects the overall rate of population growth by increasing both absolute numbers and numbers of young people having children but also by having a direct impact on the age structure of the population. Migration is a very selective process according to age. In the short run, immigration contributes to increase the active population group and hence contributes to the growth of the labor force. Population dynamics tell us that in the long run, the age structure of the population can change dramatically as the population grows. In recent years, the debate on the influence of demography on economic growth has shifted emphasis from population size and growth to the age structure of population. Because people's economic behavior varies at different stages of life, changes in a country's age structure have significant effects on its economic performance. Economic growth and population growth are related because the latter modifies the age structure of the population through the demographic transition. Dividing the population into three age groups, two of dependents (the young and the old), and one economically active, each age group in a population behaves differently with distinct economic consequences.

Children require intensive investment in health and education, prime-age adults to supply labor and savings, and the elderly again require investment in health and retirement plans.

Because immigration directly affects the age structure of the receiving population, both in the short and in the long run, it seems relevant to ask how these changes affected the Latin American countries. Did immigration increase the working-age population and thus produce a "demographic gift" for economic growth? Leaving aside the fact that policies to take advantage of this "gift" have to be in place, immigrants can be considered as a "ready-to-use" working population, thus lowering the cost of resources devoted to the care of children until they reached the working age. However, immigrants themselves, being young, can definitely contribute to increase the number of dependents because they have and raise children in the host country, hence creating a "demographic burden." It is important to establish whether the effect of immigration in Latin America represented a net demographic gift or demographic burden, and whether it was a gift in the short run and a burden in the long run.

Immigrants contributed overwhelmingly to the growth of the labor force because they concentrated primarily in the working age group and, therefore, had an impact on economic development in the long run. This implies that, in the absence of immigration, labor costs would have been higher. Real wages would have been 46 percent higher in 1910 in Argentina. The Brazilian case is not so straightforward because real wages would have been only 2 percent higher in 1910 in the absence of mass migration. Having a larger and probably better-educated labor force will only bear economic fruit if the extra workers can find jobs. Given that immigrants arrived in Latin America because of the availability of jobs, we can assume that, in the short run, the majority of the working-age immigrant population found in the population censuses in the receiving countries were contributing to economic growth. Immigrants increased the economically active population and, thus, the labor force. *Ceteris paribus* this means more output. As the population as a whole grows less than the active population, output per capita increases faster than output per worker.

All immigration statistics show that an overwhelming majority of migrants concentrated in the young population groups: 84 percent of the immigrants to Argentina between 1857 and 1924 were in the thirteen to sixty age group (54% of them were less than thirty years of age). Data from the 1914 Argentine census showed that 86 percent of foreigners were in the active population group (from fifteen to sixty-four). For natives, the same percentage was 45 percent. In Brazil, 77 percent of immigrants through the port of Santos between 1908 and 1936 were aged older than twelve, a lower percentage than in Argentina because of the larger number of children. In general, immigrants belonged everywhere to the young population cohorts.

An aspect that has been frequently neglected is the fact that many immigrants traveled in family groups, carrying dependents, mostly children, with them. Research has shown that not only was the migratory decision usually a family decision, but that very often all the family emigrated together from Europe. It is well known that the peculiarities of the Cuban labor demand pulled more male immigrants traveling alone than did Brazil. The latter attracted relatively more families with children than other countries, but it may be surprising for some to see the high numbers of family groups migrating also to Argentina. Originally, the immigration policy was designed to bring families to work on the land, but there is a tendency among historians to look at the migration flows according to gender and age and not to family groups in countries like Argentina. In 1895, 48 percent of migrants to Argentina arrived as a family group. As the inflow grew, the family share decreased, but only slightly: in 1913, immigrants' family groups were 41 percent of total immigration. It is difficult to know from these data the proportion of children within these families. It has been documented that some of these family groups, especially among the Italians, were composed entirely of working-age members (e.g., a father and three or four sons). Nevertheless, some nationalities had stronger tendencies than others to travel in family groups. The Spaniards are a case in point. Beginning in 1900, almost 40 percent of Spanish immigrants to Argentina came in family groups, with the percentage growing from the late nineteenth century. Italians presented the opposite trend: more family groups in the nineteenth century and fewer in the years before World War I. Spanish families were also larger than both those of the Italians and the average for all immigrants (3.2 members per Spanish family in 1913 compared with 2.8 for the Italians and 3.0 overall). Spanish families were also overrepresented in Brazil. A mere 18 percent of the Spanish flow arrived without family at Santos in the 1908–36 period, in contrast with 53 percent of the Portuguese. The number of children (32%) was also higher among Spanish family groups in Brazil than other nationalities (19% Portuguese children). Part of the explanation might be different migratory strategies because of the extraordinary diffusion of information about different labor markets. Spanish families opted for Brazil and Argentina, whereas individual Spanish migrants specialized in Cuba.

The data cast some doubt on the overall contribution of immigration to raising the working-age population in the countries of destination. It might be the case that, even if the majority of the population were contributing to the labor force, they were simultaneously raising the number of children. If a large number of families arrived with children, they already had higher dependency rates than individuals arriving on their own. For receiving societies, the costs associated with family immigration were higher in terms of health, education, and public services.

Permanent immigrants, either with or without family at arrival, also contributed to a rise in the birth rate because of their age structure. Did countries of immigration have higher birth rates because of the arrival of this younger population? Or did immigrants contribute to an early start of the demographic transition by lowering birth rates? Data for the first quarter of the nineteenth century suggest that the latter was the case for some countries. Birth rates were lower in Uruguay and Argentina than elsewhere in Latin America in 1900–24 and the decreasing trend is clear from 1900 onward. Cuba had also relatively low birth rates in the 1920s but not before, whereas Brazil shows the opposite trend – lower birth rates at the beginning of the century and higher rates in the early 1920s. Actually, Brazil had one of the highest birth rates in Latin America in 1930.

However, we simply do not know if it was immigration or other forces at work that explain the relatively low birth rates in the River Plate. The majority of arrivals were from high birth-rate areas in Europe (southern countries). Urbanization, education, and economic growth could also have contributed to the decline in birth rates in the River Plate areas as immigrants were influenced by the new environment. In 1895, the average number of children per woman in Argentina was 8.4 for natives and 6.1 for foreigners, but the main differences were between rural and urban women according to their literacy levels. In 1947, the figures were 3.6 children per native woman compared with 3.2 for foreign females. Populations that experience a rapid rate of increase in per capita income generally have lower mortality and lower fertility than those where per capita income grew more slowly. Sánchez-Albornoz argues that the overall high birth rates in Latin America were related to the large share of the rural population. Only the most developed and open countries had started the first phase of the demographic transition by the first quarter of the twentieth century.

With some qualifications about family immigration, immigrants contributed decisively to the growth of the labor force because of their concentration in the working-age group. It seems clear that Argentina and

Uruguay, like other countries in the New World, had a demographic advantage attributable to immigration because the economically active were growing faster than the dependent population in the years 1870 through 1913. However, it has been argued that this positive contribution was offset in the long run because of rapid population growth. Through time, immigrants, particularly if they have high fertility rates, also contribute to the growth of the dependent young.

This is the argument used by Taylor to explain Argentine economic retardation relative to Australia in the age of mass migration. High rates of immigration and more fecund immigrants in Argentina than in Australia contributed definitively to increase the dependent population group and therefore depressed savings, inhibited capital deepening, and retarded economic growth. Foreign capital imports maintained the level of output per worker in the *belle époque* before World War I. In the interwar period, when foreign capital did not arrive as before, Argentina suffered from her low domestic savings capacity because of high dependency rates driven by a fast-growing population swelled by massive immigration. Argentine dependency rates, calculated as the ratio of dependent population (0–15 age group plus those older than 64) to active population, were higher in 1914 than dependency rates in Canada, Australia, and the United States. In the 1940s, however, Argentine rates were similar to those found in Canada but still higher than Australian and U.S. dependency rates.

We do not have any research similar to Taylor's for other Latin American countries. It might be illuminating to compare dependency rates within Latin America in the long run. Table 10.5 presents dependency rates in Latin America both for massive immigration countries and for low immigration countries like Mexico and Chile. In the late nineteenth century, Cuba had the lowest dependency rates of the countries considered. Argentina and Chile, with very different immigration rates, had similar dependency rates, whereas Mexico and Uruguay had the highest. In the first decade of the twentieth century (although census dates are not the same), Argentina had the lowest dependency rate. This can clearly be attributed to the increase in the young-adult population group attributable to immigration. Brazilian immigration policy, which favored family arrivals, could have contributed to the rise in the dependency rate. But in Cuba, where immigration from Europe was predominantly male immigration with no children, native population growth and perhaps the influx of Caribbean immigrants increased the dependency rate notably. The Argentine trend to decreasing the dependency rate is clear in 1947. Even in the 1940s, when the

Table 10.5. *Dependency rates: Latin America and other New World countries (1872–1947)*

Countries

Argentina	1869	1895		1914			1947
	0.839	0.734		0.688			0.533
Brazil	1872	1890	1900		1920		1940
	0.719	0.755	0.907		0.880		0.815
Cuba		1889	1907		1919		1943
		0.643*	0.698*		0.891*		0.660
Uruguay		1900	1908				
		0.854*	0.777				
Mexico		1895	1900	1910		1930	1940
		0.813*	0.805*	0.801		0.802*	0.796
Chile		1895	1907		1920	1930	
		0.772	0.784*		0.702	0.685	
Canada	1871	1891		1911	1921	1931	1941
	0.883	0.692		0.600	0.645	0.598	0.526
Australia	1861	1891	1901	1911	1921	1933	1947
	0.610	0.666	0.643	0.520	0.567	0.500	0.496
U.S.	1870	1880	1900	1910	1920	1930	1940
	0.754	0.686	0.632	0.547	0.573	0.533	0.488

Notes:
*Age group (15–60).
The dependency rate is the ratio of dependent population (0–15) + (over 64) to active population (15–64).
Source: Calculated from Brian R. Mitchell, *International Historical Statistics. The Americas 1750–1988* (Basingtoke, 1993).

demographic transition was on its way in more Latin American countries that in the preceding period, Argentina clearly had the lowest dependency rates of all. The idea of a demographic burden in Argentina depends entirely on the basis of the comparison.

5. CONCLUSIONS

The global economy evolved slowly through the nineteenth century. Immigration flows reached their highest levels in the early decades of the twentieth century. Latin American countries like Argentina, Uruguay, Cuba, and Brazil participated actively in the international labor market. Other countries in the region, however, remained poorly integrated with the rest of the world in terms of labor flows.

Much has been written on the international mass migration of Europeans and some efforts have been made to balance the overwhelming United States coverage that has traditionally dominated migration studies. Still, the experience of the Latin American countries is not fully incorporated into current debates on historical migration, in spite of the fact that 13 million Europeans migrated to the region between 1870 and 1930. Even the Latin American country most favored by researchers, Argentina, still lags behind the research done on the United States, Australia, and Canada.

Latin America was a latecomer to the age of free mass migration. In the 1880s, when mass European immigration started in Latin America, it was clear that the region could not compete with the United States. Although mass migration started in the last decades of the nineteenth century, it was only truly massive in the early years of the twentieth century prior to World War I. The phenomenon of massive arrivals was short-lived for Latin American countries because the international labor market changed dramatically after World War I.

European immigration to Latin America from the 1880s onward presents a pattern similar to those of other destination countries. The same economic and demographic forces were at work in sending and receiving regions in the Latin American segment of the international labor market. Immigrants to Latin America were also from latecomer countries of emigration in Europe. Migrants were, to some extent, different from those who crossed the Atlantic in the first waves. However, the difference was not so much that Latin America received poorer and more backward immigrants than the United States but that poorer and less literate migrants formed a higher proportion of all immigrants in the 1880–1914 period because of the southern shift in countries of origin. Segmentation of the international labor market existed long before the mass migration era. Culture, language, and diffusion of information through early migrants' networks were powerful forces directing southern Europeans toward Latin America.

Migration policy also played a role in attracting immigrants to the region. Argentina followed an open-door immigration policy. Given the high wages and existing demand for labor, not much more was needed to pull immigrants. Labor market conditions, political stability, and personal freedom were the most powerful forces attracting immigrants. The most outstanding immigration policy in Latin America was that of Brazil. The state of São Paulo followed an active policy of subsidizing immigration from Europe

on a larger scale and for a longer time than any other country. In order
to understand the different migratory policies adopted by Latin American
governments, research should now go beyond the well-established facts to
take a new look at the received wisdom, such as the hypothesis that those
who gained most by immigration were the big landowners. The alleged
losers – traditionally neglected – should also be examined, particularly the
impact of immigration on the native labor force and unskilled labor, the
functioning of internal labor markets, and inequality trends in the long run.
The adjustment of immigrants to the host labor markets seems to have been
quite successful, particularly in the urban sector. However, future analysis
should distinguish between first- and second-generation immigrants.

Some qualifications can be made to the general characterization of immigrants to Latin America as generally unskilled and illiterate. Lack of skills
could have been an advantage in the adaptation process to new labor market, which, for the majority, was the urban labor market. Rates of literacy
were lower among Latin American immigrants immigrating to the United
States, Canada, and Australia, but migrants were positively selected from
their countries of origin, particularly in the Iberian Peninsula, according to
literacy. Immigrants had also higher literacy rates than the native population
in Latin America. Those countries that had the smallest native population
around 1870 and the largest inflow of European immigrants showed the
highest literacy rates around 1910.

Immigrants not only brought human capital with them, they also contributed to the creation of social capital in the receiving countries. The
concept of social capital, based on trust, cooperation, and shared civic values for a given society, can be very usefully applied to the role immigrants
played in associational activities in Latin America. Social capital can be
related to political outcomes, such as public commitment to education
and social cohesion. Immigrants probably contributed in some countries
to economic development in the long run by creating social capital.

Immigration had an impact on labor force and population growth.
Migrants contributed as well to raise the dependent age groups in the
population, particularly children, in the medium and long run. Because
the debate regarding the influence of demography on economic growth
has shifted the emphasis from population size and growth to the economic
consequences of the age structure of the population, the impact of large
numbers of young immigrants to Latin American countries, other than
Argentina, is a particularly promising topic for future research.

11

EDUCATION AND SOCIAL PROGRESS

FERNANDO REIMERS

OVERVIEW

Despite more than a century of intermittent progressive policy rhetoric, schools in Latin America still marginalize the children of indigenous groups, of rural populations, and of the poor. This paradox of a resilient conservative school practice and progressive education policy rhetoric is explained by conflict among policy elites, first on the priority of educating the children of the poor at high levels more generally and second on the purposes of schooling, and by the ensuing discontinuities in policy and weak implementation of progressive aspirations.

Because educational results take time (it takes a while to build new schools, to change curricula and print new books, and for teachers to learn new ways), and because the linkages between policy rhetoric and policy implementation and outcomes also take time, the conditions in Latin American educational institutions reflect the tensions between two competing education ideologies and the cumulative influences of past projects. One ideology, a series of progressive ideas and projects, espoused that schools should build an inclusive and democratic social order, whereas another ideology, a series of conservative ideas and initiatives, saw the purposes of schools as supporting an authoritarian and exclusionary social structure. This chapter examines these time lags, tensions, and coexistence of contradictory ideologies in school practice to explicate why education policy

I appreciate the generous feedback of John Coatsworth, Manuel Contreras, Sara Lawrence-Lightfoot, Julie Reuben, and Rosemary Thorp to a draft of this chapter. Susan Kenyon provided valuable editing suggestions.

implementation often trails policy talk in Latin America, and why short-term victories of progressive views in policy rhetoric had limited consequences for the actual learning opportunities of marginalized children.

Toward the end of the nineteenth century, the nations of Latin America differed from most of the nations of Europe and the United States in the relatively low level of education of their populations and, in particular, in the deep education divides that separated the elites from marginalized groups. In spite of state-led efforts to expand access to public education, the twentieth century ended with equally important educational schisms between the Latin American nations and their northern neighbors, as well as internal divides based on social class, ethnicity, and location of residence.

This failure to close internal and external education gaps resulted from the failure of economic and political elites to reach consensus on the need to provide the children of the poor with real learning chances that would prepare them to master the core subjects in the curricula, to think for themselves, and to develop political voice and agency and from the limited channels through which the poor could hold education policymakers accountable for the learning opportunities available to their children. The centralization of education decision making early in the twentieth century weakened the voice of local communities in the affairs of schools.[1] Education thus became an arena ready to be captured by powerful interests, the subject of national politics rather than of community politics. Because democratic politics were exceptional throughout the century, poor parents and local communities had limited means to hold the state accountable for the dismally low learning chances available to their children. In addition, the low levels of education of poor parents themselves limited their ability to recognize the poor quality of the instruction offered to their children. It was thus that the public purposes of school systems were captured to serve the narrow interests of economic and business groups, teacher unions, politicians, and education bureaucrats.[2]

---

[1] Carlos Newland attributes this to a profound mistrust of national governments on the part of local officials and to the structure of public financing, which depended on taxes levied on foreign trade. Carlos Newland, "Spanish American Elementary Education, 1950–1992: Bureaucracy, Growth and Decentralization," *International Journal of Educational Development* 15:2 (1995): 103–14.

[2] There are two consequences of this lack of participation by poor parents and communities in educational governance. One is that their needs could not influence the availability and type of education for their children. It was then difficult to replace existing educational institutions with local efforts reflective of community needs and aspirations. A second consequence of the centralization of educational governance, as has been pointed out by David Plank and colleagues for Brazil, is that it could then serve the private interests of politicians and bureaucrats, stimulating corruption and clientelism. David Plank, Jose Amaral, and Antonio da Ressureição Xavier, "Why Brazil Lags Behind

Education policy was shaped by three sets of political actors and processes: first, by national politics in which education reform was embedded. Second, by the political mobilization and exchanges of actors with vested interests in education: namely, parents, students, teachers, and administrators. Last, education reforms were influenced by cross-national and global forces as local political groups, social entrepreneurs, and international actors and institutions mobilized ideologies and resources to advance their objectives. Because of the centralization of educational governance, national-level politics and transnational influences played a greater role than local school or district-level politics in shaping the purposes of schools during the twentieth century.[3]

Throughout the twentieth century, the state became the most important actor in an unprecedented expansion of access to formal education in Latin America.[4] The main gains of the progressive projects were in this quantitative expansion. The struggle for equity was also played out, though with far less success, in reforms that aimed to incorporate into school the most marginalized groups. The oldest of these reforms, those directed toward indigenous and rural children, were highly contested, resulting in the persistent educational marginalization of these groups. The most recent of these reforms also competed with objectives to enhance the efficiency of the education system: reforms that were advanced preferentially by governments and politicians building alliances with external actors and institutions. Throughout the century, there was least progress in aligning the content of the curriculum with the aspiration to educate free minds and democratic citizens. This chapter discusses how politics shaped the struggle for educational opportunity in these various reforms.

To study the struggle between these two competing ideologies, I look at policy rhetoric, implementation, and outcomes as they illuminate the arenas where this struggle took place. Contestation generally began with the policy agenda. The paper trail of constitutions, laws, declarations, and

in Educational Development," in Nancy Birdsall and Richard Sabot, eds., *Opportunity Foregone. Education in Brazil* (Baltimore, MD, 1996), 117–46.

[3] It is possible that this "top heavy" emphasis of my analysis results from my focus on public education and on large-scale reform. I have not focused on small-scale, grassroots, and local educational initiatives where perhaps the politics are different. My choice of perspective is based on the fact that, as I demonstrate in this chapter, the state became the major agent in sponsoring education throughout the century.

[4] Not all education takes place in formal educational institutions. Informal and nonformal efforts play a very important role in the creation and re-creation of roles and expectations of culture and socialization and of the social and cultural capital of different social groups.

education plans is the dominant focus of analysis in this chapter. This focus is complemented by examination of implementation, particularly as reflected in specific policies, programs, and projects and in changes in quantitative indicators of opportunity to access educational institutions as well as in changes in the educational attainment and achievement of the population.

THE POLITICS OF PUBLIC EDUCATION
BEFORE THE TWENTIETH CENTURY

States became actors in the development of education because policy elites thought schools could contribute to larger social purposes, a basic tenet of the progressive education ideology. Throughout the twentieth century, states supported the development of schooling for a variety of purposes, including "modernizing" societies, preparing human resources to increase the productivity of the labor force, developing national identity, or transforming the structure of opportunity and fostering social mobility, and only rarely to form democratic citizens. The twentieth-century competition between the progressive and conservative education projects focused on those objectives, on who should be educated and how, on the duration and financing of compulsory education, and on who should attend other levels and types of education and for what purpose. More recently, the differences also revolve around whether special initiatives should be supported to reach marginalized groups.

The conservative educational ideology reflected long-term trends established in colonial times. This ideology saw education as instrumental to reinforcing existing social stratification and organization. Those who thus saw their privileges as dependent on the educational marginalization of large groups of the population supported education policies with distinct exclusionary goals.[5] These ideas were advanced by elected officials, often authoritarian rulers, educational institutions, and a dominant culture that perceived the children of the poor as inferior, thus justifying educational apartheid.

[5] For an extended discussion of the contribution of elite values, reflecting a feudal structure, to the underdevelopment of Latin American societies, see Seymour Lipset, "Values, Education and Entrepreneurship," in Seymour Lipset and Aldo Solari, eds., *Elites in Latin America* (Oxford, 1967), 3–60. For a more recent discussion, see Howard Wiarda, *The Soul of Latin America* (New Haven, CT, 2002).

During the twentieth century, this conservative ideology was challenged by a progressive alternative, which sought to expand the learning opportunities of marginalized groups. The roots of the progressive view extend back to the independence movement and to the creation of the modern republics. The operators of progressive projects were modern political parties and coalitions between an emerging group of industrialists and the newly incorporated political actors: migrants into cities and immigrants in the countries in the south. The main gains of the progressive project were the creation of public education systems; universalization of primary education; unprecedented educational expansion at all levels, with consequent intergenerational educational mobility; and a silent revolution that significantly diminished the gender gap in educational opportunity.

Whereas the conservative ideology saw education as an instrument to preserve the birth rights of elites in unequal societies, the progressive view[6] saw it as instrument to build a new social order, a new American identity, and, only episodically and more recently, a more just and inclusive society. The conservative view accepted that social origin should also be social destiny and that education would mediate this by excluding subdominant groups from certain levels of education or by expecting schools to develop a limited range of skills among the poor. In contrast, the progressive view espoused that schools could develop talent among all children and that in so doing they could alter the distribution of social opportunities. Often, progressives espoused broader expectations for the skills and dispositions that schools should develop, at times focusing on educating democratic citizens, whereas conservatives remained more interested in having schools prepare people for work.

The competition between these perspectives predates the twentieth century. The main progressive legacies of this early period were an ideology and a legal and institutional framework supportive of public education and of compulsory primary education. Conservative legacies included the social acceptance of unequal educational opportunities for different social groups and of education practices, especially at the lower levels, emphasizing

---

[6] The roots of the progressive education ideology in Europe are in the works of Jean Jacques Rousseau in the eighteenth century and of the Utopians, Thomas More and Francis Bacon, in the sixteenth century. They established the intellectual foundations to link education and social reform. In the United States, John Dewey in the late nineteenth and early twentieth centuries articulated most clearly the links between education and social change. Many see him as the main figure of Progressive Education, which is linked to a larger movement of social reform known as the Progressive Movement. The roots of Progressive Education in North America predate Dewey, extending back to the ideas of Horace Mann and Francis Parker in Massachussetts.

obedience to authority (*magister dixit*) and conformity, rather than independent and critical thinking.

The most established educational institutions in pre-Columbian times served to educate the ruling elites of the people of Mesoamerica and of the Incas.[7] This conservative ideology was replaced by another conservative set of ideas of the Spanish colonizers, who also saw the function of the (new) educational institutions as to educate the (new) elites, the Spaniards and *criollos*. A combination of royal mandates and religious initiatives laid the foundation for the first schools in the Spanish colonies in the Americas. The colonial conservative education view also sought to extend the Catholic faith among the people of the Americas and, consequently, the submission to the authority of the Roman Catholic Church. Religious orders were the first to establish and run schools and universities from the fifteenth to the eighteenth centuries.

Although it is possible to find some examples of progressive educational initiatives during this period, their scope was modest. In 1792, for example, Fray José San Alberto, Archbishop of La Plata, established the *Escuela de Niñas Pobres San Alberto* in Chuquisaca.[8] An alternative movement, led by the Jesuits, educated indigenous people in the reductions of Bolivia and Paraguay. This education for self-reliance, along with the reductions per se, was interrupted by the expulsion of the Jesuits in 1767.

The dominant policy throughout much of the colonial period was one of educating the elites, and educating them for obedience to authority. The Royal Cedula of 1785 of King Carlos IV established that it was not desirable to "illustrate the Americans." "His Majesty does not need philosophers, but good and obedient subjects."[9] This Cedula authorized boroughs (*parroquias*) to establish religious schools, which would also teach basic literacy for the children of Spaniards and *criollos*.

The creation of universities for the elites was the most significant educational development of this period. As a result, universities had long been

---

[7] In the Valley of Mexico, the Mexicas had separate schools for the nobles (*calmecac*) and the commoners (*telpochcalli*). They instructed in the arts of war, in religious rites, and possibly in trades related to the productive specialization of the *calpulli*. Outstanding educational achievement allowed some commoners to ascend in the social structure. See Pablo Escalante, *Educación e ideología en el México antiguo* (Mexico City, 1985), 17. Also see Alfredo López Austin, *La educación de los antiguos nahuas* (Mexico City, 1985), 26–8. In the Inca empire, selected women received segregated education in *Ajllawaci*. The houses of knowledge, the *Yachaywasis*, were reserved for the nobles. José Juárez and Sonia Comboni, eds., *Sistema educativo nacional de Bolivia* (La Paz, 1997).

[8] Juárez and Comboni, eds., *Sistema educativo nacional de Bolivia*.

[9] Ibid.

established and consolidated by the time national public education systems were created in the nineteenth century.

The struggle between the conservative and progressive ideologies was embedded in the larger political competition between conservatives and liberals, with liberals advocating the expansion of universal public primary education and challenging Church dominance, and conservatives espousing education controlled by the Church. In Colombia and Ecuador, for example, the dominance of the Church in the provision of education, an education that mandated teaching of Catholicism, was supported by a landed oligarchy of political conservatives.[10] In Mexico, after independence, liberals and conservatives agreed on the importance of education, but disagreed sharply after 1824 on the role of the Church and freedom of instruction. Although the Mexican liberals initially opposed the intervention of the state in education, in the 1830s, they proposed state-led education as a way to curb the dominance of the Church and of the conservatives.[11]

For the best part of the first three centuries since the establishment of the Spanish colonies in the Americas, the notion that education served to legitimate a social order and the existing social structure was unchallenged. The independence movement and the emergence of the new republics in the late 1700s and early 1800s introduced alternative expectations for schools.

The 1800s were characterized by political battles among different elite groups. In some cases, these battles resulted in changes in the structure of the economy. Economic reorganization, and the accompanying urbanization, provided a receptive context for the implementation of a different educational ideology. This new ideology no longer saw educational institutions as the bulwarks of the agricultural social order of the past. Rather, educational institutions were seen as the heralds of a new urban and industrial society and as the gateways through which new social groups would move upward to senior and mid-level leadership positions in the economy and in the new political and administrative institutions.

Two core related ideas emerged in the nineteenth century that formed the basis of the developments of the twentieth century. The first was a challenge to the dominance of the church in the conduct of education (the Church, loyal to the Spanish Crown, identified with the conservative

---

[10] José H. Serrano, ed., *Sistema educativo nacional de la República de Colombia* (Madrid, 1993), and Carlos Poveda, ed., *Sistema educativo nacional del Ecuador* (Quito, 1994).

[11] Germán Alvarez, ed., *Sistema educativo nacional de México* (Mexico City, 1994).

movement). The intellectual foundation of the independence movement, which advocated an egalitarian ethic and independence of inquiry and thought, also challenged a Church identified with an authoritarian social order and with religious dogma as superior to human reasoning as basis for the construction of truth. The second idea, originating in the early period of independence, was that all should have access to primary education and that the state had a responsibility to provide that access. This idea took hold and found its way into new education laws and, in several cases, into the constitutions of the new republics. As the independent nations consolidated during the nineteenth century, the ambition of universal, publicly provided primary education gained acceptance throughout Latin America.

The postindependence movement brought clear expectations that education be central in the formation of the new Americans' identity and in the inclusion of heretofore marginalized groups of the population for social participation. This progressive aspiration coexisted with the conservative view that saw divided education (education for the new elites, but only fundamental instruction to *mestizos* and the lower classes) as appropriate. The French Revolution influenced the South American independence movement with the ideals of Freedom, Equality, and Justice, shaping the aspiration to universalize access to primary education. Simón Bolívar, well versed in the works of Rousseau and the Utopians, wrote eloquently about the pivotal role of education in the newly independent nations. Two of his teachers and close associates, Simón Rodríguez and Andrés Bello, played key roles in shaping the new ideology of the role of education in the newly independent nations.

As first president of Bolivia, Bolívar appointed Simón Rodríguez as first Director General of Public Education. In a decree dated December 11, 1825, they established that education, which must be general and for all, is the first duty of the government and that the health of the republic rests on the moral dispositions that the citizens acquire in schools at an early age.[12] In 1835, Ecuador, another of the republics that gained independence from Spain as part of the same movement, adopted the first law of public education, establishing the directorate of education and an inspectorate system.

As a result of the influence of Bello and Sarmiento, in the mid-nineteenth century, most public schools in Chile were aimed at providing literacy skills to poor children.[13] Table 11.1 summarizes the first legal documents to recognize universal public primary education as a state responsibility.

---

[12] Juárez and Comboni, eds., *Sistema educativo nacional de Bolivia.*
[13] Ivan Nuñez, ed., *Sistema educativo nacional de Chile* (Santiago, 1993).

Table 11.1. *First legal documents proposing universal primary education in Latin America*

Country	Year	Legal instrument and purpose
Peru	1823	Constitution establishes that Congress will regulate education through periodic plans. It also indicates that instruction is a common need for all and that the Republic owes it to all citizens.
Bolivia	1825	Decree establishing general education as a government responsibility.
Peru	1828	Constitution establishes free primary instruction for all citizens.
Chile	1833	Constitution recognized freedom of teaching – from authority of the Church – while assigning to the state a strong mandate in the promotion and oversight of education. In 1920, a Primary Education Law established compulsory primary education.
Ecuador	1835	First law of public education.
Cuba	1841	Royal order establishing free education for poor children.
Bolivia	1851	Constitution establishes universal right to education. Independent education under the supervision of the state. Established creation of schools for girls. Established free primary schooling.
Mexico	1867	First Law of Public Instruction establishes primary education free and compulsory for "the poor," excludes religious instruction from the curriculum.
Costa Rica	1869	Decrees free and compulsory primary education.
Venezuela	1870	Decree of public, compulsory, and free primary instruction and creation of the Ministry of Education.
Argentina	1884	First law approving compulsory primary schooling.
Colombia	1886	Constitution establishes free primary schooling.

Sources: José Juárez and Sonia Comboni, eds., *Sistema educativo nacional de Bolivia* (La Paz, 1997); José H. Serrano, ed., *Sistema educativo nacional de la república de Colombia* (Madrid, 1993); Olman Ramírez, *Sistema educativo nacional de Costa Rica* (Madrid, 1997); Ivan Nuñez, ed., *Sistema educativo nacional de Chile* (Santiago, 1993); Germán Alvarez, ed., *Sistema educativo nacional de México* (Mexico City, 1994); Ministerio de Educación de la República del Perú, *Sistema educativo nacional del Peru* (Lima, 1994); Enid Pérez, *Sistema educativo nacional de Venezuela* (Caracas, 1995).

This victory of progressive policy was soon followed by the creation of institutions that would make it possible to implement national education policies. The second half of the nineteenth century saw the creation of incipient national education systems and structures. This was also a time when the new nation-states launched large-scale education initiatives in curriculum design, provision of educational materials, and teacher education. These initiatives provided the intellectual, legal, and organizational foundation that made possible the massive expansion of the twentieth century.

Transnational exchanges supported the development of public education as foreign educators played advisory and management roles in support of the emerging public education systems, facilitating the exchange of ideas, instructional materials, and practices. Venezuelan-born Andrés Bello was the first rector of the Universidad de Chile. At the time, the university was in charge of the supervision of the public education system. It trained teachers and developed curricula. Bello was among those who first advocated for education and cultural institutions to shape a new identity for the new Americans. The grammar of the Spanish language he developed challenged Spain's Royal Academy of the Language by recognizing how language was used in Ibero-America. As rector of the Universidad de Chile, Bello instituted a contest to encourage essays on the kind of primary education system that would best fit the American social, political, and economic project.[14]

Argentine-born Domingo Faustino Sarmiento, also working in Chile, won this contest with an essay that argued for the common school (*Educación Común*), a mandatory and free center for the formation of the political identity of all the citizens of the newly independent nations. Sarmiento's ideas on the common school were very influential in Chile (where he directed the first teacher training institution), then in Argentina (where he became Minister of Education and President) and Paraguay.[15] Through the works of some of his followers, like José Pedro Varela in Uruguay, these ideas extended to other countries as well.[16] Sarmiento visited Massachusetts, to learn firsthand of the efforts of Horace Mann to build a broad-based coalition to garner support for the "common school" and became a friend of Horace's wife Mary Peabody Mann, with whom he maintained an active correspondence focusing on educational, scientific, and political development.[17] Sarmiento brought the first teachers from the United States to

---

[14] Gregorio Weinberg, "Andrés Bello," in Zaghloul Morzy, ed., *Pensadores de la educación* (Paris, 1993), 84.

[15] Hector Bravo, "Domingo Faustino Sarmiento," in *Pensadores de la Educación*, 506–7.

[16] Marta Demarchi and Hugo Rodríguez, "Jose Pedro Varela," in *Pensadores de la Educación*, 719–34.

[17] Barry Velleman, ed., *My Dear Sir: Mary Mann's Letters to Sarmiento* (Buenos Aires, 2001).

Argentina. The first Argentine textbooks were translated from English and French.

The translation of textbooks and curricula and the reliance on education advisors from nations with more established public education systems were resources commonly used by those working to establish public education systems. In Bolivia, school curricula in 1879 were translated from Dutch curricula for primary schools and French textbooks of Guillet-Damitt were adopted as official textbooks. A Belgian educator directed the first normal school in Bolivia, established in 1909, with collaboration from a delegation of Chilean educators. Colombia received technical assistance from a group of German educators who, in 1867, advised the National Directorate of Public Instruction. Teacher training institutions were set up following the German model at the time. In the late nineteenth century, Ecuador, too, received a mission from Germany to reform teacher training institutions and demonstration schools and, later on, to reform the curricula.

In Chile, during the 1880s, German educators ran the teacher training institutions (*escuelas normales*) and reformed primary education. In 1889, they established the Pedagogical Institute to train secondary school teachers, which would later be incorporated into the Universidad de Chile as part of the faculty of philosophy and education.

Chile, in turn, through exchanges and technical assistance, supported the development of public education in other countries in Latin America. At the beginning of the twentieth century, for example, the Bolivian government provided scholarships to teachers for training in Chilean institutions. Chilean missions of education advisors worked in Bolivia at the beginning of the century with the Directorate of Primary Schools and of Languages. A group of Chilean teacher trainers also worked in teacher education. In 1935, a group of Chilean educators arrived in Costa Rica to advise on the reform of basic and secondary education and in the reestablishment of the university.

THE INTENSIFICATION OF EDUCATION POLITICS DURING THE TWENTIETH CENTURY

The first half of the twentieth century served to consolidate the national systems of public education initiated in the latter part of the previous century.

This resulted in an increasing centralization of education governance, severing existing ties between schools and local governments. The struggles between liberals and conservatives continued, with the conservatives representing the interests of the landed oligarchies under attack by the emergent industrialists. The specific education strategies advocated by each group changed as interests on the social outcomes of education changed. Over time, conservatives came to accept the emphasis of liberals in providing universal elementary instruction once it no longer challenged the distribution of social and economic privileges. As education strategies converged, the struggle between conservatives and liberals moved to new terrains. By the middle of the twentieth century, for instance, there was widespread acceptance of the desirability of providing universal primary education, originally a progressive idea, although this expansion was soon followed by a growing social segmentation of primary schools as a result of quality disparities. The consensus reached by elites on the importance of universal access to elementary education was not reached with regard to the purposes of that instruction and, consequently, with regard to issues of curriculum content or pedagogy. As a result, while there was subsequent progress in expanding the educational attainment of the population and in closing attainment gaps among social groups, there was not the same progress in addressing the quality of instruction or in closing quality gaps. With segemented tiers of quality at the elementary level, social divides moved up to secondary and tertiary levels or instruction as some primary school graduates were deficiently prepared to continue their education at higher levels. The victory of 100 years of progressive advocacy for universal primary education thus took place at a time when the most relevant educational levels for economic mobility became secondary and tertiary education.

Once national systems were established, all countries in Latin America began national programs of education reform. As had been the case since independence, education reforms had a clear political motivation and expressed larger political projects. As one reform rapidly succeeded another and as political competition increased, the gaps between policy rhetoric, implementation, and results increased.[18]

---

[18] The gaps between education policy rhetoric and implementation have been observed in other regions beyond Latin America. Tyack and Cuban, for example, examining a century of education reform in the United States, conclude that the basic grammar of schooling has proved quite resistant to policy-induced change. David Tyack and Larry Cuban, *Tinkering Toward Utopia. A Century of Public School Reform* (Cambridge, MA, 1995), 85–109. Mark Hanson suggests that the gap between policy and implementation is particularly large in Latin America and attributes this to the fact

The policy–implementation gap was particularly large with regard to those policy objectives upon which there was less social consensus, namely the incorporation of marginalized groups and rural and indigenous children, and with regard to providing high quality instruction to the poor. The achievement of equal educational opportunity was the most contentious of all goals proposed for education in the twentieth century. This is the reason for the large gap we observe today between progressive rhetoric and implementation results. Policy elites did not agree that equal opportunity and outcomes were desirable and they disagreed on what equality of educational opportunity meant.

The twentieth-century reforms directed at equality of educational opportunity have been of two kinds. The first and most significant reform was an unprecedented educational expansion, which established the supremacy of public education. This policy of state-led educational development came to be known as the *Estado Docente* and was the main victory of the progressive project during the century. The second set of reforms specifically targeted marginalized children to receive more resources, attention, and special programs. These reforms were highly contested and did not last long. The most recent iteration of these reforms was initiated during the 1990s, amidst growing emphasis on cost cutting and improving educational efficiency and competitiveness.

Undermining the gains of the quantitative expansion was a growing process of social segmentation in educational institutions. The children of dominant groups became gradually concentrated in institutions that excluded those who had gained access to education as a result of progressive victories. This social segregation occurred through patterns of residential segregation, institutional practices of discrimination in public schools, and the flight of privileged groups to private institutions. The sharp social segregation of schools struck a serious blow to the vision of the "common school" developed by the founders of public education systems, first by expanding

that the colonies had to implement laws and regulations designed in Spain. Recognizing that the rulers had imperfect knowledge of the reality they were ruling over, local authorities would resort to the practice of "se acata pero no se cumple" (we accept the ruling but do not comply). Mark Hanson, *Educational Reform and Administrative Development. The Cases of Colombia and Venezuela* (Stanford, CA, 1986), 15. Another way to interpret the facts observed by Hanson is that local elites had sufficient autonomy to advance their own agenda at the implementation stage even though the process of policy formation constrained their ability of doing so at the policy-design stage. Examples of this implementation gap were the dispositions of Kings Ferdinand the Catholic and Charles I which compelled the *encomenderos* to educate indigenous people in the *encomienda* but which were never implemented. Raul Bolaños, "Orígenes de la educación pública en México," in F. Solana, R. Cardiel, and Raul Bolaños, *Historia de la educación pública en México* (Mexico City, 1981), 13–14.

divided, rather than common, institutions, and second by allowing the development of unequal tiers of quality in these separate schools.

Progressive ideas gained space in policy rhetoric, and also action, during the first half of the century, when the confrontation with a conservative ideology was overt and when these ideas were part of a broader political struggle aimed at resolving conflicts between competing groups in society. Beginning in the 1950s, a modernizing ideology (*desarrollismo*) spread rapidly throughout Latin America. The dominant import substitution industrialization strategy, an ideology of state-led development, the growing process of urbanization, and the gradual mobilization of the emerging middle classes all supported educational expansion.[19] Important gains in access to education at all levels resulted from this convergence of social, political, and economic forces.

In the 1960s, as political elites turned to authoritarian governments to demobilize some of the most radical political groups, however, education was purposefully emptied of its progressive political content. Then a new *desarrollismo* emerged toward the late 1960s and 1970s; one that equated development with economic growth and that was silent about human rights, democracy, and social change. The purposes of schools would no longer be to form democratic citizens but obedient workers. Schools would focus on developing skills for economic industrialization while they conserved the values of a traditional authoritarian and stagnant social order. This emerging ideology weakened what had been a powerful mobilizing, organizing framework and rendered it helpless to resist the penetration of a neoconservative agenda during the 1980s. As import-substituting elites and politicians, who had made their careers under state-led development, came under siege during the 1980s, the struggle for equal educational opportunity suffered the most serious setback in the century. Expanding access to those groups not yet in school at each education level took a back seat to the concern with improving the quality of education and the efficiency of how education monies were spent. The purposes of schools narrowed in yet another way, by emphasizing fewer academic subjects and, in practice, low-order cognitive skills.

Neoconservatives advanced a renewed faith in markets as the best mechanisms to regulate collective action, including the distribution of public

---

[19] The expansion of state bureaucracy, along with the new industries created during the century, contributed to the creation of the jobs for the new middle classes, who in turn demanded more education for their children.

goods and services. With states under attack, public education was under stress. Public education funding was cut sharply under structural adjustment programs. The quality of education, which had already been stretched by the rapid expansion of the previous decades, declined. Efficiency-enhancing education reforms and a new concern with "quality" spread rapidly.[20] There was a renewed emphasis on streamlining the curriculum to basic subjects (language, math, and sciences). The new emphasis on quality was, however, intellectually flawed. In practice, quality came to mean achieving the intended objectives of the curriculum without examining whether those objectives were relevant to the new political challenges of democratic citizenship or to the new economic challenges of high value-added competitiveness. Quality was understood more as effectiveness in achieving the objectives of the curriculum than as examining the level and pertinence of those standards. Schools were again primarily to train workers that could contribute to economic competitiveness in low-productivity industries, rather than citizens who could make societies more democratic. The century ended with renewed rhetoric addressing equality as an objective and with incipient efforts to redress the growing education divides. Unlike the ideologies of the nineteenth and early twentieth centuries, however, these ideas were now embedded within larger reforms seeking to improve efficiency and were lukewarm about, when not directly opposed to, state-led educational development. They also lacked the synergies resulting from association with broader political agendas, parties, and social movements that could mobilize educationally marginalized groups.

At the beginning of the twentieth century, three countries most clearly represented those where a new economic and political order supported progressive education ideas: Argentina, Chile, and Uruguay. In these countries, the successful export-oriented economy and associated urbanization and large-scale immigration paved the way for a state-led national education system that sought to quickly develop a national, modern identity among

---

[20] These were also the emerging concerns of education elites in the leaders of the neoconservative movement in the OECD, namely the United States and Great Britain. Some have argued that the United States sought to extend this new set of priorities to countries under its political influence. John Bock and G. Arthur, "Politics of Educational Reform: The Experience of a Foreign Technical Assistance Project," *Educational Policy* 5:3 (September 1991): 312–28. Also, see Gary Orfield, "Policy and Equity: Lessons of a Third of a Century of Educational Reforms in the United States," in Fernando Reimers, ed., *Unequal Schools, Unequal Chances* (Cambridge, MA, 2002), 402. Others have suggested that international banks, such as the World Bank, reflecting interbureaucratic politics, dominated by economists who shared the tenets of the neoconservative agenda, supported reforms with very narrow objectives and strategies. See Karen Mundy, "Educational Multilateralism and World Disorder," *Comparative Education Review* 42 (1998): 448–78.

all. The purpose of elementary school was largely political. An inclusive ideology spread – one that openly espoused equality of educational opportunity as a foundation of the new society. Those distant historical influences are still reflected in the higher levels of educational attainment of people in these countries and in greater educational equality relative to other countries in the region.

In Argentina between 1914 and 1930, most children gained access to elementary school.[21] In Chile, during the second half of the nineteenth century, enrollments in primary school increased tenfold and by 1887, one in five children in the age group six to fourteen was in school. The expansion of education continued, in part as a result of the autonomy of the education system from larger social forces, and accelerated between 1965 and 1974 as part of two political projects – a Social Christian project under Eduardo Frei and a socialist project under Salvador Allende. This expansion would stop during the military regime of Augusto Pinochet.[22]

The creation of a mass-based public education system and the transition from a church-dominated to a state-dominated education system were not without conflict. Church–state relations mediated the consequences of this conflict for the new educational legislation supporting the establishment of the *Estado Docente*.[23] In Colombia, beginning in the 1930s, the state had to overcome overt resistance from the church and private groups in the integration of gender-segregated schools and in fostering greater socioeconomic integration in schools.[24] In Chile, the 1925 Constitution separated church and state and upheld the principle of freedom of teaching while establishing that education was a preferential matter of the state. These changes were opposed by the oligarchies, contributing to the political instability that led to the coup of 1931.[25]

Every political transition proclaiming radical change was accompanied by an education reform, although some of them were short-lived. In 1917, Costa Rican President Gonzalez Flores's reformist agenda included an education reform aimed at increasing the links between schools and the

---

[21] Dario Pulfer and Ana Vitar, eds., *Sistema educativo nacional de Argentina* (Buenos Aires, 1993).

[22] C. Rodríguez, "Chile: System of Education," in Torsten Husen and Neville Postlewhaite, eds., *International Encyclopedia of Education* (London, 1994), 738–46. See also Ivan Nuñez, ed., *Sistema educativo nacional de Chile*.

[23] T. Bruneau, *The Political Transformation of the Brazilian Catholic Church* (Cambridge, 1974); Daniel Levine, *Churches and Politics in Latin America* (Beverly Hills, CA, 1980); and I. Vallier, *Catholicism, Social Control and Modernization in Latin America* (New York, 1970).

[24] Serrano, ed., *Sistema educativo nacional de la República de Colombia*.

[25] Nuñez, ed., *Sistema educativo nacional de Chile*.

productivity of small farmers. It sought to generate funding in farm-schools. This reform was highly contested by teachers, parents, and public opinion, and eventually by members of Congress.[26] The 1952 Bolivian Revolution of Victor Paz Estenssoro included education reform among the four core pillars of the revolution (along with nationalization of the mines, agrarian reform, and universal voting rights). The reform's emphasis was to extend education to rural areas, to strengthen national identity. It created a code of education with participation of the confederation of workers, the church, private schools, and the National University.[27] At mid-twentieth century, the states in Costa Rica and Venezuela made educational expansion a cornerstone of democracy consolidation projects and, in the case of Cuba, of socialism. Peru would follow with an ambitious reform in 1968 that was to support a broader project of socialist political and economic restructuring. All of these countries expanded educational access significantly in the early years of the political transition.

In 1957, Costa Rica approved an education law (*Ley Fundamental de Educación*), which articulated a rationale for education as part of a democratic project. Venezuela's democracy turned to schools as an instrument to reshape the nation. Primary enrollment growth increased from 7 percent per year prior to 1958 to more than 20 percent per year in the years immediately following the democratic transition. Secondary school enrollment growth doubled in this period. Growth in university enrollments increased from 12 percent per year in 1957 to 60 percent in 1959.[28]

The Cuban socialist revolution turned to education early. A 1959 education law established the creation of ten thousand classrooms and another law of December of the same year established a framework for a comprehensive education reform. These reforms increased primary education enrollments from under 50 percent in 1959 to 90 percent in the first few years of the revolution. A massive literacy campaign in 1961 and follow-up adult education programs targeted the more than one million adults who could not read in 1959 (23% of the adult population) and virtually eliminated illiteracy. A 1962 university reform law established preferential admission policies for the children of peasants and workers.

---

[26] Olman Ramírez, *Sistema educativo nacional de Costa Rica* (Madrid, 1997).

[27] Manuel Contreras argues that the Bolivian Education Reform of 1952 was an afterthought of the revolution and that its results failed to match its rhetoric (personal communication, January 13, 2003).

[28] Fernando Reimers, "Venezuela: System of Education," in *International Encyclopedia of Education*, 6592.

The Peruvian education reform of 1968, under a socialist military government, sought to create a "new Peruvian man" in line with the aspirations of the revolution. The goals of the Peruvian education reform were to contribute to work and development, the structural transformation of society, and the creation of a self-reliant and independent Peruvian nation. This reform was highly contested, particularly its most transformative proposals calling for education for collectivist organization in farming communities and bilingual education policies. The reform restructured and expanded basic education and restructured administration in rural areas in education clusters.

Because education was so clearly perceived as serving political purposes, authoritarian governments turned to schools to facilitate acceptance of the new order. Throughout much of the twentieth century, educational institutions fulfilled their traditional role of reinforcing traditional authoritarian institutions, rather than the incipient and contested democratic practices.

Universities were particularly affected by authoritarian governments of the right or left because they often provided oppositional leadership. In Venezuela, the Central University was purged by the Christian Democratic administration in the early 1970s because the armed leftist insurgency received support from some university students and faculty. During the same period, the National University in Uruguay provided leadership to radical political opposition and was consequently targeted by security forces under authoritarian rule. The military that ruled Argentina from 1976 to 1983 also closely scrutinized university faculty members and students for ties to the insurgency that developed during the last few years of Perón's regime. Many of the "disappeared" during the *guerra sucia* were members of the university community. The military government that ruled in Chile from 1973 to 1990 targeted universities as part of efforts to demobilize political opposition. Under the intervention of military rectors, universities shut down entire social studies programs. Many members of the academic community fled Chile in fear for their safety under the military regime. In El Salvador, toward the end of twelve years of civil war, the entire leadership of the Catholic University was assassinated by elite counterinsurgency battalions because they were perceived to provide moral leadership to the opposition during the conflict, which ended in 1992. At the end of the twentieth century, the authoritarian government of President Chávez in Venezuela actively sought to control universities to demobilize political opposition and proposed legislation that greatly increased their control by the executive. The greatest levels of ideological control on the university community were those exerted by the regime of Fidel Castro in Cuba, where the Communist Party controlled faculty appointments, freedom of speech in universities, freedom of faculty members and students to associate and travel abroad, and employment prospects of graduates. The authoritarian intervention of universities, the constraints to academic freedom, the physical annihilation and prosecution of scholars and students, and the use of terror toward the university community (part of the larger political struggles that marked Latin America during the twentieth century) had dire and long-lasting consequences on the ability of public universities to fulfill their missions.

THE POLITICS OF BASIC EDUCATION EXPANSION DURING THE TWENTIETH CENTURY AND ITS RESULTS

The growth of public access was greatest in primary education because more consensus was reached among elites on the importance of extending opportunity at this level. Conflict was greater regarding the need to foster equality of access to secondary and tertiary institutions, and access in those levels correspondingly did not grow as much as it did in primary. Also, a greater percentage of students in those levels enrolled in private institutions, indicating that social demand exceeded the capacity of public institutions. But the challenges to the idea that all children should receive a quality education continued throughout the century, often overtly, most commonly in the benign neglect that produced dismal conditions in the schools attended by the children of the poor. As recently as 1991, a former minister of education of Venezuela[29] argued in a publication of the National Education Council, an advisory body of the Ministry of Education:

Faced with the choice of providing a first rate education to a third of the population or a mediocre education to all, I would not vacillate. I would choose a first rate education for a third of the population, because that third of the population would pull the country forward.[30]

Legal and constitutional changes in several countries during the 1980s and 1990s sought to reduce state responsibility for the provision of

[29] Venezuela is one of the Latin American countries that made educational expansion an important priority during the democratic transition beginning in 1958.
[30] Arturo Uslar Pietri, "Las dos opciones del arcangel," Consejo Nacional de Educacion. September 6, 1991.

education. The military government in Chile introduced drastic education reforms in the 1980s that transferred educational management to the municipalities and fostered the development of private schools through a voucher financing scheme. These, as well as the previous reforms of the national curriculum and the changes in the universities, were locked into place by an educational law passed on the last day of the military in office (March 10, 1990): the *Ley Orgánica Constitucional de Enseñanza* (Ley 18.962). This law created a public corporation, the *Consejo Superior de Educación*, which includes a representative of the armed forces and with a composition that gives limited power to the executive. This body has final authority to approve fundamental changes in education, including the curricula and the creation of universities or the approval of fields of study within universities. A legal change of this nature can only be revoked by another law that would require a majority in Congress. As a result, the governments that have been elected in Chile since 1990 have been unable to alter the structural changes made by the previous administration.

A 1991 constitutional reform in Colombia supported decentralization and the participation of private providers, while containing state responsibility for the provision of public education:

The Reform required the approval of diverse political bodies. Achieving its goals and ensuring its internal coherence meant waging simultaneous battles in sundry and changing terrains in the constitutional realm by ensuring that the text of the new Constitution agreed with the desired goals, especially those regarding the *intensifying of decentralization and free and open private participation in the education process*... (emphasis added)

The educational reform effort brought before the Constitutional Assembly was directed at obtaining two specific objectives. First, to ensure that general norms on education (contained in Title II of the Constitution, "About rights, guarantees, and obligations") would concur with the government's ideas. In this area, however, the political tasks were mostly defensive; they centered on *avoiding the approval of populist proposals such as the one that would establish "free and mandatory public education for all Colombians"* and other similar initiatives.[31]

Most of the expansion in access to primary and secondary schooling was in public institutions. By the end of the century, primary education enrollments in private schools were 42 percent in Chile; between 10 and 20 percent

---

[31] Armando Montenegro, *An Incomplete Educational Reform: The Case of Colombia* (Washington, DC, n.d.), 9–10. Emphasis added.

in the Dominican Republic, El Salvador, Guatemala, Nicaragua, Panama, Brazil, Colombia, Ecuador, Paraguay, Peru, Uruguay, and Venezuela; and less than 10 percent in Costa Rica, Cuba, and Mexico. The percentage of private enrollments was much higher for secondary education, but most students were still enrolled in public institutions.[32] Private enrollments were the highest at the university level, with 34 percent of the students enrolled in private institutions by the 1980s. This was up from 7 percent of students in private institutions in 1955.[33] The educational expansion meant that most children had the opportunity to exceed their parents' educational levels. In Mexico, for example, in 1998, 40 percent of students in the sixth grade had already exceeded their fathers' educational level.[34]

The growing number of education institutions, bringing together teachers, students, and parents, were arenas ripe for the emergence of political organization. Recognizing this potential, the emerging political parties and the state co-opted many of the new unions of teachers and students. The political mobilization of education stakeholders supported educational expansion with some autonomy from larger political forces. In Argentina, the 1940s saw schools mobilize popular sectors and the emergence of teacher unions and student unions, around the student government of secondary schools (*centros de estudiantes*). During the 1930s, teachers in Bolivia began to organize in cooperatives, credit unions, and associations, which formed the basis of the *Liga Nacional del Magisterio*. President Paz Estenssoro's education reform of 1952 included a major mobilization of the universities, trade unions, the Church, and private schools in the preparation of the first education code.[35] In Mexico, all teacher unions were unified in 1943 to create the *Sindicato Nacional de Trabajadores de la Educación* (SNTE), recognized by presidential decree in 1944 as the only entity that could represent all teachers.[36] The SNTE became a very important pillar of the dominance of the Partido Revolucionario Institucional of Mexican politics in the twentieth century, and it would grow to become the largest trade union in the hemisphere. In 1947, a teaching statute was approved in Uruguay that established the Teacher Assembly as a consultative forum for education policy. It also provides the framework for political and trade mobilization of teachers.

---

[32] UNESCO, *World Education Report. The Right to Education* (Paris, 2000).
[33] Daniel Levy, *Higher Education and the State in Latin America* (Chicago, 1986), 4–5.
[34] Reimers, *Unequal Schools, Unequal Chances.*
[35] Juárez and Comboni, eds., *Sistema educativo nacional de Bolivia.*
[36] Alvarez, ed., *Sistema educativo nacional de México.*

Although some of the politics supporting the development of mass education were domestic, these were embedded and supported by international influence and politics, as had been the case during the previous century. In the late 1940s and 1950s, a transnational coalition of interests and developments overlapped with the interests of local elites promoting import substitution industrialization to mobilize a significant educational expansion. Two powerful ideas in the field of economics would support this expansion. The first was the identification of human capital as the key factor in the economic recovery of Europe after the Second World War. The second was the idea that development could be planned. The field of international development cooperation thus emerged during the Cold War. Multilateral and bilateral development agencies began to support, with cash and technical assistance, the economic development of allies, and this included supporting educational expansion.

Somewhat independently, beginning in the 1950s, the United Nations system established an array of organizations to support the achievement of rights outlined in the Universal Declaration of Human Rights. Education was recognized as a fundamental human right and United Nations Educational, Scientific, and Cultural Organization (UNESCO) took on a central role in promoting the universalization of primary education and literacy.

UNESCO convened meetings of ministers and senior staff of Ministries of Education and stimulated exchanges of ideas on how to achieve the goal of universal primary education. The Inter-American Development Bank and the World Bank funded loans to finance some of the infrastructural expansion, initially of the universities, then the technical training institutions and vocational tracks in high schools and, last, the primary schools. The Alliance for Progress, too, marshaled support for the education development of the Latin nations. This unprecedented convergence of interests resulted in an impressive quantitative expansion during the century. It also resulted in the adoption of common planning methodologies, a growing domination of an economic rationale for education development and, eventually, the abandonment of the view that education was a means to support political democratization or the universalization of human rights.[37]

The victory of the progressive project in consolidating public education systems, albeit of low quality and focusing principally on the lower levels of education, is expressed in the fact that schools are one of the national

---

[37] This was particularly true as authoritarian governments came onto the scene as part of the struggle against communism that played out in Latin America during the Cold War.

institutions in which the public had most confidence at the end of the twentieth century. A sample survey administered to adults in 1998 found that 89 percent of Chileans had much or some confidence in schools, compared with 61 percent who had similar levels of confidence in the police, 57 percent in the press, 51 percent in the government, 53 percent in the army, 43 percent in Congress, or 27 percent in the political parties. In Mexico, with overall lower levels of confidence in all public institutions, 64 percent of those interviewed expressed much or some confidence in schools, compared with 45 percent in the army, 33 percent in the police, 30 percent in the government and political parties, 29 percent in the press, and 28 percent in Congress.[38] The preference for public provision of education services is far greater in Latin America than in the United States. Whereas 42 percent of the adults in the United States prefer government ownership of schools, the respective figures are 51 percent in Mexico, 59 percent in Ecuador and Venezuela, 62 percent in Colombia, 66 percent in Bolivia and Paraguay, 68 percent in Chile, 70 percent in Peru, 71 percent in Costa Rica, 72 percent in Argentina and Brazil, 74 percent in Guatemala, 75 percent in Panama, and 84 percent in the Dominican Republic.[39]

During the twentieth century, states extended not just access to primary education, but also the duration of compulsory education, from five or six years of schooling at the beginning of the twentieth century, to eight or nine years of basic instruction toward the end. In 1967, Chile was one of the first countries to extend the duration of basic education from six to eight years and to reduce secondary education from five to seven years to four to five.[40] By the end of the century, the duration of compulsory education was eleven years in Guatemala and Peru; ten years in Costa Rica, Dominican Republic, Ecuador, Mexico, and Uruguay; nine years in Argentina, Chile, Cuba, El Salvador, and Paraguay; eight years in Bolivia, Brazil, and Colombia; seven years in Venezuela; and six years in Haiti, Nicaragua, and Panama.[41] By comparison, the duration of compulsory schooling in Germany was thirteen years; in the United Kingdom and the United States, twelve years; and in Canada, France, and Spain, eleven years.

[38] Joseph Klesner, "Legacies of Authoritarianism," in Roderic Ai Camp, ed., *Citizen Views of Democracy in Latin America* (Pittsburgh, PA, 2001), 118–38.
[39] Kenneth Coleman, "Politics and Markets in Latin America," in Ai Camp, *Citizen Views of Democracy in Latin America*, 185–205.
[40] Rodríguez, "Chile: System of Education."
[41] UNESCO Institute of Statistics. http://www.uis.unesco.org/en/stats/statistics/database/DBIndex. htm, accessed June 19, 2003.

During the twentieth century, most Latin American states delivered on the promise of providing initial access to compulsory primary education to all children. A remarkable expansion of enrollments took place during the century, far exceeding the rapid population growth. This expansion of the incipient systems of education established in the nineteenth century was stimulated by import substitution industrialization and the associated urbanization of the Latin American population. Most of this expansion was in public institutions. For the progressives, this consolidation of the *Estado Docente* represented a victory over an education dominated by the Church, perceived to legitimize class differences (by the preferential emphasis on educating elites), differences in gender roles (by segregated education), and acceptance of the authority of the Church.[42]

The number of children enrolled in primary schools increased from 15 million in 1950 to 85 million in 1997; at the secondary level, enrollment increased from 2 million to 29 million; and at the tertiary level, from 300,000 to 9.4 million.[43]

The expansion in the capacity to enroll children in elementary school was dramatic. In 1950, none of the countries in Latin America had enough capacity to enroll all children of primary school age in school. Most could barely enroll half of them, as indicated by the gross enrollment ratios shown in Table 11.2. Only Argentina and Uruguay had gross enrollment ratios in primary school of more than 90 percent. Primary school systems were large enough to incorporate between 60 percent and 76 percent of the relevant age group in Costa Rica, Cuba, Chile, El Salvador, Panama, and Paraguay. In the remaining countries, fewer than three in five children of primary school age could attend school.

The differences in 1950 enrollment rates among countries reflect varying emphases of policy over the previous fifty years. Argentina and Uruguay developed inclusive educational ideologies earlier than the remaining countries and, as a result, expanded their education systems accordingly. At the lower end of the distribution of enrollment rates, Brazil, Nicaragua,

---

[42] The struggle between the conservative and progressive projects took place also within the Church, especially after the Puebla and Medellín Bishops' Conferences, where a preferential option for the poor was adopted as an official framework of the Latin American Church. Some of the progressive practices are those where Church-based education organizations and social movements partner to empower marginalized groups and communities. Examples of these practices are the work of the Society of Jesus, with popular education in marginalized communities through the organization Fe y Alegría. Although the educational practice of Church-related organizations have become more diverse since Puebla, the traditional role of Church-related educational institutions was to serve the needs of the most privileged members of the Latin American societies.

[43] UNESCO, *World Education Report*, 116, Tables 3.1, 3.2, and 3.3.

Table 11.2. *Enrollment rates in primary education in Latin America,*
1950–2000

	Gross enrollment rates						Net
	1950	1965	1970	1980	1990	2000	2000
Argentina	94	101	105	106	106	120	107
Uruguay	90	106	112	107	109	109	90
Panama	76	102	101	106	106	112	100
Chile	74	124	104	109	100	103	89
Paraguay	74	102	109	104	105	111	92
Peru	67	99	107	114	123	128	104
Cuba	66	121	121	106	98	102	97
Costa Rica	61	106	110	105	101	107	91
El Salvador	61	82	84	75	81	112	81
Ecuador	57	91	99	117	116	115	99
Dominican Republic	54	87	100	118	96	124	93
Mexico	53	92	106	120	114	113	103
Venezuela	51	94	97	93	96	102	88
Brazil	39	108	119	98	106	162	97
Nicaragua	39	69	78	94	94	104	81
Colombia	36	84	101	112	102	112	89
Bolivia	35	73	78	87	95	116	97
Guatemala	28	50	58	71	78	102	84
Honduras	28	80	87	98	108	106	88
Haiti	19	50	53	76	48		

Note: For the year 2000, gross and net enrollment rates are provided. See footnote 44 for a definition of gross and net enrollment rates.
Sources: Data for 1950 are from Ricardo Nassif, German Rama, and Juan Carlos Tedesco, *El sistema educativo en América Latina* (Buenos Aires, 1984). Data for 1965 are from World Bank, *Social Indicators of Development Database*. Data for 1990 are from UNESCO, *The World Education Report 2000* (Paris, 2000). All other data are from the UNESCO Statistical Database: http://www.uis.unesco.org/en/stats/statistics/database/DBIndex.htm, accessed June 19, 2003.

Colombia, Bolivia, Guatemala, Honduras, and Haiti had more exclusionary education systems. These conditions of access in 1950 influenced the ensuing development of education systems, making it more challenging for some countries to catch up with the rest in closing access gaps.

Between 1950 and 1965, the capacity of primary education systems expanded dramatically. By 1965, the gross enrollment rate exceeded

100 percent in eight countries[44] (Chile, Cuba, Brazil, Uruguay, Costa Rica, Panama, Paraguay, and Argentina) and 90 percent in an additional four (Peru, Venezuela, Mexico, and Ecuador). Only Guatemala and Haiti had lower rates, at 50 percent. By the end of the century, all countries but Haiti had achieved gross enrollment rates of 100 percent and net enrollment rates were close to or higher than 90 percent in all countries but Guatemala, El Salvador, Haiti, and Nicaragua.

Table 11.3 shows that secondary education also expanded during the twentieth century and from a much lower base than primary. However, by the end of the century, only a handful of countries were enrolling at least two thirds of the relevant age group at this level. These countries were Cuba, Argentina, Chile, Brazil, Peru, and Panama. In seven countries, fewer than two of five children were enrolled at this level (Paraguay, Venezuela, El Salvador, Guatemala, Bolivia, Haiti, and Honduras). The remaining countries enrolled between half and two thirds of the children in this age group.

Two factors constrained the expansion of secondary education. First, expansion in access at the primary level was achieved with a number of measures that reduced quality, such as reducing the duration of the school day to accommodate multiple shifts in the same building, expanding the workload of teachers to teach in multiple shifts, and reducing the quality and quantity of instructional resources per student. As a result, many of the children who gained access to primary school repeated grades multiple times; thus, the number who eventually graduated from this level was only a fraction of the number who gained initial access to primary school. Second, expansion of access to secondary school was constrained by policy. The emphasis during most of the century was on the universalization of primary education and literacy, a minimalist version of the concept of equal educational opportunity. Differences among countries at the end of the twentieth century in access to secondary school were not just a result of differences in economic resources or even of how much access had been achieved by mid-century, but reflected policy priorities. For example, Argentina, Chile, and Uruguay had the highest levels of access in 1950 and 1995; they were also among the countries with highest levels of income.

---

[44] The gross enrollment rate is the ratio of the total number of children enrolled in a level relative to the total number of children of school-going age. Because students enrolled can be younger or older than the official school-going age, this rate can exceed 100 percent. This indicator is a proxy for access and a measure of the capacity of the school system. Net enrollment rates include only children of the official school-going age in the calculations – excluding children who are overage or underage – and are therefore a better indicator of access to education. In Latin America, there are many children who are retained in the same grade from one year to the next; these repeaters who are overage explain the large discrepancy between gross and net enrollment rates.

Table 11.3. *Gross enrollment rates in secondary education (in descending order by 2000 levels in Latin America and comparator countries)*

	Gross enr. rates						Net	Gross national income per capita
	1950	1965	1970	1980	1990	2000	2000	2000/US$
Cuba	5	23	22	81	89	81.89	79.65	
Argentina	10	28	44	56	71	96.65	79.06	7,450
Chile	11	34	37	53	73	75.45	74.51	4,810
Uruguay	17	44	59	62	81	98.06	69.93	6,150
Bolivia	5	18	25	37	37	79.63	68.13	990
Panama	9	34	39	61	63	69.17	62.17	3,250
Peru	6	25	31	59	67	80.77	61.49	2,060
Mexico	3	17	23	49	53	75.31	59.66	5,100
Colombia	4	17	23	39	50	69.84	56.54	2,020
Venezuela	3	27	35	21	35	59.33	50.36	4,310
Ecuador	4	17	26	53	55	57.44	48.06	1,070
Paraguay	2	13	16	27	31	59.82	46.70	1,460
Costa Rica	6	24	28	47	42	50.94	43.37	3,820
Dominican Republic	2	12	21	42	51	59.46	40.20	2,120
Nicaragua	3	14	17	41	40	53.99	35.52	370
Guatemala	2	8	8	18	23	37.00	26.21	1,690
Brazil	6	16	26	33	38	56.00		3,630
Honduras	1	10	13	30	33			860
El Salvador	3	17	22	24	26	54.19		2,000
Haiti	1	5	6	14	21			500
Canada		56	65	88	101	102.60	97.87	21,720
Belgium		75	81	91	103			25,070
Spain		38	56	87	104	115.64	93.73	14,760
France		56	74	85	99	107.76	92.36	23,990
Korea, Republic of		35	42	78	90	94.12	90.86	9,010
Italy		47	61	72	83	95.93	90.51	20,130
United States			84	91	93	95.16	88.13	34,370
Portugal		42	56	37	67	113.65	85.19	11,190
Philippines		41	46	64	73	77.29	52.63	1,020
Singapore		45	46	60	68			23,350
Thailand		14	17	29	30	81.93		2,020

Note: See footnote 44 for a definition of enrollment rates.

Sources: Data for 1950 are from Nassif, Rama, and Tedesco, *El sistema educativo en América Latina*. Data for 1965 are from World Bank, *Social Indicators of Development Database*. Data for 1990 are from UNESCO, *World Education Report. The Right to Education* (Paris, 2000). All other data are from the UNESCO Statistical Database. Data for Gross National Income per Capita are from World Bank, World Development Indicators Database, http://devdata.worldbank.org/data-query/, accessed June 19, 2003. Gross enrollment data for Brazil in 2000 and for 1995, from UNESCO, *World Education Report*. This is because in 2000, Brazil changed the way it defined the duration of primary and secondary education for the purposes of reporting to UNESCO, lowering the first level ISCED1 from six to four years, and consequently making it impossible to compare appropriately the 2000 enrollment rates – inflated because of this definitional change – with data from previous years.

At the other extreme of the distribution, Guatemala, Haiti, and Honduras were at the low end of access and income in the 1950s and also at the end of the century. By contrast, Costa Rica, with higher enrollment rates in 1950 and a level of income comparable to Colombia, Ecuador, the Dominican Republic, Mexico, and Nicaragua, had lower enrollment rates than these countries in 1997. Another example that education policy priorities, and not just initial conditions or income, influenced expansion of enrollment rates is the difference between Brazil and Peru. Both started with enrollment rates of 6 percent in 1950, but enrollment expanded significantly more in Peru, in spite of lower levels of income.

The policies affecting primary and secondary school expansion had a significant and direct impact on the number of years of schooling attained by the population and, consequently, on literacy rates and the knowledge and skills of the labor force. Women gained significantly more than men with this expansion.

As a result of the expansion of compulsory schooling toward the end of the century, those aged fifteen to twenty-four living in urban areas in most countries had attained nine to ten years of schooling on average, as seen in Table 11.4. In rural areas, people had three years less of schooling on average than in urban areas. Women had more years of schooling than men in all countries in urban areas except in Bolivia, Guatemala, Mexico, and Paraguay. In these four countries, the differences were very small, and were largest in Bolivia. The same was true in rural areas, except in Bolivia, Guatemala, Mexico, and Peru.

Comparing the average years of schooling attained by all groups among those aged fifteen to twenty-four with those aged twenty-five to fifty-nine, it is clear that educational attainment grew most for women and it grew more for women and men in rural areas than in urban areas. Education levels for urban men, the group with the highest levels of education among those aged twenty-five to fifty-nine, were similar to the education profile of men aged fifteen to twenty-four. For urban women, in contrast, the younger group had, on average, 0.7 more years of school. Young rural males had, on average, 1.4 more years of schooling, whereas young urban women had, on average, more than two years more schooling than their older counterparts.

The ability of the state to support increases in the educational attainment of the population makes more blatant the persistent exclusion of some children from an education of quality that would allow them the opportunity to complete the levels that most mattered for economic and social mobility. Still, at the end of the twentieth century in Latin America, among the

Table 11.4. *Average number of years of school attained by different population groups circa 2000*

	Population 15 to 24 years of age				Population 25 to 59 years of age			
	Urban		Rural		Urban		Rural	
	Males	Females	Males	Females	Males	Females	Males	Females
Argentina 2000	9.7	10.5			10.2	10.3		
Bolivia 2000	10.3	9.9	6.9	5.7	10.6	8.8	5.0	2.9
Brazil 1999	7.2	7.9	4.4	5.4	6.9	7.1	3.2	3.4
Chile 2000	10.6	10.7	8.7	9.2	11.0	10.6	6.7	6.8
Colombia 1999	9.0	9.3	6.2	6.8	8.9	8.4	4.7	4.9
Costa Rica 2000	8.4	8.8	6.8	7.1	9.1	9.0	6.4	6.3
Ecuador 2000	9.7	10.0	7.0	7.2	9.9	9.6	5.7	5.3
El Salvador 2000	9.1	9.1	5.7	5.7	8.9	7.8	3.7	2.9
Guatemala 1998	7.6	7.5	4.1	3.1	7.2	5.8	2.4	1.4
Honduras 1999	7.3	7.8	4.7	5.1	7.6	7.1	3.5	3.6
Mexico 2000	9.8	9.7	7.6	7.4	9.5	8.6	5.6	5.0
Nicaragua 1998	7.2	7.8	3.8	4.6	7.4	6.6	3.2	3.2
Panama 1999	9.8	10.3	7.6	8.4	10.4	10.5	6.9	7.2
Paraguay 1999	9.5	9.4	6.4	6.5	9.6	9.0	5.0	4.5
Peru 1999	10.2	10.2	7.5	6.9	10.9	9.5	5.7	3.6
Dominican Republic 2000	8.8	9.9	6.3	7.2	8.9	8.9	5.2	5.0
Uruguay 2000	9.0	9.9			9.0	9.4		
Venezuela 2000	8.2	9.3			8.1	8.5		

Sources: Household surveys conducted in the respective countries and processed by Economic Commission of Latin America and the Caribbean (ECLAC), *Social Panorama 2001–2002* (Santiago, 2002), Tables 30 and 31. Data for Argentina are only for greater Buenos Aires. Data for urban Paraguay include only Asunción.

people aged fifteen to nineteen years, 3 percent had never attended school, 13 percent dropped out of school in elementary school, 8 percent dropped out upon completing elementary education (typically six years), and 9 percent dropped out during secondary education.[45] As a result, one in three persons did not complete a high school education.

School dropouts are disproportionately from the poorer households, first because most of them live in villages, where people are poorer, and second because, in cities, it is the poorer children who tend to drop out. There are sharp differences in the opportunities to proceed in school

[45] Economic Commission for Latin America and the Caribbean, *Social Panorama 2001–2002* (Santiago, 2002).

between urban and rural areas. In rural areas, the odds of never entering school are 3.5 times greater than in urban areas (6% vs. 1.7%), the odds of dropping out in elementary education are 2.3 times greater (23% vs. 11%), the odds of discontinuing school upon completion of elementary education are 1.9 times greater (13% vs. 7%), and those of dropping out of secondary school are the same (9% in each setting). As a result of the cumulative impact of these divides, the odds of never completing a secondary education are 89 percent greater for children in villages than for those who live in cities.[46] These rates are based on household survey data conducted in eighteen countries in the region circa 2000: Argentina, Bolivia, Brazil, Colombia, Costa Rica, Chile, Dominican Republic, Ecuador, El Salvador, Guatemala, Honduras, Mexico, Nicaragua, Panama, Paraguay, Peru, Uruguay, and Venezuela. Among those living in cities, 43 percent of the school dropouts belong to the poorest income quartile.[47]

As a result of high school dropout rates resulting from poverty and poor education quality, the levels of educational attainment of the population are low, and there are large gaps in the educational attainment of different social groups. These gaps further economic divisions – because most income inequality relates to educational inequality – as well as social and cultural gaps. Among those aged twenty-five to fifty-nine years old, the average years of schooling attained by those living in cities versus those living in rural areas was, respectively, ten and four in Bolivia, seven and three in Brazil, eleven and seven in Chile, nine and five in Colombia, nine and six in Costa Rica, ten and six in Ecuador, eight and three in El Salvador, seven and two in Guatemala, seven and four in Honduras, nine and five in Mexico, seven and three in Nicaragua, ten and seven in Panama, nine and five in Paraguay, ten and five in Peru, nine and five in the Dominican Republic, and eight and five in Venezuela.[48]

Consequent with the increase in the years of education completion, literacy rates grew significantly. Whereas by the end of the twentieth century there were still nine countries in the region where more than 10 percent of the population declared itself illiterate, Haiti, Guatemala, Nicaragua, Honduras, and El Salvador had rates in excess of 20 percent. This progress was impressive relative to the levels of illiteracy at the beginning of the century, but less so relative to the levels of illiteracy in other countries. Among the comparator countries presented in Table 11.5, only two (Singapore and

---

[46] Ibid., 25.
[47] Ibid., 114.
[48] Ibid., 251–52.

Table 11.5. *Illiteracy rate for countries in Latin America and selected comparator countries by descending order in 2000*

	Illiteracy rate, total (% of population age 15+)								
	1900	1950	1960	1970	1980	1990	2000	Males	Females
Haiti		90		79		47	50.2	48.0	52.2
Nicaragua		62		43	13		33.5	33.8	33.3
Guatemala		71	62	54		45	31.5	24.0	38.9
Honduras	67	65	55			27	25.0	25.1	25.0
El Salvador		60	51	43	33	27	21.3	18.5	23.9
Dominican Republic	57	36	33		17	16.3	16.3	16.3	
Bolivia		68				23	14.6	8.1	20.8
Brazil	65	51	39	34	26	19	13.1	13.0	13.2
Peru			39	28	18	15	10.1	5.3	14.8
Mexico	77	35	35	26	17	13	8.8	6.7	10.9
Ecuador		44	33		24	14	8.4	6.8	10.1
Colombia	58	38	27	19	14	13	8.4	8.4	8.4
Panama		30	23	22	14		8.1	7.5	8.8
Portugal	73	44		29	21	15	7.8	5.3	10.1
Singapore		54		31	18		7.7	3.8	11.7
Venezuela		48		24	15	8	7.5	7.0	8.0
Paraguay		34	25	20		10	6.7	5.6	7.8
Philippines	51	40		17	17		5.1	4.9	5.2
Thailand		48		21	12		4.5	2.9	6.1
Costa Rica		20	16	12		7	4.4	4.5	4.4
Chile	50	20	16	15		7	4.2	4.1	4.4
Cuba	57	24				6	3.3	3.2	3.4
Argentina	53	14	9	7	6	5	3.2	3.2	3.2
Uruguay			10	6		4	2.4	2.9	2.0
Spain	59	18		10	7	5	2.4	1.5	3.2
Korea, Republic of				12	7	4	2.2	0.9	3.6
Italy	48	19		5	4	2	2.0		
Belgium	20	3							
Canada	17	4							
France	17	3							
United States	11	3							

Sources: Data for 1950 and 1960 are from Nassif, Rama, and Tedesco, *El sistema educativo en america latina.* All other data are from the UNESCO Statistical Database.

Portugal) had illiteracy rates as high as 8 percent. The Philippines and Thailand, for example, which in 1950 had illiteracy rates as high as Ecuador, Mexico, and Colombia and slightly lower than Brazil, had reduced illiteracy more effectively than these countries by the end of the century. In the countries with high illiteracy rates, there were more illiterate women than men. Given the fact that educational attainment on average increased more for women than for men, this suggests that the most educationally mobile women were not the most marginalized.

In spite of the expansion in educational enrollments during the twentieth century, in 1999, levels of education for those twenty-five to sixty-four years old were still very low in Latin America relative to OECD countries. In Brazil, 63 percent of the population had only a primary education or less, with an additional 13 percent having some lower secondary education. In Chile, 31 percent had primary or less and 26 percent, lower secondary education. In Mexico, the respective figures were 59 and 21 percent; in Peru, 47 and 7 percent; and in Uruguay, 53 and 16 percent. These figures compare with averages for the OECD of 16 percent with primary or less and 20 percent secondary or less. In Canada, the figures were 7 and 13 percent, and in the United States, 5 and 8 percent. In other words, on average, three in five persons in the OECD countries have attained at least upper secondary education, and in Canada and the United States, four in five persons have done so. This compares with one in five persons in Mexico and Brazil, 1.5 in five in Uruguay, and two in five in Chile and Peru.[49]

Furthermore, the average levels of educational attainment mask deep disparities in educational opportunities of various income groups. Table 11.6 shows the different probabilities of ever enrolling in school, to be enrolled at the age of twelve, and to have completed grades six and nine at the age of between fifteen and nineteen for the richest 20 percent, the next 40 percent, and the poorest 40 percent in several countries in Latin America. Although there are disparities in the opportunity to ever enroll in school and to be enrolled at the age of twelve, the greater disparities are in the probability to have completed sixth grade or to have completed ninth grade from the age of fifteen to nineteen, suggesting how different structures of opportunity lead different income groups to have differing education profiles.

Different ethnic groups also have varying opportunities to attain higher levels of schooling. In Brazil, for example, twenty-five- to sixty-year-old

---

[49] OECD, *Education at a Glance. OECD Indicators* (Paris, 2001), 43.

Table 11.6. *Probabilities of enrollment at various levels and of attaining sixth and ninth grade by income group*

Country	Richest 20%	Middle 40%	Poorest 40%	Richest/Poorest
Ever enrolled in school (12-year-olds)				
Bolivia (1997)	0.99	0.99	0.99	100%
Brazil (1996)	0.99	0.99	0.92	108%
Colombia (2000)	0.99	0.99	0.96	103%
Dominican Republic (1996)	0.99	0.97	0.88	113%
Guatemala (1999)	1	0.97	0.87	115%
Haiti (1995)	0.9	0.93	0.69	130%
Nicaragua (1998)	0.99	0.96	0.79	125%
Peru (2000)	1	1	0.99	101%
Enrolled in school at the age of 12				
Bolivia (1997)	0.98	0.98	0.85	115%
Brazil (1996)	0.99	0.99	0.92	108%
Colombia (2000)	0.99	0.95	0.83	119%
Dominican Republic (1996)	1	0.98	0.92	109%
Guatemala (1999)	0.78	0.99	0.85	92%
Haiti (1995)	0.87	0.91	0.65	134%
Nicaragua (1998)	0.97	0.91	0.72	135%
Peru (2000)	0.99	0.99	0.94	105%
Completed grade six (15 to 19)				
Bolivia (1997)	0.93	0.89	0.55	169%
Brazil (1996)	0.81	0.69	0.33	245%
Colombia (2000)	0.92	0.88	0.52	177%
Dominican Republic (1996)	0.88	0.76	0.47	187%
Guatemala (1999)	0.91	0.6	0.22	414%
Haiti (1995)	0.6	0.36	0.1	600%
Nicaragua (1998)	0.9	0.73	0.32	281%
Peru (2000)	0.98	0.96	0.77	127%
Completed grade nine (15 to 19)				
Bolivia (1997)	0.55	0.46	0.21	262%
Brazil (1996)	0.38	0.28	0.08	475%
Colombia (2000)	0.73	0.61	0.25	292%
Dominican Republic (1996)	0.64	0.4	0.14	457%
Guatemala (1999)	0.65	0.21	0.03	2167%
Haiti (1995)	0.31	0.11	0.02	1550%
Nicaragua (1998)	0.55	0.28	0.06	917%
Peru (2000)	0.85	0.71	0.32	266%

Source: World Bank, *Educational Attainment and Enrollment Around the World*, http://www.worldbank.org/research/projects/edattain/edattain.htm, accessed June 11, 2002.

whites have, on average, seven years of schooling, compared with just over four for Afro-Brazilians. In Guatemala, indigenous people have two years of schooling, compared with more than five for nonindigenous. In Peru, indigenous people have less than six years of schooling, compared with more than nine for nonindigenous. In Bolivia, indigenous people have four years of schooling, compared with nine for nonindigenous.[50]

A 1998 survey administered to adults in Chile, Costa Rica, and Mexico found significant differences in educational attainment by skin color. Table 11.7 shows how the gaps are greater in Mexico, followed by Chile, and are less pronounced in Costa Rica. In Mexico, *morenos* are 64 percent more likely than whites to have completed only primary education, and *mulatos* are two and a half times as likely as whites to have only an elementary education. Conversely, *morenos* are 59 percent as likely as whites to have a college education, and *mulatos* only 27 percent as likely as whites to have reached college. There are corresponding similar gaps in income by color associated with these differences in educational attainment.

Along with gaps in educational attainment between the population in Latin America and those in other countries, and the equity divides in educational attainment, Latin American education systems failed to provide opportunities to learn at high levels to most students. International comparisons suggested that the quality of education in Latin America was low in literacy, math, science, and civic education.

In spite of the improvement in self-reported literacy rates, by the end of the twentieth century, the actual reading ability of Latin America students was significantly lower than that of students in other OECD and other middle-income countries. A survey of the knowledge and skills of fifteen year olds in the principal industrialized and middle-income countries conducted in 2000 and 2001 assessed to what extent students near the end of compulsory education had acquired some of the knowledge and skills that are essential for full participation in society. On average, the performance of Argentinean, Brazilian, Chilean, Mexican, and Peruvian students in reading, mathematical, and scientific literacy was at the very bottom of the achievement levels of students in all of the forty-seven countries participating in the study.[51] Twenty-three percent of the students in Argentina

[50] Inter American Development Bank, *Measuring Social Exclusion: Results from Four Countries* (2001), cited in PREAL. *Quedándonos atrás. Un informe del progreso educativo en América Latina* (Washington, DC, 2001), 10.

[51] OECD-PISA, The OECD Program for Student Assessment, http://www.pisa.oecd.org/ accessed June 11, 2002, also http://www.pisa.oecd.org/Docs/Download/ExecutiveSummaryPISAplus.pdf, accessed July 21, 2003.

Table 11.7. *Percentage of adults by highest level of education completed by color in 1998*

	White	*Moreno*	*Mulato*	*Moreno*/White	*Mulato*/White
				Ratio	
Mexico Education					
Primary	22	36	53	1.64	2.41
Secondary	32	38	30	1.19	0.94
Higher	41	24	11	0.59	0.27
Costa Rica Education					
Primary	50	54	54	1.08	1.08
Secondary	26	22	23	0.85	0.88
Higher	18	10	7	0.56	0.39
Chile Education					
Primary	35	38	50	1.09	1.43
Secondary	38	38	40	1.00	1.05
Higher	26	24	9	0.92	0.35

Source: Miguel Basanez and Pablo Paras, "Color and Democracy in Latin America," in Roderic Ai Camp, ed., *Citizen Views of Democracy in Latin America* (Pittsburgh, PA, 2001), 145.

and Brazil, 20 percent of students in Chile, 16 percent in Mexico, and 54 percent in Peru could not complete the simplest reading tasks, involving just reading words fluently, locating a single piece of information, identifying the main theme of a text, or making a simple connection. This compares with 6 percent on average for all OECD countries, and 2 percent in Canada, 4 percent in Spain, and 6 percent in the United States who could not complete the simplest reading tasks. Furthermore, only 2 percent of students in Argentina, 1 percent of students in Chile and Mexico, 0.6 percent of Brazilian students, and 0.1 percent of Peruvians are capable of completing sophisticated reading tasks. This compares with 10 percent of the students on average for the OECD countries, 17 percent in Canada, and 12 percent in the United States.[52] There are similarly large differences in mathematic and scientific literacy, with Brazilian and Mexican students scoring way below students in the remaining countries in those tests.

[52] OECD-PISA, The OECD Program for Student Assessment, Table 2.1a.

These results are consistent with those of another international study of mathematics and science achievement of students in thirty-nine countries (the Third International Mathematics and Science Study, TIMSS). Among the thirty-nine countries participating in the study, only students in South Africa, a country suffering the heavy burden of years of apartheid, scored slightly below students in Colombia.[53] The results in the science test were just as poor for Colombian students, with only South African students scoring below Colombian students.[54]

Mexico participated in the same TIMSS study but withdrew upon receiving preliminary results that placed it at the bottom of the distribution of scores. Chile participated in a repeat round of the TIMSS study, obtaining average scores far below the international average.

There is no evidence to suggest that countries that have not participated in international comparisons would fare better than those reported here. In a comparative study of student achievement in twelve Latin American countries conducted by UNESCO in 1998, the differences in average achievement between countries were less than one standard deviation. The top achievers in the fourth grade were Chile, Argentina, Brazil, Colombia, and Mexico, countries that performed poorly in international comparisons. Only Cuban students achieved at significantly higher levels than their counterparts in the rest of Latin America.[55]

The low levels of literacy and basic skills of Latin American students reflected the poor teaching conditions that resulted from ineffective and unstable policies to support opportunities to learn. In a survey of students in third and fourth grade in a number of countries in Latin America, only some of the students indicated that they understood their teachers' lessons consistently. The percentage of students who always understood their teachers was higher in private schools and higher in urban than in rural areas, as shown in Table 11.8.

The low quality of teaching was the result of insufficient instructional materials, poor preparation of teachers and principals, and poor communication between teachers and parents. These deficiencies compounded the impact of the limited circumstances in which many poor

[53] Albert Beaton et al., *Mathematics Achievement in the Middle School Years: IEA's Third International Mathematics and Science Study (TIMSS)*, (Chestnut Hill, MA, 1996), 23.

[54] Albert Beaton et al., *Science Achievement in the Middle School Years: IEA's Third International Mathematics and Science Study (TIMSS)*, (Chestnut Hill, MA, 1996), 23.

[55] UNESCO-OREALC, *Primer estudio internacional comparativo sobre lenguaje, matemática y factores asociados en tercero y cuarto grado* (Santiago, 1998).

Table 11.8. *Percentage of third- and fourth-grade students who reported they always understood the explanations of their teachers in a survey administered by ministries of education and coordinated by UNESCO*

	Large cities (>1 million)		Small cities		Rural areas
	Private (%)	Public (%)	Private (%)	Public (%)	Public (%)
Argentina	69	66	57	61	57
Bolivia	69	64	69	65	60
Brazil	53	46	53	52	49
Chile	42	46	50	51	52
Colombia	62	62	64	62	54
Cuba	0	90	0	86	87
Honduras	66	71	70	64	68
Mexico	66	60	60	62	60
Paraguay			71	74	63
Peru	56	63	69	64	53
Dominican Republic	69	67	62	63	63
Venezuela	74	65	61	71	62
	60	66	62	63	61

Source: My own calculations based on data from UNESCO-OREALC, Laboratorio Latinoamericano de la Calidad de la Educación, *Primer estudio internacional comparado* (Santiago, 1998).

children grew, without adequate early childcare, nutrition, and stimulation. Table 11.9 shows the percentage of elementary school children who had textbooks to support literacy instruction, the most basic subject of the curriculum. It is remarkable that in so many countries these rates are below 100 percent.

The emphasis of reform during the twentieth century on elementary education arguably undermined the development of a strong civic culture and democracy. A study of the relationship between education and democratic attitudes based on a cross-national survey of forty-eight societies, including Chile, Costa Rica, and Mexico, found that more-educated individuals were more likely to support democracy.[56] A separate study of the same data only for the three Latin American countries concludes that although the

[56] Alejandro Moreno, "Democracy and Mass Belief Systems in Latin America," in *Citizen Views of Democracy in Latin America*, 35.

Table 11.9. *Percentage of third- and fourth-grade students who reported they had a language textbook in a survey administered by ministries of education and coordinated by UNESCO*

	Large cities (>1 million)		Small cities		Rural areas
	Public (%)	Private (%)	Public (%)	Private (%)	Public (%)
Argentina	56	84	58	73	59
Bolivia	76	90	60	76	45
Brazil	84	76	85	93	92
Chile	90	94	93	95	92
Colombia	70	79	67	84	70
Cuba	97	0	97	0	98
Honduras	75	79	76	68	74
Mexico	96	100	94	98	96
Paraguay	0	0	76	87	75
Peru	55	84	48	62	46
Dominican Republic	57	68	57	63	53
Venezuela	71	81	76	84	70

Source: My own calculations based on data from UNESCO-OREALC, Laboratorio Latinoamericano de la Calidad de la Educación, *Primer estudio internacional comparado.*

majority of the adults polled do not trust other people (suggesting low levels of civic culture), the 30 percent who do trust others are significantly more educated and more likely to have reached secondary education and college.[57] A similar increasing marginal effect of secondary education on interpersonal trust was found by Robert Putnam in the United States.[58]

The emphasis of most public schools on rote learning and the limited opportunities for students to learn to think for themselves further limited the preparation of democratic citizens. How could those taught to parrot poorly understood ideas and to accept that truth rests on authority rather than on evidence and reasoning value the freedom to think independently?

The climate in most schools did not favor the development of relationships of trust among students and teachers. International studies

[57] Timothy Power, "Does Trust Matter?" in *Citizen Views of Democracy in Latin America*, 59.
[58] Robert Putnam, "Tuning In, Tuning Out: The Strange Disappearance of Social Capital in America," *Political Science and Politics* 27:4 (December 1995): 665.

Table 11.10. *Percentage of third- and fourth-grade students who report they trust their teacher and who say they constantly fight with classmates in a survey administered by ministries of education and coordinated by UNESCO*

Estrato	Do you trust your teacher			Constantly fight with classmates (%)
	Yes (%)	Sometimes (%)	No (%)	
Large city: Public	28	42	30	26
Large city: Private	23	47	29	19
Urban: Public	30	39	30	30
Urban: Private	26	45	29	21
Rural	33	36	31	32

Source: My own calculations based on data from UNESCO-OREALC, Laboratorio Latinoamericano de la Calidad de la Educación, *Primer estudio internacional comparado* (Santiago, 1998). Averages for all countries surveyed, unweighted. Countries in the survey are Argentina, Bolivia, Brazil, Chile, Colombia, Cuba, Honduras, Mexico, Paraguay, Dominican Republic, and Venezuela.

consistently point to classroom and school climate as important predictors of civic knowledge and participation. In a survey of elementary school students, less than a third indicated that they trusted their teacher sometimes and about a third said they did not trust their teacher. About a fourth of the students said that they constantly had fights with their classmates, as shown in Table 11.10.

Confining educational opportunity to elementary education of low quality prevented the development of civic and social capital and of democratic attitudes, which was in keeping with the conservative ideology and with the designs of authoritarian governments that saw the most important purposes of education for the masses as training workers rather than democratic citizens of good judgment, capable of independent thinking, and committed to universal human rights. Several studies of the curriculum of primary education in Latin America have found it lacking in opportunities to develop democratic attitudes or understanding of basic human rights.[59] Teachers often show disrespect to students and the social climate in many schools is one where students learn to mistrust and fear their teachers and classmates, rather than safe communities that model democratic practices. Elementary

[59] Eleonora Villegas-Reimers, *Can Schools Teach Democratic Values?* (Washington, DC, 1993), and *Civic Education and the School Systems of Latin America and the Caribbean* (Washington, DC, 1993).

school teachers were also limited role models of tolerance and acceptance of differences, important civic virtues in a democracy. A random sample survey administered to public school teachers in Mexico in 2002 revealed that one in five teachers would not allow an indigenous person or a person of another race to live in their home, a third would not accept a person of another religion, and two in five would not accept a homosexual.[60] Surveys administered to teachers in Argentina, Peru, and Uruguay found also a high prevalence of prejudice toward a number of groups. For instance, 34 percent of the teachers in Argentina had negative views toward homosexuals and 55 percent in Peru and 20 percent in Uruguay did too. In Argentina, 15 percent of the teachers, 38 percent in Peru, and 11 percent in Uruguay had negative views toward members of other nationalities or ethnic groups. Teachers also had negative views towards people who lived in slums, 52 percent in Argentina, 16 percent in Peru, and 33 percent in Uruguay."[61]

An international study of civic knowledge of fourteen-year-olds, conducted in 1998 in which Chile and Colombia participated, found that students in those countries had significant lower levels of civic knowledge and skills than students in the United States and other OECD nations. For example, almost a full decade after the transition to democracy in Chile, only half of the fourteen-year-olds in that country knew that in a democracy government is carried out by elected representatives.[62]

Illustrative of the lack of civic effectiveness of education reforms in Latin America are the declining rates of political engagement of young people in Chile and the low levels of civic knowledge of high schools students in this country, a full decade after the transition to democracy, after a major education reform that involved a complete revamping of the curriculum and the production and distribution of new textbooks. While a third of those aged eighteen to twenty-nine participated in the referendum in 1988, just over 15 percent voted in the presidential elections of 1999.[63]

---

[60] Fundación Este País, *Percepcion de la educación básica. Encuesta nacional sobre creencias, actitudes y valores de maestros y padres de familia de la educación básica en Mexico* (Mexico, 2002).

[61] Emilio Tenti Fanfani, "Les immigres a l'ecole. La xeonophobie des enseignants en Argentine, Perou et Uruguay," Instituto Internacional de Planificación de la Educación, Buenos Aires, 2003. http://www.iipe-buenosaires.org.ar/pdfs/docentes-inmigrantes_frances.pdf_page 4.

[62] Judith Torney-Purta and Joanne Amadeo, *Strengthening Democracy in the Americas through Education*, Organization of American States, Washington, DC, 2004. http://www.oas.org/udse/ingles2004/executive_summary-fin.pdf.

[63] Cristian Cox, "Formacion ciudadana y educación escolar. La experiencia chilena," presented at VII Reunión de la Red de Educación, February 17 and 18, 2005, Washington, DC.

THE POLITICS OF UNIVERSITY REFORM DURING THE TWENTIETH CENTURY AND THEIR RESULTS

Established during colonial times to prepare the religious, political, and intellectual leadership of the Americas, universities are the oldest of Latin America's educational institutions. The struggle between progressives and conservatives had limited impact in universities in that access to higher education remained elusive for the majority of the population in Latin America throughout the twentieth century. However, faculty and students at different times during the century framed the nature of the debate between progressives and conservatives and shaped ideas on how countries should develop, as well as what role universities should play in the development process. As part of this debate, universities opened limited access to the children of the emerging middle classes.

The public university emerged to challenge the dominance of the Catholic university. The university reform movement, begun in Córdoba in 1918, called for the autonomy of universities as a way to position them as critical interlocutors of the state. This reform, advocating greater academic freedom for faculty, would be gained with open and public contests for teaching positions. In the 1920s and 1930s, the "autonomous" universities emerged.

For most of the twentieth century, traditional public universities continued to be centers of recruitment and socialization of political leadership, as they had been in the past. They frequently challenged the state and accounted for more than one political transition. In Venezuela, for example, during the 1950s, much of the resistance to the military regime was organized by the university student movement. The key leaders of the modern political parties were leaders of the student movement. The same was true in Peru in the 1950s.

The progressive victory in universities during the twentieth century was in a limited expansion in access, which resulted in significant intergenerational educational mobility, not for the most excluded but for a small fraction of the urban middle classes. By the end of the century, the percentage of the population aged twenty-five to fifty-nine years with a college degree averaged 6 percent, and an additional 6 percent had some technical qualification reflecting some higher education.[64] During the century,

---

[64] Economic Commission for Latin America and the Caribbean, *Social Panorama 2001–2002*, 74.

institutional differentiation and experimentation grew, which produced, at the same time, institutions of very high and very low quality. Some of the new institutions, many of them private, served to accommodate an unmet demand at low cost. By contrast, some of the new institutions, the experimental universities, received significant financial support from the state and from the private sector, to provide high-quality instruction with less politics than traditional public universities.

The inability of the majority of the population to access higher education and the growing social segregation and isolation of public universities reflect a multifaceted victory of the conservative project through various complementary processes. One of these was the relatively low growth of enrollment in this sector. In 1997, 9.4 million students attended higher education institutions in Latin America. Although on the surface this is a remarkable increase over the 300 thousand students enrolled in 1950, it is a very modest increase relative to the 70 million increase in primary education enrollments during the same period. During the 1980s, just as a college education became more important than ever to aspire to leadership positions and for social and economic mobility, access to this level became more constrained. The ratio of primary to university students, which had declined sharply from forty-five in 1950 to thirteen in 1980, changed only slowly to nine in 1997. The corresponding changes in the ratios of secondary to university students declined from seven to three between 1950 and 1980 and did not change thereafter.[65] As shown in Table 11.11, by the end of the century, access to tertiary education in Latin America was significantly more constrained than access in comparator countries, a continuation of a trend characterizing most of the century.

In the mid-century, higher education was truly an opportunity for the elites, ranging from 6 to less than 1 percent of the relevant age group enrolled at this level. Access expanded most during the 1960s and 1970s. In spite of this expansion, by the end of the century, access to higher education was lower in Latin America than in comparator countries. Whereas more than half of the relevant age group attended a tertiary institution in Korea, the United States, Canada, Spain, Belgium, France, Portugal, and Italy, only Argentina had similar levels of access; in the rest of the countries, less than a third of the students had access to college.

Private institutions grew to fill the demand unmet by public universities. Authoritarian governments supported the expansion of private universities

---

[65] These figures are derived from Table 11.1 in this chapter.

Table 11.11. *Gross enrollment ratios in tertiary education ranked by access in 2000*

| | Gross Enrollment: Tertiary | | | | | | | | |
	1950	1960	1970	1980	1990	1995	2000	Male	Female
Korea, Republic of			7	15	39	52	77.62	97.02	57.02
United States			47	56	75	81	72.62	62.86	82.77
Canada			53	57	95	88	59.99	51.57	68.82
Spain			9	23	37	48	59.36	55.20	63.71
Belgium			17	26	40	56	56.99	53.52	60.58
France			19	25	40	51	53.58	48.16	59.24
Portugal			7	11	23	39	50.20	42.53	58.11
Italy			17	27	32	42	49.88	43.07	56.95
Argentina	5	11	13	22	38	36	47.96	36.43	59.72
Chile	2	4	9	12	21	28	37.52	39.12	35.88
Uruguay	6	8		17	30	30	36.10	25.59	46.96
Bolivia	2	4	9	15	21	23	35.66		
Thailand			3	15	19	20	35.27	38.88	31.69
Singapore			6	8	19	34			
Panama	2	5	7	21	21	30	34.90	26.23	43.82
Philippines			17	24	28	29	31.21	29.80	32.66
Peru	2	4	11	17	30	27	28.84	42.87	14.66
Venezuela	1	4	10	21	29	30	28.50	23.21	33.96
Cuba		3	4	17	21	13	24.16	22.42	25.98
Colombia	1	2	4	9	13	15	23.33	22.37	24.30
Mexico	2	3	5	14	15	15	20.71	21.14	20.27
El Salvador	1	1	3	9	16	19	18.20	16.30	20.11
Brazil	1	2	5	11	11	15	16.51	14.42	18.61
Costa Rica	2	5	9	21	27	30	16.04	14.54	17.62
Dominican Republic	1	2	6	9	18	23			
Ecuador	1	3	7	35	20	20			
Honduras	1	1	2	7	9	9	14.73	12.75	16.76
Nicaragua	1	1	5	12	8	11			
Paraguay	1	2	4	9	8	10			
Guatemala	1	2	3	8	9	8			
Haiti	1	1		1	1	1			

Source: UNESCO Statistical Database, accessed June 19, 2003.

as a convenient alternative to the more politicized and radicalized public universities, and elites saw them as convenient alternatives to protect their children from political radicalization.[66] These processes led to a growing social stratification of students in public and private universities and made it possible for economic and political elites to abandon public universities to the deadly mixture of underfunding, excessive isolationism, and management by incompetent demagogues because many public universities had systems of governance that rewarded political entrepreneurship over academic merits. The results curtailed the potential benefit of having achieved access to this level.

To sum up, some things changed while much remained the same during the twentieth century in Latin America. Education systems expanded, and the number of people declaring themselves to be literate increased. However, illiteracy levels remained higher than those of countries in Asia, Europe, and North America and the demonstrated reading proficiency and academic skills of Latin American students were at the bottom in all international comparisons. The opportunity to enroll in schools and universities also increased, but access to secondary and tertiary education was significantly lower than in other regions. The educational attainment of the population changed only modestly as a result of the educational expansion of the second half of the twentieth century. There were differences between countries in educational outcomes and access. Although some of these reflected earlier commitments to a progressive project, as in Argentina, Chile, and Uruguay, some of the greatest gains in educational opportunity were in countries where progressive education policies reflected a larger political project, such as in Costa Rica, Cuba, Peru, and Venezuela.

THE POLITICS OF TARGETED POLICIES TO REACH THE POOR

Along with the policies that supported the expansion of access to all levels of education, particularly to primary education, progressive policies sought to provide differentiated attention to marginalized populations. Initially, policies were developed to attempt to provide access to rural and indigenous children by developing alternative modalities of education. More recently, targeted policies have attempted to improve the quality of the

[66] Daniel Levy, *Higher Education and the State in Latin America* (Chicago, 1986).

education provided to marginalized children and to support their enrollment in existing modalities of education. These reforms did not last long and had disappointing results.

Because the expansion of education during the twentieth century reflected the interests of urban-based political alliances and the city-based industrialization under import substitution, rural education was largely neglected during the last century. As a result, indigenous populations, most of whom lived in rural areas, were marginalized from educational expansion.

The first of two important exceptions to this trend was the expansion of rural education in Mexico while José de Vasconcelos was Secretary of Education after the revolution. In his efforts to use education as the means to create a new Mexican identity (the *Raza Cósmica*) and to reunify the country after the war, Vasconcelos established primary schools and teacher-training institutions in rural areas and supported "cultural missions" of teachers, university graduates, and technicians who went to rural areas to work with teachers and communities in education, health, and organized campaigns to increase productivity.

Costa Rica provides another exception to the secular neglect of rural education. At several times throughout the century, reformers tried to improve the quality of rural schools, the orientation of the curriculum to improve the productivity of small rural farmers, or the links between the curriculum and rural life.

The reforms attempting to improve the options of indigenous communities through education were rare and short-lived. Supported only by their disempowered beneficiaries and by isolated politicians and social entrepreneurs, these reforms did not have the muscle to resist the fury of the landed oligarchies who saw them as all too convenient targets to express their resistance to the progressive project. Especially contested were the educational programs to reach indigenous groups with specific objectives to foster social and political organization.[67]

The Jesuit reductions were arguably the earliest initiative to provide educational opportunities to indigenous children. These larger forms of social organization included schools that sought to empower the indigenous for

[67] For an excellent discussion of the politics of indigenous education in Bolivia at the beginning of the twentieth century, see Brooke Larson, "Capturing Indian Bodies, Hearths and Minds: 'El hogar campesino' and Rural School Reform in Bolivia, 1920s–1940s," in Merilee Grindle and Pilar Domingo, eds., *Proclaiming Revolution: Bolivia in Comparative Perspective* (Cambridge, MA, 183–209).

self-reliance and collective action. The reductions of *Moxos* and *Chiquitos* in Bolivia, and the reductions in Paraguay, provided education linked to the daily needs and the local conditions where the reduction was located. There was also emphasis in artistic education, especially music. Expulsion of the Jesuits from the Americas in the eighteenth century interrupted this experiment.

At different times in Bolivia, policy elites targeted the poor in policy rhetoric. President Hernando Siles, in his inaugural speech of January 6, 1926, announced a national crusade in favor of indigenous people (*Cruzada Nacional Pro-Indio*), recognizing that education efforts until that point had excluded them. The crusade was launched in April of the same year but failed because of lack of popular support and, in particular, because of the opposition from the landlords. In 1931, a Bolivian educator, Elizardo Perez, argued that rural schools should be explicitly designed to serve the needs of indigenous children, establishing the School of Warisata. This school was designed to serve the territorial limits of the social and economic organization of the Aymara people – the *ayllu*. It was designed to promote the indigenous values of the *ayllu* and to serve the community by strengthening its traditions, ideals, and solidarity. It aimed to foster cooperative learning and action-based learning, strong links between schools and communities, and cooperation among teachers and students, among students, and among parents and students. It eliminated the school schedule and examinations, fostered bilingual education, the arts, and physical education, and eliminated content areas unrelated to life in the villages. The school was organized around a cluster. A number of small rural schools were attached to a cluster school. The clusters, named *nucleo escolar campesino*, included centers of literacy and popular education, technical schools, and teacher-training "normal" schools. This model extended to several dozen clusters, but was fiercely opposed by landowners and finally eliminated in 1941.[68]

In 1932, Mexico's Secretary of Education Moises Saenz (a former student of John Dewey at Columbia University) initiated experiments in education in indigenous languages and a pilot project to promote self-reliance, political organization, and mobilization of indigenous groups in Michoacán. This experiment, admired later by President Lázaro Cárdenas, led to the creation of a separate Department for Indigenous Affairs[69] under Cárdenas's regime. The experiment itself was short-lived.

[68] Juárez and Comboni, ed., *Sistema educativo nacional de Bolivia*.
[69] Guillermo de la Peña, "Educación y cultura en el México del siglo 20," cited by Pablo Latapi "Un siglo de educación nacional," in P. Latapi, ed., *Un siglo de educación en Mexico* (Mexico, 1998), 43–83.

In 1968, the socialist regime of General Velasco Alvarado in Peru included indigenous and rural education as an important component of the education reform. Education was to foster the process of organization of *comunidades agrícolas campesinas* through the creation of education clusters that would work as centers of adult education and organization. In addition, the content of the curricula was changed to reflect nationalistic values, which celebrated the indigenous contribution to Peruvian identity. Bilingual education was a component of this reform, including experiments to teach Quechua and Aymara as second languages to Spanish speaking children. This reform was fiercely opposed by the Peruvian urban middle and upper classes as well as by the landowners who lost their land in the associated land reform.

Progressives targeting the education of indigenous children also advocated organizing teacher-training schools specifically to educate indigenous teachers. Bolivia, in the 1931 Plan of Teacher Education, called for the creation of normal schools for indigenous teachers. With the creation of the Department of Indigenous Affairs in Mexico in the 1940s, indigenous teacher-training schools were created. These schools, and the administrative units in charge of implementing programs specifically for indigenous children, have barely survived the open and covert confrontation of the state.

Throughout most of the century, when schools reached the localities where indigenous children lived, teaching occurred in a language that the children did not understand. Language policy was assimilationist and denied the value of indigenous cultures and languages. By teaching indigenous children in a foreign language, and doing that poorly, with badly trained teachers and in impoverished conditions, schools served to legitimize the subordinate role of indigenous communities. Throughout most of the twentieth century, bilingual education programs in Latin America have been variations of a policy of "castellanization" where instruction in the mother tongue is used to transition the child into the dominant language, to eventually abandon the mother tongue.[70]

---

[70] Notice that in other parts of the world, such as Canada, Spain, Switzerland, or parts of the United States, bilingual education is not transitional but is "two-way," meaning it is designed to develop full competency in two or more languages in speakers of either language. Two-way bilingual education is predicated on a model that sees cultural diversity as a strength. Transitional bilingual education accepts the dominance of one language and one culture over another and seeks to teach children these codes of power, at the expense of their cultural identity. That I consider the introduction of transitional bilingual education as a progressive practice underscores the relativity of the concept of progressive. By reference to a status quo where indigenous children were immersed in a foreign language, the dominant practice throughout most of the century, transitional bilingual education is a progressive innovation. The progressive nature of policies to expand educational opportunity to indigenous children in ways that robbed them of an indigenous identity is clearly questionable.

Fernando Reimers

Nowhere is the large role played by broader societal values and institutions in mediating the implementation of education policy more apparent than with regard to the policies aimed at improving the opportunities of students of indigenous descent. Consequently, nowhere is the gap between policy rhetoric and implementation practice larger.

During a visit I made to Chile in June of 2003, the education representative of the Ministry of Education in Temuco (the poorest province in Chile, with the highest concentration of indigenous people, *Mapuches*) described the challenges faced by Mapuche students. He explained that there was a growing number of Mapuche high school graduates who had the necessary scores to pass the university entrance examinations but who did not have the economic means to go to college. The number of scholarships available to support these students was extremely limited and not growing. He said, "this is an issue that is politically explosive. It is only a matter of time until these students realize that they have the skills and the desire to be college educated but that they live in a society that denies them this opportunity. I can't understand how our political leadership does not see this." When pressed to explain why there were not more initiatives focused on college access of Mapuches, he expanded, "I often think that deep down we don't really believe that Mapuches have the same rights as other people. *Aqui a nadie le importan los Mapuches, y en Santiago menos.* No one will tell you this openly, perhaps we'll admit this among very close friends, but I think that is the real reason why they face such poor odds."

The view that many highly educated individuals were relatively indifferent was confirmed by the administrators and teachers of a high school for indigenous students described subsequently. They explained that most university graduates in Chile have very limited sensitivity toward the indigenous theme. This high school, run by the Catholic Church, had been selected by the Ministry of Education as one of the anticipation high schools, a flagship national program to foster excellence in secondary education (*liceos Montegrande*). The managers and teaching staff of this high school said it represented the vanguard of intercultural education in the country and that a good proportion of their students were children of Mapuche leaders. Although the quality of the facilities of this high school was impressive, the quality of instruction was not. In this high school, students were trained to be "assistant preschool teachers," "assistant nurses," and other similar occupations. No one among the staff was able to explain what the demand was for such occupations nor what kind of wages those graduates would command. It was made clear that the focus was not to prepare students for college entrance.

Amid a rhetoric of teaching students to be proud of their native language and cultural heritage and to develop self-esteem, we found a school culture of low academic expectations where students were engaged in low-order cognitive tasks. We found students in the track of assistant preschool teachers engaged doing handicrafts, and one class of students of assistant nurses playing and talking with each other as the teacher devoted his time to talk to four of them in a corner of the classroom. I interviewed a former teacher of this school, a Mapuche woman with a masters degree, who was very upfront in her criticism of the school. She said: "I know this school very well for I worked there seven years. Like the rest of the few Mapuche teachers in that school it pained me to see that we received the brightest Mapuche children and condemned them to occupations without future. Once some teachers in the school proposed creating an option to educate maids, the argument being that so many of our graduates ended up as maids in Santiago. I was furious and opposed it . . . I went to the newspapers. Eventually I was pushed out of the school . . . The option to educate maids was not approved after all but I suppose it makes no difference, that's what many of the graduates of this high school end up doing anyway." The persistence of race-based gaps in educational achievement, as well as the persistence of income-based achievement gaps, was indicative of the failure of the education reforms of the twentieth century to live up to the rhetoric of the policies promising equal educational opportunity.

In Brazil, language test scores of fourth grade black students in 2001 were two thirds of a standard deviation below the scores of white students. Whereas only 12 percent of the black students in this grade can read at an intermediate or higher level, 36 percent of the white students can read at those levels.[71]

In Mexico, language test scores of sixth-grade students in indigenous schools are two thirds of a standard deviation below the scores of students in rural schools and a full standard deviation below the scores of students in urban public schools.[72]

During the last decade of the century, a different set of targeted policies were advanced by governments with support of international agencies.

---

[71] Paula Louzano, "Racial Inequalities in Brazilian Primary Education," presented at the Annual Conference of the Comparative and International Education Society, Stanford, CA, March 22–26, 2005.

[72] Most scholarship describes the influence of multilateral organizations as a single phenomenon, characterizing it as the expression of a "neoliberal" project. I believe this aggregation fails to capture adequately the specific channels and purposes of these influences and fails to recognize the heterogeneity of points of view between and within international agencies.

The onset of the debt crisis and the adjustment era of the 1980s inaugurated a new kind of role for international actors and influence. As local elites built alliances with external groups and agencies favoring the integration of Latin America into the world economy, two related but different processes of influence on the education sector gained importance.[73] The principal mechanism of influence was the economic adjustment process itself and the international actors it empowered. Advocates of "shock therapy" to close the fiscal and trade gaps unintentionally caused significant harm to education systems. Pressed between the rock of a cartel of creditors and financial institutions and the hard place of the entrenched interests of the most powerful domestic political groups, governments slashed education budgets, often disproportionately to the budget cuts that were administered elsewhere across the public sector. The best teachers and administrators who believed they had brighter prospects elsewhere, or who were simply too demoralized to continue to teach impoverished children in deteriorating schools, left the profession. Entire education systems were set back as a result of this influence of fiscal austerity and adjustment.[74]

At the end of the twentieth century, Latin American nations were spending significantly less on education than the OECD countries. At the primary level, for example, the OECD spends 19 percent of GDP per capita per student. This is also the level of spending of the United States, compared with 12 percent in Argentina and Brazil, 17 percent in Chile, and 11 percent in Mexico, Peru, and Uruguay.[75]

A secondary, more complex, process of influence resulted from international institutions funding loans to finance education reform. Although international financing of education projects did not originate with the adjustment era, in a context of declining education budgets, the funds from loans and grants acquired a new importance. International agencies thus gained more leverage to influence the specifics of education policy, even though the proportion of education budgets funded with loans was

[73] Ernesto Trevino, and German Trevino, "Estudio sobre las desigualdades educativas en Mexico: la incidencia de la escuela en el desempeno academico de los alumnus y el rol de los docents," (Colección cuadernos de investigación #5, Instituto Nacional para la Evaluacion de la Educación, Mexico, 2004).

[74] Fernando Reimers, "The Impact of Economic Stabilization and Adjustment on Education in Latin America," *Comparative Education Review* 35:2 (May 1991): 319–53; *Deuda externa y financiamiento de la educación. Su impacto en Latinoamérica* (Santiago, 1990); and "Education and Structural Adjustment in Latin America and Sub-Saharan Africa," *International Journal of Education and Development* 14:2 (1993): 119–29.

[75] OECD, *Education at a Glance. OECD Indicators. 2001* (Paris, 2002), 68.

modest. Between 1991 and 1997, World Bank loans accounted for less than 3 percent of education budgets in Argentina, Brazil, Costa Rica, Colombia, Mexico, Panama, Peru, Uruguay, and Venezuela. The highest levels of education budgets funded with World Bank loans during the period were in Bolivia (7%), Chile (5%), Dominican Republic (6%), Nicaragua (8%), and Paraguay (12%). Latin America and the Caribbean received a total of more than US$1 billion per year for education between 1990 and 1994, with loans from the World Bank and the Inter-American Development Bank accounting for about three fourths of this total.[76]

Education specialists working in these agencies represented a diversity of views and were as likely to favor conservative as progressive projects. As a result of this diversity, these loans funded projects representing diverse objectives and approaches. They funded a number of experiments to support privatization, decentralization, and school autonomy, which converged with the efforts to tinker with efficiency that during the 1980s replaced the interest in educational expansion of the previous decades. However, they also funded projects to expand access and to improve quality in disadvantaged communities consistent with the progressive agenda.

During the last decade of the century, another set of transnational actors supported progressive initiatives. They included United Nations organizations, particularly UNESCO, UNICEF, and the Economic Commission for Latin America and the Caribbean (ECLAC), which reacted to the perception that the adjustment of the 1980s had eroded the social gains made since the 1950s. These organizations called attention to educational development worldwide, articulated in 1990 during the World Conference on Education for All convened in Jomtien, Thailand, and a series of follow-up conferences culminating with another World Conference on Education in Dakkar in 2000.[77] These institutions built coalitions with nongovernmental organizations. Together, these actors worked to influence national priorities along lines consistent with the progressive project. The last decade of the twentieth century began with a highly influential report jointly authored by the ECLAC and the regional office of UNESCO calling for renewed attention to education reform as the foundation for economic competitiveness with equity. Soon after, the governments of Argentina, Chile, Mexico, and Uruguay launched policies to improve the quality of

---

[76] Robert McMeekin, *Coordination of External Assistance to Education in Latin America and the Caribbean* (Santiago, 1995).

[77] Karen Mundy and Lynn Murphy, "Transnational Advocacy, Global Civil Society? Emerging Evidence from the Field of Education," *Comparative Education Review* (February 2001).

the schools attended by marginalized children. The emphasis on education as a strategy to reduce poverty was reiterated at every regional meeting of senior education officials. In 1998, the presidential summit of the Americas made education the key theme in its signed declaration, highlighting the links with poverty reduction.

Consistent with this new emphasis in policy as the century ended, governments in several countries supported initiatives to increase equity in education. Typically, these equity reforms were embedded in larger education reforms, which sought to increase quality and efficiency.

For example, after the demise of the military dictatorship in Chile in 1991, the Ministry of Education began to talk about positive discrimination – the disproportionate attention to marginalized schools – as a strategy to achieve equity in education. Soon after, government documents of Argentina and Mexico also explicitly highlighted compensatory policies as one of the strategies to achieve equity in education.

The actions that have been supported as part of reforms to increase equity aimed to improve the basic conditions in schools attended by low-income children. These include changes in funding formula to increase per-pupil expenditures in marginalized schools, as in Brazil; construction or repair of facilities to expand access; and more and better instructional materials. Efforts to expand access have also included developing alternative modalities to offer some educational opportunities to low-income students such as various modalities of distance secondary education in rural areas in El Salvador, Honduras, and Mexico or various forms of community-based courses to expand access in marginalized rural areas.

Other policies in this group have supported teacher education, teacher guides, and infrastructure, primarily in schools attended by the poor, such as a series of programs to improve marginalized rural and urban schools in Mexico; the *Escuela Nueva* program in Colombia to enhance the quality of rural schools; and the program to enhance the quality of the schools with lowest levels of student achievement, the P900 program in Chile.

Because these reforms have taken place embedded in larger efforts seeking overall improvement in efficiency and quality, and because the level of resources destined for inputs specifically targeted to poor students is a relatively small component of the overall level of resources for educational improvement, often these reforms have succeeded at improving the conditions of schools attended by poor children without closing the gap between these and other schools in the system. Improvements, however, have been modest. Another popular policy option to support the education of marginalized children during the 1990s was conditional cash transfers, scholarship programs intended to provide incentives to poor families to keep their children in school. These programs were implemented on a large scale during the 1990s in Brazil and Mexico, and on a smaller scale in a number of other countries, including Argentina, Colombia, Guatemala, Honduras, and Nicaragua. Aside from their welfare objectives, to provide income to families in extreme poverty, these programs were mainly intended to encourage school attendance, assuming that once in school children would learn valuable skills. In this sense, they were, as many other efforts during the twentieth century, helpful to support school attendance but limited in their effectiveness to influence learning, particularly because many of the children receiving these scholarships attended schools of dismal quality as discussed in this chapter.

CONCLUSIONS

Educational opportunity expanded during the twentieth century in Latin America. In some ways it expanded more dramatically than at any other time in the region's history. It did not, however, expand significantly enough to reduce the unequal distribution of education among different social groups or to close the gaps between Latin America and the OECD.

Absent throughout most of the century was a priority to give the children of the poor equal opportunities to attend schools, high schools, and universities where they would be supported to learn content to empower them to have significantly better options than their parents to participate in society. Toward the end of the century, policy discourse, and some action, indicated that some policy elites were once again considering this objective but mostly at the basic levels of education.

Close examination of the links between policy rhetoric and results demonstrates that education policy matters. What states and societies decide to do, how they define priorities and the programs, and actions they undertake and support have transformed, in part, schools and the education profile of the population. The citizens of Latin America have more years of schooling today than a century ago. Most of them declare themselves literate, whereas many of their ancestors a century ago could not read. Most are more likely to reach higher levels of schooling than their parents. Women have gained more than men from this intergenerational educational mobility in the region.

During the twentieth century, education systems in Latin America changed much and changed little at the same time. They changed much because they expanded – always as part of larger political projects. They changed little because they relied on a dominant model of schooling that did not help many children learn much and because internal and external educational gaps remained unchanged. The purpose to make schools teach all children at high levels so they could be competent democratic citizens was frequently challenged by the purpose to have schools either serve the narrower purpose of training workers for the jobs of the past or to educate different children for differing purposes. The tension between having schools reproduce the authoritarian past versus building a different, more democratic future undermined the ability of schools to teach much to poor children.

Educational opportunity remained an elusive concept, the result of negotiation and conflict between two competing ideologies, which had emerged at independence: a conservative set of ideas that saw education as a means to preserve privilege, and a progressive alternative that saw education as the foundation to build more inclusive societies. Politics were the dominant force that defined how these two competing views were negotiated. These politics were initially domestic, but as the region opened up (again) to integrate into the world economy, they were increasingly global. Domestic politics reflected the struggles of national stakeholders and issues as well as micro-education politics, when particular education stakeholders were mobilized to advance their interests. Domestic political actors developed transnational alliances to support their position. Domestic education politics, however, were dominated by large national corporate interests (states, political parties, businesses, and unions) and had little room for teachers, parents, students, and local communities or social movements. Transnational alliances supported renewed attention to equal educational opportunity as human rights and development organizations helped focus attention on the dismally low learning chances of poor children in a region where culture, history, and institutions were at odds with the simple democratic idea that all children can learn at high levels and to think for themselves and that it is important that they do.

Part IV

SECTORAL DEVELOPMENT
AND EQUITY

12

STRUCTURE, PERFORMANCE, AND POLICY IN AGRICULTURE

OTTO T. SOLBRIG

Agriculture is the most important and basic human economic activity. Without food, life is not possible. Yet, paradoxically, as a country develops, the economic importance of agriculture diminishes and its contribution to the Gross National Product (GNP) is reduced. This is because the income elasticity of demand for agricultural products is low. Once people have satisfied their basic needs, their attention moves to the satisfaction of other wants. Yet, as an economy develops, the productivity of agriculture increases, lowering the costs of production and freeing labor that moves to the industry and service sector.

A corollary of this fact is that a high contribution of agriculture to GNP implies a low level of development. However, agriculture can be the motor that energizes the economy. A modern agriculture, in contrast with traditional farming, has many linkages with industry, both as a user of industrial products (e.g., fertilizers, machinery, and agrochemicals) and as a source of materials for industrial enterprises (e.g., fibers, raw food products, and industrial oils). Modern agriculture is also a consumer of services (e.g., banking, transport, and research). Few countries have developed without developing first a strong agrarian base.

Latin American agriculture is very heterogeneous, reflecting the enormous diversity of landscapes, climates, soils, and local circumstances. Yet, there are some common features. The first and most striking is the importance of agriculture in the economies of Latin America. Since colonial times, the region has depended on agriculture and livestock as major sources of exports and employment. A second feature is the uneven allotment of land, the well-known *latifundio-minifundio* distribution. A final characteristic is the persistence of a large sector of small farmers poorly integrated into the economy and producing primarily food staples for local markets. They often are referred to as self-sufficient. Strictly speaking, very few farmers in Latin America are self-sufficient because they are tied to a market economy, albeit not very strongly or efficiently.

All through the long twentieth century, agriculture has been the principal source of foreign earnings in most Latin America countries. Mineral extraction (including oil) is the only other sector that rivals agriculture and, in some countries, most notably Venezuela, Mexico, Chile, and Bolivia, extractive industries have dominated the economy.

One characteristic of the Latin American agricultural export sector has been the prevalence of one or a very few products in each country: coffee in Brazil and Colombia; coffee and bananas in Central America; sugar in Cuba; wheat, maize, and cattle in Argentina. This dependence on few export products has made countries very contingent on the vagaries of external markets and vulnerable to price fluctuations. It also has led to boom and bust cycles, such as those of natural rubber in Brazil or henequen in Mexico at the beginning of the century.

Yet, in spite of the importance of agriculture in most Latin American countries, it has not been able to energize the rest of the economy and help develop other sectors. One possible reason for this situation is the concentration of the land in the hands of a small landed elite at the start of the long twentieth century.

The uneven land distribution in Latin America – the *latifundio-minifundio* duality – is a colonial heritage that became consolidated in the nineteenth century and is a persistent characteristic of the region. Land concentration endures in spite of repeated attempts at land reform. However, land concentration has many and different forms, such as the typical large *hacienda* that is labor rich and capital poor, the plantation that is also labor and land rich but also is better capitalized and more efficient than the *hacienda*, or the more capitalized large estate that prevailed in areas with labor shortages such as Argentina or northern Mexico, where there was investment in labor-saving machinery.

Traditional *latifundios* are known by different names – *hacienda, fundo, estancia* – but all share similar characteristics. Productivity per hectare or per worker is low and they normally concentrate on one product. Nevertheless, during the long twentieth century, the importance of the traditional *latifundio* has diminished significantly. A new kind of large estate dominates the rural scene in many countries, notably Argentina and Brazil: the capital-rich and labor-poor estate that takes advantage of the economies of scale of modern agriculture.

The traditional hacienda of the eighteenth and nineteenth centuries, with its powerful control over labor and quasi-independence from national law, has disappeared in Latin America.[1] Coercive labor was eliminated by the end of the nineteenth century (Brazil, the last country in the continent to abolish slavery, did so in 1888) but, for some time, debt peonage, company towns, and payments by chit kept people tied to the land. Labor laws in most countries have improved working conditions for farm workers even though salaries continue to be low. Also, inheritance laws and poor management led to the breakup of many estates, and market pressures forced modernization in the form of greater capital investments on most of the rest. Government attempts at land reform in many countries broke up some large estates and put pressure on others to modernize. Yet land concentration continues to be a characteristic of the rural sector in Latin America.

For the rural population, the transformation of the *latifundios* into modern production units was not always benign because it increased unemployment and often led to the eviction of workers from small plots they occupied in the haciendas and *latifundios*. The result has been an exodus of rural workers to the cities, where they often swell the mass of unemployed. Such migration was not exclusively caused by the modernization of agriculture because higher wages in cities were also a powerful attraction. In other cases, displaced farmers and farm workers migrated to the newly opened lands in the interior of the continent where there is an active agricultural frontier. Deforestation and land degradation has been a much deplored characteristic of these areas.

The precise extent and economic role of peasant agriculture in Latin America are matters of debate among scholars and social activists. It is undeniable that such a sector is an important component of the rural environment in Latin America. Yet, from the very beginning of Spanish and Portuguese colonial days, rural enterprises have been tied to the market, albeit often very weakly. Another characteristic of agriculture in the long twentieth century is the increasing marginalization of peasant agriculture.

Throughout the world, the twentieth century has created more changes in the rural sector than at any other time in history. From a tradition-driven and very conservative craft, agriculture has been transformed into a knowledge- and science-based enterprise. These developments have

---

[1] Tulio Halperin Donghi, "The Buenos Aires Landed Class and the Shape of Argentine Politics (1820–1930)," in E. Huber and F. Safford, eds., *Agrarian Structure and Political Power* (Pittsburgh, PA, 1995), 39–66.

augmented productivity and helped agriculture expand production to keep up with an increased demand from a growing population. They also have altered the relation of people to the land, introduced a more industrial approach to farming, increased the linkages and dependence on industry, made it more vulnerable to the vagaries of markets and commodity prices, and increased the environmental impact of farming. A majority of the population lives today in cities, another change that took place in the last fifty years. These changes in the rural environment are driven by a growth in demand resulting from population and economic growth. However, Latin America has not been able to benefit greatly from these changes in demand. The reasons and consequences are discussed throughout this chapter because they vary by commodity and by country.

In this chapter, I present an overview of the development of agriculture in Latin America during the long twentieth century, emphasizing the structural changes that have taken place. I describe the boom–bust character of some production (i.e., rubber, henequen) and its dependence on changing markets; the problems of overproduction (i.e., coffee, sugar); the vulnerability of Latin American agriculture to overseas economic conditions (i.e., meat, linseed); and the impact of modernization of the agricultural sector (i.e., fruits and vegetables). I also describe and comment on some of the transformations that have occurred during the long twentieth century. Space does not allow for a detailed, country-by-country, or commodity-by-commodity discussion of these changes, their causes, and consequences. Thus, the discussion is along general lines.

I first discuss land use and land-use changes in the last hundred years, including attempts at land reform. I follow with a discussion of the principal crops, their characteristics, and impact, including a consideration of technological change in Latin America. I close with a discussion of present trends and problems.

LAND USE IN LATIN AMERICA

Of all human economic activities, none is more intimately connected to the land than agriculture. Land use is almost synonymous with agriculture. Yet agriculture is increasingly more dependent on technology and capital than on land and labor.

But land still matters. In the first instance, soil and climate determine the type of crops that can be cultivated efficiently in any one area, and the technologies that have to be employed to bring them to harvest economically. The geographical location of an area in relation to markets sets transportation costs and affects land values. Finally, the topography, type of soil, climate, and technology employed combine in determining the environmental impact of agriculture.

The geography of Latin America has been an important determinant in its history of land use. A backbone of mountains runs along the western part of the area from northern Mexico to Tierra del Fuego, interrupted only in the Darien area of Panama. In South America, the Andes Mountains divide the continent into a Pacific group of countries (Ecuador, Peru, and Chile), an Atlantic group of countries (Guyana, French Guyana, Suriname, Brazil, Uruguay, and Argentina), and a group of Caribbean countries (Colombia and Venezuela). Two countries (Paraguay and Bolivia) are landlocked. In North and Central America, the presence of interior mountain chains were, for a long time, a barrier in the process of uniting the Pacific and Atlantic sections of the countries of the region (Mexico, Guatemala, Honduras, Nicaragua, and Costa Rica). Panama, because of the canal, is an exception, and so are El Salvador and Belize, which face only one ocean. The mountains have affected availability of overseas markets and transport costs and have acted as barriers for inter-American trade and integration. Finally, the Caribbean islands present their own peculiar characteristics.

South America extends from the Northern to the Southern Hemisphere. Consequently, it has an enormous diversity of climates that range from typically temperate climates with cold winters and hot summers in its southern end, to tropical climates close to the equator with even temperatures throughout the year and only a wet and a dry season. Furthermore, the presence of mountains creates new climatic regimes, with a tropical rainfall pattern but cool and even temperatures throughout the year, such as in the highlands of Colombia and Ecuador. Central America and Mexico repeat the South American pattern in a northerly direction, with a wet, tropical climate in Panama and temperate dry climates in northern Mexico.

The principal determinant of crop yield is water availability. Plants consume enormous quantities of water that they extract from the soil. This soil water is replenished periodically through rainfall. Water shortages reduce crop productivity. Yet excess water in the soil can also be detrimental because it deprives roots of oxygen and leads to reduced growth or even death. Sunshine is also necessary for good growth and excessively cloudy climates such as mid-altitude in mountains can also reduce growth. In Latin America, a gamut of precipitation regimes is encountered, from some of the most extreme deserts in the world, such as the Atacama desert in Chile and Baja California in Mexico, with less than fifty millimeters of rainfall a year, to some of the wettest areas in the world, such as the Chocó in Colombia or southern Chile, with more than seven meters of rainfall.

Tropical rainfall regimes create special problems for agriculture with their alternation of a rainy season with an excess of precipitation followed by a dry season with a large water deficit. The length of the dry season can vary from a few weeks in the wettest part of the Amazon Basin and the Chocó region of Colombia to seven months in the savanna regions of Brazil, Colombia, and Venezuela. The length of the dry season is the determining factor in the kind of agriculture and the type of crops grown in tropical regions. In areas with marked dry seasons, crop agriculture is only possible during the rainy season, eliminating the possibility of growing high-value perennial crops such as coffee, sugar, or cocoa unless supplemental irrigation is available during the dry season.

Temperate regions offer a more even distribution of rainfall throughout the year. Agriculture is limited in these regions by the total amount of rainfall and by winter temperatures. The Southern Hemisphere, with a higher proportion of ocean in relation to landmasses, has a more temperate climate than similar areas in the Northern Hemisphere, conditions that favor grain agriculture.

The soils in Latin America are very diverse, as is to be expected in such a vast region. The type of soil reflects the underlying geology and past and present climate. The physical and chemical characteristics of the soil affect their capacity to retain water and provide plants with needed nutrients. They also determine to a large extent their susceptibility to erosion.

Soils in the upland areas and mountain slopes of the Andes and in Central America are young soils of good quality. Soils in lowland tropical areas are, for the most part, old soils that are almost completely devoid of nutrients and quite fragile. The best soils are those of the Argentine pampas, which is an area of deposition of sediments of Andean origin. The chemical and physical characteristics of the soil can be a major constraint to agriculture in Latin America. This problem is especially serious in lowland tropical regions.

Constraints of water, slope, and soil can be overcome with technology – basically, irrigation, drainage, terracing, and fertilization. These techniques have their roots in antiquity but have been perfected over time. Their application requires capital that has been a limiting factor in the development of Latin American agriculture. They also increase production costs. They are often not applied, leading to soil erosion and land degradation. A very promising new technology to control erosion is No-Till agriculture (also known as direct seeding), which has spread very fast in Argentina, Paraguay, and southern and central Brazil in the last ten years. This consists of planting the seed directly into the stubble of the previous crop using special machinery and without plowing. It is the modern version of the Maya planting stick. It now is used in more than 50 percent of the cultivated area of Argentina, Paraguay, and southern and central Brazil.

As long as there was ample land and labor, extensive agriculture, which uses a minimum of technology, prevailed in Latin America. With the closing of the agricultural frontier in many Latin American countries (the exception being areas with remaining tropical forests), attention has increasingly been paid to ways to augment yields through intensification and replacing land and labor with capital. The history of Latin American land use during the long twentieth century, but especially in the second half, is the history of the change from extensive to intensive agriculture or, if you wish, from an agriculture based on land and labor to one that uses more capital and knowledge.

Reliable data on land use at the beginning of the long century are not available for Latin America as a whole, and individual country data are quite uneven. There are good data for the Southern Cone countries and less reliable data for the rest of the Latin American area. Good data maintained by FAO exist only since 1961. It has been calculated[2] that in the period between 1860 and 1919, 4.5 million hectares were converted to crops in Central America and 35.4 million in South America. Since then, 18.8 million hectares in Central America and 65 million hectares in South America have been transformed into cropping land. This is considerably below the 761 million hectares of potentially arable land in Latin America but close to the 133 million being cultivated in 2000. If these estimates are correct, only 10 million hectares were cultivated during colonial times. Table 12.1 lists the cultivated land by countries from 1961 to 2000 in ten-year intervals, and Table 12.2 shows land in permanent pastures.

Tables 12.1 and 12.2 show some very distinct patterns. The Southern Cone countries (Uruguay, Argentina, and Chile) show very modest increases in agricultural surface since 1961. Argentina and Uruguay, known for their cattle and sheep, show a very slight decrease in pastures, whereas Chile

---

[2] J. F. Richards, "World Environmental History and Economic Development," in W. C. Clark and R. E. Munn, eds., *Sustainable Development of the Biosphere* (Cambridge, 1986), 53–74.

Table 12.1. *Cultivated surface 1961–2000 (in 1,000 hectares) and percentage change since 1961*

	1961	1970	1980	1990	2000	1961–2000	% change
Argentina	18,277	23,851	25,000	25,000	25,000	6,723	36.78
Bolivia	1,280	1,525	1,875	1,900	1,944	664	51.88
Brazil	20,751	26,000	38,632	45,600	53,200	32,449	156.37
Chile	3,640	3,902	3,836	2,802	1,979	−1661	−45.63
Colombia	3,532	3,572	3,712	3,305	2,818	−714	−20.22
Costa Rica	285	285	283	260	225	−60	−21.05
Cuba	1,550	2,310	2,630	3,250	3,630	2,080	134.19
Dominican Republic	720	820	1,070	1,050	1,096	376	52.22
Ecuador	1,705	1,725	1,542	1,604	1,574	−131	−7.68
El Salvador	488	450	558	550	560	72	14.75
Guatemala	1,100	1,100	1,270	1,300	1,360	260	23.64
Haiti	410	505	545	555	560	150	36.59
Honduras	1,295	1,330	1,484	1,462	1,068	−227	−17.53
Mexico	22,420	21,688	23,000	24,000	24,800	2,380	10.62
Nicaragua	1,030	1,040	1,151	1,963	2,457	1,427	138.54
Panama	438	432	435	499	500	62	14.16
Paraguay	700	805	1,620	2,110	2,290	1,590	227.14
Peru	1,796	2,558	3,220	3,500	3,700	1,904	106.01
Puerto Rico	224	152	74	65	35	−189	−84.38
Uruguay	1,330	1,380	1,403	1,260	1,300	−30	−2.26
Venezuela	2,830	2,840	2,850	2,700	2,440	−390	−13.78
Latin America	85,801	98,270	116,190	124,735	132,536	46,735	54.47

Source: FAO FAOSTAT Database (Rome).

shows an increase of 35 percent. Of the countries bordering on the Amazon Basin, three (Colombia, Ecuador, and Venezuela) show a loss in agricultural area and one, Bolivia, shows a 50 percent increase in agricultural surface and modest increases in pastures. The remaining three (Paraguay, Brazil, and Peru) show substantial increases in agricultural surface and pastures (106 and −4% in Peru; 156 and 52% for Brazil, and 227 and 60% in the case of Paraguay). In Central America, Costa Rica doubled its agricultural surface in the last forty years and increased its grazing surface by 155 percent. The other countries in that region show increases between 20 and 70 percent in agricultural surface and in pastures except Honduras, which shows a loss of agricultural surface. Mexico (9.2 and 7.4 %) shows very little change.

Table 12.2. *Natural and planted grasslands (1,000 hectares)*

	1961	1970	1980	1990	2000	%
Argentina	147,000	144,500	143,200	142,200	142,000	−3.4
Bolivia	28,600	28,600	31,500	33,200	33,831	18.3
Brazil	122,135	154,138	171,414	184,200	185,000	51.5
Chile	9,550	11,000	12,800	12,850	12,935	35.4
Colombia	35,000	38,000	40,100	40,083	40,920	16.9
Costa Rica	915	1,363	2,010	2,330	2,340	155.7
Cuba	1,900	2,410	2,607	2,900	2,200	15.8
Dominican Republic	2,092	2,092	2,092	2,090	2,100	3.8
Ecuador	2,200	2,300	4,016	4,921	5,107	132.1
El Salvador	604	610	610	640	794	31.5
Guatemala	1,110	1,200	1,300	2,500	2,602	134.4
Haiti	585	635	509	497	490	−16.2
Honduras	1,500	1,500	1,500	1,500	1,508	5.3
Mexico	74,499	74,499	74,499	77,500	80,000	7.4
Nicaragua	3,900	4,100	4,600	4,815	4,815	23.5
Panama	1,060	1,100	1,260	1,400	1,477	39.3
Paraguay	13,600	14,000	15,100	17,995	21,700	59.6
Peru	28,191	27,120	27,120	27,120	27,100	−3.9
Puerto Rico	312	330	336	232	210	−32.7
Uruguay	13,847	13,697	13,630	13,520	13,543	−2.2
Venezuela	15,750	16,030	16,768	18,240	18,240	15.8
Latin America	504,350	539,224	566,971	590,733	598,912	18.8

Source: FAO FAOSTAT Database.

In summary, it is clear that the overall increase of 25 percent in agricultural surface and close to 20 percent in pastures in Latin America since 1960 was very unevenly distributed, being concentrated primarily in tropical countries. Two countries – Costa Rica and Paraguay – show the greatest increase in percentage of land allotted to agriculture and livestock raising, whereas Brazil shows the greatest absolute increase in surface dedicated to these activities. Since 1961, 246 million hectares of new land were incorporated into agriculture and livestock raising, of which 162 million hectares, 66 percent of the total, were in Brazil.

We can divide land use in the long century into two distinct periods that correspond with the time before and after World War II. During the early period, agricultural and livestock area expanded primarily in the temperate and subtropical regions (Southern Cone and southern Brazil, Mexico) and coastal tropical regions, and a second period when agricultural and grazing area increased principally in tropical and interior regions. During the first period, increases in production corresponded with increases in surface, whereas in the second, increases in production came both from increases in area cultivated and increases in yield. The change from extensive agriculture to intensive agriculture took place as the result of the occupation of most of the best agricultural land together with the availability of new technologies collectively known as the "green revolution." These consist primarily of the combination of more productive genetic varieties (High Yielding Varieties or HYV), labor-saving machinery (tractors, self-propelled machinery), and chemical inputs (herbicides, fertilizers, pesticides). The new techniques were diffused by governmental agricultural research organizations (e.g., INTA [*Instituto Nacional de Tecnología Agraria*] in Argentina, EMBRAPA [*Empresa Brasileira de Pesquisas Agropecuarias*] in Brazil, INIA [*Instituto Nacional de Investigaciones Agrícolas*] in Mexico) and by a private international network of stations known as the CGIAR [Consultative Group for International Agricultural Research] of which the CIMMYT [*Centro de Investigacion de Maiz y Trigo*] in Mexico is the best known.

Argentina is the best documented example of this shift in land use. From 1890 to 1930, cultivated surface in the pampas increased from 2,049,683 hectares in 1895 to 7,792,842 hectares in 1937 when all arable land was under cultivation. A long period of stagnation followed, and starting in the late 1960s, agricultural productivity in the pampas increased without an increase in surface. When, in the 1990s, export taxes and other controls on agriculture were lifted, record yields, especially in cereals and oilseeds, followed. Between 1960 and 2000, Argentina tripled its pampean agricultural production without increasing agricultural surface. For the country as a whole, total agricultural land in 2000 was twenty-five million hectares, seven million more than the surface cultivated in 1961. The difference is entirely attributable to the occupation of new land outside the pampas, made possible in large measure by the introduction of No-Till agriculture that allows farming in drier areas.

In Brazil, the situation is more complex. Southern Brazil (the states of São Paulo, Paraná, Santa Catarina, and Rio Grande do Sul) followed a pattern similar to that of Argentina: increases in production tied to increases in surface until the middle of the century and production increases attributable to yield increases without increases in surface in the last thirty years.

Interior regions of Brazil were very lightly settled during the first half of the century with a largely peasant agriculture, some of which was truly self-sufficient, and extractive activities, primarily rubber tapping. The modernization of agriculture in the southern states after 1960 led to the expulsion of many small holders that moved to the newly opened lands in the interior of the continent. Consequently, Brazil has two distinct types of agriculture: a very modern and highly capitalized agriculture centered in the southern states but spilling over into some new areas such as the states of Goias and Mato Grosso and also in parts of the northeast, and an extensive and poorly capitalized agriculture in frontier regions. Yet, even in these areas, there is increasing pressure to augment yields and enhance efficiency.

Central America and southern Mexico have seen, in the last fifty years, the largest transformation (in percentage) of forestland into agricultural land in Latin America. This process seems to have slowed down now because more than 80 percent of the existing tropical forest has been transformed into agricultural land or pastures (see Chapter 9).

Land use in the Andean countries with a large peasant population during the first half of the century was among the most traditional in all the Americas. Lately, there has also been a strong push in these countries to increase production and introduce modern technology aimed at small holders. The best example is Chile, which has developed the most efficient and capital-intensive agriculture in Latin America. Its limited arable land surface and its Mediterranean climate with winter rains and summer drought circumscribe agriculture in Chile. Consequently, just like in California, with which it shares many climatic characteristics, much of agriculture in Chile is irrigated. As is well known, this type of agriculture produces the highest yields.

AGRICULTURAL GROWTH STRATEGIES

In the second half of the nineteenth century, Latin America adopted a strategy of export-led growth. Because at that time the level of industrialization was extremely low, agricultural products and minerals were the main commodities available for export. This period coincides with a stage in the industrial development of Europe when there was a great demand for foodstuffs and minerals. It also coincided with the prevalence in the governing elite of Latin America at that time of a liberal economic philosophy intent on opening and economically developing their countries after the stagnation that independence and civil war had brought.

The economic growth that took place in the principal Latin American countries in the 1880–1914 period did not just happen but was the result of a vision colored by self-interest and adjusted to local circumstances. The landowning classes controlled the central governments. They were also the producers of the agricultural export commodities. Yet the infrastructure of roads and port facilities needed to bring products to market was practically nonexistent in Latin America and there was not enough capital in most countries to build them. There also was a shortage of labor in many countries.

Because Europe was interested in the growth of trade with Latin America, an unwritten collaboration developed. European and United States interests saw an opportunity for investments. European capital – primarily English – was infused into transport infrastructure (mostly railroads), finance (banks), and commerce. In some cases, such as the construction of the port of Buenos Aires, the government borrowed the money from abroad to build the necessary infrastructure.

Local interests perceived an opportunity for enrichment and kept the production of agricultural commodities firmly in their hands. According to Halperin Donghi, their earnings were higher than those of foreign investors.[3] An exception was provided by some plantation enclaves – most notably banana plantations in Central America and sugar estates in Cuba – that were foreign (mostly U.S.) owned. Yet this boom did not always increase savings nor was it necessarily invested in industry, but led often to conspicuous consumption by the landed elites, as attested by opera houses in the Amazon or palatial buildings in Mérida, Mexico, or Buenos Aires.

The owners of the land controlled the rural population (through a system of patronage and coercion). They also prevailed on the national governments to have laws enacted that favored their interests. This elite became known as the landed oligarchy. In some cases, such as in Argentina, the relationship of the landed oligarchy with English capitalists was so close that English customs and mores were adopted. Argentina became a virtual economic – but not a political – colony of Great Britain in the twenty years preceding World War I.

The development of the landed oligarchy went through three phases.[4] The first phase saw the establishment and expansion of the landed oligarchy. It started after the end of the wars of independence and the civil wars that followed. These had ended by the middle of the nineteenth century,

[3] Halperin Donghi, "The Buenos Aires Landed Class."
[4] J. Chonchol, *Sistemas agrarios en América Latina* (Mexico City, 1994).

although in some countries such as Colombia this did not happen until the end of the century. During this first phase, a group of leading families in each country obtained control over the land and the rural population. This was done in different ways according to the characteristics of each region. In most countries, one important source was the sale of fiscal lands at very low prices to a few bidders. So, for example, following the military campaign against nomad Indians in Argentina in 1879, known locally as *La conquista del desierto*, the central government obtained control over vast areas of land. Most of these were distributed to the troops in lieu of pay, the surface received being in relation to military rank. Because many of the soldiers and lower ranks were not ready to become agricultural pioneers at the frontier, they quickly sold their allotments to a few individuals for very low prices. In other countries, local ruling groups directly appropriated fiscal lands. Another source was land held by Indian villages or self-sufficient peasants that was taken over, such as in Ecuador and in Mexico, by neighboring haciendas without compensation. Finally, in some countries, most notably Mexico and Colombia, a source of land was the expropriation of estates held by the Catholic Church.

The second phase that started around 1880 and lasted until World War I was a phase of consolidation of the landed oligarchies. Taking advantage of their control of land, they monopolized the production of export commodities in their *haciendas* and plantations. In these years, the oligarchic state reaches its apogee. Yet here there are also great differences between countries. In Argentina, for example, there was an active land market during this period.[5] The third phase that lasted from World War I until the depression of 1929 is one of crisis and decadence of the oligarchic state, as it was increasingly challenged by a rising urban middle class.

The export-led growth strategy was initially quite successful, yet in the long run it was unable to match the growth of the United States for a variety of reasons.[6] In many instances, the producers of export products became very successful enclaves, not always well integrated with the rest of the economy. Their growth did not invariably translate into a similar growth in the sector producing for the domestic market. This is particularly the case in Mexico, Peru, and Brazil, but it can be seen also elsewhere. In some cases,

---

[5] Roberto Cortés Conde, *El progreso argentino 1880–1914* (Buenos Aires, 1979). O. Barsky and J. Gelman, *Historia del agro argentino* (Buenos Aires, 2001). Jeremy Adelman, *Frontier Development* (London, 1994).

[6] Victor Bulmer-Thomas, *The Economic History of Latin America Since Independence*, 2nd ed. (Cambridge, 2003).

that difference still persists. However, differences between domestic and export markets should be seen more as differences of degree than of kind.

The economic depression that enveloped the world after 1929 had a devastating effect on the growth of Latin American agriculture. Gone – or highly curtailed – were the markets for coffee, sugar, and other tropical, as well as temperate, commodities. Prices plunged severely. Latin American countries found themselves in very difficult situations and many defaulted on their debts. In order to maintain crop values, governments bought commodities at some fixed minimum price and warehoused them, waiting for better prices, or even burned them, as in the case of Brazilian coffee. Not until World War II did growth resume. By then, most Latin American countries, now attuned to the interests of urban sectors, adopted an import substitution growth strategy in the hope of developing industry. Tariffs, particularly for industrial products, were raised to favor local industries. Yet these industrial products for the most part were not internationally competitive and countries had to go back to agriculture to produce the export surplus that could earn the foreign exchange needed to supply industry with capital goods and raw materials. However, the new industries were unable to supply the rural sector, at a reasonable price, with the chemical fertilizers and pesticides or the machinery needed to modernize. The result was a slow growth of the rural sector as well.

Demographic growth in the second half of the twentieth century has been the highest in human history and population growth has been extremely high in Latin America during this period (Table 12.3). Although at the beginning there were serious doubts regarding the capacity of the world's agriculture to feed such a fast-growing population, the last forty years have seen agricultural production exceed population growth. A number of relatively simple, but powerful capital-intensive technologies were introduced such as High Yielding Varieties, low-priced chemical fertilizers, chemical herbicides and pesticides, and new labor-saving machinery. Because these technologies required less labor and had economies of scale, there was also a reduction in the relative proportion of rural labor and, occasionally, even in absolute terms (Table 12.4) as well as concentration in the ownership of land. Finally, these more intensive technologies also had negative environmental effects.

The reduced labor requirement of agriculture led to massive internal migration movements that are not yet over. In some countries, such as Argentina, Brazil, or Mexico, they coincided with a period of industrial growth that absorbed some of the rural population. In other cases, such

Table 12.3. *The population of Latin America: 1950–2005 (in thousands)*

	1950	1960	1970	1980	1990	2000	2005 (est.)
Argentina	17,150	20,616	23,962	28,094	32,527	37,032	39,302
Bolivia	2,714	3,351	4,212	5,355	6,573	8,329	9,275
Brazil	53,975	72,742	95,988	121,616	147,957	170,406	181,086
Chile	6,082	7,608	9,496	11,147	13,100	15,211	16,136
Colombia	12,568	16,857	22,561	28,447	34,970	42,105	45,580
Costa Rica	862	1,236	1,730	2,285	3,049	4,024	4,454
Cuba	5,850	6,985	8,520	9,712	10,629	11,199	11,369
Dominican Republic	2,353	3,231	4,422	5,695	7,061	8,373	9,026
Ecuador	3,387	4,439	5,970	7,961	10,264	12,646	13,798
El Salvador	1,951	2,579	3,599	4,587	5,112	6,278	6,876
Guatemala	2,969	3,963	5,243	6,820	8,749	11,385	12,952
Haiti	3,261	3,803	4,520	5,453	6,907	8,142	8,799
Honduras	1,380	1,894	2,591	3,567	4,870	6,417	7,199
Mexico	27,737	36,944	50,588	67,562	83,223	98,872	106,139
Nicaragua	1,134	1,542	2,123	2,919	3,824	5,071	5,774
Panama	860	1,126	1,506	1,950	2,398	2,856	3,067
Paraguay	1,488	1,842	2,350	3,114	4,219	5,496	6,216
Peru	7,632	9,931	13,193	17,324	21,569	25,662	27,804
Puerto Rico	2,218	2,360	2,716	3,197	3,528	3,915	4,091
Uruguay	2,239	2,538	2,808	2,914	3,106	3,337	3,455
Venezuela	5,094	7,579	10,721	15,091	19,502	24,170	26,468
Latin America	162,904	213,166	278,819	354,810	433,137	510,926	548,866

Source: FAO FAOSTAT Database.

as Peru, Bolivia, Paraguay, Costa Rica, Colombia, and Brazil, a part of the displaced rural population migrated to the frontier in search of land. This resulted in massive deforestation in frontier areas (see Chapter 9).

In the fourth section, I describe the particulars of the agricultural growth strategy in selected countries and in relation to different commodities. However, first some words regarding land reform are needed.

ATTEMPTS AT LAND REFORM

Some kind of land reform has been implemented in most Latin American countries during the long twentieth century. Land reform aimed at breaking

Table 12.4. *The rural population of Latin America: 1950–2005 (in thousands)*

	1950	1960	1970	1980	1990	2000	2005
Argentina	5,944	5,440	5,178	4,811	4,386	4,370	4,355
Bolivia	1,795	2,119	2,536	2,921	2,920	3,136	3,237
Brazil	34,268	39,560	41,741	40,366	37,347	32,119	29,161
Chile	2,529	2,447	2,352	2,091	2,191	2,162	2,086
Colombia	7,276	8,574	9,793	10,636	10,941	10,538	10,263
Costa Rica	573	812	1,058	1,214	1,412	1,649	1,710
Cuba	2,961	3,154	3,391	3,097	2,801	2,764	2,703
Dominican Republic	1,794	2,254	2,641	2,819	2,935	2,898	2,898
Ecuador	2,430	2,911	3,610	4,222	4,609	4,679	4,808
El Salvador	1,238	1,590	2,181	2,566	2,595	2,492	2,362
Guatemala	2,093	2,677	3,380	4,269	5,416	6,870	7,605
Haiti	2,864	3,212	3,631	4,161	4,871	5,236	5,373
Honduras	1,137	1,463	1,842	2,323	2,834	3,033	3,071
Mexico	15,906	18,194	20,730	22,735	22,920	25,341	26,066
Nicaragua	738	932	1,125	1,452	1,795	2,225	2,420
Panama	552	662	789	966	1,109	1,249	1,294
Paraguay	974	1,187	1,479	1,816	2,164	2,420	2,531
Peru	4,922	5,334	5,619	6,137	6,708	6,988	7,068
Puerto Rico	1,318	1,309	1,132	1,058	1,012	970	943
Uruguay	492	504	503	430	342	270	243
Venezuela	2,709	2,941	3,048	3,106	3,124	3,160	3,144
Latin America	94,513	107,276	117,759	123,196	124,432	124,569	123,341

Source: FAO FAOSTAT Database.

up large estates has been seen as an issue of social equity by many sectors in Latin American societies, especially after the decline of the power of the landed oligarchy. When large estates are not managed efficiently, land reform is also a way to increase production, and many economists advocated land reform on those grounds.[7] In practice, land reform in many cases has been a vehicle to disable rural-based political power groups, as was the case in Peru.

The hope is that land reform will help stimulate economic development by increasing production and capital accumulation that then can be invested in industry and service activities. Yet, in practice, land reform does not

[7] B. Johnston and P. Kirby, *Agriculture and Structural Transformation: Economic Strategies in Late Developing Countries* (London, 1975).

always lead to increased productivity. A case in point is Peru, where the land reform enacted by the military regime of General Velasco Alvarado did break up some very efficient estates that were replaced by less efficient cooperatives.

Land reform can be effected by expropriation or by the forced sale of large estates to the government that subsequently breaks up such estates and distributes them to smallholders, or it can be effected through tax instruments. The first attempt at land reform in Latin America was by the government of the Mexican revolution, which broke up all the large *haciendas*. The 1917 Constitution of Mexico set limits to the land area that individuals could own, and established the new juridical entity of the *ejido*. These are areas held by local communities and subdivided by them into farms that are individually worked during the life of the farmers. After that they revert back to the community, but in practice they often are passed to the farmer's heirs. *Ejido* land could not be sold or taken for debts, so that it could not be mortgaged. Although often held as an example, the Mexican land reform, after some initial successes, was an impediment to the development of modern agriculture in Mexico and was modified in the 1990s (for more details see the fourth section).

The second attempt at land reform was that effected in Bolivia after the 1952 revolution. *Haciendas* in the Bolivian *altiplano*, where most of the population was concentrated at that time, had maintained the structure of the local native communities. However, the communities that were within the jurisdiction of the *haciendas* – which were a majority – owed labor services to the estates in a system that resembled the European medieval *corvée* system. The Bolivian land reform involved breaking up those large *haciendas* that contained native communities, the abolition of the community's obligations to the estates, and giving the members of communities, which had been tied to the land until then, freedom of movement. At the time of the reforms, close to 80 percent of the Bolivian population was rural. The years following the Bolivian revolution saw a significant growth of the Bolivian population. There also were massive population movements to the cities and to the lowlands, both in the eastern escarpment of the Bolivian *altiplano* and in the northeast. This was an unintended consequence of the agrarian reform.

The Bolivian land reform did not bring back the traditional native community, as had been intended. For the most part, community land was subdivided into individual plots. It did, however, increase the living standard of the Bolivian peasant, and increase social services, especially schools and medical services. It also led to the occupation of the Bolivian lowlands, where an active agricultural frontier has resulted in extensive deforestation.

The Cuban land reform is the most drastic of all those carried out in Latin America. One of the first decisions of the Castro government upon taking over the country in 1959 was to enact the land reform act of May 1959. The law set a maximum size of thirty *caballerías* (a *caballería* is equivalent in Cuba to 13.43 hectares) for a farm, except for those whose productivity was 50 percent above the national average. These could be as large as 100 *caballerías*. Foreigners as well as sugar mills were prohibited from owning land, and tenancy, sharecropping, and similar agreements were prohibited. Former tenants, sharecroppers, and squatters got two *caballerías* of the land they had tilled free, and the owners of the land could be compelled to sell them three more *caballerías* for a total of five (some sixty hectares). Expropriated land was to be paid by government bonds, but that was never done. In 1963, a second agrarian reform was passed that expropriated all private land beyond five *caballerías*. Owners were compensated with up to 250 pesos a month for ten years.

The state in Cuba became the de facto landlord, determining to a very large extent the crops to be cultivated and the forms of production. The emphasis on sugar production continued (see the fourth section) and a high-input agriculture was implemented. When Cuba lost the support of the former Soviet Union, this kind of agriculture collapsed and has been replaced successfully by a more environmentally friendly system.

Contrary to the agrarian reforms in Mexico, Cuba, and Bolivia, which were the result of a revolution, a freely elected democratic government initiated the reform in Chile. For some time in the 1940s and 1950s, Chile's agricultural production had not kept up with population growth and the country had become a net importer of food. Many felt that the root cause was the uneven land tenure regime based on the traditional *hacienda* known as *fundo* in Chile (see the fourth section). The Frei government, in 1965, initiated a process of land reform that went through several phases in the next twelve years. The first phase, from 1965–70, was one of limited expropriation and capitalist modernization; the second phase of total expropriation and liquidation of the *hacienda* system took place under the socialist government of Salvador Allende; and the final phase, under the dictatorship of Augusto Pinochet, was one of retrenchment.

During the first phase of the Chilean agricultural reform, about 10 percent of the *fundos* were expropriated and incentives given for the rest to modernize. The expropriated *fundos* were organized into *asentamientos*, a sort of cooperative in which the former workers had rights in line with their previous role in the *fundo*. After a trial period of three to five years, hacienda workers could obtain property rights to the land of the *fundo* and could choose to divide it and farm individual plots, maintaining a loose cooperative arrangement, or could choose to farm the former *fundo* collectively. At the same time, the government tried to provide incentives for nonexpropriated *fundos* to modernize. The availability of irrigation water was increased, efforts were made to stabilize prices, and credit was provided. Land taxes were increased and *hacienda* workers were allowed to unionize. These changes forced the owners of inefficient private *fundos* to modernize or sell their estates. In this first phase, the approach was a "carrot and stick" one aimed primarily at increasing agricultural production.

The second phase took place under the government of Salvador Allende, based on the same law as the Frei government, but radicalizing its implementation by expropriating all *fundo* land. Government policy shifted from trying to increase agricultural efficiency to trying to eliminate the landlord class and transfer power to rural workers. Nevertheless, private capitalist farms in the forty to eighty hectares range survived and increased from 12 to 27 percent of all land farmed. Because of their high productivity, the importance of these farms was greater than their actual surface. Expropriated *fundos* were organized into large cooperatives that could reap benefits of scale. They were put under government management with former rural workers as wage laborers. The new units known as CERA (*Centro de Reforma Agraria*) looked more like collective farms or *haciendas* with the state as owner. In spite of hopes to the contrary, they turned out to be fairly inefficient because rural workers preferred to farm their own plots of land.

The agrarian reform in Peru has been the most peculiar one in Latin America. A military government under the leadership of General Juan Velasco Alvarado in 1971 executed it. Good-quality arable land is in short supply in Peru (see the fourth section) and it was very unequally held. On the coast, large and efficient *haciendas* and sugar estates controlled all the land and the water; in the inter-Andean valleys, a mixture of *haciendas, minifundios,* and indigenous communities competed for the land. The vast Amazonian lands were just being opened for colonization. Land conflicts were common, with occasional occupation of *haciendas* in the coast and a steady alienation of Indian lands by *haciendas* in the inter-Andean valleys.[8] The military government feared an agrarian uprising following the model

---

[8] Ably dramatized in the novel of Manuel Scorza, *Redoble por Rancas* (Barcelona, 1970).

of the Cuban revolution. There was a feeling in vast sectors of Peruvian society that a more equitable distribution of land was necessary to forestall such an uprising.

On June 24, 1968, the first agrarian reform law was approved by decree and the next day the large sugar estates on the northern coast of Peru were militarily occupied and expropriated. The new law determined a maximum of one hundred fifty hectares for coastal irrigated properties and fifty to seventy hectares for highland estates. However, owners of *haciendas* not expropriated were allowed to subdivide their estates into smaller units (usually sold to family or friends). A new decree in 1971 retroactively annulled all these subdivisions. The military government also used provisions in existing laws about absentee ownership and labor laws to expropriate holdings smaller than the one hundred fifty hectares limit. Eventually, most coastal holdings above fifty hectares were subdivided, as were those above thirty hectares in the inter-Andean valleys and beyond.

The Peruvian land reform was aimed primarily at the destruction of the power of the landholding elite that had dominated Peruvian politics for so long. In that it was successful. On the other hand, the division of the large sugar estates reduced their efficiency and productivity. Although many workers in the coastal *haciendas* and sugar estates benefited by becoming owners, those in the inter-Andean valleys did not fare so well. The largest problem in this area is not so much the large *hacienda* as the large number of *minifundistas*, which own insufficient land. The Peruvian reforms did nothing to alleviate that problem that still persists and was one of the issues in the *Sendero Luminoso* uprising in the 1980s.

Other land reform laws such as those in Venezuela, Brazil, and Argentina have had very little impact on land tenure. Those in Brazil and Venezuela have been basically colonization programs to given landless peasants access to land at the frontier. Argentina never implemented a real land reform, in part because the modernization of agriculture is fairly advanced and also because it lacks any significant population of landless peasants.

As Latin America moved from being a region with a majority of rural population to a region with a majority urban population, issues of land distribution and tenure have receded in importance. Concurrently, there has been a quiet revolution in much of the countryside. The traditional *hacienda* has disappeared and has been replaced by well-capitalized, modern production units that reap economies of scale. Ownership of the land has lost its importance and firms are as likely to rent land as to own it. The principal legacy of the various attempts at land reform has been the disappearance of rural-based power groups that existed at the beginning of the twentieth century.

LATIN AMERICAN AGRICULTURAL PRODUCTION

At the start of the long twentieth century, Latin America was the exclusive world producer of henequen (Mexico) for the cordage and twine trade and of natural rubber (Brazil) primarily for the transport industry. Today neither crop is of importance in world trade. Central America at that time was an important producer of cochineal and indigo, natural dyes no longer in use. Cacao, very important at the time, especially in Ecuador, is now of secondary importance because West Africa has become the principal producer of cocoa. Panama hats, made in Ecuador, were in universal use. Today most men go hatless. Argentina was the principal world source of linseed during the first half of the twentieth century; no longer. Some crops, such as soybeans, sorghum, and sunflowers, were unknown sixty years ago and are today among the major commodities produced in the region. Other products, which a hundred years ago were grown for local consumption, have become major export products because of advances in transport and refrigeration – among them, fruits and vegetables, flowers, and the growing of fish in aquaculture. Other agricultural commodities were and continue to be of importance: coffee, sugar, cattle, wheat, maize, bananas, cassava, cotton, potatoes, and sweet potatoes. This ability to adjust to market changes attests to the dynamism of agriculture in the region and its ability to conform to new conditions.

Latin America produces a great variety of plant and animal products for food and fiber. Yet fewer than twenty products are significant in terms of volume and commerce. This is not very different from other countries, given that about twenty commodities dominate world agricultural commerce. If individual countries are analyzed, we find that the production base is even narrower, with one to five goods dominating the statistics.

Another characteristic of Latin American agricultural production is the low level of elaboration of many of the commodities. For example, Argentina is a major world producer and exporter of wheat, yet it essentially produces flour only for the local market (some is exported to Brazil). An exception to this is the production and export of soybean oil (Argentina is the world's major exporter) or soybean meal (Brazil is the world's major

Table 12.5. *Surface, production, and yield of selected commodities in 2002 and changes since 1961 (surface in 1,000 hectares; production in metric tons; yield in kg/hectare)*

	Surface	% change	Production	% change	Yield	% change
Cereals	1,208,025	67.95	3,562,356	232.89	–	–
Maize	560,000	121.00	1,450,000	326.42	2,589.29	92.95
Rice	250,374	208.78	1,717,170	417.41	6,858.42	67.57
Coffee	228,500	158.63	158,979	272.81	695.75	44.15
Potatoes	225,538	−4.11	2,545,810	104.70	112,877.00	113.48
Wheat	160,000	104.29	190,000	123.70	1,187.50	118.61
Beans	70,000	56.77	65,000	52.83	928.57	−2.51
Sugar	60,000	14.44	7,950,000	−1.85	132.50	−14.23
Cotton	60,000	−75.39	115,422	−68.64	1,723.23	14.16
Citrus	54,650	314.96	628,186	239.74	11.49	−18.13
Oranges	23,500	197.47	280,000	135.69	119,149.00	−20.77
Oil Palm	7,800	25,061.29	190,000	68,245.32	243,590.00	171.63
Soybeans	1,900	90.00	2,800	180	14,737.00	47.37
Sorghum	13	987.50	26	987.38	2898.30	800.00

Source: Author's calculations based on FAO FAOSTAT Database.

exporter), and refined sugar. Although the region is an exporter of liquid and dry milk, it has little presence in the commerce of cheese.

Good production statistics at the beginning of the century are hard to come by. Only since the 1960s are reliable statistics available from the Food and Agricultural Organization of the United Nations (FAO). Table 12.5 lists some relevant statistics regarding the principal agricultural products and their change since 1960. Here I describe in a general way the history of the principal agricultural commodities in given regions and the economics of production.

Latin America is the world's major producer of coffee, sugar, and beef. It is the major exporter of soybeans and soybean products, and other oilseeds (sunflowers, peanuts, and palm oil). It is also a major producer and exporter of tropical fruits (principally bananas), and cereals (corn, rice, sorghum, and wheat). A booming business has developed in the production and export of vegetables, flowers, and citrus fruits. Brazil is today the principal exporter of orange-juice concentrate and Argentina, of lemons. Other important agricultural products are the staples of the Latin American diet: beans, rice, plantains, and cassava. These are produced mostly for the domestic market. The poultry industry has made great strides since the 1960s and poultry is becoming an important ingredient in the diet of Latin Americans, replacing beef in many countries. Nevertheless, the cattle herd has kept growing, especially in Brazil, where it tripled in the last fifty years and is today the largest of any country in the world. Cotton and sheep raising, which were very important fifty years ago, have seen a decline as world prices have plummeted because of competition from synthetic fibers.

Yields have improved significantly since the end of the nineteenth century, and especially in the last forty years, but very unevenly across crops and across countries. The best performance has been in cereals following the introduction of green revolution technologies. The worst performance has been in staple crops consumed locally such as plantains and cassava. Countries and regions with active agricultural frontiers – primarily tropical – show lower yields than other areas, especially temperate regions. Increases in yield are closely related to the level of agricultural research and the degree of technology transfer.

Space does not allow a detailed description of the growth and development of the many crops grown in Latin America. I therefore concentrate on a few in order to highlight their history, production, agronomic technologies, commerce, and problems. I do this in conjunction with a description of the history of agriculture in certain regions. I use coffee to illustrate agriculture in Brazil, Colombia, and Central America. Sugar is employed as an illustration of agriculture in northern Brazil and Cuba. Cereals and oilseeds are the topics when talking about agriculture in Argentina and southern Brazil. The new sectors of vegetables, fruits, and flowers are highlighted when talking about Chile. Finally, the Latin American diet's staple crops such as cassava, plantains, beans, and rice are discussed in conjunction with peasant agriculture.

THE GROWTH OF THE COFFEE ECONOMY IN BRAZIL, COLOMBIA, AND COSTA RICA

Coffee is the most important agricultural commodity in international commerce, second only to oil in terms of value. Latin America is the principal producer of coffee in the world and has been so throughout the last century. Brazil is the largest producer in the world, followed by Colombia. Other important Latin American producers are Mexico, Guatemala, Honduras, Peru, and Costa Rica.

Table 12.6. *Production (metric tons) of green coffee in Latin America and percentage change between 1961 and 2002*

	1961	1970	1980	1990	2002	% change
Bolivia	4,400	11,200	20,540	24,378	24,821	464.11
Brazil	2,228,704	754,800	1,061,195	1,464,856	2,390,390	7.25
Colombia	450,000	507,000	724,380	845,000	660,000	46.67
Costa Rica	61,769	73,192	106,389	151,100	155,200	151.26
Cuba	37,000	19,742	18,973	24,900	15,000	−59.46
Dominican Republic	36,210	42,494	60,091	59,377	35,476	−2.03
Ecuador	53,500	72,053	69,445	134,980	148,000	176.64
El Salvador	122,500	129,490	184,230	147,200	112,201	−8.41
Guatemala	100,600	126,546	177,430	202,400	235,000	133.60
Haiti	45,720	32,610	42,900	37,200	28,000	−38.76
Honduras	21,450	39,456	64,228	119,784	190,000	785.78
Mexico	126,616	185,293	220,040	440,000	319,835	152.60
Nicaragua	23,200	39,418	59,107	27,996	68,182	193.89
Panama	5,000	4,436	7,272	11,547	13,940	178.80
Paraguay	6,000	4,310	7,800	17,576	2,800	−53.33
Peru	42,643	65,368	86,177	81,142	158,979	272.81
Puerto Rico	15,876	15,422	11,884	12,927	12,800	−19.38
Venezuela	57,050	60,586	58,173	76,412	69,000	20.95
Latin America	3,438,238	2,183,416	2,980,254	3,878,775	4,639,624	34.9

Source: FAO FAOSTAT Database.

Coffee is a tropical understory shrub or small tree that cannot withstand frost. Two species are grown: Arabian coffee (*Coffea arabica*) and robusta coffee (*Coffea canephora*). Most coffee grown in Latin America is the higher quality *C. arabica*. In spite of its name, it comes originally from what is today Kenya and it thrives best in cool tropical climates. The best coffee is produced on mountain slopes between 500 and 1,500 meters above sea level. It can be grown under the shade of trees (its original habitat) or in the open sun, according to varieties. Shade-grown coffee is of higher quality and longer useful life as a crop but it is less productive. Sun-grown coffee plantations have a useful life of about twenty years and require chemical fertilization. Coffee plantations, because they are grown mostly on mountain slopes, are a major source of soil erosion. In Latin America, coffee plantations have been a major source of land degradation, especially in Brazil.

Starting in the early nineteenth century, virgin forest lands along the coast of Brazil in the state of Espiritu Santo were felled and planted with coffee. The heavy rainfall and the steep slopes combined to create heavy soil erosion, exposing the roots of the shrubs and eventually reducing productivity. At that point, the land was abandoned and the process repeated on new land. From the state of Espiritu Santo, coffee moved in Brazil to the states of Minas Gerais first and then São Paulo, which became the largest coffee-producing state of Brazil during the twentieth century. Because of this movement, coffee became known in Brazil as an itinerant crop.

During the first half of the twentieth century, coffee was the principal agricultural product of Brazil and after the collapse of the rubber boom in 1919, it accounted for more than 70 percent of Brazil's export earnings. The coffee blight that destroyed plantations in the Far East at the end of the nineteenth century was a contributing factor in Brazil's market dominance. However, overproduction in Brazil and other Latin American countries and import restrictions in Europe depressed prices that fluctuated significantly.

In an effort to stabilize prices, and given Brazil's near-monopoly position, Brazilian coffee interests convinced their government to engage in a scheme known as *valorization*. It consisted of buying and warehousing coffee when its price was below a given floor (0.15 U.S. $/Kg) and reselling it when it rose above a given ceiling. The scheme was at first successful, but during the world depression in the 1930s, the government had to burn some of its coffee reserves because of a lack of a market. The scheme also had the effect of losing market share for Brazil because other producers took advantage of times of higher prices to increase their planted surface.

After World War II, coffee producers and the United States entered into an agreement to stabilize coffee prices. Countries set production quotas with the participation of the principal consumer, the United States. However, countries could not keep production below the agreed limits, whereas other countries that were not part of the agreement gained market share. The coffee agreement failed in spite of a second attempt.

Agreements to control prices of agricultural commodities are bound to fail. It is not in the interest of consuming countries and the temptation by producing countries to free ride is too high. Such agreements can only work with nonrenewable resources – and then not always – when there is a dominant producer that can impose discipline on the smaller producer. This is not the case with agricultural commodities.

Colombia is the second producer of coffee in Latin America. Contrary to Brazil, where coffee is produced in large estates with an emphasis on high yields at the expense of quality, Colombian coffee is produced by both large estates and smallholders with an emphasis on quality in order to obtain a better price.

Coffee diffused into Colombia from Venezuela early in the nineteenth century. Coffee was first grown in the 1830s in the state of Santander and exported via Lake Maracaibo. From Santander it spread to the state of Antioquia, which became – and still is – the center of coffee growing in Colombia. From the beginning, coffee in Colombia was grown in the shade rather than in the open sun, as it was in Brazil. Although the large coffee *hacienda* dominated production, a system of sharecropping and small producers developed that distinguishes Colombia from Brazil. Shortages of labor, rather than of land, constrained the growth of coffee in Colombia. This resulted in a mixture of different types of producers that included large coffee estates, and different systems of sharecropping.

Colombia has excellent growing conditions and, given that from the start the shrubs were grown in the shade, their coffee has had a well-deserved reputation for quality. Coffee growing is a labor-intensive enterprise. Seeds are germinated in specially prepared beds and transplanted to the field after six months. The shrubs then take two years before they bear fruit. Coffee plants have to be pruned by hand yearly. Harvesting, which is also a manual operation, normally requires at least three collections when the fruits are ripening because the berries do not mature simultaneously. The fruits then undergo a process of depulping, drying, and sorting to produce the so-called "green" coffee, that is, coffee ready to be toasted and ground into the product utilized to make the drink. These last operations are normally done in the consuming countries.

Colombia's civil wars lasted longer than in other South American countries, but once a semblance of order had been established, coffee exports tripled between 1894 and the end of the century (Table 12.7). Coffee brought Colombia out of an economic slump into which it had fallen as the result of the civil wars. By 1930, Colombia was exporting more than one million bags and the country had became the second largest producer after Brazil, renowned for its mild and high-quality coffees.

Coffee producing stayed in native hands and, as mentioned, it was grown under a diversity of arrangements, from the large coffee *finca* to the small estate of a few hectares, and with a diversity of sharecropping arrangements. Contrary to other countries, coffee growers never coalesced into a landed oligarchy. Foreign capital was invested into transport (railroads) and processing and, especially, commercialization and export. The world depression

Table 12.7. *Coffee exports from Colombia in five-year averages (1880–1909)*

Year	Exports (Kg)
1880–1884	4,899,960
1885–1889	5,971,980
1890–1894	8,526,960
1895–1899	26,539,980
1906–1909	37,771,980

Source: Marco Palacios, *Coffee in Colombia 1850–1970* (Cambridge, 1980).

of 1930 ended the coffee boom as the bottom fell out of the market. Since 1961, the area dedicated to coffee has not changed although production has increased because of increases in yields. The sharp fluctuations in price have created a crisis atmosphere in Colombia. Many smallholders moved to frontier regions and switched to the growing of coca that is much more profitable in spite of the risks involved.

Coffee was introduced into Costa Rica in the 1830s. Costa Rica was then a country of smallholders, with a small population concentrated in the central plateau around the city of Cartago. Coffee was – and is – grown primarily on the Pacific slope of the mountains up to 1,500 meters. Volcanic soil is particularly valued for coffee growing. It quickly increased in worth, and soon a concentration of it in a few hands followed. This process was furthered by the need of capital to process the coffee beans. Small producers who could not obtain the equipment to process the coffee beans were unable to compete and sold their land to those with modern facilities.

The first shipments of Costa Rican coffee to Europe in 1850 went via Cape Horn because the country lacked ports and roads to the Caribbean Sea. Yet, even so, coffee exports started growing and the government encouraged its growth by giving away fiscal lands for the growth of this crop. The coffee boom began and Costa Rica, which was the most backward of the Central American countries, was transformed into one of the more prosperous. From Costa Rica, coffee growing diffused to other Central American countries, especially Guatemala and El Salvador, and to Mexico.

It is estimated that in the mid-nineteenth century there were about 4,000 hectares planted in coffee in Costa Rica. This surface grew slowly all through the long twentieth century to today's 103,500 hectares – a twenty-five–fold increase. Forty percent of that increase has taken place since 1960.

The rate of growth was damped primarily by labor shortages because there did not exist a large Indian population in the country and most farmers owned small plots. This situation resulted in better salaries and working conditions in Costa Rica than in other Central American countries (especially Guatemala). It also checked the growth of the Costa Rican coffee *haciendas* that were modest by the standards of other coffee-producing countries. Until recently, smallholders continued to dominate the rural landscape in Costa Rica (not necessarily exclusively producing coffee) and they are probably one factor that has made Costa Rica the most democratic country in Central America.

Nevertheless, coffee interests dominated the body politic in Costa Rica because coffee was such a large part of the economy, and it still plays a very important role. In the second half of the nineteenth century, coffee accounted for between 70 and 90 percent of exports.[9] The construction of a railroad to the Caribbean and building of adequate port facilities in Puerto Limón aided the development of the coffee boom. Costa Rica is now trying to increase market share by concentrating on quality and trying to sell directly to consumers in the United States through producer cooperatives and other marketing arrangements. There is also a push to produce "shade" and "organic" coffee (produced without agrochemicals) that sells at a premium to a selected public in the United States and Europe. However, soil erosion continues to be a serious problem.

Table 12.8 compares the production, surface, and yields of coffee in the last forty years in the three countries analyzed. Coffee, which was the major agricultural product of Brazil during the first half of the century, has been steadily declining in importance. Although Brazil is still the world's principal producer, production has remained steady with an increase of slightly over 7 percent in forty years, and a loss of 46 percent of the surface dedicated to this crop. Yields, however, have doubled. Colombia, which still depends heavily on coffee exports, has seen an increase of close to 50 percent in production because of greater yields with essentially no change in surface. Costa Rica has increased production by 150 percent because of a combination of a 50 percent increase in surface dedicated to the crop and a 77 percent increase in yields. Whereas Brazil has successfully reduced its dependence on coffee, Colombia and especially Costa Rica have increased theirs. Given the glut of coffee in the world and the low prices, the strategy of Costa Rica and Colombia presents definite risks. Both of these countries

---

[9] Chonchol, *Sistemas agrarios en América Latina*, 175.

Table 12.8. *Production, surface, and yields of coffee in Brazil, Colombia, and Costa Rica between 1961 and 2002*

	1961	1970	1980	1990	2002	% change
Production (metric tons)						
Brazil	2,228,704	754,800	1,061,195	1,464,856	2,390,390	7.25
Colombia	450,000	507,000	724,380	845,000	660,000	46.67
Costa Rica	61,769	73,192	106,389	151,100	155,200	151.26
Surface (hectares)						
Brazil	4,383,820	2,402,993	2,433,604	2,908,960	2,367,510	−45.99
Colombia	832,000	830,000	1,084,000	1,000,000	805,000	−3.25
Costa Rica	73,000	95,000	81,750	115,000	103,500	41.78
Yield (Kg/hectare)						
Brazil	508.39	314.11	436.06	503.57	1,009.66	98.60
Colombia	540.87	610.84	668.25	845.00	819.88	51.59
Costa Rica	846.15	770.44	1,301.39	1,313.91	1,499.52	77.22

Source: FAO FAOSTAT Database.

are trying to gain market share by emphasizing quality, and leaving the market for low-quality caturra coffee (used primarily for making instant coffees) to low-cost producers, especially Vietnam and African countries.

SUGAR AND AGRICULTURE IN NORTHERN BRAZIL AND CUBA

Columbus brought sugar cane to America on his second voyage. Yet it was in Brazil, especially in the state of Bahia, and not in the Caribbean, where it first was grown extensively and became the first major agricultural export from the Americas. Sugar has ever since been a very important high-value agricultural commodity in Latin America. The region produces almost half of all the cane sugar produced worldwide (44% in 2002, up from 43% in 1961) and almost half of the surface dedicated to this crop in the world (44% in 2002, down from 49.5% in 1961) is in Latin America. Sugar, more than any other commodity, led to the importation of African slaves and maintained this commerce for close to three centuries.

Although sugar cane is grown in almost all Latin American countries and is a major commodity in most, it is especially important in the economy of five of them: Cuba, Brazil, Mexico, Guatemala, and Peru. Argentina, the fifth largest producer in Latin America, does it behind a huge protective barrier, and in Venezuela, the sixth producer in the area, sugar growing is overshadowed in importance by oil. Because Chapter 10 of Volume I deals specifically with the production technology of sugar, we will only indicate some historical characteristics connected with this crop.

Sugar, like coffee, is a high-value commodity. Sugar is extracted from two very different plants: sugar cane and sugar beet. The sugar beet has been cultivated for only two hundred years. It is a plant of temperate regions and the costs of production and its yields make it uncompetitive with sugar cane, the most efficient crop known in converting sunlight into carbohydrate. However, given the high value of sugar, countries that grow sugar beets protect their domestic production with tariff barriers and import quotas.

Sugar is also the only agricultural food commodity that is not a necessary ingredient of the human diet. Nevertheless, people crave it. Sugar is probably the agricultural commodity that is subjected to the greatest degree of tariff and export and import controls. The United States sets strict import quotas that are allocated to countries based on political and not economic considerations. So, for example, Cuba, the principal exporter of sugar in the world, lost its U.S. quota after 1960.

Sugar is also the raw material for the production of ethanol used in the elaboration of alcoholic drinks. This alcohol has also been hailed as a sustainable alternative to gasoline. Alcohol is a better fuel than gasoline from an environmental standpoint because it burns cleaner – that is, without harmful byproducts other than carbon dioxide. The use of alcohol as fuel made the city of São Paulo, with its fifteen million inhabitants and enormous fleet of cars, almost smog-free.

In the 1970s, and following the world oil crisis, Brazil adopted a very ambitious program to replace half the gasoline used by automobiles with alcohol. For this purpose, a comprehensive production technology was developed that industrializes the entire sugar cane plant. The sugar is fermented into ethyl alcohol, whereas the bagasse is used for making paper and cardboard. The remaining part of the plant is then used as fuel in the sugar factories. In order to encourage this program, the government guaranteed a minimum price. The program has been technically very successful and Brazil replaced about half its gasoline consumption with alcohol for a fleet of cars equipped with special carburetors. However, the program has never been competitive in price, especially when oil prices have been low. The government is in the process of reducing the subsidies to the alcohol program that will eventually be phased out. This will almost certainly mean the end of this experiment.

However, it is Cuba – and not Brazil – that is most dependent on sugar. At one time, Cuba was the largest producer of sugar in the region, with more than eight million tons, but after the loss of much of its overseas markets in the 1990s, its production has plummeted as land has been turned over to food production.

Cuba is the best example of the strategy of export-led growth.[10] Sugar was produced extensively until the middle of the nineteenth century. The cane was cut by hand and taken to the factory (*ingenio*) and pressed in mills (*trapiches*) that were moved by animal or waterpower. The cane juice was then concentrated in large copper kettles over open fires. Starting in the middle of last century, this process was replaced by steam-driven mills (*centrales*) capable of crushing huge amounts of cane, which was then concentrated in vats under vacuum and then refined by passing it through charcoal filters. This process allowed the recovery of much more sugar from the cane than before and resulted in a product of higher quality. In the second half of the nineteenth century, the European and U.S. markets, together with an appetite for more foodstuffs, also developed a sweet tooth. In the United Kingdom alone, the consumption of sugar rose from 16.3 pounds per person in the 1840–4 period to 82 pounds in the 1895–9 period. Supplying this market became a huge business. The new large and efficient mills replaced and eliminated the old ones. Between 1846 and 1890, while sugar production in Cuba increased from three hundred thousand tons to one million, the number of mills was reduced from 14,421 to 400, a 12,000 percent increase in the capacity of individual mills.

The new factories had to be fed enormous quantities of sugar cane to be made to pay, and this required a better system of moving sugar from field to factory. Oxen carts were replaced by narrow-gauge railroads. At the beginning of this modernization process, cane was produced by smallholders (*colonos*) that sold the cane to the factories. But the need to count on a steady and reliable supply led the *centrales* to start acquiring the land of the *colonos*, who became, in fact, sharecroppers and eventually employees. Inevitably, a very small number of estates dominated the sugar industry of Cuba.

The cane continued to be harvested by hand with machetes, and this became the bottleneck in the new system. New immigrants flocked to Cuba primarily from other Caribbean Islands but also from Europe and even China. Over half a million persons moved to Cuba in the second half of the nineteenth and first half of the twentieth century. Capital for the construction of *ingenios* and infrastructure came from abroad, primarily the United States. Land became increasingly concentrated as estates tried to

---

[10] Roberto Cortés Conde, *The First Stages of Modernization in Spanish America* (New York, 1974), 29.

capture the entire process from sugar cane field to the commercialization of the resulting product. The profitability of the industry attracted foreigners and, increasingly, U.S. interests acquired the industry.

Labor conditions were dismal. Contrary to the situation in Brazil and other tropical regions, where sugar cane is harvested in ten out of twelve months of the year, in Cuba, a subtropical country, the sugar harvest is concentrated in four months, from August to November. At that time, the demand for labor is very high. There is also a demand for labor at the beginning of the growing season in the spring, but it is minor. Consequently, work in the cane fields is very seasonal. And, as Cuba became increasingly a monocrop economy, almost 50 percent of its labor force became seasonal, with few work opportunities during the remainder of the year.

Nevertheless, economic growth was rapid for a while. Cuba soon became the world's principal exporter of sugar, primarily to the U.S. market. The process of modernization required capital that came from abroad. Slowly, local, inefficient mills were displaced by the more modern ones, financed or owned by U.S. firms. *Centrales* became bigger and fewer as time went by. When, after World War I, demand diminished, many mills were forced into receivership.

The increasing dependency of Cuba on sugar created a vicious cycle of dependency. The capital inputs needed by the sugar industry came from abroad, especially the United States. The raw sugar was exported to be refined in the recipient countries. Cuba provided the raw material and labor. The latter was poorly paid and was employed for only a few months of the year. In turn, the monocrop agriculture degraded the land.

When Fidel Castro came to power in 1959, one of the aims of his government was to decrease Cuba's dependence on sugar by industrializing and diversifying the economy. Ironically, Cuba's increasing need for oil and industrial inputs made Cuba as dependent on sugar exports as before. It was only after the collapse of the Soviet bloc that Cuba reduced sugar production and turned land over to the growing of foodstuffs.

THE DEVELOPMENT OF THE GRAIN AND CATTLE ECONOMY
IN THE ARGENTINE PAMPAS

Argentina is known the world over as a major producer and exporter of cereals and meat. This correct perception is based entirely on the production of the fertile pampas. However, the pampas occupy only thirty million hectares – about one tenth of the country – and only about half of the pampa surface is used to produce crops. Much of the rest of the Argentine territory is too dry for agriculture without irrigation. This includes Patagonia and the center and western part of the country. Only the northern and eastern provinces have sufficient humidity for rain-fed agriculture. However, irrigated enclaves in Mendoza, San Juan, and Rio Negro are home to a thriving production of grapes and fruits. Tucumán, Jujuy, and Salta grow subsidized sugar cane, as well as tobacco, cotton, and, increasingly, soybeans.

Hides, tallow, and salted meat were the low-value exports of the nascent Argentine Republic in the first half of the nineteenth century. Herds of very primitive cattle were raised in open ranges in a coastal strip in the pampas approximately 100 miles wide that extended from 400 kilometers south of the city of Buenos Aires to some 500 kilometers north and northeast of the city. A very extensive agriculture was practiced around the few cities and served strictly the local market. At times, following bad harvests, the country was forced to import flour.[11]

Starting around 1830, sheep were introduced and they slowly started to displace cattle in the regions close to the harbors.[12] Wool increasingly became an important export product, slowly displacing the traditional products. Raising sheep required more infrastructure and more care than raising cattle in open ranges. Sheep prepared the rural society to think in terms of improving earnings by investments. A number of improvements were introduced, such as windmills and, above all, wire fencing to delimit properties and within them paddocks, because sheep could not be raised in open ranges. Fencing created a great deal of initial resistance in a rural population that was accustomed to roam freely over the open range. It also consolidated property rights, an important condition in the establishment of a landed oligarchy.

When the country became organized along democratic and republican lines in 1853, the government adopted a policy of encouraging immigration through the establishment of agricultural colonies. The early colonists at first grew cereals and found a ready market at home and abroad in spite of very low yields. A conjunction of factors followed. Europe at the end of the nineteenth century was in need of foodstuffs and became a natural market for Argentine cereal surpluses. As word of the existence of fertile land spread

---

[11] J. C. Garavaglia, *Pastores y labradores de Buenos Aires* (Buenos Aires, 1999).

[12] Hilda Sabato, *Capitalismo y ganaderia en Buenos Aires: La fiebre del lanar 1850–1890* (Buenos Aires, 1989).

through Europe, many peasants immigrated to Argentina in search of work. Yet, although some found land in the agricultural colonies, most found the land in the hands of landed families (the oligarchy) that controlled huge estates dedicated to the raising of livestock, known as *estancias*. So most immigrants became sharecroppers in the *estancias* instead.

The reason why not more immigrants became owners is a matter of debate. As Cortés Conde has shown, there was an active land market in the pampas and many immigrants became landowners.[13] An alternative explanation for the persistence of the large estate and sharecropping is that the immigrant was not interested in settling in Argentina, but was interested in earning capital to return home. He therefore was not particularly interested in investing his capital in land.

By the end of the century, refrigeration made it possible to send frozen and eventually chilled meat to Europe. The European market demanded good quality and this led to the improvement of the cattle herds by crossing them with European breeds, especially two English breeds: Shorthorns and Herefords. By then, the export of salted meat was a dying industry. The landed elite then became ranchers importing the best English animals to improve their herds and Argentina soon became known for the quality of its cattle herds.

Agriculture, especially wheat agriculture, produced profound changes in Argentine rural society. Whereas extensive cattle raising required almost no infrastructure or equipment, agriculture demands a minimum of implements. Extensive cattle raising requires little labor and much of it on a seasonal basis, whereas extensive agriculture requires much more labor, especially at harvest time. Although cattle can move to points of elaboration and export on the coast on their own hoofs, cereals require a transportation network. It was primarily the lack of labor and of cheap means of transportation that had held back agriculture in the pampas. Finally, although some knowledge is required to raise cattle extensively, agriculture requires much more.

A conjunction of forces favoring agriculture came together at the end of the nineteenth century to spur the spectacular growth of pampean agriculture. In the first place was the development of a European market for cereals. The wave of immigrants arriving in Argentina in increasing numbers after 1880, most of them experienced farmers, provided the needed labor. Finally, the development of a railroad network financed by English interests and the

---

[13] Roberto Cortés Conde, *El progreso argentino 1880–1914* (cited previously).

invention of the refrigerated steamship provided the needed transportation network.

Economic growth between 1880 and 1914 was spectacular and Argentine living standards, particularly in the city of Buenos Aires, rose to rival those of Europe. The world depression of the 1930s dealt a mortal blow to the export-led development strategy and exposed the vulnerability of Argentina to foreign markets. Although Argentina was affected by the depression less than some other Latin American countries, it nevertheless switched to an import substitution strategy that was to prove very ineffective.

The original plan was for the government to appropriate part of the agricultural surplus from exports and use it to subsidize import-substituting industry. To that effect, the Perón government (1946–55) devised a scheme by which the state bought the agricultural crop at a fixed price and exported it at world prices. The reaction of the agricultural sector was to switch from export to domestic production and to favor meat production over cereals. As agricultural production stagnated, it soon became obvious that it was necessary to introduce new technologies to increase productivity. In the 1960s, a new research and technology transfer organization – the National Institute for Agricultural Research (INTA) – was created and financed by a 1 percent tax on agricultural exports. INTA introduced High Yielding Varieties of wheat from Mexico and quickly developed a strong program of agricultural research and diffusion. Soon yields and production began to increase and Argentine agriculture was again on an upward growing curve.

Nevertheless, agriculture continued to be burdened with export taxes that reduced profitability and discouraged investment. In the 1960s, Argentina entered into a vicious cycle of inflation and devaluation that would last thirty years and that was very detrimental to the development of agriculture. In order to keep domestic food prices down, export taxes would be assessed on agricultural exports to reduce incentives to produce for export. As exports stagnated, Argentine industry, heavily dependent on imports of materials and technology, soon would create a foreign exchange crisis. To spur exports and reduce imports, the government would devalue the currency and reduce export taxes. Soon domestic food prices would start to rise and the government would again raise export taxes and the whole cycle would be repeated once more. Finally, after two episodes of hyper-inflation in 1989 and 1990, the country adopted a currency board, fixing the value of the peso at parity with the dollar and lifting almost all export taxes and controls on agriculture. An agricultural boom followed that saw agricultural production double in the last ten years, with great increases in yields and adoption of new technologies. Argentina is today one of the leaders in the use of biotechnology[14] (so-called GMF, genetically modified food) and direct seeding (also known as No-Till), an erosion-suppressing technology.

THE EVOLUTION OF CHILE'S AGRICULTURE WITH AN EMPHASIS ON THE NEW SECTORS OF VEGETABLES AND FRUITS

Chile is a country squeezed between the Andes and the Pacific Ocean. The northern third of the country is extremely dry and not fit for agriculture unless there is artificial irrigation. The center of the country has a Mediterranean type of climate with winter rains and summer droughts. Irrigation here is also necessary for growing summer crops. Below latitude thirty-eight degrees south, the climate is increasingly wet, with up to seven meters of rainfall in certain places and cold winters, the duration and harshness of which increase with latitude. Therefore, agriculture is concentrated in valleys in the center of the country where the rivers that bring the melting waters of the Cordillera are used for irrigation, or in the south-center area where there is sufficient rain throughout the year and where we find a dairy industry. Forestry, especially in the south of the country, is also important.

Chile was one of the first Latin American countries to become stabilized after independence, civil wars having been very brief. As in the rest of the area, a landed oligarchy took hold of the government and embarked on a path of export-led development. Mining rather than agriculture emerged as the principal export sector. Nevertheless, for a short period in the mid-nineteenth century, the country exported wheat, first to Peru and then to California and Australia, but that activity was short-lived and was over by the end of the nineteenth century. During most of the time under consideration, agriculture was primarily directed at the domestic market. The large *hacienda*, known as *fundo* in Chile, was the principal production unit. Labor was captured by offering plots of land to workers in the *hacienda* in exchange for work.[15]

Mining of first gold and silver, later *salitre*, and finally copper was the mainstay of the Chilean economy prior to World War II. Copper still continues to be the principal export, but it no longer is as dominant as before. There was the usual foreign investment in railroads and utilities,

[14] E. Trigo et al., *Los transgénicos en la agricultura argentina* (Buenos Aires, 2002).
[15] Arnold Bauer, *Chilean Rural Society* (Cambridge, 1975).

but also in the mining sector, especially copper that was totally foreign owned. The mining sector that was concentrated in the north and center of the country constituted an enclave with limited interaction with the domestic sector. Foreign mining concerns paid better salaries and offered better working conditions than other sectors of the economy.

In Chile – as in all areas of the world where agriculture depends on irrigation – access to water is more important than access to land. The Cordillera, with huge snowfields, is the source of irrigation water. Streams coming from the Andes are dammed and a network of canals, perfected and increased over time, distributes that water to the fields. *Fundos* in areas without access to irrigation were huge, often in the tens of thousands of hectares, and were dedicated to livestock raising, primarily sheep and goats. In the irrigation areas, however, *fundos* never exceeded 5,000 hectares, and usually were smaller, in the 500-to-1,000-hectare range. They coexisted with many independently farmed small plots of less than 10 hectares.

Because agriculture sold only to the domestic market, Chilean farming provided a great diversity of products, including cereals, vegetables, fruits, and vineyards that gave rise to a wine industry of good quality. The Mediterranean climate is particularly well suited for the production of wine.

Livestock was (and still is) raised in the nonirrigated areas of the country. In winter, it is fed on the natural grasses that thrive in the wet winter months along the hills in the coast and in the foothills of the Andes. In summer months, when these areas become parched because of the lack of rain and there is no fodder, animals are moved to the meadows at high altitudes in the Cordillera, and some of them are even transshipped to similar areas on the other side of the border. This transhumance has been going on for close to two hundered years. Nevertheless, Chile is not self-sufficient in meat products, having to import beef from Argentina.

The agricultural sector did not grow at the same rate as demand and, by the 1940s, was no longer able to supply the domestic market so that Chile had to rely on food imports. This situation was aggravated by the strife that resulted from attempts at land reform during the governments of Eduardo Frei and Salvador Allende (see the third section).

In the late 1970s, economic policy was directed at improving Chile's performance in agriculture by concentrating on high-value products, especially fruits, vegetables, and wines for export. This effort was very successful and Chile became an exporter of these products primarily to the United States, the European Union, and countries of the Pacific Rim. Export of agricultural products between 1975 and 2001 grew at an annual rate of 18 percent.

Whereas in 1975 agricultural exports were only 3.8 percent of the total, by 2001 they had grown to about 17 percent. A total of 1.613 U.S. billion dollars were exported in 2001. Of these, fruits, especially table grapes, were the most important products, representing a third of all agricultural exports (U.S. $660 million).[16] Since 1961, vegetable production has increased two and a half times, from 1 million to 2.6 million metric tons, while the surface dedicated to this activity has increased only by 30 percent, from 73 thousand hectares to 105 thousand hectares.

Chile exemplifies the modern strategy of export-led growth based on natural resources, both renewable (agriculture, forestry) and nonrenewable (copper). There is a great deal of concern that this strategy is not sustainable economically or environmentally. As with all agricultural commodities, markets become saturated, leading to reductions in price. From an environmental viewpoint, the intensification of agriculture has reduced crop rotations and increased pest loads. This in turn has increased significantly the use of pesticides that are mostly imported. Given the limited amount of agricultural land and the dependency on irrigation, land degradation poses a serious threat to Chile.[17]

THE EVOLUTION OF MEXICO'S AGRICULTURE

Geographically, Mexico is a very diverse country. Two mountain chains – the Sierra Madre Occidental and the Sierra Madre Oriental – descend from the north along both coasts and meet south of Mexico City. There, a number of large and active volcanoes delimit a number of valleys and interior basins, the so-called *meseta* that occupies the center of the country up to the Isthmus of Tehuantepec. From there south along the southwest coast, the mountains continue, whereas to the northeast there is a large, relatively flat area that extends (with some interruptions by low mountain chains) to the Yucatan peninsula.

The north of the country is dry and agriculture without irrigation is not possible. Most of the area is dedicated to cattle raising, except in areas along the foothills of the mountains where rivers have been dammed to provide irrigation. Farther south in the area of the Bajío and the valleys north of Mexico City, rainfall is adequate for growing temperate crops

---

[16] E. Figueroa et al., "Sustentabilidad ambiental del sector exportador chileno," in O. Sunkel, ed., *Sustentabilidad ambiental del crecimiento económico chileno* (Santiago, 1996).

[17] M. R. Quiroga and S. Van Hauwermeiren, *The Tiger Without a Jungle* (Santiago, 1996).

such as wheat. The southwest part of the country, where there is adequate precipitation such as in the state of Morelos, is dedicated to tropical crops such as sugar and coffee, as are the mountain slopes in the state of Veracruz. The lowlands in the southern states of Veracruz, Chiapas, and Tabasco were covered with the northern extension of the tropical rainforest until recently. However, in the last thirty years, a great part of that forest has been felled and converted into pastures. Finally, the state of Yucatan is underlined by a limestone shelf that significantly reduces the water-holding capacity of the land. Consequently, in spite of adequate rainfall, agriculture is restricted to low-lying basins.

Henequen, a cactus-like succulent native to Mexico, was grown in the area around Mérida in the nineteenth and early twentieth centuries, but that crop has almost disappeared today. In its heyday, Yucatan held a monopoly in the production of this crop, the fibers of which are used to make rope and twine. At the time, mechanical reaper-binders used for harvesting wheat in the United States used enormous quantities of twine, made mostly from henequen. The privileged situation of Yucatan producers created enormous fortunes that were invested in great part in conspicuous consumption of palatial houses and other luxuries. Henequen requires a lot of labor, and the landed elite enslaved in all but name the local Maya population. The Mexican revolution after 1910 freed labor from bondage and took over the commercialization of the crop. By then, the new combine harvesters had replaced the reaper-binders and demand (and price) dropped significantly. Henequen continued to be grown protected by government subsidies, but the introduction of synthetic fibers dealt a mortal blow to this crop. The last government-subsidized henequen factory in Mérida closed in 1999.

During colonial times, Mexico's agriculture and animal-raising activities helped to create a singular agricultural production institution that was the large *hacienda*.[18] These were quasi-feudal establishments that controlled large areas of land, grew a diversity of crops, and raised cattle, sheep, and other domestic animals. Above all, they controlled the lives of the rural population by a variety of means, including physical coercion, debt peonage, and laws and customs that created personal work obligations. *Haciendas* had their own police and jails to enforce their rule over those who worked there. Yet the Spanish legislation also protected the rights of indigenous communities to their land. Colonial authorities tried to protect

[18] F. Chevalier, *La formación de los latifundios en México* (Mexico City, 1975).

both indigenous and nonindigenous workers by keeping the *haciendas* from abusing their power in trying to capture the labor of the population through debt peonage.

Independence brought to power the landed aristocracy based on the large hacienda. It promptly changed many of the rules that protected agricultural laborers. They also encroached on indigenous communities, appropriating their land and turning them into *hacienda* laborers. So, whereas in 1854 there were approximately five thousand independent indigenous communities with their own land, language, and customs, by 1910, on the eve of the Mexican revolution, most of them had disappeared and more than 95 percent of the rural population worked in the *haciendas*. This change allowed the mobilization of Indian labor that was a condition for the growth of Mexican agriculture. It had, of course, many negative consequences for the individual welfare of the people involved.

It is estimated that in 1910 there were about eleven thousand *haciendas* in Mexico, covering a surface of approximately eighty-eight million hectares, with an average surface of 8,000 hectares per hacienda. *Haciendas* were distinguished from *ranchos*, which were smaller establishments dedicated mostly to cattle raising.

Working conditions varied in the *haciendas* according to location and type of production. In the center and south of the country, where agricultural production of export commodities prevailed (sugar, cotton, henequen) and where there tended to be a surplus of labor, salaries and working conditions were much worse than in the north of the country. Here, the emphasis was on cattle raising that required fewer workers and there was a labor shortage compared with the south. In the north, there also was the possibility for laborers to emigrate to the United States if landowners abused their power.

Different systems of production prevailed in the *haciendas*, and sometimes more than one. Basically, the owner of the *hacienda* could exploit the *hacienda* himself or he could enter into different types of sharecropping arrangements. Production for export was more likely to be done directly. In such cases, the owner might live in the *hacienda* and administer it himself or, more likely, he was an absentee owner and entrusted the running of the *hacienda* to an administrator.

Sharecropping could be done by halves or by fifths. In the first case, the proceeds of the harvest were shared equally; in the second case, the owner kept three fifths and the sharecropper, two fifths. The *hacienda* usually provided the land, the seed, and often the plow and oxen. In very dry regions where growing conditions were marginal, *haciendas* occasionally accepted arrangements that guaranteed them only one third of the harvest.

There were two types of laborers: *peones libres*, who worked for a salary or as sharecroppers and often owned a small plot of land as well, and *peones acasillados*, who lived in the *hacienda* and were permanently ascribed to it. Salaries were very low and often workers were paid by chit redeemable in the *hacienda* store. Owners advanced pay to their workers and made them beholden to them for some time. By law, if a worker accepted a year's salary in advance, that person was obliged to work for the *hacienda* for the rest of his life. This system produced a population of captive laborers who could be and often were abused. The situation was worst in the southern plantations of sugar, coffee, and henequen. In the latter ones, the local indigenous population was for all practical purposes enslaved and forced to work in what was a dangerous occupation.

During the *Porfiriato* (the period of Mexican history between 1876 and 1911, when Porfirio Díaz was president most of the time), the Mexican economy grew quite rapidly following the export-led development model already explained. Production of export commodities – coffee, sugar, cotton, henequen, and cattle – grew at a much faster rate than food staples, especially maize and beans. So, for example, maize production went from 282 Kg per head in 1877 to only 144 Kg per head in 1977. In that same period, henequen production in Yucatan increased by 300 percent. Cattle raised in enormous ranches were exported to the United States for fattening in the border states, primarily Texas. Railroads were constructed with U.S. capital that facilitated the movement of goods to the United States.

In 1910, and following the fraudulent denial by the Díaz government of the election victory of Francisco Madero, the opposition presidential candidate, there occurred an armed insurrection that signaled the start of the Mexican revolution. Armed conflicts of one sort or another would last until 1928, when finally constitutional government was established.

An important aspect of the Mexican revolution was a quest for the return of land that had been taken from indigenous people and small peasants by the haciendas. It was enshrined in the slogan *Tierra y Libertad* of Emiliano Zapata, the popular leader of the peasants of the state of Morelos. The Mexican Constitution of 1917 decreed the breaking up of the *haciendas* (many of which were destroyed during the uprising) and the return of the land to peasants and indigenous people. The Constitution established two types of land tenure: private property that could not exceed 100 hectares and communal property known as *ejidos* (see previous section).

As a result of the turmoil of the Mexican revolution, it was not until the time of the presidency of General Lázaro Cardenas in 1934–40 that agricultural production reached the levels of 1910. By then, the production conditions and the crop mixture had changed in favor of smallholders and with a greater emphasis on foodstuffs for the internal market, especially maize and beans, the basic staples of the Mexican diet. Yet the food situation was quite precarious. The Mexican government, with help from international donors, began a concerted research and education effort to increase agricultural production that was quite successful. Production increased (Table 12.9) for a number of commodities. New High Yielding Varieties of cereals were introduced, and a number of irrigation projects were completed that significantly increased the cultivated area. Yet, after a few successful years, in which agricultural production grew faster than population, production growth declined and was unable to keep up with the population.

The failure of Mexico to feed itself is complex and space does not allow a detailed analysis. For historical reasons rooted in the prerevolutionary history of the country, Mexico's rural sector has lacked the capacity to adjust fast enough to changes in technology and means of production. It is also constrained by its rugged terrain and unpredictable climate, with either too much or not enough rain. Given the low returns of agriculture, there has not been enough investment, giving rise to a vicious cycle.

The Mexican *ejido* that was set up as a legal entity by the Mexican constitution was supposed to re-create pre-Hispanic forms of land tenure. Because of the history of land expropriation by the landed oligarchy, the Mexican Constitution decreed that *ejidos* could not be alienated, particularly for debts. A community called an *ejido* held them in property. The community divided the land among its members who normally farmed the land individually. Because the land could not be alienated, it became almost impossible to raise capital through mortgages. At the time *ejidos* were set up, agriculture was mostly extensive, but as agriculture intensified in private lands throughout Mexico, the *ejido* could not compete. Furthermore, because of population growth, the surface of the *ejido* became divided into more and more people. Eventually, the combination of insufficient land and a traditional approach to farming made *ejidos* noncompetitive. In the 1990s, the Mexican Constitution was amended to allow the sale of *ejido* land. *Ejidos* also concentrated more than other establishments on the growing of staple foods, especially maize and beans.

The story of the failure of the *ejido* and the Mexican land reform to make Mexico self-sufficient in food is a sad story but also an important

Table 12.9. *Mexican agricultural production (metric tons) 1961–2002*

	1961	1970	1980	1990	2000	2002	% change
Cotton	1,191,000	890,000	1,085,013	553,335	223,844	117,238	−90.16
Oil palm	253,000	140,000	84,000	25,414	83,000	110,000	−56.52
Rice	332,944	405,385	445,364	394,388	351,447	292,000	−12.30
Soybeans	19,737	214,603	322,205	575,366	102,314	127,000	543.46
Coffee	126,616	185,293	220,040	440,000	338,170	319,835	152.60
Beans	723,340	925,041	935,174	1,287,364	887,868	1,333,730	84.38
Oranges	772,382	1,254,682	1,743,212	2,220,338	3,812,683	4,526,510	486.05
Sorghum	290,641	2,747,210	4,689,445	5,978,159	5,842,308	5,500,000	17,923.69
Citrus	971,681	1,627,154	2,667,218	3,187,783	6,061,597	6,874,517	607.49
Corn	6,246,106	8,879,385	12,374,400	14,635,439	17,556,900	19,000,000	204.19
Cereals	8,516,733	15,006,401	20,893,795	25,561,636	27,991,447	29,114,225	241.85
Sugar	19,167,984	34,651,424	35,278,624	39,919,368	44,150,000	46,000,000	139.98

Source: FAO FOSTAT Database.

lesson. To overcome the abuses of the *hacienda* system in the nineteenth century, land was overly subdivided during the first half of the twentieth century and could no longer serve the needs of intensive agriculture in the second half of the century. Private producers who were also subjected to upper limits in their holdings (that often were subverted with subterfuges) became much more efficient than the *ejidos*.

PERU AND PEASANT AGRICULTURE

Peru is the home of one of the oldest and most developed American civilizations: that of the Incas. The Incas introduced into cultivation, among other crops, cotton, potatoes, and peanuts, which are among the most important contemporary crops. During colonial times, Peru was the home to the Viceroyalty of Peru, which at one time stretched from Ecuador to the Río de la Plata. Lima was the entrepôt for the silver from Potosí during the Hapsburg period.

Geographically, Peru can be divided into three major regions. One is the coastal zone. This is one of the driest areas anywhere on Earth and agriculture is only possible with irrigation. Several rivers stream from the Andean Cordillera and their waters have been utilized for irrigation since pre-Columbian times. The second major region comprises the large inter-Andean valleys, known in Peru as the region of the Sierra. Occupied by a large Indian population, these valleys (e.g., Huancayo, Ayacucho, Andahuailas, Cuzco) are occupied by large estates as well as by a large number of very small (*minifundios*) peasant farms. Finally, beyond the large and imposing Cordillera de los Andes stretches the Amazon basin, until very recently covered by a continuous and imposing tropical rainforest.

The Incas had developed a system of agriculture that made use of all these zones, but especially the first two. Cotton and other tropical crops were cultivated in the coastal valleys under irrigation. Maize – their main food staple – as well as beans, amaranth, and quinoa were cultivated in the mountain valleys, whereas potatoes and other root crops were grown at the highest altitudes of the Peruvian–Bolivian *altiplano*. Coca leaves were the main product grown on middle elevations in the Amazonian slope. The Spaniards maintained, to a large extent, these patterns of cultivation but added some of their own crops to this mixture: sugar cane and grapes in the coastal lowlands and wheat, together with maize, in the Sierra.

The economy of the Peruvian viceroyalty was affected negatively by the Bourbon reforms. The loss of Potosí and its silver, which were incorporated into the new viceroyalty of the Río de La Plata deprived it of its principal source of revenue, and the abandonment of Lima as the entrepôt for the shipment of goods via Panama to Cuba was another. Independence did not alleviate this situation until the middle of the century, when the rich guano deposits along the coast began to be exploited.

Because of the physical constraints of the country that limit agricultural production, the export-led development could not rest on agriculture. Mining – first guano, then copper and other minerals, and even later oil – was much more important than agriculture. Nevertheless, agriculture played a role, especially the growing of sugar cane.

Along the coast of Peru north of Lima, conditions for growing sugar are very favorable, provided there is irrigation water. As mentioned, a number of rivers carry the meltdown from the Cordillera to the sea. These rivers have a torrential behavior during the rainy months from December to April but are only a trickle by the time they reach the coast during the dry months. Consequently, a number of canals, some of them dating to pre-Hispanic times, capture water at the foot of the mountains and carry it to the coast. Since colonial times, large *haciendas* had captured most of the land and especially the water rights. Sugar had not been the only crop; grapes, cotton, and cattle were also important products. The other problem for the sugar estates was labor. Indian labor during colonial times proved insufficient, so African slaves were imported. In 1854, slaves were emancipated. Emancipation benefited sugar planters because they were paid 300 pesos per emancipated person.

Demand for sugar rose considerably in Europe and the United States during the second half of the nineteenth century. This coincided with the end of the guano boom in Peru. The capital that had been invested in the export of guano was now chiefly invested in coastal agriculture and especially in sugar production. Both Peruvian capitalists and recently arrived immigrants entered the trade. A sugar boom followed, with all the characteristics seen in other countries: the consolidation of a sugar elite that controlled land and labor and especially water rights and played an important role in national politics. A shortage of labor developed that was supplied in part by the importation of indentured workers from China and Japan. Yet, by the onset of World War I, the demand for sugar grew at a slower rate than the increase in world output, bringing an end to the sugar boom.

The sugar boom helped to create savings that were invested in other sectors of the economy. It also helped create personal fortunes and political

Table 12.10. *Production (metric tons) of selected commodities in Peru (1961–2001) at five-year intervals*

	Sugar	Maize	Wheat
1961	8,100,000	340,037	153,595
1966	9,002,009	581,008	145,002
1971	8,777,762	616,368	122,225
1976	9,227,137	725,659	127,497
1981	5,653,755	590,805	116,678
1986	7,010,300	876,307	121,143
1991	6,500,000	659,779	87,275
1996	6,700,000	810,460	146,152
2001	8,000,000	1,315,870	181,877

Source: FAO FAOSTAT Database.

dynasties. They also consolidated the hold on land and water in the coastal valleys by the landed elite. Sugar production – as in Cuba – was mechanized and consolidated, with small and inefficient producers being taken over by the larger and more efficient ones.

In the 1970s, the military government of General Velasco Alvarado nationalized the sugar estates and distributed the land to smallholders. Sugar production was collectivized, yet lack of research and capital investments led to an important reduction of yields, so that although sugar surface was increased, there was a small decrease in production.

The land reform was an attempt to resolve a serious problem in Peruvian agriculture. In effect, export sectors such as sugar and cotton have modernized throughout the long twentieth century and kept up with international standards, whereas domestic agriculture has remained stagnant and increasingly unable to supply the country's food needs.

Since 1950, the population of Peru has quadrupled from seven to twenty-seven million persons. Only the production of rice, a staple of the Peruvian diet, grown under irrigation in the coastal enclaves, increased by the same amount during the period. Maize, the other important staple and a typical product of the Sierra region, only tripled, whereas wheat production barely doubled and bean production increased by a scant 50 percent (Table 12.10). Consequently, the food situation in Peru has been unsatisfactory – it is the South American country with the lowest average calorie intake per person. Only Haiti and Nicaragua have a lower average caloric intake then Peru in Latin America. Malnutrition among the poorer strata of the population is very serious. Because much food production takes place in the Sierra area and is largely produced by peasant agriculture, the problem in Peru has racial and social as well as economic ramifications.

It must be remembered also that access to food is a question of income and prices.[19] In an open economy, prices are set by the international market. A producer will always sell to the highest bidder and that is usually the international market. As the income of the poor deteriorates in relation to world prices, their capacity to purchase food diminishes. Because the poor spend a much larger percentage of purchases of food in relation to income, they are impacted more than the rest of the population when food prices increase.

Much has been written regarding "peasant" agriculture in Latin America. This term is confusing and misleading. There is no doubt a sector of farmers in Latin America that work small plots that can be less than a hectare. Many of them are descendants of the indigenous population and their farming techniques often contain elements inherited from pre-Colombian times. A good example are Mayan farmers in the state of Chiapas, Mexico, who still practice the ancient *milpa* system of corn cultivation. But these traditional techniques and customs coexist with elements of European origin, such as plows, oxen, metal tools, and introduced crops such as wheat. Seeds are likely to be from improved varieties, but not always. Bolivian potato farmers cultivate a mixture of white potatoes and local varieties, the latter mostly for home consumption. These smallholders, or *minifundistas*, are almost always connected to a market economy in many ways. The need to pay taxes and obtain cash forces these farmers to produce a surplus for the market. They are, therefore, not equivalent to the traditional European peasant.

This farming population is considerable in Peru and other Andean countries such as Ecuador and Bolivia, although the area farmed by them is less than that in commercial agriculture. Their yields can be high because they apply a lot of labor and farm the land very intensively. They lack capital and the small plots they farm usually produce enough to permit the survival of the farmer's family but leaves no room for savings. Their plots are too small and their farming techniques inappropriate given the present economic environment to produce a salable surplus. They also are poorly connected to commercialization networks. Furthermore, the class cleavages in Peru, with their racial overtones inherited from colonial times, have created a great deal of distrust that is often a barrier to communication. Finally, there is also a long history of land disputes among indigenous

---

[19] A. Sen, *Poverty and Famines* (London, 1984).

communities, *haciendas*, and mining concerns. More powerful actors have pushed smallholders increasingly into poor marginal lands.

Society has a special regard for the small farmer, which has been romanticized by writers from Thomas Jefferson to Wendell Berry as the steward of nature and the bulwark of democracy. Others – especially landed interests – consider small producers nonviable and ignorant. But "peasant farmers" in Latin America are neither great stewards of nature nor are they ignorant, although they almost always are poor. These farmers have been left out from a process of farming modernization because of their meager holdings and lack of capital. Critics who argue that these small farms are nonviable often do not consider alternatives.

Some holdings are indeed too small. In the highlands of Peru, some farmers only own one or two furrows. These people hold on to the land, but make a living selling their labor to the larger farms. But farms in the range of ten to fifty hectares are perfectly viable for growing certain crops, such as coffee, fruits, or vegetables. Smallholders require assistance with farming methods, ways to protect land from erosion and degradation, and commercializing their crops. Intermediaries often capture much of the value of their produce.

International agencies as well as national research agencies are trying to protect small farmers to increase their output, helping them to hold on to their land and capture most of the value of what they produce. Many peasant farmers lack means to transport their produce to market and have to rely on middlemen who offer only a small part of the price the farmer could obtain if he could sell directly in the market. In cases in which the plots farmed are too small to maintain a family, cooperative arrangements are needed to capture some economies of scale.

The hopeless situation of many small Peruvian farmers have led them to abandon agriculture and move to the coast, especially Lima, in search of urban employment. There, they swell the large population of the shantytowns surrounding the capital. Others have moved into the Amazon basin, to start afresh in some of the valleys at the eastern foot of the Cordillera, such as the Hualaga valley. Many have turned to growing illicit drug plants that, although a risky proposition, offer a high return.

THE PUSH INTO THE AMAZON BASIN

Latin America has the largest reserves of arable land of any area in the world. However, most of it is covered with rich and diverse tropical forests that are also worth preserving. Consequently, a conflict has arisen between the interests of conservationists in preserving the forest and agricultural interests that wish to develop it. With the growth of the population in Latin America, the conflict has become quite acute. Large areas of forests in tropical Mexico and Central and South America that once were covered with lush forests are now dedicated to agriculture or, more often, cattle raising. Nowhere is this conflict better illustrated than in Brazil.

In 1838, Charles Goodyear invented the process of vulcanization of rubber. Until then, rubber had limited uses because it became brittle when cold or wet. Vulcanization opened the way for the fabrication of rubber tires used first in bicycles and later in automobiles. To say that without rubber tires the automobile could not have been invented is not an exaggeration.

At the time, the only significant source of rubber was the latex of the rubber tree, *Hevea brasiliensis*. This majestic tree was found in the Amazon forest growing as isolated individuals. Tappers or *siringueiros* cut trails through the forests of the western Amazon, each of them connecting some 60 to 150 trees, the maximum that a person could tap in a day. The locations of these trails were kept secret. The trunks of the trees were tapped at each visit that took place every other day during the harvest season. Because the latex stopped flowing after about twenty-four hours, trees had to be tapped at each visit. Heating the juice over a forest fire then coagulated it into large rubber balls. These were then transported at the end of the tapping season by open canoe to ports on the Amazon River, principally Manaus and Belem. From there, they were shipped to Europe and the United States for processing.

Tappers worked for rubber dealers called *aviadores*, or forwarders, who furnished on credit and at high price food and supplies for six months in the jungle on condition that the tapper sell all his rubber to him and accept only his goods. On return from the jungle, the costs of supplies were deducted from the value of the rubber. Because this system was easily abused, normally tappers obtained very little monetary benefit. Capital requirements, even so, were high. The *aviadores*, in turn, were beholden to capitalists who advanced the needed money. These capitalists controlled the export of rubber. Huge fortunes were made in the thirty years before World War I that transformed Belem and Manaus from sleepy towns into rich tropical emporiums.

However, the boom did not last long. Seeds were taken from Brazil and planted in different parts of the British Empire, most notably in Malaya.

Here, plantations were established. Although it was not known at the time, rubber trees in Amazonia suffer from the attack of a fungus. Only isolated trees that escape the fungus survive. Because the fungus is not transmitted through the seed, plantations in the Far East were disease-free. Plantations allowed a much more rational and efficient handling of the trees and of labor and allowed rubber to be produced at a fraction of the cost of tapping wild trees in the Amazon. When plantations came into full production shortly before World War I, the price of wild rubber collapsed and rubber tapping in the Amazon became a marginal operation. Rubber, which had been second only to coffee as an export crop in Brazil, suddenly became a marginal product.

After World War II, Brazil moved its capital to the interior and embarked on a concerted push to develop its interior. The population was growing and moving in large numbers to the cities of the south, especially São Paulo. Government policies were promoted to encourage agricultural development. The modernization of agriculture in the southern states of São Paulo, Paraná, Santa Catarina, and Rio Grande do Sul forced many smallholders to sell their land and move to the interior in search of new land. In this, they were encouraged by an extensive program of colonization of the interior of Brazil promoted by the government. The Amazon region, which includes the savanna regions known as the *cerrado*, and the Amazon forest proper, were targeted. Between 1970 and 1990, millions of new farmers settled in these regions. EMBRAPA (*Empresa Brasileira de Pesquisa Agropecuaria*), the federal agricultural research organization, developed a number of successful new technologies for these regions. Much of Mato Grosso and southern Goias were turned over to the growing of soybeans in large estates using the most modern machinery and production methods. Smaller farmers in frontier regions grew beans, rice, maize, and manioc. However, the greatest area was dedicated to the creation of pastures and the raising of cattle. There are now more cows than people in Brazil, which now has by far the largest cattle herd in the world. New roads allowed the extraction of valuable tropical timber. Large swathes of forest and savannas were transformed into pastures or agricultural land, especially in the states of Pará, Goias, Mato Grosso, and Rondônia.

Similar advances on the Amazon forest took place in Peru, Colombia, Bolivia, and Paraguay. The fastest rate of advance (but not the absolute amount) of the agricultural frontier has been in Paraguay and Peru rather than in Brazil. It is calculated that in another fifty years, most of the Amazon forest will have been converted to other uses. Efforts are underway to protect some of the enormous diversity of plants and animals by creating natural reserves.

Among the new crops cultivated in these regions is the coca plant (*Erythroxylon coca*) that, although illegal, is adapted to this environment and is by far the most profitable crop. This is particularly so in Bolivia, Peru, and Colombia, and to a lesser extent in Ecuador.

CONCLUSIONS

Over the last century, the principal change that can be observed is the intensification of agriculture. Yet profitability per hectare is down, mainly because of the increased cost of inputs and the relative fall in international prices of most commodities.

The principal production costs of extensive agriculture practiced at the beginning of the twentieth century were labor and land amortization. Seeds were carried from one season to the next; fertilizer – if any was used – was manure, also produced on the premises. Machinery was limited – plows, seed drills, and harvesting equipment – and often produced locally. Pesticides and herbicides were unknown. Intensive agriculture, on the other hand, requires much purchased input. Seeds have to be bought, if not yearly, at very frequent intervals. The new varieties require a better land preparation that implies specialized machines. Tractors have replaced horses and oxen as sources of power and, consequently, instead of fodder produced in the premises, fuel has to be purchased. The new varieties also require the use of chemical fertilizers, herbicides, and pesticides. Although the number of agricultural workers is down, labor costs have come down much less. This is in part because today's worker has to be better prepared and in part because of new labor laws, but also because of the need of technical advice that is not cheap. Consequently, the farm's net income is only 10 to 20 percent of gross income. This makes producers that farm small areas noncompetitive with large producers who can reap benefits of scale in the use of machinery and in their capacity to obtain better prices for their inputs.

The dependence of countries on a few export commodities has not changed throughout the long twentieth century, although the commodity mix has. Coffee is still a major crop in Brazil, Colombia, and Central America; sugar continues to be an important export product in Cuba and Peru; cattle and cereals are very important in Argentina. To this list must now be added soybeans and citrus in Argentina and Brazil; fruits and vegetables in Chile and Argentina; and flowers in Colombia and Ecuador. Still, prices of agricultural commodities have continued their downward trend, especially for cereals.

Modern industrial agriculture is stacked against the small producer and the producer of commodities, especially grains, but also coffee and sugar, two high-value products. Synthetic products have also conspired against the profitability of farmers. Synthetic rubber has replaced natural rubber; synthetic fibers for cordage and twine have almost completely replaced sisal and henequen; synthetic textile fibers have reduced significantly the market for cotton and wool.

Another factor that reduces the profitability of agriculture is government intervention. In developed countries, especially the United States, Western Europe, and Japan, governments try to protect their farmers from competition from lower-cost producers. This takes many forms. In Europe, high import taxes, export subsidies, and subsidies to farmers to produce certain commodities; in the United States, minimum prices are guaranteed; in Japan, high tariffs keep imported products out. Farmers are sometimes paid for not producing certain commodities or for producing them in certain environmentally friendly ways. Export subsidies are also used generously. In Latin America, especially in countries with large agricultural exports such as Argentina, exports are taxed, thereby reducing the farmer's profits.

Behind the complex web of subsidies in developed countries is the understandable wish of all societies for food security. Depending on imports for food supply can make countries very vulnerable to external pressure. In Latin American countries, there is a long tradition of relying on customs duties as a major source of government revenue. Another tradition in Latin America is the avoidance of taxes, a situation that almost forces governments to use custom duties as a major source of revenue.

Subsidies and taxes distort markets and prices. In developing countries, subsidies increase production and lead to the farming of marginal land. The increased production lowers prices. Export taxes are equivalent to increasing production costs. The reaction of Latin American farmers is to produce more in compensation. This only makes the situation worse, leading to overproduction.

The coffee agreements showed that it is impossible to regulate production of commodities in a market with many actors and no dominant one to impose market discipline. Overproduction and low prices are likely to continue. From a Latin American point of view, the elimination of market interventions – be they subsidies or taxes – would help create a fairer situation. It also would be environmentally beneficial. This is not likely to happen soon.

Another effect of low prices caused by market interventions by governments is to eliminate small producers. As margins decrease, small producers with high fixed costs cannot compete and must find employment in larger farms or outside of agriculture. This is part of the reason that after witnessing a decrease in average farm size during most of the twentieth century, this trend has been reversed in the last thirty years.

What can we learn from the development of agriculture in Latin America during the long twentieth century and what does it tell us regarding the future? Agricultural and livestock products, together with mining, have been the principal exports of Latin America since the arrival of the Spaniards and Portuguese. During the first third of the long twentieth century, these export products were the engine that pulled the development train, and it led to rapid growth and, in some cases, most notably in the Southern Cone, created a high standard of living. Yet, although it created pockets of wealth, this phase was not sustainable. Until World War I, European countries and the United States absorbed increasing amounts of cereals and beef, sugar and coffee, rubber and henequen. But World War I brought this period to an end and the world depression of the 1930s dealt it a mortal blow. Latin America, following the analysis of the terms of trade by Prebisch and led now by a new more urban leadership, abandoned the export-led development model in favor of import-substitution industrialization. Although in its early phases the new model proved successful, it too was not sustainable and eventually was abandoned in the 1980s.

Characteristics of Latin American agriculture during the long twentieth century include change and diversity. From a traditional system based on the large estate using extensive systems based on land and labor, agriculture in the region has become much more capitalized, with a strong knowledge base. In spite of several attempts at land reform, the large estate still dominates the rural scene. Yet today's estate differs considerably from that of 100 years ago. Gone are the semifeudal labor relations that prevailed at the beginning of the twentieth century, replaced by a mechanized agriculture that uses much less labor. The *minifundio* still exists in many regions, particularly in the Andean countries of Peru, Bolivia, and Ecuador, increasingly pushed into a marginal situation both physically and socially.

Diversity was and continues to be a characteristic of the agriculture of this vast region, a result of the variety of climates, topography, history, and societies. So, not all large estates at the beginning of the twentieth century conformed to the stereotype of the traditional hacienda, nor are all large estates highly capitalized and efficient at the end of the period. The duality between a modern export sector and a less developed domestic sector varied considerably among countries and, in many cases, such as in Argentina, did not exist.

The population of the world is still growing and so is its standard of living. Future demand for agricultural products will therefore continue. The big question is whether demand will grow faster than supply. Farmers, helped by scientific research and new technologies, have been able to increase food and fiber production at a rate faster than demand. Whether this kind of agriculture is sustainable is debatable. And in the future, markets are likely to demand sustainable production methods, presenting Latin America with one more challenge.

13

THE POLITICAL ECONOMY
OF INDUSTRIALIZATION

STEPHEN HABER

This chapter builds on recent research by scholars across a broad number of countries and disciplines to offer a reinterpretation of the history of Latin American industrialization. It departs from the standard view that underlies much of the literature on Latin America's economic history: that Latin America had open, "export economies" from the 1870s to the 1930s, and that these export economies were then dramatically transformed into "import-substituting" economies during the period 1930–80.

Obviously, the history of industrialization was not the same in Bolivia as it was in Brazil – there was considerable variation from country to country, with the smaller economies of the region generally industrializing later and less completely than the larger economies. Capturing both the general trends and the specifics of each case would exceed the space limitations of a single chapter. I therefore concentrate my analysis on four cases: Argentina, Brazil, Chile, and Mexico. I have chosen these cases because they account for three quarters of total Latin American gross domestic product (GDP) and because they are (and historically were) the most heavily industrialized countries in the region. Other countries certainly have (and had) manufacturing sectors but, as a practical matter, when we speak about Latin American industry, we are really speaking about the manufacturing sectors of Argentina, Brazil, Chile, and Mexico.

The reinterpretation that I offer contains four arguments. First, I argue that there was substantial industry in Latin America well before 1930. In fact, in the countries that we focus on in this chapter, the development

The author acknowledges helpful discussions with Herbert Klein, James Robinson, Kenneth Sokoloff, and Barry Weingast, whose insights contributed to this chapter.

of large-scale, mechanized industry can be dated from the 1890s. Second, one logical implication of this argument is that there must have been policies favorable to industrialization – particularly protective tariffs – during the so-called era of export-led growth.[1] Third, Latin American governments, both before and after 1930, were protectionist not because of vague economic goals, but because there were political benefits to supporting manufacturers. The research by Raúl Prebisch and the United Nations Economic Commission for Latin America (ECLA) economists in the 1950s gave intellectual legitimacy to developments already taking place: their research did not, in and of itself, cause governments to adopt policies designed to protect and subsidize manufacturing. Fourth, the ultimate outcome of import-substituting industrialization (ISI) is as depicted in the standard literature: highly protected and woefully inefficient industries. The difference in the interpretation advanced here is that this outcome was not the product of the rise of "developmentalist" states. It was the product of a historically longer political process that involved economic agents making specific demands on politicians who were not accountable to broad constituencies. In particular, politicians were not accountable to the group that ultimately paid the cost of protectionism: consumers, who tended to be politically unorganized and who typically lacked electoral mechanisms that would allow them to sanction public officials for policies inimical to their interests.

This is not to argue that there were no differences between the pre- and post-1930 periods of Latin American industrial development. First, manufacturing was quantitatively larger in the post-1930 period. Second, in the pre-1930 period, virtually all industry was domestically owned. In the post-1930 period (and especially after 1950), domestic firms were joined by multinational enterprises. Third, after 1930, industrialists had a powerful political ally in organized labor. Industrialists and labor unions may not have liked one another (indeed, they actively abhorred one another), but they did have a common interest in trade protection. They therefore formed coalitions that would only be broken with the collapse of import substitution in the 1980s. Even noting these differences, however, it is clear that there is no neat divide between the pre- and post-1930 periods in terms

---

[1] One could dispense with this logical implication by arguing that Latin American countries had a comparative advantage in manufacturing in the early twentieth century. Such an argument would, however, be difficult to sustain. Indeed, the evidence all points the other way. See, for example, Gregory Clark, "Why Isn't the Whole World Developed? Lessons from the Cotton Mills," *Journal of Economic History* 47, 1 (1987): 141–74.

of government policies, the adoption of mechanized technologies, the scale of enterprise, or the inward-looking nature of industry.

Pushing back the point at which governments initiated pro-industry policies creates somewhat of a conundrum. Latin American governments were supposedly great supporters of *laissez faire* in the late nineteenth and early twentieth centuries. How, then, could governments simultaneously embrace *laissez faire* and protectionism? The answer is that governments do not have to frame coherent policies. The notion that governments are "autonomous" entities that frame development "strategies" is social-science fiction. A more realistic view is that self-interested economic agents make endless demands on public officials to create policies that confer an economic benefit on them and them alone. When granting those policies is in the self-interest of public officials, they do so. The accretion of ad hoc policies means that the overall package of regulations, laws, and tax codes that comprise a property rights system may work at cross-purposes to one another. The policies that supported industrial development in Latin America – both during the so-called periods of "export-led growth" and "import-substituting industrialization" – were not an exception to this general rule.

INDUSTRIAL DEVELOPMENT AMIDST EXPORT-LED GROWTH, 1890–1930

There had been, at least since the mid-nineteenth century, precocious attempts at industrial development in a number of Latin American countries. Nevertheless, the available quantitative evidence indicates that whatever industry had been founded grew at a very modest pace. Per capita incomes were too low, and markets were too isolated by high transport costs, to support modern manufacturing.[2]

The pace of industrial growth accelerated rapidly in the 1890s. Circa 1914, the larger countries of the region – particularly Brazil, Mexico, Chile, and

---

[2] See, for example, Stanley Stein, *The Brazilian Cotton Manufacture: Textile Enterprise in an Underdeveloped Area, 1850–1950* (Cambridge, MA, 1957); Stephen Haber, "Assessing the Obstacles to Industrial Development, The Mexican Economy," *Journal of Latin American Studies* 24, 1 (1992): 1–32; Armando Razo and Stephen Haber, "The Rate of Growth of Productivity in Mexico, 1850–1933: Evidence from the Cotton Textile Industry," *Journal of Latin American Studies* 30, 3 (1998): 481–517; Fernando Rocchi, "Building a Nation, Building a Market: Industrial Growth and the Domestic Economy in Turn-of-the-Century Argentina" (Ph.D. dissertation, University of California, Santa Barbara, CA, 1997).

Argentina – boasted sizable manufacturing sectors, which produced a broad range of consumer nondurables (particularly beer, cigarettes, soap, matches, hats, paper, footwear, and cotton cloth). In some cases, domestic firms had also moved into the production of intermediate inputs (basic chemicals, glass bottles) and construction goods (particularly cement, explosives, bricks, steel rails, and iron and steel structural shapes).

The impetus for industrial development came from the expansion of foreign trade. Driving the growth of foreign trade were two factors. The first was that most Latin American countries were on the silver standard, and silver fell in value relative to gold in the last two decades of the nineteenth century. Most Latin American countries, therefore, saw their currencies depreciate in real terms relative to the gold-backed currencies of the economies of the North Atlantic. As international trade theory would predict, real exchange rate depreciation resulted in the expansion of the tradables sectors at the expense of nontradables. Second, the late nineteenth century also saw a dramatic decline in the international costs of transport, as steel-hulled steamships came to replace wood and sail.

Real exchange rate depreciation and falling costs of maritime transport kick-started Latin American economic growth. Latin American countries could now produce and ship goods at a price low enough to be competitive in the United States and Western Europe. These exports included minerals (particularly copper and lead), industrial fibers (cotton, wool, jute, and sisal), staple agricultural goods (primarily beef and wheat), and nonstaple agricultural commodities (the most important of which were coffee, bananas, and sugar). The result was a wave of foreign direct investment in precisely those sectors. In order for these investments to bear fruit, however, there had to be a means to move commodities from their point of production to the ports or, in the case of Mexico, to the U.S. border. Trade therefore gave rise to the construction of railroad networks (also financed by foreign investment) that crisscrossed Latin America, linking major cities and integrating markets.[3]

---

[3] Most of the best work done to date on railroads focuses on the cases of Brazil and Mexico. See, for example, the chapter in this volume by William Summerhill. Also see his "Transport Improvements and Economic Growth in Brazil and Mexico," in Stephen Haber, ed., *How Latin America Fell Behind: Essays on the Economic Histories of Brazil and Mexico, 1800–1914* (Stanford, CA, 1997), 93–117, and *Order Against Progress: Government, Foreign Investment, and Railroads in Brazil, 1854–1913* (Stanford, CA, 2003). On Mexico, see Sandra Kuntz Ficker, *Empresa extranjera y mercado interno: el Ferrocarril Central Mexicano, 1880–1907* (Mexico City, 1995); Sandra Kuntz Ficker and Paolo Riguzzi, eds., *Ferrocarriles y vida económica en México, 1850–1950: Del surgimiento tardío al decaimiento precoz* (Mexico City, 1996); and John H. Coatsworth, *Growth Against Development: The Economic Impact of Railroads in Porfirian Mexico* (Dekalb, IL, 1981).

The growth of the export sector, the concomitant growth of railway networks, and implicit trade protection created by depreciating real exchange rates created the conditions conducive to industrial development. First, there came into existence a wage-earning population of ranch hands, miners, plantation workers, stevedores, and railway men that generated considerable demand for consumer goods. Second, this growing population of working-class consumers was not made up of isolated pockets of workers toiling away in enclaves: they were part of a national market that was linked by railways. In fact, as William Summerhill has shown for Brazil and Sandra Kuntz Ficker has shown for Mexico, most of the commodities carried by Latin American railways were destined for domestic (not international) markets.[4] Finally, depreciating real exchange rates operated exactly the same as an across-the-board increase in import tariffs: they raised the domestic price of imported goods.

Latin America's merchants, who earlier had been importing manufactured goods, quickly realized the potential created by growing markets and implicit trade protection. They soon began to erect textile mills, beer breweries, cigarette factories, soap works, and other manufacturing enterprises. The production of consumer goods, in turn, produced demand for intermediate inputs, such as glass bottles, paper, and basic chemicals. At the same time, the growth of ports and railways meant that there was demand for construction goods, such as steel and cement. Almost immediately, Latin America's nascent industrialists began to pressure their governments for high tariffs on the final goods they produced (in order to further protect them from foreign competition) and for low or zero tariffs on the capital and intermediate goods they needed in order to ramp up production.

This process of industrial development as a consequence of the growth of the export sector has been most intensively studied in the case of Mexico. Prior to the 1880s Mexican manufacturing was hampered by low per capita incomes and by the lack of long-distance transport. Beginning in the 1880s and accelerating in the 1890s, "export-led growth" removed these obstacles to industrial development. As a consequence, industry expanded at a dramatic pace.[5]

---

[4] William Summerhill, "Transport Improvements and Economic Growth in Brazil and Mexico," and *Order Against Progress*, ch. 6; Sandra Kuntz Ficker, *Empresa extranjera y mercado interno*.

[5] For a detailed discussion, see Stephen Haber, *Industry and Underdevelopment: The Industrialization of Mexico, 1890–1940* (Stanford, CA, 1989), and "Assessing the Obstacles to Industrial Development;" Mario Cerutti, *Burguesía, capitales, e industria en el norte de México* (Monterrey, Mexico, 1992); Dawn Keremetsis, *La industria textil mexicana en el siglo XIX* (Mexico City, 1973); Carlos Marichal and Mario Cerutti, eds., *Historia de las grandes empresas en México, 1850–1930* (Mexico City, 1997); Aurora

Table 13.1. *Size estimates of the cotton textile industries of Mexico, Brazil, India, and the U.S.*

Year	Mexico	Brazil	India	U.S.
Circa 1850	135,538			
Circa 1865	154,822	14,875	285,524	
Circa 1875		45,830	886,098	
Circa 1880	249,294	84,956		10,653,435
Circa 1885–90	277,784	78,908	2,145,646	
Circa 1895	411,090	260,842		14,384,180
Circa 1900	588,474		4,945,783	19,436,984
Circa 1905	678,058	778,224		
Circa 1910	702,874	823,343	6,357,460	28,178,862
Circa 1914	752,804	1,634,449		
Circa 1921	770,945	1,621,300	6,763,036	34,603,471
Circa 1927	821,211	2,692,077		
Circa 1930–34	803,873	2,507,126	9,124,768	33,009,323

Source: Stephen Haber, "Banks, Financial Markets, and Industrial Development: Lessons from the Economic Histories of Brazil and Mexico," in Anne O. Krueger, ed., *Latin American Macroeconomic Reform: The Second Generation* (Chicago, 2003).

A description of the rapid growth and transformation of the cotton textile industry gives a sense of the process. Circa 1888, the Mexican cotton textile industry was small, much of it still operated on water power, and characterized by a slow rate of productivity growth. In the next decade, the industry more than doubled in size. By 1911, the industry had grown an additional 50 percent (see Table 13.1). The quantitative expansion of the textile industry was accompanied by a qualitative change in the methods of production. Mexico's mills now employed high-velocity, electric-powered looms and spindles, which were a far cry from the old water-, steam-, horse-, or human-powered machinery. The new enterprises also operated on a tremendous scale, employing hundreds of workers and thousands of machines. Mexico's leading firms were not only large relative to the small Mexican market, they were enormous even by U.S. standards. Finally, an industry that had been characterized by stagnant productivity growth now began to enjoy rapid productivity gains.[6]

Gómez Galvarriato, "The Impact of Revolution: Business and Labor in the Mexican Textile Industry, Orizaba, Veracruz, 1900–1930" (Ph.D. dissertation, Harvard University, 1999).

[6] Armando Razo and Stephen Haber, "The Rate of Growth of Productivity in Mexico, 1850–1933."

Equally dramatic transformations took place in other manufacturing industries. Mexico's first integrated steel mill (*Fundidora Monterrey*) was founded in 1900. Its U.S.-designed blast furnace, Bessemer converters, and rolling mills allowed it to rapidly establish a domestic monopoly in the production of structural shapes, rails, and other products. In the paper industry, one giant, vertically integrated firm brought in high-speed, Swiss-made machinery with a capacity three times that of all its competitors combined, bought out its actual and potential rivals, and established a national monopoly in the market for newsprint and other low-value-to-bulk paper products. In the cigarette industry, two giant firms, employing automated cigarette-rolling machines and thousands of workers, pushed out the hundreds of artisan shops that had characterized the tobacco industry. These two firms, *El Buen Tono* and *La Tabacalera Mexicana*, controlled more than 60 percent of the market by 1910. In beer brewing, a domestic industry was created almost overnight, with local monopolies established in virtually every major city by the turn of the century. One of the industry's leading firms (the *Cervecería Cuauhtémoc*) soon came to control 28 percent of the national market. It went on to spin off a glass-bottle-making company (*Vidriera Monterrey*) that quickly established itself as a domestic glass monopoly that persisted until the 1990s. A similar situation developed in the cement industry. Until the turn of the century, Mexico produced no cement at all. By 1911, there were three firms in operation with a combined capacity of 150,000 metric tons per year. In soap and glycerin, Mexico's hundreds of artisan producers were forced out of business by the mammoth *Compañía Industrial Jabonera de la Laguna* – one of the four largest soap factories in the world. La Laguna later turned its expertise in basic chemicals toward the establishment of a spin-off firm, the *Compañía Nacional Mexicana de Dinamita y Explosivos*, which monopolized the production and distribution of dynamite.[7] A similar process took place in shoe and boot manufacturing, where large-scale factories (particularly those of United Shoe and Leather) began to replace the artisan shops that had dominated leather working in the nineteenth century.

Brazil underwent a very similar process of industrial development during the period 1890–1914. As was the case in Mexico, the development of industry was strongly linked to the growth of the export sector. In fact, the areas that industrialized the first and the fastest were exactly those that were most

7 Stephen Haber, Armando Razo, and Noel Maurer, *The Politics of Property Rights: Political Instability, Credible Commitments, and Economic Growth in Mexico, 1876–1929* (Cambridge, 2003), ch. 5.

clearly tied to the so-called export economy – namely, the coffee-growing states of São Paulo, Rio de Janeiro, and Minas Gerais. As was also the case in Mexico, Brazil's railroads, which putatively were created in order to move exports to ports, actually played a major role in integrating markets, thereby allowing domestic manufacturing firms to take advantage of economies of scale in production. The end result was that Brazil industrialized at a rapid pace in the two decades prior to World War I.

Brazil's early industrial development was strongly weighted toward the production of consumer nondurables. Cotton textiles, wool textiles, leather working, hat making, paper making, and beer brewing (and its associated industry of glass bottle making), all expanded well before World War I. Some industries, such as beer brewing, were almost identical in their development to Mexico: a small number of large, modern breweries (*Antartica* and *Brahma*) dominated the market by the turn of the century. The available estimates indicate that on the eve of World War I, domestic production of consumer goods accounted for 80 percent of total domestic consumption.[8]

Some industries, particularly those linked to construction, were slower to develop in Brazil than in Mexico. This was particularly the case for steel and cement, which did not develop in any sizable way in Brazil until the late 1910s and early 1920s.[9] Other intermediate goods industries did develop, however. These included jute sack manufacturing (an adjunct to the coffee industry) and wheat milling, in addition to the aforementioned glass-bottle industry. There were also some capital goods producers, including shipbuilding and machinery industries of modest scale.[10]

Brazil's largest industry, and its most intensively studied, was cotton textile manufacturing. Circa 1890, Brazil had a miniscule textile industry, small in size even by the standards of Mexico. By 1905, it had the largest cotton textile industry in Latin America. Its textile industry continued to grow at a dramatic rate to 1914, when it was roughly double the size of Mexico's textile industry (see Table 13.1). Its growth was then slowed by World War I (a subject we return to momentarily), but it continued growing in

[8] Bill Albert, *South America and the First World War: The Impact of the War on Brazil, Argentina, Peru, and Chile* (Cambridge, 1988), 186.

[9] For a discussion of individual industries, see Wilson Suzigan, *Indústria brasileira: origem e desenvolvimento* (São Paulo, 1986), 108–15; Werner Baer, *The Development of the Brazilian Steel Industry* (Nashville, TN, 1969); Stanley Stein, *The Brazilian Cotton Manufacture*, Nathaniel H. Leff, *The Brazilian Capital Goods Industry, 1929–1964* (Cambridge, MA, 1968); and Warren Dean, *The Industrialization of São Paulo, 1880–1945* (Austin, TX, 1969).

[10] Bill Albert, *South America and the First World War: The Impact of the War on Brazil, Argentina, Peru, and Chile* (Cambridge, 1988), 186.

the early 1920s. Circa 1927, it was roughly three times the size (measured in spindlage) of the Mexican cotton textile industry.[11] Nevertheless, in both the Mexican and the Brazilian cases, the domestic cotton textile industries had, for all intents and purposes, pushed aside imported cloth by 1914. For the most part, the only foreign cloth imported was fine-weave, high-quality cloth.

Argentina underwent a similar process of industrial development during the period 1890–1914. The expansion of the export economy and the construction of railroads created a growing market for all manner of consumer goods. Local entrepreneurs (many of whom began as merchants) quickly erected manufacturing plants to satisfy that growing demand.

One of the myths of early Argentine industrialization is that, with the exception of meat packing, firms were of very small size and resembled artisan shops more than modern factories. Like most myths, this one has *some basis* in fact. First, there is no doubt that Argentina had a very large and concentrated meat-packing industry. Second, it is also true that the *average size* of Argentine manufacturing firms circa 1913 was fewer than eight workers (see Table 13.2).

The problem with this view, however, is that the average size of firms is a very misleading measure of industrial development or of the presence of large firms in the process of industrialization. In 1964, for example, 40 percent of Argentina's manufacturing workers were employed by firms of more than 200 workers. These large firms accounted for only 0.6 percent of all firms, and they produced 42 percent of all output. Obviously, large-scale firms played a major role in Argentine industry. The average size of manufacturing firms, however, was only 7.2 workers – a lower number than in 1913 (see Table 13.2). What was true in 1964 was also true at the turn of the century. The average firm was of very small size, but that does not mean that a large proportion of industrial production did not take place in large, mechanized, and modern factories. As Fernando Rocchi has demonstrated, large-scale factories characterized the beer, glass-bottle, tobacco products, soap, chemical, footwear, match, paper, cotton hosiery, construction materials, hat, food-processing, and metal-working industries.[12] On balance, the evidence indicates that Argentine industry looked a

---

[11] Studies on textiles tend to use the number of spindles as a proxy for industry size because spindles (the machines that spin combed cotton into yarn) constituted the most important capital input for the production of cotton textile goods. See, for example, Nancy F. Kane, *Textiles in Transition: Technology, Wages, and Industry Relocation in the U.S. Textile Industry, 1880–1930* (Westport, CT, 1988).

[12] Fernando Rocchi, "Building a Nation, Building a Market," 40, 86, 95, 100, 108, 109, 113, 119; Paul H. Lewis, *The Crisis of Argentine Capitalism* (Chapel Hill, NC, 1990), 298–9.

Table 13.2. *The growth of Argentine industry, 1895–1974*

Year	Number of establishments	Number of workers	Installed horsepower	Workers per establishment	Horsepower per worker
1895	24,114	174,782	30,033	7.2	0.2
1913	47,343	363,771	237,817	7.7	0.7
1935	37,362	437,816	1,026,086	11.7	2.3
1937	45,263	539,525	1,190,493	11.9	2.2
1939	49,100	581,599	1,423,872	11.8	2.4
1941	52,445	684,497	1,645,041	13.1	2.4
1943	59,765	820,470	1,836,453	13.7	2.2
1946	84,905	1,058,673	2,076,531	12.5	2.0
1950	81,599	1,035,765	2,661,922	12.7	2.6
1954	148,371	1,217,844	3,570,037	8.2	2.9
1964	190,892	1,370,483	5,115,913	7.2	3.7
1974	126,388	1,525,221	6,753,375	12.1	4.4

Source: Paul Lewis, *The Crisis of Argentine Capitalism* (Chapel Hill, NC, 1990), 36, 37, 299.

lot like that of Brazil and Mexico: industries that could not take advantage of economies of scale in production or distribution were made up of hundreds of very small workshops, whereas industries that could take advantage of economies of scale were characterized by a small number of extremely large firms.

The Argentine beer industry provides an example of the rapid growth of large-scale manufacturing. Rising incomes, increasing population, and market integration during the so-called period of export-led growth produced a dramatic increase in the demand for beer. Beer consumption grew eightfold from 13 million to 109 million liters between 1891 to 1913. Two giant firms, *Quilmes* and *Biekert*, each producing tens of millions of liters of beer annually, quickly emerged and dominated the industry. Circa 1911, these two firms accounted for 67 percent of domestic beer production.[13]

A similar process occurred in the cigarette industry. Cigarettes had traditionally been rolled by hand in artisan workshops or nonmechanized factories and were of irregular quality. The dramatic expansion of the Argentine economy during the late 1880s and early 1890s increased the demand for cigarettes, thereby allowing firms to adopt technologies that permitted them to capture scale economies. As early as 1889, the first Bonsack automatic cigarette-rolling machine was introduced. The spread of mechanized technology quickly drove small firms out of business. Within a

[13] Fernando Rocchi, "Building a Nation, Building a Market," 40, 144, 412.

decade, cigarette production was concentrated in a single conglomerate, the *Compañía Nacional de Tobacos*, which employed 2,800 workers and had a capacity of 400,000 cigarettes per day.[14]

Argentina did not develop a cotton textile industry of the size and complexity of those found in Brazil and Mexico. With a few notable exceptions, such as the giant *Compañía Dell'Acqua* (which produced 1.5 million meters of cloth per year), most cotton factories in Argentina imported yarn that they then knit into hosiery. Argentina's cotton knitwear factories, however, operated on a tremendous scale. The rapid expansion of the industry can be seen by the dramatic increase in the volume of yarn imported, which grew sixteenfold between 1893 and 1904, from 298,392 kilos to 4,759,000 kilos. Circa 1908, domestic production of all cotton goods was valued at seventeen million pesos – 22 percent of total consumption.[15]

Overall, the growth of Argentine industry during the belle époque was dramatic. Circa 1869, Argentina had virtually no manufacturing industry to speak of. By 1895, it had 24,114 firms employing almost 175,000 workers. By 1913, the number of firms had doubled (to 48,779), the number of workers had grown by 135 percent (to 410,221), and the value of total fixed capital quintupled (to 1.8 billion pesos) (see Table 13.2).[16]

Chile underwent a similar process of industrial development. As Henry Kirsch has demonstrated, by 1914, much of Chilean industry was characterized by large-scale producers employing mechanized techniques of production.[17] In fact, Chile had a nascent capital goods industry that was tied, in particular, to the production of railway cars. The same firm that pioneered this industry later moved on to shipbuilding and other metal-working industries. In addition, Chile had roughly the same mix of consumer goods industries found in Argentina: beer, shoes, paper, and cigarettes. It also produced some intermediate goods (basic chemicals, glass) and construction goods. Indeed, it had a large and thriving cement industry.[18]

Latin American industry circa 1890–1914 may have been modern in the sense that it used mechanized production technologies and in the sense

---

[14] Fernando Rocchi, "Building a Nation, Building a Market," 43–4, 87, 113.

[15] Ibid., 50, 57, 95.

[16] Paul H. Lewis, *The Crisis of Argentine Capitalism*, 31.

[17] Henry Kirsch, *Industrial Development in a Traditional Society: The Conflict of Entrepreneurship and Modernization in Chile* (Gainesville, FL, 1977).

[18] Bill Albert, *South America and the First World War: The Impact of the War on Brazil, Argentina, Peru, and Chile* (Cambridge, 1988), 200–2; Henry Kirsch, *Industrial Development in a Traditional Society;* Gabriel Palma, "From an Export-Led to an Import-Substituting Economy: Chile 1914–39," in Rosemary Thorp, ed., *An Economic History of Latin America*, vol. 2, *Latin America in the 1930s: The Role of the Periphery in World Crisis* (London, 2000), 44–5.

that it operated on a tremendous scale. It was not modern, however, in the sense that it could compete effectively against producers in the United States and Great Britain. This had two ramifications. First, it meant that virtually none of Latin America's manufactured goods was exported, even to other Latin American markets. Second, it meant that virtually none of it would have existed had it not been for tariff protection.

In point of fact, the larger economies of Latin America had the highest tariffs in the world prior to World War I. Average tariff rates in Latin America were, on average, five times higher than those of the industrialized countries of Western Europe. They were an order of magnitude higher than those of East Asian countries.[19]

Not only were average tariffs high, but they were also structured so as to provide effective protection. There is a difference between protectionism and uniformly high import tariffs. Protectionism is characterized by high tariffs on a select group of targeted goods and low or zero tariffs on the raw materials, intermediate, and capital goods that are necessary inputs to production. If countries have the same tariff rates on inputs to production as they have on final products, the rate of effective protection might well approach zero (whatever benefit is conferred by the tariff on final goods is reduced by the higher cost of inputs created by tariffs on those products). What we in fact observe for the larger economies of Latin America is precisely the pattern that one would associate with protectionism: average tariffs tended to decline, while the tariffs on selected final goods were rising dramatically.

In no other Latin American country have tariffs and tariff policies been as intensively studied as in the case of Mexico. Beginning in 1891, the Mexican government honed the tariff system with an eye toward protecting domestic manufacturers *and* maximizing government revenues. On the one hand, the government drove down the tariffs on manufactured goods that Mexico did not produce – the goal being to reduce the costs facing the users of those goods and to increase the government's revenues from import taxes. On the other hand, the government drove up the tariffs on goods produced by Mexico's new and rapidly growing industries, the goal being to protect firms from international competition. Thus, tariff rates on a select group of

---

[19] John H. Coatsworth and Jeffrey G. Williamson, "The Roots of Latin American Protectionism: Looking before the Great Depression" (National Bureau of Economic Research Working Paper 8999); Michael Clemens and Jeffrey G. Williamson, "Closed Jaguar, Open Dragon: Comparing Tariffs in Latin America and Asia before World War II" (National Bureau of Economic Research Working Paper 9401).

products were extraordinarily high: 76 percent for bottled beer, 72 percent for common cloth, 88 percent for fine cloth, 198 percent for printing paper, 225 percent for candles, and 234 percent for soap, to cite a few examples. Over the course of the 1890s, the level of tariff protection declined because the tariff was specific, not ad valorem, and the peso was depreciating against gold-backed currencies. Declines in nominal tariffs, however, were more than mitigated by the fact that the peso was depreciating in real terms – which provided implicit protection. Given the government's commitment to protecting specific industries, when Mexico finally switched to the gold standard in 1905, it revised its tariff schedules upward to ensure that favored industries would continue to receive protection.[20]

In addition, the demands of manufacturers for low-cost inputs produced a "cascading" tariff structure: duties on final manufactured goods were high whereas duties on the inputs to produce those final goods were low or zero. Trade protection in steel illustrates the case clearly. In 1909, the tariff on steel products produced by Mexico's sole integrated steel manufacturer, *Fundidora Monterrey*, was 43.7 percent. The tariff on products that *Fundidora Monterrey* did not produce was roughly half that: 22.9 percent. The tariff on the imported inputs that *Fundidora Monterrey* consumed was 3.4 percent.[21] This was true in the textile industry as well. The tariff on imported cloth tended to be twice that of the tariff on imported raw cotton. The result was an effective rate of protection that varied from 39 to 78 percent (the variance driven by movements in the real exchange rate, which affected the peso price of imports).[22]

The mechanism by which manufacturers obtained protective tariffs was purely selective and individual. From 1887 to 1905, Mexico's Congress delegated the authority to legislate on tariffs to the executive branch. Beginning with the 1905 tariff reform, Congress once again voted on the tariff, but it could only accept or reject proposals made by the executive branch – not initiate tariff legislation. This meant that for all intents and purposes,

---

[20] Edward Beatty, *Institutions and Investment: The Political Basis of Industrialization in Mexico Before 1911*, ch. 3 and 4 (Stanford, CA, 2001); Sandra Kuntz Ficker, "Institutional Change and Foreign Trade in Mexico, 1870–1911"; and Edward Beatty, "Commercial Policy in Porfirian Mexico: The Structure of Protection," both in Jeffrey L. Bortz and Stephen Haber, eds., *The Mexican Economy, 1870–1930: Essays on the Economic History of Institutions, Revolution, and Growth* (Stanford, CA, 2002); Graciela Marquez, "The Political Economy of Mexican Protectionism, 1868–1911" (Ph.D. dissertation, Harvard University, 2002); Aurora Gómez-Galvarriato, "The Impact of Revolution."

[21] Aurora Gómez Galvarriato, "El desempeño de la Fundidora de Hierro y Acero de Monterrey durante el Porfiriato. Acerca de los obstáculos a la industrialización en México," in *Historia de las grandes empresas en México, 1850–1930* (Mexico City, 1997) 216.

[22] Aurora Gómez Galvarriato, "The Impact of Revolution," 604.

the power to raise (or lower) tariffs resided in a single person – José Y. Limantour, Mexico's Secretary of the Treasury from 1893 to 1911. Limantour appears to have operated under a single guiding principal in making these decisions: manufacturers who were part of the political coalition that supported the dictator Porfirio Díaz were granted protection; everyone else was out in the cold.[23] Not surprisingly, companies that received high levels of trade protection tended to have members of Díaz's cabinet or congress on their boards of directors.[24]

We do not yet have the kind of detailed research on the political economy of trade protection in Brazil that we have for Mexico. Nevertheless, it is clear that what took place in Brazil conforms to the Mexican pattern in at least two dimensions. First, there was no global policy to protect industry. Rather, individual industries lobbied for protection. Second, some industries were extremely successful in this game and obtained tariffs that effectively drove foreign goods from the market.

One industry that has been studied in considerable detail is cotton textiles. The evidence is unambiguous: beginning in the late 1880s, the government began to push up the tariff on finished cotton cloth at the same time that it reduced tariffs on raw materials and eliminated the tariffs on cotton textile machinery. In other words, it introduced a cascading tariff structure that allowed for effective protection. As occurred in Mexico, inflation in the 1890s eroded the tariff (tariffs were specific, not ad valorem), but the real depreciation of the exchange rate compensated for the reduction in the tariff. Between 1898 and 1905, the depreciation of the real exchange rate was reversed – the *milreis* appreciated. As a result, the government increased nominal tariffs. Calculated as ad valorem equivalents, Brazilian textile tariffs increased from 22.4 percent in 1895 to 49.7 percent in 1906.[25]

The evidence about Brazil's industrial tariffs, generally speaking, conforms to what we know about cotton textiles. They rose in the 1880s and declined in the 1890s because of inflation. The real depreciation of the exchange rate, however, compensated for the decline in nominal

---

[23] Graciela Marquez Colin, "The Political Economy of Mexican Protectionism, 1868–1911."

[24] Stephen Haber, Armando Razo, and Noel Maurer, *The Politics of Property Rights: Political Instability, Credible Commitments, and Economic Growth in Mexico, 1876–1929*, ch. 3 (Cambridge, 2003); Armando Razo, "Social Networks and Credible Commitments in Dictatorships: Political Organization and Economic Growth in Porifiran Mexico, 1876–1991," ch. 8 and 9 (Ph.D. dissertation, Stanford University, 2003).

[25] Wilson Suzigan, *Indústria brasileira: origem e desenvolvimento*, 143–5.

tariffs. When the exchange rate appreciated, compensatory tariffs were established.[26]

Research to date on Argentine trade protection lacks the econometric bells and whistles that characterize research on Mexico and Brazil. It does, however, make it clear that manufacturers were able to obtain protective tariffs on an industry-by-industry basis. As Rocchi's work makes clear, there was both an organized "industrial lobby" that pushed for protection and a protectionist coalition in the Argentine congress that log-rolled specific tariff increases for a wide variety of industries.[27] The available evidence indicates that in some classes of goods, such as foodstuffs and beverages, the nominal tariff rates were over 50 percent. In some other goods, particularly cloth, the rates were substantially lower – just over 20 percent.[28]

Industrial development requires, of course, more than protective tariffs. It also requires the ability to develop or adapt technology and the ability to mobilize capital to purchase the capital goods that are the embodiment of that technology. That is, unless there is a financial system that connects those who have liquid wealth with those who can employ it in productive investments, the growth of industry can be no faster than that permitted by the reinvestment of profits.

A detailed discussion of the political economy of financial system development across Latin America would take us well beyond the space and thematic constraints of this chapter on industry. We can offer nothing more than a brief summary of a rapidly growing literature. In broad strokes, there are five major requirements for an efficient financial system: sound public finances, a stable currency, a banking system, a central bank, and well-developed securities markets. Some Latin American countries, at some points in time, managed to have some of these features. For example, Mexico in the late nineteenth century had a stable currency and sound public finances, but it did not have well-developed securities markets, it had a miniscule banking system, and it lacked a central bank.[29] Similarly, during

---

[26] Wilson Suzigan, *Indústria brasileira: origem e desenvolvimento*, 204–5.

[27] Fernando Rocchi, "Building a Nation, Building a Market," 54, 72, 100, 140, 330, 336, 337, 404.

[28] The low rate on cloth explains why Argentina's cotton textile industry remained small relative to that of Brazil and Mexico. Victor Bulmer-Thomas, *The Economic History of Latin America Since Independence*, 2nd ed. (Cambridge, 2003), 145.

[29] Noel Maurer, "Banking Regulation and Banking Performance in Porfirian Mexico," in *The Mexican Economy, 1870–1930*; Maurer, *The Power and the Money: The Mexican Financial System, 1876–1928* (Stanford, CA, 2002); Maurer, "Banks and Entrepreneurs in Porfirian Mexico: Inside Exploitation or Sound Business Strategy?" *Journal of Latin American Studies* 31 (1999):331–61; Maurer and Stephen Haber, "Institutional Change and Economic Growth: Banks, Financial Markets, and Mexican Industrialization," in *The Mexican Economy, 1870–1930*; Stephen Haber, "Banks, Financial Markets, and

the period 1890–1914, Brazil had well-developed securities markets, but it did not have any of the other requisites of an efficient financial system. This allowed a boom in industrial development financed by the sale of securities, but this system broke down in the long run because the lack of sound public finances produced an inflationary spiral that undermined the stock and bond markets.[30] Argentina, for its part, had virtually none of the requisites of a sound financial system. Rather, in the years prior to 1914, it essentially free rode on the British financial system.[31] On the whole, Latin American countries tended to be under-banked and to have very underdeveloped securities markets. Manufacturers, therefore, tended to be liquidity constrained, which had negative effects on the extensive growth of industry, the adoption of new technologies and, hence, productivity growth.

This is not to say that industrial firms could *never* call on domestic securities markets or banks to finance investment. The large, mechanized firms that dominated product markets in most countries tended to be able to obtain working capital from banks to which they were connected by overlapping boards of directors.[32] Some of them were also able to mobilize long-term investment capital by selling equity or bonded debt on organized exchanges. This was particularly the case in Brazil during the period 1890–1914, when the securities markets flourished.[33] It is to say, however, that as a general rule there was differential access to capital: only a limited number of entrepreneurs were able to make use of the financial system to mobilize

Industrial Development: Lessons from the Economic Histories of Brazil and Mexico," in José Antonio González et al., eds., *Macroeconomic Reform in Latin America: The Second Stage* (Chicago, 2003); Carlos Marichal, "El nacimiento de la banca mexicana en el contexto latinoamericano: problemas de periodización," in Leonor Ludlow and Carlos Marichal, eds., *La banca en México, 1820–1920* (Mexico City, 1998).

[30] Anne Hanley, "Capital Markets in the Coffee Economy: Financial Institutions and Economic Change in São Paulo, Brazil, 1850–1905" (Ph.D. dissertation, Stanford University, 1995); Gail Triner, *Banking and Economic Development: Brazil, 1889–1930* (New York, 2000); Stephen Haber, "Banks, Financial Markets, and Industrial Development: Lessons from the Economic Histories of Brazil and Mexico," in *Macroeconomic Reform in Latin America: The Second Stage*.

[31] Lance E. Davis and Robert E. Gallman, *Evolving Financial Markets and International Capital Flows: Britain, the Americas, and Australia, 1865–1914*, ch. 6 (Cambridge, 2001); Andrés Regalsky, "Banking, Trade, and the Rise of Capitalism in Argentina, 1850–1930," in Alice Teichova, Ginette Kurgan-Van Hentenryk, and Dieter Ziegler, eds., *Banking, Trade, and Industry, Europe, America, and Asia from the Thirteenth to the Twentieth Century* (Cambridge, 1997).

[32] Noel Maurer and Stephen Haber, "Institutional Change and Economic Growth."

[33] Stephen Haber, "The Efficiency Consequences of Institutional Change: Financial Market Regulation and Industrial Productivity Growth in Brazil, 1866–1934," in John H. Coatsworth and Alan M. Taylor, eds., *Latin America and the World Economy Since 1800* (Cambridge, MA, 1998), 275–322; Raghuram G. Rajan and Luigi Zingales, "The Great Reversals: The Politics of Financial Development in the Twentieth Century," *Journal of Financial Economics* 69:1 (July 2003); Aldo Musacchio, "Ordem (na corte) e Progresso: O poder judiciário e o mercado financeiro na transformação econômica republicana," *Acervo: Revista do Arquivo Nacional* 15:1 (November 2002).

capital, while everyone else was starved for funds. Differential access to capital explains, in large part, the tendency of Latin American industry toward high levels of concentration, even in industries that were characterized by modest returns to scale technologies: capital market imperfections essentially operated as a barrier to entry.[34]

Nevertheless, by 1913–14, the largest countries in the region had already built substantial industrial sectors. Although the estimates are rough, the available estimates indicate that manufacturing accounted for 19.4 percent of total value added in Brazil, 16.6 percent in Argentina, 14.5 percent in Chile, and 12.3 percent in Mexico.[35]

FROM WORLD WAR I TO THE GREAT DEPRESSION

The interruption of international capital and product markets with the onset of World War I did not produce a major disruption in Latin America's industrial development. On the one hand, Latin American industry was helped by the fact that the European economies had turned to war production. Thus, even those industries that lacked the political clout to obtain tariff protection during the 1890–1914 period now obtained implicit protection as foreign-produced consumer goods disappeared from the market. On the other hand, Latin American industry was hurt by the war in two senses. First, Latin American economic growth prior to 1914 had been financed in large part by foreign capital inflows – particularly from Great Britain. These flows dried up in 1914, and with their disappearance came the stalling of the overall process of growth. Second, Latin American industry tended to import most of its capital and intermediate goods from the advanced industrial economies of the North Atlantic. With the war, these inputs became extremely difficult to obtain. To a very small degree, domestic producers moved into the production of some of these goods. Until the United States entered the war, some inputs could also be obtained there. Nevertheless, spare parts for machines (as well as new machinery), coal, and chemicals (used for tanning, explosive manufacturing, and textile dyeing and finishing) were all hard to come by. The end result was that Latin American industry continued to grow, but at a modest pace, until the war's end.

[34] Stephen Haber, "Banks, Financial Markets, and Industrial Development."
[35] Brazilian data from Bill Albert, *South America and the First World War: The Impact of the War on Brazil, Argentina, Peru, and Chile* (Cambridge, 1988), 185. Data for other countries from Victor Bulmer-Thomas, *The Economic History of Latin America Since Independence*, 134.

The slowdown in industrial development during 1914–18 can be clearly seen in the Brazilian case, where we have excellent serial data. Table 13.1 presents data on the size of Brazil's cotton textile industry. From 1907 to 1914, the textile industry, measured in spindlage, doubled in size. From 1914 to 1921, the industry grew not at all. It then resumed growing after 1921, roughly increasing in size by 50 percent by the end of the decade. A skeptical reader might argue that this pattern is peculiar to the cotton textile industry. That argument does not stand up, however, to data assembled by Wilson Suzigan on the real value of machinery imports to Brazil. Note that the data set measures flows, not stocks. Also note that Brazil produced virtually no industrial machinery during the period in question: virtually everything was imported from the United States, the United Kingdom, France, and Germany. The data set, presented in Table 13.3, is thus an excellent estimator of new spending on capital equipment by manufacturing firms. The data are unambiguous: the war produced a dramatic contraction in new investment. In 1914, total machinery imports were only 41 percent of their 1913 level. From 1915 to 1918, machinery imports oscillated between 12 and 17 percent of their 1913 levels.

An even more skeptical reader might argue that the contraction in new spending on capital equipment does not mean that Brazilian industry did not earn windfall profits during the war – profits that could be reinvested later, once it was possible to import capital equipment. In Table 13.4, I test this hypothesis directly by presenting estimates of the profitability of Brazilian cotton textile manufacturing. I present four different measures of profits, each one capturing different concepts of what profits are and who receives them: the nominal rate of return on owner's equity, the real rate of return on owner's equity, the real market rate of return to stockholders, and the real market rate of return to stock and bondholders.[36] The sampling

---

[36] The first two measures (the nominal and real rate of return on owners' equity) treat profits as the *book value* of income owned by shareholders divided by the *book value* of capital owned by shareholders. Income is calculated as dividends plus directors' fees plus changes in reserve accounts. Capital is measured as the value of reserve accounts plus the par value of outstanding shares. The only difference in the two measures is that the first is unadjusted for inflation, whereas the second adjusts both income and changes to the value of reserve accounts in the owner's equity calculation for inflation. The second two measures (real financial returns to stockholders and real financial returns to stock and bondholders) treat profits as the *market value* of financial returns to stockholders or to stock and bondholders divided by *the market value* of those investments. Both are adjusted for inflation. In calculating financial profits to shareholders, income is measured as changes in the real market value of stock plus real dividends, and capital is measured as the real market value of stock. In calculating financial profits to stock and bondholders, we assume that investors hold a portfolio of stocks and bonds (weighted by their market capitalization).

Table 13.3. *Brazilian industrial machinery imports, 1900–1939[a]*
(Real, 1913, £ sterling)

Year	Textile machines	Index 1913 = 100	Total industrial machinery[1]	Index 1913 = 100
1900	126,743	22	535,963	19
1901	96,266	17	410,308	14
1902	170,822	30	509,999	18
1903	175,434	30	582,390	20
1904	222,508	39	738,712	26
1905	161,262	28	891,185	31
1906	201,017	35	1,136,843	40
1907	405,519	70	1,591,120	56
1908	421,303	73	1,457,111	51
1909	388,217	67	1,476,458	52
1910	423,990	73	1,733,234	61
1911	503,017	87	2,222,300	78
1912	667,605	116	2,963,600	104
1913	577,919	100	2,857,718	100
1914	172,874	30	1,157,885	41
1915	100,684	17	337,491	12
1916	113,612	20	375,121	13
1917	102,091	18	487,195	17
1918	122,520	21	424,971	15
1919	140,964	24	794,953	28
1920	131,674	23	1,271,030	44
1921	385,041	67	1,607,563	56
1922	583,579	101	1,453,184	51
1923	439,932	76	1,322,218	46
1924	634,953	110	1,939,346	68
1925	1,039,711	180	2,609,991	91
1926	638,609	111	2,167,597	76
1927	546,863	95	2,144,788	75
1928	517,749	90	2,281,960	80
1929	408,474	71	2,863,740	100
1930	215,078	37	1,605,285	56
1931	208,576	36	703,717	25
1932	246,965	43	777,451	27
1933	355,360	61	1,242,563	43
1934	435,122	75	1,543,216	54
1935	536,892	93	1,929,352	68
1936	605,101	105	1,925,418	67
1937	709,731	123	2,412,365	84
1938	811,770	140	2,836,861	99
1939	507,433	88	2,428,693	85

Notes:
[a] Exports of industrial machinery from Great Britain, the United States, France, and Germany to Brazil, converted to real pounds.
[1] Includes textile machines, as well as generators, electric motors, metal-working machines, wood-working machines, shoe-making machines, sugar mills, sugar-processing equipment, refrigeration, brewing equipment, typesetting equipment, spare parts, and other industrial machinery not specified by type.
Source: Wilson Suzigan, *Indústria brasileira: Origem e Desenvolvimento* (São Paulo, 1986), 360–4.

Table 13.4. *Estimates of rates of return to the Brazilian cotton textile industry*[1] *(Divisia index of all firms listed on the Rio de Janeiro and São Paulo exchanges)*

Year	Nominal rate of return on owner's equity	Real rate of return on owner's equity	Real financial returns to stockholders	Real financial returns to stock and bondholders
1900	9.8	3.7	15.1	18.6
1901	1.7	0.8	2	20.1
1902	9.8	4.8	55.4	21.6
1903	8	4.1	16.1	9.1
1904	15.2	8.6	− 4.3	9.6
1905	10.1	6.8	10.3	26.8
1906	6.9	2.4	8.3	0.5
1907	10	6.1	12.4	2.5
1908	6.9	4.2	−12.8	2.8
1909	5.7	4.4	0.2	16.7
1910	7.2	5.1	8.5	8.2
1911	12.7	8.1	5.8	1.9
1912	7.7	5.1	−9.5	−4.5
1913	6.3	4.5	−6.5	9.6
1914	3.3	3.2	− 1	15.5
1915	10.5	4.2	−24.2	−7.7
1916	6.9	4.7	−8.1	−15.5
1917	7.5	4	−1.3	−3.1
1918	12.3	5.3	8.7	2.3
1919	7.1	4	−5.6	−3.1
1920	12.9	7.1	−6.4	−8.8
1921	3.1	2.1	11.2	17.7
1922	10.9	5.9	21.2	−0.2
1923	14.6	6.9	−15.6	−17.8
1924	8	3.9	−5.3	−4.1
1925	2.7	2.6	−17.4	−15.1
1926	4.5	2.8	4.8	21.8
1927	2.7	1.9	0.5	4.6
1928	2.9	1.2	−5.4	−9.2
1929	−2	−0.1	−12.2	2.7
1930	−1.3	−0.6	−4.3	10.9
1931	1.7	1.3	12.4	12.3
1932	3.7	2.2	1.5	1.7
1933	4.6	2.7	3.4	5.5
1934	−4	−0.3	6.8	−9.5
1935	1.9	0.5	3.1	−2.7
1936	−14	−4.7	2.7	−16.2

Year	Nominal rate of return on owner's equity	Real rate of return on owner's equity	Real financial returns to stockholders	Real financial returns to stock and bondholders
1937	3.9	1.5	−0.4	−6.2
1938	4.1	1.8	−3.8	0
1939	1.8	0.6	−7.1	0.8

Notes:

[1] The nominal and real rate of return on owner's equity treat profits as the book value of income owned by shareholders, divided by the book value of capital owned by shareholders. Income is calculated as dividends plus directors' fees plus changes in reserve accounts. Capital is measured as the value of reserve accounts plus the par value of outstanding shares. Real financial returns to stockholders and real financial returns to stock and bondholders treat profits as the market value of financial returns to stockholders or to stock and bondholders divided by the market value of those investments. In calculating financial profits to shareholders, income is measured as changes in the real market value of stock plus real dividends, and capital is measured as the real market value of stock. In calculating financial profits to stock and bondholders, we assume that investors hold a portfolio of stocks and bonds (weighted by their market capitalization).

Source: Calculated from data in *Jornal do Commercio* and *O Estado de São Paulo*, various years.

technique employed was to gather observations on all cotton textile firms listed on the São Paulo and Rio de Janeiro stock markets, and to then construct a *Divisia* (shifting weight) Index. The smallest number of firms in any year was thirty. The largest number of firms was sixty-six.

The results are clear: there were no windfall profits during the war. The real rate of return on owner's equity fell during 1914–18 to an annual average of 4.3 percent, compared with 4.9 percent for the period 1900–13. The decline in market rates of return was even more severe: real financial returns to stockholders fell from 7.2 percent to negative 5.2 percent. A stockholder who bought a portfolio of cotton textile stocks at the end of 1914, reinvested all dividends, and rebalanced the portfolio every year would have lost 25 percent of his investment by the end of 1918. An investor who took the more conservative approach of buying a weighted portfolio of textile stocks and bonds, who reinvested all dividends, and who rebalanced the portfolio every year would have done somewhat better, but would still have lost money. The real financial returns to such an investor would have been negative 1.7 percent per year from 1914 to 1918, compared with 10.3 percent from 1900 to 1913.

The available evidence indicates that Argentina had an experience similar to that of Brazil. Barbero and Rocchi's estimates indicate that industrial output stagnated from 1914 to 1918. The lack of imported raw materials and intermediate goods strangled most Argentine manufacturing firms. Only those firms that had sufficient capacity and that employed domestic raw materials – such as the wool textile industry – benefited from the war.[37] Not surprisingly, urban unemployment increased from 6.7 percent to 19.4 percent between 1913 and 1919. We also know that there was a sharp increase in the number of business failures.[38]

We do not, as yet, have the kinds of systematic data sets for Chile that we do for Argentina and Brazil. Nevertheless, Bill Albert's careful (and critical) evaluation of the secondary literatures indicates that Chile's experience was not dissimilar to that of its neighbors. Industrial output, investment, and employment fell during the early years of the war and then slowly recovered to its 1913 levels.[39]

One implication that emerges from the evidence about Brazil, Argentina, and Chile is that Mexico did not forego an opportunity for rapid industrial expansion because of the Mexican Revolution of 1910–20. The detailed analysis of the Mexican case by Haber, Razo, and Maurer clearly indicates that industrial output and investment contracted sharply in Mexico during the years of civil war (1913–17).[40] Their analysis also indicates little in the way of the destruction of physical plant, as well as a swift recovery of output and investment as soon as the civil war ended. In fact, data on the importation of industrial machinery to Mexico (Table 13.5) demonstrate more or less the same pattern as do the data on Brazil (see Table 13.3): a severe contraction in 1914–17 followed by a dramatic recovery. The implication is that even had there been no revolution to interrupt factor and product markets, Mexican output and investment would have been depressed because of the shortage of raw materials, machines, and spare parts.

With the end of hostilities in 1918, the same process that had permitted the expansion of industry prior to 1914 began anew. Great Britain was no longer the dominant consumer of Latin American export goods, the dominant source of foreign capital flows, and the dominant source of machinery and equipment. The United States had taken over all of those roles. From

---

[37] María Inés Barbero and Fernando Rocchi, "Industry," in Gerardo della Paolera and Alan M. Taylor, eds., *A New Economic History of Argentina* (Cambridge, 2003), 261, 265.

[38] Paul H. Lewis, *The Crisis of Argentine Capitalism* (Chapel Hill, NC, 1990), 35.

[39] Bill Albert, *South America and the First World War*, 202–10.

[40] Stephen Haber, Armando Razo, and Noel Maurer, *The Politics of Property Rights*, ch. 5.

Table 13.5. *Exports of manufacturing machinery from the United States and United Kingdom to Mexico, in 1929 U.S. dollars*

Year	Total manufacturing machinery	Index 1913 = 100	Textile machinery	Index 1913 = 100
1900	734,770	51	468,115	1,806
1901	402,167	28	183,564	708
1902	386,609	27	248,021	957
1903	521,033	36	147,243	568
1904	789,190	55	395,789	1,527
1905	890,938	62	265,632	1,025
1906	1,158,405	80	354,592	1,368
1907	1,474,894	102	471,916	1,821
1908	1,441,350	100	472,963	1,825
1909	1,154,146	80	525,028	2,025
1910	1,017,436	71	349,919	1,350
1911	1,372,511	95	331,188	1,278
1912	1,111,385	77	391,488	1,510
1913	1,442,572	100	25,922	100
1914	300,418	21	6,274	24
1915	115,660	8	3,405	13
1916	428,426	30	8,521	33
1917	895,278	62	35,552	137
1918	1,543,712	107	85,800	331
1919	2,891,556	200	164,364	634
1920	4,960,427	344	457,035	1,763
1921	4,056,181	281	138,966	536
1922	2,779,865	193	1,112,938	4,293
1923	2,050,045	142	595,872	2,299
1924	2,011,632	139	634,439	2,447
1925	2,699,575	187	916,903	3,537
1926	7,298,838	506	1,111,451	4,288
1927	6,604,369	458	1,066,284	4,113
1928	6,263,526	434	1,123,659	4,335
1929	8,615,809	597	680,932	2,627
1930	8,179,263	567	643,881	2,484
1931	1,089,077	75	426,688	1,646
1932	546,913	38	163,623	631
1933	957,090	66	415,211	1,602
1934	1,421,132	99	532,113	2,053
1935	1,778,275	123	694,107	2,678

Source: Stephen Haber, Armando Razo, and Noel Maurer, *The Politics of Property Rights: Political Instability, Credible Commitments and Economic Growth in Mexico, 1876–1929* (Cambridge, 2003), ch. 5.

the point of view of industrial development, however, this change made little difference: foreign investment and foreign markets drove an overall growth process, one of the outcomes of which was the rapid expansion of domestic manufacturing industry.

Brazil provides a relevant (and intensively studied) case in point. As Table 13.1 indicates, its cotton textile industry, the growth of which had stalled from 1914 to 1921, grew by 66 percent from 1921 to 1927. By this point, with 2.7 million spindles in operation, it dwarfed the cotton textile industry of any other Latin American country. New manufacturing investment was not just confined to cotton textiles. As Table 13.3 indicates, roughly 75 percent of new machinery imports during the 1920s were in industries other than textiles. Moreover, during the 1920s, the average annual flow of industrial machine imports was 44 percent higher than it had been from 1900 to 1913. Output increased with the growth of new investment. The available estimates indicate that between 1920 and 1928, total industrial output grew anywhere from 28 percent (the Villela-Suzigan estimates) to 57 percent (the Haddad estimates).[41]

The increase in investment and output was, in part, the consequence of investments in established lines of manufacturing, such as textiles, beverages, hats, and footwear. The growth of investment and production, however, went far beyond established industries and even included the production of some intermediate and capital goods. These new industries included chemicals, iron and steel, gas appliances, cement, electrical hardware, rayon textiles, tobacco products, tires, and machinery of various types including electric motors, sugar-processing equipment, and textile spinning and weaving machines.[42] Many of the machinery manufacturers had started out as repair shops and had moved into machine fabrication during and after World War I. Some of them, however, were subsidiaries of U.S. and European firms that were now beginning to open factories abroad. These included General Electric, RCA, IBM, Ericsson, Philips, and Standard Electric. In addition, during the 1920s, foreign companies – particularly Ford and General Motors – erected automobile assembly plants in Brazil.[43]

Mexico's experience during the 1920s was similar to that of Brazil. Firm- and industry-level data from the cotton textile, steel, cement, and

---

[41] Flavio Rabelo Versiani, "Before the Depression: Brazilian Industry in the 1920s," in Rosemary Thorp, ed., *An Economic History of Latin America*, vol. 2, *Latin America in the 1930s: The Role of the Periphery in World Crisis* (London, 2000), 145.

[42] Ibid., 145–7, 155.

[43] Ibid., 156.

cigarette industries all point in the same direction: there was substantial new investment in plants and equipment from 1918 through the late 1920s.[44] Data on the export of industrial machinery from the United States and Great Britain to Mexico provide independent verification of the data from individual industries. As Table 13.5 indicates, during the 1920s, industrial machinery exports to Mexico were anywhere from twice (in the case of textile machines) to six times (manufacturing machines other than textiles) what they had been during the period 1900–10. In part, the growth of investment took place in domestic firms that had been established before 1910. In part, there was also the founding of new firms that manufactured products that previously had been imported, such as cotton knitwear and rayon cloth. Finally, the growth of investment also included the establishment of subsidiaries of foreign corporations. These included the British-American Tobacco Company, the International Match Company, the Dupont de Nemours Company, the Palmolive Company, and the Ford Motor Company.[45]

As investment climbed, so did output. The data sets put together by Haber, Razo, and Maurer on the steel, cement, cigarette, beer, cotton textile, and dynamite industries all point in the same direction: sustained and dramatic growth from 1918 through the 1920s. In all six industries, national firms satisfied all of Mexican demand, pushing imports out of the market. Data on small-scale manufacturing, such as hats, shoes and boots, and the confection of clothing, cannot be retrieved directly. Data are available, however, on one of the most important inputs into all of these industries: electric power consumption in Mexico City for commercial purposes. To the degree that this proxies output in small-scale industries (the data exclude power generated for the water, tramway, or public lighting systems), the evidence is unambiguous: power consumption increased by 60 percent from 1910 to 1920, and then doubled from 1920 to 1927.[46]

Data on Chilean industrial investment and production tell much the same story. Palma's estimates of Chilean manufacturing output not only indicate that production increased during the 1920s but also that Chilean industrialists were diversifying beyond the production of consumer non-durables. Total manufacturing output grew 24 percent between 1918 and 1925. Even more striking, the share of consumer durable, intermediate, and

[44] Stephen Haber, Armando Razo, and Noel Maurer, *The Politics of Property Rights*, ch. 5.
[45] Ibid.
[46] Ibid.

capital goods in total output increased from 18 percent to 24 percent. The rate of growth of total manufacturing output slowed during the latter half of the 1920s, but the diversification into more complex goods continued. By 1929, 29 percent of Chilean industrial production was made up of consumer durables, intermediate, and capital goods. The two fastest growing industries were chemicals (the output of which nearly doubled from 1918 to 1929) and metal machinery and transport equipment (the output of which nearly tripled during the same period).[47]

Argentina's experience parallels that of Chile. Argentine industry continued to expand in the 1920s but at a slower pace than it had prior to 1914. At the same time, industrial production began to shift away from beverages and foodstuffs and toward chemicals, metal products, and textiles. Circa 1914, chemicals and oils accounted for only 3 percent of output. By 1935, they were 10 percent. Over the same period, metals and machinery jumped from 5 percent of industrial output to 14 percent, while textiles grew from 11 percent to 21 percent.[48]

INDUSTRIAL DEVELOPMENT DURING THE GREAT DEPRESSION

The growth of manufacturing industry after 1930 was a broadening and elaboration of a process that had been going on for quite some time. Moreover, just as was the case during the 1890–1930 period, the post-1930 period was also characterized by ad hoc policy responses to changes in the economic environment. Politicians, businessmen, and organized labor responded to events as they were overtaken by them. The result was tariff protection, multiple exchange rate systems, quantitative restrictions on imports, government-owned industrial development banks, parastate enterprises, and a style of industrial development that was decidedly inward-looking, technologically backward, and inefficient. It should be kept in mind, however, that these were the ex-post outcomes of an ad hoc process rather than the result of carefully thought-out plans or "growth strategies."

The Great Depression hit Latin America hard and early. Well before Wall Street's Black Friday in October 1929, the prices of most Latin American exports had been steadily falling. With the contraction of the U.S.

---

[47] Gabriel Palma, "From an Export-Led to an Import-Substituting Economy," 51–3.
[48] María Inés Barbero and Fernando Rocchi, "Industry," 272–3.

and European economies during 1930–2, export prices, as well as export volumes, went into free fall. The result was a dramatic contraction of Latin American export earnings. In Mexico, to cite a relevant example, total export earnings in 1932 were only one third their 1928 level.[49] Chile, to cite another example, was even harder hit: its export earnings in 1932 were only one sixth their 1929 level.[50]

In the short run, the collapse in exports caused a dramatic contraction of the manufacturing sector. Consider, for example, the case of Mexico. Cárdenas's estimates of total industrial output indicate a decline of 31 percent from 1929 to 1932.[51] Data from individual industries provide independent confirmation of these aggregate estimates: steel output fell by 67 percent, beer by 41 percent, cotton textiles by 22 percent, cement by 13 percent, and cigarettes by 8 percent. In industries in which there had been substantial investment in new plant and equipment in the 1920s, the results were catastrophic. In the cigarette industry, for example, the leading firm (a subsidiary of the British American Tobacco Company) was able to operate at only 37 percent of capacity. The cement industry (where capacity had close to doubled in the late 1920s) was even more hard hit: it operated at only 34 percent of capacity in 1932.[52] As sales collapsed, so too did the financial statements and share prices of manufacturing firms. Estimates by Haber of real financial returns indicate that an investor who purchased a portfolio of common stock in Mexico's largest, publicly traded manufacturing companies would have sustained a loss of 7.8 percent per year from 1926 to 1932.[53]

The experiences of other Latin American countries mirror that of Mexico. From 1929 to 1932, total manufacturing output fell by 22 percent in Chile and by 7 percent in Brazil.[54] The latter figure is almost certainly a gross underestimate.[55] Much as happened in Mexico, the profitability of

---

[49] Stephen Haber, *Industry and Underdevelopment*," 153.

[50] Gabriel Palma, "From an Export-Led to an Import-Substituting Economy," 55.

[51] Enrique Cárdenas, "The Process of Accelerated Industrialization in Mexico, 1929–1982," in Enrique Cárdenas, José Antonio Ocampo, and Rosemary Thorp, eds., *An Economic History of Twentieth Century Latin America*, vol. 3, *Industrialization and the State in Latin America, The Postwar Years* (London, 2000), 179.

[52] Stephen Haber, *Industry and Underdevelopment*, 158, 163, 165.

[53] Ibid., 169.

[54] Flavio Rabelo Versiani, "Before the Depression," 159; Gabriel Palma, "From an Export-Led to an Import-Substituting Economy," 60.

[55] Data from individual manufacturing industries indicate that the 7 percent decline is a probably misleading. Output fell by 23 percent in beverages, 24 percent in shoes and boots, 58 percent in hats, and 29 percent in furniture, for example. See Flavio Rabelo Versiani, "Before the Depression," 159.

manufacturing firms fell sharply. Our index of real rates of return on owner's equity in the Brazilian cotton textile industry indicates that firms, on average, lost money in 1929 and 1930, and barely managed to turn a profit in 1931 (see Table 13.4).

In the medium term, however, the Depression created conditions that were favorable to industrial development. The response of governments around the world during the Depression was to abandon the gold standard. In the context of a major decline in Latin American exports, the resulting system of freely floating exchange rates produced sharp currency devaluations. These devaluations did not produce concomitant jumps in domestic inflation. The result was that virtually every Latin American country saw its currency devalued in real terms during the 1930s.

Real exchange rate depreciation kick-started Latin American economic growth. First, it made the region's exports extremely competitive in international markets. Second, it created high levels of implicit protection for the manufacturing sector.[56]

The result was the rapid growth in manufacturing output. Output growth was not only high compared with the rest of the world (in the United States and Canada, industrial growth was near zero during the 1930s), but was also high compared with the rate of growth of Latin America's other economic sectors.[57] In Brazil, for example, manufacturing output increased by 82 percent from 1928 to 1939. Solis's estimates for Mexico indicate that total manufacturing output in 1939 was roughly double that in 1925, with most of the growth coming after 1934.[58] The story was much the same in Chile: total manufacturing output grew by 30 percent from 1929 to 1939,

---

The reason for the discrepancy between individual industries and the aggregate series likely resides in the fact that the latter are strongly influenced by cotton textiles (the largest industry in Brazil). As I have shown elsewhere, the standard IBGE series on textile output seriously understate the dimensions of the downturn in that industry. The reason is that the textile "output" series are, in fact, series on textile sales. Sales actually fell less far than output because manufacturers applied steep discounts in order to move unsold textiles, which had been accumulating since the late 1920s, out of their warehouses. Textile output did, in fact, decline dramatically – by some 39 percent from 1927 to 1930 – but this decline is not picked up in the standard series. See Stephen Haber, "Business Enterprise and the Great Depression in Brazil: A Study of Profits and Losses in Textile Manufacturing," *Business History Review* 66 (Summer 1992): 335–63.

[56] A real depreciation of the exchange rate causes the prices of imported goods to increase in terms of domestic currency. It therefore has the same effect as an across-the-board increase in import tariffs.

[57] Carlos F. Díaz Alejandro, "Latin America in the 1930s," in *An Economic History of Latin America in the 1930s*, vol. 2, 34.

[58] E. V. K. Fitzgerald, "Restructuring through the Depression: The State and Capital Accumulation in Mexico, 1925–1940," in *Latin America in the 1930s*, vol. 2, 241.

at the same time that GDP growth was flat for the economy in general.[59] The result was that by 1939, manufacturing accounted for 16.5 percent of Latin America's total GDP.[60]

In some industries, particularly those associated with construction or metal-working, output growth during the 1930s was staggering. In the cement industry, for example, between the late 1920s and the late 1930s, cement production grew more than fourteenfold in Colombia, sixfold in Brazil, fourfold in Argentina, and twofold in Mexico.[61] The result was that by the end of the 1930s, domestic cement production pushed imported cement completely out of the market. A similar process occurred in the Brazilian steel industry where, from 1929 to 1939, the output of steel ingots increased more than fourfold (to 114,000 tons) and the output of rolled steel products increased threefold (to 101,000 tons).[62] Thus, even before the founding of the much-vaunted *Volta Redonda* works in the 1940s, Brazil was already the largest steel producer in Latin America, dwarfing even Mexico's well-established industry by a factor of three.[63] It had also pushed foreign-produced steel ingots from the market and had captured 23 percent of the domestic market for rolled shapes.[64]

Much of the increase in output during the 1930s was accomplished by running capacity that had been installed in earlier decades on an intensive basis.[65] Suzigan's estimates of the importation of manufacturing machinery to Brazil, for example, indicate that flows of new machinery were 11 percent lower in real terms during the ten-year period 1930–9 than they had been during 1920–9, and were no higher than they had been during the ten years prior to World War I (see Table 13.3). In the steel industry, which witnessed impressive output growth in the 1930s, virtually all of the output in 1939 was produced by firms that had been founded during the 1920s.[66] Data from Mexico indicate much the same pattern. The flow of new manufacturing machinery during 1930–5 was roughly half of what it had been from 1920 to 1929. Even in 1935, when the output recovery was in full swing, the

---

[59] Gabriel Palma, "From an Export-Led to an Import-Substituting Economy: Chile 1914–39," 60.

[60] Enrique Cárdenas, José Antonio Ocampo, and Rosemary Thorp, "Introduction," in *An Economic History of Twentieth Century Latin America*, vol. 3, 17.

[61] Carlos F. Díaz Alejandro, "Latin America in the 1930s," 35; Stephen Haber, *Industry and Underdevelopment*, 169.

[62] Werner Baer, *The Development of the Brazilian Steel Industry* (Nashville, TN, 1969), 61.

[63] Mexico data from Stephen Haber, *Industry and Underdevelopment*, 177.

[64] Werner Baer, *The Development of the Brazilian Steel Industry*, 61.

[65] Carlos F. Díaz Alejandro, "Latin America in the 1930s," 36.

[66] Calculated from data in Werner Baer, *The Development of the Brazilian Steel Industry*, 65.

Table 13.6. *Argentine industrial firms in 1946*

Period of founding	Percentage of establishments	Percentage of workers	Percentage of output by value	Relative output per firm (percent output divided by percent of establishments)
Before 1871	0.3	1.7	2.0	6.67
1871–90	1.4	6.4	6.8	4.86
1891–00	2.1	6.8	7.8	3.71
1901–10	4.6	10.5	10.1	2.20
1911–20	8.9	12.5	14.2	1.60
1921–30	19.7	18.7	20.5	1.04
Subtotal (before 1931)	37.0	56.6	61.4	1.66
1931–40	32.5	25.6	25.2	0.78
1941–46	29.1	15.2	11.4	0.39
Subtotal (1931–46)	61.6	40.8	36.6	0.59
Unknown	1.4	2.5	2.0	1.43

Source: Calculated from Paul Lewis, *The Crisis of Argentine Capitalism*, 40.

flow of new manufacturing machinery was only a fifth of what it had been during the latter part of the 1920s (see Table 13.5). The data on Argentina's industrial plant yield similar results. In 1935, 78 percent of industrial output was produced by firms that had been founded before 1930.[67] Similar data for 1946 indicate that there was not a tremendous amount of investment in the period after 1935. As late as 1946, 61 percent of industrial output was produced by firms that had been founded before 1930 (Table 13.6).

This is not to argue that there were no new firms founded and no new industries developed during the 1930s. There were individual industries that underwent substantial capacity growth in the 1930s. One such case was the Brazilian metal-working and machinery industry, in which many new firms were established. These firms produced agricultural machinery, textile

[67] Jorge Katz and Bernardo Kosacoff, "Import-Substituting Industrialization in Argentina, 1940–1980: Its Achievements and Shortcomings," in *An Economic History of Twentieth Century Latin America*, vol. 3, 282.

spinning and weaving machinery, wood-working machinery, refrigeration equipment, boilers, elevators, and printing equipment, along with a host of other products.[68] These new industries included consumer goods as well. In Mexico, for example, literally hundreds of small firms sprang up during the latter part of the 1930s, producing goods such as silk and rayon flat crepes, cotton knitwear, rayon knitwear, and hosiery.[69] Data from Chile indicate that a similar process took place: thousands of firms with workforces from five to one hundred were founded between 1927 and 1937.[70] The Argentine data on industrial production in 1946, presented in Table 13.6, tell the same story. There were many new firms founded from 1931 to 1946 (they accounted for 62 percent of firms operating in 1946). These firms accounted, however, for only 37 percent of output. If we take the ratio of firms to output for the periods before and after 1931, we generate a rather striking result: firms founded during 1931–46 were roughly one-third the size of firms founded before 1931.

The evidence strongly contradicts the thesis that Latin America's industrial development can be dated from the 1930s. In fact, not only were many of the firms and much of the capacity in the 1930s inherited from earlier decades, but the basic business model of Latin American industry was inherited from those decades as well. In those earlier decades, real exchange rate depreciation produced conditions that favored the development of domestic manufacturing industries. Once exchange rate depreciation stopped or was reversed, manufacturers lobbied their governments for tariff protection.

The political process by which tariff protection had been awarded to favored manufacturers during the years before 1914 continued throughout the 1920s and then accelerated in the 1930s. In Chile, for example, there were multiple revisions of the tariffs after 1914. The 1928 tariff revision not only increased the number of goods subject to import duties, it also gave the president the right to raise tariffs on any product without the need to consult congress. Not surprisingly, within two years, President Ibañez had used this provision to increase import taxes on 440 different customs classifications. On average, tariffs increased by 71 percent from 1928 to 1930 and covered 73 percent of imports. The Chilean government

[68] Wilson Suzigan, *Indústria brasileira: origem e desenvolvimento*, 281.
[69] Stephen Haber, *Industry and Underdevelopment*, 186.
[70] Gabriel Palma, "From an Export-Led to an Import-Substituting Economy: Chile 1914–39," 60.

increased tariffs again in 1931. In 1933, President Alessandri put through an across-the-board tariff increase of 50 percent. A year later, he replaced that increase with a tariff surcharge of 100 percent, which was further increased in 1935 to 300 percent.[71]

The history of Mexican tariff setting is much the same. Mexico, as we discussed earlier, had been extremely protectionist during the Díaz dictatorship. During the 1910–20 Revolution, the Mexican government had tried to lower tariff rates, and had achieved some success. Near as they can be measured, tariffs in 1920 were at roughly half their 1910 level.[72] Under intense pressure from manufacturers (and from Mexico's politically powerful labor federation – the *Confederación Regional Obrera de México*), in the mid-1920s, textile tariffs climbed back to their Porfirian levels. Aurora Gómez-Galvarriato's careful estimates indicate that the effective rate of protection for common cotton cloth was 38 percent in 1923, 46 percent in 1927, and 345 percent in 1930. Tariffs on fine weave goods rose even faster: the effective rate of protection was 53 percent in 1923, 65 percent in 1927, and 397 percent in 1930.[73] These results are consistent with those obtained by Graciela Márquez for a broader range of goods. Her estimates indicate that for consumer goods as a whole (not including foodstuffs), the average nominal tariff in 1924 was 38 percent. In 1930, the average tariff on that same group of products had increased to 47 percent. In some individual product lines, the average tariff had increased even more dramatically. In textiles, for example, the tariff increased from 45 to 59 percent. In manufactured clothing, the tariff increased from 43 to 69 percent. Moreover, in intermediate goods, the average tariff (36 percent in 1930) was lower than in nonagricultural consumer goods (47 percent in 1930), suggesting a cascading tariff structure.[74] Márquez's estimates of intermediate goods tariffs, it should be pointed out, are most likely upwardly biased, because they are strongly driven by chemicals and iron and steel products – industries that

---

[71] Gabriel Palma, "From an Export-Led to an Import-Substituting Economy: Chile 1914–39," 48, 58.

[72] For the coefficient of protection before and after the Revolution, see Daniel Cosio Villegas, *La cuestión arancelaria en México* (Mexico City, 1989), 58. Aurora Gómez Galvarriato's estimates for the cotton textile industry indicate the same magnitude of change. See "The Impact of Revolution," 604–8. For a discussion of the political battles surrounding the tariff in 1920, see María del Carmen Collado Herrera, *Empresarios y políticos, entre la Restauración y la Revolución 1920–1924* (Mexico City, 1996), 208.

[73] Aurora Gómez-Galvarriato, "The Impact of Revolution," 604–8.

[74] Graciela Márquez, "Protección y cambio institucional: la política arancelaria del Porfiriato a la Gran Depresión." (Working Paper, El Colegio de México, Centro de Investigaciones Económicas, 2001).

existed in Mexico and that demanded protection from foreign competition. A sample drawn on intermediate goods that were not manufactured domestically would probably indicate even lower tariffs on intermediate goods. In short, the evidence indicates that the same trend that we saw in textiles – of increasing rates of effective protection – almost certainly held across manufacturing as a whole.

The evidence on other Latin American countries, although less plentiful, runs in the same direction as that for Chile and Mexico. In Brazil, for example, the evidence regarding cotton textiles indicates that tariffs fell during World War I (when industry received implicit protection from the war), but then were raised by the government in the 1920s. Circa 1928, the tariff on common cotton cloth was 100 percent. Tariffs on capital and intermediate goods were high as well, although they were not at the astronomical level of textiles. This suggests a cascading tariff structure and thus positive effective rates of protection.[75] In some countries, governments began to substitute quantitative restrictions for tariffs, essentially not letting in foreign produced goods at any price. This was the case, for example, in Argentina, where the government successively revised tariffs upwards, devalued the currency, and introduced quantitative restrictions on imports.[76]

The broad range of tariff and nontariff barriers to trade that governments put into place in the 1930s were not conceived by policymakers as permanent. Rather, they were ad hoc responses to short-term crises. In fact, from the point of view of governments, tariff and nontariff barriers made a great deal of economic sense – without even considering the political benefits of protecting domestic manufacturing. The collapse of export revenues meant that governments faced balance of payments problems. Negative trade balances could not be offset by positive balances on the capital account, because sources of foreign lending and foreign direct investment had largely dried up during the Depression. Thus, governments needed to find ways to stop hemorrhaging foreign exchange to pay for imports – tariffs and quantitative restrictions were the obvious instruments to bring about this result.[77]

---

[75] Marcelo de P. Abreu, Alfonso S. Bevilaqua, and Demosthenes M. Pinho, "Import Substitution and Growth in Brazil, 1890s–1970s," in *An Economic History of Twentieth Century Latin America*, vol. 3, 157.

[76] Jorge Katz and Bernardo Kosacoff, "Import-Substituting Industrialization in Argentina, 1940–1980," in *An Economic History of Twentieth Century Latin America*, vol. 3, 283.

[77] Enrique Cárdenas, José Antonio Ocampo, and Rosemary Thorp, "Introduction," 10.

POST-1940 INDUSTRIAL DEVELOPMENT

In the ensuing decades, the ad hoc protectionist policies of the 1890s through the 1930s were deepened, broadened, given intellectual justification by development economists,[78] and made into quasipermanent features of the region's political economy. The reasons were several fold: implicit protection from World War II, chronic shortages of foreign exchange, and the political power of organized industrialists and organized industrial workers. Let us take up each of these in turn.

As we have already seen, the experience with implicit protection via exchange rate depreciation during the early 1930s was soon followed in many countries by explicit protection in the form of tariff increases and quantitative restrictions on imports. Because tariffs in most countries were specific, not ad valorem, one would expect domestic price inflation to have gradually eaten away at the protection afforded by these tariffs. That did not occur, however, because the protectionist 1930s were followed by another long period of implicit protection – this one provided by World War II.

The specific effects of the war cut two ways. On the one hand, the war meant that manufacturers of consumer goods were protected from foreign imports. On the other hand, the war also meant that they had difficulty obtaining imported machinery, spare parts, and intermediate inputs. During World War I, the latter effect had dominated the former and accounts, in part, for the sluggish performance of industry during 1914–18. By the 1940s, however, the situation was different: Latin America had substantially greater industrial capacity than had been the case in 1914. Moreover, most of the larger countries also had metal-working industries that were capable of repairing, if not copying, manufacturing machinery. This was particularly the case in Argentina and Brazil, where machine repair and fabrication had been taking place on a modest scale since the 1920s. There had also been the development of some intermediate goods industries during the 1920s – particularly basic chemicals.

The result was that it was possible to run a good deal, although certainly not all, of the already installed plant and equipment around the clock, even if it was not possible to import new capital equipment. This appears to have been particularly true in the Mexican case where, as Clark

---

[78] For a discussion of how development economists came to embrace protectionism in developing countries, see Anne O. Krueger, "Trade Policy and Economic Development: How We Learn," *American Economic Review* 87, 1 (March 1997): 1–22.

Reynolds has shown, most output growth in the 1940s came from running capacity installed in the decades before World War II.[79] It was also true in Argentina, where the ability to run existing plant intensively allowed manufacturers to grab market share from imports. In textiles, for example, domestic manufacturers increased their market share from 50 percent to 88 percent. Much the same happened in the paper industry (where domestic manufacturing increased from 55% to 67% of the market), in the chemical industry (where domestic manufacturers increased their market shares from 75% to 85%), and in electrical machinery production (where domestic manufacturers increased their share from 67% to 90%).[80] Regardless of the intensity with which firms ran old factories during World War II, the end result was the same: there was lots of time – roughly the fifteen years from the onset of the Great Depression to the end of World War II – for Latin American manufacturers to become *very accustomed* to captive domestic markets.

Manufacturers were not the only group that had come to view trade protection – either implicit or explicit – as a given: Latin America's politically powerful industrial workers had as well. In part, the growing influence of labor was a function of numbers: there were simply more miners, stevedores, railway-men, and factory workers in the 1930s than there had been in 1900. In equal part, however, workers had, by the 1930s, become increasingly well organized. In some countries, Mexico being perhaps the archetypal case, they had begun to fuse unions together into national labor federations that were affiliated with political parties. The economic crisis of the early 1930s had brought down many of the governments of the interwar period, or had thrust those governments into crisis. The response, not just in Latin America but around the world, was that politicians had to search for groups that could be part of new coalitions. Given the fact that unions had quantitatively large memberships, were able to mobilize supporters and coordinate their actions, and often had leaderships who were not ideologically opposed to capitalism, they were natural coalition partners for the governments that came to power in the 1930s and 1940s. That is, Latin America's "populist"

[79] Clark W. Reynolds, *The Mexican Economy: Twentieth Century Structure and Growth* (New Haven, CT, 1970), 161–8. Enrique Cárdenas notes that Mexico was somewhat unique among Latin American countries during World War II in that it was able to export a good deal of its output. His calculations indicate that 79 percent of the increase in output during the war can be attributed to exports. Enrique Cárdenas, "The Process of Accelerated Industrialization in Mexico, 1929–1982," in *An Economic History of Twentieth Century Latin America*, vol. 3, 84–5.

[80] Paul H. Lewis, *The Crisis of Argentine Capitalism*, 95.

governments, which historians often identify with particular political leaders such as Getulio Vargas, Juan Perón, and Lazaro Cárdenas, were the product of a more fundamental and larger political process by which some *organized subset* of the working class traded its political support for job security and upward mobility for *its membership alone.*

Once organized labor had been brought into the governing coalitions of most countries, its leadership quickly became strong advocates of trade protection. This is not to say that the relationship between labor unions and manufacturers was not acrimonious, conflictive, and adversarial. It was deeply so. It is to say, however, that both groups saw it in their interest to defend the protection that afforded them stable jobs, stable profits, and (for union leaders) a stable flow of revenues from their rank and file. In fact, the informal coalitions that came to exist between organized labor and organized industrialists were so powerful that even the military governments of the 1960s and 1970s – with the notable exception of Chile's Pinochet government – did not attempt to tinker with protectionism in any serious manner.

One might consider it odd that even right-wing military governments were so easily swayed by protectionist lobbying from industrialists and (left-leaning) labor unions, until you consider that the incentives of governments, regardless of their ideological stripe, were also aligned with trade protection. Latin American governments during the postwar period were confronted by chronic balance of payments problems. On the one hand, Latin American countries were losing market share to other developing countries in their major mineral and agricultural exports. Some sense of this can be gleaned from the following four data points: in 1946, Latin America accounted for 13.5 percent of world exports; by 1955, that figure stood at 8.9 percent; by 1965, at 6.2 percent; and by 1975, at 4.4 percent.[81] On the other hand, Latin America could not substitute net capital inflows for decreasing export revenues. Prior to 1914, trade deficits were financed by positive balances on the capital account – as a result of foreign direct investment and foreign loans. In the postwar period, those sources of finance were no longer as freely available. The extent to which capital flows decreased can be seen in Table 13.7. Circa 1914, the shock of foreign direct investment (FDI) in the larger countries of the region was a large multiple of their GDPs: FDI was 2.6 times GDP in Argentina, 2.96 times in Brazil,

---

[81] Alan M. Taylor, "On the Costs of Inward-Looking Development: Price Distortions, Growth, and Divergence in Latin America," *Journal of Economic History* 58 (March 1998): 1–28.

Table 13.7. *Foreign investment in Latin America as a percent of GDP*

Country	Year							
	1900	1914	1929	1938	1950	1970	1980	1990
Argentina	4.15	2.6	1.12	0.87	0.12	0.14	0.23	0.64
Brazil	2.55	2.96	0.92	0.7	0.18	0.17	0.32	0.36
Chile	1.88	2.11	1.56	1.63	0.49	0.38	0.27	0.4
Colombia	0.74	0.27	0.34	0.35	0.24	0.19	0.13	0.21
Mexico	1.55	1.83	1.28	0.79	0.17	0.12	0.23	0.32
Peru	1.78	1.21	0.64	0.46	0.22	0.22	0.32	0.48
Uruguay	3.14	1.62	0.67	0.59	0.18	0.13		0.31
Venezuela	2.52	0.98	1.05	0.73	0.55	0.36	0.32	0.47

Source: Alan M. Taylor, "Latin America and Foreign Capital in the 20th Century," in Stephen Haber, ed., *Political Institutions and Economic Growth in Latin America: Essays in Policy, History, and Political Economy* (Stanford, CA, 2000), 129.

1.63 times in Chile, and 1.83 times in Mexico. By 1929, these ratios, as well as those for smaller economies, had fallen substantially: FDI in these economies was now roughly equal to GDP. The ratios decreased even further during the 1930s, and then collapsed almost completely thereafter. Circa 1950, FDI was only a small fraction of GDP: 0.12 in Argentina, 0.18 in Brazil, 0.49 in Chile, and 0.17 in Mexico (Table 13.7). It then stayed at that level until the 1970s.

The upshot was that Latin American governments had to find ways to either increase exports or decrease imports. Given the political costs associated with each option, governments tended to chose the latter: boosting exports typically requires the politically unpopular step of a major currency devaluation; decreasing imports simply requires a tariff. In addition, there were time-horizon considerations: increasing exports takes years; decreasing imports can be done overnight. This was even true of military governments, which one might assume to operate with longer time horizons. In Argentina, for example, the military government of Martínez de Hoz tried to lower tariffs and eliminate nontariff barriers when it came to power in the spring of 1976. In the short run it was successful, driving down average tariffs from 94 percent when it came to power to 53 percent before the year was out. It also eliminated quotas and other nontariff restrictions. In the next several years, it pushed tariffs down even further, reaching 26 percent in 1979, with an announced goal of 15 percent for 1981. It could not stay the course, however. By 1980, Argentina was running current account

Table 13.8. *Nominal rates of protection, circa 1960*

Country	Consumer non-durables	Consumer durables	Semi-manufactures	Industrial raw materials	Capital goods
Argentina	176%	266%	95%	55%	98%
Brazil	260%	328%	80%	106%	84%
Chile	328%	90%	98%	111%	45%
Colombia	247%	108%	28%	57%	18%
Mexico	114%	147%	28%	38%	14%
Uruguay	23%	24%	23%	14%	27%
EEC	17%	19%	7%	1%	13%

Source: Alan M. Taylor, "On the Costs of Inward Looking Development: Price Distortions, Divergence, and Growth in Latin America," *Journal of Economic History* 58 (March 1998): 1–28.

deficits, as imported goods flooded the market. Investors came to believe that the government would have to devalue in order to check the tide of imports. The result was capital flight. Part of the response was predictable: the government was forced to devalue the currency. Part of the response was somewhat less predictable: the government completely reversed course on trade liberalization; it returned to protectionism, and embraced high tariffs, quantitative restrictions on imports, and exchange controls.[82]

The conjuncture of political and economic constraints meant that once Latin American governments put protective tariffs or nontariff barriers into place, they did not subsequently remove them. As one author has put it: protectionism was not a time-bound process; instead, every ad hoc protectionist policy became a "permanent conquest."[83] The result was that the ad hoc policies of the 1940s and 1950s became enshrined until the economic collapse of the 1980s. Just how protectionist the Latin American economies were can be gleaned from Table 13.8, on nominal rates of protection, circa 1960. There are two striking patterns to the data. First, import tariffs on manufactures were astronomically high relative to those of the European Economic Community (EEC). In consumer goods, tariffs were almost always in excess of 100 percent and were as high as 328 percent. Second, the lower tariffs on capital goods, semi-manufactures, and industrial raw

[82] Jorge Katz and Bernardo Kosacoff, "Import-Substituting Industrialization in Argentina, 1940–1980," 301.
[83] Enrique Cárdenas, José Antonio Ocampo, and Rosemary Thorp, "Introduction," 16.

materials, although still high by EEC standards, were significantly lower than the tariffs on consumer goods. The implication is that effective rates of protection were also extremely high. Joel Bergsman's detailed study of Brazilian effective rates of protection bears this out. In 1967, after a reform that drastically *lowered* tariffs, the average effective rate of protection on Brazilian manufactures was 117 percent.[84] The available evidence for other countries runs in the same direction: circa 1960, the effective rate of protection on consumer durable goods was 285 percent in Brazil, 123 percent in Chile, and 85 percent in Mexico.[85] The available data on Argentina tell the same story: the average effective rate of protection in 1969 was 97 percent.[86]

In addition to tariff walls, virtually every Latin American country also had quantitative restrictions on imports. These required importers to obtain permits from the government, in addition to paying the tariff, in order to bring a particular product or input into the country. From the point of view of governments, such permit systems were advantageous because permits could be used as patronage to maintain the loyalty of the individuals who were doing the importing. Like most protectionist policies, these began on an ad hoc, temporary basis. Consider, for example, the Mexican experience. Facing enormous pressure on its trade account, the Mexican government imposed quantitative restrictions on imports in 1947. At first, the restrictions only applied to "luxury goods," but a year later the Ministry of the National Economy was given the authority to increase the range of restricted goods – the only requirement being that it had to first consult with the Secretary of the Treasury to assess the impact of the restriction on government revenues. As a practical matter, this meant that manufacturers could lobby the executive branch of government, which could then, without the need to seek legislative approval, restrict the importation of competing products. During the 1950s, these mechanisms were used to obtain quotas on a wide variety of domestically produced goods. As soon as a new industry appeared, the government provided it with import quotas.[87]

[84] Joel Bergsman, "A política comercial no pós-guerra," in Flavio Rabelo Versiani and José Roberto Mendonca de Barros, eds., *Formação econômica do Brasil: a experiência da industrializaçao* (São Paulo, 1977), 396.

[85] Alan M. Taylor, "On the Costs of Inward-Looking Development," 1–28.

[86] Julio Berlinski, "International Trade and Commercial Policy," in Gerardo della Paolera and Alan M. Taylor, *A New Economic History of Argentina* (Cambridge, 2003), 214.

[87] Enrique Cárdenas, "The Process of Accelerated Industrialization in Mexico, 1929–1982," 187. For detailed discussions of protectionism in the Mexican case, see Robert Bruce Wallace et al., *La política de protección en el desarrollo económico de México* (Mexico City, 1979); and Timothy King, *Mexico: Industrialization and Trade Policies Since 1940* (London, 1970).

By 1956, 28 percent of imports were limited by a system of import permits. The proportion of restricted goods grew to 65 percent in 1965, and to 74 percent in 1974.[88] Similar quantitative restrictions, with similarly ad hoc decree mechanisms, were created in Argentina and Chile.[89]

A third protectionist instrument that governments had at their disposal was the use of multiple exchange rates. Manufacturers could import necessary capital goods at special exchange rates that lowered the domestic currency cost of imported machinery and other inputs, but foreign-produced manufactured goods had to come into the country subject to an entirely different exchange rate that made competing imports look extremely expensive in local currency terms. Governments had similar latitude in determining the exchange rate for exports. In fact, governments used "exchange rate management" in any number of ways, depending on their goals at the moment: if they wanted to help exporters compete in foreign markets, they granted them a favorable exchange rate; if they wanted to tax exports to subsidize industry, then the government granted exporters an unfavorable exchange rate – and kept the difference between the international market-determined rate and the official exchange rate. In short, multiple exchange rate systems amounted to a set of complicated implicit taxes and implicit subsidies.

Once governments went down the road of "exchange rate management" there was no end. In Chile, to cite a notorious example, in 1952 there was a system of five multiple exchange rates and three "free" exchange rates, as well as various combinations of both. The government board (CONDECOR), which oversaw this system, not only had the authority to determine exchange rates, it also had the power to ban outright specific imports or exports.[90] Argentina had a similar system of multiple exchange rates that were designed to subsidize industry by implicitly taxing agricultural exports. This was the *Instituto Argentino para la Promoción de Intercambio* (the Argentine Institute for the Promotion of Trade, IAPI), which was created in 1946. IAPI was anything but an export promotion institution. Instead, the Argentine government nationalized all foreign trade, forcing it through IAPI. IAPI then taxed exporters and subsidized industrialists via

---

[88] Robert Bruce Wallace et al., *La política de protección en el desarrollo económico de México*, 94.
[89] Ricardo French Davis et al., "The Industrialization of Chile during Protectionism, 1940–1982," in *An Economic History of Twentieth Century Latin America*, vol. 3, 130–1; Julio Berlinski, "International Trade and Commercial Policy," in *A New Economic History of Argentina*, 213.
[90] Ricardo French Davis et al., "The Industrialization of Chile during Protectionism, 1940–1982," 130.

a system of multiple exchange rates.[91] The use of multiple exchange rates, unlike tariffs and quantitative restrictions, waxed and waned. They were particularly popular in the 1940s and 1950s. Their use, under International Monetary Fund (IMF) pressure, subsided during the 1960s. In the late 1970s and 1980s, however, they made a comeback because they allowed governments to promote exports (and earn foreign exchange) without having to suffer the political consequences of major currency devaluation.

In the medium term, these policies spurred industrial development. In the three decades that followed World War II, Latin American GDP grew 5.6 percent per annum. Manufacturing outgrew the rest of the economy, increasing by 6.8 percent per year. Manufacturing as a share of total Latin American GDP, therefore, rose from 19 percent in 1945 to 26 percent in 1974 – about the same share as in the United States.[92]

The growth of Latin American manufacturing during the postwar period was largely accomplished by the growth of firms that produced consumer durables, such as household appliances and, most particularly, automobiles. This period also saw the flourishing of industries that produced construction goods, most notably steel, cement, and flat-rolled glass, in order to meet the demand of the region's rapidly growing cities. By the 1970s, the range of industrial production expanded even further, including basic petrochemicals, diesel trucks, and aluminum. Some countries, most notably Brazil and Argentina, even developed (with considerable government support) sizable armaments industries that produced low-cost, low-tech aircraft, armored vehicles, and light weapons. This required, of course, the development of their machine tool and other capital goods industries.

It is not clear, however, that the increase in the *size* of Latin American industry necessarily translated into an increase in the *productivity* of Latin American industry. Clark Reynold's estimates for Mexico, for example, indicate that productivity growth in manufacturing during the period after 1940 was quite modest. Mexican industrial output increased at the rate of 8 percent per year from 1940 to 1950 and 7.3 percent per year from 1950 to 1960. But the percentage of that output increase that was not accounted for by the growth of capital and labor was only 0.2 percent per year from 1940 to 1950 and 0.7 percent per year from 1950 to 1960.[93]

[91] Jorge Katz and Bernardo Kosacoff, "Import-Substituting Industrialization in Argentina, 1940–1980," 286.

[92] Data from Enrique Cárdenas, José Antonio Ocampo, and Rosemary Thorp, "Introduction," 16.

[93] Clark W. Reynolds, *The Mexican Economy: Twentieth Century Structure and Growth* (New Haven, CT, 1970), 166. Barbero and Rocchi obtain similar results for Argentina from 1935 to 1954. María Inés Barbero and Fernando Rocchi, "Industry," in *A New Economic History of Argentina*, 274.

The whole point of protectionism was to create distortions that favored manufacturers over other economic sectors. These distortionary policies – tariffs, quantitative restrictions, and multiple exchange rates – generated, however, unintended and perverse consequences. Governments tended to respond to these perverse outcomes with another round of ad hoc policies, which, in turn, gave rise to other unintended and perverse outcomes. Let us examine these briefly.

One of the outcomes of protectionism was that it exacerbated Latin America's balance of payments problem, rather than solving it. Governments embraced quantitative import restrictions and tariffs in the late 1940s because of the rapid dwindling of their foreign exchange reserves. In the short run, the strategy worked. Nobody had thought, however, about the consequences of the growth of consumer goods industries in the context of societies that had historically invested little in education and had little in the way of social overhead capital. It soon became obvious that most capital goods – and in many industries, a good deal of the intermediate goods – were going to have to be imported. In the medium and long terms, this created, perversely, tremendous pressures on the balance of payments.

One solution to this problem was yet more trade protection – now on intermediate and some capital goods. These steps, of course, lowered the effective rate of protection on consumer goods, so it was necessary to increase nominal rates of protection or increase quantitative restrictions on imports for those industries as well. A second solution to the balance of payments problem was to increase export earnings. The only readily available mechanism to do that was to increase traditional exports – mineral and agricultural products. This meant that industrial development required the promotion of the traditional export sector. As is often the case, increasing exports required its own set of ad hoc policies, which, too, were distortionary.

There was, in short, really no such thing as "import-substituting industrialization." In the first place, many of the products that were produced by domestic manufacturers had never really been imported in sizable quantities before. What was really taking place in Latin America was the growth of domestic markets, not the substitution of one set of producers for another in order to satisfy a preexisting market. Second, and even more fundamentally, the process of industrial development required foreign exchange earnings. In the long run, these might have been generated by exporting manufactured goods. In the short run, however, that was not an option – and the short run was the time horizon that mattered to governments.

Once governments committed to short-run, ad hoc solutions to the balance of payments problem, the long-run solution of creating manufacturing industries that were capable of exporting became less and less obtainable. The result was a set of policies that in the aggregate worked against one another: trade protection for consumer goods producers, trade protection for intermediate and capital goods producers, preferential exchange rates for the importers of capital goods; and preferential exchange rates for the exporters of agricultural and mineral products.

A second perverse consequence of protectionism was that it transferred rents from domestic consumers to multinational companies (MNCs). One of the features of trade protection is that it tends to be nonexcludable: all producers are protected by the tariff wall. The response of foreign firms to protectionism was, therefore, to jump over the tariff wall by erecting local plants. This was a process that had begun in the 1920s, with the arrival of automobile assembly operations in Argentina, Brazil, and Mexico. By the 1950s, it was in full swing. Data from Argentina provide some sense of the overall process. Circa 1950, FDI accounted for only 3 percent of total manufacturing investment. By the end of the decade, it accounted for almost 20 percent. Well over half of this investment was in the automobile industry.[94] The rest clustered in chemicals, farm machinery, electric motors, rubber, pharmaceuticals, plastics, and synthetic fibers. In fact, the only heavy industries not dominated by MNCs were steel and paper.[95] Data on MNC investment in Mexico yield similar – if more muted – results. As of 1959, 47 percent of U.S. FDI in Mexico was in manufacturing. In fact, virtually all of the growth of U.S. FDI in Mexico between 1950 and 1959 was in the manufacturing sector. The result was that in 1959, U.S. investors held claims on 8 percent of total Mexican manufacturing investment.[96]

MNC investment tended to cluster in particular industries in which the advantages of foreign firms – their access to overseas capital markets and their knowledge of particular technologies – outweighed the advantages of domestic firms – their knowledge of local markets and their political connections. Not surprisingly, the end result, after a period of intense competition, was segmented markets: MNCs tended to completely dominate particular lines of manufacturing (automobiles, office equipment, consumer electronics, pharmaceuticals), but were almost completely absent

[94] Jorge Katz and Bernardo Kosacoff, "Import-Substituting Industrialization in Argentina, 1940–1980," 298–9.
[95] Paul H. Lewis, *The Crisis of Argentine Capitalism*, 299.
[96] Clark W. Reynolds, *The Mexican Economy*, 190–1.

in others (textiles, clothing, leather goods, steel, cement, glass, household appliances).

Trade protection created a third set of unforeseen problems. Industrial technology tended to be designed for large and deep markets, such as those of Western Europe and the United States. Latin America's markets tended, however, to be small and shallow. This meant that Latin American manufacturing companies – including the MNCs – were going to be inefficient producers. Either they could employ technologies that were less efficient than the world standard, or they could employ the most efficient technologies but operate them at far less than capacity. Many producers chose the first option, purchasing second-hand machinery and outmoded product designs. Others chose the second option, employing world-class facilities that they operated at far less than the minimum efficient scale of production. Both choices implied that Latin American firms produced at a higher cost than those elsewhere. The latter choice also implied that the structure of the market would be characterized by monopoly or oligopoly. The net result of both sets of choices was that consumers paid higher prices for manufactured products than they would have under free trade.

One of the reasons for the presence of MNCs in much of heavy industry was the lack of adequate banking systems and securities markets to mobilize domestic capital. The lack of adequate financial systems had plagued Latin American industry since the pre-1914 period. Over time, as the scale and cost of industrial technology increased, these problems grew increasingly severe. Although there was a good deal of variation from country to country, the basic pattern was that Latin American countries tended to be under-banked and to have small and thin securities markets.[97] Under-banking tended to be a product of explicit government policies designed to repress financial development as a means of subsidizing the fisc (banks could only obtain charters from central governments, central governments kept the number of charters low and required high reserve ratios, and then required banks to hold much of their reserves in the form of government bonds).[98] Thin securities markets tended to be a product of the fact that bondholders

---

[97] For a detailed study of the Mexican case, see Gustavo del Angel, "Paradoxes of Financial Development: The Construction of the Mexican Banking System, 1941–1982" (Ph.D. dissertation, Stanford University, 2002). For a general discussion of the thinness of Latin American Financial Systems, see: Ross Levine, "Bank-Based or Market-Based Financial Systems: Which Is Better," *Journal of Financial Intermediation* 11 (2002): 1–30.

[98] For a discussion of financial repression, see Ronald McKinnon, *Money and Capital in Economic Development* (Washington, DC, 1973).

had little protection in the case of bankruptcy, and that there was little in the way of external auditing of public companies in Latin America until the late 1970s – when the largest firms started borrowing money from foreign banks, which demanded audited financial statements. Until that point, stockholders had little to go on in making investment decisions other than the firm's past record of dividend payments and the reputation of the firm's principals. On top of this, high inflation, particularly in the Brazilian and Argentine cases but elsewhere as well, made the evaluation of a firm's financial statements difficult, even had there been other protections for shareholders. Not surprisingly, very few firms could actually sell shares to the public.

Latin American governments could have addressed these problems by rewriting securities laws, by creating a stable macroeconomic environment, by making it easier to obtain a bank charter, and by reducing reserve requirements for banks. Those choices, however, all came with short-run political costs, which public officials did not want to bear. Governments therefore addressed the problem of inadequate financial intermediation by creating intermediaries of their own, which took the form of government-owned industrial finance banks. The first of these was Mexico's *Nacional Financiera* (founded in 1934). Virtually every other country with substantial industry soon created similar banks, such as Chile's *Corporación de Fomento de la Producción* (founded in 1939), Argentina's *Banco de Crédito Industrial* (founded in 1944), and Brazil's *Banco Nacional de Desenvolvimento Econômico* (founded in 1952).

These government banks were supposed to lend to small- and medium-sized firms. As a practical matter, however, they rarely did so. The political pressure to lend to large firms, which tended to have large, unionized, and politically organized labor forces, simply outweighed whatever original mandate the banks may have had. This was particularly the case in Mexico, but was true in other countries as well.[99] In fact, as Noemi Girbal-Blacha's work on Argentina's *Banco de Crédito Industrial* and *Banco Nacional* makes clear, virtually all the bank's capital was allocated to large firms.[100]

Latin America's industrial development banks did more, however, than make loans. They also took equity stakes in firms. In theory, this is not

[99] Enrique Cárdenas, "The Process of Accelerated Industrialization in Mexico, 1929–1982," 190.
[100] Noemi Girbal-Blacha, "Viejos actores, nuevas functiones: Bancos y crédito al la producción en la Argentina, 1946–1955" (Paper presented at the XIII Congreso de la Asociación Internacional de Historia Económica, Buenos Aires).

necessarily a bad thing to do. The problem was that, in practice, they tended to invest a disproportionate share of their resources in large firms that lost money. In Mexico, for example, *Nacional Financiera* typically took a minority shareholder position in companies to which it was also making loans. If the firm performed well, *Nacional Financiera's* stake would, over time, become purely nominal. If the firm performed badly, however, *Nacional Financiera* typically bought out the other shareholders. From the point of view of the government, many of these enterprises were simply too big to fail, or had unionized workforces that were politically crucial. This policy of bailouts not only prevented the bank from deploying its capital more effectively elsewhere, it also encouraged moral hazard: knowing that they would be bailed out, manufacturers undertook enterprises of doubtful profitability.[101]

The relentless logic of subsidies ultimately produced government ownership of a wide range of manufacturing industries, financed of course through government development banks. Government ownership tended to cluster in the production of so-called strategic goods, such as steel, basic petrochemicals, and fertilizers. Government ownership in these industries was rationalized on the basis that these were high-risk, capital-intensive industries characterized by large minimum efficient scales of production and capital indivisibilities. Although this is true, it was also the case that these firms tended to produce inputs for other industries. Given the fact that there were no private shareholders, the prices of the firms' outputs were determined on political grounds: government-owned firms wound up charging below-market prices. In other words, taxpayers subsidized the privately owned enterprises that purchased the steel, electricity, chemicals, and other inputs produced by so-called parastate firms.

By the late 1960s and early 1970s, it was becoming increasingly clear that protectionism and "state-led development" had created endless distortions. Consumers paid high prices for badly made goods. Entrepreneurs found it difficult to evaluate projects and make investment decisions because so much of their calculus turned on political, rather than market, signals. Governments were providing increasingly larger subsidies, via the exchange rate system, government banks, and parastate firms – and the benefits of many of those subsidies were being captured by foreign-owned manufacturing firms.

By the 1970s, Latin America's governments were faced with a set of hard decisions: end subsidies and market distortions by opening up to foreign

---

[101] Enrique Cárdenas, "The Process of Accelerated Industrialization in Mexico, 1929–1982," 195.

trade, or take advantage of the boom in international capital markets to subsidize a system that had run into decreasing marginal returns. With the notable exception of Chile, governments throughout Latin America, "democratic" and authoritarian alike, opted to buy time by borrowing abroad. The outcome of that experience is well known: the debt crisis of the 1980s not only produced an economic and social disaster, it also brought about a dissolution of the political coalitions that had supported protectionism and subsidization since the 1890s. The result was the end of trade protection, the privatization of government-owned firms, and the shifting of Latin American manufacturing increasingly toward export markets. The full details of that transformation are the subject, however, of the chapter in this volume by Victor Bulmer-Thomas.

CONCLUSIONS

Beginning in the 1890s, the largest economies of Latin America conducted a 100-year experiment in which they built substantial manufacturing sectors behind barriers to trade. This experiment was not carried out because public officials were ideologically committed to industrialization or because of economic theories that challenged free trade. Indeed, the growth of large-scale manufacturing industry predated structuralist theories by sixty years. Rather, Latin America's industrialization was kick-started by an endogenous process of economic development, the roots of which were found in the growth of the so-called export economy. Once industrialists got a foothold, they lost no time in seeking tariff protection. Governments granted this protection because it came at virtually no political cost: the one class that stood to lose from trade protection, consumers, had no political voice. The result was that by 1914, all of the larger countries of Latin America had become increasingly protectionist and were undergoing a rapid process of industrial growth.

The next six decades brought long periods of prosperity and short periods of stagnation or decline. Over the long term, however, industry outgrew the rest of the economy. Circa 1975, when this style of industrial development had reached its zenith, the manufacturing sector's share of Latin American GDP was comparable to that in the United States.

Over time, governments played larger roles in the process of industrial growth. They devised increasingly complicated systems designed to simultaneously tax imported manufactures and subsidize the cost of imported inputs to the production of those goods. They also became financiers, partners, and even direct owners of manufacturing firms.

This does not mean, however, that Latin American post-1930 industrial development was "state led" or that it was somehow fundamentally different from the industrial growth of the pre-1930 period. The process of Latin American industrial development was always ad hoc. Governments did not grant trade protection because they were committed to a particular vision of industrial development. They did it because they were rewarding politically powerful constituents, some of whom were industrialists and some of whom were industrial unions. They also did it because balance of payments crises often presented them with difficult political choices: suffer the negative fallout of devaluation (the effects of which are obvious and immediate) or impose restraints on trade (the effects of which are more difficult to detect and understand for the average voter). Similarly, governments did not create industrial finance banks and buy equity in manufacturing firms because they had some ideological commitment to government ownership. They did it because government financial policies repressed the development of banking systems and securities markets that could mobilize adequate capital for industrial development. Charting a different course in terms of financial market regulation would have come at sizable short-run political and economic costs: governments would have had to adhere to stable fiscal policies, create independent central banks, and undo the segmented monopolies and oligopolies that characterized Latin American banking. Governments, therefore, chose the second-best solution of government financing of private firms. Once this started, however, government loans became like trade protection: it was a permanent prize to be captured. Finally, governments did not become direct owners of manufacturing firms because public officials were convinced of the superiority of state ownership. They did it because many private firms, especially ones that the government had lent money to, were simply too big to fail. In short, governments increasingly intervened in support of industry because it was in the self-interest of industrialists, industrial unions, and public officials to do so. This was an outcome of the ad hoc nature of Latin American industrial development, not the product of carefully thought-out plans or strategies. This was as true of Latin America's industrial development from 1890 to 1930 as it was from 1930 to 1980.

14

POVERTY AND INEQUALITY

MIGUEL SZÉKELY AND ANDRÉS MONTES

INTRODUCTION

Poverty and inequality have been deeply rooted in Latin American societies since the early colonial era. With the arrival of Spanish and Portuguese conquerors, the diverse resources of the region in terms of land and other factor endowments were carved up in ways that favored the few at the expense of the many. Later, the intensification of colonization brought the development of economic structures that cemented these inequalities in place. Both the diversity of factor endowments in the region and the way in which they have been distributed have therefore played a heavy hand in predisposing Latin America toward certain paths of development – paths characterized by wide-ranging degrees of inequality in wealth, human capital, and political power.[1]

The severity of inequality has varied across the continent, depending on many factors. Generally speaking, however, patterns of production, land distribution, and schooling that Latin America has followed have consistently fostered high degrees of inequality. Many of these patterns

The authors would like to thank Adriana Argaiz for her excellent research assistance. The opinions expressed in this chapter are the authors' and should not be attributed to the institution to which they are affiliated.

[1] Kenneth L. Sokoloff and Stanley L. Engerman, "History Lessons Institutions, Factor Endowments, and Paths of Development in the New World," *Journal of Economic Perspectives* 14, 3 (Summer 2000): 217–32.

were formed in the early colonial era, when indigenous populations were denied rights while a select number of elites of European descent were given the lion's share of wealth, land, and power to administer their conquered territories.

The early differences in the extent of inequality persisted and were reproduced in the way economic and social institutions evolved over time; these institutions, in turn, exerted their own influence on the path of economic development. In cases of extreme inequality, institutions favored elites and limited the access of much of the population to economic opportunities. Having attained high socioeconomic status, elites were thus in an advantageous position to maintain that status over time, with the rest of society paying the price of underdevelopment. Overall, in regions in which wealth, human capital, and political influence were highly concentrated in the hands of the elites, competition was restricted.

During the past century, most Latin American countries, in one way or another, pursued policies aimed at addressing these social inequalities. These policies were not created in a vacuum but were strongly shaped by the macroeconomic environment. As the macroeconomic environment evolved over the course of the century in fundamental (as well as unpredictable and unforgiving) ways, these changes were mirrored in the evolution of development policies.

This chapter takes a close look at the historical progress of poverty and inequality in order to grasp the reasons behind their stubborn persistence. Only with this knowledge can sound recommendations for future policies be made. The chapter is organized as follows. The next section summarizes the available evidence on poverty and inequality in the region, underscoring the limitations of those data. The third section provides an overview of the main explanations of long-run evolution of poverty and inequality given in the literature. The fourth section outlines the conceptual framework used to analyze the evolution of income-earning assets that form the basis of this chapter. Using this framework, sections four, five, and six take an in-depth look at the behavior of assets in Latin America over the course of the past century, delving into issues surrounding their accumulation, utilization, and returns. The following section draws lessons on the historical roles that assets have played in Latin American development in the past, and the last section provides the conclusion.

HISTORICAL TRENDS: THE EVOLUTION OF POVERTY AND INEQUALITY DURING THE TWENTIETH CENTURY

DATA LIMITATIONS

An important challenge in analyzing the evolution of poverty and inequality in Latin America is data quality and availability. Clearly, any study attempting to assess the progress of poverty and inequality over long periods should be aware of the shortcomings of the existing information – and, consequently, of the assumptions made by its analysis – and strive to tackle this issue.

There are at least five different sources of information on income for Latin America: tax records, social security records, establishment statistics, population censuses, and household surveys. Still, there is no reliable source on income because most of these sources present various problems, including coverage, accuracy, detail, and the specificity of sectors. Because of these problems, it is normally agreed that the ideal source for estimating poverty and inequality is household surveys. However, most countries only started implementing these surveys at the beginning of the 1970s and many are not even comparable within countries.

Recently, there has been a renewed interest in the use of these kinds of income and expenditure surveys because they present an invaluable source for examining changes in income distribution and observing household behavior relating to expenditure and different forms of income (e.g., financial assets, wages, bequests). Nevertheless, the quality of surveys containing more or less detailed information on expenditure and income varies across a wide spectrum. Furthermore, various methodological differences make the comparison between surveys even more difficult.

It is essential that inequality analysis take three factors into account, which are, as described in Deaton: (1) the characteristics of the sample, (2) differences in survey quality and coverage of population groups, and (3) differential coverage of income sources and geographic areas.[2] Regarding the first factor, among the most important elements that have to be taken into account when using income and expenditure surveys are the sampling

---

[2] Deaton Angus, *The Analysis of Household Surveys: A Microeconometric Approach to Development Policy* (Baltimore, 1997).

frame and size. This is relevant because weights can overstate or diminish the importance of population subgroups, leading to inaccurate results. The same is valid for the sample size of a survey because the larger the sample size, the smaller the standard error of any estimate.

The quality and coverage of the surveys are also of vital importance for making cross-country comparisons. In this respect, income misreporting and underreporting are the most common problems. Additionally, household surveys use samples in which some groups are likely to be underrepresented. In particular, wealthier individuals are not normally sampled; hence, the true level of inequality is usually higher than what surveys inform.

Analyzing poverty and inequality using cross-country comparisons leads to several problems, such as the definition of economies of scale at the household level, the treatment of missing or zero incomes, accounting for regional price variations, and so on. Székely and Hilgert engage in a detailed discussion of these issues and argue that country rankings may be strongly influenced by parameter choices rather than genuine distributive differences.[3]

An additional complication is that there are only a few countries in Latin America for which data are available to document the evolution of poverty and inequality over long periods of the twentieth century. The earliest comparative study of poverty trends in Latin America and the Caribbean was done by Altimir in the late 1970s.[4] The author identifies considerable variations regarding poverty levels in urban households. These ranged from 5 percent in Argentina to 38 percent in Colombia. On the other hand, rural poverty registered even more dramatic variations. It varied from 19 percent in Argentina to 73 percent in Brazil. Altimir's estimates show a generalized improvement in the 1960s and 1970s that halted, and in some cases reversed, in the 1980s.

As is discussed later, the 1980s and 1990s were years of economic volatility and increasing poverty and inequality in the region. There is no country in Latin America – based on the limited data available – for which it can confidently be said that income inequality improved during the 1990s. The main factor driving the lack of distributive progress was wage inequality. Increasing income inequality was driven by the widening wage gaps. Furthermore, macroeconomic shocks such as the debt crisis and economic

[3] Székely, Miguel, and Marianne Hilgert, "What's Behind the Inequality We Measure? An Investigation Using Latin American Data" (OCE Working Paper Series no. 409, Inter-American Development Bank, 1999).
[4] Oscar Altimir, *La dimensión de la pobreza en América Latina* (Santiago, 1979).

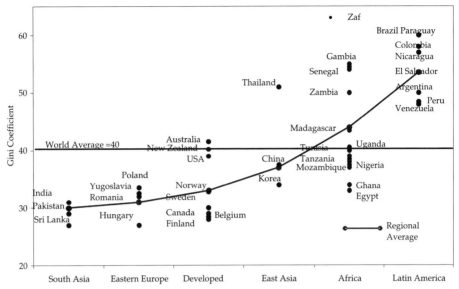

Figure 14.1. Gini index for countries with good-quality data for the 1990s.
Sources: Miguel Székely and Marianne Hilgert, "What's Behind the Inequality We Measure? An Investigation Using Latin American Data" (OCE Working Paper Series no. 409, Inter–American Development Bank, 1999); Klaus Deininger and Lyn Squire, "A New Data Set Measuring Income Inequality," *World Bank Economic Review* 10, 3 (September 1996): 565–91.

reforms of the 1980s also played a role in driving a larger wedge between the wages of some groups vis-a-vis others.

LATIN AMERICA: THE MOST UNEQUAL REGION IN THE WORLD

Figure 14.1 shows the Gini index for a set of Latin American countries, in addition to countries worldwide, for which information around 1995 is available. We note that the average world Gini index is approximately 0.4 (the Gini ranges from 0 to 1, with 1 being the highest and most unequal value). On average, South Asia had the lowest inequality level, with a Gini index of 0.3, followed by Eastern Europe. Next are the developed countries, with an average of 0.32. Although these three regions have similar average inequality indices, it is interesting to note that the variance is greater among developed countries. Although all Eastern European and South Asian countries for which data are available are found to have lower-than-world-average inequality levels, rich countries such as the United States,

Australia, and New Zealand are found to have inequality levels that are very similar to the world average. The situation of the East Asian countries is comparable, with inequality levels below the world average, though with a higher variance. Furthermore, the latter region includes Thailand, which has a relatively high level of inequality.

Africa is fifth in terms of regional averages. Its average inequality level exceeds the world average, although with substantial variability among countries. This area includes South Africa (coded *Zaf*), which has the highest inequality level of all countries in the world, and Egypt, which has a relatively low inequality level. Therefore, in this case, the average tells us little about the situation of individual countries.

Last, as shown in the figure, Latin America has the highest average Gini index, with a value of approximately 0.54. It is the only region in which all countries in the sample exceed the world average inequality level. It is also interesting to note that South Africa's high inequality index is followed by a substantial number of countries, all Latin American.

THE EVOLUTION OF POVERTY AND INEQUALITY IN LATIN AMERICA, 1970–2000

It has been made clear that many limitations hinder comparisons of income distribution and poverty in Latin America. Nevertheless, some efforts have been made to collect within-country comparable information on income and expenditure in order to analyze the evolution of inequality and poverty at the regional level for the last twenty-five years. Londoño and Székely gathered a large number of household surveys from the region to analyze progress from 1970 to 1995.[5] In their analysis, the authors face the standard comparability problems between countries, as well as the underreporting for some income variables. However, their analysis allows for a study of the evolution of poverty and inequality for the largest countries in the region, which is described herein.

Figure 14.2 illustrates the economic performance after the 1960s.[6] Extreme and moderate poverty declined, while inequality also registered a

---

[5] Juan Luis Londoño and Miguel Székely, "Persistent Poverty and Excess Inequality: Latin America 1970–1995," *Journal of Applied Economics* 3, 1 (May 2000): 93–134.

[6] For the purposes of this chapter, two definitions of the poverty line are used: a 1985 Purchasing Power Parity (PPP)-adjusted dollar-a-day line to measure extreme poverty, and US $2 1985 PPP-adjusted dollars per capita per day for moderate poverty. Regarding the discussion on the definition of poverty lines, there are significant differences in consumption patterns across countries and through time, which make it difficult to establish common criteria. Other scholars, such as Montek Ahluwalia, Nicholas Carter, and Hollis Chenery, "Growth and Poverty in Developing Countries," *Journal of*

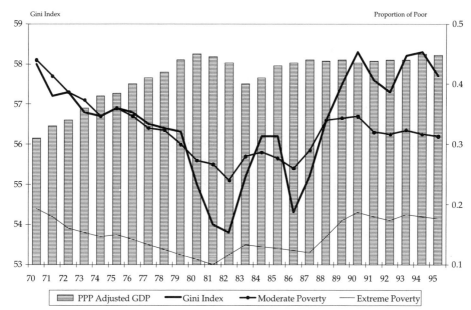

Figure 14.2. Inequality and poverty in Latin America: 1970–1995 (GDP per capita).
Source: Juan Luis Londoño and Miguel Székely, "Persistent Poverty and Excess Inequality: Latin America 1970–1995," *Journal of Applied Economics* 3, 1 (May 2000): 93–134. Purchasing Power Parity states that exchange rates between currencies are in equilibrium when their purchasing power is the same in each of the two countries. This means that the exchange rate between two countries should equal the ratio of the two countries' price level of a fixed basket of goods and services. When a country's domestic price level is increasing (i.e., a country experiences inflation), that country's exchange rate must depreciate in order to return to PPP.

constant decline that ended in the early 1980s. The early 1980s were characterized first by recession and later by stagnation, whereas the 1990s show a recovery. Also, income distribution improved substantially from 1970 to 1982 (the Gini index was reduced by four points), whereas the 1980s coincided with a sharp deterioration in income distribution (the Gini peaked at 58.3 in 1990). Even though the 1990s were years of recovery, extreme and moderate poverty did not show any improvement during this period. Inequality increased substantially.

Development Economics" 6 (1979): 299–341; Michael Bruno et al., "Equity and Growth in Developing Countries: Old and New Perspectives in the Policy Issues," in Vito Tanzi and K. Y. Chu, eds., *Income Distribution and High Quality Growth* (Cambridge, MA, 1998); Martin Ravallion and Shaohua Chen, "What Can New Survey Data Tell Us about Recent Changes in Distribution and Poverty?" *The World Bank Economic Review* 11, 2 (1997): 357–82, focus on producing internationally comparable estimates for each of the world regions.

Table 14.1. *Poverty measures for Latin America, 1970–1995*

Year	Moderate poverty				Extreme poverty			
	Head count ratio	Poverty gap	FGT(2) index	Million of poor	Head count ratio	Poverty gap	FGT(2) index	Million of poor
1970	43.6	18.7	11.2	117.1	19.2	6.5	4.0	51.4
1975	36.2	15.5	9.3	110.1	14.8	4.5	3.4	44.9
1980	27.5	11.1	6.9	93.8	10.5	2.6	2.6	36.0
1985	28.3	11.3	5.8	107.8	11.4	2.9	1.3	43.3
1990	35.2	16.4	9.7	147.9	17.4	6.3	3.6	73.1
1995	33.1	15.4	9.2	152.5	16.2	6.1	3.7	74.5

Note: Foster, Greer, and Thorbecke index with parameter value = 2.
Source: Juan Luis Londoño and Miguel Székely, "Persistent Poverty and Excess Inequality: Latin America 1970–1995."

As argued by Londoño and Székely, the 1970s were characterized by an expansion of the incomes of the poor and the middle classes at the expense of the richest 20 percent of the population.[7] The 1980s show the opposite: the income share of the poorest 90 percent decreased considerably while the income share of the richest 10 percent expanded by about 10 percent. The 1990s show yet another picture, with the poorest and the richest deciles losing part of their shares, and the middle class expanding theirs.

The economic expansion in Latin America during the 1970s helped reduce not only inequality but also poverty. The data observed in Table 14.1 indicate that between 1970 and 1980, both moderate and extreme poverty declined from 117.1 million to 93.8 million people and from 51.4 million to 36 million, respectively. For the most part, this trend and improvement in income distribution are attributed in various studies to the high growth rates experienced during those years. The poverty gap and the Foster, Greer, and Thorbecke (FGT) index, which is more sensitive to the changes taking place at the bottom of the distribution, also declined during the 1970s, indicating that there were not only fewer poor but that these were less poor than before.[8]

In order to assess the impact on poverty of economic expansion and changes in inequality, Londoño and Székely decompose changes in poverty

[7] See note 5.
[8] James Foster, Joel Greer, and Erik Thorbecke, "A Class of Decomposable Poverty Indices," *Econométrica* 52 (1984): 761–6, designed a family of poverty measures that are given by the

into growth and distribution effects (Figure 14.3 presents the results). Poverty declined during the 1970s because of the high growth rates and more equitable income distribution; however, this was not the case for the 1980s. Most of the rise in poverty during that decade can be attributed to changes in inequality and not, contrary to conventional wisdom, only to the economic stagnation observed during those years.

Despite the fact that GDP per capita increased by almost 6 percent in real terms between 1990 and 1995 in Latin America, poverty levels appeared to remain stubbornly persistent. These results are, in part, attributable to the low impact of growth on poverty reduction because of the lack of distributive progress.

Table 14.2 shows changes in absolute poverty for the period between 1970 and 1995, by country. During the 1970s, Latin America achieved a decrease in the numbers of moderately poor of 23.3 million as well as in extreme poverty of 15.5 million. In particular, Brazil, Colombia, and Mexico made important strides, although most of this reduction came more from the upper ranks of the poor in Colombia and Mexico than from the poorest of the poor as was the case in Brazil. Nevertheless, the economic crisis of the lost decade of the 1980s brought a considerable increase in the number of poor, both at the moderate and the extreme levels.

Between 1980 and 1990, moderate poverty increased by 54.1 million people, and 37.1 million individuals slipped into the category of extreme poor. The most alarming increase in the numbers of extreme poor happened in Brazil, where 23.8 million people became poorer during this period. Other countries where poverty increased significantly in contrast to the previous decade were Guatemala and Peru, where the number of moderately

following formula:

$$P_\alpha = \frac{1}{n} \sum_{y_i < p} \left(\frac{p - y_i}{p} \right)^\alpha$$

where P is the poverty line, α is the sensitivity measure, n is the total population, y_i is the income of the *i-th* individual, and $p - y_i$ is the poverty gap. For this index, widely known as the FGT index, α can take different values, giving place to various poverty measures. In the case $\alpha = 0$, the index is the *head-count ratio*, which indicates the share of the population whose income or consumption is below the poverty line. In the case $\alpha = 1$, we obtain the *poverty gap*, which provides information regarding how far off households are from the poverty line. In other words, the poverty gap captures the mean aggregate income or consumption shortfall relative to the poverty line across the whole population and is obtained by adding up all the shortfalls of all the poor and dividing it by the total population. In the case $\alpha = 2$, we obtain the poverty severity, also denominated FGT(2), which takes into account not only the distance separating the poor from the poverty line but also the inequality among the poor, that is, a higher weight is placed on those households who are farther away from the poverty line.

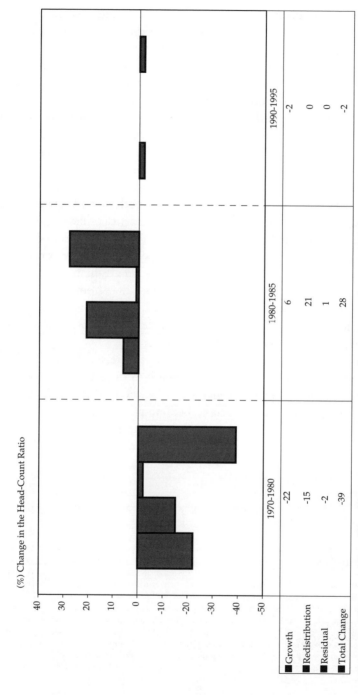

Figure 14.3. Decomposition of the change in poverty into growth and redistribution effects for Latin America: 1870–1995.
Source: Juan Luis Londoño and Miguel Székely, "Persistent Poverty and Excess Inequality: Latin America 1970–1995."

Table 14.2. *Changes in absolute poverty in Latin America, by country*

Country	Moderate poverty			Extreme poverty		
	1970–1980	1980–1990	1990–1995	1970–1980	1980–1990	1990–1995
Latin America	−23.30	54.11	4.56	−15.46	37.14	1.14
Bahamas	−0.01	0.01	0.01	−0.01	0.01	0.01
Brazil	−13.12	34.75	1.24	−10.10	23.75	0.51
Chile	0.38	1.47	−1.04	0.23	0.21	0.62
Colombia	−4.21	0.67	−0.21	−1.51	0.57	−0.52
Costa Rica	0.19	0.11	0.01	0.23	0.00	−0.03
Dominican Republic	−0.51	1.34	−0.14	−0.61	0.86	−0.20
Guatemala	0.43	2.38	0.33	0.17	1.57	0.20
Honduras	0.52	0.97	0.40	0.21	0.49	0.24
Jamaica	0.10	−0.12	−0.01	0.01	−0.15	−0.03
Mexico	−2.23	−1.25	4.00	−0.12	1.49	0.42
Panama	0.00	0.49	−0.07	−0.16	0.41	−0.06
Peru	1.41	3.18	−0.70	−0.33	0.86	0.02
Venezuela	−0.88	1.10	0.10	−0.14	0.72	−0.01
Other Countries	−5.37	9.00	0.63	−3.32	6.36	1.2

*Millions.

Source: Juan Luis Londoño and Miguel Székely, "Persistent Poverty and Excess Inequality: Latin America 1970–1995," *Journal of Applied Economics* 31 (May 2000): 93–134.

Table 14.3. *Poverty and inequality in Latin America, 1989–2000*

Country	Index	1989–1990	1991–1992	1993–1994	1995	1996	1997	1998	1999	2000
Argentina	Gini Index					0.4771		0.4935		
	Head-Count Ratio					18.40		17.90		
	FGT(2) Index					2.27		2.26		
Bolivia	Gini Index	0.5449		0.5323	0.5274	0.5877	0.5890		0.6014	
	Head-Count Ratio	65.63		63.40	63.60	62.14	62.34		61.36	
	FGT(2) Index	20.19		18.27	17.37	24.84	24.18		27.40	
Brazil	Gini Index		0.5728	0.5952	0.5911	0.5907	0.5919	0.5901	0.5847	
	Head-Count Ratio		48.26	49.68	44.66	41.55	41.25	41.92	41.26	
	FGT(2) Index		15.03	15.51	12.91	11.98	11.91	11.52	11.11	
Chile	Gini Index	0.5470	0.5220	0.5558		0.5638		0.5587		
	Head-Count Ratio	32.37	19.78	22.70		18.32		16.11		
	FGT(2) Index	6.12	2.77	3.69		2.91		2.60		
Colombia	Gini Index		0.5670	0.6038	0.5697		0.5756	0.5679	0.5620	
	Head-Count Ratio		42.39	44.67	38.79		38.37	37.79	39.37	
	FGT(2) Index		10.73	11.94	8.83		10.78	9.94	10.14	
Costa Rica	Gini Index	0.4596	0.4598	0.4549	0.4570		0.4589	0.4612		
	Head-Count Ratio	35.89	34.23	29.20	28.70		30.86	30.47		
	FGT(2) Index	8.87	8.07	6.11	6.11		6.33	5.88		
Dominican Republic	Gini Index					0.4810		0.4778		
	Head-Count Ratio					38.13		34.56		
	FGT(2) Index					8.05		5.32		
Ecuador	Gini Index				0.5600			0.5616		
	Head-Count Ratio				49.53			47.98		
	FGT(2) Index				17.15			15.41		

Country	Index							
El Salvador	Gini Index				0.5052	0.5195	0.5589	0.5455
	Head-Count Ratio				58.60	61.25	63.98	63.98
	FGT(2) Index				14.54	15.84	21.34	21.29
Honduras	Gini Index	0.5703	0.5489		0.5284	0.5908	0.5852	0.5843
	Head-Count Ratio	77.20	75.94		76.30	74.73	74.85	75.25
	FGT(2) Index	32.25	31.48		30.15	35.43	34.88	35.42
Mexico	Gini Index	0.5309	0.5341	0.5361	0.5276		0.5377	
	Head-Count Ratio	19.74	16.17	15.34	21.22		21.17	
	FGT(2) Index	3.28	2.29	2.13	3.62		4.15	
Nicaragua	Gini Index			0.5669			0.6024	
	Head-Count Ratio			70.67			72.68	
	FGT(2) Index			28.88			28.14	
Panama	Gini Index		0.5625		0.5602	0.5755	0.5652	0.5631
	Head-Count Ratio		47.75		47.81	43.53	38.05	36.61
	FGT(2) Index		17.04		16.43	14.37	11.92	10.80
Paraguay	Gini Index				0.5700		0.5692	0.5942
	Head-Count Ratio				52.09		51.00	61.12
	FGT(2) Index				17.96		19.48	23.28
Peru	Gini Index		0.4643	0.4832		0.5055		0.4933
	Head-Count Ratio		41.86	43.98		43.23		42.43
	FGT(2) Index		10.33	10.82		11.40		12.22
Uruguay	Gini Index	0.4064	0.4319		0.4209	0.4300	0.4388	
	Head-Count Ratio	23.15	19.55		16.61	11.69	13.59	
	FGT(2) Index	2.70	2.91		2.09	1.46	1.78	
Venezuela	Gini Index	0.4396		0.4288	0.4669	0.4863	0.4705	0.4675
	Head-Count Ratio	12.55		8.68	15.23	17.95	18.87	20.63
	FGT(2) Index	2.13		1.08	2.53	3.48	3.46	4.08

Source: Miguel Székely, *The 1990s in Latin America: Another Decade of Persistent Inequality, but with Somewhat Lower Poverty* (Mexico City, 2001).

597

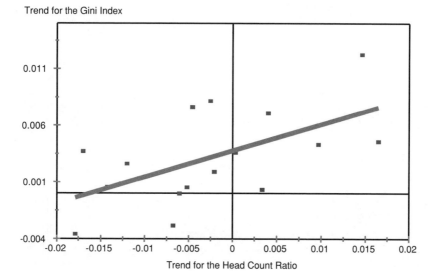

Figure 14.4. Trends in poverty and inequality in Latin America during the 1990s.

poor increased by 2.4 million and 3.2 million, respectively. The 1990s proved to be a period of recovery, except for Mexico, where more than 4 million individuals slipped into the ranks of the moderately poor because of the 1994–5 economic crises.

Székely finds that despite the stabilization and macroeconomic growth enjoyed during the second half of the 1990s, the region's well-being did not improve.[9] Both inequality and the number of poor increased between the early and late 1990s, not only in the region as a whole but also on a country-by-country basis. As shown in Figure 14.4, poverty and inequality grew hand in hand during the 1990s. The figure plots the trend in the Gini index on the vertical axis versus the trend for the head count ratio, showing a clear positive relationship between increases in inequality and increases in poverty.

Furthermore, Table 14.3 shows how inequality increased considerably in a number of countries. The Gini index grew by four points between 1993 and 1998 in El Salvador, Nicaragua, Peru, and Venezuela, and by about six points in Bolivia during the decade. In other countries such as Chile, Colombia, Ecuador, Mexico, and Panama, inequality showed no trend.

[9] Miguel Székely, *The 1990s in Latin America: Another Decade of Persistent Inequality, but with Somewhat Lower Poverty* (Mexico City, 2001).

However, despite economic growth and a stabilization of prices, inequality was not reduced in most of the region.

The same can be said for poverty. In some countries, such as Paraguay and Venezuela, poverty increased sharply during the 1990s. Paraguay underwent a 10 percent increase between 1995 and 1999, whereas in Venezuela the increase represented by the head count ratio was of the order of almost 8 percent over the course of the decade. Moreover, the FGT index confirms that the increase in poverty not only increased the number of poor in those countries, but also made the poorest worse off than before. This is also the case for other countries, such as El Salvador, Mexico, and Peru, where even though poverty remained more or less constant, the FGT index increased, signaling a worsening of the situation of the poor. This could explain the relationship between inequality and poverty for those countries where poverty did not increase while inequality did. That is, although poverty did not rise in absolute terms, the poorest suffered further welfare losses.

Despite a strong increase in inequality in Latin America and the persistently high inequality levels, there were a number of exceptions to these trends. Brazil, Chile, and Uruguay saw a reduction in the numbers of poor during the 1990s, as illustrated in Table 14.3. Brazil and Uruguay reduced poverty by almost 10 percent during the decade, and in Chile poverty halved, from 32.4 percent at the beginning of the 1990s to 16.1 percent in 1998. Still, it is too early for optimism because the only success story of overall economic progress in Latin America seems to have been the case of Chile.

ECONOMIC GROWTH, POVERTY, AND INEQUALITY

Why has Latin America been plagued by persistently high inequality and poverty levels? This section offers and critiques some of the traditional explanations for the long-term prevalence of these phenomena, particularly the Kuznets inverted U hypothesis, and presents a brief assessment of the growth-inequality-poverty nexus.

THE KUZNETS HYPOTHESIS

The widespread adoption of the belief that economic growth is the main vehicle for poverty reduction and improvement in living standards spawned many different theories regarding poverty and inequality. Among the most well known and influential is the one elaborated by Nobel laureate, Simon Kuznets, in 1955. Kuznets's studies of distributional changes during the development process hinged on population shifts from traditional to modern activities, specifically the dynamics of the transition during the initial stages of development to a modern industrial sector with higher wages. Kuznets concluded that at low income levels, economic growth tended to create more inequality. Once a critical threshold level of income was reached, however, further economic growth tended to reduce inequality. In other words, Kuznets predicted that inequality would grow during the first stages of development and industrialization, but decline consistently after reaching a turning point. This hump-shaped relationship between per capita income and income inequality has come to be known as the Kuznets inverted U hypothesis.

The empirical background for the Kuznets hypothesis came from research on inequality indicators for the United Kingdom, West Germany, and the United States. During the 1950s, when the research took place, inequality was falling in those countries, after having risen earlier. The economic mechanism thought to underlie these nonlinear trend lines was the transfer of labor from low-productivity (medium inequality) sectors to high-productivity (low inequality) sectors – namely, the transfer from agriculture to industry. The changes in income distribution observed suggested that inequality between these two sectors was substantially greater than the inequality within them and, given the data available for that period of time, that conclusion seemed unassailable.

Kuznets therefore formally introduced the idea of a link between inequality and development by acknowledging that total inequality is the result of the combined income distributions of the rural and urban populations. Kuznets argued that the income gap between these two groups presents the following two issues: (a) the average per capita income of the rural population is usually lower than that of the urban, and (b) within-group inequality for the rural population is somewhat narrower than that for the urban population.

Based on these two statements, he reached the following conclusions: first, that all other conditions being equal, the increasing weight of urban populations means an increasing share for the more unequal of the two component distributions; and second, the relative difference in per capita income between the rural and urban populations does not necessarily drift downward in the process of economic growth. Indeed, there is some evidence to suggest that it is stable at best, and, in fact, tends to widen because per capita productivity in urban economic pursuits increases more rapidly than in agriculture. If this were so, inequality in the total income distribution would increase during the beginning stages of the industrialization process.

After a certain period of time, the theory predicts, inequality will decline as rural–urban migration drives down the remunerations received by the expanding modern sector while driving up those received in the traditional sector. The effects of these two processes narrow the rural–urban income gap.

Comprehensive tests of the Kuznets hypothesis have been recently made possible by the compilation, in 1995–6, of the highly regarded Deninger-Squire[10] International Inequality Database, which contains 682 observations of Gini coefficients and quintile shares for 108 countries. Deninger-Squire concluded that these data provided little support for an inverted U relationship between levels of income and inequality when tested on a country-by-country basis, with no support for the existence of a Kuznets curve in approximately 90 percent of the countries researched. In light of the much more plentiful information available to today's empirical researchers, one might expect the support for the Kuznets hypothesis to have largely eroded.

In fact, with the availability of improved econometric techniques, the debate on the relation between inequality and economic growth has continued. For instance, Anand and Kanbur argue that if the econometric specification is improved, the inverted U shape relationship between inequality and growth vanishes.[11] Bruno et al., Li et al., and Ravallion and Chen use an improved data set and argue that there is no systematic relation between the Gini inequality index and GDP per capita growth.[12] Nevertheless, according to Barro, inequality and growth do follow the inverted U shape relationship suggested by Kuznets. De Janvry and Sadoulet and Morley arrive at the same conclusion by using a data set that includes only

[10] Klaus Deininger and Lyn Squire, "A New Data Set Measuring Income Inequality," *World Bank Economic Review* 10, 3 (September 1996): 565–91.

[11] Sudhir, Anand, and S.M.R. Kanbur, "The Kuznets Process and the Inequality-Development Relationship" *Journal of Development Economics* 40 (1993): 25–52.

[12] Michael Bruno et al., "Equity and Growth in Developing Countries: Old and New Perspectives in the Policy Issues"; Hong Yi Li et al., "Explaining International and Intertemporal Variations in Income Inequality," *The Economic Journal* 108, 446 (1998): 26–43; Martin Ravallion and Shaohua Chen, "What Can New Survey Data Tell Us about Recent Changes in Distribution and Poverty?" *The World Bank Economic Review* 11, 2 (1997): 357–82.

Latin American countries.[13] A recent paper by Lundberg and Squire argues that changes in GDP and in income inequality are jointly determined and should therefore be examined in a system of simultaneous equations in which the direct relationship between these two variables is of secondary interest.[14]

Therefore, after considerable controversy and empirical testing, the jury is still out on the relationship between development levels and inequality as postulated by Kuznets. Many scholars have devoted their efforts to trying to either prove or disqualify this hypothesis, opening the door for many questions. Given the scarcity of evidence, the only verifiable – and alarming – conclusion is that Latin America seems to have remained on the top part of the curve for many years already, without showing any decline in the inequality trend, but rather a constant and upward-rising trend toward more poverty and inequality.

POVERTY, INEQUALITY, AND GROWTH

As for poverty, the straightforward explanation is that its evolution depends mainly on economic growth.[15] To engage in this analysis, first one must identify who counts as belonging to the group of "poor" and then determine how to measure the incomes of that group to track changes in their conditions over time.

One approach widely followed for defining the poor is a relative definition, such as all people in the lowest quintile or decile. The central question this approach seeks to address is the nature of the relationship between economic growth and growth in the income standard of the poor, and whether the growth elasticity of this income standard exceeds, equals, or falls below unity. The earlier papers in this strand of literature – including Adelman and Morris; Ahluwalia; and Ahluwalia, Carter, and Chenery – were

---

[13] Robert Barro, "Inequality and Growth in a Panel of Countries" (Mimeograph, Harvard University, 1999); Alain De Janvry and Elizabeth Sadoulet, "Growth, Poverty and Inequality in Latin America: A Causal Analysis, 1970–1994," *Review of Income and Wealth* 46, 3 (2000): 267–87; Samuel Morley, *La distribución del ingreso en América Latina y el Caribe* (Mexico City, 2000).

[14] Mattias Lundberg and Lyn Squire, "The Simultaneous Evolution of Growth and Inequality," (Mimeograph, Washington, DC, 2000).

[15] Many other factors have been considered to be of influence regarding poverty and inequality in Latin America. This includes macroeconomic fluctuations such as high inflation periods, as well as structural and demographical trends like migration. Although these trends have certainly influenced the evolution of poverty in the region, the main objective of the current study is to first observe the relationship between economic growth and poverty alleviation and, second, to study the development of physical and human assets and its incidence in the well-being of Latin America.

primarily interested in the growth–inequality relationship (with one inequality measure being the income share of the poor group), but they also asked whether the poorest 20 percent of the population shared the benefits of growth proportionally.[16] These authors conclude that the income share of the poor tends to decline in the early stages of development but increases in the long run.

This approach has received renewed attention recently. Romer and Gugerty, Gallup, and Dollar and Kraay state that the growth elasticity of the incomes of individuals in the bottom quintile is essentially equal to one.[17] Timmer obtains a more modest elasticity of around 0.9.[18] Even though these studies use the same data and similar econometric techniques, they disagree on the issue of whether growth leads to a proportional increase in the income of the poor – in other words, if the gains for the poor are smaller than those of other groups.

The second approach to poverty and inequality measurement tracks income poverty levels using an absolute poverty line and a standard poverty measure. Ravallion, Ravallion and Chen, and Bruno employ absolute poverty lines of one and two dollars a day to identify the poor and then aggregate, using the most common measures of poverty, the head count ratio and the per capita poverty gap.[19] These studies find that the growth elasticity of the head count ratio is normally below a minus-two level. In other words, when average income increases by 1 percent, the proportion of poor declines by more than 2 percent. Hence, the results not only show that the relation between growth and poverty reduction does not function on a merely one-to-one basis, but they further imply that growth is the main vehicle for poverty reduction.

Other authors such as Morley, De Janvry and Sadoulet, and Smolensky also use poverty lines that combine an absolute and a relative component, but their elasticities are highly sensitive to the location of the poverty

---

[16] Irma Adelman and Albert Morris, *Economic Growth and Social Equity in Developing Countries* (Stanford, CA, 1973); Montek Ahluwalia, "Inequality, Poverty and Development," *Journal of Development Economics* 2 (1976): 307–42; Montek Ahluwalia, Nicholas Carter, and Hollis Chenery, "Growth and Poverty in Developing Countries," *Journal of Development Economics* 6 (1979): 299–341.

[17] Michael Roemer and Mary Kay Gugerty, "Does Economic Growth Reduce Poverty?" (Discussion Paper no. 4, Harvard Institute for International Development, Harvard University, 1997); John Luke Gallup et al., "Economic Growth and the Income of the Poor" (Harvard Institute for International Development, Discussion Paper no. 36, Harvard University, 1999); David Dollar and Aart Kraay "Growth Is Good for the Poor" (Mimeograph, Washington, DC).

[18] Peter Timmer, *How Well Do the Poor Connect to the Growth Process* (Cambridge, MA, 1997).

[19] Martin Ravallion, "Growth and Poverty: Making Sense of the Current Debate" (Mimeograph, World Bank, Washington, DC, 2000).

line.[20] The growth elasticity of poverty ranges from −2.59 to −0.69, depending on whether the threshold is established at 50 percent or 100 percent of the average income at the initial period of observation.

Foster and Székely propose an alternative methodology to track low incomes, based on Atkinson's family of "equally distributed equivalent income" functions denominated "general means."[21] Based on this methodology, they estimate the growth elasticity of the general means and use 144 household surveys from twenty countries that cover the last twenty-five years of the twentieth century. Among other results, they found that poor individual incomes do not grow on a one-to-one basis with the increases in mean income. Therefore, their conclusions differ from others that use per capita income of individuals in the first quintile as an income standard of the poor and argue that the growth elasticity of this income standard is unity. Foster and Székely estimate the relationship for a set of Latin American countries and conclude that the elasticity of the income of the poor to economic growth is also lower than one.

In sum, even though the relationship between growth and poverty is evidently close, the available evidence indicates that growth itself cannot fully explain changes in poverty in the region.

SOME FINAL CONSIDERATIONS

From the previous discussion, it is possible to assert that even in cases where the inequality–development relationship does seem to follow the inverted U pattern suggested by the main development theories, extreme poverty has not declined consistently as a natural outcome of the development process, contrary to expectations. Moreover, the mechanisms through which poverty was supposed to change were actually only observed during a relatively short subperiod (1977–84).

In some cases (e.g., Mexico) it can be found that, contrary to what the theory predicts, the main cause of the change in the standard of living of the extremely poor after the turning point in the inequality-development relationship was that the rural–urban gap continued to expand, generating

[20] Alain De Janvry and Elizabeth Sadoulet, "Growth, Poverty and Inequality in Latin America: A Causal Analysis, 1970–1994"; Eugene Smolensky et al., "Growth Inequality and Poverty: A Cautionary Note," *Review of Income and Wealth Series* 40, 2 (1994): 217–22.

[21] James E. Foster and Miguel Székely, "Is Economic Growth Good for the Poor? Tracking Low Incomes Using General Means" (Working Paper no. 453, Inter-American Development Bank, 2001).

significant poverty-increasing effects. The distribution of income within the subgroups, implicitly assumed constant, also changed considerably in most of the years.

Overall, this implies that, at least in some cases, the results are not in line with the Kuznets hypothesis, which would have predicted a consistent improvement in the standard of living of the poor after the turning point. Even in the context of positive economic growth and declining inequalities, a deterioration in the standard of living of the poorest is observed. Uncertainty about the accuracy of the Kuznets hypothesis could be well extrapolated to an entire region such as Latin America, which has borne the twin burdens of poverty and inequality for a long period of time, despite extended periods of economic growth.

INCOME-EARNING ASSETS IN LATIN AMERICA

ASSETS, PRICES, AND RETURNS: AN ASSET-BASED APPROACH

Traditional explanations arguing that economic growth can explain the evolution of poverty and inequality in Latin America and the Caribbean are clearly insufficient for understanding the persistently high levels in the region. In the spirit of Engermann and Sokoloff, one could argue that the main factor driving the persistently disparate income levels is the skewed distribution of factor endowments, or income-earning assets, among individuals.

One way to pursue this analysis is to acknowledge that the income of each individual in a society is a function of the combination of four essential elements: first, the stock of income-earning assets owned by each individual (classified as either human or physical capital); second, the extent to which these assets are employed in producing income; third, the market value of income-earning assets; and fourth, the income received independently of income-earning assets, which may include transfers, gifts, and bequests, among others. Consequently, family per capita income can be expressed in the following equation:

$$y_i = \frac{\left(\sum_{i=\ell}^{j} \sum_{a=\ell}^{i} A_{a.i} R_{a.i} P_a \right) + \sum_{i=\ell}^{k} T_i}{n}$$

where y represents the household per capita income of the individual i; A is a variable representing the stock of asset type a, owned by an individual i; R is a variable representing the rate at which asset type a is used by individual i; and P is the market value per unit of asset type a. The variable j represents the number of income-earners in the household to which the individual i belongs, l is the number of different types of assets, and k is the number of individuals in the household obtaining income from transfers and bequests, whereas n is the size of the household to which i belongs.

For simplicity, here we classify income-earning assets into human and physical capital. Human capital assets are the set of skills endowed by individuals – such as knowledge, capability, or expertise – and the health that enables them to produce any good or service. The most widely used proxy for quantifying knowledge is years of formal education. Other types of skills acquired through experience or training programs are not always available and are more difficult to measure. Information on labor market experience is also seldom available. Therefore, the definition of human capital is restricted to years of schooling and health.

On the other hand, physical capital refers to the monetary value of any form of financial asset, be it money holdings, property, rents, capital stock used for production, or any other form of physical capital used to produce a good or service. These stocks can be used in several ways; they can either be invested for production or accumulated to function as savings.

In terms of opportunity to use the assets productively, the two clear areas are employment and investment opportunities. Employment opportunities refer to the conditions, costs, and incentives in the labor market that influence the demand for different kinds of labor and the demand for skills. Investment opportunity comes from the existence of an efficient financial market that gives access to credit. Credit can be used to create economic activity and to take advantage of the economic environment to generate income.

Ownership, or other avenues of access to any of these income-earning assets, implies that an individual has the potential capacity to generate income at some point in time, but the income that is actually generated depends on the use of the asset. For instance, in the case of human capital, the years of schooling of an individual will only be translated into income when that person becomes gainfully employed. Regarding physical capital, it will only produce income when the dividend or return generated by the asset is made liquid.

Turning to the third income component, prices and returns for each income-earning asset, the behavior of prices is somewhat unique because it is determined by supply and demand, as well as by institutional factors. Prices and returns are therefore set by the economic system, and the individual responds to them in the process of deciding whether to seek income and accumulate a certain type of capital. Unlike the other two income components, the individual exercises very little control over prices and returns.

Finally, the fourth element in the income-generating process described earlier is transfers, bequests, and gifts that a household receives and that are not directly related to income, prices, or returns.

There is certainly a link between assets, their use, and poverty. As we show subsequently – for instance, in the case of human capital – the poor have smaller stocks. They receive the lowest rewards not only for having a small stock, but also because the returns are nonlinear and increase with the size of the stock. Finally, because of the low returns, the poor and, specifically, women ultimately end up using these assets at a much lower rate.

In an attempt to improve our understanding about why poverty and inequality in Latin America have historically been so high, we explore long-term trends in the underlying factors determining incomes: assets, use, and returns. This section examines the process of human and physical capital accumulation in Latin America in order to assess how the distribution of these assets evolved in the region during the past century.

HUMAN CAPITAL ACCUMULATION THROUGH SCHOOLING ATTAINMENT

Because Latin America is characterized by increasingly high wage inequality, it is essential to know how human capital is distributed as well as how its distribution changes over time. This section establishes some of the more general trends followed by Latin America throughout the century, examining changes in both the flows and stocks of schooling. South Korea and Taiwan are interesting cases for comparison because they are regarded as having achieved outstanding schooling progress during the twentieth century. Comparisons of Taiwan and the Latin American region are presented subsequently.

Figure 14.5, taken from Behrman, Duryea, and Székely, plots schooling attainment for Taiwan and the average Latin American country for all

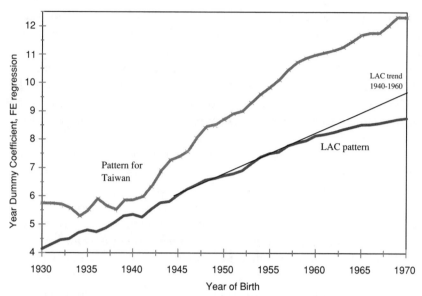

Figure 14.5. Pattern of schooling progress in Taiwan and Latin America.
Source: Jere Behrman, Suzanne Duryea, and Miguel Székely, "Schooling Investments and Aggregate Conditions: A Household-Survey Approach for Latin America and the Caribbean" (Working Paper no. 407, Inter-American Development Bank, Washington, DC, 1999).

cohorts (or groups of individuals) born between 1930 and 1970.[22] The figure shows that, on average, Latin America and Taiwan had very similar levels of schooling among cohorts born before 1940, but from that year on, progress in Taiwan shot upward. Thirty years later, cohorts in Taiwan were registering attainment levels almost 50 percent greater than the average Latin American country. The figure also shows the slowdown in Latin America for the 1960–70 birth cohorts. Cohorts born in those years were making schooling decisions that coincided with the early years of the debt crisis in the region. The figure also plots a trend line in Latin America from

[22] Household surveys for years around 1995 are used to produce this figure. Therefore, cohorts born in 1930 were about 65 years of age at the time of the survey, whereas those born in 1970 were around the age of 25. The figure does not include information on more recent cohorts (born after 1970) because a considerable share of individuals born after 1970 have not yet completed their schooling; hence, it is not clear what their attainments will be. The Latin America and the Caribbean (LAC) pattern was obtained by pooling all the information on the average years of schooling by year of birth, for 18 countries, and estimating a country fixed-effects regression using the average schooling of each cohort as the dependent variable and dummy variables for each year as the right-side variables. The figure plots the coefficients for the year dummies.

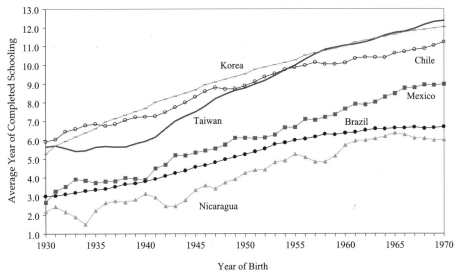

Figure 14.6. Mean years of schooling by cohort.
Source: Jere Behrman, Suzanne Duryea, and Miguel Székely, "Schooling Investments and Aggregate Conditions: A Household-Survey Approach for Latin America and the Caribbean."

1940 to 1960. Had the same trend continued for cohorts born after 1960, the average years of schooling for the last cohort would have been close to 10 years, rather than around 8.5.

Figure 14.6 plots information on cohorts born between 1930 and 1970 for a selected group of countries: Chile (one of the countries in Latin America with the highest current schooling levels and second only to Argentina for the 1970 birth cohort), Mexico (the country in Latin America with the greatest growth in mean years of schooling between the 1930 and 1970 birth cohorts), Brazil and Nicaragua (two of the countries in Latin America with the poorest schooling performances), and Korea and Taiwan. All of these countries display significant improvements in mean schooling for individuals born between 1940 and 1960, though more for Taiwan than for the others. Yet in Taiwan and South Korea, schooling increased at faster rates for persons born after 1960 than did most of Latin America, with the exceptions of Mexico and the Dominican Republic. For example, Chile and Taiwan had similar mean schooling for people born between 1950 and 1955, but those born in 1970 in Taiwan have, on average, one more grade of schooling than their Chilean counterparts. On the other hand, the large differences between Mexico and the Dominican Republic versus South Korea and Taiwan that can be observed today are not attributable to greater progress in these two East Asian countries for the most recent cohorts but rather to their much higher levels at the start of the period covered.

Not all countries in the Latin American region registered the same spread of education progress. For example, Honduras reported no increases in educational attainment for more than a decade for the cohorts born between 1925 and 1940, and it was not until the early 1950s that significant increases were reported.

In Table 14.4, information on the average years of schooling is presented for various cohorts. Seventeen countries in Latin America are listed in increasing order of mean schooling attainment for those born in 1930. Similar data for South Korea, Taiwan, and the United States are given at the bottom of the table. This table clearly portrays the upward trend for new generations of Latin Americans. Although advancements are notable for all countries, there is considerable disparity among nations. Brazil entered the century with one of the lowest levels, much like those of Honduras. Chile and Panama, on the other hand, had educational attainments almost three times higher than those of Brazil at the turn of the last century. Notwithstanding the progress reported, the table shows that many countries have suffered important setbacks regarding education.

On average, there was an increase of 4.6 years of schooling in the seventeen Latin American countries from the cohort born in 1930 to the one born in 1970. The largest increases were in Mexico, the Dominican Republic, Chile, Ecuador, Bolivia, and Venezuela, all of which boasted a gain of more than five years during the period. The smallest changes were in Jamaica, Paraguay, Brazil, and Nicaragua, all with less than four years. In contrast, South Korea and Taiwan made impressive strides in schooling attainment, boosting average years of education by 6.8 and 6.5 years, respectively, during the same period. Recent generations in these nations are approaching the schooling attainment levels of the United States.

Educational attainment levels in Latin America improved by only one year per decade in the region. Given this sluggish growth, the supply of the highest skills has also been quite slow to increase and has not been able to keep pace with the growing demand. This predicament has been a common one across the region and, as a result, the wages of highly educated individuals relative to unskilled employees have risen (see the

Table 14.4. *Average years of schooling by birth cohort*

Country	Year of birth					Change		
	1930	1940	1950	1960	1970	1930–1950	1950–1970	1930–1970
Honduras	1.4	3.2	4.6	5.6	6.1	3.2	1.4	4.7
Nicaragua	2	3.2	4.3	5.8	5.8	2.2	1.6	3.8
El Salvador	2.1	3.2	4.1	5.7	7	2	2.9	4.9
Brazil	2.8	3.6	5.2	6.2	6.7	2.4	1.5	3.9
Mexico	2.9	4.2	6.7	8.2	9.3	3.8	2.6	6.4
Dominican Republic	3.2	4.2	7	8.6	9.1	3.9	2.1	5.9
Venezuela	3.2	5.1	6.9	7.9	8.3	3.7	1.4	5.1
Bolivia	3.3	4.5	6.3	7	8.6	2.9	2.3	5.2
Ecuador	3.9	4.5	6.5	8.5	9.5	2.6	3	5.6
Colombia	3.9	4.4	6.2	7.7	8.4	2.3	2.2	4.4
Costa Rica	4.3	5.7	7.1	8.8	8.4	2.8	1.3	4.1
Chile	5.2	7.1	8.9	10.1	11.1	3.7	2.1	5.8
Panama	5.8	6.9	8.8	10.3	10.1	3.1	1.3	4.4
Peru	6	6.3	7.4	9.4	10	1.4	2.6	4
Uruguay*	6.3	7.4	8.8	10	10.7	2.5	1.9	4.4
Jamaica	6.9	7.9	8.3	9.6	10.6	1.4	2.3	3.7
Argentina*	7.5	8.3	10	11	11.3	2.5	1.3	3.8
Average LAC	4.1	5.3	6.9	8.2	8.8	2.7	1.9	4.6
Korea	5.3	7.7	9.5	11	12	4.3	2.5	6.8
Taiwan	5.8	5.8	8.9	11	12.3	3.2	3.3	6.5
USA	12.3	12.9	13.6	13.3	13.4	1.3	−0.2	1.1

*The survey for Argentina includes only Gran Buenos Aires; the survey from Uruguay covers only urban areas.
Sources: Suzanne Duryea and Miguel Székely, "The Determinants of Schooling in Latin America: A Micro-Macro Approach" (Working Paper, Inter-American Development Bank, 1999). Data from Korea were taken from *UNESCO Statistical Yearbook*, (New York, 1997).

fourth section), thereby contributing to the ever-widening income gap between highly and poorly educated individuals.

Schooling progress in Latin America was considerably greater for the generations born between 1930 and 1950 – a gain of 2.7 years – than for those born between 1950 and 1970 – a gain of 1.9. The deceleration appears to be steeper in Honduras, Dominican Republic, Venezuela, and Panama, where progress for cohorts born between 1930 and 1950 was more than 1.5

Table 14.5. *Average year of schooling by birth cohort for males and females*

Country	Year of birth					Change		
	1930	1940	1950	1960	1970	1930–1950	1950–1970	1930–1970
Average LAC (Latin America and the Caribbean)								
Male	4.6	5.7	7.2	8.4	8.8	2.6	1.5	4.1
Female	3.7	4.9	6.6	8	8.9	2.9	2.3	5.2
Taiwan								
Male	7.1	7.5	9.8	11.5	12.3	2.6	2.6	5.2
Female	3.7	4.4	8.2	10.5	12.2	4.5	4.1	8.5

Source: Suzanne Duryea and Miguel Székely, "The Determinants of Schooling in Latin America: A Micro-Macro Approach."

years greater than for those born in the following two decades. South Korea also had a much greater apparent increase between the 1930 and 1950 birth cohorts (4.3 years) than between the 1950 and 1970 birth cohorts (2.5 years).

The case of Taiwan is quite different. Measured schooling progress in this country for cohorts born between 1930 and 1950 was 3.2 years, which is only 0.5 years greater than the average Latin America country. Four Latin American countries (Mexico, Dominican Republic, Venezuela, and Chile) had gains of about 0.5 years greater than Taiwan for individuals born in the same years. However, unlike most of Latin America, Taiwan did not experience a slowdown in the next two decades. The gain for cohorts born between 1950 and 1970 was 3.3 years, which far exceeds the average 1.9-year gain in Latin America. There is only one country in the Latin American region (Ecuador) that had progress similar to Taiwan's for cohorts born during those two decades.

Table 14.5 shows similar data for the whole region subdivided by gender. On average, in Latin America, females had 1.1 years less schooling than males for the cohort born in 1930, but registered a gain of 1.1 years more for cohorts born forty years later. For both males and females, there was a general pattern of greater progress during 1930–50 than during the following two decades, but in the case of females, the slowdown was minor. In four countries, Colombia, Ecuador, El Salvador, and Peru, the gains for females between the 1950 and 1970 birth cohorts were even greater than the gains between the 1930 and 1950 birth cohorts.

Taiwan experienced a similar pattern. Females in Taiwan started out 2.4 years behind males for the 1930 birth cohort, but the 1970 birth cohort has

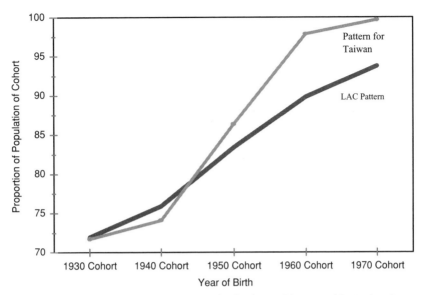

Figure 14.7. Proportion of the population with schooling in Taiwan and Latin America. *Source:* Jere Behrman, Suzanne Duryea, and Miguel Székely, "Schooling Investments and Aggregate Conditions: A Household-Survey Approach for Latin America and the Caribbean."

practically caught up to their male counterparts. The increase in schooling attainment for females in Taiwan between the 1930 and 1970 birth cohorts was 8.3 years, 3.3 years more than the increase for females in Latin America. For males, in contrast, the increase of 5.2 for males in Taiwan was only 1.1 years greater than for males in Latin America. Therefore, despite the relatively greater school progress in Latin America for females relative to males, it is females more than males that fell relatively farther behind Taiwan.

An interesting feature of the dynamics of schooling progress is that most Latin American countries had wider educational coverage – defined here as successful completion of at least the first grade – than Taiwan and South Korea among cohorts born before 1950. However, there is a stark contrast between the two East Asian nations and the Latin American region with respect to the proportion of the population that has completed primary schooling. Figure 14.7 plots the proportion of individuals in each age cohort that has completed at least one year of schooling in Taiwan and the average Latin American country. For cohorts born between 1930 and 1950, there is practically no difference. For the 1970 cohort, Taiwan reached practically

Table 14.6. *Average years of schooling; 25–65 years*

	Income decile									
	I	II	III	IV	V	VI	VII	VIII	IX	X
Argentina	7.1	7.7	7.84	8.28	8.84	9.39	9.65	11.28	11.73	14.24
Bolivia	6.44	7.31	7.73	8.15	8.14	8.58	9.2	9.61	10.83	12.12
Brazil	2.41	3.2	3.38	3.82	4.32	7.84	5.68	6.37	7.5	10.33
Colombia	4.86	5.62	5.93	6.37	6.63	6.96	7.18	7.73	7.75	6.68
Costa Rica	4.51	5.01	5.61	6.01	6.33	6.67	7.37	7.83	9.01	11.85
Chile	6.31	7.16	7.64	8.02	8.45	8.91	9.43	10.3	11.3	13.12
Ecuador	3.92	4.77	5.39	5.67	6.63	7.36	8.1	8.37	9.44	11.76
El Salvador	2.1	2.4	2.78	3.17	3.53	4.1	5.2	6.19	7.58	11.02
Honduras	2.73	2.95	3.25	3.71	4.21	4.46	4.88	5.92	6.74	8.98
Mexico	3.08	3.52	4.39	5.43	5.93	6.53	7.31	7.83	8.66	11.24
Panama	3.62	3.8	4.33	4.93	5.15	5.69	6.67	7.35	8.19	10.75
Paraguay	3.62	3.8	4.33	4.93	5.15	5.69	6.67	7.35	8.19	10.75
Peru	5.85	6.31	6.47	6.19	6.29	6.83	7.4	8.27	9.06	10.84
Uruguay	6.3	6.83	7.22	7.49	7.81	8.28	8.99	9.53	10.64	12.68
Veuezuela	5.85	6.31	6.6	6.86	6.76	7.32	7.17	7.72	8.21	9.93

Source: Suzanne Duryea and Miguel Székely, "The Determinants of Schooling in Latin America: A Micro-Macro Approach."

full coverage, whereas the average Latin American country lagged, with around 94 percent coverage.

Within decades in Latin America, there are important disparities in schooling attainment. Table 14.6 plots the average years of schooling by income decile for the active population of fifteen Latin American countries around the nineties. The huge educational gap is quite astonishing. This holds especially true for countries such as Argentina, Chile, and Mexico, where the difference between the highest income decile and the poorest is about seven years of schooling. These gaps hold the key to the analysis of inequality because those individuals with the highest incomes have also attained the highest levels of education, thereby perpetuating the vicious cycle of considerable disparities in income and well-being. Nevertheless, differences among income deciles are not the sole problem related to schooling attainment in the Latin American region.

Table 14.7 presents for each country the percentages of population by year of birth who have completed primary and secondary schooling. This

Table 14.7. *Proportion of the population in each birth cohort completing at least primary education*

Country	1930 pri	1930 sec	1940 pri	1940 sec	1950 pri	1950 sec	1960 pri	1960 sec	1970 pri	1970 sec
Argentina*	73.0	31.7	82.5	45.2	88.7	55.7	94.2	63.0	97.5	74.1
Bolivia	27.3	42.4	37.5	20.8	48.9	33.5	63.5	40.1	79.1	62.2
Brazil	15.0	14.0	20.4	19.1	34.1	32.0	48.8	44.4	55.2	58.3
Colombia	41.4	17.2	49.7	25.1	60.6	39.4	76.0	58.2	82.5	49.1
Costa Rica	32.7	14.1	51.6	26.7	72.7	37.2	84.3	52.6	87.0	66.3
Chile	32.9	28.1	42.3	36.2	60.6	50.7	77.7	65.8	85.3	48.2
Dominican Republic	21.6	11.1	23.6	15.0	44.3	31.2	59.3	47.5	67.2	76.4
Ecuador	33.8	12.9	38.8	17.8	58.1	31.4	77.3	50.4	86.9	55.3
El Salvador	14.5	8.7	28.0	16.3	36.5	21.8	53.3	41.4	59.3	64.2
Honduras	11.7	3.9	22.2	11.1	36.4	18.0	48.5	24.6	64.2	50.6
Jamaica	74.6	42.0	85.8	57.4	93.5	66.2	95.9	90.0	95.9	32.3
Mexico	22.3	8.1	33.2	15.7	52.5	32.5	70.0	47.1	83.1	95.3
Nicaragua	16.3	6.7	24.6	11.9	34.8	22.6	49.4	36.9	57.8	98.9
Panama	50.8	27.6	62.6	40.3	77.4	52.5	90.1	69.3	91.8	66.3
Paraguay	26.7	13.8	36.4	17.5	51.0	28.2	65.2	37.3	72.6	42.7
Peru	49.3	28.8	61.6	36.8	68.4	49.1	83.2	67.6	89.1	72.7
Uruguay*	59.5	25.9	73.0	40.7	84.3	55.8	93.0	71.1	96.5	44.2
Venezuela	40.0	13.0	57.0	22.7	73.4	41.7	84.0	58.4	87.2	75.4
Average LAC (Latin America and the Caribbean)	35.7	19.4	46.2	26.5	59.8	38.9	73.0	53.7	79.9	97.7
Korea	66.2	27.3	88.6	51.6	97.9	77.6	99.4	93.4	99.7	81.2
Taiwan	68.3	26.1	71.6	24.6	92.7	48.8	98.9	85.3	99.6	98
USA	97.3	97.5	97.9	95.5	98.7	97.2	99.1	97.6	99.3	66.8

Note: pri = primary; sec = secondary school
Source: Suzanne Duryea and Miguel Székely, "The Determinants of Schooling in Latin America: A Micro-Macro Approach."

exercise proves extremely useful in illustrating the huge disparities among countries in the region, as well as the gap between the region and Taiwan, South Korea, and the United States. For example, in Honduras, the country with the poorest track record, 11.7 and 3.9 percent of the population born in 1930 have completed at least primary and secondary education, respectively. For the same birth cohort, almost 70 percent of the Korean and Taiwanese populations have completed primary and approximately 30 percent have completed secondary. This immense disparity is reflected in almost every generation for all Latin American countries, until the 1960 and 1970 cohorts. The countries in Latin America most likely to achieve levels of education on a par with the East Asian countries are Argentina and Uruguay. Still, the sad fact remains that even when a few Latin American countries win the struggle to achieve high levels of education, the bulk of their regional neighbors are left behind.

PHYSICAL CAPITAL

Specific measurement of physical capital accumulation is generally problematic. Even when information is available regarding physical capital, it is rarely useful for comparisons over time. For that reason, and to allow for a longer time horizon, we use a proxy for physical capital, namely, capital per worker. This indicator portrays the total value of the physical capital of an enterprise, including inventories and fixed equipment, per each unit of labor employed.

Figure 14.8 presents the ratios of capital stock per worker for Latin America, South Korea, and Thailand. As shown, the Latin American region accounted for more than two times, even three in the case of Thailand, the capital per worker in 1965. Despite this clear head start, South Korea overtook the region in the following years. Growth continued steadily during the 1970s until 1982, when Latin America's capital per worker decreased during the crisis of the 1980s, and South Korea's capital accumulation expanded. By the 1990s, South Korea's capital per worker was almost two times greater than Latin America's, whereas the gap between Latin America and Thailand narrowed considerably between 1965 and 1992.

These data are broken down by country for the Latin American region in Table 14.8. As is apparent, the capital per worker ratio grew substantially between 1965 and 1975. The ratio doubled in countries such as Bolivia, Mexico, Panama, and Paraguay, whereas the smallest, although still positive, growth rate took place in Peru and Venezuela. From 1975 to 1985, however, although growth rates remained positive, they slowed drastically throughout the region in comparison to the previous decade. This paved the way for a sharp reduction in the capital-stock-per-worker ratio during most of the 1980s and the beginning of the 1990s, when Chile was among the only few to experience positive growth as the rest of the region headed into a decline.

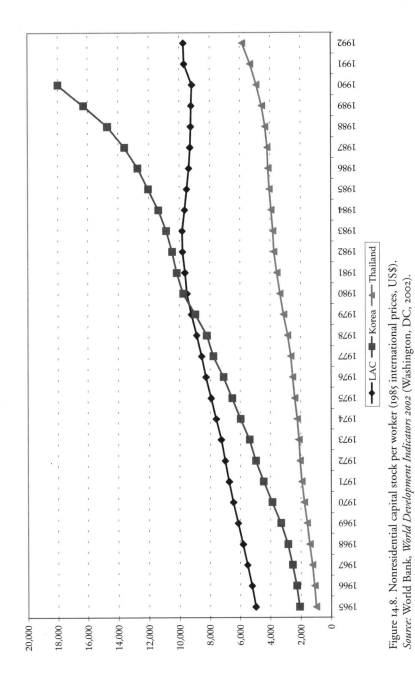

Figure 14.8. Nonresidential capital stock per worker (1985 international prices, US$).
Source: World Bank, *World Development Indicators 2002* (Washington, DC, 2002).

617

Table 14.8. *Percentage changes in nonresidential capital stock per worker in Latin America (1965–1992)*

	1965–1975	1975–1985	1985–1992
Argentina	70.03	27.94	−9.36
Bolivia	119.72	19.01	−23.64
Chile	36.42	2.22	61.14
Colombia	54.71	20.77	−0.38
Dominican Republic	106.87	56.55	17.82
Ecuador	64.81	58.85	1.75
Guatemala	43.26	31.09	−10.31
Honduras	65.37	0.60	−11.03
Mexico	93.28	18.92	−2.28
Panama	122.60	18.89	−2.29
Paraguay	135.29	76.88	19.08
Peru	34.19	8.84	−10.12
Venezuela	16.26	19.99	−10.40

Source: Authors' own calculations taken from data of the Penn World Table.

These figures provide a clear picture of the slowdown in the accumulation of capital in Latin America at the national level. In terms of its effect over inequality, small capital stocks are usually associated with high returns and, because this factor is normally concentrated among the rich, the effect of low accumulation rates would be expected to be inequality increasing. In order to explore this possibility further, we would need to have data on capital ownership at the household level. Unfortunately, this kind of information is highly scarce.

Finally, we present data on the use of arable land, which relates to the use of physical capital. As is observed in Figure 14.9, in the case of various countries of Latin America such as Argentina, Brazil, Colombia, and Panama, inequality in arable land has been high in comparison to other developing countries such as India, South Korea, and Thailand. As shown in Figure 14.9, during the fifties and sixties, only Mexico presented a Gini coefficient on arable land of around 0.6, similar to India or Thailand during the same decades, whereas the other Latin American countries had Gini levels of around 0.8 and 0.9 points.

Thailand was able to reduce this inequality in the 1980s, reaching Gini levels near to 0.4 and 0.3 (similar to South Korea), whereas in most of Latin

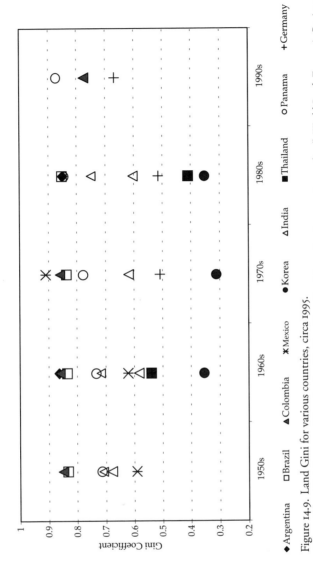

Figure 14.9. Land Gini for various countries, circa 1995.
Source: Klaus Deininger and Lyn Squire, "A New Data Set Measuring Income Inequality," *World Bank Economic Review* 10, 3 (September 1996): 565–91.

America, inequality remained constant and, in some cases, such as in Mexico during the 1970s and Panama during the 1980s and 1990s, it even increased. The only country with a decrease in its land Gini was Colombia, to around 0.75 points, although this level was still double the one from the East Asian developing countries. In sum, according to the available evidence, statistics show that similar to the case of education, physical capital assets in Latin America are concentrated in a few hands.

USE OF ASSETS

The accumulation of human and physical capital in Latin America has not only been slow compared with other regions, but the distribution of these income-earning assets has been highly skewed toward the rich. The second element in the process of income-formation is the use of assets. This section examines this component. First, we concentrate on human capital and then we present a brief analysis of the use of physical capital and land.

LABOR FORCE PARTICIPATION IN LATIN AMERICA: THE USE OF HUMAN CAPITAL

Latin America has been characterized by deep changes in terms of the possibilities of using human capital to generate income during the past decades. This has been especially so in the case of women. Figure 14.10 shows that total labor market participation in Latin America increased from around 64 percent in 1970 to 70 percent during the 1980s, continuing to rise at a much slower pace during the 1990s. The figure also shows that practically the entire shift was caused by the substantial increase in female participation. Women accounted for only 23 percent of the labor force in 1970, but their share increased to 36 percent over the next twenty-six years.

To assess the magnitudes of demographic and schooling effects on female labor force participation, Duryea and Székely estimate a regression in which changes in women's labor supply are a function of changes in education, fertility, and other variables.[23] Their results indicate that reductions in fertility and increases in average education are, in fact, associated with increases in female participation. The authors also find that the change

---

[23] Suzanne Duryea and Miguel Székely, "The Determinants of Schooling in Latin America: A Micro-Macro Approach" (Mimeograph, Inter-American Development Bank, 1999).

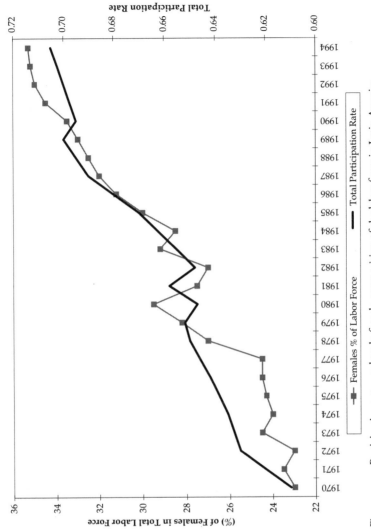

Figure 14.10. Participation rates and male-female composition of the labor force in Latin America. *Source:* Suzanne Duryea and Miguel Székely, "The Determinants of Schooling in Latin America: A Micro-Macro Approach" (Mimeograph, Inter-American Development Bank, 1999).

in the age structure, triggered by the demographic transition, has a strong association with the sharp rise in female participation rates. Thus, the aging of Latin America's population is another factor that would affect female labor force participation and a more intensive use of income-earning assets.

The connection between schooling and participation has several channels. If schooling of women increases their awareness and use of contraceptive methods or increases their bargaining power relative to men's (should men prefer more children), then more educated women will have fewer undesired births.[24] If women enjoy better economic opportunities because of educational attainment, the opportunity cost of their time invested in child care increases with their schooling level. Consequently, they tend to have fewer children if the increased opportunity cost is large enough to offset the potential positive income effect.[25]

Similarly, if the reward paid in the labor market for a fixed amount of schooling increases, the opportunity cost of the time invested in raising children increases, and the desired number of children tends to decline (with the net effect depending on the income versus the price effects once again). Conventional wisdom and much of the past empirical literature suggest that women's schooling is the dominant factor associated with fertility declines, though in most studies exactly what causal role women's schooling is playing is not identified.

In fact, Table 14.9 shows that participation rates in Latin America increase considerably with education.[26] For instance, in Honduras, women with no schooling have participation rates of about 32 percent, whereas those with higher education have a participation rate of 72 percent. The average ratio between the participation rates of women in the lowest education category to those in the highest category is approximately one to three.

According to Duryea and Székely, around 30 percentage points of the increase in participation rates are associated with the change in the age composition of the population. Specifically, the relative size of the thirty to thirty-nine age group increased by 15 percent during the decade and, because this is the group that registers the highest participation rates, total female

[24] Mark Rosenzweig and Paul Schultz, "The Supply and Demand for Births: Fertility and Its Life Cycle Consequence," *American Economic Review* 75, 5 (1985): 992–1015; Mark Rosenzweig and Paul Schultz, "Fertility and Investments in Human Capital: Estimates of the Consequences of Imperfect Fertility Control in Malaysia," *Journal of Econometrics* 36 (1987): 163–84.
[25] Michael Kremer and Daniel Chen, "Income Distribution Dynamics with Endogenous Fertility," *American Economic Review* (May 1999).
[26] The only exception is Peru in 1985.

participation increased. The relative size of the forty to forty-nine group – which registers lower participation rates – also expanded and this tended to reduce participation. However, because this expansion was smaller (around 8%), it was offset by the change in the thirty to thirty-nine age group. With respect to the 1990s, female participation continued to expand, although at a slower pace. In the 1980s, the average annual increase was 3.4 percent; in the 1990s, it fell to 2.4 percent.

What are the forces causing the changes in the age structure that affect the use of human capital through female labor force participation? Shifts in age structure are mainly triggered by changes in fertility and mortality that have taken place some years before becoming manifest. With constant age-specific fertility and mortality rates, a population grows at a steady rate and the age structure remains stable. However, if fertility and mortality decline at different rates, as is the case during the stereotypical demographic transition from a high-fertility/high-mortality steady state to a low-fertility/low-mortality steady state, population growth and dependency ratios vary. Differences in age structures and dependency ratios across countries today are attributable mainly to differences in fertility rates and to the varying paces at which they have declined over time.

Decreased fertility is typically associated with increased female schooling. Surveys of the literature on fertility repeatedly suggest that the strongest empirical association between fertility declines and observed variables in micro and aggregate studies is the inverse one between women's schooling and fertility. In a summary of the empirical literature, Birdsall finds that female education of over four years bears one of the strongest and most consistent negative relationships to fertility, and that empirical work has strongly confirmed the hypothesis that parents' education – especially a mother's education above the primary level – is associated with lower fertility.[27] Schultz also implies that increasing educational attainment of women is generally associated with reduced fertility.[28]

Another factor affecting fertility is health. The more precarious are health conditions, the lower the probability of the survival of each child and, therefore, the larger the number of pregnancies required to be able to meet the target number of adult children. If health conditions improve, thereby reducing infant mortality rates and increasing life expectancies, people will

[27] Nancy Birdsall et al., "Why Low Inequality Spurs Growth: Saving and Investment by the Poor," in Andrés Solimano, ed., *Social Inequalities: Values, Growth and the State* (Ann Arbor, MI, 1998).

[28] Schultz, "Inequality in the Distribution of Personal Income in the World: How It Is Changing and Why" (Mimeograph, Yale University, 1997).

Table 14.9. *Participation rates for men and women ages 30–45 by level of completed schooling (percent)*

Country and year	Women				Men			
	A No education	B Primary	C Secondary	D Higher	A No education	B Primary	C Secondary	D Higher
Brazil 81	0.34	0.37	0.53	0.82	0.95	0.97	0.97	0.98
Brazil 95	0.5	0.57	0.67	0.87	0.92	0.95	0.97	0.987
Chile 87	0.25	0.3	0.39	0.7	0.81	0.94	0.96	0.98
Chile 94	0.34	0.36	0.46	0.74	0.8	0.95	0.98	0.98
Colombia 95	0.42	0.46	0.61	0.87	0.92	0.98	0.98	0.98
Costa Rica 81	0.87	0.91	0.93	0.93	0.91	0.96	0.98	0.93
Costa Rica 95	0.34	0.35	0.48	0.7	0.87	0.97	0.98	0.97
Ecuador 95	0.68	0.61	0.62	0.81	0.88	0.96	0.98	0.98
El Salvador 95	0.41	0.57	0.7	0.9	0.89	0.93	0.94	0.94
Honduras 89	0.26	0.4	0.61	0.76	0.96	0.98	0.95	0.97
Honduras 96	0.32	0.49	0.6	0.72	0.95	0.98	0.98	0.97
Mexico 84	0.37	0.39	0.47	0.72	0.74	0.97	0.98	0.98
Mexico 94	0.37	0.39	0.47	0.72	0.74	0.97	0.98	0.98
Nicaragua 93	0.33	0.49	0.66	0.72	0.9	0.89	0.89	0.95

Panama 95	0.2	0.34	0.55	0.83	0.84	0.96	0.96	0.97
Paraguay 95	0.72	0.72	0.73	0.86	0.79	0.98	0.99	0.99
Peru 85/6	0.82	0.78	0.66	0.78	0.92	0.98	0.96	0.97
Peru 96	0.77	0.71	0.64	0.72	0.89	0.98	0.94	0.97
Venezuela 81	0.23	0.33	0.52	0.76	0.95	0.98	0.98	0.97
Venezuela 95	0.31	0.41	0.6	0.83	0.9	0.97	0.97	0.96
Argentina 81*	0.63	0.34	0.42	0.71	0.98	0.98	0.98	0.97
Argentina 96	0.64	0.48	0.56	0.8	0.75	0.96	0.98	0.99
Bolivia 86*	0.45	0.43	0.48	0.61	0.87	0.96	0.97	0.87
Bolivia 95	0.68	0.68	0.63	0.8	0.95	0.98	0.97	0.96
Uruguay 81*	0.47	0.47	0.52	0.8	0.63	0.97	0.98	0.99
Uruguay 95	0.34	0.59	0.73	0.91	0.4	0.97	0.99	0.99

* The surveys for Argentina include only Gran Buenos Aires. The surveys for Bolivia include only urban. The surveys for Uruguay include only urban.

Source: Suzanne Duryea and Miguel Székely, "Schooling Investments and Aggregate Conditions: A Household-Survey Approach for Latin America and the Caribbean" (Working Paper no. 407, Inter-American Development Bank, 1999).

perceive these changes. They will then respond rationally to the knowledge that they will be able to achieve their expected desired family size with fewer births because of increased probabilities of survival to adulthood. Furthermore, with longer expected life spans, the returns to human resource investments are greater. This shifts the incentives toward investing more in each child – and having fewer of them – and away from having a high number of children.

According to estimates of Behrman, Duryea, and Székely for Latin America as well as other regions, the two key variables that affect fertility trends are the differences in female schooling and in health. Female schooling differentials are consistent with about three-quarters of the difference in fertility, with secondary school being most important, followed by tertiary. Better health in the developed than in the developing world as represented by the life-expectancy-at-age-one variable is consistent with about one quarter of the difference.

In the case of Latin America, the association with female schooling is larger and with health smaller than for all developing countries combined. For female schooling in Latin America, differences in secondary schooling have particularly strong associations and those for tertiary schooling also are relatively large. Because Latin America has a higher proportion of its female population over twenty-five years of age with completed schooling only at the primary level than do the developed countries, differences in this schooling level are associated negatively with the fertility difference.

In sum, the main change taking place in Latin America with regard to the use of human capital in the region is the increase in female participation rates. Whereas male participation is fairly stable across age groups and across the income distribution, female participation is highly influenced directly by education, fertility, and demographic changes. Among these three factors, education plays a major role because it affects participation indirectly through its effects on fertility and on future age structures, in addition to its direct impact.

This is an important conclusion because it reveals that education may have affected income inequality and poverty in Latin America during the past century through various channels. The most direct channel has been that education is an asset in itself and, therefore, it determines the potential that an individual has for generating income. Indirectly, schooling affects income by influencing the possibilities of using the income-earning assets acquired. The analysis in this section reveals that the possibilities of putting human capital to work are highly influenced by schooling. The greater the education level, the greater the chances of using education in the labor market to generate income.

INVESTMENT: THE USE OF CAPITAL ASSETS

Physical capital in Latin America has been as unevenly distributed and used as human capital. The behavior of this asset in terms of investment in productive activity (*use* of physical capital) in the region has been one of constant instability. Foreign Direct Investment (FDI) stagnation characterized the region for more than two decades, until the 1980s, when the debt crisis hit. Instead of following a recovery trend at the beginning of the 1990s, investment rates went into a steep slide, leaving the region far behind other countries that had had similar levels.

As shown in Figure 14.11, Latin America entered the 1950s with similar ratios of real investment to GDP as those of Southeast Asian countries such as South Korea and Thailand. Economic upheavals then induced Latin America to raise its levels of investment from 10 percent to 15 percent of GDP in only a decade, while South Korea and Thailand were only investing 8 percent and 11 percent, respectively. Nonetheless, within a brief period of time, this situation had changed dramatically.

The 1960s were a stagnant decade for Latin America, during which economic inactivity with respect to FDI was a feature distinguishing the region. Investment did not fall, with some years showing no growth or very low growth rates and others showing modest increases at best. South Korea and Thailand, on the other hand, took the opposite course. South Korea showed an exponential investment rise over the course of the 1960s. By the 1970s, while Latin America was experiencing an investment rate of 16 percent, South Korea was leaps and bounds ahead, at 27 percent. Thailand followed a somewhat similar trend, but its investment growth rates were not as impressive as those of South Korea. Thailand's shares continued to grow steadily, however, and by the 1970s, its rate was 21 percent – low in comparison to Korea's 27 percent but higher than Latin America's 16 percent.

Latin America and Thailand performed similarly during the 1970s, going through ups and downs, while Korea continued to increase its investment rate. By the 1980s, Korea's share was almost 35 percent whereas Latin America and Thailand were still stuck in the 20 percent range. The 1990s brought economic crises that inflicted critical setbacks on all three countries. Although investment shares diminished across the board, recovery

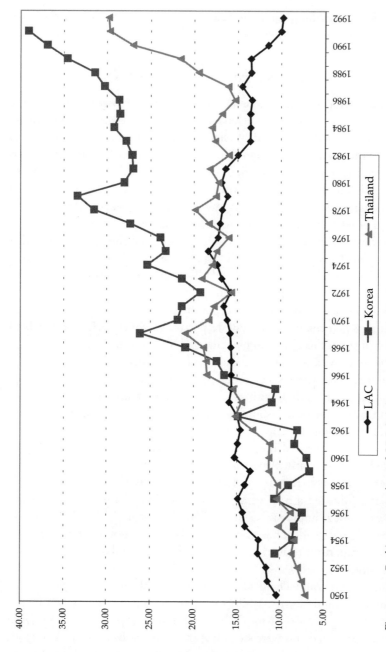

Figure 14.11. Real investment share of GDP (%) (1995 international prices).
Source: Penn World Table 1994.

628

came sooner for the Asian countries. Latin America's rates continued their downward slide, widening the ever-expanding gap between the Latin American region and the two Southeast Asian countries.

As for the use of land, the percentage of arable land used in agriculture in Latin America is not particularly high (Figure 14.12). In fact, it is low compared to other regions. It accounted for only 4 percent of the total land area at the beginning of the sixties, when the average for the world was more than twice that number. The share remained relatively constant (reaching 6.5%) at the end of the twentieth century, when the percentage for East Asia reached 12 percent. Consequently, the rate of use of this income-earning asset has been rather modest. As shown in the previous section, land is highly concentrated in the few countries for which data are available. Given its low rate of use and high returns, this would be expected.

ASSETS, PRICES, AND RETURNS

Prices reflect the rate of return that assets earn when they are put to work in the market. For the purposes of this section, the focus is on the returns to education as reflected in income and the returns to capital as reflected in interest rates. Unlike other variables such as levels of education or fertility, returns to assets are not nearly as heavily influenced by individual decisions. Rather, they are determined to a large extent by supply and demand, as well as by institutional factors, on which each individual exerts a negligible degree of influence. Prices are therefore mostly set by the economic system, and their interaction with the individual begins when he or she embarks on the process of seeking income or accumulating a certain type of capital.

RETURNS TO EDUCATION: THE PRICE RECEIVED FOR PUTTING HUMAN CAPITAL TO WORK

If the relative demand for different skills had remained the same over time, even meager improvements in school attainment by the Latin American population should have been associated with a relative decline in the earnings of the more educated. However, the evidence shows that this was not so.

Table 14.10 gives the coefficient estimates for the trend followed by the (log) wage gap between individuals with higher, secondary, and primary education for fifteen Latin American countries for years between 1977 and

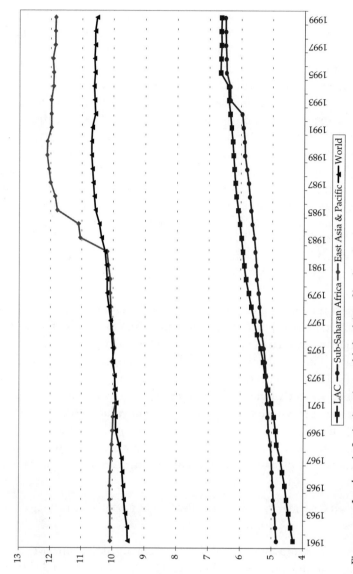

Figure 14.12. Land use in Latin America, arable land (% of land area).
Source: World Bank, *World Development Indicators 2002* (Washington, DC, 2002).

Table 14.10. *Country trends for wage gaps and overall policy*

Country	Higher to secondary wage gap	Higher to primary wage gap
Paraguay	0.1008	0.1482
El Salvador	0.0736	0.0942
Colombia	0.0181	0.0661
Mexico	0.0152	0.0287
Ecuador	0.0177	0.0283
Chile	0.0146	0.0241
Nicaragua	0.0561	0.0209
Costa Rica	0.0198	0.0198
Peru	0.0061	0.017
Uruguay	0.0074	0.0129
Panama	0.0103	0.0082
Bolivia	0.0097	0.0065
Argentina	0.0093	0.0012
Venezuela	0.0064	−0.0009
Honduras	0.0102	−0.0017
Average all LAC	0.0155	0.01817

Source: Jere Behrman, Nancy Birdsall, and Miguel Székely, *Poverty and Income Inequality in Developing Countries: A Policy Dialogue on the Effects of Globalization* (Paris, 1999).

1998. A positive trend means that the gap has been expanding. Interestingly, the higher-education-to-secondary-school wage gap has augmented in all fifteen countries during the past two decades. The countries where the higher–primary wage gap (second column) increased the most are Paraguay, El Salvador, and Colombia. The only three countries where the gap narrowed are Argentina, Venezuela, and Honduras. Paraguay and El Salvador are also the countries where the higher–secondary wage gap increased the most, while Colombia registered a more moderate increase than in the higher–primary gap. Peru and Argentina are the two countries where the increase in the higher–secondary gap was smallest, but there is no country where the gap narrowed. The correlation between the coefficients in Table 14.10 is 0.86, which indicates a high (although not perfect) correspondence between changes in the higher–primary and higher–secondary wage gaps.

On average, wage differentials in the region have increased substantially during the 1990s. Figure 14.13 shows that the average differential among the same fifteen counties expanded considerably during the first half of the decade and remained fairly stable thereafter. The higher-to-secondary

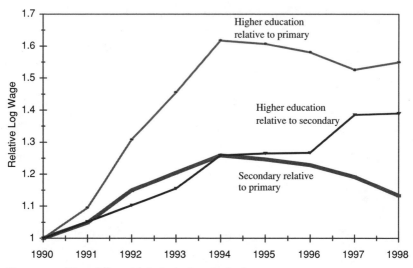

Figure 14.13. Wage differentials in Latin America in the 1990s.
Source: Jere Behrman, Suzanne Duryea, and Miguel Székely, "Schooling Investments and Aggregate Conditions: A Household-Survey Approach for Latin America and the Caribbean."

differential shows a similar pattern, while the secondary-to-primary gap increased during the first five years of the decade and decreased during the second half.

Figure 14.14 summarizes the country-year information for the marginal return to each level of schooling for the years between 1990 and 1998 (profiles normalized to the value of the coefficient for 1990).[29] The generally positive slope for the linear return reflects the fact that the return to an extra year of schooling in Latin America has increased by about 7 percent during the 1990s. The disaggregation by schooling levels reveals that the increase is totally driven by the large rise in the marginal return to higher (post-secondary) schooling. The returns to primary and secondary schooling declined after the early 1990s, though with partial recovery in the late 1990s.

Table 14.11 provides some evidence on the returns to education by country.[30] According to the table, having incomplete primary schooling implies,

---

[29] The estimates are the regional average for the returns to schooling from log-wage regressions for each household survey.

[30] The table shows the coefficients of a standard Ordinary Least Squares (OLS) Mincer regression where the dependent variable is the log hourly wage of each individual and the independent variables are experience (proxied by age six minus years of schooling), experience squared, and a vector of dummies representing five different education levels. The returns on education are determined

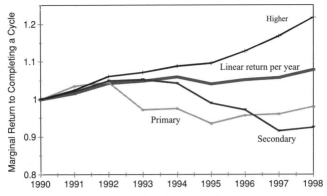

Figure 14.14. Marginal returns to education: Latin America in the 1990s.
Source: Jere Behrman, Nancy Birdsall, and Miguel Székely, "Economic Reform and Wage Differentials in Latin America" (Working Paper, Inter-American Development Bank, 2000).

on average, an income 18 percent higher than that for people with no schooling. Complete primary education yields a return of 37 percent, whereas incomplete and complete secondary education have returns of 61 percent and 95 percent, respectively. The greatest returns are observed for higher education, with 152 percent on average. The largest differences in returns between the lowest and highest schooling levels are observed in Brazil, Chile, Colombia, and Mexico.

This evidence illustrates the circularity between asset ownership, use, and return. The poor have the smallest stocks of human capital. In the case of females, those with fewer assets tend to use them to a lower extent. Furthermore, those with the smallest stocks of human capital receive the lowest rewards not only for having a small stock but also because the returns are nonlinear and increase with the size of the stock. Finally, because of the low returns, the poor (especially women) ultimately earn lower rates on their assets.

RETURNS TO PHYSICAL CAPITAL

The return on an asset such as physical capital has many components, a fact that complicates the analysis. This chapter's treatment of physical capital

by a variety of factors and are less subject to individual preferences and decisions. The regression is estimated for adults in the 25–65 age range and does not correct for sample selection biases attributable to participation. However, the conclusions about the changes in the returns to education and the differences between low and high schooling levels do not change substantially when corrections for the bias are attempted.

Table 14.11. *Returns to education in Latin America during the 1990s*

Country	Year	Coefficients from ordinary least squares (OLS) regression				
		Primary incomplete	Primary complete	Secondary incomplete	Secondary complete	Higher education
Argentina*	1996	0.12	0.21	0.34	0.6	1.03
Bolivia*	1990	−0.14	−0.06	0.11	0.21	0.49
	1991	−0.14	−0.06	0.11	0.21	0.49
	1993	0.09	0.17	0.36	0.66	1.11
	1995	0.06	0.16	0.25	0.56	1.13
Brazil	1992	0.12	0.26	0.47	0.84	1.54
	1993	0.1	0.24	0.47	0.82	1.5
	1995	0.45	0.82	1.17	1.72	2.5
	1996	0.41	0.76	1.13	1.65	2.39
Chile	1990	0.19	0.36	0.66	0.97	1.72
	1992	0.2	0.33	0.61	1.02	1.83
	1994	0.27	0.44	0.67	1.11	1.87
	1996	0.19	0.38	0.67	1.08	1.92
Colombia	1997	0.19	0.55	0.82	1.28	2.1
Costa Rica	1989	0.22	0.42	0.7	1.04	1.51
	1991	0.11	0.27	0.53	0.84	1.47
	1993	0.3	0.43	0.65	0.88	1.55
	1995	0.21	0.37	0.57	0.84	1.44
Dom. Rep.	1996	0.3	0.49	0.63	0.75	1.39
Ecuador	1995	0.23	0.49	0.9	1.26	1.64
El Salvador	1995	0.26	0.49	0.73	1.17	1.77
Honduras	1992	0.15	0.38	0.71	1.11	1.82
	1996	0.24	0.54	0.7	1.23	1.9
	1998	0.17	0.4	0.59	1.79	1.92
Mexico	1989	0.33	0.68	1.05	1.47	1.9
	1992	0.43	0.82	1.27	1.72	2.37
	1994	0.24	0.52	0.88	1.39	2.05
	1996	0.09	0.4	0.93	1.65	2.43
Nicaragua	1993	0.4	0.55	0.71	0.99	1.47
Panama	1991	−0.07	0.04	0.22	0.47	0.96
	1995	0.06	0.14	0.33	0.56	1.09
	1997	−0.03	−0.06	0	0.23	0.96
Paraguay	1995	0.32	0.71	1.07	1.63	2.26
Peru	1991	0	−0.02	0.08	0.12	0.31
	1994	0.03	0.08	0.27	0.34	0.73
	1997	0.22	0.29	0.5	0.56	1.09
Uruguay*	1989	0.03	0.12	0.27	0.32	0.52
	1992	0.27	0.51	0.81	0.99	1.47
	1995	0.18	0.36	0.73	0.93	1.46
Venezuela	1995	0.35	0.55	0.73	0.98	1.44
	1997	0.27	0.43	0.58	0.88	1.59
Average LAC	1997	0.18	0.37	0.61	0.95	1.52

* Surveys with urban coverage.
Source: Orazio Attanasio and Miguel Székely, eds., *Portrait of the Poor* (Washington, DC, 2001).

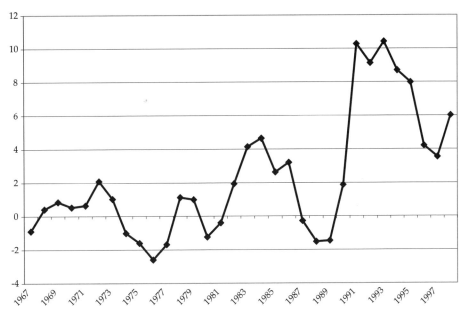

Figure 14.15. Real interest rates for five Latin American countries.
Source: World Bank *Global Development Finance & World Development Indicators* (Washington, DC, 2002).

has focused more on its investment component than its infrastructure one. Because there is no single price that can be used to describe the evolution of the returns to physical capital investment, this subsection concentrates on the evolution of interest rates as a general price indicating the behavior of returns to physical capital, specifically investment.

Figure 14.15 shows the average real interest rate for five Latin American countries (Brazil, Colombia, Chile, Mexico, and Venezuela) for the period 1965–99.[31] As can be seen, with only few exceptions (eight years out of the thirty-five spanning the 1965–99 period), real interest rates are positive and high in many cases. Average real interest rates fluctuated around 1 to 2 percent during the 1960s and early 1970s, were generally low during the late 1970s, and were positive during practically all the following twenty years, reaching levels above 10 percent during the mid-1990s. Real interest rates are a lower-bound indicator of the returns to capital in an economy,

---

[31] Because of the high volatility of real interest rates in most countries, we concentrate only on these five cases. The data correspond to three-year moving averages for each of the five countries (this is why the figure plots the data from 1967 on).

so the data reveal that those owning physical capital assets were most likely obtaining considerable rewards for putting them to work.

Another way of determining whether returns to capital are attractive in an international context is the flow of foreign investment to a country. Presumably, if all other factors remain the same, capital will flow to a country when its returns (e.g., corrected by risk factors) exceed those that would be obtained elsewhere. Latin America did attract foreign investment during the 1990s. This is in stark contrast with the previous two decades, when hardly any flows took place. The levels of FDI during the 1970s and 1980s were very small because the region was largely closed to capital flows, but the relatively high levels during the 1990s suggest that returns to capital in the region were, in fact, attractive.

FACTOR ENDOWMENTS AND INCOME DISTRIBUTION

The evidence presented in the previous three sections suggests that the factors underlying the historical persistence of inequality and poverty in Latin America are the following: (1) income-earning assets in the region have historically been unevenly distributed among the population; (2) those who have fewer assets also find fewer opportunities to use these assets to generate income; and (3) asset returns are lower on a per-unit basis for those with smaller stocks of assets, so that the poor incur a double financial penalty.

These conclusions may come as a surprise to those arguing that trade liberalization processes – which have been pursued by most of the countries in the region since the 1980s – tend to raise the demand for unskilled labor in unskilled labor-abundant countries such as those in Latin America. This increased demand is expected, in turn, to reduce inequality and poverty by boosting the wages for workers with lower schooling levels. Similarly, one would expect that countries in which physical capital is relatively scarce – again, as in Latin America – would experience positive capital inflows with trade openness and capital account liberalization, precisely because of the initially high returns inherent in a closed economy. This would tend to reduce the returns to capital, which would ultimately improve income distribution, given that capital is usually concentrated among the rich. Under the same argument, if a country that is land-abundant relative to the rest of the world opens up to trade, the returns on this asset will tend to increase. The effect on income distribution will depend on how stocks of land are distributed, so for Latin America this would have been expected to be inequality-increasing.

Why does an apparent contradiction arise between the expected results from economic liberalization processes in Latin America, on the one hand, and the empirical evidence presented in the second section on the other? Is standard trade theory not useful for understanding the current reality in Latin America? Or is it that perhaps Latin America is not what it seems? What if, for instance, the region is not as abundant in unskilled labor as is widely believed? This section develops the argument that the key to the apparent paradox might be the following: the theory is valid, but the perceptions are flawed. What seems to be unfounded are the beliefs that the region has an advantage in producing unskilled labor-intensive goods at low cost, that capital is significantly scarcer than in the rest of the world, and that land is a considerably abundant factor. In fact, this section proposes that Latin America is caught between two worlds. On the one hand, it is not the most unskilled labor-abundant region. On the other, however, schooling progress has been so sluggish in the past few decades that the region has not effected the "big push" observed in other countries (e.g., East Asia) to reach the point at which comparative advantages in semiskilled labor were achieved. In a similar vein, capital is certainly not as abundant as in the most developed economies but, at the same time, it is not as scarce a factor as in the average developing country. Furthermore, with technical progress, land does not appear to be as abundant a factor as is commonly supposed.

The region has arrived at this state because at the time that the region's endowments were changing, the world was also evolving. Large countries such as China and India entered the global markets during the 1980s, causing sizable shifts in the world effective factor endowments. These countries have a large abundance of relatively unskilled labor, scarce capital, and relatively abundant land. In bringing these factor endowments to the world market, they have modified the amount of factors of production that are available on a global scale and, in open competition for world markets, this has had enormous effects over the prices paid for human and physical capital in the international arena.

In order to develop this argument, the calculations and estimations by Spilimbergo, Londoño, and Székely are updated and presented subsequently.[32] These authors obtain world average values for factor

---

[32] Antonio Spilimbergo, Juan Luis Londoño, and Miguel Székely, "Income Distribution, Factor Endowments and Trade Openness," *Journal of Development Economics* 59 (1997): 77–101.

endowments by computing each country's share in world trade and multiplying this share by the factor endowment (human capital, physical capital, and land) to obtain a trade-weighted average.[33] The weights are used because the factor endowments of a country only compete in the world market if the country actually trades. Therefore, endowments of countries totally closed to international trade have no weight in the average, whereas those that do trade are weighted by their importance in international markets.[34]

TRADE AND HUMAN CAPITAL ENDOWMENTS

The story of the evolution of human capital is illustrated in Figure 14.16, which plots the endowment of the most unskilled labor available for production – that is, the share of workers with no schooling among the population over twenty-five years of age.[35] As can be seen, Latin America has a much larger share of working-age population with no schooling than the East Asian economies or the world average but has a considerably lower share than South Asia, the most populous region in the world.

[33] These authors estimate country and world endowments up to 1992. Here we update the figures to 1996. We use the same estimation methods and (updated) data sources as these authors.

[34] There are some other studies addressing the trade–inequality relationship. Francois Bourguignon and C. Morrison, eds., *External Trade and Income Distribution* (Paris, 1989), develop a model in which income distribution depends on factor endowments and the degree of trade openness of each country. By using a cross-country analysis of thirty-six observations in 1970, they conclude that factor endowments can explain 60 percent of the difference in income shares of the bottom decile across countries. Sebastian Edwards, "Openness, Trade Liberalization and Growth in Developing Countries," *Journal of Economic Literature* 31 (1997): 1358–93, uses a larger sample of countries with time-series observations, but does not find any significant effect of trade on income distribution. There is a larger number of studies addressing the trade–wage inequality relationship. For example, see Donald Robbins, "HOS Hits Facts: Facts Win: Evidence on Trade and Wages in the Developing World" (Development Discussion Paper 557, Harvard Institute for International Development, Harvard University, 1996); Adrian Wood, *North-South Trade Employment and Inequality: Changing Fortunes in a Skill-Driven World*, (London, 1994), and "Openness and Wage Inequality in Developing Countries: The Latin American Challenge to East Asian Conventional Wisdom," *The World Bank Economic Review* (1996); George Borjas and Valerie Ramey, "Foreign Competition, Market Power and Wage Inequalities," *The Quarterly Journal of Economics* XC (1995): 1075–1110; Richard Freeman and Lawrence Katz, eds., *Differences and Changes in Wage Structure* (Chicago, 1995). We chose the methodology by Spilimbergo, Londoño, and Székely for two reasons. The first is that they use more adequate trade openness measure and estimation methods, and the second is that rather than focusing on wage inequality, they consider the distribution of total household income.

[35] These figures use the share of adults with no schooling, primary, secondary, and higher education from the updated Barro-Lee database. See Jong Wha Lee and Robert Barro, "International Data on Educational Attainment: Updates and Implications," (Working Paper no. 42, Center for International Development, Harvard University, April 2000) to measure the human capital endowment of each country. East Asia, according to the definition adopted here, comprises the four fastest growing East Asian countries.

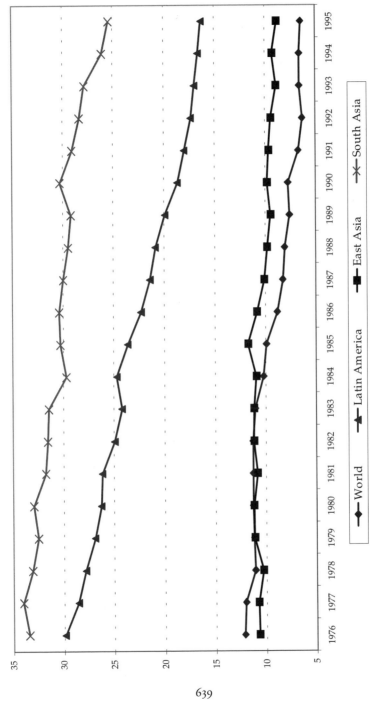

Figure 14.16. Percentage of workers with no schooling among the population over twenty-five years of age by region. *Source:* Authors' own calculations.

Where Latin America stands out is in the abundance of workers with primary schooling. The bulk of the working-age population in Latin America has only achieved some level of primary education. That is not the case in South Asia, where primary schooling still seems to be a "luxury good" for most. It is not the case in East Asia, either, but for the opposite reason that considerable strides have been made in schooling progress. The share of population that has either no schooling or only primary in that region is very low.

On the other hand, Latin America falls far behind East Asia, South Asia, and the world average with respect to the endowment of workers with secondary schooling. Whereas in South Asia, about 33 percent of the working-age population has achieved secondary schooling, only 20 percent have done so in Latin America. Because the factor is scarcer in Latin America, it would be expected that local wages for workers with secondary school would be relatively high; their wages would be relatively low in South Asia because of greater abundance. The contrast with East Asia and the world average is even starker.

Latin America is also not well-endowed with workers with higher education. Although it has caught up with the rest of Asia, its endowments are still well below those in East Asia and the world average. Thus, the returns to these skills in the labor market would be expected to be relatively high in the region and, consequently, the global demand for them relatively low.

Figure 14.17 plots the world's effective endowment of skilled labor from 1965 to 1995.[36] The figure demonstrates that the rate of change of the world endowment declines between 1960 and 1980. This is because of the entry of China and India into world markets. Because these two countries have high numbers of unskilled labor, they drive the world average down. Given this change, Latin America by 1996 seemed to be a region with human capital endowments very similar to the world endowment, with no particular advantage in international markets. At the dawn of the twenty-first century, Latin America neither belongs to the group of countries in which unskilled labor is highly abundant, nor does it belong to the group of countries that have made enough schooling progress so as to have an abundant semiskilled labor work that can compete and be highly rewarded in world markets.

---

[36] Following Spilimbergo, Londoño, and Székely, *effective* endowments are calculated by obtaining the weighted average of country endowments, where the weight is given by the participation of the country in world trade (low weights imply that the country's endowments compete less in world markets). These authors' calculations are extended to include the 1992–6 period.

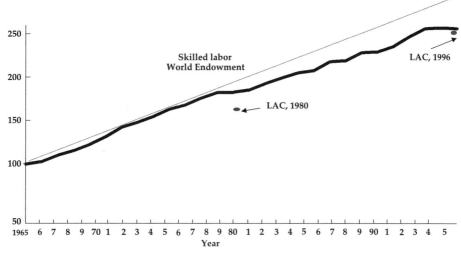

Figure 14.17. Effective world skilled labor endowments.
Sources: Data for 1965–92 are reproduced from Antonio Spilimbergo, Juan Luis Londoño, and Miguel Székely, "Income Distribution, Factor Endowments and Trade Openness," *Journal of Development Economics* 59 (1997): 77–101; 1992–7 data are authors' calculations using the same methodology and updated data sources.

In the 1980s, the endowment of unskilled labor in Latin America was higher than the world average (there was relative scarcity of skilled labor), which suggests that had the region been open to international trade during the previous decades, it would have been able to exploit its comparative advantage in goods produced with relative intensity of unskilled labor. Presumably, this would have reduced the wage gap between the skilled and unskilled in the region, and could have resulted in inequality and poverty reductions. As shown in the second section, the evidence indicates that the opposite happened in reality because the 1980s were years of significant increases in inequality. Thus, it seems that the region had the right endowments but the wrong policies at that time. Paradoxically, it is the opposite: the region had the right policies in terms of benefiting from comparative advantage, but it had the "wrong" human capital endowments.

TRADE AND ENDOWMENTS OF PHYSICAL CAPITAL AND LAND

A similar story applies to the case of physical capital, represented here by the endowment of capital per worker in each country. Figure 14.18

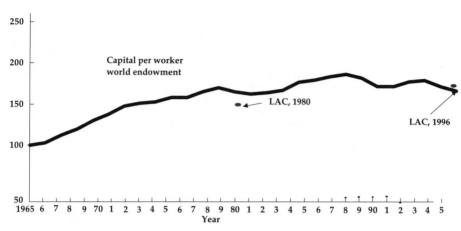

Figure 14.18. Effective world capital endowments.
Sources: Data for 1965–92 are reproduced from Antonio Spilimbergo, Juan Luis Londoño, and Miguel Székely, "Income Distribution, Factor Endowments and Trade Openness"; 1992–7 data are authors' calculations using the same methodology and updated data sources.

shows that the world's effective endowment of this factor increased steadily from 1965 to 1980, and remained fairly stable thereafter with the entry of additional (capital-scarce) countries into the arena of international trade. Latin America had an effective endowment that was below the world average around the 1980s (indicating that the factor was relatively scarce in the region, and earning high returns), but by the second half of the 1990s, the region's endowment was almost identical to the average world endowment.

As with human capital, the proposed explanation for persistently high levels of inequality in Latin America is that it had the right endowment at the wrong time. Had the region been more open to trade during the 1980s, presumably capital flows would have been attracted by the region's high returns, eventually reducing the "excess" returns to capital that are typical of semiclosed economies. The window of opportunity to reap the distributional benefits was missed because by the time the region opened to trade in the 1990s, its endowment of physical capital no longer provided the same advantages.

CONCLUSION

This chapter has summarized evidence on the persistence of poverty and inequality in Latin America during the second half of the twentieth century.

This feature of the region seems to have been present for a long time, perhaps for all of the modern history of the countries in the region.

Here we have argued that there are three long-run underlying reasons for the high levels of poverty and inequality: the accumulation of income-earning assets (namely, human capital, physical capital, and land) has been slow and highly unequal in relation to the population of each country; the individuals with the lowest stocks end up using them at a lower rate because the economic environment has provided fewer opportunities for them, as compared to those with more assets; and the price that is paid in the market for putting assets to work depends, among other factors, on the size of the stock one can offer. In sum, the individuals with greater stocks of income-earning assets have been able to obtain higher incomes not only because they have more assets, but because by having more assets, they have had more chances to use them productively, and they have received a higher return for each unit of asset owned.

In turn, this unfortunate combination is attributable to a mix of two critical factors. The first is policy. Latin America followed an import sub-stitution industrialization strategy for at least three decades (1950s–70s), during which the most abundant factor in the region (unskilled labor) received relatively low returns precisely because of its relative abundance in a closed economy. In contrast, physical capital, which was relatively scarce, reaped the benefits by receiving high returns because of its scarcity. During these years, the factor endowments of the region could have resulted in improvements in income distribution and poverty reduction had the region opened up more to international markets because the returns to unskilled labor in the international environment of the 1960s–70s would have presumably increased with trade given that this factor of production was relatively scarce internationally. Physical capital, which is concentrated among the rich, would have seen its rates of return reduced in this setting, with additional progressive effects on income distribution.

The second factor is that the world changed in significant ways during the 1980s. On the one hand, the Latin American countries started opening up to international trade, but at the same time, other countries did the same and this changed the world supply of factors. With the entry of countries such as China and India – which together are five times the size of Latin America – into the international arena, Latin America lost attractiveness as a region with abundance of the lowest skills and scarcity of physical capital because these newcomers to the world scene have considerably larger comparative advantages in these areas. At the same time, countries in East Asia exploited their considerable strides in schooling progress, with which they could reap the benefits of belonging to the few countries with relative abundance of semiskilled labor. The result is that in most Latin American countries today, relative prices of labor and capital are working against the majority of the population: low wages for the relatively unskilled and high returns to physical capital because of relatively small flows of this factor to the region.

What about the future? For some time now, the Latin American region has been "investing" in its young because approximately 40 percent of its population was of school age, a group that is normally supported by other household members who are of working age. However, during the first decades of this century, the share of individuals aged nineteen years or more will increase, and so total dependency rates will fall. The population weight of the elderly (defined as individuals sixty-five and older) – who are not economically active – is also increasing, so eventually the share of "dependents" in the population will grow again.

Because of the evolution of the total dependency rate in the region, Latin America is entering a "window of opportunity" during which the share of the working-age population will be growing relative to the share of dependents, whether young or old. This "window" represents an opportunity because when a higher proportion of household members are of working age, more investment per child and greater savings for retirement can be made. However, this window will begin to close as the population ages. The total dependency rate will rise again to its current level by approximately 2040. The region's "window of opportunity" (defined as the years of low dependency) will last on average for the next forty years.[37] However, the share of the elderly is already increasing very rapidly in several countries relative to the working-age population, and this will require a faster accumulation of private or public resources in the near future to provide for retirement and medical expenditures. Pressure on pension systems, social security programs, and families who support elderly members will be felt strongly within the next fifteen years in Cuba, Uruguay, and Brazil; and within the next twenty years in Chile, Colombia, Argentina, and Costa Rica.

---

[37] Calculations from the population data and projections in UNESCO Statistical Yearbook (1997). Our dependency ratios give different weights to the elderly (aged 65 or more) and to children (aged 0–19) because it is relatively more expensive to finance the cost of supporting the elderly (i.e., because of high medical costs) than the investment needed to support a child. To calculate the relative weights, we compared public expenditures per capita in education and public expenditures per capita in social security for the elderly, obtained from Inter-American Development Bank (1996). The result was that one elderly person absorbs, on average, four times more public resources than a child.

The "window of opportunity" is relevant for education because it provides an excellent chance for improving the quality of schooling. As the population share of school-age children begins to decline, simply maintaining the same tax contribution per worker and the level of overall educational spending represents more resources per student. If more resources per child can be translated into better schooling quality, there is an opportunity for closing the education gap in the region. Similarly, if greater shares of the population enter into working age and start saving, capital stocks may rise and, with it, the returns to capital may decline. These are only two of the channels by which the demographic window of opportunity may materialize into improvements in the standard of living for the Latin American population through changes in the factor endowments of the region. However, the key to the future is to combine the recovery of the "right" factor endowments with the right policies.

BIBLIOGRAPHICAL ESSAYS

CHAPTER 1 (LUIS BÉRTOLA AND JEFFREY G. WILLIAMSON)

If not a new concept, globalization is a relatively new word. In a narrow sense, not much was written about globalization in Latin America prior to 1940. Since then, the historical literature on globalization has boomed. Furthermore, Latin American economic history, and work on the Latin American globalization experience in particular, have undergone two major shifts, both in the last two decades. The first shift has been manifested by a diminished role played by Latin American scholars in the production of comparative and general economic histories, and an augmented role by Anglophone scholars and editors directing big projects. The second shift entailed a move away from dependency and developmental or structuralist approaches toward mainstream economic theory (the new economic history), the new institutional economics, and the new political economy. In some cases, this new trend implied a revisionist attempt to show the achievements of export-led growth. In others, the work looked to domestic factors in order to explain why the benefits of globalization were not adequately exploited. Still others incorporated the contributions made by dependency and structuralist thinking and the new approaches in assessing the evolution of the domestic economy.

The First Shift

The publication of *The Cambridge History of Latin America* in the mid-1980s initiated a change in the way general works covering the whole Latin American region have been written. Before that date, the most outstanding works were usually written by Latin American scholars, typically in Spanish or Portuguese, and often by social scientists and not historians. Since the mid-1980s, the main general works on Latin America have been written in English. Leslie Bethell, ed., *The Cambridge History of Latin America*, vol. 6, *Latin America Since 1930: Economy,*

Society and Politics (Cambridge, 1994), contains two key chapters written by Rosemary Thorp and Victor Bulmer-Thomas. These authors are responsible for two of the most important comprehensive works that have been published since then. Bulmer-Thomas, *The Economic History of Latin America Since Independence*, 2nd ed. (Cambridge, 2003) is analytically strong and penetrating, and exploits a dualistic model to assess the performance of different Latin American countries in the export-led era. Rosemary Thorp, *Progress, Poverty and Exclusion: An Economic History of Latin America in the 20th Century* (Inter-American Development Bank, 1998) is the result of a research project financed by the Inter-American Development Bank, in which more than thirty outstanding scholars were involved. The contributions of these scholars were collected in three satellite volumes. Of special interest for this bibliographic essay is Enrique Cárdenas, José Antonio Ocampo, and Rosemary Thorp, eds., *The Export Age: The Latin American Economies in the Nineteenth and Early Twentieth Centuries* (Basingstoke, 2001). The book contains eight chapters with national studies and one on Central America. The introductory chapter written by the three editors is an attempt to draw general features from national and regional studies. Although the book is descriptive, the text makes stimulating use of new institutional and political economy approaches to tackle the different ways in which factor markets were built and the role of the state in this process.

In short, it seems that Latin American scholars are not, by themselves, producing as many comprehensive works on Latin American economic history (and history in general). This kind of comparative analysis requires the leadership of editors who can coordinate many authors; comprehensive works written by individual English scholars were based directly (Thorp) or indirectly (Bulmer-Thomas) on the initiative of editors promoting collective works. The present volume seems to confirm this trend.

The Second Shift

DATA ON GDP, REAL WAGES, PRICES, AND LIVING STANDARDS

The ebb in dependency approaches has been associated with the application of more economic theory and with an enormous increase in available data. Latin America may still lag behind in terms of the availability of reliable historical statistics, but very impressive improvements have taken place, especially in the 1990s.

New GDP estimates and related national income statistics have been the point of departure of a new generation of research in economic history that has served to offer a reinterpretation of Latin American performance during the first globalization boom. Some of the new series are as follows. **Argentina**: Roberto Cortés Conde and Marcela Harriague, "Estimaciones del producto bruto interno de Argentina 1875–1935" (Documento de Trabajo, Departamento de Economía, Universidad de San Andrés, 1994). **Brazil**: Claudio Contador and Claudio Haddad, "Produto real, moeda e preços: a experiência brasileira no período 1861–1970," *Revista brasileira de estatística* 36 (1975); Claudio Haddad, *O crescimento do produto real no*

Brasil, 1900–1947 (Río de Janeiro, 1979); Raymond Goldsmith, *Brasil 1850–1984: desenvolvimento financieiro sob um século de inflaçao* (São Paulo, 1986); Instituto Brasileiro de Geografia e Estatística, *Estadísticas históricas do Brasil: series econômicas, demográficas e socias de 1550–1988* (Rio de Janeiro, 1990). **Chile:** José Díaz, Rolf Lüders, and Gert Wagner, "Economía chilena 1810–1995: evolución cuantitativa del producto total y sectorial" (Documento de Trabajo 186, Pontífica Universidad Católica, 1998); José Jofre, Rolf Lüders, and Gert Wagner, "Economía chilena 1810–1995. Cuentas fiscales" (Documento de Trabajo 188, Pontífica Universidad Católica, 1998); Juan Braun et al., "Economía chilena 1810–1995. Estadísticas históricas" (Documento de Trabajo 187, Pontífica Universidad Católica, 1998). **Mexico:** John Coastworth, "Obstacles to Economic Growth in Nineteenth Century Mexico," *American Historical Review* (February 1978); Instituto Nacional de Estadística, Geografía e Informática, *Estadísticas Históricas de México I* (México City, 1986); Sandra Kuntz-Ficker, "Nuevas series del comercio exterior de México," *Revista de Historia Económica* (Primavera-Verano 2001). **Uruguay:** Luis Bértola et al., *El PBI de Uruguay 1870–1936 y otras estimaciones* (Montevideo, 1999); Magdalena Bertino and Héctor Tajam, *El PBI de Uruguay 1900–1955* (Montevideo, 1999). **Venezuela:** Asdrúbal Baptista, *Bases cuantitativas de la economía Venezolana 1830–1995* (Caracas, 1997).

Surveys for the whole of Latin America may be found in Naciones Unidas, Comisión Económica para América Latina (CEPAL), *Series históricas del crecimiento de América Latina* (Santiago de Chile, 1978); Angus Maddison, *The World Economy: A Millennial Perspective* (París, 2001); Pablo Astorga, Ame R. Bergés, and Valpy FitzGerald, "The Standard of Living in Latin America During the Twentieth Century" (Queen Elizabeth House Working Paper Series 103, March 2003); and André Hofman, *The Economic Development of Latin America in the Twentieth Century* (Cheltenham, 2000).

Relative factor and commodity prices have been systematically collected and studied by Jeffrey Williamson. His first attempt, with only limited treatment of Latin America, was "The Evolution of Global Labor Markets Since 1830: Background Evidence and Hypothesis," *Explorations in Economic History* 3 (1995). In a trilogy bearing the common name "Real Wages and Relative Factor Prices in the Third World 1820–1940," Williamson expanded the database on wages, land prices, and terms of trade to Asia, the Mediterranean basin, and Latin America (Harvard Institute of Economic Research Discussion Papers nos. 1842, 1844, and 1853, all produced in 1998). An upgraded version of the Latin America paper was published with the title "Real Wages, Inequality and Globalization in Latin America before 1940," *Revista de Historia Económica*, Número Especial (1999). For national or regional studies on the topic, see Eulalia María Lahmeyer Lobo, "Condiciones de vida de los artesanos y de la clase obrera en Rio de Janeiro en la decada de 1880 hasta 1920," *HISLA, Revista Latinoamericana de Historia Económica y Social* 5 (1985); C. W. Brading, "Un análisis comparativo del costo de la vida en diversas capitales de hispanoamérica," *Boletín Histórico de la Fundación John Boulton* 20 (1969); Miguel Urrutia and Mario Arrubla, *Compendio de estadísticas históricas de Colombia* (Bogotá, 1970); Oscar Zanetti and Alejandro García, *United Fruit Company: un caso de dominio imperialista en Cuba* (Habana, 1976); Aurora Gómez Galvarriato,

"The Evolution of Prices and Real Wages in Mexico from the Porfiriato to the Revolution," in John Coatsworth and Alan Taylor, eds., *Latin America and the World Economy Since 1800* (Cambridge, MA, 1998); Instituto Nacional de Estadística, Geografía e Informática, *Estadísticas Históricas de México I* (México City, 1986); Luis Bértola et al., "Southern Cone Real Wages Compared: A Purchasing Power Parity Approach to Convergence and Divergence Trends, 1870–1996," in XXVII Encontro Nacional de Economia, *Anais III* (Belem do Pará, 1999); and Luis Bértola, María Camou, and Gabriel Porcile, "Comparación Internacional del Poder Adquisitivo de los Salarios Reales de los Países del Cono Sur, 1870–1945," Asociación Uruguaya de Historia Económica, *Segundas Jornadas de Historia Económica* (Montevideo, 1999).

Terms of trade estimates have been collected in CEPAL, *Los términos de intercambio de américa latina* (Santiago de Chile, 1978). Recently, Yael Hadass and Jeffrey Williamson provided a compilation and discussion of terms of trade performance, including some new series for Latin America, in "Terms-of-Trade Shocks and Economic Performance, 1870–1940: Prebisch and Singer Revisited," *Economic Development and Cultural Change* 51 (2003). Country studies are found in R. Gonçalvez and A. Coelho Barros, "Tendências dos termos da troca: a tese de Prebisch e a economia brasileira: 1850–1979," *Pesquisa e Planejamento Econômico* 12 (1982); and Belén Baptista and Luis Bértola, "Uruguay 1870–1913: indicadores de comercio exterior" (Asociación Uruguaya de Historia Económica, *Segundas Jornadas de Historia Económica*, Montevideo, 1999). See also the terms of trade citations by Leandro Prados in this volume.

NEW APPROACHES

As quantitative evidence accumulated, an increasing number of studies have tackled the periodization of export-led growth, evaluated its achievements and shortcomings, and enhanced the comparative perspective. The dominant feature of this new work is its critique of the dependency approach, the increasing role given to domestic forces and circumstances, the progressive expansion of the new economic history dominated by mainstream neoclassical thinking, and more recently by neo-institutional approaches. In some works, neostructuralist, post-Keynesian, and neo-Schumpeterian approaches have also emerged, prompted by the revival of the Economic Commission of Latin American and the Caribbean (ECLAC) as an active center for studies on Latin American development. Nevertheless, the old *Annales*-like style of historical analysis still constitutes the paradigm for several valuable contributions, offering a considerable amount of empirical research loosely related to any theoretical reference, with the risks this always implies.

Most of these new data have produced new interpretations of economic performance in relation to globalization. Export-led performance is studied in Roberto Cortés Conde and Jane Hunt, eds., *The Latin American Economies: Growth and the Export Sector 1880–1930* (New York, 1985), and Sergio Silva and Tamás Szmrecsányi, eds., *Historia econômica da primeira república*, part 1 (São Paulo, 1996). Roberto Cortés Conde, "El crecimiento de las economías latinoamericanas, 1880–1930," *Historia Mexicana* XLII:3 (1993), makes a neoclassical defense of the achievements of export-led growth. Alan Taylor, "Tres fases del crecimiento económico argentino," *Revista de Historia Económica* 3 (1994), dates the Argentine decline in the 1910s, prior to the protectionist policies of the 1930s. Other discussions of Argentine performance are found in Antonio Santamaría and Marcela García, "El crecimiento económico argentino en perspectiva histórica," *Revista de Historia Económica* 3 (1994); Roberto Cortés Conde, *La economía argentina en el largo plazo: Ensayos de historia económica de los siglos XIX y XX* (Buenos Aires, 1997); and Mario Rapoport, Andres Mussachio, and Eduardo Madrid, *Historia económica, política y social de la Argentina (1880–2000)* (Buenos Aires, 2001). Stephen Haber, "Introduction: Economic Growth and Latin American Economic Historiography" in Stephen Haber, ed., *How Latin America Fell Behind. Essays on the Economic Histories of Brazil and Mexico 1800–1914* (Stanford, 1997), offers a frontal attack on the dependency approach and moves toward neo-institutional thinking in order to answer the question in the title of the book. Other relevant contributions in this volume are: Nathaniel Leff, "Economic Development in Brazil, 1822–1913"; Enrique Cárdenas, "A Macroeconomic Interpetation of Nineteenth-Century Mexico"; and Stanley Engerman and Kenneth Sokoloff, "Factor Endowments, Institutions, and Different Paths of Growth Among New World Economies: A View from Economic Historians of the United States." This latter contribution stresses the role of original factor endowments in shaping institutions that help account for different growth patterns. Other important contributions are José Antonio Ocampo, *Colombia y la economía mundial 1830–1900* (Bogotá, 1984); Patricio Meller, "Una perspectiva de largo plazo del desarrollo económico chileno, 1880–1990" in Magnus Blomström and Patricio Meller, eds., *Trayectorias divergentes: comparación de un siglo de desarrollo latinoamericano y escandinavo* (Santiago, 1990); Luis Bértola and Gabriel Porcile, "Argentina, Brasil, Uruguay y la economía mundial: una aproximación a diferentes regímenes de convergencia y divergencia," in Luis Bértola, *Ensayos de Historia Económica: Uruguay y la Región en la Economía Mundial 1870–1990* (Montevideo, 2000); also by the same authors, see "Argentina, Brazil, Uruguay and the World Economy: An Approach to Different Convergence and Divergence Regimes" (Documento de Trabajo, Unidad Multidisciplinaria-FCS, 42, Montevideo, 1998). This latter work stresses the existence of different historical patterns for the relation between globalization and convergence, depending on specialization patterns and technology in relation to world demand. Jeffrey L. Bortz and Stephen Haber, eds., *The Mexican Economy, 1870–1930: Essays on the Economic History of Institutions* (Stanford, 2002) tackles the relation between economic growth under autocratic forms, including banking, finance, trade, and labor relations.

GLOBALIZATION AND INCOME DISTRIBUTION

Income distribution was a central topic in the structuralist and dependency approaches, in terms of both the international and the domestic economies: the outflow of resources and the concentration of property and income were considered to be permanent features of the export-led model, having a strong negative impact on development.

Interest in this topic receded in the 1980s and 1990s. Perhaps because of the intense political debate over who gains from recent globalization experience, there has been a revival of historical interest in income distribution in the last few years, both theoretically and empirically. The joint book by Phillip Aghion and Jeffrey Williamson, *Growth, Inequality and Globalization* (Cambridge, 1998) is a good example of that revival. Income distribution during the first globalization boom has been a recurrent topic in Jeffrey Williamson's recent works, which increasingly have included Latin America. For example, see "Growth, Distribution and Demography: Some Lessons from History," *Explorations in Economic History* 35 (1998); "Real Wages, Inequality, and Globalization in Latin America before 1940," *Revista de Historia Economica*, 17: Número Especial (1999); "Land, Labor, and Globalization in the Third World, 1870–1940," *Journal of Economic History* 62 (March, 2002); and with Peter Lindert, "Does Globalization Make the World More Unequal?" in *Globalization in Historical Perspective*. Williamson's main conclusions are that globalization implied price movements that worsened income distribution in the resource-abundant parts of the periphery, thus strengthening the political backlash against globalization there. Finally, the existence of the Kuznets curve is discussed in Jeffrey G. Williamson, *Inequality, Poverty, and History: The Kuznets Memorial Lecture* (Oxford, 1991), and in Luis Bértola, "Income Distribution and the Kuznets Curve: Argentina and Uruguay since the 1870s" (Documento de Trabajo #52, Unidad Multidisciplinaria-FCS, Montevideo, 2002).

The connections among globalization, school enrollment, economic growth, political participation, and income distribution have also been at the center of comparative studies, such as that of Elisa Mariscal and Kenneth Sokoloff, "Schooling, Suffrage, and the Persistency of Inequality in the Americas, 1800–1945," in Stephen Haber, ed., *Political Institutions and Economic Growth in Latin America* (Stanford, 2000). Luis Bértola and Reto Bertoni, "Educación y aprendizaje en escenarios de convergencia y divergencia" (Documento de Trabajo #46, Unidad Multidisciplinaria-FCS, Montevideo, 1998), tackles school enrollment both as a proxy for income distribution and for domestic efforts to develop social capabilities in Argentina, Brazil, and Uruguay compared with the core countries.

Globalization and Economic Instability

Latin American economic instability has always attracted scholarly attention. The structuralist and dependency approaches stressed the existence of an asymmetric relation between cycles in the core and the periphery – for example, see Osvaldo Sunkel and Pedro Paz, *El subdesarrollo latinoamericano y la teoría del desarrollo* (Mexico City, 1982) – similar to the way in which previous scholars had found those cycles to be inversely related on both sides of the Atlantic economy – for example, see Brinley Thomas, *Migration and Urban Development: A Reappraisal of British and American Long Cycles* (London, 1972).

On the basis of the new data produced mainly in the 1990s and by applying new econometric techniques, a new generation of studies on instability has appeared. In all cases, the existence of long Kuznets-like swings is confirmed and it is argued that the impact of this instability on aggregate long-run performance has been important. Some contributions are Claudio Contador, *Ciclos econômicos e indicadores de atividade no Brasil* (Rio de Janeiro, 1977); Francisco Cribari-Neto, "The Cyclical Component in Brazilian GDP," *Revista de Econometría* 1 (1993); C. K. Harley, "Transportation, the World Wheat Trade, and the Kuznets Cycle, 1850–1913," *Explorations in Economic History* 17 (1980); Luis Catão, "The Transmission of Long Cycles between 'Core' and 'Periphery' Economies. A Case Study of Brazil and Mexico, 1870–1940" (Ph.D. dissertation, Darwin College, Cambridge University, 1991); Luis Bértola, "Fases, tendencias y ciclos en las economías de Argentina, Brasil y Uruguay (1870–1990)," *Ciclos* 10 (1996); and Luis Bértola and Fernando Lorenzo, "Componentes tendenciales y cíclicos en el PBI per capita de Argentina, Brasil, Uruguay 1870–1988," in Luis Bértola, ed., *Ensayos de Historia Económica: Uruguay y la Región en la Economía Mundial 1870–1990* (Montevideo, 2000). Daniel Lederman concentrates on political cycles in Chile in *The Political Economy of Protection: Theory and Chilean Experience* (Stanford, CA, 2005).

Globalization, Industrial Performance, and Policy

Industrial growth prior to 1930 was a neglected issue in Latin American historiography thirty years ago. Most of the work written in the 1950s, 1960s, and early 1970s concentrated on mining and the agrarian sector during the first globalization boom, whereas industrial growth was thought to be a product of the 1930s, the result of new industrial policy and protectionism, reinforced by weakened competition from the industrial countries. Thus, industrialization has been connected with antiglobal delinking.

Criticisms of dependency theory and more empirical research both generated a new interest in what has come to be called "early industry." A good review of the achievements of this early revisionist wave may be found in Colin Lewis, "Industry in Latin America before 1930" in Leslie Bethell, ed., *The Cambridge History of Latin America, Vol. 4, c 1870 to 1930* (Cambridge, 1986). This debate continued into the 1990s, although the questions were framed more sharply: Under what conditions did domestic industrial growth take place? What role did protectionist policies play? How did movements in the exchange rate affect industrial protection? What role did industrial elites and industrial entrepreneurs play? These questions are addressed in the chapters in this work by Aurora Gomez, Richard Salvucci, and Stephen Haber.

CHAPTER 2 (ALAN M. TAYLOR)

The chapter takes as given certain aspects of macroeconomic history in the region and the wider world. For a survey of economic performance in Latin America over the long run, see John H. Coatsworth, "Economic and Institutional Trajectories in Pre-Modern Latin America," in John H. Coatsworth and Alan M. Taylor, eds., *Latin America and the World Economy Since 1800* (Cambridge, MA, 1999), and "Cycles of Globalization, Economic Growth, and Human Welfare in Latin America," in Otto T. Solbrig, Robert L. Paarlberg, and Francesco Di Castri, eds., *Globalization and the Rural Environment* (Cambridge, MA, 2001); Victor Bulmer-Thomas, *The Economic History of Latin America Since Independence*, 2nd ed. (Cambridge, 2003). On the global economy in the long run, see Angus Maddison, *Monitoring the World Economy* (Paris, 1995), and *The World Economy: A Millennial Perspective* (Paris, 2001). On the origins of modern financial markets, see Larry Neal, *The Rise of Financial Capitalism: International Capital Markets in the Age of Reason* (Cambridge, 1990).

By the same token, space requires that we gloss over the details on the general evolution of global capital markets. For a survey of major players in the pre-1914 era, see Lance E. Davis and Robert E. Gallman, *Evolving Financial Markets and International Capital Flows: Britain, The Americas, and Australia, 1865–1914* (Cambridge, 2001). An historical overview of the entire period since 1870 is given by Barry J. Eichengreen, *Globalizing Capital: A History of the International Monetary System* (Princeton, NJ, 1996). Comparisons on past and present also inform Albert Fishlow, "Lessons from the Past: Capital Markets During the 19th Century and the Interwar Periods," *International Organization* 39 (1985): 383–416. The Great Depression is singled out as a turning point by Maurice Obstfeld and Alan M. Taylor, "The Great Depression as a Watershed: International Capital Mobility in the Long Run," in Michael D. Bordo, Claudia D. Goldin, and Eugene N. White, eds., *The Defining Moment: The Great Depression and the American Economy in the Twentieth Century* (Chicago, 1998), and "Globalization and Capital Markets," in Michael D. Bordo, Alan M. Taylor, and Jeffrey G. Williamson, eds., *Globalization in Historical Perspective* (Chicago, 2003). A complete historical account appears in Obsteld and Taylor, *Global Capital Markets: Integration, Crisis, and Growth* (Cambridge, 2004). In the postwar period, the liberalization of capital markets has been very slow and uneven. See Dennis P. Quinn, "The Correlates of Change in International Financial Regulation," *American Political Science Review* 91 (1997): 531–51. On the state of global capital markets today, see International Monetary Fund, *International Capital Markets: Developments, Prospects, and Key Policy Issues* (Washington, DC, 1997), and IMF, *World Economic Outlook* (Washington, DC, October 2001).

Much has been written recently on the long-run integration of the world economy more generally. For example, see Michael D. Bordo, Barry Eichengreen, and Douglas A. Irwin, "Is Globalization Today Really Different Than Globalization a Hundred Years Ago?" *Brookings Trade Forum* (Washington, DC, 1999); Kevin H. O'Rourke and Jeffrey G. Williamson, *Globalization and History: The Evolution of a Nineteenth-Century Atlantic Economy* (Cambridge, MA, 1999); Alan M. Taylor and Jeffrey G. Williamson, "Convergence in the Age of Mass Migration," *European Review of Economic History* 1, 1 (1997): 27–63; and the various chapters in *Globalization in Historical Perspective* (cited previously).

On the impact of British capital in Latin America in the nineteenth and early twentieth centuries, the standard reference is J. Fred Rippy, *British Investments in Latin America, 1822–1949: A Case Study in the Operations of Private Enterprise in Retarded Regions* (Minneapolis, MN, 1959). On government debt and crises, see Carlos Marichal, *A Century of Debt Crises in Latin America: From Independence to the Great Depression, 1820–1930* (Princeton, NJ, 1989).

Data on nineteenth-century British capital exports can be found in Charles H. Feinstein, "Sources and Methods of Estimation for Domestic Reproducible Fixed Assets and Works in Progress, Overseas Assets, and Land," in Charles H. Feinstein and Sidney Pollard, eds., *Studies in Capital Formation in the United Kingdom: 1750–1920* (Oxford, 1988); D.C. M. Platt, *Britain's Investment Overseas on the Eve of the First World War: The Use and Abuse of Numbers* (New York, 1986); Irving Stone, "British Direct and Portfolio Investment in Latin America Before 1914," *Journal of Economic History* 37 (1977): 690–722; and *The Global Export of Capital from Great Britain, 1865–1914: A Statistical Survey* (New York, 1999). On European capital exports as a whole, see Herbert Feis, *Europe, The World's Banker, 1870–1914: An Account of European Foreign Investment and the Connection of World Finance with Diplomacy Before the War* (New Haven, CT, 1931). On U.S. capital exports in the twentieth century, see Barbara Stallings, *Banker to the Third World: U.S. Portfolio Investment in Latin America, 1900–1986* (Berkeley, CA, 1987). For a long-run look at foreign investment stocks and especially foreign direct investment, see also Michael J. Twomey, "Patterns of Foreign Investment in Latin America in the Twentieth Century," in *Latin America and the World Economy Since 1800* (cited previously), and *A Century of Foreign Investment in the Third World* (London, 2000); and William Woodruff, *Impact of Western Man: A Study of Europe's Role in the World Economy 1750–1960* (New York, 1967).

Quantitative historians are now beginning to model foreign investment patterns, seeking to identify the determinants of British capital export, its quantities, and prices. See Michael D. Bordo and Hugh Rockoff, "The Gold Standard as a 'Good Housekeeping Seal of Approval,' " *Journal of Economic History* 56, 2 (1996): 389–428; Michael Clemens and Jeffrey G. Williamson, "Wealth Bias in the First Global Capital Market Boom, 1870–1913," *Economic Journal* 114 (2004): 304–37; Michael Edelstein, *Overseas Investment in the Age of High Imperialism* (New York, 1982); Niall Ferguson, "Globalization with Gunboats: The Costs and Benefits: The British Empire Revisited" (Oxford, April 2002, photocopy); and Maurice Obstfeld and Alan M. Taylor, "Sovereign Risk, Credibility, and the Gold Standard: 1870–1913 versus 1925–31," *Economic Journal* 113 (2003): 1–35.

The problems of sovereign debt, default, and reputation constitute a major theme in the literature. See Peter H. Lindert and Peter J. Morton, "How Sovereign Debt Has Worked," in Jeffrey D. Sachs, ed., *Developing Country Debt and the World Economy* (Chicago, 1989), and Michael Tomz, "How Do Reputations Form? New and Seasoned Borrowers in International Capital Markets" (paper presented at the 2001 Annual Meeting of the American Political Association, San Francisco); and *Sovereign Debt and International Cooperation* (forthcoming). On the debt crisis of the 1820s, see Frank G. Dawson, *The First Latin American Debt Crisis: The City of London and the 1822–25 Loan Bubble* (New Haven, CT, 1990).

On Brazil's crises, see Eliana A. Cardoso and Rudiger Dornbusch, "Brazilian Debt Crises: Past and Present," in Barry J. Eichengreen and Peter H. Lindert, eds., *The International Debt Crisis in Historical Perspective* (Cambridge, MA, 1989); Gail D. Triner, "International Capital and the Brazilian Encilhamento, 1889–1892: An Early Example of Contagion among Emerging Capital Markets?" (paper presented at the Economic History Association Conference, Philadelphia, PA, October 2001). On Argentina's crises, see W. H. Bishop, "The Argentine Crisis," *Economic Journal*

1 (1891): 533–8; Roberto Cortés Conde, *Dinero, deuda y crisis: evolución fiscal y monetaria en la Argentina, 1862–1890* (Buenos Aires, 1989); Gerardo della Paolera and Alan M. Taylor, *Straining at the Anchor: The Argentine Currency Board and the Search for Macroeconomic Stability, 1880–1935*, NBER Series on Long-Term Factors in Economic Growth (Chicago, 2001), and "Gaucho Banking Redux," *Economía* 3 (2003): 1–42; Barry J. Eichengreen, "The Baring Crisis in a Mexican Mirror" (University of California, Berkeley, February 1997); and John H. Williams, *Argentine International Trade Under Inconvertible Paper Currency, 1880–1900* (Cambridge, MA, 1920).

The interwar crisis has been studied exhaustively, including its implications for global capital markets. On the role of the gold standard, see Barry J. Eichengreen, *Golden Fetters: The Gold Standard and The Great Depression 1919–1939* (Oxford, 1992), and Barry J. Eichengreen and Jeffrey D. Sachs, "Exchange Rates and Economic Recovery in the 1930s," *Journal of Economic History* 45, 4 (1985): 925–46. For a regional perspective, see José Manuel Campa, "Exchange Rates and Economic Recovery in the 1930s: An Extension to Latin America," *Journal of Economic History* 50, 3 (1990): 677–82. Debt and default are treated in Barry J. Eichengreen and Richard Portes, "After the Deluge: Default, Negotiation, and Readjustment during the Interwar Years," in *The International Debt Crisis in Historical Perspective* (cited previously). A seminal account of the depression on the periphery remains that of Charles P. Kindleberger, *The World in Depression, 1929–1939* (Berkeley, CA, republished 1986), as well as "Commercial Policy Between the Wars," in Peter Mathias and Sidney Pollard, eds., *The Cambridge Economic History of Europe* (Cambridge, 1989).

On debt crises as a whole, see Carlos F. Díaz Alejandro, "Stories of the 1930s for the 1980s," in Pedro Aspe Armella, Rudiger Dornbusch, and Maurice Obstfeld, eds., *Financial Policies and the World Capital Market: The Problem of Latin American Countries* (Chicago, 1983), and "Good-Bye Financial Repression, Hello Financial Crash," *Journal of Development Economics* 19 (1985): 1–24; Albert Fishlow, "Conditionality and Willingness to Pay: Some Parallels from the 1890s," and Erika Jorgensen and Jeffrey Sachs, "Default and Renegotiation of Latin American Foreign Bonds in the Interwar Period," both in *The International Debt Crisis in Historical Perspective* (cited previously); and Jeffrey D. Sachs, ed., *Developing Country Debt and the World Economy* (Chicago, 1989). For a discussion of crises and their costs, see Michael D. Bordo et al., "Is the Crisis Problem Growing More Severe?" *Economic Policy* 32 (2001): 51–82.

The problems of the interwar period for capital markets have been well explored by scholars. On the export of capital from Britain between the wars and the restrictions thereon, see John Michael Atkin, *British Overseas Investment, 1918–1931* (New York, 1977). On the appearance of exchange control in interwar Latin America, see Herbert M. Bratter, "Foreign Exchange Control in Latin America," *Foreign Policy Reports* 14, 23 (1939): 274–88. On the political and ideological reaction against free markets starting in the 1930s, see Deepak Lal, *The Poverty of Development Economics* (Cambridge, MA, 1985); Ragnar Nurkse, "International Investment Today in the Light of Nineteenth-Century Experience," *Economic Journal* 64 (1954): 744–58; and Karl Polanyi, *The Great Transformation* (New York, 1944).

On the problems of categorizing postwar exchange rate regimes, see Eduardo Levy Yeyati and Federico Sturzenegger, "Classifying Exchange Rate Regimes: Deeds vs. Words," *European Economic Review* 49 (2005): 1603–35, and Carmen M. Reinhart and Kenneth S. Rogoff, "The Modern History of Exchange Rate Arrangements: A Reinterpretation," *Quarterly Journal of Economics* 119 (2004): 1–48.

The sources of growth in Latin America and the contribution of capital accumulation have been studied in a growth accounting framework by Victor J. Elias, *Sources of Growth: A Study of Seven Latin American Economies* (San Francisco, 1992), and André A. Hofman, *The Economic Development of Latin America in the Twentieth Century* (Northampton, MA, 2000). Investment has also been found to be a robust determinant of growth in regression analyses. See, for example, Ross Levine and David Renelt, "A Sensitivity Analysis of Cross-Country Growth Regressions," *American Economic Review* 82 (1992): 942–63; and Francisco Rodríguez and Dani Rodrik, "Trade Policy and Economic Growth: A Skeptic's Guide to Cross-National Evidence," in Ben S. Bernanke and Kenneth Rogoff, eds., *NBER Macroeconomics Annual 2001* (2000). The question as to why more capital does not flow to poor countries, if technology is transferable, was posed by Robert E. Lucas, Jr., "Why Doesn't Capital Flow from Rich to Poor Countries?" *American Economic Review* 80, 2 (1990): 92–6. Technology is likely not very transferable. On how much capital accumulation and technology transfer might counterfactually contribute to narrowing the gap between rich and poor nations, see Robert E. Hall and Charles I. Jones, "Why Do Some Countries Produce So Much More Output per Worker than Others?" *Quarterly Journal of Economics* 114, 1 (1999): 83–116. Even with low technology levels, which, in turn, imply low capital stocks, distortions in capital markets could be the source of considerable retardation in the periphery. See Pierre-Olivier Gourinchas and Olivier Jeanne, "The Elusive Gains from International Financial Integration," NBER Woring Paper no. 9684 (Cambridge, MA, 2003).

On postwar capital market policies, see Pedro Aspe Armella, Rudiger Dornbusch, and Maurice Obstfeld, *Financial Policies and the World Capital Market: The Problem of Latin American Countries* (Chicago, 1983). On other possible causes of foreign capital exclusion from Latin America, see Charles I. Jones, "Economic Growth and the Relative Price of Capital," *Journal of Monetary Economics* 34 (1994): 359–82; Alan M. Taylor, "Tres fases del crecimiento económico argentino," *Revista de Historia Económica* 12 (1994): 649–83; "Debt, Dependence, and the Demographic Transition: Latin America into the Next Century," *World Development* 23, 5 (1995): 869–79; "Argentina and the World Capital Market: Saving, Investment, and International Capital Mobility in the Twentieth Century," *Journal of Development Economics* 57, 1 (1998): 147–84; "On the Costs of Inward-Looking Development: Price Distortions, Growth, and Divergence in Latin America," *Journal of Economic History* 58, 1 (1998): 1–28; and "Latin America and Foreign Capital in the Twentieth Century: Economics, Politics, and Institutional Change," in Stephen Haber, ed., *Institutions and Latin American Economic Growth* (Stanford, 2000).

On the role of institutions in economic performance, see Daron Acemoglu, Simon Johnson, and James A. Robinson, "The Colonial Origins of Comparative Development: An Empirical Investigation," *American Economic Review* 91

(December 2001): 1369–96, and Dani Rodrik, Arvind Subramanian, and Francesco Trebbi, "Institutions Rule: The Primacy of Institutions over Geography and Integration in Economic Development" (National Bureau of Economic Research, Working Paper Series no. 9305, November 2002).

CHAPTER 3 (MARCELO DE PAIVA ABREU)

This bibliographic essay is necessarily incomplete given space limitations, the long time span covered, and the large number of economies involved. This is particularly true for the smaller economies. It should be complemented by the three bibliographical essays covering economic matters in post-1929 Latin America as a whole, included in Leslie Bethell, ed., *The Cambridge History of Latin America*, vol. 9, *Bibliographical Essays* (Cambridge, 1995).

To put Latin America in the global context, reference to general works on the world economy is necessary. For financial developments in the world economy over the whole period, see Barry Eichengreen, *Globalizing Capital: A History of the International Monetary System* (Princeton, NJ, 1996). Other relevant books on financial matters in specific subperiods include Barry Eichengreen, *Golden Fetters: The Gold Standard and the Great Depression, 1919–1939* (London, 1996); Richard Gardner, *Sterling-Dollar Diplomacy: The Origins and Prospects of Our International Economic Order* (New York, 1969); and Robert Solomon, *The International Monetary System 1945–1981* (New York, 1982). For the relations of the International Monetary Fund with Latin America, see J. Keith Horsefield, ed., *The International Monetary Fund, 1945–1965: Twenty Years of International Monetary Cooperation*, 3 vols. (Washington, DC, 1969); Margaret de Vries, *The International Monetary Fund, 1966–1971: The System Under Stress*, 2 vols. (Washington, DC, 1976); and *The International Monetary Fund, 1972–1978: Cooperation on Trial*, 3 vols. (Washington, DC, 1985). On the relations of Latin America with the World Bank, the standard histories are Edward S. Mason and Robert E. Asher, *The World Bank Since Bretton Woods* (Washington, DC, 1973); and Devesh Kapur, John P. Lewis, and Richard Webb, eds., *The World Bank: Its First Half Century*, vol. 1, *History* (Washington, DC, 1997). For operations of the Inter-American Development Bank, see Sidney Dell, *The Inter-American Bank: A Study in Development Financing* (New York, 1972), and Diana Tussie, *El BID* (Buenos Aires, 1997).

Relevant works on trade or trade-related policies in the 1930s are Henry J. Tasca, *The Reciprocal Trade Policy of the United States: A Study in Trade Philosophy* (Philadelphia, 1938); Howard S. Ellis, *Exchange Control in Central Europe* (Cambridge, MA, 1941); and Larry Neal, "The Economics and Finance of Bilateral Clearing Agreements: Germany, 1934–8," *Economic History Review* 32, 2 (1979): 391–404. After World War II, the focus changed to export and import structures. On primary commodities, see J. W. F. Rowe, *Primary Commodities in International Trade* (Cambridge, 1965). On exports of manufactures, see Alfred Maizels, "Recent Trends in Latin America's Exports to the Industrialized Countries," in Victor L. Urquidi and Rosemary Thorp, eds., *Latin America in the World Economy*

(London, 1973), and Gustav Ranis, "Challenges and Opportunities Posed by Asia's Superexporters: Implications for Manufactured Exports from Latin America," in Werner Baer and Malcolm Gillis, eds., *Export Diversification and the New Protectionism* (Urbana, IL, 1981). Robert Hudec, *Developing Countries in the GATT Legal System* (London, 1988), is useful on Latin America and the General Agreement on Tariffs and Trade.

From the late 1940s, the Economic Commission for Latin America (ECLAC) is a major source of data and studies on Latin American economies. For example, see ECLAC, *Economic Survey of Latin America* (New York, several years), especially 1948 and 1949, and *The Economic Development of Latin America and its Principal Problems* (Lake Success, NY, 1950). On Raúl Prebisch's contributions, see Adolfo Gurriere, ed., *La obra de Prebisch en la CEPAL*, 2 vols. (Mexico City, 1982), and Arturo O'Connell, "The Return of the 'Vulnerability' and Raúl Prebisch's Early Thinking on the Argentine Business Cycle," *Cepal Review 75* (2001): 51–65. In the mid-1950s, a series of extremely influential reports on the main Latin American economies was published by ECLAC under the general title of *Análisis y proyecciones del desarrollo económico*. Articles published in the *Economic Bulletin for Latin America*, and later in the *Cepal Review*, have also been influential. For example, see "The Growth and Decline of Import Substitution in Brazil," *Economic Bulletin for Latin America* 9 (1964): 1–61.

Brian R. Mitchell, *International Historical Statistics: The Americas, 1750–1993* (New York, 1998) is a useful compilation to be handled with care. Angus Maddison, *Monitoring the World Economy, 1820–1992* (Paris, 1995), includes world GDP estimates since 1820. But see the much more detailed official historical statistics from country sources, such as *Estatísticas históricas brasileiras. Séries econômicas, demográficas e sociais de 1550 a 1988* (Rio de Janeiro, 1990); *Estadísticas históricas de México* (Mexico City, 1994); and Miguel Urrutia and Mario Arrubla, eds., *Compendio de estadísticas históricas de Colombia* (Bogotá, 1970). For many countries, there are databases that include historical data in the Internet sites of central banks or ministries of the economy. For Chile, see Juan Braun et al., "Economía chilena 1810–1995: Estadísticas históricas" (*Documento de Trabajo* 187, Pontificia Universidad Católica de Chile, Instituto de Economía, Santiago de Chile, 2000). There are unofficial, less satisfactory sources of historical data such as V. Vásquez-Presedo, *Estadísticas históricas argentinas II (Comparadas). Segunda Parte 1914–1939* (Buenos Aires, 1976).

The economic history of Latin America as a whole is analyzed in three chapters of Leslie Bethell, ed., *The Cambridge History of Latin America*, vol. 6, *Latin America since 1930. Economy, Society and Politics*, part 1, *Economy and Society* (Cambridge, 1994): Victor Bulmer-Thomas, "The Latin American Economies, 1929–1939"; Rosemary Thorp, "The Latin American Economies, 1939–c.1950"; and Ricardo French-Davis, Oscar Muñoz, and José Gabriel Palma, "The Latin American Economies, 1950–1990." They cover many aspects related to Latin America and the world economy. Victor Bulmer-Thomas, *The Economic History of Latin America since Independence*, 2nd ed. (Cambridge, 2003) is the standard general economic history. Other contributions on Latin America as a whole, arranged in the chronological order of periods analyzed, are John H. Williams, "American Foreign Exchange

Problems in Brazil, Argentina, Chile and Uruguay, 1934," in *Foreign Relations of the United States 1934. The American Republics*, vol. 4 (Washington, DC, 1951), 390–422; Carlos F. Díaz-Alejandro, "Latin America in the 1930s," in Rosemary Thorp, ed., *An Economic History of Twentieth-Century Latin America*, vol. 2, *Latin America in the 1930s: The Role of the Periphery in World Crisis* (Basingstoke, 2000); Robert Triffin, "Central Banking and Monetary Management in Latin America," in Seymour Harris, ed., *Economic Problems of Latin America* (New York, 1944); Angus Maddison, *Two Crises: Latin America and Asia 1929–38 and 1973–83* (Paris, 1991); Celso Furtado, *Economic Development of Latin America: A Survey from Colonial Times to the Cuban Revolution* (Cambridge, 1970); Albert Hirschman, *A Bias for Hope. Essays on Development and Latin America* (New Haven, CT, 1971); and Rosemary Thorp and Laurence Whitehead, eds., *Inflation and Stabilisation in Latin America* (Basingstoke, 1979). On economic integration, see Sidney Dell, *A Latin American Common Market?* (London, 1966); and M. H. J. Finch, "The Latin American Free Trade Association," in Ali M. El-Agraa, ed., *International Economic Integration* (Basingstoke, 1988). There are other chapters of interest on subregional integration in the latter book.

For a good source on long-term capital flows, see United Nations, Department of Economic and Social Affairs, *External Financing in Latin America* (New York, 1965). For a useful collection of essays on financial advisors, see Paul W. Drake, ed., *Money Doctors, Foreign Debts, and Economic Reforms in Latin America from the 1890s to the Present* (Wilmington, DE, 1994). Barbara Stallings, *Banker to the Third World. United States Portfolio Investment in Latin America, 1900–1986* (Berkeley, CA, 1987) is the standard source on U.S. portfolio investment. Also, see Cleona Lewis, *America's Stake in International Investments* (Washington, DC, 1938). William H. Wynne, *State Insolvency and Foreign Bondholders*, vol. 2, *Selected Case Histories of Governmental Foreign Bond Defaults and Debt Readjustments* (New Haven, CT, 1951); Marcelo de Paiva Abreu, "Debt Policies in South America, 1929–1945," *Brazilian Journal of Political Economy* 20 (2000): 63–75; and selected chapters of Barry Eichengreen and Peter Lindert, eds., *The International Debt Crisis in International Perspective* (Cambridge, MA, 1989), analyze the policies adopted by different Latin American economies on the foreign debt following the shock in the late 1920s. For the more recent period, see Robert Devlin, *Debt and Crisis in Latin America. The Supply Side of the Story* (Princeton, NJ, 1989); and World Bank, *World Debt Tables*. Giorgio Fodor, "The Origin of Argentina's Sterling Balances, 1939–1943," in Guido di Tella and Christopher Platt, eds., *The Political Economy of Argentina, 1880–1946* (Basingstoke, 1985); and Marcelo de Paiva Abreu, "Brazil as a Creditor: Sterling Balances, 1940–1952," *Economic History Review* 43, 2 (1990): 450–469, consider the unusual experience of Latin American countries as creditors.

D. M. Phelps, *The Migration of Industry to Latin America* (New York, 1936) is excellent on early foreign direct investment. For early data, see U.S. Department of Commerce, Office of Business Economics, *U.S. Investments in the Latin American Economy* (Washington, DC, 1957). Data presented in Fred J. Rippy, *British Investments in Latin America, 1822–1949. A Case Study in the Operations of Private Enterprise in Retarded Regions* (Minneapolis, MN, 1959), should be complemented with the more reliable Bank of England, *United Kingdom Overseas Investments 1938 to 1948* (London, 1950). Also, see Mira Wilkins, *The Maturing of Multinational Enterprise. American Business Abroad from 1914 to 1970* (Cambridge, MA, 1974).

For Argentina, the whole period is well covered by Guido di Tella and Christopher Platt, eds., *The Political Economy of Argentina, 1880–1946* (Basingstoke, 1985); Guido di Tella, *Argentina under Perón, 1973–76: The Nation's Experience with a Labour-based Government* (Basingstoke, 1983); and Guido di Tella and Rudiger Dornbusch, eds., *The Political Economy of Argentina, 1976–1983* (Basingstoke, 1989). Carlos F. Díaz-Alejandro, *Essays on the Economic History of the Argentine Republic* (New Haven, CT, 1970) is a classic source. Pablo Gerchunoff and Lucas Llach, *El ciclo de la ilusión del crecimiento: Un siglo de políticas económicas argentinas* (Buenos Aires, 1998) covers the whole 1928–1982 period and more, as does Marie-Ange Veganzones and Carlos Winograd, *Argentina in the 20th Century: An Account of Long-Awaited Growth* (Paris, 1997).

On the 1930s, see also Jorge Fodor and Arturo O'Connell, "La Argentina y la economía atlántica en la primera mitad del siglo XX," *Desarollo Económico* 13 (1973): 1–67; Gerardo della Paolera and Alan Taylor, "Economic Recovery from the Argentine Great Depression: Institutions, Expectations and the Change of Macroeconomic Regime," *Journal of Economic History* 59 (1999): 567–99; and Arturo O'Connell, "Argentina into the Depression: Problems of an Open Economy," in Rosemary Thorp, ed., *Economic History of Twentieth-Century Latin America*, vol. 2, *Latin America in the 1930s* (Basingstoke, 2000). Virgil Salera, *Exchange Control and the Argentine Market* (New York, 1941) is a classic. For balance of payments data, see Manuel Balboa, "La evolución del balance de pagos de la República Argentina, 1913–1950," *Desarollo Económico* 12 (1972): 153–172. For the initial Perón years, see Jorge Fodor, "Perón's Policies for Agricultural Exports, 1946–1948: Dogmatism or Common Sense?" in David Rock, ed., *Argentina in the Twentieth Century* (London, 1975). For the 1950s, see Carlos Díaz-Alejandro, *Exchange Rate Devaluation in a Semi-Industrialized Country: The Argentine Experience, 1955–1961* (Cambridge, MA, 1965); and Richard Mallon and Juan Sourrouille, *Economic Policymaking in a Conflict Society. The Argentine Case* (Cambridge, MA, 1975).

On Brazil, see the essays in Marcelo de Paiva Abreu, ed., *A ordem do progresso: Cem anos de política econômica republicana 1889–1989* (Rio de Janeiro, 1990), which cover the whole 1928–1982 period. Albert Fishlow, "Origins and Consequences of Import Substitution in Brazil," in L. E. DiMarco, ed., *International Economics and Development: Essays in Honor of Raúl Prebisch* (New York, 1972), deals with import substitution in the long term, as does Marcelo de Paiva Abreu, Afonso Bevilaqua, and Demosthenes Madureira de Pinho Netto, "Import Substitution and Growth in Brazil, 1890s–1970s," in Enrique Cárdenas, José Antonio Ocampo, and Rosemary Thorp, eds., *An Economic History of Twentieth-Century Latin America*, vol. 3, *Industrialization and the State in Latin America: The Postwar Years* (Basingstoke, 2000). Antonio Delfim Netto, *O problema do café no Brasil* (São Paulo, 1959), is the classic source on coffee.

On the 1930s, see Marcelo de Paiva Abreu, "Argentina and Brazil during the 1930s: The Impact of British and US International Economic Policies," in Rosemary Thorp, ed., *An Economic History of Twentieth-Century Latin America*, vol. 2, *Latin America in the 1930s: The Role of the Periphery in World Crisis* (cited previously).

Celso Furtado, *The Economic Growth of Brazil: A Survey from Colonial to Modern Times* (Berkeley, CA, 1963), is a classic treatment of the 1930s and 1940s. For later periods, see Pedro S. Malan and Regis Bonelli, "The Brazilian Economy in the Seventies: Old and New Developments," *World Development* 5 (1977): 19–45; Edmar L. Bacha, *El milagro y la crisis: Economia brasileña y latinoamericana* (Mexico City, 1986); Edmar L. Bacha, "Issues and Evidence on Recent Brazilian Growth," *World Development* 5 (1977): 47–67; Peter Evans, *Dependent Development: The Alliance of Multinational, State and Local Capital in Brazil* (Princeton, NJ, 1979); World Bank, *Brazil: Industrial Policies and Manufactured Exports* (Washington, DC, 1983); John Wells, "Brazil and the Post-1973 Crisis in the International Economy," in Rosemary Thorp and Laurence Whitehead, eds., *Inflation and Stabilisation in Latin America* (Basingstoke, 1979); and Dionísio Dias Carneiro, "Long-Run Adjustment, the Debt Crisis and the Changing Role of Stabilization Policies in the Recent Brazilian Experience," in Rosemary Thorp and Lawrence Whitehead, eds., *Latin American Debt and the Adjustment Crisis.*

On Mexico, see Enrique Cárdenas, ed., *Historia económica de México*, vol. 5 (Mexico City, 1994); Leopoldo Solís, ed., *La economía mexicana*, vol. 1, *Análisis por sector y distribución*, and vol. 2, *Política y desarrollo* (Mexico City, 1973); Rolando Cordera, ed., *Desarollo y crisis de la economía mexicana. Ensayos de interpretación histórica* (Mexico City, 1981); and Carlos Bazdresch et al., eds., *México: Auge, crisis y ajuste* (Mexico City, 1993). On Mexico's long-term foreign economic policies, see Leopoldo Solís Manjarrez, *La realidad económica mexicana: retrovisión y perspectivas* (Mexico City, 2000), ch. 6. On import substitution in the long term, see Enrique Cárdenas, "The Process of Accelerated Industrialization in Mexico, 1929–1982," in *An Economic History of Twentieth-Century Latin America*, vol. 3, *Industrialization and the State in Latin America: The Postwar Years* (cited previously). On foreign economic policies in specific periods, see on the 1930s, Enrique Cárdenas, "The Great Depression and Industrialisation: The Case of Mexico," in Rosemary Thorp, ed., *An Economic History of Latin America*, vol. 2, *Latin America in the 1930s: The Role of the Periphery in World Crisis* (cited previously); Antonio Ortiz Mena, *El Desarrollo estabilizador: Reflexiones sobre una epoca* (Mexico City, 1998); Jaime Ros, "Mexico from Oil Boom to the Debt Crisis: An Analysis of Policy Response to External Shocks, 1978–85," in *Latin American Debt and the Adjustment Crisis* (cited previously); and Carlos M. Urzúa, "Five Decades Between the World Bank and Mexico," in Devesh Kapur, John P. Lewis, and Richard Webb, eds., *The World Bank*, vol. 2 (Washington, DC, 1997).

On Chile in the 1930s, see Gabriel Palma, "From an Export-Led to an Import-Substituting Economy: Chile 1914–1939," in Rosemary Thorp, ed., *An Economic History of Twentieth-Century Latin America*, vol. 2. *Latin America in the 1930s: The Role of the Periphery in World Crisis* (cited previously); and Manuel Marfán, "Politicas reactivadoras y recesion externa: Chile 1929–1938," in Oscar Muñoz, ed., *Perspectivas históricas de la economía chilena: del siglo XIX a la crisis del 30* (Santiago de Chile, 1984). For the 1950s and 1960s, see Aníbal Pinto, *Chile: un caso de desarrollo frustrado* (Santiago de Chile, 1964); and Markos Mamalakis and Clark Winston Reynolds, *Essays on the Chilean Economy* (Homewood, IL, 1965). On the 1970s, see World Bank, *Chile. An Economy in Transition* (Washington,

DC, 1979); Alejandro Foxley, *Latin American Experiments in Neo-conservative Economics* (Berkeley, CA, 1983); and Sebastian Edwards and Alejandra Cox Edwards, *Monetarism and Liberalization: The Chilean Experiment* (Chicago, 1991).

On Central America and the Caribbean, see Victor Bulmer-Thomas, *The Political Economy of Central America since 1920* (Cambridge, 1987); and "The Wider Caribbean in the 20th Century: A Long-Run Development Perspective," *Integration & Trade* 15 (2001): 5–56. On the Caribbean, see Antonio Santamaría García, "Alteration, Crisis and Adjustment in the Cuban Export Economy, 1898–1939," in Enrique Cardenas, José Antonio Ocampo, and Rosemary Thorp, eds., *An Economic History of Twentieth-Century Latin America*, vol. 1, *The Export Age* (Basingstoke, 2000), 32–54; and for Cuba before the 1940s, see Henry Wallich, *Monetary Problems of an Export Economy* (Cambridge, MA, 1950). Carmela Mesa-Lago, *Market, Socialist, and Mixed Economies. Comparative Policy and Performance. Chile, Cuba, and Costa Rica* (Baltimore, 2000), is useful, especially on post-1959 Cuba and postwar Costa Rica. On bananas in the Caribbean in the long term, see Peter Clegg, *The Caribbean Banana Trade* (Basingstoke, 2000). Also, see Paul W. Ashley, "The Commonwealth Caribbean and the Contemporary World Order: The Cases of Jamaica and Trinidad," in Paget Henry and Carl Stone, eds., *The Newer Caribbean: Decolonization. Democracy, and Development* (Philadelphia, PA, 1983); Jennifer Sharply, "Jamaica, 1972–1980," in Tony Killick, ed., *The IMF and Stabilization: Developing Country Experiences* (New York, 1984); and Anthony Payne and Paul Sutton, eds., *Dependency under Challenge: The Political Economy of the Commonwealth Caribbean* (Manchester, 1984).

On Colombia, see José Antonio Ocampo et al., "Consolidación del capitalismo moderno (1945–1986)," in José Antonio Ocampo, ed., *História económica de Colombia* (Bogotá, 1987). Also, see José Antonio Ocampo, "The Colombian Economy in the 1930s," in Rosemary Thorp, ed., *An Economic History of Twentieth-Century Latin America*, vol. 2. *Latin America in the 1930s: The Role of the Periphery in World Crisis* (cited previously); José Antonio Ocampo and Santiago Montenegro, *Crisis mundial, protección e industrialización: Ensayos de história económica colombiana* (Bogotá, 1984); José Antonio Ocampo and Camilo Tovar, "Colombia in the Classical Era of Inward-Looking Development," in Enrique Cárdenas, José Antonio Ocampo, and Rosemary Thorp, eds., *An Economic History of Twentieth-Century Latin America*, vol. 3. *Industrialization and the State in Latin America: The Postwar Years* (cited previously); and Carlos Díaz-Alejandro, *Foreign Trade Regimes and Economic Development. Colombia* (New York, 1976). Marco Palacios, *El café en Colombia: Una historia económica, social y política* (Mexico City, 1983) is a classic on coffee.

On Peru, see Rosemary Thorp and Geoffrey Bertram, *Peru 1890–1977. Growth and Policy in an Open Economy* (London, 1978). Also, see Rosemary Thorp and Carlos Londoño, "The Effect of the Great Depression on the Economies of Peru and Colombia," in Rosemary Thorp, ed., *An Economic History of Twentieth-Century Latin America*, vol. 2. *Latin America in the 1930s: The Role of the Periphery in World Crisis* (cited previously); Pablo Kuczynki, *Peruvian Democracy Under Stress: An Account of the Belaunde Administration, 1963–1968* (Princeton, NJ, 1977); Shane Hunt, "Direct Foreign Investment in Peru: New Rules for an Old Game," in

Abraham Loewenthal, ed., *The Peruvian Experiment: Continuity and Change under Military Rule* (Princeton, NJ, 1975); and several of the essays included in Cynthia McClintock and Abraham Loewenthal, eds., *The Peruvian Experiment Reconsidered* (Princeton, NJ, 1983).

On Venezuela, see Sergio Aranda, *La economía venezolana* (Mexico City, 1977), and Pablo Astorga, "Industrialization in Venezuela: The Problem of Abundance, 1936–1983," in Enrique Cárdenas, José Antonio Ocampo, and Rosemary Thorp, eds., *An Economic History of Twentieth-Century Latin America*, vol. 3. *Industrialization and the State in Latin America: The Postwar Years* (cited previously). Also on Venezuela and the oil industry is Jorge Salazar-Carrillo, *Oil and Development in Venezuela during the Twentieth Century* (Westport, CT, 1994); and Franklin Tugwell, *The Politics of Oil in Venezuela* (Stanford, CA, 1975).

On the smaller economies not considered previously, references are necessarily limited. On Bolivia, see Walter Gómez, *La minería en el desarrollo económico de Bolivia* (La Paz, 1978); and Juan Antonio Morales and Napoleón Pacheco, "El retorno de los liberales," in *Bolivia en el Siglo XX. La formación de la Bolivia contemporánea* (La Paz, 1999). On Ecuador, see Fernando Velasco Abad, *Ecuador: Subdesarollo y dependencia* (Quito, 1981); and Leonardo Vicuña, *Economia ecuatoriana: Problemas, tendencias y proyecciones* (Guayaquil, 1980). On Paraguay, see Carlos Fletschner et al., *Economía del Paraguay contemporáneo* (Asunción, 1984); and Joseph Pincus, *The Economy of Paraguay* (New York, 1968). On Uruguay, see Instituto de Economía, *El proceso económico del Uruguay: Contribución al estudio de su evolución y perspectivas* (Montevideo, 1969); and Jorge Notaro, *La política económica del Uruguay, 1968–1984* (Montevideo, 1984).

CHAPTER 4 (VICTOR BULMER-THOMAS)

The economic history of Latin America since the end of inward-looking development has been shaped by two events: globalization and the debt crisis. On both of these, there is a substantial literature. In the case of the debt crisis, the literature focuses heavily on the region. However, the literature on globalization – still growing rapidly – is much more general in nature and Latin America does not always feature prominently. Despite this, it is essential reading for those seeking to understand the nature and character of the New Economic Model that took shape in Latin America from the 1980s onward.

A good starting point for the debt crisis in Latin America is R. Devlin, *Debt and Crisis in Latin America: The Supply Side of the Story* (Princeton, NJ, 1989). Case studies of most of the worst-affected countries can be found in Rosemary Thorp and Lawrence Whitehead, eds., *Latin American Debt and the Adjustment Crisis* (Pittsburgh, PA, 1987). Both these books were published while the debt crisis was still developing and do not therefore take account of the issue of Brady bonds that was widely credited with ending the crisis. The reader should therefore also consult a number of references that look back over the 1980s debt crisis from the perspective of the 1990s. These include G. Kaminsky and A. Pereira, *The Debt*

Crisis: Lessons of the 1980s for the 1990s (Washington, DC, 1994); J. Boughton, *The IMF and the Latin American Debt Crisis: Seven Common Criticisms* (Washington, DC, 1994); W. Cline, *International Debt Re-examined* (Washington, DC, 1995); and R. Grosse, ed., *Government Responses to the Latin American Debt Problem* (New Brunswick, NJ, 1995).

Globalization in its modern form is often compared with earlier periods. To gain a sense of historical perspective, the reader should consult Barry Eichengreen, *Globalizing Capital: A History of the International Monetary System* (Princeton, NJ, 1996); and Michael Bordo, Alan Taylor, and Jeffrey Williamson, eds., *Globalization in Historical Perspective* (Chicago, 2003). An elegant statement in favor of globalization can be found in S. Fischer, "Globalization and Its Challenges," *American Economic Review* (May 2003); and a strong critique by a former chief economist at the World Bank is provided by Joseph Stiglitz, *Globalization and Its Discontents* (New York, 2002). A. Guerra-Borges, *Globalización e integración latinoamericana* (Mexico City, 2002) is a thoughtful book that recognizes the historical inevitability of globalization and asks how Latin America can adjust to the new reality. A similar approach, although not limited to Latin America, is taken by many of the authors in R. Baldwin and L. Alan Winters, eds., *Challenges to Globalization* (Chicago, 2003). See also D. Baker, G. Epstein, and R. Pollin, eds., *Globalization and Progressive Economic Policy: What Are the Real Constraints and Opportunities?* (Cambridge, 1998).

Trade liberalization is only one part of globalization, but it has been a very important part for Latin America. Trade liberalization was at first driven forward by GATT and is now promoted by its successor, the World Trade Organization. There is a good literature on this topic, which is very relevant for Latin America. See John H. Jackson, *The World Trade Organization: Constitution and Jurisprudence* (London, 1998). See also D. Tussie, "Trade Policy Within the Context of the World Trade Organization," *CEPAL Review*, no. 62 (August 1997); and Patricia Gray Rich, ed., *Latin America: Its Future in the Global Economy* (Basingstoke, 2002). On trade liberalization more generally, the reader should consult S. Edwards, "Openness, Trade Liberalization, and Growth in Developing Countries," *Journal of Economic Literature* 31:2 (September 1998); and J. Frankel and D. Romer, "Does Trade Cause Growth?" *American Economic Review* 89:3 (June 1999). A much more sceptical note on the benefits of free trade is struck by G. Gereffi, D. Spener, and J. Bair, eds., *Free Trade and Uneven Development* (Philadelphia, 2002).

Capital account liberalization is another key part of globalization. The literature that analyzes this phenomenon in relation to Latin America is discussed subsequently. However, the general issues are considered in H. Edison et al., "Capital Account Liberalization and Economic Performance: Survey and Synthesis" (International Monetary Fund Working Paper No. 02/120, Washington, DC, 2002); and S. Fischer et al., *Should the IMF Pursue Capital Account Convertibility?* (Princeton, NJ, 1998). The specific problems of capital account liberalization in emerging markets are well reviewed in D. Beim and C. Calomiris, *Emerging Financial Markets* (New York, 2001); and A. Demirguc-Kunt and E. Detragiache, "The Determinants of Banking Crises: Evidence from Developing and Developed Countries," *IMF Staff Papers* 45:1 (March 1998).

The region with which Latin America has been most compared since the debt crisis erupted is Asia. Latin America's economic performance has often been compared unfavorably with many Asian countries and an understanding of the transformation of the Asian economies is therefore important in order to establish whether this criticism is justified. A classic text on South Korea, perhaps the most successful Asian tiger, is Alice Amsden, *Asia's Next Giant: South Korea and Late Industrialization* (Oxford, 1989). Because this was written before the 1997 Asian financial crisis, it is necessary to also consider more recent writings. These include Joseph. E. Stiglitz and S. Yusuf, eds., *Rethinking the East Asian Miracle* (New York and Washington, DC, 2001); Alice Amsden, *The Rise of "the Rest": Challenges to the West from Late-Industrialization Economies* (New York, 2001); M. Goldstein, *The Asian Financial Crisis: Causes, Cures and Systemic Implications* (Washington, DC, 1998); and Ha-Joon Chang, "The East Asian Model of Economic Policy," in E. Huber, ed., *Models of Capitalism: Lessons from Latin America* (Chapel Hill, NC, 2002). Comparisons with Latin America can be found in Nancy Birdsall and F. Jaspersen, *Pathways to Growth: Comparing East Asia and Latin America* (Washington, DC, 1997).

There are a number of very useful statistical sources that allow comparisons between Latin America and other parts of the world during the recent phase of globalization. See, in particular, the World Bank, *World Development Indicators* (Washington, DC), which is produced each year as a CD-ROM covering the period from 1960 to the present. Although it covers a much longer period, Angus Maddison, *The World Economy: A Millennial Perspective* (Paris, 2002) is also invaluable. The United Nations produces a large range of relevant statistics, including an annual report on multinational companies. See United Nations, *World Investment Report* (New York). Various regular publications of the International Monetary Fund are also very helpful for understanding the forces of globalization. See, for example, International Monetary Fund, *World Economic Outlook* (Washington, DC).

The New Economic Model is the name given to the set of policies that shaped Latin America in the 1980s and 1990s. See Victor Bulmer-Thomas, ed., *The New Economic Model in Latin America and Its Impact on Income Distribution and Poverty* (New York, 1996). See also Barbara Stallings and W. Peres, *Growth, Employment and Equity: The Impact of the Economic Reforms in Latin America and the Caribbean* (Washington, DC, 2000). The New Economic Model is also analyzed in depth in a special issue of *World Development*. See N. Reinhardt and W. Peres, "Latin America's New Economic Model: Micro Responses and Economic Restructuring," *World Development* 28:9 (September 2000) and the other articles in the same issue.

The set of policies that make up the New Economic Model were also known in the 1990s as the Washington Consensus. See J. Williamson, ed., *Latin American Adjustment: How Much Has Happened?* (Washington, DC, 1990). The limitations of the Washington Consensus began to be widely acknowledged in the second half of the 1990s, when growth started to falter in Latin America and more emphasis was put on "second generation" reforms (sometimes called "reform of the reforms") that included greater attention to institutions and the rule of law. See Jeffrey Williamson and P. Kuczynski, eds., *After the Washington Consensus: Restarting*

Growth and Reform in Latin America (Washington, DC, 2003). The shortcomings of the Washington Consensus are also discussed in R. Vos, L. Taylor, and R. Paes de Barros, eds., *Economic Liberalization, Distribution and Poverty: Latin America in the 1990s* (Cheltenham, 2002). See also Ricardo Ffrench-Davis, *Reforming the Reforms in Latin America: Macroeconomics, Trade, Finance* (Basingstoke, 1999).

The structural reforms in Latin America are covered in general terms in a number of good studies. See Sebastian Edwards, *Crisis and Reform in Latin America: From Despair to Hope* (Oxford, 1995). An optimistic note is struck in S. Burki and G. Perry, *The Long March: A Reform Agenda for Latin America and the Caribbean in the Next Decade* (Washington, DC, 1997), although this was written before the decline of capital flows to Latin America that began in 1998. The most successful country in Latin America in terms of economic performance (growth and equity) has been Chile, and this has been extensively analyzed. See, for example, Ricardo Ffrench-Davis, *Economic Reforms in Chile: From Dictatorship to Democracy* (Ann Arbor, MI, 2002).

There has been a strong correlation in Latin America between economic performance and capital inflows. Not surprisingly, therefore, this topic has figured prominently in the recent economic history of Latin America. See Felipe Larraín, ed., *Capital Flows, Capital Controls, and Currency Crises: Latin America in the 1990s* (Ann Arbor, MI, 2000). Ricardo Ffrench-Davis and S. Griffith Jones, eds., *Coping with Capital Surges: The Return of Finance to Latin America* (Boulder, CO, 1995) examines the phenomenon of capital inflows at a time when they were booming. This raised the question of capital controls to stem inflows rather than outflows and this increasingly relevant topic is explored in J. De Gregorio, Sebastian Edwards, and R. Valdés, "Controls on Capital Inflows: Do They Work?" *Journal of Development Economics* 63:1 (October 2000). Spanish investment, which in flow terms became more important than U.S. investment for a short period at the end of the 1990s, is considered in P. Toral, *The Reconquest of the New World: Multinational Enterprises and Spain's Direct Investment in Latin America* (Aldershot, 2001). Chile also features prominently in the literature on capital inflows and capital controls. See B. Bosworth, Rudiger Dornbusch, and R. Labán, eds., *The Chilean Economy: Policy Lessons and Challenges* (Washington, DC, 1994).

The investment and savings processes in Latin America have also come under close scrutiny. A careful study of investment can be found in G. Moguillansky and R. Bielschowsky, *Investment and Economic Reform in Latin America* (Santiago, 2001). Analyses of savings can be found in Ricardo Hausmann and H. Reisen, eds., *Promoting Savings in Latin America* (Paris, 1997); L. Rojas-Suárez and S. Weisbrod, *Financial Markets and the Behavior of Private Savings in Latin America* (Washington, DC, 1997); and C. Reinhart, *Accounting for Saving: Financial Liberalization, Capital Flows and Growth in Latin America and Europe* (Washington, DC, 1999). See also M. Agosín, *Saving and Investment in Latin America* (Geneva, 1994).

Investment in Latin America, particularly DFI, has been closely linked to privatization since the 1980s. This phenomenon has been widely discussed in the region from different angles. The impact on distribution is the subject of D. McKenzie and D. Mookherjee, *The Distributive Impact of Privatization in Latin America: Evidence from Four Countries* (Boston, 2003). A more general study can be found in L. Manzetti, *Privatization South America Style* (Oxford, 1999); and M. Birch and J. Haar, eds., *The Impact of Privatization in the Americas* (Coral Gables, FL, 2000). A good case study of telecommunications is provided in J. Clifton, *The Politics of Telecommunications in Mexico: Privatization and State-Labour Relations, 1982–95* (Basingstoke, 2000). The privatization debate also includes pension reform. See A. Barrientos, *Pension Reform in Latin America* (Aldershot, 1998).

Trade policy has been a dominant feature of work on Latin America since the debt crisis. See M. Agosín and Ricardo Ffrench-Davis, "Trade Liberalization and Growth: Recent Experiences in Latin America," *Journal of Interamerican Studies and World Affairs* 37:3 (1995); G. Dijsktra, "Trade Liberalization and Industrial Development in Latin America," *World Development* 28:9 (September 2000); and R. Robertson, "Trade Liberalization and Wage Inequality: Lessons From the Mexican Experience," *World Economy* 23:6 (June 2000). A great deal of attention has also been paid to hemispheric integration. The main schemes are covered in Victor Bulmer-Thomas, ed., *Regional Integration in Latin America and the Caribbean: The Political Economy of Open Regionalism* (London, 2001). The concept of "open" regionalism is analyzed in ECLAC, *Open Regionalism in Latin America and the Caribbean – Economic Integration as a Contribution to Changing Patterns with Social Equity* (Santiago, 1994). The Free Trade Area of the Americas is the subject of J. Salazar-Xirinachs and M. Robert, eds., *Toward Free Trade in the Americas* (Washington, DC, 2001).

Exchange rate policy has become increasingly important in Latin America as a result of the devastating effect of financial crises. The Brazilian experience is discussed by a former President of the Central Bank in Gerardo Franco, *The Real Plan and the Exchange Rate* (Princeton, NJ, 2000); and in A. Ferreira and G. Tullio, "The Brazilian Exchange Rate Crisis of January 1999," *Journal of Latin American Studies* 34:1 (2002); whereas Argentina's failed Convertibility Law is analyzed in Michael Mussa, *Argentina and the Fund: From Triumph to Tragedy* (Washington, DC, 2002). An overview is provided in M. Falcão Silva, *Modern Exchange Rate Regimes, Stabilisation Programmes and Coordination of Macroeconomic Policies: Recent Experiences of Selected Developing Latin American Economies* (Aldershot, 1999). The politics of exchange rate policy is the subject of C. Wise and Riordan Roett, eds., *Exchange Rate Politics in Latin America* (Washington, DC, 2000). The financial crises of the 1990s are explored in a number of publications. A good study of Mexico can be found in Stanley Weintraub, *Financial Decision-Making in Mexico: To Bet a Nation* (Pittsburgh, PA, 2000); and of Brazil in M. Arruda, *External Debt: Brazil and the International Financial Crisis* (London, 2000). The Argentine financial crisis is very well dissected in the study by Michael Mussa cited previously.

Fiscal and labor market policies have received a certain amount of attention, although not as much as they deserve. An excellent analysis of fiscal policy can be found in M. Cárdenas and S. Montenegro, eds., *La economía política de las finanzas públicas en américa latina* (Bogotá, 1999). Social spending is explored in R. Cominetti and G. Ruiz, *Evolución del gasto público social en América Latina, 1980–95* (Santiago, 1998). The labor market is explored in some depth in Sebastian Edwards and Nora Lustig, eds., *Labor Markets in Latin America: Combining Social Protection with Market Flexibility* (Washington, DC, 1997). Another good study is J. Weller, *Reformas económicas, crecimiento y empleo: los mercados de trabajo en américa latina y el caribe* (Santiago, 2000).

The overall performance of Latin America under the New Economic Model is explored in the last two chapters of Victor Bulmer-Thomas, *The Economic History of Latin America since Independence*, 2nd ed. (Cambridge, 2003); and in the last two chapters of Rosemary Thorp, *Progress, Poverty and Exclusion: An Economic History of Latin America in the 20ᵗʰ Century* (Washington, DC, 1998). Export performance is examined in C. Macario, *Export Growth in Latin America: Policies and Performance* (Boulder, CO, 2000). The Brazilian experience is covered in Werner Baer, *The Brazilian Economy: Growth and Development*, 5th ed. (Westport, CT, 2001), whereas Mexico is the subject of Enrique Dussel Peters, *Polarizing Mexico: The Impact of Liberalization Strategy* (Boulder, CO, 2000). There are also four interesting case studies in M. de Miranda, ed., *Alternativas de política económica y social en américa latina y el caribe: cuatro casos de estudio: Colombia, Costa Rica, Cuba y México* (Bogotá, 2002).

CHAPTER 5 (ALAN DYE)

Most of the contributions to the study of Latin American institutions presuppose a basic knowledge of the concepts of the new institutional economics or positive political economy, or if not, they adopt the less rigorous definitions of "institution" characteristic of literature that preceded the "new institutionalism." This bibliography surveys the major new institutionalist contributions to Latin American economic history, including some references to empirical or theoretical works that do not deal directly with Latin America but are valuable resources for concepts and theoretical tools relevant to the study of institutions in Latin America. It is intended as an introduction to the most important works on the subject matter covered in the chapter, but it is by no means exhaustive.

An insightful, comprehensive study of Latin American institutions is William P. Glade, *The Latin American Economies: A Study of Their Institutional Evolution* (New York, 1969), which gives a rich synthesis of their evolution from the viewpoint of the American institutionalist school. Claudio Véliz, *The Centralist Tradition in Latin America* (Princeton, NJ, 1980) gives a compelling, though loosely argued, structuralist thesis of Latin American centralist bias. Familiarity with the new institutional economics, especially North (discussed subsequently), brings greater analytical clarity to many of Véliz's inductive insights, which preceded their theoretical explanation. Useful methodological surveys of new institutionalist methods as applied to Latin America are in the editor's introduction to Stephen Haber, ed., *How Latin America Fell Behind: Essays on the Economic Histories of Brazil and Mexico, 1800–1914* (Stanford, CA, 1997); and Jeffrey L. Bortz and Stephen Haber, "The New Institutional Economics and Latin American Economic History," in Jeffrey L. Bortz and Stephen Haber, eds., *The Mexican Economy, 1870–1930: Essays on the Economic History of Institutions, Revolutions, and Growth* (Stanford, CA, 2002),

1–22. These two collections, along with John H. Coatsworth and Alan Taylor, eds., *Latin America and the World Economy Since 1800* (Cambridge, MA, 1998), offer rich collections of articles that apply the tools of the new economic history and new institutionalist analysis to questions central to Latin American economic history.

The reader who wishes to develop proficiency in the methods of the new institutional economics should begin with Douglass C. North, *Institutions, Institutional Change and Economic Performance* (Cambridge, 1990) and *Structure and Change in Economic History* (New York, 1981) as the most accessible and comprehensive treatments of the central theoretical concepts. A valuable collection that focuses on empirical methods and applications is Lee Alston, Thráinn Eggertsson, and Douglass North, eds., *Empirical Studies in the New Institutional Economics* (Cambridge, 1996). Thráinn Eggertsson, "A Note on the Economics of Institutions," in that volume, gives an excellent short overview of the main theoretical ideas, and Lee Alston, "Empirical Work in Institutional Economics: An Overview," gives a pragmatic and insightful survey of empirical strategies that have been used to test or apply the new institutional economics in practice. Important complements to this literature are the bodies of work by institutional economists on the transaction-cost theory of organizations, bargaining, and contracting. The most engaging treatments of organizational theory are Oliver E. Williamson, *The Economic Institutions of Capitalism* (New York, 1985), and *The Mechanisms of Governance* (New York, 1996). A masterful survey of the fields of organization, bargaining, and contracting theory and application is Paul Milgrom and John Roberts, *Economics, Organization and Management* (Upper Saddle River, NJ, 1992).

There are many critiques of this literature coming from related social science disciplines. Two of particular value are Mark Granovetter, "Social Embeddedness," *American Journal of Sociology* 91 (1985): 481–510, and Jack Knight, *Institutions and Social Conflict* (Cambridge, 1992).

The theoretical literature on self-enforcing institutions is rapidly changing. At the writing of this chapter, the most up-to-date, comprehensive, and forward-looking treatment is Masahiko Aoki, *Toward a Comparative Institutional Analysis* (Cambridge, MA, 2001). Much of literature on this question is relatively inaccessible to the nonspecialist, but Aoki includes an accessible survey of the most significant contributions and a lucid analytical synthesis with considerable foresight into the broad significance of this theoretical literature, refreshingly international in scope, addressing a variety of types of institutional and organizational patterns found in Latin America and elsewhere in world. Many of the seminal papers were authored by Avner Greif and co-authors, of which the works most relevant to this chapter on culturally or ideologically self-enforcing institutions are Avner Greif, "Reputation and Coalitions in Medieval Trade: Evidence on the Maghribi Traders," *Journal of Economic History* 49 (1989): 857–82; "Cultural Beliefs and the Organization of Society: A Historical and Theoretical Reflection on Collectivist and Individualist Societies," *Journal of Political Economy* 102 (1994): 912–50; Avner Greif, "On the Interrelations and Economic Implications of Economic, Social, Political and Normative Factors: Reflections from Two Late Medieval Societies," in John N. Drobak and John V. C. Nye, eds., *The Frontiers of the New*

Institutional Economics (San Diego, 1997), 57–94; and Avner Greif, Paul Milgrom, and Barry Weingast, "Coordination, Commitment, and Enforcement: The Case of the Merchant Guild," *Journal of Political Economy* 102 (1994): 745–76.

Applications of positive political economy to Latin America has made important advances in recent years. The most important work is Stephen Haber, Armando Razo, and Noel Maurer, *The Politics of Property Rights: Political Instability, Credible Commitments, and Economic Growth in Mexico, 1876–1929* (Cambridge, 2003). Jeffrey L. Bortz and Stephen Haber, eds., *The Mexican Economy, 1870–1930: Essays on the Economic History of Institutions, Revolutions, and Growth* (Stanford, CA, 2002) is an outstanding collection of articles giving careful analyses of specific sectors. A masterfully concise summary of the theoretical commitment problem in the Latin American political institutions is Stephen Haber, "The Commitment Problem and Mexican Economic History," in that volume. For additional analysis and empirical application, see Stephen Haber and Armando Razo, "Political Instability and Economic Performance: Evidence from Revolutionary Mexico," *World Politics* 51, 1 (1998): 99–143; and Stephen Haber, Noel Maurer, and Armando Razo, "When the Law Does Not Matter: The Rise and Decline of the Mexican Oil Industry," *Journal of Economic History* 63 (2003): 1–32. The comparison of the postrevolutionary emergence of limited government in the United States against political disorder in Latin America is developed in Douglass C. North, William Summerhill, and Barry R. Weingast, "Order, Disorder and Economic Change: Latin American versus North America," in Bruce Bueno de Mesquita and Hilton L. Root, eds., *Governing for Prosperity* (New Haven, 2000), 59–84. This work employs a game-theoretic model of constitutional commitment developed in Barry Weingast, "The Economic Role of Political Institutions: Market-Preserving Federalism and Economic Development," *The Journal of Law, Economics and Organization* 11, 1 (1995): 1–31; "Constitutions as Governance Structures: The Political Foundations of Secure Markets," *Journal of Institutional and Theoretical Economics* 149, 1 (1993): 286–311; and "The Political Foundations of Democracy and the Rule of Law," *The American Political Science Review* 91, 2 (June 1997): 245–63. The most frequently cited empirical application of this theory is Douglass C. North and Barry R. Weingast, "Constitutions and Commitments: The Evolution of Institutions Governing Public Choice in Seventeenth-Century England," *Journal of Economic History* 49, 4 (1989), 803–32, an indispensable read in positive political economy.

Useful surveys of the positive theory of political economy and institutions are Kenneth A. Shepsle and Barry R. Weingast, eds., *Positive Theories of Congressional Institutions* (Ann Arbor, MI, 1995); and James A. Alt and Kenneth A. Shepsle, eds., *Perspectives on Positive Political Economy* (Cambridge, 1990). From an economist's transaction-cost viewpoint, see Avinash K. Dixit, *The Making of Economic Policy: A Transaction-Cost Politics Perspective* (Cambridge, MA, 1996). A tractable approach to political bargaining is developed in Gary Libecap, "Distributional Issues in Bargaining for Property Rights," *Journal of Institutional and Theoretical Economics* 145, 1 (1989): 6–24, with empirical applications in Libecap, *Contracting for Property Rights* (Cambridge, 1989). This work and Elinor Ostrom, *Governing the Commons: The Evolution of Institutions for Collective Action* (Cambridge, 1990) focus on common pool problems from poorly defined or communal property and explore formal and informal institutional mechanisms that resolve them. Although they do not directly address Latin America, they offer useful insights into questions of communal landholding and untitled claims relevant to Latin American history.

The debate on endogeneity versus exogeneity in institutional change and the role of factor endowments was spurred by Stanley L. Engerman and Kenneth L. Sokoloff, "Factor Endowments, Institutions, and Differential Paths of Growth Among New World Economies: A View from Economic Historians of the United States," in *How Latin America Fell Behind* (cited previously), 260–304. Empirical support by these authors and a co-author are in Engerman and Sokoloff, "The Evolution of Suffrage in the New World" (National Bureau of Economic Research Working Paper 8512, October 2001); and Elisa Mariscal and Kenneth L. Sokoloff, "Schooling, Suffrage, and the Persistence of Inequality in the Americas, 1800–1945," in Stephen Haber, ed., *Political Institutions and Economic Growth in Latin America* (Stanford, CA, 2000), 159–218. A related hypothesis about factor endowments and political institutions in Central America is Jeffery M. Paige, *Coffee and Power: Revolution and the Rise of Democracy in Central America* (Cambridge, MA, 1997). An empirical test of the Engerman-Sokoloff factor-endowments hypothesis in coffee-producing economies is Jeffrey Nugent and James A. Robinson, "Are Endowments Fate?" (CEPR Discussion Papers 3206, 2002). Analytical and empirical models of global processes with relation to the Engerman-Sokoloff approach are Jean-Marie Baland and James A. Robinson, "Land and Power" (CEPR Discussion Papers 3800, 2003); and Daron Acemoglu, Simon Johnson, and James A. Robinson, "Reversal of Fortune: Geography and Institutions in the Making of the Modern World Income Distribution" (Working Paper, August 2001).

The argument that independence lifted imperialist constraints, making liberalization, along with multiple other paths, possible is best developed in John H. Coatsworth, "Notes on the Comparative Economic History of Latin America and the United States," in Walter L. Bernecker and Hans Werner Tobler, eds., *Development and Underdevelopment in America: Contrasts of Economic Growth in North and Latin America in Historical Perspective* (New York, 1993); and "Economic and Institutional Trajectories in Nineteenth-Century Latin America," in *Latin America and the World Economy Since 1800* (cited previously), 23–54. It is useful to read his "Obstacles to Economic Growth in Nineteenth-Century Mexico," *American Historical Review* 83, 1 (1978): 80–100, along with these works for concreteness in a specific national context. This piece, along with Stephen Haber, *Industry and Underdevelopment: Industry and Underdevelopment: The Industrialization of Mexico, 1890–1940* (Stanford, CA, 1989), is indispensable for the study of long-run economic process in Mexico. A variety of alternative views about long-run process or "the problem of persistence" in Latin America are found in Jeremy Adelman, ed., *Colonial Legacies: The Problem of Persistence in Latin American History* (New York, 1999). Two provocative and controversial examinations of long-run institutional evolution are Robert H. Bates, *Prosperity and Violence: The Political Economy of Development* (New York, 2001); and Hernando de Soto, *The Mystery of Capital: Why Capitalism Triumphs in the West and Fails Everywhere Else* (New York, 2000). When reading about long-run evolutionary processes, one cannot overlook the dependency approach or its critics. There is no representative work in a field fraught with acrimonious disagreement, but the most important contribution is widely considered to be Fernando Henrique Cardoso and Enzo Faletto, *Dependency and Development in Latin America* (Berkeley, CA, 1971). A comprehensive bibliography and critique is Robert A. Packenham, *The Dependency Movement: Scholarship and Politics in Development Studies* (Cambridge, MA, 1992). Another valuable critique and dialogue is John Sheahan, *Patterns of Development in Latin America: Poverty, Repression, and Economic Strategy* (Princeton, NJ, 1987).

On the rise of liberalism and its significance for institutions after independence, see Jeremy Adelman *Republic of Capital: Buenos Aires and the Legal Transformation of the Atlantic World* (Stanford, CA, 1999); Gabriel L. Negretto and José Antonio Aguilar-Rivera, "Rethinking the Legacy of the Liberal State in Latin America: The Cases of Argentina (1853–1916) and Mexico (1857–1910)," *Journal of Latin American Studies* 32 (2000): 361–97; Gabriel L. Negretto, "Constitution-Making and Institutional Design: Distributing Power Between Government and Opposition in Three Argentine Constitutions (1853–60, 1949, 1994)" (Ph.D. dissertation, Columbia University, 2000). An important contribution to the study of institutional mechanisms that supported dictatorial regimes in Latin America is Brian Loveman, *Constitution of Tyranny: Regimes of Exception in Latin America* (Pittsburgh, PA, 1993). On the problem of learning and political stability, see Frank Safford, "Politics, Ideology, and Society in Post-Independence Spanish America," in Leslie Bethell, ed., *The Cambridge History of Latin America*, vol. 3 (Cambridge, 1985). Examinations of the intellectual and political actors in the framing of liberal constitutionalism and reforms are Charles A. Hale, *Mexican Liberalism in the Age of Mora, 1821–1853* (New Haven, CT, 1968), and *The Transformation of Liberalism in Late Nineteenth-Century* (Princeton, NJ, 1989); Richard N. Sinkin, *The Mexican Reform, 1855–1876: A Study in Liberal Nation-Building* (Austin, TX, 1979); and Tortcuato S. Di Tella, *National Popular Politics in Early Independent Mexico, 1820–1847* (Albuquerque, NM, 1996).

Surveys, synthesis, and analysis of Latin American constitutions are in William W. Pierson and Federico G. Gil, *Governments of Latin America* (New York, 1957); Jonathan Hartlyn and Arturo Valenzuela, "Democracy in Latin America since 1930," in Leslie Bethell, ed., *The Cambridge History of Latin America*, vol. 4 (Cambridge, 1994), 99–162; and J. Lloyd Mecham, "Latin American Constitutions, Nominal and Real," *Journal of Politics* 21, 2 (May 1959): 258–75. Valuable summaries of national constitutional histories are found in articles by country under the subtitle "Constitutions" in Barbara Tenebaum, ed., *Encyclopedia of Latin American History and Culture*, 5 vols. (New York, 1996). An accessible source of primary constitutional documents for each Spanish American country is the Web site of the Biblioteca Virtual Miguel de Cervantes, "Constituciones hispanoamericanas," *http://cervantesvirtual.com/portal/constituciones/constituciones.html.* The literature on the constitutional histories in Latin America is more extensive than can be covered here. Works that were of specific value to this chapter include José Pareja Paz-Soldan, *Las constituciones del Peru* (Madrid, 1954); Ramiro Borja y Borja, *Las constituciones del Ecuador* (Madrid, 1951); Hernan G. Peralta, *Las constituciones de Costa Rica* (Instituto de Estudios Políticos, 1962); Ricardo Gallardo, *Las constituciones de El Salvador*, 2 vols. (Madrid, 1961); Jorge Mario García Laguardia, *La defensa de la constitución* (Universidad de San Carlos de Guatemala, 1983); Jorge Mario García Laguardia, *La reforma liberal en Guatemala: Vida política y orden constitucional* (Mexico City, 1980); Luis Mariñas Otero, *Las constituciones de Honduras* (Madrid, 1962); Antonio Esquiva Gómez, *Las constituciones políticas y sus reformas en la historia de Nicaragua*, 2 vols. (Editorial IHNCA(UCA), 2000).

Theories of public choice and positive political economy have emphasized the significance of centralism or federalism. For theoretical perspectives, a useful general survey is Robert P. Inman and Daniel L. Rubinfeld, "The Political Economy of Federalism," in Dennis Mueller, ed., *Perspective on Public Choice: A Handbook* (Cambridge, 1997), 73–105; William Riker, *Federalism: Origin, Operation, Significance* (Boston, 1964); Yingyi Qian and Barry R. Weingast, "Federalism as a Commitment to Preserving Market Incentives," *Journal of Economic Perspectives* 11 (1997): 83–92; and Weingast, "Economic Role of Political Institutions" (cited previously). An insightful historical analysis of the controversy over federalism in postrevolutionary Argentina is Mirón Burgín, *Economic Aspects of Argentine Federalism, 1820–1852* (Cambridge, MA, 1946). Other studies of federalism in specific countries are found in J. Lloyd Mecham, "The Origins of Federalism in Mexico," *Hispanic American Historical Review* 18, 2 (1938), 164–182; Percy Alvin Martin, "Federalism in Brazil," *Hispanic American Historical Review* 18, 2 (1938), 143–163; Marcello Carmagnani, ed., *Federalismos latinoamericanos: Mexico, Brasil, Argentina* (Mexico, 1993); William R. Summerhill, "Market Intervention in a Backward Economy: Railway Subsidy in Brazil, 1854–1913," *Economic History Review* 51 (1998): 542–68, and "Institutional Determinants of Railroad Subsidy and Regulation in Imperial Brazil, 1866–1934," in *Political Institutions and Economic Growth in Latin America* (cited previously), 21–68.

Indispensable as an introduction to the public policy question of the bureaucracy is Hernando de Soto, *The Other Path* (New York, 1989). Two valuable surveys of the economics and institutionalist theoretical literature are Terry M. Moe, "The Positive Theory of Public Bureaucracy," and Ronald Wintrobe, "Modern Bureaucratic Theory," in Dennis C. Mueller, ed., *Perspectives on Public Choice: A Handbook* (Cambridge, 1997), 429–54. Important contributions on its application to Latin American bureaucracies are found in Barbara Geddes, "Building 'State' Autonomy in Brazil, 1930–64," *Comparative Politics* 22, 1 (January 1990): 217–35; and *Politician's Dilemma: Building State Capacity in Latin America* (Berkeley, CA, 1994). On the role of twentieth-century corporatism and bureaucracy, see Jeffrey L. Bortz, "The Legal and Contractual Limits to Private Property Rights in Mexican Industry During the Revolution," and Aurora Gómez Galvarriato, "Measuring the Impact of Institutional Change in Capital-Labor Relations in the Mexican Textile Industry, 1900–1930," both in Jeffrey L. Bortz and Stephen Haber, eds., *The Mexican Economy* (cited previously), 255–88 and 289–323; and Auroran Gómez Galvarriato, "The Impact of Revolution: Business and Labor in the Mexican Textile Industry, Orizaba, Veracruz, 1900–1930 (Ph.D. dissertation, Harvard University, 1999). For examinations of corporatism in international relations, see Robert H. Bates, *Open-Economy Politics: The Political Economy of the World Coffee Trade* (Princeton, NJ, 1997); and Alan Dye and Richard Sicotte, "How Did Brinkmanship Save Chadbourne?: Credibility and the International Sugar Agreement of 1931,"

Explorations in Economic History (forthcoming, 2005). Charles A. Hale, "Political Ideas and Ideologies in Latin America, 1870–1930," in Leslie Bethell, ed., *Ideas and Ideologies in Twentieth Century Latin America* (Cambridge, 1996), 133–206, analyzes the ideological basis of twentieth-century corporatism. Compare and contrast with Joseph L. Love, "Economic Ideas in Latin America since 1930," 207–70, in the same volume. A valuable essay of significance to the question of bureaucracy and its significance to the middle classes is Michael F. Jiménez, "Elision of the Middle Classes and Beyond: History, Politics, and Development Studies in Latin America's 'Short Twentieth Century,'" in *Colonial Legacies* (cited previously), 207–28.

On the history of the judiciary, see Eduardo Zimmermann, ed., *Judicial Institutions in Nineteenth-Century Latin America* (London, 1999), especially Zimmermann, "The Education of Lawyers and Judges in Argentina's *Organización Nacional*"; Linda Arnold, "Privileged Justice? The *Fuero Militar* in Early National Mexico"; and Osvaldo Barreneche, "Criminal Justice and State Formation in Early Nineteenth-Century Buenos Aires." Related works are Frank Safford, *The Ideal of the Practical: Colombia's Struggles to Train a Technical Elite* (Austin, TX, 1978), and Victor M. Uribe Uran, *Honorable Lives: Lawyers, Family, and Politics in Colombia, 1780–1850* (Pittsburgh, PA, 2000). Theoretical explanations of occurrence or nonoccurrence of judicial independence are in William M. Landes and Richard A. Posner, "The Independent Judiciary in an Interest-Group Perspective," *Journal of Law and Economics* 18, 3 (1975): 875–901; J. Mark Ramseyer, "The Puzzling (In)Dependence of Courts: A Comparative Approach," *Journal of Legal Studies* 23, 2 (1994): 721–47; and Matthew C. Stephenson, "'When the Devil Turns . . .': The Political Foundations of Independent Judicial Review," *Journal of Legal Studies* 32, 1 (2003): 59–89. Other provocative analyses of the significance of judicial institutions in Argentine political economy are Matías Iaryczower, Pablo Spiller, and Mariano Tommasi, "Judicial Independence in Unstable Environments, Argentina 1935–1998," *American Journal of Political Science* 46.4 (2002), pp. 669–716; and Lee Alston and Andrés Gallo, "The Erosion of Limited Government: Argentina 1930–1947" (SSRN Working Paper, June 2003).

On the question of the civil law tradition in Latin American political economy, indispensable is the short, insightful book by John Henry Merryman, *The Civil Law Tradition: An Introduction to the Legal Systems of Western Europe and Latin America* (Stanford, CA, 1969). Analysis of the persistent institutional constraints from the absolutist Spanish legal tradition is in John H. Coatsworth and Gabriel Tortella Casares, "Institutions and Long-Run Economic Performance in Mexico and Spain, 1800–2000" (David Rockefeller Center for Latin American Studies, Working Papers on Latin America, No. 02/03-1). George M. Armstrong, Jr., *Law and Market Society in Mexico* (New York, 1989) has assembled a detailed examination of the evolution and influence of Spanish colonial legal tradition on Mexican society, which reaches different conclusions but complements Coatsworth and Tortella.

Table 5.2 in the chapter was constructed using a valuable reference series for the historical study of Latin American law and legal history; see Edwin M. Borchard, *Guide to the Law and Legal Literature of Argentina, Brazil and Chile* (Washington, 1917); Edward Schuster, *Guide to Law and Legal Literature of Central American*

Republics (New York, 1937); Richard C. Backus and Phanor J. Eder, *A Guide to the Law and Legal Literature of Colombia* (Washington, DC, 1943); Crawford M. Bishop and Anyda Marchant, *A Guide to the Law and Legal Literature of Cuba, the Dominican Republic and Haiti* (Washington, DC, 1944); John T. Vance and Helen L. Clagett, *A Guide to the Law and Legal Literature of Mexico* (Washington, DC, 1945).

On the land question and the relationships among property rights in land, violence, and social justice, William Glade, *The Latin American Economies* (cited previously) gives a valuable overview. Friedrich Katz, ed., *Riots, Rebellion, and Revolution: Rural Social Conflict in Mexico* (Princeton, NJ, 1988) is a rich collection of essays focusing on the question of conflicts over land between indigenous communities and creoles. In particular, see John H. Coatsworth's contribution, "Patterns of Rural Rebellion in Latin America: Mexico in Comparative Perspective," which surveys the history and literature on agrarian conflict and violence over land. For a comparison of violence and seizures of land in Mexico before and after Porfirio Díaz, see John H. Coatsworth, "Railroads, Landholding, and Agrarian Protest in the Early Porfiriato," *Hispanic American Historical Review* 54, 1 (1974): 48–71, which is one of the earliest and highly original applications of the new institutional economics to Latin America. Of value for understanding the problems of making effective claims to public lands is Robert Holden, *Mexico and the Survey of Public Lands: The Management of Modernization 1876–1911* (DeKalb, IL, 1994). Among the large literature on Mexican land reforms, see especially Jesús Silva Herzog, *El agrarismo mexicano y la reforma agraria* (Mexico City, 1959). On the question of property rights in land after the transfer of Mexican California to the United States in 1848, see Karen Clay, "Property Rights and Institutions: Congress and the California Land Act of 1851," *Journal of Economic History* 59, 1 (1999): 122–42, and Karen Clay and Werner Troesken, "Squatting and the Settlement of the United States: New Evidence from Post-Gold Rush California," *Advances in Agricultural Economic History* 1 (2000): 207–34.

An interesting contrast with Mexican rural conflict is found in the Bolivian question, for which the best analysis is Herbert S. Klein, *Haciendas and 'Ayllus': Rural Society in the Bolivian Andes in the Eighteenth and Nineteenth Centuries* (Stanford, CA, 1993). Several excellent studies of the Central American countries focus on the land questions in relation to the indigenous agrarian institutions. See especially Hector Lindo-Fuentes, *Weak Foundations: The Economy of El Salvador in the Nineteenth Century* (Berkeley, CA, 1990); David McCreery, *Rural Guatemala 1760–1940* (Stanford, CA, 1994); and Paige, *Coffee and Power* (cited previously). A series of monographs by George McCutchen McBride, *The Agrarian Indian Communities of Highland Bolivia* (1921); *The Land Systems of Mexico* (New York, 1923); and *Chile: Land and Society* (1936), offer valuable explanations of the legal and customary frameworks of national "land systems," which offer particularly valuable insights into the evolution and functioning of customary communal property rights.

An analysis of the evolution of rural unrest and land reform in Colombia is Albert O. Hirschman, "Land Use and Land Reform in Colombia," in *Journeys Toward Progress* (Garden City, NY, 1965). James T. Parsons, *Antiqueño Colonization in Western Colombia* (Berkeley, CA, 1968) is the main work documenting the relatively egalitarian Antioqueño settlement and landholding patterns. Of related interest are Marco Palacios, *Coffee in Colombia 1850–1970: An Economic, Social and Political History* (Cambridge, 1980), and José Antonio Ocampo, *Colombia y la economía mundial, 1830–1910* (Mexico City, 1984).

On land reform, legal disputes, and violence in Brazil, see Lee J. Alston, Gary D. Libecap, and Bernardo Mueller, *Titles, Conflict and Land Use: The Development of Property Rights and Land Reform on the Brazilian Amazon Frontier* (Ann Arbor, MI, 1999), and "Property Rights and Land Conflict: A Comparison of Settlement of the U.S. Western and Brazilian Amazon Frontiers," in *Latin America and the World Economy Since 1800* (cited previously), 24–84, which gives a comparative analysis of ambiguities in property rights in land in the twentieth century. Bernardo Mueller, "The Economic History, Political Economy and Frontier Settlement of Land in Brazil" (cited previously) examines the historical roots of differences in the United States relative to Brazilian treatment of property rights in land. A related work is Warren Dean, "Latifundia and Land Policy in Nineteenth Century Brazil," *Hispanic American Historical Review* 51 (November 1971): 602–25.

On the evolution of land privatization in Argentina, see Miguel Angel Cárcano, *Evolución histórica del régimen de la tierra públic, 1810–1916* (Buenos Aires, 1917). Roberto Cortés Conde, *El progreso argentino: 1880–1914* (Buenos Aires, 1979); Samuel Amaral, *The Rise of Capitalism on the Pampas* (Cambridge, 1997); Hilda Sábato, *Agrarian Capitalism and the World Market: Buenos Aires in the Pastoral Age, 1840–1890* (Albuquerque, NM, 1990); and Alan M. Taylor, "*Latifundia* as Malefactor in Economic Development? Scale, Tenancy, and Agriculture on the Pampas, 1880–1914," *Research in Economic History* 17 (1997): 261–300, address the question of land concentration and the development of the land market in Argentina. Comparative analyses of Argentina and Canada are Jeremy Adelman, *Frontier Development: Land, Labour, and Capital on the Wheatlands of Argentina and Canada 1890–1914* (Oxford, 1994); "The Social Bases of Technical Change: Mechanization of the Wheatlands of Argentina and Canada, 1890–1914," *Comparative Studies in Society and History* 34, 2 (1992): 271–300; Carl Solberg, *The Prairies and the Pampas: Agrarian Policy in Canada and Argentina* (Stanford, 1987); and D. C. M. Platt and Guido Di Tella, eds., *Argentina, Australia, and Canada: Studies in Comparative Development, 1870–1965* (London, 1985). On the weakness of fiscal and monetary institutions, see Roberto Cortés Conde and George T. McCandless, "Argentina: From Colony to Nation: Fiscal and Monetary Experience of the Eighteenth and Nineteenth Centuries," in Michael D. Bordo and Roberto Cortés Conde, eds., *Transferring Wealth and Power from the Old to the New World: Monetary and Fiscal Institutions in the 17th Through the 19th Centuries* (Cambridge, 2001), 378–413; and Gerardo della Paolera and Alan M. Taylor, *Straining at the Anchor: The Argentine Currency Board and the Search for Macroeconomic Stability, 1880–1935* (Chicago, 2001).

On the Cuban sugar industry and contracts with cane growers, see Alan Dye, *Cuban Sugar in the Age of Mass Production: Technology and the Sugar Central, 1899–1929* (Stanford, CA, 1998); "Why Did Cuban Cane Growers Lose Autonomy? 1889–1929, in *Latin America and the World Economy* (cited previously), 323–46; "Avoiding Holdup: Asset Specificity and Technical Change in the Cuban Sugar Industry, 1899–1929," *Journal of Economic History* 54 (1994): 628–52; and Alan

Dye and Richard Sicotte, "The U.S. Sugar Program and the Cuban Revolution" (Barnard College Working Paper, 2003). Also, see Antonio Santamaría García, *Sin azúcar no hay país: La industria azucarera y la economía cubana (1919–1939)* (Seville, 2001), and Oscar Zanetti and Alejandro García, *United Fruit Company: Un caso del dominio imperialista en Cuba* (Havana, 1976). For an alternative analysis, see Ramiro Guerra y Sánchez, *Azúcar y población en las Antillas*, 2nd ed. (Havana, 1944).

The new institutionalist literature on credit markets and banking has focused mostly on Mexico and Brazil. Stephen H. Haber, "Financial Markets and Industrial Development: A Comparative Study of Governmental Regulation, Financial Innovation, and Industrial Structure in Brazil and Mexico, 1840–1930," in *How Latin America Fell Behind* (cited previously), 146–78; and "Industrial Concentration and the Capital Markets: A Comparative Study of Brazil, Mexico, and the United States, 1830–1930," *Journal of Economic History* 51, 3 (1991): 559–80, compare Mexico and Brazil and benchmark them against institutional change in early U.S. banking. For examinations of the governance of banking in Mexico, see Noel Maurer, *The Power and the Money: The Mexican Financial System, 1876–1932* (Stanford, 2003); Maurer, "The Internal Consequence of External Credibility: Banking Regulation and Banking Performance in Porfirian Mexico," and Maurer and Stephen Haber, "Institutional Change and Economic Growth: Banks, Financial Markets, and Mexican Industrialization, 1878–1913," both in *The Mexican Economy* (cited previously), 50–92 and 23–49; Carlos Marichal, "Obstacles to the Development of Capital Markets in Nineteenth-Century Mexico," in *How Latin America Fell Behind* (cited previously), 118–45; and Noel Maurer and Tridib Sharma, "Enforcing Property Rights Through Reputation: Mexico's Early Industrialization, 1878–1913," *Journal of Economic History* 61, 4 (2001): 950–73. For valuable examinations of lending in traditional and modern mortgage markets and in extended kinship networks, see Paulo Riguzzi, "The Legal System, Institutional Change, and Financial Regulation in Mexico, 1870–1910: Mortgage Contracts and Long-Term Credit," in *The Mexican Economy* (cited previously), 120–60; and David W. Walker, *Kinship, Business, and Politics: The Martínez del Río Family in Mexico 1823–1867* (Austin, TX, 1986). For Brazil, see Gail D. Triner, *Banking and Economic Development: Brazil, 1889–1930* (New York, 2000); and Stephen Haber, "The Efficiency Consequences of Institutional Change: Financial Market Regulation and Industrial Productivity Growth in Brazil, 1866–1934"; and Anne Hanley, "Business Finance and the São Paulo Bolsa, 1886–1917," both in *Latin America and the World Economy* (cited previously), 275–322 and 115–38. For Peru, see Alfonso W. Quiroz, *Domestic and Foreign Finance in Modern Peru, 1850–1950* (Pittsburgh, PA, 1993).

CHAPTER 6 (ROBERTO CORTÉS CONDE)

There is no general work dealing in a comprehensive way with the fiscal and monetary regimes of the Latin American countries in the long twentieth century. Only Victor Bulmer-Thomas's *The Economic History of Latin America Since*

Independence, 2nd ed. (New York, 2003) deals with fiscal and monetary policies in several chapters. Although it is a work of a general nature, it goes quite deeply into this topic throughout the several periods under analysis, principally during the expansion of the export economies and the era of industrialization with state intervention. It provides a necessary and useful introduction for those interested in the subject.

Needless to say, general works on the evolution of Latin American economies do refer to the fiscal and monetary policies, but from a more general macroeconomic approach. Among them, we may mention the most recent one by Rosemary Thorp, *Progress, Poverty and Exclusion* (Washington, DC, 1998), the chapters related to the various countries in Enrique Cárdenas, José Antonio Ocampo, and Rosemary Thorp, eds., *An Economic History of Twentieth Century Latin America* (London, 2000), and some of the country chapters in Roberto Cortés Conde and Shane Hunt, eds., *The Latin American Economies* (New York, 1985). References can also be found in Reinhardt Liehr, *The Public Debt in Latin America in Historical Perspective* (Madrid, 1995). Finally, some specific issues related to fiscal problems such as the Latin American debt are dealt with in Carlos Marichal, *Historia de la Deuda Externa de América Latina* (Madrid, 1988).

Country Studies

The published materials on fiscal and monetary regimes of individual Latin American countries are quite uneven. Those devoted to monetary and banking regimes are more numerous, whereas those dealing with fiscal institutions are few and only exist as parts of other studies. In spite of the fact that both aspects were interrelated because of the governments' repeated use of money issue as a source of financing, monetary and banking questions seem to have been more interesting than fiscal ones for contemporary businessmen, and as a result, more studies have been devoted to monetary and banking issues. Besides, there are not many works dealing jointly with both aspects.

MEXICO

Although it covers a period beyond that addressed by this chapter, the work by Marcelo Carmagnani, *Estado y Mercado. La Economía Pública del Liberalismo Mexicano, 1850–1911* (Mexico City, 1994), which extends to the end of the Porfiriato, provides a detailed analysis of the preparation of the budget, taking into consideration the political and economic aspects involved, and comparing the revenue and expenditure budgeted with what actually happened. It provides statistical information on expenditure and revenue at a disaggregated level based on primary sources, which is very valuable for those interested in analyzing the subject on the basis of the data contained in the Annual Reports of the Secretariat of Finance and Public Credit for the 1867/68–1910/11 period and other official sources. Upon comparing this information with other sources, in particular with the *Historical Statistics of Mexico*, differences were detected in some periods. The fact that

Carmagnani's work is based on primary and official sources led us to take him as the main reference in all cases where it was possible.

The work by James W. Wilkie, *La Revolución Mexicana, gasto federal y cambio social* (Mexico City, 1967), includes a valuable collection of data on budgeted and realized expenditure rearranged by the author by replacing the official classifications used in the administrative sources with another set of categories organized by expenditure targets, with the aim of revealing the policies' possible aims in each case, and how these could vary from the budgeted sums to the actual expenditures. This modern classification, perhaps the most useful aspect of his work, was criticized for implying that the government was pursuing the same goals at the end of the nineteenth and the beginning of the twentieth century as after World War II.

On the Porfiriato, we find Fernando Rosenweig's articles on currency in Daniel Cosio Villegas, ed., *Historia Moderna de México* (Mexico City, 1965), and the studies on banking by Leanor Ludlow and Carlos Marichal, eds., *La Banca en México 1820–1920* (Mexico City, 1998). See also the works on the banking system by Charles Conant, *The Banking System of México* (Washington, DC, 1910), and the doctoral thesis on banks of issue by Mónica Gómez, "Un Sistema Bancario con Emisión de Billetes por Empresarios Privados: El Comportamiento del Banco Nacional de México en el Proceso de Creación de Dinero. México 1884–1910" (Ph.D. dissertation, El Colegio de México, 2001), which is an indispensable tool to learn about an important case of a bank of issue in a country with a metallic standard.

Information on the revolutionary period is very scarce because of the fact that the state was undergoing a crisis and each revolutionary leader had his own center of power. A relevant work is that by Estela Zabala, "Los Impuestos y los Problemas Financieros de los Primeros Años de la Revolución," *Historia Mexicana* 31, 3 (1982), and also the article by Francisco Rodríguez Garza, "La reforma fiscal Federal en el México de entre guerra," in *Tiempo y Devenir en la Historia Económica de México* (Mexico City, 2002), and that by Luis Aboites Aguilar, "Imposición directa, combate a la anarquía y cambios en la relación federación-estados. Una caracterización general de los impuestos internos en México 1920–1950" (Mexico City, 2001). These last two works, showing the special characteristics of the postrevolutionary tax system in Mexico, are key to understanding the evolution of the fiscal regime and the debate on fiscal powers, especially the old opposition between centralizing trends and those granting more power to the states. This tension lasted for a long time, as evidenced in the struggle to abolish the *alcabalas* (tariffs imposed by states on interstate commerce) and the problems of double taxation, anarchy in the tax regime, and the central government's share of the revenues the states collected.

On monetary regimes, the work by Edwin Walter Kemmerer is essential; E. W. Kemmerer, *Inflation and Revolution. The Mexican Experience 1912–1917* (Princeton, NJ, 1940). Kemmerer was a professor at Princeton and a renowned advisor in the Andean countries, where he contributed to the creation of central banks. His work deals with the different revolutionary money issues and inflation. Although aimed at a different purpose, there are useful references also in Emilio Zebadúa, *Banqueros y Revolucionarios. La Soberanía Financiera de México, 1914–1929* (Mexico City, 1994).

The most comprehensive work on monetary policy for most of the twentieth century is the Annual Report by the Banco de México. See also *Cincuenta Años de Banca Central. Ensayos Conmemorativos 1925–1975* (Mexico City, 1976), published for the fiftieth anniversary of the Bank, especially the chapters by Ernesto Fernández Hurtado, "Reflexiones sobre aspectos fundamentales de la Banca Central en México," and by Manuel Cavazos Lerma, "Cincuenta años de Política Monetaria," which analyze the several functions the bank performed, including bank of issue and commercial bank, in addition to specialized Central Bank. Also relevant is the work by Dwight Brothers and Leopoldo Solís, *Evolución Financiera de México* (Mexico City, 1967), with explanations about the reasons why the Bank of Mexico did not fulfill the classic functions of a central bank by using tools such as the interest rate and open-market transactions. This might have been because of the lack of a debt market that forced the bank to regulate reserves and handle credit in a selective way by operating with rediscounts. The authors also show how the Banco de México was subordinate to the Secretariat of Finance, and that fiscal policy relied on financing of government deficits through the financial system.

On the postrevolutionary period, the book by Enrique Cárdenas, *La Hacienda Pública y la Política Económica, 1929–1958* (Mexico City, 1994), is very valuable with its analysis of the behavior of revenue and expenditure and the resulting deficits in relation to the different economic policies pursued in the period under study.

On the stabilizing development period, the article by its main architect, Antonio Ortiz Mena, is still essential; although involved in its implementation, he offers a balanced description of the policy purposes and development in "El Desarrollo Estabilizador," *El Trimestre Económico* 146 (1970).

On the most recent period, and in spite of its subjective criticism, there is a good article by Marcos Chávez, "Las Finanzas Públicas de México, 1970–2000. Crónica del Fracaso de la Política Fiscal" in *Programa de Ciencia, Tecnología y Desarrollo (Procientec)* (Mexico City, 2001).

BRAZIL

The most complete work on the evolution of fiscal variables is that by Raymond Goldsmith, *Desenvolvimento Financeiro sob um Século de Inflaçao* (Brasilia, 1984). He undertook the task of rearranging a number of series and made estimations – of GDP, among others – to show the importance of finance. It is a strictly quantitative work, which does not provide much information about the main institutional facts and economic policies. To complement the study by Goldsmith, a suitable work is Marcelo de Paiva Abreu, ed., *A Ordem do Progresso. Cem anos de política econômica republicana 1889–1989* (Río de Janeiro, 1990), which, although dealing with economic problems of a general nature, makes reference to the fiscal and monetary policies in each of the periods under consideration.

The book by Winston Fritsch, *External Constraints on Economic Policy in Brazil, 1889–1930* (Pittsburgh, PA, 1988), although also dealing with the general aspects of the economic policies from the Old Republic to the 1930 revolution, is the most complete work from the point of view of the description of the successive fiscal and monetary policies applied during that period and the circumstances that led to their implementation. Fritsch challenges the well-known hypothesis that fiscal and monetary policies were the result of the pressure exerted by the hegemonic interests of the São Paulo coffee sector through polices aimed at supporting the coffee industry financed by debt or inflation and the continuous depreciation of the *milreís*. He also opposes the contrary hypothesis that claims that Brazilian administrations had a strong orthodox bias. Fritsch reveals a more complex situation in which Brazil is affected by exogenous circumstances, such as the evolution of the coffee harvest and changing world demand and the fluctuations in the capital markets. He analyzes how policies responded to a set of external and internal circumstances, including the interests of all the states (not only São Paulo), the interests of foreign creditors to whom the government resorted for financing with the aim of withholding exports, and who, in turn, exerted pressure for the adoption of austere fiscal and monetary stability measures that limited government freedom. The work covers the evolution of such policies from the big monetary expansion with a plurality of banks of issue in 1891 through the orthodox reaction of adjustment and stabilization, the adoption of the gold standard in 1906 with a Conversion Board, and its suspension during World War I until its return in 1926.

The article by André Lara Resende, "Estabilização e reforma 1964–1967," in *A Ordem do Progreso* (cited previously) contains a very good description of the 1964 reforms (The Government Economic Action Plan, "PAEG"), and compares them with the former stabilization plans, including President Goulart's Triennial Plan formulated by Celso Furtado. It deals with monetary and fiscal policies, and wage and salary policy and its consequences for prices and GDP growth, pointing out that these policies were conditioned to a great extent by difficulties in the balance of payments, and concluding that – contrary to what is often said – the program was not an orthodox one.

As regards the monetary regime, it is indispensable to consult Carlos Peláez y Wilson Suzigan, *Historia Monetaria do Brasil* (Brasilia, 1976), the best monetary history of a Latin American country published to this date. It includes monetary series and analyzes the variables determining supply, prices, and GDP from the nineteenth century to the 1970s. It provides a detailed and sound analysis of the different monetary policies on the basis of the empirical evidence and monetary theory, evaluating the opinion of "metallists" (orthodox) and those in favor of depreciation, with the understanding that there was an oscillation from one view to the other, and that it was orthodox tendencies that prevailed because of the need for external financing. It also considers the financial debates centering on World War II and the 1930 crisis.

The book by Steven Topik, *The Political Economy of the Brazilian State: 1889– 1930* (Austin, TX, 1987), which covers the Empire's final period to the 1930 crisis, provides a detailed analysis of fiscal and monetary policies and challenges the thesis that such policies had always been shaped by the government's dependence on the coffee sector, showing that the state had a relative autonomy and that the pressure exerted by foreign creditors also had an important role; whereas the coffee sector was striving for a depreciation of the local currency, foreign creditors supported orthodox measures, which prevailed every time the Brazilian government was in need of credit. Finally, it claims that the enlargement of the state was not the result of the collapse of the export economy but the product of its very expansion.

Thomas Skidmore, *The Politics of Military Rule in Brazil 1964–85* (London, 1998) illuminates the sociopolitical framework within which economic decisions were made and implemented.

CHILE

The article by José Jofré, Rolf Luders, and Gert Wagner, "Economía Chilena 1810–1995. Cuentas Fiscales," *Pontificia Universidad Católica de Chile, Instituto de Economía, Documento de Trabajo* 188 (2000), has series for fiscal revenue and expenditure for the 1810–1995 period; the series are treated in detail and very conscientiously, with an excellent methodological handling of the data. The article by Gabriel Palma, "Trying to Tax and Spend Oneself out of the Dutch Disease: The Chilean Economy from the War of the Pacific to the Great Depression," in *An Economic History of Twentieth-Century Latin America* (cited previously), 234–56, provides a new explanation of the fiscal policy in the era of the nitrate expansion and claims that the expenditure on infrastructure and education served to prevent an overvaluation of money (Dutch disease).

Guillermo Subercasseaux, *El Sistema Monetario y la Organización Bancaria de Chile* (Santiago de Chile, 1920), is the best known work on banking regimes in Chile from colonial times to the first years of the twentieth century. In turn, the work by Frank Whitson Fetter, "Monetary Inflation in Chile" (Princeton, NJ, 1931) – especially after the attention given to it by Albert Hirschman in *Journeys Toward Progress: Studies of Economic Policymaking in Latin America* (Buenos Aires, 1963) – is one of the best explanations of inflation in Chile, emphasizing the basis of political and social interests (those of the landed gentry, exporters who collected revenue in hard currency and paid in depreciated local currency). This was a recurrent argument in the debate about inflation in Latin America in the 1970s. The chapter by Paul W. Drake (1989) on "La Creación de los Bancos Centrales en los Países Andinos," in Pedro Tedde and Carlos Marichal, eds., *La Formación de los Bancos Centrales en España y América Latina; siglos XIX y XX* (Madrid, 1994) about the Kemmerer mission, which also covers other Andean countries, deals with the projects for the creation of central banks. As regards Chile's monetary statistics, two works of great use to us may be mentioned: Marcos Mamalakis, *Historical Statistics of Chile: Money, Prices and Credit Services* (Westport, 1983), and Juan Braun et al., "Economía Chilena 1810–1995. Estadísticas Históricas," in *Pontificia Universidad Católica de Chile, Instituto de Economía, Documento de Trabajo* 187 (2000), both providing excellent treatment of the series. The work by Patricio Meller, *Un siglo de política económica chilena: 1890–1990* (Santiago, 1996), also provides references on fiscal policies for several periods in the long twentieth century.

ARGENTINA

The works on monetary and banking questions in Argentina are more complete and numerous than those on the fiscal regimes. There are references to the latter in the articles published in Javier Ortiz's *Nueva Historia de la Nación Argentina*

(Buenos Aires, 2000) and in the chapter by Roberto Cortés Conde, "The Vicis-situdes of an Exporting Economy: Argentina (1875–1930)," in *An Economic His-tory of Twentieth-Century Latin America* (cited previously); and in Roberto Cortés Conde, "Finanzas Públicas, Moneda y Bancos (1810–1899)," in *Nueva Historia de la Nación Argentina* (Buenos Aires, 2000). See also the excellent book by Pablo Gerchunoff and Lucas Llach, *El Ciclo de la Ilusión y el Desencanto: Un Siglo de Políticas Económicas Argentinas* (Buenos Aires, 1998). There is also an important article on fiscal issues in Federico Herschel and Samuel Itzcovich, "Fiscal Policy in Argentina," *Ciclos* 9 (1969).

For later periods, we may mention Atilio Elizagaray, "Taxes, Expenditures and Government Economic Surplus in Argentina (1946–55)" (Documento de Trabajo 1984, Instituto Torcuato Di Tella – Centro de Investigaciones Económicas, Buenos Aires); Ricardo López Murphy, Jorge Avila, and Roberto Zorgno, "Crec-imiento Económico, Políticas Públicas y Reforma Fiscal" (Documento de Trabajo 1988, 6ta. Convención de Bancos Privados Nacionales – Asociación de Bancos Argentinos [ADEBA], Buenos Aires); and Cristina Vargas de Flood and María Marcela Harriague, "El Gasto Público Consolidado" (Documento de Trabajo 1993, Secretaría de Programación Económica, Ministerio de Economía y Obras y Servicios Públicos).

With reference to statistical information, the oldest data were derived from the annual Yearly Statistical Reports and from the Statistical Excerpt of 1915, published by the General Directorate of Statistics of the Nation (belonging to the Ministry of Economy). The *Anuario Geográfico Argentino* (Buenos Aires, 1942) is also a good source of data. Later on, data were collected from the series published by the Comision Económica Para América Latina on revenue and expenditure, which were transcribed by Instituto de Estudios Económicos de la Realidad Latino Americano, and disaggregated tax information from the Dirección General Impositiva.

We can also mention the valuable work on monetary regimes by Gerardo Della Paolera and Javier Ortiz, "Money, Financial Intermediation and the Level of Activ-ity in 110 Years of Argentine Economic History," Documento de Trabajo Nro. 36, (Universidad Torcuato Di Tella, Buenos Aires, 1995); reference should also be made to Marie-Ange Véganzonès and Carlos Winograd, *Argentina en el Siglo XX : Crónica de un Crecimiento Anunciado* (Paris, 1997), and to Pablo Gerchunoff and Lucas Llach (cited earlier).

On monetary and banking issues, the following were very useful: Aldo Arnaudo, *Cincuenta Años de Política Financiera Argentina: 1934–1983* (Buenos Aires, 1987) is an essential work to understand the main aspects of monetary policies in Argentina. Rafael Olarra Jiménez, *Evolución Monetaria Argentina* (Buenos Aires, 1968), pro-vides a summary of events in that field. Adolfo Diz, "La experiencia monetaria y bancaria de la década del 70" (Valores en la sociedad industrial, Setiembre 1994 – AÑO XII / Nro.30, Centro de Estudios de la Sociedad Industrial – Universidad Católica Argentina, Buenos Aires), contains a very important thesis on the factors that determine the monetary supply. Raul Prebisch, "La orientación del crédito en el sistema financiero durante la vigencia de efectivos mínimos fraccionarios," in *El Banco Central de la República Argentina en su 50 aniversario: 1935–1985* (Buenos Aires, 1986), explains some of the goals of monetary policies. On specific issues, such as public debt and inflation, we may mention Domingo Cavallo and Angel Peña, "Déficit fiscal, endeudamiento del gobierno y tasa de inflación: Argentina 1940–1982," *Revista Estudios* (Buenos Aires) And for a panorama of the public sector, it is advisable to read Osvaldo Schenone, "Public Sector Behavior in Argentina," in Felipe Larraín and Marcelo Selowsky, *The Public Sector and the Latin American Crisis* (San Francisco, 1991).

CHAPTER 7 (RICHARD SALVUCCI)

There are several indispensable surveys of the period. Foremost is Victor Bulmer-Thomas, *The Economic History of Latin America Since Independence*, 2nd ed. (Cambridge, 2003). For long-term GDP and capital formation estimates, see André A. Hofman, *The Economic Development of Latin America in the Twentieth Century* (Cheltenham, UK, 2000). A valuable addition to the literature on "export-led growth" that draws a number of revisionist conclusions is Enrique Cárdenas, José Antonio Ocampo, and Rosemary Thorp, eds., *An Economic History of Twentieth-Century Latin America: The Export Age* (Hampshire, UK, 2000). Still worthwhile are Roberto Cortés Conde and Shane J. Hunt, eds., *The Latin American Economies. Growth and the Export Sector, 1880–1930* (New York, 1985), and Cortés Conde's classic, *The First Stages of Modernization in Latin America* (New York, 1974). Rory Miller, *Britain and Latin America in the Nineteenth and Twentieth Centuries* (London, 1993) contains a valuable discussion of British trade with Latin America in the period under consideration.

The literature on the gold standard in Latin America has grown considerably in recent years. One most often thinks of Alec Ford's pioneering *The Gold Standard 1880–1914: Britain and Argentina* (Oxford, 1962), but there has been much of value published since. Ford himself reprised and amplified his work in "International Financial Policy and the Gold Standard, 1870–1914," in *The Cambridge Economic History of Europe*, vol. 8 (Cambridge, 1989). But for detailed criticism, see Roberto Cortés Conde, *La economía Argentina en el largo plazo* (Buenos Aires, 1997), or Barry Eichengreen, "The Gold Standard Since Alec Ford," in S. N. Broadberry and N. F. R. Crafts, eds., *Britain in the International Economy* (Cambridge, 1992). There is also the important contribution of Michael Bordo (with Anna J. Schwartz), "The Operation of the Specie Standard: Evidence for Core and Peripheral Countries, 1880–1990," in Michael D. Bordo, ed., *The Gold Standard and Related Regimes* (Cambridge, 1999), 238–317, and Bordo, "The Gold Standard: The Traditional Approach," in Michael D. Bordo and Anna J. Schwartz, eds., *A Retrospective on the Classical Gold Standard, 1821–1931* (Chicago, 1984), 23–119. Bordo and Eichengreen have also collaborated on an important reconsideration of the gold standard in "The Rise and Fall of a Barbarous Relic: The Role of Gold in the International Monetary System," in Guillermo A. Calvo, Rudi Dornbusch, and Maurice Obstfeld, eds., *Money, Capital Mobility and Trade. Essays in Honor of Robert Mundell* (Cambridge, MA, 2001), 53–121. A recent monograph emphasizing the monetary approach to the balance of payments is Gerardo della Paolera and

Alan M. Taylor, *Straining at the Anchor. The Argentine Currency Board and the Search for Macroeconomic Stability, 1880–1935* (Chicago, 2001). A provocative paper with implications for Latin America is Jeffrey B. Nugent, "Exchange-Rate Movements and Economic Development in the Late Nineteenth Century," *The Journal of Political Economy* 81, 5 (1973): 1110–35. Of equal interest are Albert Fishlow, "Market Forces or Group Interests: Inconvertible Currency in Pre-1914 Latin America" (working paper, Berkeley, CA, 1987); Barry Eichengreen, "The Baring Crisis in a Mexican Mirror" (http://repositories.cdlib.org/iber/cider/C87-084); and Jeffry Frieden, "Monetary Populism in Nineteenth-Century America: An Open Economy Interpretation," *The Journal of Economic History* 57, 2 (1997): 367–95. Also, see Jeffry Frieden and Ernesto Stein, eds., *The Currency Game. Exchange Rate Politics in Latin America* (Washington, DC, 2001). Barry Eichengreen, *The Gold Standard in Theory and History* (New York, 1985), remains an indispensable historical introduction.

Pablo Martin Aceña and Jaime Reis, eds., *Monetary Standards in the Periphery. Paper, Silver, Gold, 1854–1933* (London, 2000), contains specific studies of the gold standard in Brazil (Winston Fritsch and Gustavo H. B. Franco), Chile (Agustín Llona), and Colombia (José Antonio Ocampo). Fritsch deals with the gold standard in greater detail in *External Constraints on Economic Policy in Brazil, 1889–1930* (Pittsburgh, PA, 1988), and in his summary chapter in Marcelo de Paiva Abreu, ed., *A Ordem do progresso. Cem anos de política econômico republicana, 1889–1989* (Rio de Janeiro, 1990). For Peru, see Alfonso W. Quiroz, *Domestic and Foreign Finance in Modern Peru, 1850–1950* (Pittsburgh, PA, 1993). The classic study for Mexico is Joaquín Casasus, *La reforma monetaria en México* (Mexico City, 1905), but it should be supplemented by the modern work of Aldo Mussachio, "Entre el oro y la plata: un estudio de las causas de la adopción del patrón oro en México," (BA thesis, Instituto Tecnológico Autónomo Mexicano, Mexico City, 1998). A useful survey of the Dominican Republic is J. Laurence Laughlin, "Gold and Silver in Santo Domingo," *The Journal of Political Economy* 2, 4 (1894): 536–60. For the peculiarities of the gold standard in Colombia, see José Antonio Ocampo's remarkably comprehensive *Colombia y la economía mundial 1830–1910* (Bogotá, 1984).

Another valuable study that deals with the operation of the gold standard in peripheral economies is Jorge Braga de Macedo, Barry Eichengreen, and Jaime Reis, eds., *Currency Convertibility: The Gold Standard and Beyond* (London, 1996). Also, see the important paper on Spain and Portugal by Agustín Llona in Maria Cristina Marcuzzo, Lawrence H. Officer, and Annalisa Rosselli, eds., *Monetary Standards and Exchange Rates* (London, 1997). Also useful is Michael D. Bordo and Forest Capie, eds., *Monetary Regimes in Transition* (Cambridge, 1993). Finally, it would be difficult to overstate the value of David George Cowen, "A World of Difference: Exchange Rate Regime Choice and Economic Performance in the Interwar Years" (Ph.D. dissertation, The University of Texas at Austin, 1995).

Commercial policy per sé is discussed in a number of places. A valuable comparative study is Marcelo De Paiva Abreu, "Contrasting Histories in the Political Economy of Protectionism: Argentina and Brazil, 1880–1930" (working paper, Rio de Janeiro). For Colombia, see José Antonio Ocampo and Santiago Montenegro, *Crisis mundial, protección e industrialización. Ensayos de historia económica colombiana* (Bogotá, 1984), and William Paul McGreevey's classic, *An Economic History of Colombia, 1845–1930* (Cambridge, 1971). For a superb account of Porfirian Mexico, see Edward Beatty, "Commercial Policy in Porfirian Mexico: The Structure of Protection," in Jeffrey L. Bortz and Stephen Haber, eds., *The Mexican Economy, 1870–1930. Essays on the Economic History of Institutions, Revolution and Growth* (Stanford, CA, 2002), 205–52; and "The Impact of Foreign Trade on the Mexican Economy: Terms of Trade and the Rise of Industry 1880–1923," *Journal of Latin American Studies* 32 (2000): 399–433. Also, see Stephen Haber, *Industry and Underdevelopment. The Industrialization of Mexico, 1890–1940* (Stanford, CA, 1989).

Trade and production statistics are notoriously unreliable, but there have been some major efforts at systematic collection and consideration. For a useful general overview, see Victor Bulmer-Thomas, "British Trade with Latin America in the Nineteenth and Twentieth Centuries" (working paper, London, 1998; available at http://www.peruembassy-uk.com/TraInv/britishtrade.pdf). Among the more important (by country) are Roberto Cortés Conde, "Estimaciones del producto bruto interno de Argentina, 1875–1935" (working paper, Buenos Aires, 1994); Alan Taylor, "Argentina and the World Capital Market: Saving, Investment, and International Capital Mobility in the Twentieth Century," *Journal of Development Economics* 57 (1998): 147–84; Ana María Cerro, "La conducta cíclica de la actividad económica de Argentina en el período 1820–1970" (working paper, Tucumán); Roberto A. Domenech, "Estadísticas de la evolución económica de Argentina, 1913–1984," *Estudios* 9 (1986): 103–84; Nathaniel H. Leff, *Underdevelopment and Development in Brazil*, 2 vols. (1982); Anníbal Villanova Villela and Wilson Suzigan, *Política do governo e crescimento da economia brasilierea, 1889–1945* (Rio de Janeiro, 1975); Claudio L. S. Haddad, *Crescimento do produto real no Brasil, 1900–1947* (Rio de Janeiro, 1978); *Estatísticas históricas do Brasil* (Rio de Janeiro, 1987); Gail D. Triner, *Banking and Economic Development: Brazil, 1889–1930* (New York, 2000); the excellent Web site of the Instituto Brasileiro de Geografia e Estatística (www.ibge.net); Thomas and Ebba Schoonover, "Statistics for an Understanding of Foreign Intrusions into Central America from the 1820s to 1930," *Anuario de Estudios Centroamericanos* 15, 1 (1989): 93–117, 16, 1 (1990): 135–56, and 197, 2 (1991): 77–119; Markos J. Mamalakis, *The Growth and Structure of the Chilean Economy: From Independence to Allende* (New Haven, CT, 1976); Patricio Meller, *Un siglo de economía política chilena (1890–1990)* (Santiago, 1996); Juan Braun et al., "Economía Chilena 1810–1995: Estadísticas Históricas" (working paper, Santiago, 2000), a major statistical source that came to my attention only after this chapter was completed; Sandra Kuntz Ficker, "Nuevas series del comercio exterior de Mexico, 1870–1929," *Revista de Historia Económica* 20, 2 (2002): 213–70, and her "El comercio México-Estados Unidos, 1870–1929: Reconstrucción estadística y tendencias generales," *Mexican Studies/Estudios Mexicanos* 17, 1 (2001): 71–107. For Mexican prices under silver and (on and off) gold, see Aurora Gómez-Galvarriato and Aldo Musacchio, "Un nuevo índice de precios para México, 1886–1929," *El*

Trimestre Económico 67, 1 (2000): 47–91; Bruno Seminario and Arlette Beltrán, *Crecimiento económico en el Perú: 1896–1995. Nuevas evidencias estadísticas* (Lima, 1998); Luis Bértola, *El PBI de Uruguay, 1870–1936, y otras estimaciones* (Montevideo, 1998); Asdrúbal Baptista, *Bases cuantitativas de la economía venezolana, 1830–1995* (Caracas, 1997); D. C. M. Platt, *Latin America and British Trade, 1806–1914* (New York, 1973), primarily for the statistical appendices; and Leandro Prados de la Escosura, "International Comparisons of Real Product, 1820–1990: An Alternative Data Set," *Explorations in Economic History* 37 (2000): 1–41. Angus Maddison, *The World Economy: A Millennial Perspective* (Paris, 2001) provides contemporary data. Some of the early historical data for Latin America, particularly Mexico, are questionable.

The terms of trade controversy has generated a vast literature. An important paper on the income terms of trade is T. Wilson, R. P. Sinha, and J. R. Castree, "The Income Terms of Trade of Developed and Developing Countries," *The Economic Journal* 79 (1969): 813–32. For the net barter terms of trade, see John T. Cuddington and Carlos M. Urzua, "Trends and Cycles in the Net Barter Terms of Trade: A New Approach," *The Economic Journal* 99 (1989): 426–42. Regarding the important issue of volatility in the terms of trade, see Matthias Lutz, "The Effect of Volatility in the Terms of Trade on the Growth of Output: New Evidence," *World Development* 22, 12 (1994), 1959–1975; Parantap Basu and Daryl McLeod, "Terms of Trade Fluctuations and Economic Growth in Developing Countries," *Journal of Development Economics* 37 (1992), 89–110; and Enrique G. Mendoza, "Terms-of-Trade Uncertainty and Economic Growth," *Journal of Development Economics*, 54 (1997), 323–56. But also see Angus Deaton, "Commodity Prices and Growth in Africa," *Journal of Economic Perspectives* 13, 3 (1999): 23–40. The canonical modern study of the terms of trade is Enzo R. Grilli and M. C. Yang, "Primary Commodity Prices, Manufactured Goods Prices, and the Terms of Trade of Developing Countries: What the Long Run Shows," *The World Bank Economic Review* 2 (1988): 1–47. On the entire subject of macroeconomic volatility in Latin America, see *Overcoming Volatility: Economic and Social Progress in Latin America. 1995 Report of the Inter-American Development Bank* (Washington, DC, 1995).

Any consideration of railroads in this period should begin with José Sanz Fernández, ed., *Historia de los ferrocarriles de Iberoamérica (1838–1995)* (Madrid, 1998), which includes an invaluable database on CD-ROM. Colin Lewis, *British Railways in Argentina, 1857–1914. A Case Study of Foreign Investment* (London, 1983) remains very useful. The measurement of social savings for railroads in Latin America has been pioneered by a small band of scholars. The first to appear was John Coatsworth's, "Indispensable Railroads in a Backward Economy: The Case of Mexico," *Journal of Economic History* 39 (1979): 939–60. William Summerhill's "Transport Improvements and Economic Growth in Brazil and Mexico," in Stephen Haber, ed., *How Latin America Fell Behind. Essays on the Economic History of Brazil and Mexico* (Stanford, CA, 1997), 93–117, offered alternative estimates, and Summerhill's work on Brazil is fundamental. See, for instance, "Market Intervention in a Backward Economy: Railway Subsidy in Brazil, 1854–1913," *Economic History Review* 51, 3 (1998): 542–68; and for Argentina, his "Profit and Productivity on Argentine Railroads, 1857–1913" (unpublished paper, Los Angeles). For Colombia, see María Teresa Ramírez, "Los ferrocarriles y su impacto sobre la economía colombiana," *Revista de Historia Económica* 19, 1 (2001). A major revisionist study of railroad building and its local impact in southern Mexico is Theresa Miriam van Hoy, "The Railroad as Public Utility and the Public: Land, Labor and Rail Services in Southern Mexico" (Ph.D. dissertation, The University of Texas at Austin, 2000).

On the general subject of land, labor, and the consolidation of markets in various countries, see the following: Ezequiel Gallo, *La pampa gringa. La colonización agrícola en Santa Fe (1870–1895)* (Buenos Aires, 1984); Carl E. Solberg, *The Prairies and the Pampas. Agrarian Policy in Canada and Argentina, 1880–1930* (Stanford, CA, 1987), and *Immigration and Nationalism. Argentina and Chile, 1890–1914* (Austin, TX, 1970); Simon G. Hanson, *Argentine Meat and the British Market. Chapters in the History of the Argentine Meat Industry* (London, 1938); "Brasil: 500 anos de povoamento" (www1.ibge.gov.br/brasil500/index2.html); Lowell Gudmundson and Héctor Lindo-Fuentes, *Central America, 1821–1871. Liberalism Before Liberal Reform* (Tuscaloosa, AL, 1995); Arnold Bauer, *Chilean Rural Society from the Spanish Conquest to 1930* (Cambridge, 1975); Catherine LeGrand, *Frontier Expansion and Peasant Protest in Colombia, 1830–1936* (Albuquerque, NM, 1986); José Antonio Ocampo, ed., *Historia económica de Colombia* (Bogotá, 1987); J. C. Cambranes, *Coffee and Peasants in Guatemala* (South Woodstock, VT, 1985); Robert H. Holden, *Mexico and the Survey of Public Lands. The Management of Modernization, 1876–1911* (DeKalb, IL, 1994); Roberto Melville, *Crecimiento y rebelión. El desarrollo económico de las haciendas azucareras en Morelos (1880–1910)* (Mexico City, 1979); Manuel Burga, *De la encomienda a la hacienda capitalista. El Valle de Jequetepeque del Siglo XVI al XX* (Lima, 1976); Michael Gonzales, *Plantation Agriculture and Social Control in Northern Peru, 1875–1933* (Austin, TX, 1985); Peter Klarén, *Modernization, Dislocation and Aprismo. Origins of the Peruvian Aprista Party, 1870–1932* (Austin, TX, 1973); and Héctor Lindo-Fuentes, *Weak Foundations. The Economy of El Salvador in the Nineteenth Century* (Berkeley, CA, 1990).

CHAPTER 8 (WILLIAM R. SUMMERHILL)

Few topics receive as much attention from amateur and professional historians alike as do railroads. The amount of relevant source materials available to any investigator can be nearly overwhelming, as many historians can attest. Several types of sources are worth mentioning in a general way because they are too voluminous to even begin to provide much detail. The first is the contemporary periodical press, both local and foreign. Railroad notices garnered ample attention in the newspapers of major Latin American cities. In both Britain and the United States, a press specializing in railroad news and financial reporting appeared in the nineteenth century. With respect to Latin American railways, the U.S. periodicals focused principally on affairs in Mexico, whereas in Britain, the South American railways were the object of frequent reports that today remain of great value to historians. A local specialized railway press emerged in several countries. In Brazil, by way of example, the *Revista de Estradas de Ferro* first appeared in 1885, and *Brasil*

Ferrocarril began publication in the early twentieth century. The *South American Journal and River Plate Mail* circulated widely among the expatriate business community in Latin America and frequently provided coverage of railway questions as well as foreign-owned enterprise more generally. The *Railway Age, Railway Gazette,* and *Railway Times* stand out among the examples of the contemporary overseas English-language railway periodicals that devoted some attention to Latin American railway questions.

The second type of source material that is too extensive to discuss in detail is the pamphlet literature, which was geared mainly toward promoting specific railroad projects. These publications sometimes went the other direction, as grievances of one sort or another, often over rate setting or the route of proposed extensions, gave rise to published jeremiad. Limited in their initial printings and circulation, many such pamphlets survive in major research libraries throughout Latin America, and are valuable both for the information they present on the prospects of a particular railroad that is proposed and for the insight they provide on attitudes and opinions on commercial affairs and the problem of material progress more generally.

An important reference on all Latin American economic questions, including railways and infrastructure more generally, is Roberto Cortés Conde et al., *Latin America: A Guide to Economic History, 1830–1930* (Berkeley, CA, 1977). Examples of articles providing detailed information on the sources available in particular countries include Sandra Kuntz Ficker, "Fuentes para el estudio de los ferrocarriles durante el porfiriato," *América Latina en la Historia Económica: Boletín de Fuentes* 13–14 (January–December 2000): 137–48; and Sonia Pinto Vallejos, "Historia de los ferrocarriles de Chile: Volumenes da carga y cantidad de pasajeros transportados (1901–1929)," *Cuadernos de Historia* 6 (July 1986): 49–66. Evidence, both of a quantitative and qualitative nature, on railway finance and operations is abundant in the serial publications of the railway companies themselves and in government publications dedicated to monitoring railway services. Railway companies, including those owned by governments, commonly reported their operations and financial results to the relevant government ministries. Companies that were listed on stock exchanges also generated reports, on either an annual or semester basis, to their shareholders. Both types of publications carry a wealth of information that has proven indispensable for historical research. In Mexico and Argentina, by way of example, these reports survive in reasonably complete manner. Further, for the British-owned railways in Latin America that sold equity or bonds on the London Stock Exchange, company reports are available from 1880 onward in Guildhall Library, Corporation of London.

By the late nineteenth century, the largest countries were publishing, often on an annual basis, the basic operating and financial figures of their railway systems. Key examples here are Argentina, Brazil, Mexico, and Peru. For Argentina, the national government initiated full annual statistical coverage of the rail sector for 1892 in the *Estadistica de los ferrocarriles en explotación* (Buenos Aires), which it published for decades thereafter. Data also appeared in a variety of reports of both national and provincial governments for earlier years. By the first decade of the twentieth century, the Argentine *Estadistica* volumes further provided retrospective summary figures on railway operations going back to the 1850s. Consistent but incomplete annual coverage of the operations of Brazilian railways, focusing on those lines whose concession were awarded by the central government, first appeared for the year 1898 in *Estatística das estradas de ferro do Brasil* (Rio de Janeiro). The government provided less detailed information, before the appearance of the annual statistical volumes, in the publications of the Ministry of Communications and Public Works. In Mexico, a series of volumes appeared near the end of the nineteenth century that not only initiated regular publishing of railway operating figures but also provided a valuable retrospective going back to the earliest railways: *Reseña histórica y estadística de los ferrocarriles de jurisdicción federal desde Agosto de 1837 hasta Diciembre de 1894* (Mexico City, 1895); *Reseña histórica y estadística de los ferrocarriles de jurisdicción federal, 1895–1899* (Mexico City, 1900); *Reseña histórica y estadística de los ferrocarriles de jurisdicción federal, 1900–1903* (Mexico City, 1905); *Reseña histórica y estadística de los ferrocarriles de jurisdicción federal, 1904–1906* (Mexico City, 1907), which were complemented until the revolution by a rich array of *Memórias* and related government volumes. Some evidence for Peru is found in Federico Costa y Laurent, *Reseña historica de los ferrocarriles del Perú* (Lima, 1908). A major contribution, of more recent vintage, is the book and accompanying CD-ROM edited by Jesús Sanz Fernández, *Historia de los ferrocarriles de Iberoamérica, 1837–1995* (Madrid, 1998).

Early railway studies, often by contemporaries, provide important information and serve as valuable research guides. Two that strove to encompass multiple countries were Juan José Castro, *Treatise on the South American Railways and the Great International Lines* (Montevideo, 1893) published by the Uruguayan government for the Columbian exposition; and Frederic M. Halsey, *Railway Expansion in Latin America: Descriptive and Narrative History of the Railroad Systems of Argentina, Peru, Venezuela, Brazil, Chile, Bolivia and All Other Countries of South and Central America* (New York, 1916). A short list of country-specific classics includes Bernard Moses, *The Railway Revolution in Mexico* (San Francisco, 1895); Emilio Schickendantz and Emilio Rebuelto, *Los ferrocarriles en la Argentina, 1857–1910* (Buenos Aires, reprint 1994); and Julian Smith Duncan, *Public and Private Operation of Railways in Brazil* (New York, 1932), an impressive early work of scholarship that relied heavily on the Brazilian *Estatística* volumes.

The modern monographic literature on the economic role of railways has progressed impressively over the last half century. The Argentine experience justifiably garners attention commensurate with its high level of railway density per capita in this period. In short, the narrative and analytic historiography has come a very long way since Scalabrini Ortiz's impressionistic *Historia de los ferrocarriles argentinos* (Buenos Aires, 1958). The history of British-owned railways during the better part of a century is addressed by Paul B. Goodwin in *Los ferrocarriles británicos y la U.C.R., 1916–1930* (Buenos Aires, 1974); and Colin M. Lewis, *British Railways in Argentina, 1857–1914: A Case Study of Foreign Investment* (London, 1983). The former gives more emphasis to political issues, whereas the latter is especially strong on economic questions and the unique relationship between the London capital market and railway development on the pampa. The French took up a secondary but nonetheless important position in financing Argentine railways, which is studied by Andrés Martín Regalsky in "Las inversiones francesas en los ferrocarriles argentinos, 1887–1900," *Siglo XIX* 3:5 (January–June 1988): 125–66; and "Foreign Capital, Local Interests, and Railway Development in Argentina: French Investments in Railways, 1900–1914," *Journal of Latin American Studies* 21:3 (October 1989): 425–52. Mario Justo López's impressive trilogy examines domestic and foreign-owned railways alike: *Historia de los ferrocarriles de la provincia de Buenos aires, 1857–1886* (Buenos Aires, 1991); *Historia de los ferrocarriles nacionales: incluyendo los de Santa Fé, Entre Ríos y Córdoba, 1866–1886* (Buenos Aires, 1994); and *Ferrocarriles, deuda y crisis: historia de los ferrocarriles en la Argentina, 1887–1896* (Buenos Aires, 2000). An interesting debate erupted over how to characterize the economic consequences of early Argentine railway development, which can be found in Paul B. Goodwin, "The Central Argentine Railway and the Economic Development of Argentina, 1854–1881," *Hispanic American Historical Review* 57:4 (November 1977): 613–32; and Sylvester Damus, "Critique of Paul B. Goodwin's 'The Central Argentine Railway and the Economic Development of Argentina, 1854–1881,'" *Hispanic American Historical Review* 58:3 (August 1978): 468–73. Cliometric assessments of several aspects of the Argentine railway experience are found in Sylvester Damus, "An Evaluation of Ramsey Pricing: Argentine Railways ca. 1905," *Transportation Research Forum. Proceedings* 24:1 (1983): 418–28; and in William Summerhill, "Economic Consequences of Argentine Railroad Development" (mimeograph, 2001).

The historiography on Brazilian railways has grown as well, and only the broad outlines of the last thirty or so years are sketched here. For several decades, some of the best historical research in Brazilian universities took the form of master's degree theses. Fortunately, a number of these on railroads made it into print, and two of them address the opposing ends of the spectrum of ownership. The first decade of what would become Brazil's largest railway is recounted admirably in Almir Chaiban El-Kareh, *Filha branca de mãe preta: a Companhia da Estrada de Ferro D. Pedro II (1855–1865)* (Petrópolis, 1982). The definitive economic history of the major domestically owned joint-stock railways in São Paulo is the pioneering study by Flávio Azevedo Marques de Saes, *As ferrovias de São Paulo, 1870–1940* (São Paulo, 1981). The largest of those companies is also thoroughly examined through the end of the nineteenth century by Robert H. Mattoon, "The Companhia Paulista de Estradas de Ferro, 1868–1900: A Local Railway Enterprise in São Paulo, Brazil," (Ph.D. dissertation, Yale University, 1972). Colin M. Lewis impressively turned his sights from Argentina to Brazil, with an emphasis on policy-making: *Public Policy and Private Initiative Railway Building in São Paulo 1860–1889* (London, 1991). Steven Topik moved beyond Duncan's classic study to analyze the increasing role of government in railway ownership in *The Political Economy of the Brazilian State, 1889–1930* (Austin, TX, 1987). More recently, the economic impact of railway development is taken up in William R. Summerhill, *Order Against Progress: Government, Foreign Investment, and Railroads in Brazil, 1854–1913* (Stanford, CA, 2003). Research on the experience of specific lines and various regions is ongoing in Brazilian graduate programs, so there is sure to be a continued stream of new findings on the topic.

Work on Mexican railways steams ahead at full speed and on both sides of the border. Studies of the railway's economic impact and railway policy have been most evident in recent decades. John H. Coatsworth, *Growth Against Development: The Economic Impact of Railroads in Porfirian Mexico* (DeKalb, IL, 1981) led the way with the first cliometric foray into the question of the railway's consequences in a Latin American setting. Arthur Schmidt dealt with the same era but with a tighter focus on specific regional questions in *The Social and Economic Effect of the Railroad in Puebla and Veracruz, Mexico, 1867–1911* (New York, 1987). Arturo Grunstein took up the major political and regulatory questions in "Railroads and Sovereignty: Policymaking in Porfirian Mexico" (Ph.D. dissertation, UCLA, 1994). The economic impact of Mexico's major trunk line has been reexamined and significantly revised, with a much greater focus on its consequences for the internal market than had been previously understood, by Sandra Kuntz Ficker, *Empresa extranjera y mercado interno el ferrocarril central mexicano, 1880–1907* (Mexico City, 1995). Complementing that study are the chapters viewing Mexican railways in a century-long perspective in the edited volume by Sandra Kuntz Ficker and Paolo Riguzzi, eds., *Ferrocarriles y vida económica en México, 1850–1950, del surgimiento tardío al decaimiento precoz* (Mexico City, 1996).

The surface of the corpus of studies for the rest of Latin America can barely be scratched here. Several works on Chilean railways stand out as especially worthy of attention, including what is, in effect, a company biography by Harold Blakemore, *From the Pacific to La Paz the Antofagasta (Chile) and Bolivia Railway Company 1888–1988* (London, 1990); and the broader assessment of early effects by Robert Oppenheimer, "Chilean Transportation Development: The Railroad and Socio-Economic Change in the Central Valley, 1840–1885," (Ph.D. dissertation, UCLA, 1976). The important connection between railways and mining gets some attention, as do port conditions, in Joanne Fox Przeworski, *The Decline of the Copper Industry in Chile and the Entrance of North American Capital, 1870–1916* (New York, 1980). Some of the linkages between railways and the activities that provisioned them are provided, in a comparative setting, by Guillermo Guajardo Soto, "Nuevos datos para un viejo debate: los vínculos entre ferrocarriles e industrialización en Chile y México, 1860–1950," *El Trimestre Económico* 65:258 (April–June 1998): 213–61. Colombian railways are addressed in the insightful study by Hernan Horna, *Transport Modernization and Entrepreneurship in Nineteenth Century Colombia: Cisneros and Friends* (Stockholm, 1992); in a more cliometric vein by William Paul McGreevey, *An Economic History of Colombia 1845–1930* (Cambridge, 1971), which remains one of the most ambitious and interesting studies of Latin American economic history yet written; and more recently in Maria Teresa Ramirez, "Los ferrocarriles y su impacto sobre la economía colombiana," *Revista de Historia Económica* 19:1 (2001): 81–119. Peru's experience with railways was likely much less developmental than found elsewhere. Examining various features of it are Heraclio Bonilla, "El impacto de los ferrocarriles: algunas proposiciones," *Historia y Cultura* 6 (1972): 93–120; Guido A. Pennano, "Desarrollo regional y ferrocarriles en el Perú, 1850–1879," *Apuntes* 5:9 (1979): 131–50; and Rory Miller "Railways and Economic Development in Central Peru," in Rory Miller et al., *Social and Economic Change in Modern Peru* (Liverpool, 1976), 27–52. Many studies of Cuba address its railway sector, but there is no substitute for Oscar Zanetti Lecuona and Alejandro Garcia Alvarez, *Caminos para el azucar* (Habana, 1987), which is now available in English as *Sugar and Railroads: A Cuban History, 1837–1959* (Chapel Hill, NC, 1998).

Once one moves beyond railways, the modern economic history literature on transport improvements grows considerably thinner, which suggests that there is a large amount of knowledge still waiting to be gleaned from research on these other forms of infrastructure. Studies of streetcars and early utilities exist, but not many. A clear standout is Durcan McDowell's *The Light: Brazilian Traction, Light, and Power Company Limited, 1899–1945* (Toronto, 1988). Ports and shipping have garnered somewhat more attention and were certainly more important to the growth of Latin American economies. For a key Colombian port, see Eduardo Posada-Carbó, "El puerto de Barranquilla: entre el auge exportador y el aislamiento, 1850–1950," *Caravelle* 69 (1997): 119–32. An important and comprehensive reference on Brazilian ports for this period is the government publication, *Portos do Brasil* (Rio de Janeiro, 1926). A social history of the modernization of port facilities in Brazil that offers considerable insight for economic historians is Sergio Lamarão, *Dos trapiches ao porto: um estudo sobre a área portuária do Rio de Janeiro* (Rio de Janeiro, 1991). Inland navigation is studied in pioneering work on the early commercial activities in the Plate River, *The Growth of the Shipping Industry in the Rio de la Plata Region, 1794–1860* (Madison, WI, 1957). One personalistic account that proves valuable in the absence of more scholarly work is Luis Dodero, *La navegación en la cuenca del plata y sus propulsores, memorias personales origen e historia de la más grande compañía de navegación fluvial y marítima privada* (Buenos Aires, 1961). An impressive study of public and private port improvements is provided by Silvia B. Lázzaro, *Estado, capital extranjero y sistema portuario argentino, 1880–1914* (Buenos Aires, 1992). Also valuable to historians is Edgardo J. Rocca, *El puerto de Buenos Aires en la historia* (Buenos Aires, 1996), and his *Cronología histórica del puerto de la ciudad de Buenos Aires siglos* XV–XX (Buenos Aires, 2000).

Finally, the early motor roads deserve far more attention than they have received, given that they were both complements and substitutes for railways. Most economic studies of roads focus on the period of the 1940s and later. A tremendously insightful treatment of the early period, which deserves emulation for other countries, is Richard Downes' study of early motor roads and automobiles in Brazil: "Autos over Rails: How U.S. Business Supplanted the British in Brazil, 1910–1928," *Journal of Latin American Studies* 24:3 (October 1992), 551–83.

CHAPTER 9 (OTTO T. SOLBRIG)

The economic history of the environment in Latin America was not a topic of interest until recently. Most of the literature, aside from the treatises on the biology and ecology of plants and animals, is very recent. There is only one comprehensive study documenting the changes that have occurred in the environment in Latin

America since European occupation that comes close to being an economic history of land use and the environment. This is the electronic book by Guillermo Sarmiento, *La transformación de los ecosistemas de la américa latina* (Buenos Aires, 2000). However, for partial accounts, see Alan Baker, ed., *Progress in Historical Geography* (1972), and J. D. Henshall and R. P. Momsen, *A Geography of Brazilian Development* (London, 1976). Of general interest is also the comprehensive review by W. B. Meyer and B. L. Turner, "Human Population Growth and Global Land-Use/Cover Change," *Annual Review of Ecology and Systematics* 23 (1992): 39–57. Finally, a delightful book is G. G. Whitney, *From Coastal Wilderness to Fruited Plain. A History of Environmental Change in Temperate North America: 1500 to the Present* (Cambridge, 1994).

A number of books and articles deal with aspects of the physical environment in Latin America. For example, see Jorge Morello, *Perfil ecológico de sudámerica* (Madrid, 1984); J. Aubouin et al., "Esquisse paléo-géographique et structurale des Andes méridionales," *Revue de Géographie Physique et Géologie Dynamique* 15 (1973): 11–72; and H. J. Harrington, "Paleogeographic Development of South America," *American Association of Petroleum Geologists* 46 (1962): 1773–1814. Other articles and books on the subject are R. S. Dietz and J. C. Holden, "The Breakup of Pangaea," in *Continents Adrift and Continents Aground* (San Francisco, 1976), 102–13; C. W. Stearn, R. L. Carroll, and T. H. Clark, *Geological Evolution of North America*, 3rd ed. (New York, 1979); Tim Flannery, *The Eternal Frontier* (New York, 2001); A.N. Ab'Saber, *The Paleoclimate and Paleoecology of Brazilian Amazonia*, in G. T. Prance, ed., *Biological Diversification in the Tropics* (New York, 1982), 41–59; R. A. Houghton, D. S. Lefkowitz, and D. L. Skole, "Changes in the Landscape of Latin America between 1850 and 1985. I. Progressive Loss of Forests," and "II. Net Release of CO_2 to the Atmosphere," *Forest Ecology and Management* 38 (1991): 143–72; 173–99.

The distribution of plants, animals, and ecosystems is summarized in a number of works. Gonzalo Halffter has edited a monumental work, *La diversidad biológica de Iberoamérica*, 3 vols. (Mexico City, 1998), that documents the biological diversity in Latin American countries. A comprehensive ecogeographic description of South America can be found in E. J. Fiskau et al., eds., *Biogeography and Ecology of South America*, 2 vols. (The Hague, 1968–9). Also useful are Harold Blakemore and Clifford T. Smith, *Latin America: Geographical Perspectives* (London, 1971); and T. A. Stone et al., "A Map of the Vegetation of South America Based on Satellite Imagery," *Photogrammetric Engineering & Remote Sensing* 60 (1994): 541–51. An assessment of resources and trends in their use can be found in M. J. Dourojeanni, *Situation and Trends of Renewable Natural Resources of Latin America and the Caribbean* (Lima, 1980).

For individual countries, see, for Cuba, A. Borhidi, "The Main Vegetation Units of Cuba," *Acta Botanica Hungarica* 3–4 (1987): 151–85; and *The Phytogeography and Ecology of Cuba* (Budapest, 1989). For the Choco forest of Colombia, see R. C. West, *The Pacific Lowlands of Colombia* (Baton Rouge, LA, 1957). For savannas, see Guillermo Sarmiento, *The Ecology of Neotropical Savannas* (Cambridge, MA, 1984); for the Brazilian savannas, see George Eiten, "The Cerrado Vegetation of Brazil," *Botanical Review* 38 (1972): 201–341; for the Argentine desert areas, see Gordon Orians and Otto T. Solbrig, eds., *Convergent Evolution in Warm Deserts* (Stroudsburg, PA, 1977); for Patagonia, see Alberto Soriano, Clara Movia, and Rolando León, "Deserts and Semideserts of Patagonia," in N. E. West, ed., *Temperate Deserts and Semi-Deserts* (Amsterdam, 1983), 440–54; for the Argentine pampa, see Alberto Soriano et al., "Río de la Plata Grasslands," in R. T. Coupland, ed., *Ecosystems of the World* (Amsterdam, 1991).

On the relation between environment and economic growth, we can mention J. Grunwald and P. Musgrove, *Natural Resources in Latin American Development* (Baltimore, 1970); D. Goodman and M. Redclift, *Environment and Development in Latin America* (Manchester, 1991); W. Sachs, "Global Ecology and the Shadow of Development," in W. Sachs, ed., *Global Ecology* (Halifax, 1993); and Hermann Daly, *Beyond Growth* (Boston, 1996). Another critical book is Arturo Escobar, *Encountering Development. The Making and Unmaking of the Third World* (Princeton, NJ, 1995). The relation between environment and life style is discussed by a number of authors in Osvaldo Sunkel and Nicolo Gligo, eds., *Estilos de desarrollo y medio ambiente en la América Latina*, 2 vols. (Mexico City, 1980). H. J. Leonard discusses *Natural Resources and Economic Development in Central America* (Washington, DC, 1987).

A large number of works deal with the relation between agricultural development and environmental change, usually in a negative vein. See C. J. R. Alho and E. Souza Martins, *De grão em grão, o Cerrado perde espaço* (Brasilia, 1995), which documents the environmental change in the Brazilian savannas, as do Carlos Klink, Adriana Moreira, and Otto T. Solbrig in "Ecological Impact of Agricultural Development in the Brazilian Cerrados," in M. D. Young and O. T. Solbrig, eds., *The World's Savannas* (Carnforth, 1993); and also E. Wagner "Desenvolvimento da região dos Cerrados," in W. Goedert, ed., *Solos dos Cerrados. Tecnologias e estrategias de manejo* (São Paulo, 1984). Otto T. Solbrig and Ernesto Viglizzo address the issue of agriculture and environment for the Argentine pampas in "Sustainable Farming in the Argentine Pampas: History, Society, Economy and Ecology," (The David Rockefeller Center for Latin American Studies, Harvard University, Working Papers on Latin America No. 99/00-1, Cambridge MA, 1999); and in Ernesto Viglizzo et al., "Environmental Sustainability of Argentine Agriculture: Patterns, Gradients and Tendencies 1960–2000" (Working Papers on Latin America No. 01/02-2, The David Rockefeller Center for Latin American Studies, Harvard University, 2002). Otto T. Solbrig and Raul Vera address the impact of Globalization in "Impact of Globalization on the Grasslands in the Southern Cone of South America" (Working Papers on Latin America No. 00/01-2, The David Rockefeller Center for Latin American Studies, Harvard University, 2001). Carl F. Jordan has studied the relation between nutrients and slash-and-burn agriculture in *An Amazonian Rain Forest* (Carnforth, 1989).

Deforestation and its consequences have produced a number of scholarly works. Deforestation in the Amazon basin has attracted most of the attention. Worthy of mention are Anthony Anderson, "Deforestation in Amazonia: Dynamics, Causes, and Alternatives," in A.B. Anderson, ed., *Alternatives to Deforestation: Steps Towards Sustainable Use of Amazon Rain Forest* (New York, 1990); D. Bryant, D. Nielsen, and Laura Tangley, *The Last Frontier Forest: Ecosystems and Economy at the Edge* (Washington, DC, 1997); and Keith S. Brown and G. G. Brown,

"Habitat Alteration and Species Loss in Brazilian Forests," in T. C. Whitmore and J. A. Sayer, eds., *Tropical Deforestation and Species Extinction* (London, 1992). Phillip M. Fearnside has been one of the most active students of Amazonian deforestation. See his "Deforestation in the Brazilian Amazon: How Fast Is It Occurring," *Interciencia* 7 (1982): 82–8; "Development Alternatives in the Brazilian Amazon: An Ecological Evaluation," *Interciencia* 8 (1983): 65–78; "Spatial Concentration of Deforestation in the Brazilian Amazon," *Ambio* 15 (1986): 74–81; and "Forest Management in Amazonia: The Need for New Criteria in Evaluating Development Options," *Forest Ecology and Management* 27 (1989): 61–79. Another very important book is UNESCO's (United Nations Envirnoment, Science and Culture Organization) State of Knowledge Report *Tropical Forest Ecosystems* (Paris, 1978), now slightly out of date. UNESCO has also published a symposium volume edited by Arturo Gómez Pompa, T. C. Whitmore, and Malcolm Hadley, *Rain Forest Regeneration and Management* (Carnforth, 1991). Another work is D. Skole, et al., "Physical and Human Dimensions of Deforestation in Amazonia," *BioScience* 44 (1994): 314–22. Carl Jordan has edited two important books on Amazonian deforestation and its consequences: *Amazonian Rain Forests: Ecosystem Disturbance and Recovery* (New York, 1987) and *An Amazonian Rain Forest: The Structure and Function of a Nutrient Stressed Ecosystem and the Impact of Slash-and-Burn Agriculture* (Paris, 1989). Finally, two other important multiauthored volumes are D. Goodman and A. Hall, eds., *The Future of the Amazon. Destruction or Sustainable Development* (London, 1990); and M. Clüsener-Godt and I. Sachs, eds., *Brazilian Perspectives on Sustainable Development of the Amazon Region* (Paris, 1995).

Deforestation outside the Amazon Basin is also well documented. For Central America and Mexico, see R. P. Tucker, "Foreign Investors, Timber Extraction and Forest Depletion in Central America Before 1941," in H. K. Steen and R. P. Tucker, eds., *Changing Tropical Forests* (Durham, NC, 1992); R. Daubenmire, "Some Ecological Consequences of Converting Forest to Savanna in Northwestern Costa Rica," *Tropical Ecology* 13 (1972): 31–51; Rodolfo Dirzo and M. G. Garcia, "Rates of Deforestation in Los Tuxtlas, A Neotropical Area in Southeast Mexico," *Biological Conservation* (1991); S. Harrison, "Population Growth, Land Use and Deforestation in Costa Rica, 1950–1984," *Interciencia* 16 (1991): 83–93; S.A. Sader and A.T. Joyce, "Deforestation Rates and Trends in Costa Rica," *Biotropica* 20 (1988): 11–19; S.A. Sader et al., "Forest Change Estimates for the Northern Petén Region of Guatemala," *Human Ecology* 22 (1994): 317–32; and M.P. Lehman, "Deforestation and Changing Land-Use Patterns in Costa Rica," in H.K. Steen and R.P. Tucker, eds., *Changing Tropical Forests* (Durham, NC, 1992). Norman Myers has pointed out the relation between deforestation and cattle-raising in "The Hamburger Connection: How Central American Forests Become North America's Hamburgers," *Ambio* 10 (1981): 3–8. See also his earlier study, *Conversion Rates in Tropical Moist Forests* (Washington, DC, 1979).

Finally, deforestation in South America outside of Amazonia is discussed, among others, by P. Aldhous, "Tropical Deforestation: Not Just a Problem in Amazonia," *Science* 259 (1993): 1390–1; C.J.R. Alho, T. Lacher, and H. Gonçalves, "Environmental Degradation in the Pantanal Ecosystem," *BioScience* 38 (1988): 164–71; P. Boomgaard, "Exploitation and Management of the Surinam Forests," in Steen and Tucker, *Changing Tropical Forests* (cited previously); W. Dean, "Deforestation in Southeastern Brazil," in C. Tucker and R. Richards, eds., *Global Deforestation and the Nineteenth Century World Economy* (Durham, NC, 1983); J.M.G. Kleinpenning and E.B. Zoomers, "Environmental Degradation in Latin America: The Example of Paraguay," *Tijdschrift voor Economische en Sociale Geografie* 78 (1987): 242–50; T. T. Veblen, "Degradation of Native Forest Resources in Southern Chile," in H. K. Steen, ed., *History of Sustained-Yield Forestry. A Symposium* (Durham, NC, 1984); J. Veillon, "Deforestation in the Western Llanos of Venezuela between 1950 and 1975," in Hamilton et al., eds., *Tropical Rain Forest Use and Preservation. A Study of Problems and Practice in Venezuela* (Washington, DC, 1976).

A comprehensive modeling effort of the environmental impact of development by a number of researchers under the direction of Gilberto Gallopin is detailed in *El futuro ecológico de un continente. Una visión prospectiva de la américa latina*, 2 vols. (Tokyo, 1995).

Economic aspects of deforestation are discussed by F. B. Barbier et al., "The Economics of Tropical Deforestation," *Ambio* 20 (1991): 55–9; and E. B. Barbier and J. C. Burgess, "The Economics of Tropical Forest Land Use," *Land Economics* 73 (1997): 174–95. Also see Chris Uhl and G. Parker, "Is a Quarter-Pound Hamburger Worth a Half-Ton of Rain Forest?," *Interciencia* 11 (1986): 210; and B. Gibson, "The Environmental Consequences of Stagnation in Nicaragua," *World Development* 24 (1996): 325–39.

J. O. Browder discusses social aspects of deforestation in "The Social Costs of Rain Forest Destruction: A Critique and Economic Analysis of the 'Hamburger Debate,'" *Interciencia* 13 (1988): 115–20; as does S. Stonich in "The Dynamics of Social Processes and Environmental Destruction: A Central American Case Study," *Population and Development Review* 19 (1989): 269–96. Also see R. B. Norgaard, "Sociosystem and Ecosystem Coevolution in the Amazon," *Journal of Environmental Economics and Management* 8 (1981): 238–54; and "Beyond Materialism: A Coevolutionary Reinterpretation of the Environmental Crisis," *Review of Social Economy* 53 (1995): 475–92. The same topics are the subject of M. Painter and W. H. Durham, eds., *The Social Causes of Environmental Destruction in Latin America* (Ann Arbor, MI, 1995). Juan Martínez Alier, "Ecological Economics and Ecosocialism," in M. O'Connor, ed., *Is Capitalism Sustainable?* (New York, 1994) introduces a Marxist perspective. The relation between social sciences and environment is discussed further in two symposia books: Enrique Leff, ed., *Ciencias sociales y formación ambiental* (Barcelona, 1995); and Enrique Leff and Julia Carabias, eds., *Cultura y manejo de los recursos naturales sustentables*, 2 vols. (Mexico City, 1993). Roberto Guimaraes discusses the politics of the environment in Brazil in *The Ecopolitics of Development in the Third World. Politics and Environment in Brazil* (Boulder, CO, 1991). Enrique Leff has also edited a volume dealing with knowledge and environment, *Los problemas del conocimiento y la perspectiva ambiental del desarrollo* (Mexico City, 1986). Finally, I mention a book that deals with the interphase between theology and environment; Leonardo Boff, *Dignitas Terrae. Ecologia: Grito da Terra, grito dos pobres* (São Paulo, 1995).

The relation of deforestation and climate change is the subject of several studies, among them, F. A. B. Eltahir and R. L. Bras, "Sensitivity of Regional Climate to

Deforestation in the Amazon Basin," *Advances in Water Resources* 17 (1994): 101–15; J. Shukla, C. Nobre, and P. Sellers, "Amazon Deforestation and Climate Change," *Science* 247 (1990): 1322–5; Eneas Salati and B. Vose, "Amazon Basin: A System in Equilibrium," *Science* 225 (1984): 129–38: and Eneas Salati, "The Climatology and Hydrology of Amazonia," in G. T. Prance and T. Lovejoy, eds., *Amazonia* (London, 1985); C. A. Nobre, P. J. Sellers, and J. Shukla, "Amazonian Deforestation and Regional Climatic Change," *Journal of Climatology* 4 (1991): 957–88; J. Lean, and D. A. Warrilow, "Simulation of the Regional Climatic Impact of Amazon Deforestation," *Nature* 342 (1989): 411–13; and J. Lean and P. R. Rowntree, "A GCM Simulation of the Impact of Amazonian Deforestation on Climate Using Improved Canopy Representation," *Quarterly Journal of the Royal Meteorological Society* 119 (1993): 509–30.

The very serious issue of water resources is tackled by C. Barrow, "The Impact of Hydroelectric Development on the Amazonian Environment: With Particular Reference to the Tacuruí Project," *Journal of Biogeography* 15 (1988): 67–78; C. J. Bauer, "Bringing Water Markets Down to Earth: The Political Economy of Water Rights in Chile 1976–95," *World Development* 25 (1997): 639–56; E. Monosowski, "Brazil's Tacuruí Dam: Development at Environmental Cost," in E. Goldsmith and N. Hildyard, eds., *The Social and Environmental Effects of Large Dams*, vol. 2, *Case Studies* (San Francisco, CA, 1986); P. D. Vaux and C. R. Goldman, "Dams and Development in the Topics: The Role of Applied Ecology," in R. Goodland, ed., *Race to Save the Tropics* (Washington, DC, 1991).

Soil management, erosion, and degradation are dealt with in a number of publications, among them J. M. Maass, Carl Jordan, and José Sarukhan, "Soil Erosion and Nutrient Losses in Seasonal Tropical Agroecosystems Under Various Management Techniques," *Journal of Applied Ecology* 25 (1988): 595–607; R. J. Buschbacher, Chris Uhl, and E. A. Serrão, "Abandoned Pastures in Amazonia. II. Nutrient Stocks in the Soil and Vegetation," *Journal of Ecology* 76 (1988): 682–99; R. P. Detwiler, "Land Use Change and the Global Carbon Cycle: The Role of Tropical Soils," *Biogeochemistry* 2 (1986): 67–93; Wenceslau Goedert, "Management of the Cerrado Soils of Brazil: A Review," *Journal of Soil Science* 34 (1983): 405–28.

E. Dinnerstein et al., *Conservation Assessment of the Terrestrial Ecoregions of Latin America and the Caribbean* (Washington, DC, 1995), provides a very useful and timely assessment of conservation needs for Latin America. A different approach is that of assessing change through selected indicators, as done by Manuel Winograd, *Environmental Indicators for Latin American and the Caribbean: Toward Land-Use Sustainability* (Cali, 1995); and Manuel Winograd, A. Farrow, and J. Eade, *Atlas de indicadores para América Latina y el Caribe* (Cali, 1998).

Data on land transformation and deforestation rates are very difficult to obtain. One source is the FAO FAOSTAT database in Rome [http://www.fao.org]. FAO (Food and Agriculture Organization of the United Nations) has published a series of assessments of tropical forests: FAO/UNEP *Tropical Forest Resources Assessment Project*, vol. 1, *Los recursos forestales de américa tropical* (Rome, 1981); FAO, *Tropical Forest Resources* (FAO Forestry Paper 30, Rome, 1982); FAO, *Forest Resources Assessment 1990: Global Synthesis* (Rome, 1995); FAO, *Forest Resources Assessment 1990. Survey of Tropical Forest Cover and Study of Change Processes* (FAO Forestry

Paper No. 130, Rome, 1996); FAO, *State of the World's Forests 1997* (Rome, 1997); S. Brown, *Estimating Biomass and Biomass Change of Tropical Forests. A Primer* (FAO Forestry Paper No. 134, Rome, 1997). Another source is the annual survey on *World Resources* published by The World Resources Institute and Oxford University Press (Washington, DC).

CHAPTER 10 (BLANCA SÁNCHEZ-ALONSO)

This bibliographical essay is divided in four parts according to the sections of the chapter. Each part contains the basic bibliographical material used in writing the chapter and some other useful references. For obvious reasons, not all the countries in Latin America have been subjects of research. Immigration to Argentina and the Argentine experience is, by far, the best known case and the number of titles and monographs for this country is much higher than for Brazil, Uruguay, or Cuba.

This essay is also intended to get the reader started on particular topics and is by no means exhaustive.

Section I

Data on immigration have always been the subject of criticism because legal definitions of migrants varied from country to country. It is always discussed whether the figures actually reflect the true number of migrants because of various reasons: clandestine emigration from European ports, re-emigration movements across countries of destination, passengers arriving by sea versus migrants according to the legal definition, and so on. Arrival data for countries of immigration have always been thought to be more reliable than departure data (and the other way around for source countries) and there are many problems in estimating net migration data. The most widely used collection of migration statistics is Imre Ferenczi and Walter F. Willcox, *International Migrations*, 2 vols. (New York, 1929, 1931). The first volume presents in a very detailed way migration statistics for a large group of countries according to official figures of each country. The second volume contains chapters for individual countries discussing the main characteristics of particular migratory flows.

Particularly relevant for the major countries of immigration in Latin America is the volume *Inmigración y estadísticas en el cono sur de América. Argentina, Brasil, Chile y Uruguay*. Instituto Panamericano de Geografía e Historia. Organización de los Estados Americanos. Serie Inmigración, vol. VI (México, 1990). It not only includes official statistics but census data as well. Data on immigration and other demographic variables for Latin American countries can also be found in Brian R. Mitchell, *International Historical Statistics. The Americas 1750–1988* (Basingtoke, England, 1993).

It is also useful to consult other official sources such as Instituto Brasileiro de Geografía e Estadística, *Estadísticas históricas do Brasil: Series Económicas,*

Demográficas e Sociais, 2nd ed. (Sao Paulo, 1988); República de Cuba, *Inmigración y movimiento de pasajeros*, Secretaría de Hacienda, Sección Estadísticas (La Habana 1902–1932); Dirección General de Inmigración, *Resumen estadístico del movimiento migratorio de la República argentina, 1857–1924*, Ministerio de Agricultura (Buenos Aires, 1925). A useful collection of statistics for Argentina is Vicente Vázquez Presedo (1971 and 1976), *Estadísticas Históricas Argentinas* (comparadas), vol. 1, 1875–1914; vol. 2, 1914–1939 (Buenos Aires, 1976).

As regards the major source countries in Europe of immigrants to Latin America, some scholars have attempted to refine the available statistics. Among others, see Joachim Costa Leite, "Emigraçao portuguesa; a lei e os numeros (1855–1914)," *Analise Social* XXIII, 97 (1987), 463–80, and Maria Baghana, *Portuguese Emigration to the United States, 1820–1930* (New York, 1990), for the Portuguese case; Blanca Sánchez-Alonso, "Una nueva serie anual de la emigración española, 1882–1930," *Revista de Historia Económica* VIII, 1 (1990), 133–72, for the Spanish case; Gianfausto Rosoli, ed., *Un secolo di emigrazione italiana, 1876–1976* (Roma, 1978); and Marcello Carmagnani and Giovanna Mantelli, "Fonti quantitative italiane relative all'emigrazione italiana verso l'America Latina (1902–1914). Analisi critica," *Annali della Fondazione Luigi Einaudi* 9 (1975), 283–301.

Data on real wages used in this chapter come from Jeffrey G. Williamson, "Real Wages Inequality and Globalization in Latin America before 1940," in Pablo Martín Aceña, Adolfo Meisel, and Carlos Newland, eds., *La historia económica en América Latina, Revista de Historia Económica*, Special issue (1999), 101–42. All the sources and data are included also in Jeffrey Williamson, "Real Wages and Relative Factor Prices in the Third World, 1820–1940: Latin America," (Discussion Paper no. 1853, Harvard Institute of Economic Research, October 1998). Although Williamson's real wages can be criticized, data come from well-know sources for individual countries such as Roberto Cortés Conde, *El progreso argentino, 1880–1914* (Buenos Aires, 1979), for Argentina; Luis Bertola et al., "Southern Cone Real Wages Compared: A Purchasing Power Parity Approach to Convergence and Divergence Trends, 1870–1996" (Working Paper, Unidad Multidisciplinaria, Facultad de Ciencias Sociales, Montevideo, February 1998), for Uruguay; Gustavo M. Gomes, *The Roots of State Intervention in the Brazilian Economy* (New York, 1986), for Brazil (wages for Rio de Janeiro can also be found in Raymond Goldsmith, *Brazil, 1850–1984*. [Sao Paulo, 1981]); and Oscar Zanetti and Alejandro García, *United Fruit Company: Un caso del dominio imperialista en Cuba* (La Habana, 1976), for Cuba. For immigrants' sources of income other than wages in the coffee plantations of southeast Brazil, see Thomas Holloway, *Immigrants on the Land. Coffee and Society in São Paulo, 1886–1934* (Chapel Hill, NC, 1980). A very useful work for wages and gross domestic product in Latin America in the twentieth century is Pablo Astorga and Valpy Fitzgerald, "The Standard of Living in Latin America during the Twentieth Century" (Working Paper, Queen Elizabeth House Development Studies, no. 117, May 1997).

Data for passage fares to Latin America are scarce. Alejandro Vázquez Gonzalez, "La emigración gallega a América, 1830–1930" (Ph.D. dissertation, Universidad de Santiago de Compostela, 1999), provides annual data for passage fares from Spanish ports, but similar information is not available for Portugal or Italy.

The discussion about Latin American countries experiencing unlimited supplies of labor along the lines of Lewis's model of economic development can be found in Nathaniel Leff, *Underdevelopment and Development in Brazil. Economic Structure and Change, 1822–1947*, 2 vols. (London, 1982); and Carlos Díaz Alejandro, *Essays on the Economic History of the Argentine Republic* (New Haven, CT, 1970) (Spanish translation, *Ensayos sobre historia económica argentina* [Buenos Aires, 1975]), for Brazil and Argentina, respectively. The same argument can be found in Roberto Cortés Conde, *El progreso económico argentino, 1880–1914* (Buenos Aires, 1979). For a different view, see Hatton and Williamson, "Latecomers to Mass Migration: The Latin Experience," in Timothy J. Hatton and Jeffrey G. Williamson, *Migration and the International Labor Market, 1850–1939* (New York, 1994), 5–71. Lewis' seminal work is W. Arthur Lewis, *Growth and Fluctuations, 1870-1913* (London, 1978).

General studies about Latin American economic development in the nineteenth and twentieth centuries include chapters or references to labor and immigration. See Victor Bulmer-Thomas, *The Economic History of Latin America Since Independence*, 2nd ed. (Cambridge, 2003); Leslie Bethell, ed., *The Cambridge History of Latin America*, vol. 4, c.1870–1930 (Cambridge, 1986), particularly chapters by James R. Scobie on urbanization in Latin America, 1870–1930; Manuel Moreno Fraginals on the economy and society in Caribbean plantations; William Glade, on Latin America and the international economy; and Nicolás Sánchez-Albornoz on the evolution of Latin American population. A seminal work for population in Latin America is Nicolás Sánchez-Albornoz, *The Population of Latin America: A History* (Berkeley, CA, 1974).

Magnus Mörner, *Adventurers and Proletarians. The Story of Migrants in Latin America* (Paris, 1985), is a classical and general study on immigration in Latin America. See also Boris Fausto, ed., *Fazer a America: a immigraçao em massa para a America Latina* (Sao Paulo, 2000). Very useful as a bibliographical guide is Oliver Marshall, *European Immigration and Ethnicity in Latin America: A Bibliography* (London, 1991).

Research on migration in the nineteenth and twentieth centuries is very much biased toward the United States and it is not so easy to find references to Latin American countries (Argentina being the exception) in the general accounts of European migrations. Rudolph J. Vecoli and Suzanne M. S. Sinke, eds., *A Century of European Migrations, 1830–1930* (Chicago, 1991), includes the classical essay by Frank Thistlewhite, "Migration from Europe Overseas in the Nineteenth and Twentieth Century," presented at the Eleventh International Congress of Historical Sciences in Stockholm in 1960. This author was the first in claiming against the American-centeredness of migration studies and was praised for the inclusion of destinations other than the United States. The emphasis was also in favor of a "more European" and micro approach to European emigration from the point of view of villages and towns. John D. Gould is another exception in considering destinations other than the United States in his series of three articles on European emigration in the *Journal of European Economic History* ("European Inter-Continental Emigration, 1815–1914: Patterns and Causes" 8, 3 (1979), 593–679; "European Inter-Continental Emigration. The Road Home: Return Migration from the USA" 9, 1 (1980), 41–113; and "European Inter-Continental Emigration: The Role of 'Diffusion' and

'Feedback'" 9, 2 (1980), 267–317. Gould's survey of the major problems in the study of emigration is still useful as a starting reading for those interested in migration. However, the basic reading to understand the causes and consequences of migration movements is Timothy J. Hatton and Jeffrey G. Williamson, *The Age of Mass Migration. Causes and Economic Impact* (New York, 1998). It is a fundamental text on the determinants of European emigration and the economic effects in the receiving countries, particularly in the United States but with very illuminating insights on Argentina, Uruguay, and Brazil. Also useful is the collective volume edited by Timothy J. Hatton and Jeffrey G. Williamson, *Migration and the International Labor Market, 1850–1939* (New York, 1994), particularly chapters by Alan M. Taylor, "Mass Migration to Distant Southern Shores. Argentina and Australia, 1870–1939," 91–118; and Riccardo Faini and Alessandra Venturini, "Italian Emigration in the Pre-War Period," 72–90.

Although research has been focused on the main receiving countries, there are some references useful to study the efforts of other Latin American countries to attract foreign immigration and the era of the European colonies in the central decades of the nineteenth century. Joseph W. Fretz, *Immigrant Group Settlement in Paraguay* (North Newton, KS, 1962) is one example. There is a special issue of the *Jahrbuch für Geschichte von Staat, Wirtschaft und Gesellschaft Lateinamerikas*, 13 (1976), dedicated to Latin America immigration that includes articles on less known countries of emigration to Latin America such as Russia, Scandinavia, and the Welsh and French colonies in Patagonia. Italian colonies in Argentina are carefully studied by Ezequiel Gallo, *La pampa gringa. La colonización agrícola en Santa Fé, 1870–1895* (Buenos Aires, 1983).

The study of the transition from African slavery to free European immigration in Latin America has been the object of many articles and monographs. The classic study is by David Eltis, "Free and Coerced Transatlantic Migrations: Some Comparisons," *American Historical Review* 88, 2 (1983), 251–80, and his book, *Economic Growth and the Ending of the Transatlantic Slave Trade* (New York, 1987). Herbert Klein, *The Atlantic Slave Trade* (Cambridge, 1999), includes some very useful chapters on the transition from slavery to free labor in Brazil. David W. Galenson, "The Rise and Fall of Indentured Servitude in the Americas: An Economic Analysis," *Journal of Economic History* XLIV, 1 (1984), 1–26, explores the reasons why indentured servitude declined in the United States while it reappeared in the Caribbean and South America in the early twentieth century. Pieter C. Emmer and Magnus Mörner, eds., *European Expansion and Migration. Essays on the Intercontinental Migration from Africa, Asia and Europe* (New York, 1992), includes useful chapters on emigration from Western Africa and Chinese and indentured East Asian labor in the Caribbean.

For the Caribbean, see also Manuel Moreno Fraginals, Frank Moya Pons, and Stanley J. Engerman, *Between Slavery and Free Labor. The Spanish Speaking Caribbean in the Nineteenth Century* (Baltimore, 1985), and Rebecca J. Scott, *Slave Emancipation in Cuba. The Transition to Free Labor, 1860–1899* (Princeton, NJ, 1985).

For the major countries of origin of immigrants to Latin America, there are several monographs: Ercole Sori, *L'emigrazione italiana dall'Unità alla seconda Guerra mondiale* (Bolonia, 1979), for Italy; Blanca Sánchez-Alonso, *Las causas de la emigración española, 1880–1930* (Madrid, 1995) (also the article "Those Who Left and Those Who Stayed Behind: Explaining Emigration from the Regions of Spain, 1880–1914," *Journal of Economic History* 60, 3 [2000], 730–55) for Spain; and Joachim Costa Leite, "Portugal and Emigration, 1855–1914," (Ph.D. dissertation, Columbia University, 1993).

Section II

Immigration policies in Latin America have been studied from national perspectives and there is not any comparative study. Ashley Timmer and Jeffrey G. Williamson, "Immigration Policy Prior to the 1930s: Labor Markets, Policy Interactions, and Globalization Backlash," *Population and Development Review* 24, 4 (1998), 739–71 include Argentina and Brazil in their index of migratory policies in the New World. James Foreman-Peck also provides a general analysis of immigration policies (James Foreman-Peck, "A Political Economy Model of International Migration, 1815–1914," *The Manchester School* 60, 4 [1992], 359–76).

A basic reading on legislation and immigration policies for Southern Cone countries is Hernán A. Silva, ed., *Legislación y política inmigratoria en el cono sur de América: Argentina, Brasil, Uruguay* (México, 1987). Both Argentinean and Brazilian policies have received special attention, particularly the Brazilian program of subsidized immigration. See Thomas H. Holloway, "Creating the Reserve Army? The Immigration Program of Sao Paulo, 1886–1930," *International Migration Review* 22, 2 (1978), 187–209; Holloway, *Immigrants on the Land. Coffee and Society in São Paulo, 1886–1934* (Chapel Hill, 1980); and Fernando J. Devoto, "Políticas migratorias argentinas y flujo de población europea, 1876–1925," in F. Devoto, ed., *Estudios sobre la emigración italiana a la Argentina en la segunda mitad del siglo XIX* (Napoli, 1991). See also Chiara Evangelista, *La braccia per la fazenda: immigrati e "caipiras" nella formazione del mercato di lavoro paulista (1850–1930)* (Milan, 1982), for an interesting comparison on the distortion in the immigration flow caused by Brazilian subsidies. The short-lived Argentinean program for subsidizing immigration in the late 1880s is analyzed by M. Silvia Ospital, "La inmigración subsidiada y las oficinas de información, 1887–1890," in *Jornadas de Inmigración* (Buenos Aires, 1985), 441–56.

The consequences of different immigration policies for the receiving countries are analyzed by Alan M. Taylor, "Mass Migration to Distant Southern Shores. Argentina and Australia, 1870–1939," (previously cited); and Alan M. Taylor, "External Dependence, Demographic Burden and Argentine Economic Development After the Belle Epoque," *Journal of Economic History* 52 (1992), 907–36, comparing Argentina and Australia.

For comparisons with the United States and Australian policies, see Claudia Goldin, "The Political Economy of Immigration Restriction in the United States, 1890 to 1921," in Claudia Goldin and Gary Libecap, eds., *The Regulated Economy, A Historical Approach to Political Economy* (Chicago, 1994), 223–57; Roger Daniels and Otis L. Graham, *Debating American Immigration, 1882–Present* (Lanham, MD, 2001); and David Pope, "Population and Australian Economic Development,

1900–1930," in R. Maddock and I. W. McLean, eds., *The Australian Economy in the Long Run* (Cambridge, 1987), 33–60.

Blanca Sánchez-Alonso, "European Emigration in the Late Nineteenth Century: The Paradoxical Case of Spain," *Economic History Review* 52, 2 (2000), 309–29, analyzes the effects of monetary and protectionist policies in Spain and their impact in the timing and volume of Spanish emigration. Roberto Cortés Conde, "Migración, cambio agrícola y políticas de protección. El caso argentino," in Nicolás Sánchez-Albornoz, ed., *Españoles hacia América. La emigración en masa, 1880–1930* (Madrid, 1988), 235–48, also discusses the effects of protectionist policies for agriculture in Spain and their effects on the migratory flow. For Portuguese policy and regulations, see Joachim Costa Leite, "Emigraçao portuguesa; a lei e os numeros (1855–1914)," *Analise Social*, 23, 97 (1987), 463–80; and Miriam Halpern Pereira, *A política portuguesa de emigraçâo, 1850–1930* (Lisbon, 1981).

Section III

Information about occupation and demographic characteristics of migrants can be found in the official statistics of each country of immigration and official population censuses. The analysis of passenger-ship lists has been hardly explored for the Latin American case, in contrast with research done for the United States and Australia. There is an extensive literature for the main immigration country, Argentina, followed by research done on Brazil, Uruguay, and Cuba.

A classical study of immigration in Argentina using the censuses material is Gino Germani, *Estructura social de la Argentina* (Buenos Aires, 1955). See also Gino Germani, "Mass Immigration and Modernization in Argentina," in I. L. Horowitz, *Masses in Latin America* (New York, 1970), 289–331. Fernando Devoto, *Historia de la inmigración en la Argentina* (Buenos Aires, 2003) is the most recent title on inmigration in Argentina.

Roberto Cortés Conde, *El progreso argentino, 1880–1914* (Buenos Aires, 1979), is a classical reference on Argentinean economic growth and one of the pioneers in analyzing immigration from a modern economic perspective. It is also one of the first, with Ezequiel Gallo, *La Pampa Gringa. La colonización agrícola en Santa Fé, 1870–1895* (Buenos Aires, 1983), in challenging the traditional view about the inability of immigrants in Argentina to access landownership. For the traditional view, see James R. Scobie, *Revolution on the Pampas: A Social History of Argentine Wheat* (Austin, TX, 1964). The more recent approach to the topic of latifundia versus the tenancy system in agriculture is Alan M. Taylor, "Latifundia as a Malefactor in Economic Development? Scale, Tenancy and Agriculture on the Pampas, 1880–1914," *Research in Economic History* 17 (1997), 261–300. A general and comparative picture of Argentine agricultural development can be found in Jeremy Adelman, *Frontier Development: Land, Labour and Capital on the Wheatlands of Argentina and Canada, 1890–1914* (Oxford, 1994).

For the impact of immigration in Brazil, and more specifically in the state of São Paulo, there are general and useful titles such as Thomas W. Merrick and Douglas H. Graham, *Population and Economic Development in Brazil, 1800 to the*

Present (Baltimore, 1979); and Warren Dean, *The Industrialization of São Paulo, 1880–1945* (Austin, 1969), for the absorption of the immigrant labor force in the industrial labor market. Among the most important studies for Brazilian economic development are Nathaniel Leff, *Underdevelopment and Development in Brazil. Economic Structure and Change, 1822–1947*, vol. I (London, 1982). A summary of Leff's main arguments can be read in his chapter, "Economic Development in Brazil, 1822–1913," in Stephen Haber, ed., *How Latin America Fell Behind. Essays on the Economic Histories of Brazil and Mexico, 1800–1914* (Stanford, CA, 1997), 34–64. Thomas H. Holloway, *Immigrants on the Land. Coffee and Society in São Paulo, 1886–1934* (Chapel Hill, NC, 1980), is the classical study for immigration in the coffee areas in Brazil.

For Cuba, see Abel F. Losada, *Cuba: población y economía entre la independencia y la revolución* (Vigo, 1999); and José Luis Luzón, *Economía, población y territorio en Cuba (1899–1983)* (Madrid, 1987).

Although not dealing directly with immigration, an important title for Uruguay is Luis Bertola, *Ensayos de historia económica: Uruguay y la región en la economía mundial, 1870–1990* (Montevideo, 2000). In the collective volume edited by Nicolás Sánchez-Albornoz, *Españoles hacia América. La emigración en masa, 1880–1930* (previously cited), the first part is dedicated to the regional origins of Spanish emigrants and the second includes very useful chapters on some Latin American countries of destination for immigrants: Argentina, Brazil, Cuba, Puerto Rico, and Mexico. Also useful is Nicolás Sánchez-Albornoz, ed., *Población y mano de obra en América Latina* (Madrid, 1985), with interesting chapters on the Uruguayan labor market by Juan Rial, and the Brazilian labor market by Chiara Evangelista and José Souza-Martins.

In the last years, a growing number of titles on Spanish immigration have balanced the research done for the Italians in Latin America. Among others, it is useful to consult Herbert S. Klein, *La inmigración española en Brasil* (Gijón, 1996) (Portuguese translation, *A imigraçao española do Brasil* [São Paulo, 1994]); Blanca Sánchez Alonso, *La inmigración española en Argentina. Siglos XIX y XX* (Gijón, 1992); Jordi Maluquer de Motes, *Nación e inmigración: los españoles en Cuba (siglos XIX y XX)* (Gijón, 1992); and Abel F. Losada, "The Cuban Labor Market and Immigration from Spain, 1900–1930," *Cuban Studies* 25 (1995), 147–64. Carlos Zubillaga, ed., *Españoles en el Uruguay: características demográficas, socials y económicas de la inmigración masiva* (Montevideo, 1997); and Clara E. Lida, ed., *Una inmigración privilegiada. Comerciantes, empresarios y profesionales españoles en México en los siglos XIX y XX* (Madrid, 1994) for a less well-known case such as Mexico.

Jose C. Moya, *Cousins and Strangers. Spanish Immigration in Buenos Aires, 1850–1930* (Berkeley, CA, 1998), analyzes occupational and personal characteristics of Spaniards in the city of Buenos Aires with a great variety of sources: national and municipal censuses, mutual-aid societies' records, and literary sources among others. Mark D. Szuchman was one of the first in studying a Spanish community in Argentina in *Mobility and Integration in Urban Argentina. Cordoba in the Liberal Era* (Austin, TX, 1980).

William A. Douglass and Jon Bilbao, *Amerikanuak: Basques in the New World* (Reno, NV, 1975), deals mostly with the United States but includes a chapter on Basque immigration in Latin America.

Following the pioneer work written in 1919 by Robert F. Foerster, *The Italian Emigration of Our Times* (Cambridge, MA, 1919), the study of the Italian migratory experience in the New World has generated a substantial literature. For a general view, see Emilio Franzina, *Gli Italiani al nuovo mondo: l'emigrazione italiana in America, 1492–1942* (Milan, 1995).

In Argentina, Fernando J. Devoto and a group of scholars around him have specialized in the study of the Italian community. The journal *Estudios Migratorios Latinoamericanos* is a basic reference for articles on immigration in Argentina and in other Latin American countries. Among other titles, see Fernando J. Devoto and Gianfausto Rosoli, eds., *La inmigración italiana en la Argentina* (Buenos Aires, 1985); and Fernando J. Devoto and Gianfausto Rosoli, eds., *L'Italia nella società argentina* (Roma, 1988). See also Maria Cristina Cacopardo y José Luis Moreno, "Características demográficas y ocupacionales de los migrantes italianos hacia Argentina, 1880–1930," *Studie Emigrazione* 21, 75 (1984), 277–92; and Mario Mascimbene, *Historia de los italianos en la Argentina, 1835–1920* (Buenos Aires, 1986), with comparative data on Spanish and Italian immigration. For Italian immigration in Uruguay, Fernando J. Devoto et al., *L'emigrazione italiana e la formazione dell'Uruguay moderno* (Torino, 1993). Italians in Brazil have been studied, among others, by Angelo Trento, *Do outro lado do Atlântico: um seculo de imigraçao italiana no Brazil* (São Paulo, 1989).

A very fruitful line of research has been the comparative studies between the Italians in Argentina and in the United States. Samuel Baily has been the leading scholar in this field: Samuel L. Baily, "Marriage Patterns and Immigrant Assimilation in Buenos Aires 1882–1923," *Hispanic American Historical Review* 60 (1980), 32–48; Samuel L. Baily, "Patrones de residencia de los italianos en Buenos Aires y Nueva York," *Estudios Migratorios Latinoamericanos* 1, 1 (1985), 8–47. Particularly important is his book, *Immigrants in the Land of Promise: Italians in Buenos Aires and New York City, 1870 to 1914* (Ithaca, NY, 1999). Herbert S. Klein, "The Integration of Italian Immigrants in to the United States and Argentina: A Comparative Analysis," *American Historical Review* 88, 2 (1983), 306–29, provides very interesting data for both migratory flows.

A substantial literature on chain migration and migratory networks has evolved from the pioneer article by John and Leatrice Macdonald, "Chain Migration, Ethnic Neighborhood Formation and Social Networks," *Milbank Memorial Fund Quarterly* 13, 42 (1964), 82–95. Both Jose C. Moya, *Cousins and Strangers. Spanish Immigration in Buenos Aires, 1850–1930* (cited previously), in his study of Spaniards in Buenos Aires, and Samuel Baily, in his research on the Italians (*Immigrants in the Land of Promise: Italians in Buenos Aires and New York City, 1870 to 1914* [cited previously] stress the importance of locality and migration networks in shaping migratory flows. They also ponder the importance of the social and institutional capital that facilitated the insertion of Italians and Spaniards into Argentine society and culture. Immigrants in Latin America created different kinds of organizations

Other relevant studies of particular problems at a country level are Arnold Bauer and A. Hagerman Johnson. "Land and Labour in Rural Chile, 1850–1935," in K. Duncan and I. Rutledge, eds., *Land and Labour in Latin America* (Cambridge, 1977), 83–101; Eugenio Figueroa et al. "Sustentabilidad ambiental del sector exportador chileno," in O. Sunkel, ed., *Sustentabilidad Ambiental del Crecimiento Económico Chileno* (Santiago, 1996); Cristóbal Kay, "The Development of the Chilean Hacienda System," in K. Duncan and I. Rutledge, eds., *Land and Labour in Latin America* (Cambridge, 1977), 103–40; Rayén Quiroga and Saar Van Hauwermeiren, *The Tiger Without a Jungle* (Santiago, 1996). For Peru, see P. Klaren, "The Social and Economic Consequences of Modernization in the Peruvian Sugar-Industry, 1870–1930," in K. Duncan and I. Rutledge, eds., *Land and Labour in Latin America* (Cambridge, 1977), 239–51. Interesting studies are also J. T. Brannon and G. Joseph, eds., *Land, Labor, and Capital in Modern Yucatán: Essays in Regional History and Political Economy* (Tuscaloosa, AL, 1987); S. Harrison, "Population Growth, Land Use and Deforestation in Costa Rica, 1950–1984," *Interciencia* 16 (1991): 83–93. On peasant agriculture, see Victor Toledo, "The Ecological Rationality of Peasant Production," in M. Altieri and S. Hecht, eds., *Agro-Ecology and Small Farm Development* (1990), 51–8.

Nicolo Gligo, in "El estilo de desarrollo de la América Latina desde la perspectiva ambiental," in O. Sunkel & N. Gligo, eds., *Estilos de Desarrollo y Medio Ambiente en la América Latina* (Mexico, 1980), 379–432, reviews the environmental impact of agriculture. The same subject from a world perspective is developed by J. F. Richards in "World Environmental History and Economic Development," in W. C. Clark and R. E. Munn, eds., *Sustainable Development of the Biosphere* (Cambridge, 1986), 53–74.

The relation between natural resources and agriculture is dealt with by M. J. Dourojeanni, in *Situation and Trends of Renewable Natural Resources of Latin America and the Caribbean* (Lima, 1980). The problems of water for irrigation are dealt with in C. J. Bauer, "Bringing Water Markets Down to Earth: The Political Economy of Water Rights in Chile 1976–95," *World Development* 25 (1997), 639–56. Soil management is the topic of Wenceslao Goedert, "Management of the Cerrado Soils of Brazil: A Review," *Journal of Soil Science* 34 (1983), 405–28; and J. A. Posner, "Cropping Systems and Soil Conservation in the Hill Areas of Tropical America," *Turrialba* 32 (1982), 287–99.

The history and economics of coffee growing are detailed in several studies, such as C. W. Berquist, *Coffee and Conflict in Colombia, 1886–1910* (Durham, NC, 1978); M. Palacios, *Coffee in Colombia 1850–1970* (Cambridge, 1980); C. F. S. Cardoso, "The Formation of the Coffee Estate in Nineteenth-Century Costa Rica," in K. Duncan and I. Rutledge, eds., *Land and Labour in Latin America* (Cambridge, 1977), 165–201; T. H. Holloway, "The Coffee Colono of São Paulo, Brazil: Migration and Mobility, 1880–1930," in K. Duncan and I. Rutledge, eds., *Land and Labour in Latin America* (previously cited), 301–21; Stanley J. Stein, *Vassouras. A Brazilian Coffee County, 1850–1900* (Cambridge, MA, 1976); W. Roseberry, *Coffee and Capitalism in the Venezuelan Andes* (Austin, TX, 1983).

James Scobie in *Revolution in the Pampas: A Social History of Argentine Wheat 1860–1910* (Austin, TX, 1964), describes the agricultural boom in the Argentine pampas at the turn of the twentieth century. Warren Dean details the Amazonian rubber boom in *Brazil and the Struggle for Rubber* (Cambridge, 1987), and S. B. Schwartz details the development of the Brazilian sugar industry in *Sugar Plantations in the Formation of Brazilian Society. Bahia 1550–1835* (Cambridge, 1985). Two works detail the development of henequen growing in the Yucatán peninsula of Mexico: A. Wells, *Yucatán's Gilded Age. Haciendas, Henequén, and International Harvester, 1860–1915* (Albuquerque, NM, 1985); and G. M. Joseph, *Revolution from Without: Yucatan, Mexico and the United States 1880–1924* (Cambridge, 1982). Philip Warnken deals with the modern soybean boom in *The Development and Growth of the Soybean Industry in Brazil* (Ames, IA, 1999).

Agricultural statistics since 1961 can be obtained on the Internet from the FAOSTAT Database of FAO (Food and Agricultural Organization of the United Nations in Rome) at http://www.fao.org, as well as from the Web Pages of the departments of agriculture of most Latin American countries. Another source of historical statistics is agricultural censuses that are carried out now in most countries, but only Argentina has agricultural censuses stretching back to 1890. The reliability of census data varies with the census and the country. IICA (Instituto Interamericano de Cooperación Agrícola) publishes data for many countries, as do many countries' agricultural and statistical offices. IICA has also published an essay on the history of agronomic research and teaching institutions, *Las ciencias agrícolas en América Latina* (San José, Costa Rica, 1967). More recent published statistics can be found in World Bank publications, *The World Resources Institute Yearbook* (Washington, DC), and others.

CHAPTER 13 (STEPHEN HABER)

The first scholars to address the history of Latin American industrialization in a systematic manner were a group of historians and economists who were strongly influenced by the growth economics tradition of the 1950s and 1960s. These scholars set out to understand both the causes of and the obstacles to Latin American economic growth, and did so by testing hypotheses against carefully assembled bodies of evidence. Some of this work, such as Stanley Stein, *The Brazilian Cotton Manufacture: Textile Enterprise in an Underdeveloped Area, 1850–1950* (Cambridge, MA, 1957); Nathaniel Leff, *The Brazilian Capital Goods Industry, 1929–1964* (Cambridge, MA, 1968); Werner Baer, *The Development of the Brazilian Steel Industry* (Nashville, TN, 1969); and Warren Dean, *The Industrialization of São Paulo, 1880–1945* (Austin, TX, 1969), were directly concerned with industrialization. Another strand of this literature focused on the related issue of trade protection in the process of industrial development. Two classics of this genre are Joel Bergsman, *Brazil: Industrialization and Trade Policies* (London, 1970) and Timothy King, *Mexico: Industrialization and Trade Policies Since 1940* (London, 1970). These were both published as part of a broad Organization for Economic Cooperation and Development (OECD) initiative on commercial policies and industrial development since World War II that also included studies of Pakistan,

India, and the Philippines. A third strand of the literature focused on the broader process of growth, of which industrialization was an important part. Nevertheless, industrialization was a major theme of this work. Two of the most notable of these studies, both sponsored by Yale's Economic Growth Center, are Clark Reynolds, *The Mexican Economy: Twentieth Century Structure and Growth* (New Haven, CT, 1970), and Carlos Díaz Alejandro, *Essays on the Economic History of the Argentine Republic* (New Haven, CT, 1970).

Two major themes emerged from this literature. The first was that Latin American economies grew rapidly from the 1940s to the mid-1960s, and that industry led the way. The second was that Latin America's industrial development in the post-1940 period had long antecedents. In some studies, such as Stein's *The Brazilian Cotton Manufacture*, this theme was highlighted. In others, such as Díaz Alejandro's *Essays on the Economic History of the Argentine Republic* or Reynolds's *The Mexican Economy*, this theme was more subtly advanced.

This literature, tied to mainstream economics, was soon elbowed aside by a literature influenced by dependency theory. The problems with dependency theory need not detain us here – for critiques of dependency, see Robert Packenham, *The Dependency Movement: Scholarship and Politics in Development Studies* (Cambridge, MA, 1992), and Stephen Haber, "Introduction: Economic Growth and Latin American Economic Historiography," in Stephen Haber, ed., *How Latin America Fell Behind: Essays on the Economic Histories of Brazil and Mexico, 1800–1914* (Stanford, CA, 1997). Nevertheless, one of the effects of dependency was a loosening of the requirement that arguments had to be sustained with evidence – if you know the truth based on theory, then there is no need to do systematic empirical research. Thus, for a time, Latin American economic history took a turn toward a style of work that was decidedly more impressionistic. Indeed, this style of scholarship sought, as Aldo Ferrer put it, to differentiate "historical stages within the economic system" without "the traditional economic historian's mass of data." See Aldo Ferrer, *The Argentine Economy* (Berkeley, CA, 1967), 1.

In terms of the literature on industrialization, dependency therefore gave the field very little in the way of empirical research, but it did leave us with some fairly rigid categories of analysis such as "export economies" and "import substituting industrialization." These were never really defined or operationalized in an analytically meaningful way. Nevertheless, these categories of analysis were soon transformed into stylized facts that were accepted at face value by a broad range of scholars. The fairly subtle analyses about the long trajectory of Latin American industrial development that was to be found in such works as Stein's *The Brazilian Cotton Textile Manufacture*, Reynolds's *The Mexican Economy*, or Díaz Alejandro's *Essays on the Economic History of the Argentine Republic* were replaced by a far less subtle view in which industrialization was a product of state-directed growth in the mid-twentieth century.

Any academic project that has no empirical basis can only stand for so long, and dependency was no exception to this general rule. Thus, beginning in the 1970s and accelerating in the 1980s, a new wave of empirical research on the history of Latin American industrialization began to appear. The first of these works was Carlos

Manuel Peláez, *História da industrialização brasileira* (Rio de Janeiro, 1972), whose introductory essay by Denio Nogueira celebrated the fact that Peláez embraced monetarism, rather than dependency and structuralism. Other influential works on Brazil included Flavio Versiani and José Roberto Mendonça de Barros, *Formação econômica do Brasil: a experiência da industrializaçao* (São Paulo, 1977); Nathaniel Leff, *Underdevelopment and Development in Brazil*, 2 vols. (London, 1982); and Wilson Suzigan, *Indústria brasileira: origem e desenvolvimento* (São Paulo, 1986). This work on Brazil was accompanied by studies of Chile and Mexico. See, for example, Henry Kirsch, *Industrial Development in a Traditional Society: The Conflict of Entrepreneurship and Modernization in Chile* (Gainesville, FL, 1977); Enrique Cárdenas, *La industrialización mexicana durante la Gran Depresión* (Mexico City, 1987); and Stephen Haber, *Industry and Underdevelopment: The Industrialization of Mexico, 1890–1940* (Stanford, CA, 1989). Some of the research that came out of this period can be found in abbreviated form in an extremely useful volume edited by Rosemary Thorp, *An Economic History of Twentieth Century Latin America*, vol. 2, *Latin America in the 1930s: The Role of the Periphery in World Crisis* (New York, 2000).

By the late 1980s and early 1990s, the revival of empirical research on Latin America's economic development was once again in full swing. Scholars now began to take on a broad range of topics related to the long history of industrial development, including tariffs and trade protection, industrial finance, the integration of markets, entrepreneurship, and the political basis of government support of industry.

Latin America's industrial development during the century from 1880 to 1980 could not have taken place without barriers to foreign trade. Beginning in the 1990s, scholars began to build on Bergsman and King's work on the postwar period, and began to study trade protection in the nineteenth and early twentieth centuries. The vast majority of this research has focused on Mexico. Notable works include Edward Beatty, *Institutions and Investment: The Political Basis of Industrialization in Mexico Before 1911* (Stanford, CA, 2001), particularly chapters 3 and 4; Sandra Kuntz Ficker, "Institutional Change and Foreign Trade in Mexico, 1870–1911," in Jeffrey L. Bortz and Stephen Haber, eds., *The Mexican Economy, 1870–1930: Essays on the Economic History of Institutions, Revolution, and Growth* (Stanford, CA, 2002); Edward Beatty, "Commercial Policy in Porfirian Mexico: The Structure of Protection," in *The Mexican Economy, 1870–1930*; Graciela Marquez, "The Political Economy of Mexican Protectionism, 1868–1911" (Ph.D. dissertation, Harvard University, 2002); and Richard J. Salvucci, "The Origins and Progress of U.S.-Mexican Trade, 1825–1884: 'Hoc Opus, hic labor est,'" *Hispanic American Historical Review* 71, 4 (November 1991): 697–735. Readers will also find an extremely useful and econometrically sophisticated discussion of the trade protection awarded to Mexico's second largest textile firm in Aurora Gómez-Galvarriato, "The Impact of Revolution: Business and Labor in the Mexican Textile Industry, Orizaba, Veracruz, 1900–1930" (Ph.D. dissertation, Harvard University, 1999).

The support that industrialists received from governments in the way of tariffs and other barriers to trade did not, of course, come out of thin air. Industrial development was an intensely political process that required entrepreneurs to convince public officials that it was in their interest to transfer rents from the rest of society to industrialists and industrial workers. Aligning the incentives of public officials with those of industrialists was abetted by the fact that Latin American governments (particularly in the 1940s and 1950s) faced severe balance of payments problems. Tariffs and quotas were an obvious way to stanch the flow of foreign exchange out of the country. This point is clearly made in the very useful set of country studies contained in the edited volume by Enrique Cárdenas, José Antonio Ocampo, and Rosemary Thorp, *An Economic History of Twentieth-Century Latin America*, vol. 3, *Industrialization and the State in Latin America – The Postwar Years* (New York, 2000).

Protectionism also required direct political action by industrialists. Two recent studies on Argentine industrialization make this point clearly: Fernando Rocchi, "Building a Nation, Building a Market: Industrial Growth and the Domestic Economy in Turn-of-the-Century Argentina" (Ph.D. dissertation, University of California, Santa Barbara, 1997), covers the period prior to 1914; Paul H. Lewis, *The Crisis of Argentine Capitalism* (Chapel Hill, NC, 1990), covers the entire sweep of Argentine political economy in the twentieth century. For Brazil, readers should consult Steven Topik, *The Political Economy of the Brazilian State, 1889–1930* (Austin, TX, 1987). Finally, four recent studies shed light on the politics of tariff setting in Mexico. One of these, Graciela Marquez, "The Political Economy of Mexican Protectionism, 1868–1911" (cited previously), focuses on the Porfiriato. Two others, Mario Ramírez Rancaño, *Burguesía textil y política en la Revolución Mexicana* (Mexico City, 1987) and María del Carmen Collado Herrera, *Empresarios y políticos, entre la Restauración y la Revolución 1920–1924* (Mexico City, 1996), cover the revolution and the immediate postrevolutionary period. A fourth, Stephen Haber, Armando Razo, and Noel Maurer, *The Politics of Property Rights: Political Instability, Credible Commitments, and Economic Growth in Mexico, 1876–1929* (Cambridge, 2003), draws on these works and others to analyze the entire period from the Porfiriato to the Great Depression.

Industrial development also could not have taken place without the integration of markets. Most Latin American countries are not naturally blessed with long stretches of navigable waterways that flow through their major population areas. The logical implication is that, contrary to the view that emerged from dependency theory, railroads must have played a significant role in integrating domestic markets. Two scholars working independently, Sandra Kuntz Ficker and William Summerhill, both produced similar qualitative results in strong support of this hypothesis. Kuntz Ficker's work on Mexico, *Empresa extranjera y mercado interno: el Ferrocarril Central Mexicano, 1880–1907* (Mexico City, 1995), demonstrated that most traffic on the Mexican Central Railway was short haul and destined for local markets. Summerhill, *Order Against Progress: Government, Foreign Investment, and Railroads in Brazil, 1854–1913* (Stanford, CA, 2003), makes it clear that a similar phenomenon took place in Brazil: most of the freight on Brazil's railroads was destined for domestic uses, and the vast majority of this freight would not have been transported had railroads not been constructed. A comparative article by Summerhill, "Transport Improvements and Economic Growth in Brazil and Mexico," in

Stephen Haber, ed., *How Latin America Fell Behind: Essays on the Economic Histories of Brazil and Mexico, 1800–1914* (Stanford, CA, 1997), draws parallels between the Brazilian and Mexican cases.

Industrial development also requires entrepreneurs who can combine factors of production and take advantage of market opportunities. There is a long tradition of such studies in the Latin American historiography, in large part owing to the fact that such studies are extremely amenable to the tools of traditional, nonquantitative historical analysis. Among the very first of these studies was Sanford Mosk, *Industrial Revolution in Mexico* (Berkeley, CA, 1950). The study of entrepreneurs and their social origins also figured prominently in Stein, *The Brazilian Textile Manufacture*; Dean, *The Industrialization of São Paulo*; Kirsch, *Industrial Development in a Traditional Society*; and Haber, *Industry and Underdevelopment* (all cited earlier). A systematic cross-sectional study of entrepreneurs, which is an extremely useful complement to the more prosopographical accounts found in historical literature, was carried out in the mid-1960s by Flavia DeRossi and was published as *The Mexican Entrepreneur* (Paris, 1971).

In recent years, the literature on entrepreneurs, their social and economic origins, and the history of their business enterprises has boomed. One of the most systematic of these studies, which combines aspects of both biography and business history, is Elisabeth von der Weid and Ana Marta Rodrigues Bastos, *O Fio da meada: Estratégia de expansão de uma indústria têxtil: Companhia América Fabril, 1878–1930* (Rio de Janeiro, 1986). The recent dissertation by Fernando Rocchi, "Building a Nation, Building a Market" (cited earlier), employs a similar approach. The literature on Mexico is voluminous. Among the most impressive of the works on Mexican entrepreneurs are Leticia Gamboa Ojeda, *Los empresarios de ayer: el grupo dominante en la industria textil de Puebla, 1906–1929* (Puebla, 1985), and María del Carmen Collado Herrera, *La burguesía mexicana: el emporio Braniff y su participación política, 1865–1920* (Mexico City, 1987). For studies that combine both entrepreneurial and business history, see Mario Cerutti, *Burguesía, capitales, e industria en el norte de México* (Monterrey, Mexico, 1992), and Carlos Marichal and Mario Cerutti, *Historia de las grandes empresas en México, 1850–1930* (Mexico City, 1997).

Entrepreneurs cannot accomplish much in the absence of banks and securities markets that can mobilize capital for their enterprises. In recent years, the study of banks and securities markets in Latin American economic development has become in and of itself a growth industry. For an introduction to this growing body of work, see María Bárbara Levy, *História da bolsa de valores do Rio de Janeiro* (Rio de Janeiro, 1977); Flávio Azevedo Marques de Saes, *Crédito e bancos no desenvolvimento da economia paulista, 1850–1930* (São Paulo, 1986); Anne Hanley, "Capital Markets in the Coffee Economy: Financial Institutions and Economic Change in São Paulo, Brazil, 1850–1905" (Ph.D. dissertation, Stanford University, 1995); Gail Triner, *Banking and Economic Development: Brazil, 1889–1930* (New York, 2000); Noel Maurer, *The Power and the Money: The Mexican Financial System, 1876–1928*, (Stanford, CA, 2002); Lance E. Davis and Robert E. Gallman, *Evolving Financial Markets and International Capital Flows: Britain, the Americas, and Australia, 1865–1914* (Cambridge, 2001); and Andrés Regalsky, "Banking, Trade, and the Rise of Capitalism in Argentina, 1850–1930," in Alice Teichova, Ginette Kurgan-Van Hentenryk, and Dieter Ziegler, eds., *Banking, Trade, and Industry, Europe, America, and Asia from the Thirteenth to the Twentieth Century* (Cambridge, 1997).

There are also a number of articles that employ econometric techniques to measure the independent impact of banks and securities markets on Latin American industrial structure and productivity growth. See, for example, Stephen Haber, "Banks, Financial Markets, and Industrial Development: Lessons from the Economic Histories of Brazil and Mexico," in José Antonio González et al., eds., *Macroeconomic Reform in Latin America: The Second Stage* (Chicago, 2003); Noel Maurer and Stephen Haber, "Institutional Change and Economic Growth: Banks, Financial Markets, and Mexican Industrialization," in Jeffrey L. Bortz and Stephen H. Haber, eds., *The Mexican Economy, 1870–1930*; and Stephen Haber, "The Efficiency Consequences of Institutional Change: Financial Market Regulation and Industrial Productivity Growth in Brazil, 1866–1934," in John H. Coatsworth and Alan M. Taylor, eds., *Latin America and the World Economy Since 1800* (Cambridge, MA, 1998).

One of the most interesting features of the literature produced over the past fifteen years is that so much of it focuses on the period prior to 1940. The period since World War II has received surprisingly little attention. In large part, this is a function of the fact that Latin American governments opened their markets to foreign-produced manufactures in the 1980s, thereby bringing to an end a century-long experiment with industrial development behind protective tariffs. The result has been a complete reorientation of Latin American industry (the subject of the article in this volume by Victor Bulmer-Thomas). As a consequence, economists have been more keen to study the effects of trade openness than they have been to study the failed history of protectionism. One notable (and very welcome) exception to this trend is the recent volume edited by Enrique Cárdenas, José Antonio Ocampo, and Rosemary Thorp, *An Economic History of Twentieth-Century Latin America*, vol. 3, *Industrialization and the State in Latin America – The Postwar Years* (cited earlier). This volume is an extremely useful jumping-off point for further research into the post-1940 period, as are the relevant chapters of Victor Bulmer-Thomas, *The Economic History of Latin America Since Independence*, 2nd ed. (Cambridge, 2003).

CHAPTER 14 (MIGUEL SZÉKELY AND ANDRÉS MONTES)

Many references are possible for a subject as broad as poverty in Latin America. The ones cited here aim to provide only a general overview of the bibliography on the topic. The sources selected are considered the most significant for the objectives given in our chapter.

The lack of reliable historical data on poverty for Latin America appears as the first and most important obstacle for undertaking time-series studies of the region. Flawed or scarce information is a common problem in the analysis of long-term trends in poverty, inequality, and income distribution. Oscar Altimir, "Income Distribution Statistics in Latin America and Their Reliability," *Revista de la Asociación Internacional para la Investigación de la Riqueza y el Ingreso* 33 (1987), provides important insights on this topic. Altimir offers deeper analysis of the difficulties of elaborating assessments or comparisons presented by data unavailability or unreliability over long periods of time. Data on poverty and inequality in the region did not appear until the second half of the twentieth century, and many countries do not undertake periodic surveying practices or statistical analysis. Articles containing information regarding household-survey practices throughout the world include Klaus Deininger and Lyn Squire, "A New Data Set Measuring Income Inequality," *World Bank Economic Review* 10, 3 (September 1996): 565–91; Angus Deaton, *The Analysis of Household Surveys: A Microeconometric Approach to Development Policy* (Baltimore, MD, 1997); and Martin Ravallion and Shaohua Chen, "What Can New Survey Data Tell Us about Recent Changes in Distribution and Poverty?," *The World Bank Economic Review* 11,2 (1997): 357–82.

Even though data are scarce, there are many books about Latin American economic history. For example, Rosemary Thorp, *Progreso, pobreza y exclusión: una historia económica de América Latina en el siglo XX* (Washington, DC, 1998) is one of the most detailed analyses and among the most useful sources for building on the historical trends of the evolution of poverty and inequality in Latin America and the Caribbean during the twentieth century. It provides a complete assessment of social, political, and economic indicators within the region.

There are also numerous historical studies related to poverty and inequality in Latin America. For the researcher interested in country comparisons for the whole region and examinations over broad time periods, a key paper is Oscar Altimir, "Long-Term Trends of Poverty in Latin American Countries," *Revista de la Universidad de Chile* (2001): 115–55. This article reviews the research on long-term evolution of poverty undertaken in four selected Latin American countries: Chile, Argentina, Colombia, and Mexico. These countries were chosen mainly because of data availability, but also because they constitute a representative sample of distinct Latin American trends on poverty. Other valuable sources consulted on this topic include Oscar Altimir, "Cambios en la Desigualdad y la Pobreza en América Latina," *El Trimestre Económico* 19, 241 (1994): 85–133; Alain De Janvry and Elizabeth Sadoulet, "Growth, Poverty and Inequality in Latin America: A Causal Analysis, 1970–1994," *Review of Income and Wealth* 46, 3 (2000): 267–87; Kenneth L. Sokoloff and Stanley L. Engerman, "History Lessons: Institutions, Factor Endowments, and Paths of Development in the New World," *Journal of Economic Perspectives* 14, 3 (Summer 2000): 217–32; and Juan Luis Londoño and Miguel Székely, "Persistent Poverty and Excess Inequality: Latin America 1970–1995," *Journal of Applied Economics* 3, 1 (May 2000): 93–134.

On this topic, Juan Luis Londoño and Miguel Székely, "Persistent Poverty and Excess Inequality: Latin America 1970–1995" (cited previously) is useful for understanding the analysis of poverty throughout the second half of the twentieth century. This article contains abundant statistical evidence on poverty and inequality during this period of time and assesses the changes in aggregate poverty and inequality that have taken place in Latin America during the past twenty-six years. The authors reach the conclusion that poverty and inequality have not declined during the 1990s despite remarkable improvements at the macroeconomic level. Other poverty, inequality, and income distribution studies and analyses in the region, although not particularly considering specific time periods, include Oscar Altimir, *La dimensión de la pobreza en América Latina* (Santiago, 1979); Orazio Attanasio and Miguel Székely, "An Asset-Based Approach to the Analysis of Poverty in Latin America" (Working Paper no. 376, Inter-American Development Bank, 1999); and Samuel Morley, *La distribución del ingreso en América Latina y el Caribe* (Mexico City, 2000).

There is also a wide array of studies on poverty and inequality for specific countries in Latin America and the Caribbean. For specific country-case discussions, the following sources were consulted. For Brazil: Albert Fishlow, "Brazilian Size Distribution of Income," *American Economic Review* 62, 2 (1972): 391–402; Marcelo Cortés Neri, Alexandre Pinto Carvalho, and Edward Joaquim Amadeo, "Assets, Markets and Poverty in Brazil," in Orazio Attanasio and Miguel Székely, eds., *Portrait of the Poor* (Washington, DC, 2001); and Angus Maddison, *The Political Economy of Poverty, Equity and Growth in Brazil and Mexico* (London, 1992). For Colombia: Juan Luis Londoño, *Distribución del ingreso y desarrollo económico: Colombia en el siglo XX* (Bogotá, 1995). For Peru: Javier Escobal, Jaime Saavedra, and Máximo Torero, "Distribution, Access and Complementarity: Capital of the Poor in Peru," in *Portrait of the Poor* (cited previously). For Bolivia: consult George Gray-Molina et al., "Poverty and Assets in Bolivia: What Role Does Social Capital Play?" in *Portrait of the Poor*. Oscar Altimir and Luis Beccaria do a thorough study of the Argentinian situation in "El persistente deterioro de la distribución del ingreso en la Argentina," *Desarrollo Económico* 40, 160 (2001): 589–618. For Mexico, see Miguel Székely, *Hacia una nueva generación de política social* (Mexico City, 2002); "Poverty and Equity Under ISI: Can Anything Be Said about It?" (working paper, St. Antony's College, Oxford University, 1997), and *The Economics of Poverty: Inequality and Wealth Accumulation in Mexico* (London, 1998). Also, see Humberto Pánuco-Laguette and Miguel Székely, "Income Distribution and Poverty in Mexico," in Victor Bulmer-Thomas, ed., *The New Economic Model in Latin America and Its Impact on Income Distribution and Poverty* (London, 1996); Garcia Rocha, "Note on Mexican Economic Development and Income Distribution" (Documento de Trabajo no. VII-90, Centro de Estudios Económicos, El Colegio de México, 1990); Joel Bergsman, "Income Distribution and Poverty in Mexico" (Staff Working Paper no. 395, World Bank, Washington, DC, 1980); Orazio Attanasio and Miguel Székely, "Ahorro de los hogares y distribución del Ingreso en México," *Economia Mexicana* 3, 2 (July–December 1999): 267–338; and Pedro Aspe and Javier Beristain, "Toward a First Estimate of the Evolution of Inequality in Mexico," in Pedro Aspe and Paul Sigmund, eds., *The Political Economy of Income Distribution in Mexico* (New York, 1984).

One of the most discussed issues among poverty and inequality scholars is the debate on whether growth reduces or increases inequality. Many theories have emerged through time; however, no consensus has been reached yet. Some countries' experiences tend to support some hypotheses whereas other country cases refute them. This topic has been widely discussed over time, starting in the beginning of the second half of the twentieth century. To build on our argument, an ample bibliography was consulted. Among the sources we found supporting an argument for the "one-to-one growth-equality relationship" developed by Simon Kuznets is Sudhir Anand and S. M. R. Kanbur, "The Kuznets Process and the Inequality-Development Relationship," *Journal of Development Economics* 40 (1993): 25–52. Other studies addressing the growth-development relationship include Irma Adelman and Albert Morris, *Economic Growth and Social Equity in Developing Countries* (Stanford, CA, 1973); Barbara Stallings and Wilson Peres, *Growth, Employment and Equity: The Impact of the Economic Reforms in Latin America and the Caribbean* (Washington, DC, 2000); Montek Ahluwalia, "Inequality, Poverty and Development," *Journal of Development Economics* 2 (1976): 307–42; Montek Ahluwalia, Nicholas Carter, and Hollis Chenery, "Growth and Poverty in Developing Countries," *Journal of Development Economics*" 6 (1979): 299–341; Nancy Birdsall et al., "Why Low Inequality Spurs Growth: Saving and Investment by the Poor," in Andrés Solimano, ed., *Social Inequalities: Values, Growth and the State* (Ann Arbor, MI, 1998); David Dollar and Aart Kraay, "Growth Is Good for the Poor" (Mimeo, Washington, DC); Mattias Lundberg and Lyn Squire, "The Simultaneous Evolution of Growth and Inequality" (Mimeograph, Washington, DC, 2000); Eugene Smolensky et al., "Growth Inequality and Poverty: A Cautionary Note," *Review of Income and Wealth Series* 40, 2 (1994): 217–22; John Luke Gallup et al., "Economic Growth and the Income of the Poor" (Discussion Paper no. 36, Harvard Institute for International Development, Harvard University, 1999); Martin Ravallion, "Growth and Poverty: Making Sense of the Current Debate" (Mimeograph, World Bank Development Research Group, Washington, DC, 2000); Robert Barro, "Inequality and Growth in a Panel of Countries" (Mimeograph, Harvard University, 1999); Michael Roemer and Mary Kay Gugerty, "Does Economic Growth Reduce Poverty?" (Discussion Paper no. 4, Harvard Institute for International Development, Harvard University, 1997); Michael Bruno et al., "Equity and Growth in Developing Countries: Old and New Perspectives in the Policy Issues," in Vito Tanzi and K. Y. Chu, eds., *Income Distribution and High Quality Growth* (Cambridge, MA, 1998); James Foster and Anthony Shorrocks, "Poverty Orderings," *Econométrica* 56, 1 (1998): 173–7; Jere Behrman, *The Debt Crisis, Structural Adjustment and the Rural Poor* (Williamstown, MA, 1990); Stanley Engerman and Kenneth Sokoloff, *Factor Endowments, Inequality, and Paths of Development Among New World Economies* (Cambridge, MA, 2002).

Valuable succinct discussions on Latin America and the Caribbean growth-development are included in James E. Foster and Miguel Székely, "Is Economic Growth Good for the Poor? Tracking Low Incomes Using General Means" (Working Paper no. 453, Inter-American Development Bank, 2001). The authors propose a new method for evaluating growth effects on poor incomes based on a comparison of growth rates for two standards of living: the ordinary mean and a bottom sensitive general mean. Among other results, they concluded that the incomes of the poor do *not* grow on a "one-to-one" basis with increases in average income.

Other papers and collections of essays addressing poverty and inequality are Anthony Atkinson, "On the Measurement of Inequality," *Journal of Economic Theory* 2 (1970): 224–63; Jere Behrman, Nancy Birdsall, and Miguel Székely, *Poverty and Income Inequality in Developing Countries: A Policy Dialogue on the Effects of Globalization* (Paris, 1999); Hollis Chenery and Moshe Syrquin, *Patterns of Development: 1950–1970* (London, 1975); Amartya Sen, *On Economic Inequality* (London, 1997); Paul Schultz, "Inequality in the Distribution of Personal Incomes in the World: How Is It Changing and Why" (Mimeograph, Yale University, 1997); Amartya Sen, "Poverty: An Ordinal Approach," *Econométrica* 44 (1976): 219–31; Miguel Székely and Marianne Hilgert, "What's Behind the Inequality We Measure? An Investigation Using Latin American Data" (OCE Working Paper Series no. 409, Inter-American Development Bank, 1999); Peter Timmer, *How Well Do the Poor Connect to the Growth Process* (Cambridge, MA, 1997); James Foster, Joel Greer, and Erik Thorbecke, "A Class of Decomposable Poverty Indices," *Econométrica* 52 (1984): 761–6; James Foster and Anthony Shorrocks, "Sub-group Consistent Poverty Measures," *Econométrica* 59, 3 (1991): 6870–9; Hong Yi Li et al., "Explaining International and Intertemporal Variations in Income Inequality," *The Economic Journal* 108, 446 (1998): 26–43; and Orazio Attanasio and Miguel Székely, "An Asset-Based Approach to the Analysis of Poverty in Latin America" (Working Paper no. 376, Inter-American Development Bank, 1999).

Orazio Attanasio and Miguel Székely, eds., *Portrait of the Poor: An Asset-Based Approach* (cited previously) is a comprehensive sourcebook on the condition of the poor in various Latin American countries. Its main argument is that poverty, or at least "excess poverty," in the region is a problem caused mainly by high inequality. However, income inequality in the region is, to a large extent, a reflection of a very skewed distribution of income-earning assets, human capital being the most important. This book provides an in-depth explanation of the highly unequal distribution of income-earning assets in the region. The asset-based approach considers education as one of the most important human capital assets for overcoming poverty. For a wider panorama on the changes in educational attainments through time, or to assess how the distribution of these assets evolved in the region during the past century and to examine the process of human and physical capital asset accumulation in Latin America, we relied on the following. On the topic of education, Suzanne Duryea and Miguel Székely, "The Determinants of Schooling in Latin America: A Micro-Macro Approach" (Mimeograph, Inter-American Development Bank, 1999) provides a valuable approach to the issue of schooling attainment by examining the changes in both the stocks and flows of schooling. For data on specific regions, see Jere Behrman, Suzanne Duryea, and Miguel Székely, "Schooling Investments and Aggregate Conditions: A Household-Survey Approach for Latin America and the Caribbean" (Working Paper no. 407, Inter-American Development Bank, 1999), which assesses the effect of macro conditions on schooling attainment trends throughout the world. Jere Behrman, Nancy Birdsall, and Miguel Székely, "Economic Reform and Wage Differentials in Latin America" (Working Paper, Inter-American Development Bank, 2000) portrays wage differentials in the region (depending on the schooling attainment), hence completing information for the former section and providing a very important hint about the returns to each educational degree. Also, George Psacharopulos, "Time Trends of the Returns to Education: Cross National Evidence," *Economics of Education Review* 8, 3 (1989): 225–31; and "Returns to Education: A Further International Update and Implications," *The Journal of Human Resources* 20, 4 (Autumn 1985): 583–604 provide valuable information. An updated and succinct account of the returns to education by the same author is found in *Returns to Investment in Education: A Global Update* (Washington, DC, 1993). For the Brazilian case, see Nancy Birdsall, "Public Inputs and Child Schooling in Brazil," *Journal of Development Economics* 18, 1 (May–June 1985): 67–86.

For analyzing the use of assets throughout the region, consult Suzanne Duryea and Miguel Székely, "Labor Markets in Latin America: A Look at the Supply Side," *Emerging Markets Review* 1, 3 (2000), in which the authors present facts about the connection between demographic transitions and educational changes (size and quality of labor force) with respect to labor supply, inequality, and unemployment. The conclusion is that demographics and education significantly improve our understanding of the overall decline in employment, its changing pattern, and the rises in wage inequality. The authors prove that Latin America has undergone significant changes in its age structure and educational profile during the last thirty years. Also, because there is scarce information on physical capital, the most useful sources were the *World Bank Development Indicators* as well as the *Penn Tables*. These two sources are user-friendly and provide periodic summary tables and extended time series in easy-to-manipulate formats, which proved convenient for statistical processing.

There are a number of studies that provide overviews on demographic transitions and education. For discussions on this topic, consult Jere Behrman, "Education, Health and Demography in Latin America Around the End of the Century: What Do We Know? What Questions Should Be Explored?" (Mimeograph, Washington, DC, 1999); Jere Behrman, Suzanne Duryea, and Miguel Székely, "Decomposing Fertility Differences Across Regions and Over Time: Is Improved Health More Important Than Women's Schooling?" and "Aging and Economic Opportunities: Major World Regions at the Turn of the Century," both in Orazio Attanasio and Miguel Székely, eds., *Dynamic Analysis of Household Decision Making in Latin America* (Washington, DC, forthcoming), chapters 7 and 8; Nancy Birdsall, "Economic Approaches to Population Growth," in Hollis Chenery and T. N. Srinivasan, eds., *Handbook on Development Economics* (Amsterdam, 1988), 477–542; Michael Kremer and Daniel Chen, "Income Distribution Dynamics with Endogenous Fertility," *American Economic Review* (May 1999); Mark Rosenzweig and Paul Schultz, "The Supply and Demand for Births: Fertility and Its Life Cycle Consequence," *American Economic Review* 75, 5 (1985): 992–1015; Mark Rosenzweig and Paul Schultz, "Fertility and Investments in Human Capital: Estimates of the Consequences of Imperfect Fertility Control in Malaysia," *Journal of Econometrics* 36 (1987): 163–84; Orazio Attanasio and Fernando Reimers, *Unequal School, Unequal Chances: The Challenge to Equal Opportunity in the Americas* (Cambridge, MA, 2000); and Miguel Székely, "Household Saving in Developing Countries: Demographics, Inequality and All That," in Boris Pleskovic and N. H. Stern, eds., *Annual World Bank Conference in Development Economics 2000* (Washington, DC, 2001).

Even though there has been little research on the link between factor endowments and income distribution, there are some good comparative data. Antonio Spilimbergo, Juan Luis Londoño, and Miguel Székely, "Income Distribution, Factor Endowments and Trade Openness," *Journal of Development Economics* 59 (1997): 77–101, provide the basis to support this argument. They study the empirical links among factor endowments, trade, and personal income distribution, showing that land- and capital-intensive countries have less equal income distributions, whereas skill-intensive countries have more equal income distributions. Other studies including comparative evidence on the effects of trade and markets liberalization are George Borjas and Valerie Ramey, "Foreign Competition, Market Power and Wage Inequalities," *The Quarterly Journal of Economics* XC (1995): 1075–110; Francois Bourgignon and C. Morrison, eds., *External Trade and Income Distribution* (Paris, 1989); Sebastian Edwards, "Openness, Trade Liberalization and Growth in Developing Countries," *Journal of Economic Literature* 31 (1993) 1358–93; Richard Freeman and Lawrence Katz, eds., *Differences and Changes in Wage Structure* (Chicago, 1995); Donald Robbins, "HOS Hits Facts: Facts Win: Evidence on Trade and Wages in the Developing World" (Harvard Institute for International Development), Development Discussion Paper no. 557, Harvard University, 1996); Adrian Wood, "North-South Trade Employment and Inequality: Changing Fortunes in a Skill Driven World" (London, 1994); and "Openness and Wage Inequality in Developing Countries: The Latin American Challenge to East Asian Conventional Wisdom," *The World Bank Economic Review* (1996).

INDEX

ARCHBISHOP ALEMANY LIBRARY
DOMINICAN UNIVERSITY
SAN RAFAEL, CALIFORNIA 94901